MW00770676

Praise for *Author Under Sail: The Imagination of Jack London, 1893–1902*

"In his groundbreaking and comprehensive biography of Jack London, *Author Under Sail: The Imagination of Jack London,* Jay Williams approaches London's writing life in a way that no other biographer or scholar has previously endeavored."

—Iris Dunkle, *Journal of Popular Culture*

"*Author Under Sail* offers a paradigm-shifting approach to Jack London studies. . . . Williams has the gift of explaining complex ideas in straightforward, clear language and is also a storyteller adept at tracing the human connections behind the texts and shaping them into an engrossing tale. *Author Under Sail* will become an indispensable source for all serious London scholars."

—Chris Gair, author of *Complicity and Resistance in Jack London's Novels: From Naturalism to Nature*

"Thoroughly documented and cogently argued, *Author Under Sail* heralds a departure from all scholars who thought they knew about Jack London and promises a wealth of new directions in London scholarship."

—S. M. Nuernberg, *Choice*

"Indispensable for Jack London scholars."

—Anita Duneer, *Studies in American Naturalism*

"A stunning new story of the authorial development that undergirds Jack London's prolific fiction and nonfiction. This book offers a far richer U.S. socioliterary vein than any mined to date by critics and researchers of London's life and career. Jay Williams, what's more, presents a new model of close reading, not a formalist plea for artistic unity but a showcase of literary-critical focal power. For admirers of Jack London, for students of American literature, and for historians of the book, *Author Under Sail* is a must."

—Cecelia Tichi, author of *Exposés and Excess: Muckraking in America, 1900–2000*

AUTHOR UNDER SAIL

Author Under Sail

THE IMAGINATION OF **JACK LONDON**, 1902–1907

JAY WILLIAMS

UNIVERSITY OF NEBRASKA PRESS Lincoln

Library of Congress Cataloging-in-Publication Data
Williams, Jay (James W.)
Author under sail: the imagination of Jack London /
James (Jay) W. Williams.
pages cm
Includes bibliographical references and index.
ISBN 9780803249912 (v. 1: hardback)
ISBN 9780803256835 (v. 1: epub)
ISBN 9780803256842 (v. 1: mobi)
ISBN 9780803249929 (v. 2: hardback)
ISBN 9781496223029 (v. 2: epub)
ISBN 9781496223036 (v. 2: mobi)
1. London, Jack, 1876–1916. 2. Authors, American—
19th century—Biography. 3. Authors, American—20th
century—Biography. 4. London, Jack, 1876–1916—
Criticism and interpretation. 5. Imagination in
literature. 6. Realism in literature I. Title. II. Title:
Imagination of Jack London, 1893–1902.
PS3523.O46Z9955 2014
813'.52–dc23
[B]

                    2014020276

Set in Utopia and Geogrotesque types
by Mikala R. Kolander.
Designed by Richard Hendel.

Frontispiece: Painting on board by unknown artist
outside tent at the Bohemian Grove in California,
1905. Photographer unknown. JLP 462 Alb. 24, Jack
London Photographs and Negatives, The Huntington
Library, San Marino, California.

For Patsy, always

CONTENTS

ACKNOWLEDGMENTS

I wrote this book in two different places: the University of Chicago and the Huntington Library in San Marino, California. At the university, Pat Monahan, a now-retired dean in the Division of the Humanities, provided me with the necessary quiet space—my own office—to write. Mike Zmija, the division's facilities coordinator, was also extremely helpful. Richard Neer, Haun Saussy, Lauren Berlant, and Arnold I. Davidson provided a different, equally valuable means of support. They cared. For thirty years, Arnold directly and indirectly made me a better thinker. My gratitude toward these scholars is unbounded.

At the Huntington Library, I have been fortunate to work closely with Sue Hodson since 1983; she has been a constant and encouraging presence at the library and listened to my tales of discovery. Steve Hindle, the library's Director of Research, was very supportive, and I thank the fellowship committee for providing me with a second fellowship. Happy were the days in the library when I worked with Anne Blecksmith, Catherine Wehrey-Miller, Juan Gomez, Allee Monheim, Michael Fish, Kevin Miller, James Kitahara, Natalie Russell, Emmy Zhang, Sara Couch, Samuel Wiley, Stephanie Arias, Morex Arai, Lisa Caprino, Leslie Jobsky, Jaeda Snow, Mark Fleming, and Karina Sanchez. Mary Catherine Kinniburgh at the New York Public Library's Berg Collection and Tal Nadan and John Cordovez at the Brooke Russell Astor Reading Room were particularly accommodating, as were David Pedrero, Victor Ou, and Nikolas Swihart. I also want to thank everyone who helped me navigate the London material at the Clifton Waller Barrett Library in the University of Virginia's Special Collections.

I want to thank a number of scholars for their special friendship: Alan Marcus, Melody Graulich, Aleta George, Jason de Stefano, Iris Dunkle, and Amy Tucker.

So much of my work is indebted to London scholarship, especially work by Ken Brandt, Anita Duneer, Paul Crumbley, John Hay, Keith Newlin, Jonah Raskin, Kevin Swafford, Charles Watson, and Daniel J. Wichlan. Three longtime friends and scholars have been especially helpful, in so many ways. I will always be thanking Susan Nuernberg, Clarice Stasz, and Chris Gair.

I want to thank E. Morris Potter, chair of the Rose Valley Museum and Historical Society, for an enlightening tour and talk about the American Arts and Crafts Movement. Melissa Bush at the University of Georgia Library helped with the correspondence between London and Corra Harris. Claudia Keenan has done phenomenal research and blog writing on J. Howard Moore, Parker Sercombe, Oscar Lovell Triggs, and the Chicago Arts and Crafts scene. Tjiska Van Wyk, former director of Jack London Park Partners, provided me with the opportunity to publically present chapter 11.

I am grateful to be a part of the professional team at the University of Nebraska Press. Matt Bokovoy and Heather Stauffer believe in this project and have given it a life beyond the four walls of my office. There really is no adequate way to thank them. I also want to thank, again, Joeth Zucco and Tish Fobben for their valuable support. Karen Brown returned as well to copyedit this volume, providing insights, queries, and rewrites.

I owe an immense personal debt to Clare Leary for years of support. Jan Tappan provided an affordable and comfortable headquarters. John McColpin, Cynthia Archer, and Helen McColpin redeemed the hours of solitude with kindly refreshing, reinvigorating company. Chris Kotowski and Bridget Moore enabled my research in New York City, but since the early eighties, they have given me so much more. Mark Williams, Anne Williams, Cathie McGowan, and Amy Nickoloff—my brother and sisters—cheered every little progressive step taken toward completion. Here's to Joanne Spector, who lived to see the first volume and the writing of the second, and to Leo Spector, who will see the second in print.

Alison Archer has listened for years to me working out my ideas. Her expertise in London studies has motivated me, and her love sustained me.

Patsy will always be there for me, carrying the holiday in her eye.

INTRODUCTION

In volume 1 on the authorial career of Jack London, I ended the narrative with his return from England. Having completed *The People of the Abyss*, he met with George Brett, head of the Macmillan Publishing Company in the United States, and they began a professional relationship that would last for fourteen years. In the fall of 1902, they were ready to sign a two-year contract with the understanding that they would continue publishing books together on an exclusive basis. This agreement would make London internationally famous. In the present volume, we track London's rise to fame as he writes several works that continue to attract an international audience: *The Call of the Wild*, *The Sea-Wolf*, *White Fang*, *The Iron Heel*, and *The Road*.

The security of a long-term contract for multiple works did not mean that London's relationship to his creative imagination had reached a comfortable level. Consider London's attendance at the Bohemian Club's annual High Jinks among the redwoods of Sonoma County. In the Bohemian Grove, artists had set up an outdoor studio for multiple painters to work on canvases in an atmosphere of bonhomie and collaboration. A 1905 photograph from one of London's personal photograph albums is labeled "Bohemian Club 'High Jinks' Placard."[1] The placard is an approximately waist-high piece of wood or stiff cardboard. An unknown artist painted a white formal shirt with a high collar and large cuffs, one arm raised, the whole shirt floating in the air like something the Invisible Man would wear. The title of the painting is *The White Silence*. We shouldn't be surprised at how London's contemporaries read his work. They knew his Klondike stories—like "The White Silence"—were mostly about ghosts in ghostland. It is only we who have lost touch with this fundamental aspect of his writing.

Besides tracking his fame, this current volume uncovers how London's conception of his ghostly imagination became unmoored from the Northland and moved south. No longer located only in an abyss in the icy white landscape, his imagination found a home in similar locations in seemingly more hospitable habitations: inside an oak tree (*The Iron Heel*) or a green "abyss" in Sonoma County ("Planchette" and "All Gold Canyon"). Despite his international success, despite becoming a household name as both an author and a socialist, London could not come to an easy relationship to his imagination. It would always be a source of conflict. Richard Wilbur, in "Walking to Sleep," tells his reader, "Step off assuredly into the blank of your mind / Something will come to you." For London, "assuredly" was never a given, and blankness was always something to be feared.

One way he dealt with this inner, psychological conflict was to ground his fiction in fact. He often pulled stories from the newspapers and magazines, sometimes taking material from his sources, word for word, without attribution. During this period of his career, he was accused of plagiarism at least three times in the mainstream media. Given London's work habits, I anticipate a particular reaction to the title of this work. "Didn't know he had an imagination," the informed reader might say. "Didn't he say it didn't exist?" London did proffer the nonexistence or unimportance or overrating of the faculty of the imagination. In "Getting into Print," London writes that one must dig in order to write. One cannot sit and wait for inspiration. One must light out after it with a club. It's a powerfully contradictory injunction, coming as it does from the author of *The Call of the Wild*. We remember how often Buck and other dogs are beaten into submission by men with clubs, and if my thesis is true—that London's faculty of the imagination is fictionally represented by various author figures as well as by animals such as the ghost-dog Buck—then we wonder what madness drove London to beat his imagination into submission with his author's club. This madness is not the fear all writers face when they stare at a blank white page. It is something much more horrifying, a recognition of an interior force that will destroy him if it is not tamed with words. This work, then, is an exploration into London's deeply conflicted relationship with his own authorial inner life.

It is not strictly speaking a work of biography, though elements of London's life do creep in. It simply was impossible to ignore new information that I discovered while researching his writerly life; for example, I discovered his early relationship with a woman newspaper reporter that ran concurrently with his relationship with the supposed love of his young adulthood, Mabel Applegarth. Such a relationship, in a study like this, bears directly on the question of London's knowledge of the world of writers and not on his romantic proclivities. Further, it is almost impossible to resist detailing parts of the life of a man who once told his best friend that "I once rode a saddle horse from Fresno to the Yosemite Valley, clad in almost tropical nudity, with a ball room fan and a silk parasol. It was amusing to witness the countryside turn out as I went along. Some of my party who lagged behind, heard guesses hazarded as to whether I was male or female."[2] Sister Unity of Los Angeles's Sisters of Perpetual Indulgence once told me that it is important to bring into the conversation London's possible bisexuality, not only to better understand London but also our own times and how we as a society are grappling with sexual identities. Amy Tucker pointed out to me that this little self-revelation on London's part is congruent with what she calls Jack's living through Charmian's clothing and accouterments. Jack as much as Charmian loved her lacy clothing. Again, this bit of biography impacts our understanding of his authorial career. After their marriage, Jack allowed Charmian into his compositional process. It was a symbiotic professional relationship as well as a satisfyingly personal one. Their reading, which was daily, and for hours, and often out loud, bound them as they shared the same books. Her corrections of his word choices and punctuation appear in every typescript she made; scholars imagine, and I agree, that they discussed at least some of them. He occasionally wrote notes to her in his manuscripts, asking her to contribute sentences to his manuscript that described landscape or women's clothing and other matters as well. It may be fanciful to call Jack London a cross-dresser, but not wholly inappropriate. Clothing plays an important role in London's public persona, a kind of material representation of the ghostly true self that he always denied. Hence, I feature Jack on the cover of this book in his famous white negligee shirt. Hence, the cover photo for the previous volume features him in his getup for documenting life in the East End of London. Clothing not only served as camouflage but also as a material presence for the inner self he was afraid might dry up and disappear, as he once confessed to Charmian.

London's authorial career may be read apart from his life, but it certainly should not be read apart from the sociocultural and political life of his nation. In fact, coincidentally, his career followed a similar trajectory to America's from 1876 to 1916. He moved from a small, stable, parochial beginning to a middle period of expansion and chaos to a stable but transformed and mature identity at the end. In general, he went from submitting material and being accepted by local publications to submitting and being accepted by multiple local and national publications to settling on two national publishers and routinely being translated worldwide.

America, too, moved from a parochial to an international sensibility in a number of decisive ways, which both paralleled and contrasted with London's. In 1916 the United States was more urban. It was no longer looking simply to the East for its identity but had become more and more a part of the newly formed Pacific Rim consciousness. It would definitely be a capitalistic society, not socialistic. Its culture would be formed by multiple medias, not just print. It would be multiracial. Women's rights would increase. Expansionist and militaristic, America would insist on becoming an international power. London fought against the capitalistic, expansionist character of his nation, and in this work we see him at his angriest. He believed, with George Bernard Shaw, that socialism should be the basis of all art. Between 1902 and 1907 he wrote the five major works—*The Call of the Wild, The Sea-Wolf, White Fang, The Iron Heel,* and *The Road*—that effectively represented this belief.

These works are commonly understood as masterworks of American realism and naturalism. Yet not only are the terms *realism* and *naturalism* impossible to disentangle but so are the terms *realism, naturalism,* and *romanticism.* Many have acknowledged the problem, and critical consensus now seems to be that they function well only as period markers. To address this problem I apply two terms from Michael Fried (derived from Denis Diderot)—*absorption* and *theatricality*—to American literature of the time period. Part of my warrant for borrowing terms from a different discipline comes from Tom Gunning's use of the same terms to better understand the impact of early cinema on audiences.

But the more impactful warrant stems from the long history of ut pictura poesis ("as is painting so is poetry"), taken from Horace's "Ars Poetica." Philosophers and critics have linked poetry's and painting's concerns and attributes, and classic studies such as Jean Hagstrum's *The Sister Arts* trace this history. It seems, however, that the field of American literature has been left out of this history, unless photography and film are included. London, however, was very much a part of his time period's discussion of the relationship between painting and fiction writing. Many essays in magazines aimed toward authors carried instructions about how to paint with words, and how words created pictures. In 1893 London's award-winning essay "Story of a Typhoon off the Coast of Japan" was described as "word-painting" that consisted of "little touches of absolute realism."[3]

Robert Louis Stevenson argues that high literary art consists of precision in language and unity of effect. He employs an analogy to painting to make his point: "Nothing would find room in such a picture that did not serve, at once, to complete the composition, to accentuate the scheme of colour, to distinguish the planes of distance, and to strike the note of the selected sentiment; nothing would be allowed in such a story that did not, at the same time, expedite the progress of the fable, build up the characters, and strike home the moral or the philosophical design."[4] Stevenson also argued for a blend of idealism and realism. Here and in the characterization of London's "Story of a Typhoon" we see the advocacy for a synthesis of beauty and realism that many an editor desired. Beauty attracted the reader, and realism assured the reader that what was written was true, a truth based on personal observation. Paintings appear from time to time in London's works and they function as questions about the truth of representation. What is the mode for the most accurate portrayal of life? Painting? Writing? Or some combination of the two?

In general, Michael Fried defines absorption as Denis Diderot's proposed solution to the fundamental problem of pictorial representation: "The fundamental question addressed by him [Diderot] . . . concerned the conditions that had to be fulfilled in order for the art of painting successfully to persuade its audience of the truthfulness of its representations. . . . He concluded that nothing was more abortive of that act of persuasion than when a painter's dramatis personae seemed . . . to evince even a partial consciousness of being beheld, and that the immediate task of the painter was therefore to extinguish or forestall that consciousness by entirely engrossing or . . . *absorbing* his dramatis personae in their actions and states of mind."[5] Representation seeks validation or else its truth claims are unfounded. Subjects who are deeply engrossed in what they are doing best convey those truth claims. When we view a man playing cards, a woman blowing bubbles, we are convinced they are true representations of what the painter saw because the subjects appear completely unaware of us.

Ut pictura poesis. The link to poetry (and, I assume, prose writing) can be illustrated by considering the first of the "cardinal points of poetry" that Coleridge and Wordsworth discussed as they plotted the formation of *Lyrical Ballads*: "the power of exciting the sympathy of the reader by a faithful adherence to the truth of nature." This is a principle of absorption. The second point was "the power of giving the interest of novelty by the modifying colours of imagination."[6] To make the everyday interesting (Wordsworth's task in this dual poetic endeavor) or to make the "supernatural" believable (Coleridge's task) was a common injunction for writers. For an author like London, who was so concerned with the supernatural both as a genre of writing and as an intellectual construction of the identity of the imagination, Coleridge and his great Boswellian intellectual historian Jonathan Livingston Lowes are key figures. But American writers of the turn of the century had two further concerns if they were to hold their readers' attention. The proliferation of magazines, of print culture itself, made the competition for a reader's attention very keen. Add to this competition the element of the speed of modernity. That is, given that people live their lives at breakneck speed, it is crucial to consider how one can catch and hold a reader's attention and then to convey such a profound truth that the reader stops his modern life, puts it on hold, to become absorbed in the story. When a person reads a profound truth in a story, it causes the reader to stop, to reflect, to become absorbed. To become the man on trail.

When Fried begins his study of absorption in the work of Gustave Courbet and how it disrupted the history of art, he begins with Courbet's friend, Charles Baudelaire. Baudelaire turned against Courbet's realism in painting because realism did not allow for the imagination to work. Fried argues that Baudelaire was wrong, and the reason bears directly on our understanding of London: Baudelaire could not understand that Courbet's art "could be both realistic in effect and imaginative or metaphorical in its relation to its materials." Courbet's art, according to Baudelaire, was based on mirroring life, not "projection," which would characterize art as "comparison, metaphor, and allegory."[7] In other words, there are two kinds of imagination, mirroring and projecting, and only the latter produces great art.

Intentionally or not, Fried is drawing on M. H. Abrams's classic study *The Mirror and the Lamp*, and I think this combination of Fried and Abrams is productive for the study of London's work. I hear echoes of this critique in criticisms of London's work as too brutal, too violent, too real. London's response was that he imaginatively selected and reconstructed details from life. He created human documents, not documents. When London criticized Frank Norris and social scientists like William Dall he did so because their epistemological claims to truth rested on as literal a representation of reality as possible. For example, the problem with Dall's critique of London's portrayal of First Nation people, said London, was "that he does not see with a pictorial eye. He merely looks upon a scene and sees every bit of it; but he does not see the true picture in that scene. He does not understand that mine is not realism but is *idealized realism*; that artistically I am an emotional materialist." Note the difference that London draws between seeing and looking. Seeing is an imaginative embrace of the scene before one's eyes. Looking is simply mirroring. London embraced photography, the most realistic of media, but only as he would a newspaper article. It itself was not a work of art, but it aided art's construction. For fiction had to be reliable to truth, but not to facts, or a complete set of facts. So he regarded his own photographs as mere reproductions of what lay in front of him. They were important as the first stage in the creation of art, if he so chose them to be.

Fried's terms *absorption* and *theatricality* help address these aesthetic concerns. I hope that absorption and theatricality may act together as a magnet, its twin yet opposite poles pulling this element to the right, this one to the left, realigning the mess of iron filings that has become our study of turn-of-the-century American literature. Theatricality in painting is posing, a self-conscious presentation of the self. Because the subjects are aware of the beholder, they are afforded the chance to present a public, perhaps even insincere self. Whereas in absorptive paintings, the subject looks just as he or she would look if we were to sneak up on them and stare. We thus see them as they really are. In theatrical painting we see them as they want to be seen, and thus, insincerely.

That is one kind of theatricality. There is another, which is not offensive to absorption. Theatricality is characteristic of London's nonfiction. In effect, London himself turns to face the audience to deliver a message, a message that requires the reader to be not just aware of the world in which he or she lives but engaged in it. It is an aesthetic similar to history painting. Here truth in representation must be argued, it cannot simply be shown. The arguments are staged, marshaled like troops. The link to the theater and plays is obvious, and London's war correspondence from Korea brings theater, history, politics, and theatricality all together.

Absorption is characteristic of London's fiction. It is the antithesis of argument. With his emphasis on conveying feeling and emotions through words, he wants to complete the identification of the reader with his narrative. The reader must forget the world to enter a new one. Absorption encourages the reader to enter something like a dream state, and in this state he or she comes in closest contact with the workings of the imagination and therefore accepts its truthfulness, its truth-effects.

If we imagine a ledger, on one side would be mirror, realism, photography, and theatricality. On the other, projection, analogy, the imagination, painting, writing, and absorption. Fried's argument for Courbet, and mine for London, insists on our respective subjects incorporating techniques and elements from both columns. Theatricality enters into some of London's fiction, and, at times absorptive gestures or elements appear in his nonfiction. Generally speaking, when the theatrical elements appear in short stories they are weakened, though the reverse is not true. As in Fried's definitions, once a reader becomes aware that the subject or narrator is addressing him or her directly in a short story, then the narrative loses its sense of truthfulness. This dynamic is similar to Henry James's use of *telling* and *showing*. London, too, embraced this distinction. Sincerity, one of London's key terms to describe good fiction, cannot be told. It must be shown.

At the same time, London believed in the Shavian declaration that socialism underlies all good art. I work under the assumption that both absorptive and theatrical works can express the truth of socialism. When these overtly socialistic works become didactic or intensely theatrical, they fail. As I examine his work chronologically, by date composed, I show not only how he suffused in subtle and not so subtle ways his absorptive fiction with the theatricality of socialism but also how his oscillation between genres declares how important both modes of writing were to him. Further, by blending the theatrical with the absorptive, he was able to play with genre, sometimes eliminating the boundary between fact and fiction, between essay and short story, between autobiography and drama. I know of no other author who approached authorship in this way. What sort of author was this, then? How did he conceive of authorship? What was his conception of an authorial self? And, finally, what was the relationship between this self and the imagination? These are my principal concerns in *Author Under Sail*.

Thus I became interested in concepts of the self and identity and thought to apply these theories to the idea of an authorial self, of an identity of an author. I turned to the work of Akeel Bilgrami. He posited that a core self is composed of fundamental commitments, not acts. I am who I am because if I were not committed to this one thing I would not be myself. If I applied this concept to an author, I could come up with the constituent parts of his authorial identity. I also looked to Martha Woodmansee and her models of authorship. I wanted to incorporate those models into the general description of London's authorial identity, for I was sure that whatever commitments he made he was undoubtedly duplicating other commitments authors in the past had made. But I thought, too, that there were more models than Woodmansee considered, especially idiosyncratic ones that London may have devised. Another important thread in this volume is tracking how London slowly divested himself from the model of the hobo-author and created the model of the sailor-author.

One of the reasons I believe that the dialectic of absorption and theatricality works as an explanatory model for London's work is that it helps us to understand a natural consequence of London's success as an author. He began life as a proletariat and ended in the upper class, but without disavowing his socialism. Many biographers and critics before me claim that this cannot happen, that he, like his friend Jim Whitaker and others, discarded or silenced their political beliefs as they became more successful as artists. Austin Lewis may have been the first to promulgate this thesis. In his unpublished memoir, he writes, "To be a socialist writer is one thing. It is something which implies a life of struggle and that the world calls martyrdom." That is, "a socialist writer" cannot make a living wage because there simply is no market for political science, philosophy, or sociology. "To be a professional writer," continues Lewis, "selling one's work for the market and consumed with a notion that success lies in gaining a high price for one's wares is quite another. To try and combine the two produces an utterly impossible position."

Actually, it doesn't. If Lewis had been privy to the various minutia of authorship that I deal with in this volume—the tracking of every sale, of nearly every rejection, of nearly every daily choice London made to write what he did—he might have seen how London—at times not so successfully—balanced his theatrical writings with his absorptive. It would never have occurred to Lewis that London's imagination governed all his writings, that the same impulse and necessity to write accounted for *The Call of the Wild* as well as "Revolution," for *The Road* as "Getting into Print." Of course London was a stronger writer than a thinker, but that issue is beside the point. The question is, What sort of writer was he? Lewis, on the other hand puts the question differently: What sort of socialist was he? Perhaps there is a way to understand the two questions as the same.

The goal of London's absorptive writing is to create a state of mind in the reader that is similar to that state of mind of the author when he creates from this first source of the imagination. Let us travel, London says, hand in hand through the land of the shadows, of ghosts, of the imagination. But it is also a coercive attempt, in a way. It became almost a cliché among editors and reviewers to challenge London on the truthfulness of his fiction, of its adherence to reality. London, feeling the distrust of the reader, puts him in the position of the author so that he sees what London sees and so dispels the initial distrust of reading about ghost-dogs and ghost-men. But while one is absorbed, paralyzed, one cannot act politically, and so the goal of London's theatrical writing, in contrast, is to bring the reader out of the dream state and into the political realm.

The theatrical writings also serve a personal interest of his, and this volume uncovers how dedicated, especially between 1904 and 1906, London was to the literal theater. They function as a rest from the dilemma of the imagination's source. Theatricality, for London, is a postponement of the problem of the origin of writing, for one locates the origin of theatrical writing in the writings of others, not in oneself. For the source and nature of the imagination is a mystery. It is unexplainable by science. To him, it was on par with hauntedness, ghosts, automatic writing, mesmerism, dreams, and the unconscious. It was also a violent being—wild, primitive, uncontrollable. It had a mind of its own. It had to be beaten with a club. The disciplining of the imagination yielded a disciplined form of writing, not fanciful and airy, but grounded. The incorporation of theatrical elements in his fiction—of footnotes, of documentation, of newspapers as sources for story plots—is an attempt to tame the imagination, to domesticate it. We see this most apparently in his speculative fiction, like *The Iron Heel*. And yet he is never not struggling with that force that drives him to write. Theatrical writing thus provides a relief from a near-daily battle with a metaphysical entity that his brass-tacks philosophy sought to deny. It protects him from the ghostly imagination.

Understanding the nature of his imagination was London's principal task as an author. Given its metaphysical nature, he wavered between asserting it didn't exist and picturing it as a ghost, and authors who were inhabited by the ghostly imagination became ghosts themselves. The presence of ghosts in his work is staggering; it's as if he couldn't help himself. Even when there is no call for it, a ghost will appear. I'm thinking of a scene in

Martin Eden. Eden has decided to drink away his day off from the laundry. He buys rounds for everyone in the bar, including "the furtive hobo who slid in like a shadow and like a shadow hovered at the end of the bar." The hobo as figure for an author is a classic portrayal in both London's fiction and in contemporaneous critiques of his work. The ghostly hobo-author figure appears when Eden, who hasn't written a word in weeks, drinks and "his dreams came back to him. . . . His mirror of vision was silver-clear" [123].

Alone in ghostland, London sought to form a bond with his readers. The reader becomes ghostly, inhabited by the ghost of the author, who in turn had become ghostly, inhabited by the ghost of his imagination. Thus a spiritual as well as material bond is formed between reader and author. But their similarity is not boundless, and, in fact, two crucial distinctions separate them, which makes the plight of a tormented author like London even worse. First, the reader, solitary in his or her room, retains the knowledge that he or she is not alone, that there might be millions reading the same book at the same time. People desire a bestseller in part because they aren't then reading alone. And, unlike the author, the reader leaves the ghost behind. The reader can wake up from the book. The day dawns, the body warms up, the blanket is cast aside, and the reader's own interior voice resumes speaking. The author's voice meekly retreats. But for the haunted London there is no such relief. His interior voice is the ghost. He writes to join a community of readers, but as soon as his book is put down he is alone again. He can never escape the ghost inside his head. *Author Under Sail*, then, is all about the tragedy of London's existence as an author.

AUTHOR UNDER SAIL

HOWL, O HEAV'NLY MUSE!

"I believe, now, that the first period of my career has been
completed, and that I am about to enter a second period."
—Jack London to George Brett, 21 November 1902

THE END OF THE FAMILY DRAMA

On 13 November 1902, Jack London returned to Piedmont, California, his bohemian home. He had spent two and a half months away in Europe, having completed *The People of the Abyss*. He also had taken a vacation on the Continent, slept with a woman either in London or on the Continent who gave him gonorrhea, which he then gave to his wife, Bessie London, when he returned.[1] As an author, he set sail almost immediately. On 17 November 1902, less than a week after his return to California, in the middle of an early winter rainstorm, London stood with hundreds to watch William Randolph Hearst's mother, Phoebe A. Hearst, dedicate a new campus building at the University of California. He wrote "Simple Impressive Rite at Corner-Stone Emplacement of Hearst Memorial Mining Building" for Hearst's *San Francisco Examiner*. His very next work, begun a few weeks later, was *The Call of the Wild*.[2]

The newspaper article may be somewhat of a surprise when juxtaposed with his most famous novel; one might think he didn't need to write for newspapers at this point in his career. But he had multiple authorial needs. He took the assignment because he wanted to reestablish himself immediately with the newspaper publisher and because he had a lifelong fascination with mining and other ways of working the earth. For example, in 1905, when discussing a new contract with George Brett, president of Macmillan Company and by 1903 London's inseparable business partner, he likened the publication of a cheap edition of *The Sea-Wolf* to mining: "I imagine, if successful, it should pay as a large body of low-grade ore pays the modern mining engineer."[3] His farming career later in life can be seen on a continuum with his brief stint as a Yukon gold miner.

[1

Initially, the newspaper paid him $16.70; he asked for more and received another $13.30. This same mining building becomes the site for the murder of Professor Haskell by Darrell Standing, the central character of *The Star Rover*. With that novel, it's as if London is announcing his turn—begun a number of years previous—from valorizing mining to agriculture.

We don't know exactly how London got these assignments from the *Examiner*, a question that will come up periodically, especially in regard to his job as foreign-war reporter in 1904. In July 1903, however, he gives us a clue; he writes to Joaquin Miller to praise his newest volume of poetry, *As It Was in the Beginning*, and tells him that "I am writing the *Examiner* for the privilege of reviewing it."[4] He never published the review, but his letter indicates that for these newspaper assignments he was the instigating agent. In 1907 he outlined his process for writing book reviews to Arthur Brisbane, saying that "for some time it had been my custom, when I ran across a book I wanted to review, to drop a line to Mr. [Jack] Barrett asking him whether or not he wanted the review."[5] Barrett, the news editor, was his principal contact at the paper.

London had a long memory, and while he wrote his mining-building article, he remembered that Edwin Clough, aka Yorick, his fierce critic who was syndicated in the rival *San Francisco Evening Post*, had criticized his use of certain words (like *primordial*) and phrases in his newspaper writing. So he hoped that Yorick was reading when he wrote, "If there be anything in Mr. John Galen Howard's idea that the expression of mining in architecture should be essentially elementary and primordial (and there certainly is)," London reasoned, then it's natural that the stormy weather should accompany the dedication. The dedication of the university building triggered thoughts of nationalism and pride in the West. "This College of Mines and the Greater University which it heralds is the triumph of a young and vigorous people. It is the advertisement that they are keeping abreast of the times." London had told an editor friend a few days previous that "I am all in a whirl since my return home. . . . I feel so good, and love America and things American so much."[6] But in this brief newspaper article London—both a patriot and a socialist, a lover of the land (not the homeland) and a strident and tireless critic of American social inequality—sees more widely than nationalism: "With the world become a workshop, the Greater University will train men for that workshop. Dead tongues may be well enough to mumble, but they lead to death. The language of life to-day is the language of cogs and wheels and pistons, of steam and electricity."[7] London celebrates the mining building because it expresses what he—and others—called the Machine Age. Here in architecture he finds a mirror of his own prose (a link he would explore again in his 1906 essay "The House Beautiful"). He then went home and began *The Call of the Wild*.

But before he started writing his second novel (I am not including *The Kempton-Wace Letters* in this count because it was coauthored, or *The Cruise of* The Dazzler, because it was not written as a novel, only enlarged as one), he wrote to Brett on 21 November 1902 about his plans for the next period of his career. They might be summed up in one of his Machine Age declarative sentences: "I want to get away from the Klondike." How ironic! He never stopped writing Klondike stories, and *The Call of the Wild* was a popular and sustained success.[8] But there is another irony. London, having conflated in his mind the Klondike with the act of writing short stories, was telling Brett not that he never wanted to write about the Klondike again, but that he wanted to write novels.

Brett would have been very pleased to hear this; short-story collections never had been best sellers.[9] George Platt Brett was the son of George Edward Brett, who had built the American branch of Macmillan Company. When the elder Brett died in in 1890 at sixty-one, his son took over and transformed a $50,000-a-year business into a $9-million-a-year business. He did it largely by combining high modernists—Joseph Conrad, William Butler Yeats—and more middle-brow, popular authors such as Owen Wister, Maurice Hewlett, and Winston Churchill; Churchill's *Richard Carvel* (1899) sold 500,000 copies in its first printing. (In contrast, *The Call of the Wild* sold 8,500 copies in its first printing.)[10] But Brett also favored textbooks and eventually expanded the educational department of Macmillan. He published standard American histories and reference books in sociology, psychology, and medicine. He also championed progressive causes, and though he was not as radical as London—few people in business would be—he nonetheless was at least agnostic about London's politics. He saw their value, and more than just their monetary value. However, it is difficult to pin down exactly what his political beliefs were; he certainly does not let on in the massive, fourteen-year correspondence he carried on almost monthly with London. He only betrays enough sympathy to the cause to keep his bond with London intact. One of Macmillan's directors called him an "'autocrat' whose influence was felt everywhere through the [Macmillan] building."

Some in the Macmillan family in England thought him "'a martinet, 'non-cooperative,' 'unreasonable,' who 'never bothered to give the reason for his actions.'" Most likely, "he was essentially a shy man, rather austere (a 'lone wolf')." Having lived in the West on a ranch, he was no stranger to London's western ways.[11] Though they were not his ways, he was tolerant of them. He wanted London to be just who he was—except a progressively better seller.

London recognized professionalism and high competency and was proud—thrilled—to be a part of Brett's sphere. In his November 1902 letter, turning from what he had just accomplished to what he would write in the future, he wanted to impress his new partner, and he wanted to make him proud. One way was to show off both his range and his productivity as an author. He was acutely aware of being labeled by the press as a Klondike writer. So in his letter to Brett he quickly discounted *A Daughter of the Snows* by lumping it together, in a way, with all the Klondike stories he had written so far. He had served his "apprenticeship at writing in that field, and I feel that I am better fitted now to attempt a larger and more generally interesting field." Though the Northland now seemed less interesting, he did not believe that he had exhausted the Northland as a subject. He was not saying that he was ready to move on to other, more "mature" locales. For London this momentous change in authorial direction that he was proposing to Brett did not concern locale. It concerned genre. He was ready to write longer, sustained fiction. He had more and broader tales to tell: "I have half a dozen books, fiction all, which I want to write. They are not collections of short stories, but novels. I believe I can turn out a novel now."[12] The Klondike had become synonymous with short-story writing—especially after dismissing *A Daughter of the Snows*—and why shouldn't it have? After all, by April 1904 he had published four collections of Klondike stories in four years.

Still, this profession that he was ready to abandon the Klondike in order to write a novel is truly ironic because in two weeks he would begin writing his second novel of the Northland, *The Call of the Wild*. But what is more fascinating than the irony is the silence he maintained about his new novel in the next several months. He began *The Call of the Wild* on 1 December 1902 and completed it on 26 January 1903.[13] During that time he wrote at least three letters about his future to Brett and one on the day after he finished *The Call of the Wild*. In none of these letters did he explicitly mention it at all, even though he consumes considerable letter space detailing future novels to his new publisher. Brett even came west and visited London at home in the first week of the New Year; it was only their second meeting face-to-face. The only business they discussed was *The People of the Abyss* and *The Kempton-Wace Letters*. When he finally told Brett about *The Call of the Wild*, in February, he says, "Remember you found me at work on a story when you visited me[?]" (We can almost hear London interjecting at this point. Surprise! I actually wrote a novel!) "It is large enough to make a book."[14]

His silence is partly due to his contractual relationship with Brett. First, when London pitched his need for a contract in November, his insistence that he was ready to write longer fiction was preparation, a kind of running start that he took before he actually began the novel. "I have done a great deal of studying and a great deal of thinking in the last two years [about writing novels], and I am confident that I can to-day write something worth while."[15] But he needed the financial stability and freedom necessary to write long fiction, fiction that would not materialize into payment almost immediately upon completion, as short stories did, but only after a year or so. So, as he had done with McClure and Phillips when he wanted to write *A Daughter of the Snows*, he approached a publisher about receiving advances in the form of monthly payments. "Now here comes the rub," he wrote to Brett. "I have no income save what my pen brings me in the magazine and newspaper field." (Note that *field* is not plural; here he is thinking of both yellow journalism and yellow magazinism). "The returns from a book, from the moment of beginning the first chapter, do not arrive for a year or two, but the tradesmen's bills arrive the first of each month." Then, in typical Londonian fashion, he attempts to convince his publisher by presenting a half-truthful, half-fictional autobiography. I've always worked hard, he tells Brett, ever since the age of ten. True. "When I first began to write I had no art-concepts whatever." True, if he is referring to 1893–94. "When I returned from the Klondike I began to write." Sort of true, sort of false; he is of course leaving out the first five years he was writing and sending out material to be published and talking with newspaper and magazine editors in the Bay Area and while he was on the road in Boston. This account may be labeled the no-mentor-but-myself account, boilerplate poor-mouthing that presents himself as deserving help in the publishing world, not because he has published five books and written one other, but because he imagines himself having taught himself how to write without help from the outside world and would now appreciate a little acknowledgment, say in the form of $150 a month for the next year, so that he could write a new novel.

His request becomes confusing when he next informs Brett that he has a collection of short stories he wants to finish—Klondike short stories. His magazine editors loved his short stories, when they fit with their conception of what their audiences liked, and London clearly enjoyed writing them. He took great pleasure in his skill, which at this point was considerable. Still, this pleasure does not motivate his telling Brett that by December 1903 he will send him two novels and "two other books" because, after all, he had just told Brett that he wants to temporarily stop writing short stories. Yet these "two other books" are indeed collections of short stories. One book is *Tales of the Fish Patrol*, which was four stories away from completion; he would finish it in one month of concerted effort, February 1903, as soon as he had finished *The Call of the Wild*. But the other book's genre as well as locale may strike us as baffling. After spending five paragraphs in his letter explaining to Brett that he wanted to take a break from writing short stories and about the Klondike, London then tells him that "one book is a collection of Klondike stories, similar to the ones I have already brought out." True, as he tells Brett, he has completed thirty-three thousand words of the collection (this would turn out to be *The Faith of Men, and Other Stories*), and he estimates that he needs to complete but seventeen thousand words more. But Brett couldn't help but be puzzled. Why would this young man say that he was going to "get away from the Klondike" but first complete three to four more short stories "similar to the ones" he has written, a process that could take several months? Why delay? Just to complete yet another collection that wouldn't sell well? Why not leave them uncollected? Did he really want to write a novel? We will see that it indicates London's anxiety about writing a successful novel.

London's letter is also an attempt to overwhelm Brett with the number of projects he has in mind, as if his proficiency in writing would help justify earning a contract. But as London would learn soon enough, that was the wrong tack to take. Brett would later tell him that he should write less, not more, that he was giving him a contract based on the promise of quality, not quantity. London thought it was about making a trade. If he gave Brett six books (*The Kempton-Wace Letters*, *The People of the Abyss*, two new novels, and two collections of short stories), and Brett gave him a monthly income of $150 a month for a year, then general happiness would ensue.

"Against your $1800 I will balance six books. Granting an average earning power of $300 to each book, the six books will equal the $1800."[16] Brett, however, wanted to persuade London that their relationship was not, from his end, based on economic fair trade. In his response to this letter, he told London that he would prefer to extend the length of the contract from one year to two because "I do not think that the two novels ought to be written in so short a time as one year; and, moreover, if you get these two novels ready during this time, i.e., during the two years, it will still leave six books bearing your name to be published between now and the first of December 1904, and this is more, in my opinion, than you ought to publish in justice to yourself." Brett's idea of London's potential, of the "justice" he owed himself, was nothing short of grand. "There is no real place in the permanent world of literature for anything but the very best that a man can do and as you know my belief is that you have the power to do the best work. I need only urge upon you the necessity of doing nothing, at any rate for the next two years, but what will represent the very best that is in you to do."[17] It's an injunction guaranteed to generate anxiety.

Brett's phrase "permanent world of literature" is synonymous with our term *canon*. Brett's ideas about the new American canon can be found in an essay he wrote for his friend Hamilton Wright Mabie called "A Publisher's View." He concludes by noting the increase in education, taste, and tolerance for difficult work in the United States that "presages . . . our growth toward a National literature, a literature more truly American than much that has gone before." Because Americans do not read "a literature of pessimism and decadence," the country will soon achieve a high "place . . . in literature and in art."[18] Brett saw London's work as distinctly American and part of the engine that would drive American literature to the highest place in world literature. London quickly took Brett's objectives to heart, and, emboldened by Brett's faith in his abilities, he would aim for such heights in the next few months with *The Sea-Wolf.*

He may have wanted to meet Brett's expectations with *The Call of the Wild*, but something kept him from being honest about his intentions. Because he was secretive and deceitful with Brett, it is somewhat difficult to re-create his writerly progress with his new novel. He begins *The Call of the Wild* on 1 December. *Call*, by London's count, is 32,168 words long, so he was averaging 670 words a day, taking into account the week between the first of December and 26 January that he says he lost to an accident that put him in bed, probably with a swollen foot, injured when he dropped a heavy box on it; most likely, he wasn't writing between 20 December and 1 January. This average of 670 words a day jibes with what he told Brett in his 21 November letter: "My hope," he wrote, after he outlined his fair-trade agreement of six books for $1,800 in advances, "once I am on my feet [financially], is not to write prolifically, but to turn out one book, and a good book, a year. Even as it is, I am not a prolific writer. I write very slowly."[19] He used almost exactly the same language in a letter a few weeks later to his English publisher, H. Perry Robinson. He said that he was lucky to complete four thousand words a week, "working hard all week." "I am not a fast writer," he tells Robinson.[20]

There is a slight defensive valence to these statements that render them fictional. He was sensitive to charges in the past that he had hurried through his writing, that he had overproduced. That is why in part he responded so positively to Brett's insistence on slowing down, on extending the contract. With Robinson, because London had been telling him that Isbister and Company needs to get out all his books—they were new in their relationship of American author and British publisher—and since he had a number of volumes completed, he was slightly nervous about Robinson's reaction to the amount of London material he would be publishing in a short period of time. He wanted to reassure Robinson that this would be an exceptional period: "Once you have caught up," he tells Robinson, "there will be no difficulty to stay caught up." He would work more slowly in the future.[21] Yet in September of the next year, 1904, he completed *The Game* in approximately ten days. It is nearly half the length of *The Call of the Wild*, but it took him a fifth of the time to write it.

London told a fictitious story about the writing of *The Call of the Wild* twice, once to Brett and then, several days later, to Anna Strunsky Walling. To Brett, he wrote, "The whole history of this story has been very rapid." It's as if he is apologizing for something, something that in fact Brett, or for that matter Strunsky, would have a difficult time seeing as wrong. "On my return from England I sat down to write it [*Call*] into a 4000 word yarn, but it got away from me & I was forced to expand it to its present length."[22] To Anna, he wrote three days later, "I started it as a companion to my other dog story 'Batard,' which you may remember; but it got away from me, & Instead of 4000 words it ran 32000 before I could call I [*sic*] halt."[23] As a side note, it may be a coincidence that he used the same number—four thousand—to

Brett and Strunsky to describe the length of the story and to Robinson to define how much he was able to write in a week, but it does seem likely that it serves as a kind of fictional replacement—not exactly a lie—for the truth. I believe the technical philosophical term is *bullshit*, an artful deception short of lying.[24] Or we might describe it as a kind of creation myth. Either way, the bullshit story functioned for him in the same way as his silences about the novel. Just on the basis of word counts, we can see that this story is untrue.

He seemed to have had only dog names in mind when he started; no notes survive.[25] By the third day, after two thousand words, he intentionally had not gotten to the turn, that moment in the action of a short story that takes the reader directly to the end of the story. And this third day was crucial, for on 3 December he received a telegraph from Brett saying that he wanted to sign London to a two-year contract, and on that same day Brett sent him the letter encouraging him to aim for a "permanent place" in American literature. By 6 December he had reached the four-thousand-word mark, approximately the end of chapter 1. Nothing in the first chapter indicates a shift in genre. From the very first, he knew he was not writing a short story.

If we look for a moment at the length of London's short stories, we can get a better idea of his composition process for short stories. Up to this point in his career, by far the longest story is "An Odyssey of the North," written originally in 12,500 words; when the *Atlantic Monthly* asked him to cut it by 3,000, not only did he (almost) comply (it came in around 10,000), he decided not to write such long stories. His next longest is "Wit of Porportuk" at 9,728 words, and "Finis" is 9,465, but there are no others above 9,000. There are a number of stories in the 8,000-word range, like "Love of Life" and "The Sun-Dog Trail." Both are in the collection entitled *Love of Life*, where the average length of story is 6,215 words. The average for *Moon-Face* is similar. *Children of the Frost*'s average is much lower—4,700 words—and his second collection, *The God of His Fathers*, as originally conceived, averages exactly the same, 4,700. And London's original table of contents for *The Faith of Men*, which he was writing on either side of *Call*, so to speak, is slightly higher than *Love of Life*: 6,356. So by the time that London's talent for writing short stories matured with experience, his stories ran on average around 5,500 words. Thus, again, by the first week of December in 1902 he knew he was writing something more than a short story and that he was probably testing himself against Brett's expectations.

He may also have been reticent with Brett because he was so unfamiliar with the process of writing a novel. Just as he couldn't tell Brett what exactly he was writing, so he didn't really know himself. Again, we have to remember that *The Call of the Wild* wasn't simply his second Northland novel. It was only the second novel he had ever attempted, and, given that his first was a disaster of sorts, he was in fact starting over; he had told Brett in the 21 November letter that he was starting over "on the publishing side," but he was also starting over as a novelist. In other words, he had only a vague idea about what form he was writing in and how to do it. He was caught in between. He had told Brett that he was going to write short stories for the unfinished collections and a novel that would be something called *The Flight of the Duchess*.[26] He turned away from those ideas and deliberately undertook the writing of *The Call of the Wild*. He hoped that the novel was the story's true form. But he was too inexperienced to have much confidence. Partly to protect this writing process, he publicly turned it into something that it was not.

So not only did he tell Brett (and Strunsky) that he had started out writing a short story (that is to say, not-a-novel), but he also told Brett—much earlier, and twice in the same letter, on 11 December—that he was working on a short story when he was in fact writing *The Call of the Wild*. Having signed the new contract, he mailed it back to Brett with a progress report on the work he had promised to get done by the end of 1903: "*Collection of Klondike Stories*—I have already brought the 33000 words written up to 43000 words." And then for his conclusion to the letter, he wrote, "I have several thousand words to do to finish this Klondike short story I am now at work upon. Then I shall put my undivided thought upon *The Flight of the Duchess* and other motifs for novels till I have made my choice."[27] Actually, by 11 December, he would be 7,300 words along on *Call*; London wasn't above rounding up. And it is simply impossible to imagine that he was intending to write another ten-thousand-word short story like "An Odyssey of the North." It is only slightly less imaginable to think that he would lie to his publisher about the genre in which he was writing, especially as he was telling him that once he finished the "short story" he would devote his time to plotting out his new novel.

But dissemble he did, though I do not think he was trying to trick Brett or cover up an activity that Brett would have found objectionable. In fact, after his 11 December letter about writing a short story, he simply stops telling Brett anything about his current work. By 30 December, when he tells Brett that he hears Brett will be coming west, he has almost twenty thousand words done. He then sustains an injury, which consigned him to bed for at least a week. However, a little over three weeks later, on 26 January, he had completed his novel.

When Brett visited him at the Piedmont bungalow, he almost let the dog off the chain. London wanted to tell him about the new novel, but, again, he kept quiet, another silence instead of the little white lie that he was working on a short story, not a novel. "I was working on it when you came to see me in January," he wrote to Brett when he finally told him the truth. "At the time I had made up my mind to let you carry the uncompleted duplicate away with you; but somehow the conversation did not lead up to it & I became diffident."[28] He could not bring himself to tell either Brett or Strunsky that his confidence in his own ability to write a novel was so low that he had lied or kept silent about it. He was not as confident as Brett (or probably as Strunsky) that he was so great a writer that he would always be included in the canon. Now that the novel was done, it was too late to tell the truth, and thus the creation myth and insistence on being "diffident."

But his diffidence was also motivated by a professional concern, his contractual status with Brett. When he tells Brett about *Call* after he had finished it, he also says, "This story I had begun . . . before my contract with you was signed."[29] First, this means that London wrote his novel on spec, just as he had with *The Kempton-Wace Letters*. He undertook it without the least concern for its earning power. One might even call it a private affair, something between the author and his resident ghostly imagination. Small wonder, then, as we shall see, that the novel can be read as a narrative about just such a private interior conversation.

Second, London wanted to make sure that Brett understood that he was under no contractual obligation to Brett for a story written before their written agreement took effect. In business terms, it seems almost petty for London to make this point, especially since he then gives with one hand what the other hand seems to withhold: "and of course I shall want you to bring it out some day if it should prove available," those final words being almost sarcastic in tone; how many editors for the last ten years had told him that his stories had proved "unavailable," a euphemism for flat-out rejected. He tells Brett that the *Saturday Evening Post* had just accepted the story for serialization and that he expected to receive enough money to pay off debts and go on a trip through the South Seas. So he must have felt confident in the story's value. His bragging rights to the story's acceptance by the *Post* contains a hint of aggressive defensiveness. No amount of cheerleading from his new American publisher could diffuse this defensive posture. Years of rejection made guaranteed acceptance of anything by anybody a mere fantasy, and this would continue to be true until the end of his career. To counterbalance the vagaries of publishing, even when it came to Brett and the new contract, as almost an act of revenge for his past treatment by tens and tens of editors—a motivation that would last long enough in the year to prompt him in part to write a new series of essays on writing—and as an act to defend himself, he remained circumspect until the last moment. Surprise! he in effect says to Brett. I have what looks like a very successful new novel! "It is an animal story, utterly different in subject & treatment from the rest of the animal stories which have been so successful."[30] A mere three weeks previous, London had told Brett, "Concerning the first novel I write, I have made up my mind that it shall be a sea story."[31] And even though, at that moment, 20 January 1903, he was one week away from completing *Call*, he still could not tell Brett the true nature of things until the last possible moment. Out of a complex of revenge, defensiveness, pride, and a willingness to please his new publisher—coupled with the insecurities generated by attempting to write a better novel than *A Daughter of the Snows*, a new novel so superior that it would earn him "a permanent place" in American literature—London pitches his new story to Brett. The irony is of course that Brett, so confident in his young new author, was happy to publish whatever London wrote, though London, at this early stage either could not or would not believe it. Brett must have felt that he still had a ways to go before he could domesticate this wild, new, western author of his.

London told Strunsky that *The Call of the Wild* began as a "companion" to "Bâtard," which would be true if it were a short story; so it was true for London to call *White Fang* a "companion" to *The Call of the Wild*.[32] *The Call of the Wild*'s relationship to "Bâtard" or to any previously written short story is tenuous at best, even if we ignore the evidence of the word count. It isn't a portrait of an angelic mongrel-human relationship in counterpoint to that between Bâtard and Black Leclère. It is a portrait of the adult life of Buck, whose human ownership seems incidental when compared to that of Bâtard's. In terms of genre, there is no compression in the scales of time and space in the first several paragraphs, as the form of a short story would dictate. Instead, it is a leisurely beginning, filled with details about Buck's life on the Santa Clara Valley ranch. The first chapter only takes us as far as the docking of the *Narwhal* off Dyea Beach, and we are already three thousand words into the story. The moment of congruity with "Bâtard" comes rather late, thirty-one paragraphs into the story. That is, this supposed short-story companion begins long before "Bâtard" begins. Bâtard was a "devil" from the very first sentence, though London says that "with a proper master Bâtard might have made an ordinary, fairly efficient sled-dog. He never got the chance."[33] Here's the possible prompt from the earlier story for the plot of *The Call of the Wild*. Let's take a devil-dog and make him into a decent, domesticated dog. But London doesn't start where "Bâtard" starts, something he would have done if he had intended to write a "companion" short story. He starts with Buck as a law-abiding, family animal who is turned into a "a red-eyed devil," as London plays it out in *Call*. And as he adjusts to his harsher existence, Buck doesn't become what "Bâtard" never had a chance to become. London realized that it was too late, too unrealistic, for that kind of transformation to occur.

Buck, instead, "remembered back to the youth of the breed, to the time the wild dogs ranged in packs through the primeval forest. . . . The ancient song surged through him and he came into his own again." Here, at the end of chapter 2, the story circles back to its beginning: "He came into his own again . . . because men had found a yellow metal in the North, and because Manuel was a gardener's helper whose wages did not lap over the needs of his wife and divers small copies of himself." But, rather than a circle, a fully coherent, compressed story, *Call*, as London must have known from the very beginning, begins as a novelistic spiral, looping back toward itself, through that repetition of the phrase "men had found a yellow metal" (which appears in the second sentence of the entire novel), and then carries us forward and outward and beyond. In terms of structure, this is what London meant when he said the story got away from him. Unfamiliar with the actual writing of a novel, he got to a point that was familiar—for it seemed like the end of a short story—but then had to trust his writerly instincts to continue forward into the unknown space of the novelistic form that he had set up from the beginning.

What is so strikingly different between London's first and second novels—between *Daughter of the Snows* and *The Call of the Wild*—is their form. The first is radically and unintentionally fragmented, disjointed, and amateurish. The second is beautifully unified in an Aristotelian sense. There is one action or arc—the gradual wilding of Buck—and very little in terms of subplot to distract us from that action. We may recall what London told his friend Charles Warren Stoddard about why he liked "The Son of the Wolf": it had "unity and sustained effort."[34] London took the singleness of purpose that characterizes a good short story and applied it to the novel form. If nothing else, he achieved in *The Call of the Wild* a purity of form that he had failed to achieve in his first novel.

Another striking feature of the novel is its apparent lack of printed source material. Not all his stories, of course, began with an idea culled from the daily press. But many did. In 1907, when he justified an apparent act of plagiarism in *The Call of the Wild*, he insisted on the centrality of his combination of prose reading and fiction writing: "Fiction-writers have always considered actual experiences of life to be a lawful field of exploitation—in fact, every historical novel is an sample of fictional exploitation of published narratives of fact."[35] London drew on Egerton R. Young's *My Dogs in the Northland*, but what he garnered from Young was "merely 'available data in a technical field,'" which "had little effect on plot, less on theme, and none at all on overtones and allegory."[36] As far as can be told, no book, pamphlet, or clipping survives that would show London's sources for the novel.[37]

Perhaps this absence of printed source material is conveyed in the novel's first sentence: "Buck did not read the newspapers." And the significance of this sentence grows with repetition. London repeats it five paragraphs later, probably on the second day of composition. For the reader of *The Call of the Wild* in 1903, Buck, at least according to the novel's first sentence, would be a man who read short stories and novels, not newspapers. And as a reader of novels, he did not heed the call of the newsboy: "Extra, extra!" He followed the more exalted call of the wild, that which tended toward the eternal (not the daily disposable), the "primitive" (not the "fugitive"), which is where the first chapter's title points: "Into the Primitive."

If he had read the newspapers, Buck would not have missed the "key" to his own story, the first quatrain of John O'Hara's "Atavism," the epigraph to

The Call of the Wild. In London's first letter to O'Hara, he wrote, "I ran across those lines . . . in a detached fragment . . . . Of all the poetry I know, there were no four lines . . . as appropriate for the key to *The Call of the Wild*": "Old longings nomadic leap, / Chafing at custom's chain; / Again from its brumal sleep / Wakens the ferine strain." Later, London wrote that he had "found your lines in the sea of fugitive newspaper verse."[38] Buck may not have read newspapers and their ephemeral verse and prose, but, by implication, he read short stories and novels. Or, perhaps, the emphasis should fall, not on *newspapers*, but on *read*. He doesn't read the newspapers, he just . . . what? *Writes* for the newspapers? Writes novels? Poetry? Short stories? *Inspires* novels? Poetry? Short stories? It must be the latter. After all, if he wrote for newspapers or wrote novels and stories he would certainly read them as well. So we have someone who has left the quotidian for the permanent. And we have someone who is deeply involved in the written word. Either he read it, wrote it, or inspired it, or some combination of the three. London would not have specified what Buck did not read if Buck were disinclined to read and write in a serious way.

And, moving more deeply into the sentence, we see that when London says Buck does not read newspapers, that effectively eliminates him as an author in the way that London understood authorship. Buck could not be a writer because he was not out there, amid the daily lives of peoples, reading about their problems and the ethical choices they were forced to make even in the most mundane of lives.

Oh, but wait. Buck is a dog. He doesn't read or write anything at all.

This species confusion throws us deeper into questions of authorship and, especially, of audience than if we were just concerned with similarities between newspapers and novels. We have to return to the history of the novel's composition and the question that that history begged to be raised. That is, if we accept the proposition that London was not as confident as Brett and Strunsky in his literary abilities, then why wasn't he? What was the source of his insecurity? I would argue that it is the very nature of his imagination that kept him off balance in his professional relationships.[39] That is, because he conceived of his imagination as a ghost, a haunting presence that was both benign and destructive, both tame and savage, he had no choice but to wonder what he could possibly achieve with such a capricious force inside him.

At this mention of London's ghostly imagination, it is well to remember a letter he wrote to Strunsky back in 1901. He was grasping at the ways he and Anna, so very different, were actually the same. His ulterior motive was to sleep with her—natch!—but something inchoately philosophical was at work as well: "The one gleam of sanity through it all is that we are both large temperamentally, large enough to often understand. True, we often understand but in vague glimmering ways, by dim perceptions, like ghosts, which, while we doubt, haunt us with their truths."[40] What a marvelous statement! The word *ghosts* works in two ways. First, we would not be amiss in thinking that *ghosts* refers to us. We are ghosts who "understand in vague glimmering ways." As we sort out how London knows how ghosts think, we finish the sentence and realize that, no, *ghosts* refers to *perceptions*. Perceptions are like ghosts that "haunt us with their truths." Finally, we step back and see the sentence as a whole. *Ghosts* refers to both *us* and *perceptions*. We are ghosts in ghostland, and we are humans with the ghosts of perceptions inside us, perpetually haunting us. He is linking writing, the imagination, ghosts, emotions, and the early twentieth-century psychological understanding of emotions, memory, and the structure of the mind. We see how London could come to the conclusion that ghostly perceptions and the ghostly imagination could be one and the same. The faculty of the mind that perceives and the faculty of the mind that imagines are one and the same.

Buck, as all critics point out, becomes undomesticated. But what exactly does this mean, apart from the obvious biological and evolutionary themes present in the novel? He is detached from the routine of daily life that the newspaper both instantiates and symbolizes. Not only has he escaped from the quotidian life that newspapers document, he has escaped the economics of daily life as well. Buck is an escapee from economics. That's what truly marks the unconscious, the muse, the imagination. It lives in a world without economics. And that is Buck's trajectory, from work to no work. He goes from bourgeois ranch overseer (a "king," the narrator calls him, twice), to a work beast (like those in the abyss) with a flash of divinity, to a no-work beast composed of all divinity, wild in nature. Without the call of the newsboy in his ears, he can hear this other call, a call that he hears and then gives to others (like the author London) to voice.

Buck is not only the subject of the novel but also its object. London told an early reader of the novel, his wife's niece, that Buck "could sing only the *song* of the wild, not the *call* of the wild. There is a distinction. The song of the wild was the call to him, but he could not very well sing his own call."[41] No, but he would become it. London means to say that if one writes a book, the book and the inspiration for the book are not the same. The author is called to write a book, but the book and the faculty that enables its production are not the same. I should stress that the call for London is also the summons of his vocation.[42] Like a priest, London is called (by the spirit) to be an author. To refuse this call is to die, either figuratively as a work beast or literally as a suicide, as he said, in 1898, that he would do if his mother had passed and he had not succeeded in publishing his stories. Writing, as I intentionally say over and over, is a life-and-death affair. The call calls him until he becomes the ghost that merges with the wild and becomes the subject—the imagination—that calls other objects, including the author within whom that call of the ghost resides. Buck not only hears the call of the wild, he not only voices the call, he becomes the call of the wild for the next cheechako dog, and for the author named Jack London. The title of this novel might as well be *The Imagination of the Author*.

Another way of looking at this conflation of object and subject comes at the beginning of chapter 3, the title of which is "The Dominant Primordial Beast." At this point in the story, because Buck has gone full wild, we expect that the "beast" is Buck himself. He does in fact become that beast at the end of the novel. But the first sentence of chapter 3 is not "Buck is the beast" but rather "the dominant primordial beast was strong in Buck, and . . . it grew and grew" (67). The beast within grows until it becomes congruent with its vehicle. Buck becomes the beast within. The beast within becomes Buck.

This phenomenology of the call makes an early appearance in previously published work by London. In one of his earliest essays, "The Tramp" (1900), two subheads—"The Call of the 'Road'" and "The Lash of the Master"— anticipate themes in Buck's story. The road and the wild exert such a magnetic influence that they have their own, similar calls. In one story notebook, dating from 1898, under a heading of "Malemute Kid Series," London typed a list of possible titles, including these three in a row: "The Call of the North-land The Summons—finis The Trump of doom." A fourth title comes a little further down in the list: "When the Sun Dogs Give Tongue." It is interesting that in 1898 or 1899 he had almost thought of his most famous title, but it is even more interesting that he was then linking, as he did when he wrote the novel, "call" and its synonyms "summons" and "trump" (short for *trumpet*) with catastrophe, "finis," and "doom." A little later in the notebook he writes,

> He who hears for the first time this wierd [*sic*] song, like the plaint of tortured souls, hears the first secret of the Northland; and to him who has heard it often, it bears an ever varying tale of misery and death. Since first the Northland stirred with life, this knell has rung—to the pinch of famine, to the quick death midst jamming ice, to the roar of the avalanche, to the hunter beneath the bald-faced grizzly, to the frozen grave beside the river, and always to the pitiless White Silence ["which mocks" is crossed out] which never answers back.[43]

In "Husky," he repeats this analysis: the howling of dogs is "a wail of lost and tortured souls."[44] Thus the Northland and *wild* equal doom, death, the end—in French and English. How interesting that *Call* ends with the word "finis."

The road's call is similar, and in "The Road" London likens its call to the song that the mariners sing in Alfred Tennyson's "The Lotos-Eaters." London's American lotus eaters "swore and kept and oath:—'In the hollow lotus-land to live and lie reclined / On the hills like gods together, careless of mankind.'"[45] The lotus is to the hobo as gold is to the miner.

In this essay, London focuses on the winter tramp, who chooses an urban life during winter. Tramps wander from job to job, food source to food source, pictured as if they were a herd of deer or a pack of wolf-dogs. He becomes a beast if he stays in the slums. He becomes primordial, not because of some internal deficiency, but "through modification by environment."[46] Buck may not literally be a hobo, but his time on the road/trail leads him to the life of a prisoner and the brutality of subservient life, the life of a trapped animal.

Trapped, that is, until the penultimate chapter. There is another, bohemian dimension to the tramp, and here is where Buck walks side by side with the hobo-miner. When Buck wins the big bet pulling the sled for John Thorton, he doesn't just endear himself to him, he also frees them both from the economic realm so that they can live the life fantastic that London describes in "The Tramp": "He flings his challenge in the face of society, imposes a valorous boycott on all work, and joins the far-wanderers of Hobo-land, the gypsy-folk of this latter day" (134). Buck and his cohort tramp to "a fabled lost mine" (193): "To Buck it was boundless delight, this hunting, fishing, and indefinite wandering through strange places. For weeks at a time they would hold on steadily, day after day; and for weeks upon end they would camp, here and there, the dogs loafing and the men burning holes through frozen muck" (195). Addicted to the gold-drug, the men die, as many bohemians do from overdoses and other forms of excess, but Buck lives, transformed into the spirit of that free and easy life.

In London's mind the world of the hobo—whether man or dog—is easily transposed to the world of the Arctic. Buck is the hobo-miner's familiar, their totem, and they are sons of the wolf. It's a sympathetic relationship whose highest attainment is the love between man and dog. But *The Call of the Wild* is about more than the love between species. It is about an identification between species, and now we see another dimension to the first sentence of the novel. London confuses his reader about the identity of Buck so that we can more easily bring together two disparate beings into focus as one, as if using a stereoscope.

The Call of the Wild is emphatically not allegorical. London had something much more modern in mind. In 1905 he was asked by a reporter, "Have you not attempted [introduced?] into many of your books your Socialistic theories?" (The righthand side of the text of this newspaper article is cut off in London's scrapbook.) "Not intentionally," London replied. "I suppose they crop out now and then [because they] are a part of me. A man has [to have?] a philosophy of life in order to [?] right and interpret and that [is?] to be expressed. For instance, I have been accused of making The Call of the Wild as allegory. [?] It may or may not be an allegory, that was not my intention [as?] I wrote it. I was simply [saying?] what I believed to be the [truth?]."[47] Absorptive fiction's meaning is open-ended; there is no one-to-one correspondence as in an allegory.

London himself most likely wanted to encourage multiple readings and thus discussion and controversy. In the originary debate over the allegorical quality of the book, two newspaper reviewers—L. Clare Davis and Johannes Reimers—took opposites sides of the question in 1903. In a letter to the *Stockton Evening Mail*, London wrote,

> I have been greatly interested in the discussion in your columns over the "Call of the Wild." In fact it has made me do some thinking, and I have reached the conclusion that both L. Clare Davis and Johannes Reimers are right. Mrs. Davis is certainly right when she says I wrote

a straight dog story. That was all I intended to write—just the story of the experiences of a dog. But Mr. Reimers is right when he says the story contains, or is, a human allegory. I have been reading the story over and I find the allegory there. I plead guilty, but I was unconscious of it at the time. I did not mean to do it. But since my very good friend Johannes Reimers and many others are pleased, I am glad I did it.[48]

Besides relying on "The Tramp" and "The Road," London drew directly on quite a bit of other previously published and unpublished material from his own archive that connects to the writing of *The Call of the Wild*. (Perhaps Buck read Jack London.) The connection is not merely of preview or foreshadowing. It is more substantial than that. In previously written stories and essays and in notebook trial runs for his new novel, London recognized phrases and themes that were eternal to his work, things he would never tire of representing. These are his rough drafts for the novel.

The most obvious is the essay "Husky—Wolf Dog of the North" (completed in January 1900). Using it as if it were a newspaper account of one moment in the life of Dawson, circa 1898—a human document—London writes in *Call*,

> Matthewson's sled, loaded with a thousand pounds of flour, had been standing for a couple of hours, and in the intense cold (it was sixty below zero) the runners had frozen fast to the hard-packed snow. . . . A quibble arose concerning the phrase "break out." . . . Matthewson insisted that the phrase included breaking the runners from the frozen grip of the snow. . . . The team of ten dogs was unhitched, and Buck, with his own harness, was put into the sled. . . . "Gee!" Thorton's voice rang out, sharp in the tense silence. Buck swung to the right, ending the movement in a plunge that took up the slack and with a sudden jerk arrested his one hundred and fifty pounds. . . . "Haw!" Thorton commanded. Buck duplicated the manoeuvre, this time to the left. . . . The sled was broken out. . . . "Now, MUSH!" Buck threw himself forward. . . . . His great chest was low to the ground, his head forward and down, while his feet were flying like mad, the claws scarring the hard-packed snow in parallel grooves. The sled swayed and trembled, half-started forward. . . . The jerks perceptibly diminished; as the sled gained momentum, he caught them up, till it was moving steadily along (182–89).

And his first draft—that is, of "Husky"—reads,

> In the annals of the country may be found the history of one dog-driver who wagered a thousand dollars that his favorite husky could start a thousand pounds on a level trail. Now the steel runners of a stationary sled will quickly freeze to the surface, and but the terms of the bet he was even denied the privilege of breaking the runners loose. But it was stipulated that the dog was to have three trials. The whole camp staked its dust upon one side or the other of the issue, and on the day of the trial turned out *en masse*. The dog was hitched to the loaded sled, and everything made ready. "Gee!" the master commanded from a distance. The dog swung obediently to the right, shrewdly throwing his whole weight upon the traces. "Haw!" The manoeuvre was duplicated to the left and the sled broken out. And then, "Mush on!" (the vernacular for "get up!"). The dog whined softly, driving his claws into the frozen trail, calling every muscle into play, digging away like mad. And in answer to this tremendous exertion, the sled slowly got into motion and was dragged several lengths.[49]

And at the end of the contest, as Thorton kneels beside Buck, "those who hurried up heard him cursing Buck, and he cursed him long and fervently, and softly and lovingly" (188–89). And if we are attentive readers we would know that, according to Jack London in "Husky," "no man is a fit person to drive a team of huskies who cannot command the intensive adjectives and abjurations of at least two vernaculars, besides the one drunk in with his mother's milk."[50] That is, if you haven't a facility with language, then you don't deserve the muse. True, London exaggerates the length Buck pulls the sled, but it feels true. It is sincere.

The short story "A Northland Miracle" features John Thorton, saved, not by a red-eyed dog named Buck, but by an "utterly bad" Bertram Cornell. This tale features Cornell's self-sacrifice so that Thorton may live.[51] It's not a religious story, but it does run counter to London's usual insistence that nothing good comes out of the North, and so Thorton dies in *The Call of the Wild* to correct London's "mistake" in "A Northland Miracle." On a somewhat larger scale he borrowed from "Where the Trail Forks." A miner-author figure named Sigmund owns a shepherd named Shep; Buck's mother, of course, is named Shep. Sigmund's dog survives a Native American slaughter of Sigmund and his fellow miners at their camp; Buck, of course, survives the slaughter of his human companions by the Yeehats. Shep's role in his story is to provide a coda to a tale of white–Native American encounter and misunderstanding. He, not the Native Americans, understands and thus mourns the dead miners, and as the final sentences of the story say, "The shepherd dog crept back to the deserted camp, and all the night long and a day it wailed the dead. After that it disappeared, though the years were not many before the Indian hunters noted a change in the breed of timber wolves, and there were dashes of bright color and variegated markings such as no wolf bore before."[52] London (or Buck) read that final paragraph and then wrote the fourth-to-last paragraph of *Call*: "The years were not many when the Yeehats noted a change in the breed of timber wolves; for some were seen with splashes of brown on head and muzzle, and with a rift of white centering down the chest" (227). How startling to see London borrow so exactly from his previous work. We cannot condemn this practice as a lack of inspiration, a trait of an author at a loss for words. In fact, the case is quite the opposite. Author Jack London struggled to get this scene exactly right, and it took two tries to accomplish it.

But he most significantly borrows from his very first Klondike story—"The Devil's Dice Box"—which is also a rough draft of sorts for "An Odyssey of the North." In "The Devil's Dice Box," in a cabin at the bottom of the "pit of hell," money, writing, and death unite (126). It is the wellspring of London's imagination, a deep recess—an abyss. In December 1902, back from overseas, ready to embark on his new fictional output—he hadn't written fiction since July 1902, and he hadn't written a Klondike story since May 1902—he returns in *Call* to his "fabled lost mine, the history of which was as old as the history of the country" (193) at the start of this new period in his career. He needed his satanic refreshment, a reminder of the life-and-death stakes that writing entailed. The lost mine in *Call*, so the miners believe, includes a cabin as well, and so far we feel as if we are back in the world of "The Devil's Dice Box" and "An Odyssey of the North." Again, in *Call*, there is a long and perilous search for the lost mine with its "nuggets that were unlike any known grade of gold in the Northland" (193–94). Mine, cabin, gold, mystery, a long journey, and death. All the elements are present, all except one, that is: writing. The miners never find the Lost Mine, but they find something like it, "a shallow placer," a depression in the earth formed by a streambed. Neither as deep nor as hellish as an abyss, the placer is rich enough to hold their attention. But it is not the real deal. These miners are not hobo-author figures.

In "An Odyssey of the North," we remember that Naass is the faceless, wolf-author-ghost who found imagination's wellspring. In *Call*, London goes deeper than portraying an author figure. He reaches for the story of the birth of his own creative imagination, the source of that facelessness, of the words that fight against the White Silence. And the story goes like this: Once upon a time there was a dog, an exceptional dog of great vitality and an elemental anger, a Red Wrath. His name was Buck. His vitality increased through the love of a man, for love is the most valuable of the feelings we have. But the man succumbed to a gold addiction that led him to fight and die among Native Americans. The dog, his primordial anger taking over, killed those Native Americans. He escaped into the wild, never returning to civilization. He became the ghost-dog, haunting the Northland forever.

But he was a ghost even before he died, paradoxically enough, because he was made up of "the shades of all manner of dogs, half-wolves and wild wolves . . . dreaming with him and beyond him and becoming themselves the stuff of his dreams" (168). The conflation of dreamer and the dream reenacts a larger merging: "He was older than the days he had seen and the breaths he had drawn. He linked the past with the present, and the eternity behind him throbbed through him in a mighty rhythm" (168). The past—all past time, "eternity" backward—melds with the present in this figure for the imagination, meaning that the author who can harness him and make him deliver the mail (writing) has access to any story.

The past, "eternity," turns out to be crucial for the formation of the creative imagination. When Buck dreams by the fire while helping to carry mail (dogs dream like men and see moving pictures in their dreams just as men do, which happens in *Before Adam*), he sees "the hairy man," an early hominid who both walks and swings in trees. "Far more potent [than memories of the immediate past of his life in California] were the memories of his heredity that gave things he had never seen before a seeming familiarity; the instincts (which were but the memories of his ancestors become habits) which had lapsed in later days, and still later, in him, quickened and become alive again" (112–13). Halfway through *The Call of the Wild*, we have Buck beginning to access the eternal, the time-space from where and when the call of the wild comes. The rest of the novel is a steady movement toward the moment when all claims of man cease to hold him and he releases himself fully into the present wild that is the same as the eternal wild. As John Thorton and his mates load up on gold, Buck dreams again, and again "the hairy man" returns: "And closely akin to the visions of the hairy man was the call still sounding in the depths of the forest" (199). We recall that before he got in touch with the earliest days of human history he had found and then became "the dominant primordial beast." This is the progression of the wilding of Buck: from domestic king, to beast, to companion to primitive man, to singer of the call of the wild, to the ghost who embodies the wild.

Buck's one great attribute, the thing that places him above all others, the thing that connects to his dreams and visions and stories (for who else is making the story of "the hairy man" come alive) is his imagination: "Buck possessed a quality that made for greatness—imagination" (97). The men, including Thorton, with whom Buck associates have no imagination. They simply hunt gold, find it, and bag it. But Buck is after bigger game: "This song of the huskies might have been the defiance of life, only it was pitched in minor key, with long-drawn wailings and half-sobs, and was more the pleading of life, the articulate travail of existence." In the face of death, life pleads its case through song—"one of the first songs of the younger world in a day when songs were sad. It was invested with the woe of unnumbered generations. . . . . When he moaned and sobbed, it was with the pain of living that was of old the pain of his wild fathers, and the fear and mystery of the cold and dark that was to them fear and mystery" (86–87). After the death of the miners, Buck meets the wolf pack and "now the call came to Buck in unmistakable accents. He, too, sat down and howled" (226–27). That is, first the call is outside of him; he is the object, the call the subject. Then the call enters him and he sings the call. The conflation of subject and object is complete. Just as the beast had been outside of him and then entered, now the call works the same magic. And because he has the call within him, he can mate with the wolves and produce offspring.

Before Buck meets a member of the wolf pack for the first time, he is seized by "irresistible impulses." It was the call that did it to him. "It filled him with a great unrest and strange desires." Here is London describing his authorial self at work on his writing. "It caused him to feel a vague, sweet gladness, and he was aware of wild yearnings and stirrings for he knew not what." As London traveled the world over, finding new material for his writings, so Buck "pursued the call into the forest, looking for it as though it were a tangible thing. . . . He hoped to surprise this call he could not understand. But he did not know why he did these various things. He was impelled to do them, and did not reason about them at all." He's a dog, so he wouldn't have this consciousness about the mystery within and without. But, like London who has this same "unrest" and these same "strange desires," he continues to search in the wild, "reading signs and sounds as man may read a book, and seeking for the mysterious something that called—called, waking or sleeping, at all times, for him to come" (200-1). Buck and London both searched the outside world, both nature and printed matter—novels and newspapers—for that on which to work their imaginations.

It turns out that Buck after all is a reader, but a reader of nature, not newspapers. Nature is the news to Buck. After he kills the moose in the final chapter and heads back to Thorton's camp, "he became more and more conscious of the new stir in the land" (218). "The news of it was borne in upon him" (217). His consciousness is informed by the spoken language of nature: "The birds talked of it, the squirrels chattered about it, the very breeze whispered of it." By breathing in the air, he "read a message which made him leap on with greater speed" (218). In London's authorial universe, especially in the deeply absorptive one we enter in *The Call of the Wild*, the reader becomes a writer, for the imagination—the call of the wild—is at work in both.

HEARING *THE CALL OF THE WILD*

In the most general sense, like the Native American woman acting as an amanuensis for James Ralington in "The Devil's Dice Box," Jack London acts as Buck's amanuensis. Buck howls, Jack writes. As London told his wife's niece, Buck is called to sing, and when he sings, the call is within him. When he dies, he becomes the ghostly call of the North. The wild is not simply the Yukon, or a mythological place, or even a primordial zone. It is the place where the muse lives. The muse and its locale are untamable, unknowable, like the ghost within that dictates the story. The ghost calls the tune.

The *Saturday Evening Post* got to hear the call first because London was "diffident" with Brett. In the spring and summer of 1902 London had tried to place material with the popular magazine, first with "The Golden Poppy," then "The Tramp." Both were quickly rejected. George Horace Lorimer was not London's type of editor. His first job was at the Armour Meatpacking Plant in Chicago, working as a clerk. When the workers went on strike one year, "a supply train ran through the picket lines into a siding in the Armour yards, carrying food to besieged strikebreakers. Lorimer rode the locomotive, a fact he referred to with pride in later years."[53] According to his biographer, "The magazine had to be edited for a broad middle class of readership, but he wanted to reach the upper level, too. . . . They had to be stories, however; he was scornful of intellectuality for its own sake." He wanted it to be "entertaining," in contrast to S. S. McClure who wanted his magazine to be "interesting."[54] He was especially enamored of "business fiction. To him business was a wonderful, romantic adventure."[55] Lorimer made himself famous by writing and publishing in his magazine *Letters from a Self-Made Merchant to His Son* (1902). Accepting *The Call of the Wild* was a gimme—it did not wear its anticapitalistic, bohemian economics on its sleeve—but London was not guaranteed a regular relationship with Lorimer.[56] In fact, its acceptance marks the novel as a shrewd maneuver on London's part. He was able to recognize how popular this novel would be and so sent it to the most appropriate outlet. As London told Brett, "It seems popular enough for the *Saturday Evening Post*, for they snapped it up right away. They were the first people I offered it to."[57] He must have known how politically conservative Lorimer was. It must have been extremely distasteful to him to publish a known socialist, and a great joke for London.

Lorimer may have been a strikebreaker and a middle-class Tory, but he instituted a new policy at The *Saturday Evening Post* when he took it over in 1899, and it impressed all authors, including London. He was determined to return a manuscript within three days and to pay on acceptance; he was the first editor to do the latter.[58] It did take him three weeks to write back to London. He accepted it on condition that London cut 5,000 words from the original 32,168; London cut it down to 27,000 words, but within a week of acceptance Lorimer paid seven hundred and fifty dollars (not quite London's asking price of three cents per word, but close). That's roughly twenty thousand dollars today. In seven years London would be receiving ten cents a word from Lorimer.

Brett, as is well known, paid approximately fifty-one thousand dollars (two thousand dollars in 1903) for the rights to the novel, and I will discuss the exact terms and Brett's reasoning for them a little later.[59] First, though, it is important to recall the hectic and oversaturated state of affairs in his office in the winter of 1903. When he received the letter from London announcing that he had completed "an animal story" called *The Call of the Wild*, Brett was busy with publishing details for *The Kempton-Wace Letters* and *The People of the Abyss*, including complicated negotiations with H. Perry Robinson at Isbister in London. He had just brought out *Children of the Frost*, and he was expecting London to complete *The Faith of Men, and Other Stories*, *Tales of the Fish Patrol*, and a sea story; in fact, before he had received the manuscript of *The Call of the Wild*, his response to London's description of "an animal story" was polite, but he really wanted that damn sea story: "I am delighted to hear of the story 'The Call of the Wild' and I hope you will let me read it as soon as it is finished. . . . [But] I have felt very great hopes for the sea story and your plan of working it. . . . A really good sea story at the present time would, without question, achieve a very remarkable success," not like another animal story.[60] He was too busy to recall that London had said it was finished and submitted to the *Saturday Evening Post*.

Besides all the received and planned work London had outlined and that Brett expected, Brett also had decided to publish a series of pamphlets by Macmillan authors "to be entitled, say, Little Novels by Favourite Authors." He wanted either a new story or a previously published one, the whole series "to be published, say, fortnightly during the summer."[61] London immediately sent him the uncollected "The Story of Jees Uck." Partly it was his own fault, but Brett must have felt overwhelmed. Within two months of signing their contract, he was already receiving new work, and this was work he had not contracted. This young man couldn't stop writing. Overproduction, so crucial to London's conception of his authorial identity, could be a blessing and a curse to his publishers.

When he received the manuscript of *Call*, Brett sent it out to two readers; perhaps the second reader's reports for the earlier works simply don't survive but sending it out to two readers seems a departure from his usual practice. Because the work was not under contract, he wanted to act conservatively. The first reader, who only signed with the initials M. C. J., was extremely positive.

> This is the story of a large dog, half St. Bernard and half collie, who, on account of his size and strength, is stolen and sold to be a sledge-dog when the rush for the Klondyke begins. He has very hard experiences, naturally, and in the end he finds a friend in the shape of a man who saves his life, and to whom he devotes himself. One of the best things

in the book is the account of the way in which he wins sixteen hundred dollars for his master. In the end, his master is killed by the Indians, and he joins the wandering bands of wolves, and relapses into semi-savagery. The whole thing is exceedingly clever, and while there is full sympathy shown for the dog, and he is left well-off, so far as freedom and masterfulness are concerned, there is nothing maudlin about the writer's point of view, nor any attempt to make out that a dog feels as a man would under punishment or suffering. Altogether, I think it a very remarkable piece of work, cleverer than anything that Seton Thompson has ever done, and I advise you to take it, and push it, for I believe it can be made a success. The thing is real, both as to the men and the beasts—the author has lived among them, and knows what he is talking about. Parts of it are pretty grim, but so is the Virginian, and this is nearer the actual thing.[62]

M. C. J. is not squeamish, and it is telling that he or she singles out the sled-pulling incident as particularly well written; it's as if he or she knew it was London's second attempt at telling the story. George Carpenter, the second and usual reader for Brett, was just as convinced of the quality of the story and wholeheartedly recommended publication. At first, and in a sly fashion, he determines that Jack London, and not someone else, wrote this novel; it would have been a fair question to ask—could the same person who wrote *A Daughter of the Snows* turn out as accomplished a novel as *The Call of the Wild*?—and he answered it by looking at the style: "The style is very clearly the author's own, and is remarkably consistent." He sounds like a modern-day professor checking for plagiarism. What really concerned him was the swearing: "Occasionally, there are adjectives and the like which are not, perhaps, in the best possible taste, but after all they are expressive and go with the author's whole method. I do wish, however, that you could induce him, in this special case, to strike out the two or three instances of profanity."[63] Brett sent Carpenter's namby-pamby concerns to London, making it clear that it was up to him to revise or not, but to do so would be in his best interest:

> There is one matter in connection with "The Call of the Wild" which I should like to have you consider very seriously indeed, i.e. as to whether it is possible for you to remove the two or three cases of profanity from the story and still have it retain the virility which is now

one of its distinguishing marks. I rather hope, I must confess, that you will be able to remove these few instances of profanity in the story, because, in addition to the grown-up audience for the book, there is undoubtedly possible for it a very considerable school audience, i.e. through the recommendation of teachers, and through library lists, etc. etc., and the people who have the making up of these lists, and the recommendation of these books to children will *NOT* recommend a book which had any profanity in it whatever. Do not remove the profanity if it will spoil the book in any way from your standpoint, but if it can *safely* be done please leave the profanity out.[64]

London had an aesthetic reason to keep the profanity; it was a language that a hobo-miner-author needed in order to succeed. So he told Brett, "Concerning the oaths. Inside the back cover [of the proof copy of the book] I have given the pages & lines of the book wherein oaths occur. I have a feeling that some of the less vigorous ones (two or three at any rate) should remain. But I have been both loth & unable to tackle their elimination. This I leave to you, and you have my full permission to do whatever you please with all the oaths in the book—only, if possible, I pray you leave me two or three."[65] Brett took the yellow light for green and raced ahead with linguistic and aesthetic destruction. "'Rest be blanked,' said Hal, with his beardless lips; and Mercedes said, 'Oh!' in pain and sorrow at the oath" so unnecessarily censored.[66]

Later, soon after publication in July 1903, Frederick Macmillan, the old man himself, from overseas, sent his version of a reader's report: "I am obliged to you for sending me a copy of Mr. Jack London's 'Call of the Wild' which I have read with much pleasure. He probably errs in making the dog too human, that is to say, unlike the animals in Kipling's books, he looks at everything not from the point of view of a dog but of a man. It is however an exceedingly attractive volume and ought to do well. It is very different from the vulgar ignorant stuff which the same author produced in 'The People of the Abyss.'"[67] Ah, the upper-class British were *still* upset about that book. And what would he have said about the aesthetics of profanity?

But even before Brett knew that *The Call of the Wild* would become a profitable book he was touched personally as well as professionally by this new submission from London. His letter explaining his reservations about cuss words begins with a new form of address: "My dear London"; before this it had always been "Dear Mr. London." He truly wanted to do right by Jack. On the same day he received the report from M. C. J., Brett wrote to London, saying, first, that he did not like the title (a matter to get into a little later) and, second, forgetting (maybe he wasn't forgetting after all) again that London had told him the serial rights had been sold, "In case you have not already arranged for the serial publication of this story would you like to sell me the entire copyright in the story? the title to be changed by mutual agreement. The story could then be published at any time that we saw fit, and as it is only generally covered by our specific publishing contract. The work could be made an exception very readily, by mutual agreement, to the general blanket-contract." Brett not only wanted to do right by his new author, he also wanted all that he could get. He recognized the novel's impact immediately, and he strove to be coy. He continued in the same letter:

> If you cared to consider this aspect of the matter, i.e. selling all the rights in the story, I should be glad to give you two thousand dollars ($2000) in cash for such rights, which is about six cents a word and which, as I do not know at all whether the story could be serialized, and as I have not the remotest idea as to whether it will be successful, seems to me under the circumstances a fair offer.
>
> My reason for making a different offer in this way is that I would like to try an experiment with the story, i.e. publish it in a little different form to the ordinary run of stories and possibly this might help, not only the book itself, but the general reputation of your books as well.[68]

He really didn't know how experienced London was in the business of authorship: "I'm glad you like the *Call of the Wild*," he told Brett; he knew it was good, too. "But, unfortunately, I cannot accept your offer for all rights in it. You see, the *Saturday Evening Post* bought the American serial rights of it, and already have sent me over half of the proof-sheets; while Watt & Son are handling the English serial sale of it."[69] In other words, he was doubling down and getting away with it. More than doubling. He was getting nine cents a word total from American publishers alone.

Undeterred by London's independently conceived business plan, Brett told him he didn't need the serial rights after all because he had had no intention of using them. He wanted this book, and he had two options for London. Either London could accept the cash offer, sign a one-off contract for *The Call of the Wild,* and see the book come out that summer, or they could fit it within the terms of the "general contract." Either way, he said, was fine by him, though London could feel the anxiety to get started right away. Letting the *Post* prepare the ground was sound business practice. London's plan could work because it made money for everybody. But Brett also wanted to remain on the very best terms with London. So he left it to the author: "Don't let me overpersuade you in the matter. I make the offer again because I think that it may perhaps be to both our interests that it should be accepted and that the experiment in question should be tried, but of course the decision in the whole matter is entirely in your hands and if you decide not to accept the cash offer we will publish the book in due course under the terms of our general agreement." The "cash offer" included

> putting it out in a very attractive typographic form and spending a
> very large sum of money, comparatively speaking, in endeavouring
> to give it a wide circulation and thus assist the sale of not only your
> already published books but of those still to come and for which we
> have, of course, with you already a publishing agreement.
>
> It was for the reasons of this experiment that I made you an offer of
> a definite sum for the copyright in the story and now that I know that
> serial publication is to end in time for me to try that experiment this
> summer I am willing still to let my offer in relation to this book hold
> good, proposing that if you accept this offer of a cash payment for the
> copyright (you, of course, reserving all sums received for serial publi-
> cation prior to book publication, whether here or abroad) that we shall
> publish in book form on July 8th as proposed above, really endeav-
> our, by spending an unusually large sum of money on the book, to see
> what can be done in the way of making a very decidedly large reading
> public for your future work; and, of course, in the event of your accept-
> ing the cash offer, releasing this book from the terms of our general
> agreement in relation to your unpublished volumes.[70]

London was relieved. He accepted the offer by telegraph and then wrote, saying, "I had thought, previous to receiving this last letter from you, that my already having disposed of serial rights had knocked in the head what-ever plan you had entertained for the publishing of the book. I cannot tell how glad I am to find that I was mistaken. I am sure that pushing the book in the manner you mention will be of the utmost value to me, giving me as you say, an audience for subsequent books. It is the audience already gathered, as I do hope you will gather in this case, that counts."[71] The very next day Brett sent him the check and the contract. The rapidity with which Brett and Lorimer paid for the novel must have made London's head spin after all these years of dunning publishers for payment for stories. He knew he was among professionals.

The proofs came quickly, a matter of days, and, contrary to Lorimer, Brett asked him if he would be interested in expanding the novel: "If in the revision of the proofs you find that you could add slightly in length to the book so that it would be say five or ten percent longer than at present it would be better than to cut out any part of the story, which is already quite short enough for the purpose that I have in view." He also wanted London to add a "superscription" for all the chapters, like the poem from O'Hara that opens the books as a whole.[72] Yet Brett quickly changed his mind. Please don't make any big changes, he wrote several days later, "as the book seems to me to be pretty perfect as it is and to be not likely to need much done to it."[73] Carpenter had just sent in his report, and he liked it just the way it was. Two weeks later, London concurred. "I have not added to it, or cut out from it; but merely contented myself with minor alterations," a practice he would continue, with a number of exceptions, for the rest of his career: obey the magazine's need to cut, but save the whole for book publication. He continued: "I have searched in vain for appropriate legends for the various chapters. I do not believe they exist. I have even tried to compose some myself, but not being a poet, have failed lamentably." Truly he knew his strengths as a writer. He had become content to allow whatever poetry he felt within him to infiltrate his prose. He did want to work with Brett, though, so he made a subtle change; in the original manuscript, he had placed the O'Hara stanza at the beginning of both the first and last chapters. Now, he placed it at the beginning of the book as a whole.[74]

London had been both smart and honest. He had told Brett exactly what Lorimer was paying him. Brett, in his turn, had been up-front. He told London that he had discussed the matter with Lorimer, and Macmillan would bring out the hardcover edition in July, four days after the final installment appeared in the *Saturday Evening Post*. The New York businessmen were all very anxious to get this story out in the public. London went sailing on a boat he bought with the *Post*'s money. Originally, as he told Brett, the plan was to "engage cabin passage in a sailing vessel for the South Seas, take a typewriter, plenty of paper & ink, and the plot for my sea story along, and thus get the sea atmosphere on which I have during the last several years gone stale."[75] He had told Johns in the past that a good writer puts himself into the atmosphere of a story. But despite the amount of money he was being paid, he still had family to worry about; he couldn't leave the country. So he bought a sloop. Not to worry, he told Brett: "I shall live on it a great deal, and on it I shall write the greater part of my sea-novel."[76] Author under sail, indeed. Going to sea equals writing a novel.

Despite all this goodwill and enthusiasm for publishing the book as quickly as possible, London's insecurity as a novelist arises again when he and Brett discuss a possible change of title. First, when Brett read the novel in early March he told London that he disliked the title because it was too close to Charles G. D. Roberts's *Kindred of the Wild* and because readers wouldn't understand its meaning until after they finished the book. Further, "I am afraid it is too true to nature and too good a work to be really popular with the sentimentalist public which swallows Seton Thompson or Thompson Seton, (whichever he calls himself for the moment) with acclamation and delight."[77]

In response, London agreed. The *Post* didn't like the title either, nor did they like London's second choice, *The Sleeping Wolf*.[78] That word *sleeping* is significant because it signals the extreme absorptive quality of the work. It invokes a complex of related psychological concepts—sleeping, dreaming, envisioning, mirroring, projecting—that are related as well to the workings of the imagination. It is effective on the surface, as a plot indicator: this will be the story of a dog that wakes the sleeping wolf inside himself, or, rather, more subtly, this will be the story of a dog that is transformed into the sleeping wolf that has always lived within him. But when Brett heard of the alternatives, he only became more assured that London had chosen correctly at the beginning.[79] Now London insisted that he, too, liked the original title more "but, under any circumstance, I want the decision of the title to rest with you. You know the publishing end of it, and the market value of titles, as I could not dream to know."[80] It's not that he wholeheartedly endorsed the financial reasons behind the choice of a title. It's that, absent a rock-hard confidence in his ability to choose a title for a novel, he was willing to accede to the demands of the marketplace. Besides, it wasn't about the money alone. It was also about the trust between author and publisher: "I cannot convey to you the greatness of my pleasure at knowing that the book has struck you favorably; for I feel, therefore, that it is an earnest of the work I hope to do for you when I find myself. And find myself I will, some day."[81] Two years later he claimed "it was in the Klondyke I found myself. There nobody talks. Everybody thinks. You get your true perspective. I got mine."[82] He is talking, not about his career as an author, but as an individual. Finding himself as an author was more complicated, and he needed the affirmation of a dedicated publisher to complete the process.

So after the dust settled and Macmillan printed up the copies for deposit in the Library of Congress, London noted that "on outside of paper book brought out for copyright purposes, that the title is printed *Call of the Wild*. To me this seems far less effective than *The Call of the Wild*. Somehow, the 'The' seems to give it a different & more definite meaning."[83] You bet it does. Suddenly, he has his mojo back. Here's the same Jack who understood the power of his short-story writing and got angry at *Overland Monthly* when they changed "To the Man on Trail" to "To the Man on the Trail."[84] Six months later when Richard Gilder of *Century* wanted to change the title of *The Sea-Wolf*, London complained to Brett. "*The Sea Wolf* is a strong and brief title," he wrote Brett, strongly and briefly.[85] London had seized control of the aesthetics of all of his writing completely, and Brett wisely acceded. London may have wondered until the end of his career whether each individual piece would be accepted, or would sell, or would last, but by the fall of 1903, arguing with one of the best-known magazine editors in the country, he knew what it meant to be a novelist.

The artwork on the cover and spine of his first successful novel is at once extremely pleasing and deeply troubling. London did not choose the design, but it's as if Macmillan's designer knew the inner conflict that drove London to write this novel. At first glance symmetry and color please us so much that we agree with London that this may well be the most beautiful of his covers.[86] The Christmas colors of red and green and white prompt a sense of celebration, love, and gift giving, but if we know the history of London and Christmas, we know there's a deep sense of loneliness, abandonment, and doubt about his authorial abilities at the heart of the holiday. Perhaps we register that the sky in this illustration is red—unreal, weird. The white is the white of the White Silence, not snowmen and snowballs. The three strips picturing sled dogs and their drivers appear as if they were classical bas reliefs, a modern rendition of decorations on, say, the Parthenon, and we are struck by the Greek beauty of them. They alternate with the title and then the author's name in gold. Uh-oh. Gold means trouble. The title and London's name are set in bright gold lettering, gold that the strips of dogs, men, and sled wander past, first from left to right, then right to left, and then left to right again, as if lost and never able to reach that which they desire above all else. To further intensify the conflict and turmoil, the artwork repeats the illustrations from the chapter "The Toil of Trace and Trail." The dogs' heads are down, one has his tongue out, they look beaten, and one of the men has his whip raised, ready to strike again, and again. After we read the book, we realize that what we see on the cover is the team of Buck, Joe, Sol-leks, Teek, and Pike being driven to their deaths by Charley and Hal.[87]

The book was done, its title became a catch phrase (you didn't actually have to read the book to know who Jack London was or what he thought), and now came fame to an author who had no idea that kind of fame existed. Such a famous author might think about a different firm with which to publish, so, to further tighten the bonds of trust between publisher and author, Brett for the first and only time in their relationship informed London of the financial details involved in publishing the book. He had printed twenty thousand at $6,000 and had spent at least that much in advertising. Adding in London's payment and other publishing costs, Brett feared they would lose money on the book.[88]

Brett, it turns out, had no need to worry about the public reception of "the dog story." A month later, he told London that "the second edition" sold out as hoped and "that when the fall trade opens it may take a real start from the point of view of numbers. It is mentioned among the best-selling books but books unfortunately do not seem to be selling quite as well this year as they have for several years past."[89] A year later, Brett would tell London that "the sale of *The Call of the Wild* goes on steadily. The book never succeeded quite as well as I had hoped nor as I believe it deserved to succeed but it certainly answered the purpose which I intended it should from the time I first saw it, vis. In making a reputation for your work which will stand you in good stead for anything that you like to publish."[90] Brett would stand by that statement, even when he knew London had written a least seller like *Revolution, and Other Essays*, or *Theft*, or even *The Game*. To London the sale of *The Call of the Wild* seemed enormous compared to his previous numbers, but Brett wanted him to put it all in perspective. The title, it seems, was circulating more widely than the actual book. As Frank Luther Mott summed up its first forty-five years of sales, "It did very well from the start; though it made no impression on the best seller lists, it had a steady and growing sale."[91] And seemingly never ending. By 1975 it had sold almost 1.8 million copies. Only one other work of fiction for adults published in his lifetime had sold as many—Charles Sheldon's *In His Steps*—and no other novel created as sensational and labile a phrase as *the call of the wild*.[92]

JESUS IN THE THEATER
OF SOCIALISM

London finished *The Call of the Wild* on 26 January 1903, and he began *The Sea-Wolf* around ten weeks later. Not only was he productive in this interregnum between the two novels that made him famous, his work ranges across multiple genres, employing multiple themes. Some essays and stories were written on spec; some fulfill contractual obligations to George Brett. Some subtly play off *The Call of the Wild*; some are declaratively socialist. Some are absorptive short stories, but most are theatrically minded. The essays mark his return to explicit espousal of socialist principles, or they instruct beginning writers in the mechanics of getting published. Some of his best-known essays were written during this period: "Getting into Print," "How I Became a Socialist," "The Terrible and Tragic," and "The Class Struggle."

Analyzing these essays leads us to a major work of fiction, never completed, based on the life of Jesus that first accepted and then rejected the idea that Jesus was a socialist. We might seem to drift far afield from the main thrust of the narrative of London's authorial career, but his interests were manifold, untidy, and so was the reception of his work and the various relationships he had with editors. It is of course important to track the progression of his fame. London, however, was much more than the author of *The Call of the Wild* and *The Sea-Wolf*. If we ignore this brief but intense period of writing, we risk ignoring his politics and how they were fundamental to his fiction. We need also pay particular attention to the rhythm of what he chose to write. He has just finished a major work of absorptive fiction. Instead of plunging into another, and also for other reasons that we will turn to next, he chose to delay writing *The Sea-Wolf* and turn to the theatrical mode. It was time, too, to advance the socialist cause in print.

It is a paradox well worth stressing that London, unencumbered by the demands of a contract, felt free enough to write the uncontracted *The Call of the Wild.* As with his short stories, as with *The Kempton-Wace Letters*, and as with the essays and uncompleted novel next under discussion, London wrote one of his most famous works without the financial safety net of a contract. This is an author, after all, who, upon receiving his first piece of fan mail, wrote in reply, "It's the first word of cheer I have received (a cheer, far more potent than publisher's checks)."[1] It seems the contract could cut both ways. Having promised George Brett several titles by the end of the year (and two by July), he turned his back on his sound business plan, obeyed the call to write what his imaginative voice called him to write, and dared to submit work on spec to the always fickle marketplace. He knew he was playing with Brett. In a rare moment of candor about other, secretive plans for writing, he told Anna Strunsky, who was in New York City, in March 1903, that he had just completed "The Scab" and "The Class Struggle," "each 6000 words long & something like the 'Tramp.' . . . Do not tell Mr. Brett, for he may think I am neglecting his work which I really am not."[2] Of course he was, but he did not want to endanger his contractual relationship. The freedom of writing without a contract had to be balanced with the freedom that the money from a contract could allow. A contract could protect him from the market's fickleness and guarantee him a living. The contract, so deeply desired, was both a gift and a hindrance.

The Sea-Wolf, on the other hand, was his first new contracted work with Brett, and again, the anxiety of authorship, of novel writing in particular, rose to an impactful level. Although a contract guaranteed an income, an income did not guarantee literary merit. With a new boat under his feet bought with the money from the sale of *Call*, though, London was ready to sail and write the successful sea story that he and his publisher—especially his publisher—hoped would elevate him to the status of one of America's most respected authors.

But he didn't start the novel right away. Partly from anxiety, but also from a sense of accomplishment, he felt secure enough to turn his attention to fulfilling other stipulations of his contract with George Brett. Procrastination meant three things: giving him more time to contemplate the sea novel, more time to pick the low-hanging fruit required by the contract, and more time to achieve what his inner imperative drove him to accomplish—a balance between fiction and nonfiction writing, between absorption and theatricality. After the intensity of writing a fictional work like *The Call of the Wild* he needed to remind himself—and, just as important, his audience—that he was a socialist who desired a role in the political public sphere. But the latter goal was not something he could confide to his publisher. He had told Brett in December 1902 that he would finish the fish patrol stories and the new collection of Klondike stories by July 1903. Allowing himself a week of inactivity after completing *The Call of the Wild*, he got busy. He wrote "The Marriage of Lit-Lit" (to be collected in *The Faith of Men, and Other Stories*) and mailed it on 2 February. Written in a comic mode with none of the ghostly atmosphere of his usual Northland fiction, he moved from the absorptive to the theatrical mode in his writing.

THE PRESENT STATE OF SOCIALISM IN AMERICA

But he couldn't bring himself to finish one more Klondike story and so complete the collection. Instead, he alternated between writing the last of the fish patrol stories ("The Siege of the 'Lancashire Queen,'" "Charley's Coup," "Demetrios Contos," and "Yellow Handkerchief") and essays and reviews. By the end of February he had mailed his sailing short-story collection to Brett, finished off one more story for *The Faith of Men*, and completed seven essays. He had not been exhausted by writing *The Call of the Wild*; instead, he was invigorated. He was getting to know the demands of his interior life better and better.

The essays and one review easily break into two genres: socialist/autobiographical essays and tips for beginning writers. They also can be seen as all of one piece; that is, they are concerned with beginnings (not origins, a distinction I will address later), a motivation organically connected to his sense of embarking on his second period of authorship. "How I Became a Socialist," the first of his essays and his first piece of writing after completing "The Marriage of Lit-Lit," is the title of a series dreamt up by John Spargo and the other editors of the *Comrade*, a new arts and politics journal that would in 1905 merge with the *International Socialist Review*, the unofficial organ of the Socialist Party of America. They may have been inspired by the book collection of essays by the same title, most of which first appeared in their ally the British Social-Democratic Foundation's journal *Justice* and sold in the U.S. by the Socialist Literature Company, an advertiser for the *Comrade*. Spargo, who had taken over the editorship from Leonard Abbott, had approached London for an essay in the summer of 1902. "Shall be glad to tell how I became a socialist, & I think it may differ very interestingly from the causes given by most men," London told Spargo from New York, on his way to England.[3] Spargo pursued him in January 1903, and London again begged for more time; he was close to finishing *The Call of the Wild*.[4] It is a measure of London's respect for Spargo (despite their differing political philosophies) that he turned to the task the very next month, fully aware that he was writing it for free.[5]

"It is quite fair to say," begins London in his first avowedly socialist essay since May 1901 ("Wanted: A New Law of Economic Development"), "that I became a Socialist in a fashion somewhat similar to the way in which the Teutonic pagans became Christians—it was hammered into me. Not only was I not looking for Socialism at the time of my conversion, but I was fighting it." We will return to the question of why he was "fighting it," but it is crucial to focus on that word *conversion*. William Morris, whose *News from Nowhere* was serialized in the *Comrade*, began his own "How I Became a Socialist" (written for *Justice* in 1884) with the same word: "I am asked by the Editor to give some sort of a history of the above conversion." Morris was regarded both in England and in the U.S. as someone whose greatness was measured by his combination, both in life and in his writings, of art and politics.[6] For the editors of the *Comrade* he was the artist who professed revolutionary politics, but he was exactly the kind of national figure they so desired who could help promote socialism. As the editors stated in their very first editorial, they were unconcerned with the economic basis of society. "Our mission is rather to present to our readers such literary and artistic productions as reflect the soundness of the Socialist philosophy. *The Comrade* will endeavor to mirror Socialist thought as it finds expression in art and Literature."[7] And, remember, this invitation to London came before his success with *The People of the Abyss* (which was enthusiastically reviewed in the *Comrade*) and *The Call of the Wild*. His byline includes "author of *Daughter of the Snows*, etc."

This is not to say that every socialist underwent a conversion experience; Job Harriman, for example, emphatically did not: "The intellectual process involved in one's transition from an advocate of the capitalist system to that of the socialist system is profoundly different from the process by which a sinner is transformed into a religious devotee. The former is purely intellectual, while the latter is almost entirely emotional."[8] No one ever accused London of being unemotional. Harriman's own account, however, cannot escape the language of a conversion experience, especially since he had been a minister for a number of years until he, too, had his moment of change in life, left the church, became a lawyer, and ran for mayor of Los Angeles: "On the day that I felt free from fear and secure in my right to doubt, I experienced a new sense of intellectual liberty that is absolutely unknown to the devotee of religious thought. It was on that day that life of itself became of interest to me. . . . I found that the premise from which I had previously reasoned was completely changed. I had passed from the dualistic to the monistic philosophy" (170). Although his change is in his intellectual framework, it is a conversion, nonetheless. Also consider the beginning of Frederick O. MacCartney's essay; MacCartney, too, began his professional life as a minister and then resigned to devote his full life to the cause: "While Socialism is based in economics and is primarily an interpretation of industrial development, it is nevertheless an inclusive philosophy—nay, more, it is a religion, the new religion of humanity."[9] Even Henry George's popular *Progress and Poverty*, as Alan Trachtenberg notes, is infused with religious rhetoric: It "fuses evangelical fervor with simplified Ricardian economic theory."[10]

The religious tenor of London's opening line rang harmoniously with the editors' first editorial in the *Comrade*. It begins with a quotation from Walt Whitman's *Leaves of Grass*: "With the love of comrades, With the life-long love of comrades. I will plant companionship thick as trees . . . I will make inseparable cities with their arms about each other's necks, by the love of comrades, by the manly love of comrades." The editors called this passage the "Psalm of Comradeship." They meant a secular psalm, as did Whitman. Their mission was not only to publish new artistic work by socialists but to find socialism in the literature of the past. The magazine's "function," said Abbott, "will be to develop the aesthetic impulse in the Socialist movement."[11] London's work for the cause must be seen in this larger light. In fact, the first issue of the *Comrade* included his "The Worker and the Tramp." As he said in his endorsement of the new magazine, "My congratulations upon your noteworthy first number. It is excellent. What, with the 'International Socialist Review' and 'The Comrade,' I really feel a respectable member of society, able to say to the most finicky: 'Behold the literature of my party!'"[12] For London, authorship was inseparable from politics.

His story infuses his life with other theological metaphors. Before he came to believe in socialism, he says he "formulated a gospel of work." He was "faithful" to his bosses, unaware that his success as a "wage slave" was mostly attributable to the accident of good health. "To shirk or malinger on the man who paid me my wages was a sin, first, against myself, and second, against him." When he has his moment of conversion, he invokes God's wrath if he should ever revert to his former work-beast life. Finally, he characterizes his postrevelation life as being "reborn, but not renamed." Without being religious, he effectively narrates the loss of faith and the discovery of a new faith. This new faith is complicated, though. It is not simply a belief in the correctness of a new political philosophy. Almost every other contributor to the series details the books that led to their discovery of socialism, and the most often cited book is Robert Blatchford's *Merrie England*, one of London's sources for *The People of the Abyss*. But in "The Worker and the Tramp," London locates his conversion on a different, experiential plane: "I ran back to California and opened the books. . . . I was already It, whatever It was, and by aid of the books I discovered that It was a Socialist. Since that day I have opened many books, but no economic argument, no lucid demonstration of the logic and inevitableness of Socialism affects me as profoundly and convincingly as I was affected on the day when I first saw the walls of the Social Pit rise around me and felt myself slipping down, down, into the shambles at the bottom" (278).

London's conversion did not require a new intellectual framework. Recalling his tramping days in 1894, he compares his healthy, bodily work before he encounters those at the "bottom of the Pit" to the "sailor-men, soldier-men, labor-men, all wrenched and distorted and twisted out of shape by toil and hardship and accident, and cast adrift by their masters like so many old horses." It's not just that they have been ill-treated by employers and the economic system. It's that they have no more strength; their will to live and ability to work in the same, manly way has been depleted. London doesn't say that therefore he would fight injustice and help make the lives of the workingman better. Reborn, he now swears to God that he will never *"do another day's hard work with my body. . . .* And I have been busy ever since running away from hard work" (275).[13] London converts from an apolitical thug to a socialist, bohemian artist.

The essay is filled with his rebellious, fighting spirit in his pursuit of a new beginning: against work, against capitalism, against a life of unremitting suffering and toil. He even rebels against trade unionism. While imagining himself as a strikebreaker, he sees his fate in that occupation in dire terms: "my head and my earning power irrevocably smashed by a club in the hands of some militant trades-unionist" (272). Not just foreshadowing the violent strike scene in *The Valley of the Moon*, this passage recalls the book he just completed. The man in the red sweater teaches Buck a lesson in work life just as a trade unionist would teach Jack, the work beast, a lesson in capitalism. It's all about the club. The interior life of ideas and the imagination is just as violent as the exterior social world. Both are inhabited by figures with clubs and hammers. London says his individualism was "hammered" out of him and that, most surprising, socialism was "hammered" into him. We know who did the hammering in the first instance, but who wielded the hammer of socialism? It's too easy to say that the social ills he witnessed were responsible; the social world, as London repeatedly avowed, had no interest in individual salvation. In some sense he doesn't need to ascribe agential force to the moment of his conversion. Initially, he resisted his turn to socialism and then succumbed. The hammering is actually a measure of his fight against radical personal change.

But there is another dimension to his beating. The narrative of "How I Became a Socialist" concerns not just a political awakening but more generally the embrace of a new political system, not for its own sake, but for the professional benefit that would accrue. Socialism would save him from poverty so that he could write his way out of the pit permanently. His identification of Buck as the figure of his imagination thus continues into his essay writing and then gets even more complicated, as we will see in his essays on writing produced in the same month. To escape a beating, whether by club or hammer, he must become an author. To escape the pit or abyss—whether it was located in the North or in the South, in the Klondike or in England—he must rise like a bohemian ghost-dog to run free in the wild. The spirit of God becomes simply a spirit.

On the same day he wrote "How I Became a Socialist," he also completed his reviews of two books, *Our Benevolent Feudalism* by William Ghent and *The Social Unrest* by John Graham Brooks. On 30 January, he told Brett that he had received both books (Macmillan published them) and was making notes on them.[14] He sent the article to the *Bookman*, the *Critic*, the *Independent, Outlook*, the *San Francisco Examiner*, and *Pilgrim*; all of them rejected it. Writing without a contract, he could just as easily get an immediate acceptance from *Saturday Evening Post* as he could get rejected by six outlets. He had already published "Wanted: A New Law of Economic Development" in the *International Socialist Review*, the principal publication of the Socialist Party and edited by A. M. Simons, so he reserved them for his last resort, and they accepted it and published it in May 1903 under the title "Contradictory Teachers."

Ghent was principally an author and public advocate for socialism. His book forecasts a reformed American economic system that seeks to balance the recent prognostications of H. G. Wells, Benjamin Kidd, Peter Kropotkin, Tolstoy, the neo-Jeffersonians, and Henry George and the single taxers. Starting from a succinct and accurate assessment of the American economy as monopolistic and thus feudal, it looks forward to a deeper entrenchment of feudalism. Ghent is surprisingly perceptive and prescient. Take but one example, his focus on the importance of communication technologies to the expansion of capital: "Capitalistic atoms of low valency—to use a term from chemistry—such as those invested in some of the hand trades, custom and repairing and the like [and, we might add, fiction writing]— may continue their course, but those of a high valency are sooner or later brought into association. . . . It needs no modern Newton to proclaim that in finance, commerce, and industry, as in the physical world, all bodies attract one another in direct proportion to their mass. Distance provides a limitation, it is true . . . but . . . such is the perfection of our means of communication that they provide a more transmissible medium to capital than is the pervading ether to light and gravitation" (15–16). The newly formed combination of paper and lumber companies at the turn of the century is simply a preview of the combination of, say, Anheuser-Busch (with its nearly 50 percent share of U.S. beer sales) and the St. Louis Cardinals and Major League Baseball. Ghent is one word away—the *internet*—from describing our current economic world.

Philanthropy and financial success are two more targets. "The new barons seek a public sanction through conspicuous giving, and they avoid a too obvious exercise of their power upon political institutions" (9). The words "conspicuous giving" are taken from Thorstein Veblen's "keen satire" *The Theory of the Leisure Class*, which Ghent quotes from and enlists for his work. Bill Gates's philanthropy and simultaneous efforts to change the nature of primary and secondary education, to take one example, is thus predictable using Ghent's (and Veblen's) analysis: "Out of the tremendous revenues that flow to them some of them return a part in benefactions to the public . . . always shrewdly disposed with an eye to the allayment of pain and the quieting of discontent. They are given to hospitals; to colleges and churches which teach reverence for the existing regime. . . . They are never given, even by accident, to any of the movements making for the correction of what reformers term unjustice. . . . It is a paternal, Benevolent Feudalism." (9-10). *Benevolent Feudalism* became a catchphrase in London's time.

Ghent deplores the emphasis placed on Horatio Alger–like models for personal success; in fact, whenever Ghent uses the word *success* he puts it in quotation marks. "A powerful auxiliary to the preaching of the sanctity of custom is the extolling of individual 'success.' At the very time when socio-industrial processes are settling to a fixed routine and socio-industrial forms to a fixed status—when day by day there is found less room at the top and more room at the bottom—the chorus of exhortation to the men of the land to bestir themselves reaches its highest pitch" (156-57). Ghent's book may or may not have been central to London's composition of *The Iron Heel*, but it seems its influence extended over a number of years to even the composition of *Martin Eden*, whose initial title (as it has often been noted) was *Success*. Further, in this same chapter, Ghent discusses the awful repercussions of relying on material success, including the solidification of class consciousness; the combination of plutocrats, religious figures, and the media; and the isolation and alienation of the workingman that results in passivity (he marks the high point of labor revolt as 1896), drunkenness, gambling, and, most significantly for Martin Eden, suicide.

In his review, London first sums up Ghent's book and then shows how Brooks's book proves Ghent right: "To keep down the rising tide of socialism, [Brooks] preaches greater meekness and benevolence to the capitalists. . . . And if the capitalists do not become more meek and benevolent in their dealings with labor, labor will be antagonized and will proceed to wreak terrible political vengeance, and the present social flux will harden into a status of socialism."[15] Brooks, who was a Unitarian minister, an instructor at Harvard University, and a Department of Labor field researcher, is a mere accommodationist, says London. He sees how trade unions can be maintained as simply another department of ownership's organizational structure. As London points out, Brooks fears the class struggle most of all. Convince the working class that they have a stake in the capitalistic status quo and it won't matter if they are called socialists or not. Cooptation is the key. This is why London was not a trade unionist, a position he consistently held, even in 1916 when he did want the membership of the Author's League of America to affiliate with a union.[16]

Brooks discusses the centrality of machinery to the fight between capitalists and socialists. Settling the question of who should own the means (the machines) of production is the central obstacle to domestic peace and the avoidance of class warfare. In identifying the times as the Machine Age, Brooks and London are in agreement. But Brooks advocates better controls, more attentive legislation, even military force to placate the work force. The rule of the monied class remains intact. In fact, in stark contrast to Ghent's analysis, the trusts are in themselves neutral, neither good nor bad for the general public. It is all a matter of how they conduct themselves. As Brooks puts it in *The Social Unrest*, "The trust comes into the industrial struggle with privileges and powers greater than ever have been exercised in the world's commerce. To use these powers with such prudence and fairness as not to outrage the sentiment of the community, will prove the severest test to which these combinations must submit" (62–63). As London sums it up in his review, "Which is to say, that to withstand the advance of socialism, a great and greater measure of Mr. Ghent's BENEVOLENCE will be required" (208).

When London put this review together with "War of the Classes" and other essays and sent them in the fall of 1903 to Macmillan, Brett asked his friend Hamilton Wright Mabie to be the reader. Mabie complained that this review was "largely made up of quotations" and short on analysis.[17] But that was a conscious choice by London, effective or not. He took two contrasting books and concluded with a simple objective observation: "Mr. Ghent beholds the capitalist class rising to dominate the state and the working class; Mr. Brooks beholds the working class rising to dominate the state and the capitalist class. One fears the paternalism of a class; the other, the tyranny of the mass" (214). We may want this prominent socialist to more emphatically side with labor and Ghent, but he refuses to even tip his hand to his own politics—as if they weren't already so well known. The idea was to get these two books into a mainstream journal through selective presentation of block quotations. He failed, but that is why he both deemphasized his own role in American politics and emphasized the actual words of Brooks and Ghent. He didn't need to persuade. He thought Ghent's "cunningly contrived and arrayed" (203) argument (he never characterizes Brooks's work) could stand on its own merits and would in contrast show how dangerous Brooks was.

What little religious rhetoric is employed in both books is drawn out in London's review. He quotes a passage from Ghent that he also marked in his copy:

> Efficiency—the faculty of getting things—is at last rewarded as it should be, for the efficient have inherited the earth and its fulness. The lowly, whose happiness is greater and whose welfare is more thoroughly conserved when governed than when governing, as a twentieth-century philosopher said of them, are settled and happy in the state which reason and experience teach is their God-appointed lot. They are comfortable too; and if the patriarchal ideal of a vine and fig tree for each is not yet attained, at least each has his rented patch in the country or his rented cell in a city building. (205-6)

For Ghent, the biblical allusions only help convey the passivity of an oppressed population. Brooks, wanting to argue for the "real" religious nature of capitalism (principally illustrated by its philanthropy and charitable relief organizations), goes to great lengths to show that socialism is not like a religion. But London wants to retain something of Christian ethics in his own understanding of socialism.

This is not to say that London was an informal member of or even sympathetic to the Christian Socialist movement. As Ghent told Joan London, "In the main the term Christian Socialists was a misnomer. Most of these persons should have called themselves Socialistically Inclined Christians. . . . I do not think that the Christian Socialist movement had much influence among the rank and file of the Socialist party. The general feeling—at least in New York—was one of annoyance and sometimes antipathy."[18] London could not completely separate himself from the Christian Socialist movement because he did believe in the importance of Jesus as a forerunner to socialism and because he felt beholden to his close friend and Christian Socialist Fred Bamford.

"The Scab," his next socialist essay, begins in a roundabout way, focusing on what London surprisingly calls "generosity." "In a competitive society," he writes, and we know right away that we are dealing with facts, not the socialist dream of a cooperative commonwealth. "In a tooth-and-nail society"—another realistic or theatrical definition—a scab is more "generous" (101) than a striking worker. This reversal, one of several in the essay, jars the reader from established and conventional views of the current economic system. Rhetorically, it's a brilliant way to draw the reader into his argument. It also allows London to present himself as simply an objective analyst. It's crucial to winning his case that he not be identified as a socialist. Just as he kept his own politics out of his review of Brooks's and Ghent's books to maintain his objectivity, so here he doesn't want the reader to assume he or she knows already what London will say.[19]

London doesn't say to whom the scab is generous. That, too, would color our understanding of the facts. We understand only by implication that the scab is generous because he gives his time to an employer for less money than the striker. With all that in mind, the accompanying reversal is both startling and sensible. In a capitalistic society, generosity—a Christian ethic—is met with murder: "In a competitive society . . . what is more natural than that generosity . . . should be held an accursed thing." Thus, "the generous laborer [and because we associate generosity with goodness and we know London the socialist would regard the striker as good, we are still confused by London's 'generous' treatment of the scab] threatens the life of his less generous brother laborer." And so the striker tries to kill the scab, the scab assaults the striker. Thus, London can rise to an objective level and emphasize the humanity of the scab as well as the striking laborers. Both have to work, both have to eat, both have to support families. The point is that capitalism drives the perversion of Christian ethics. The scab is a scab because of natural forces, too. He has to take someone else's job because he isn't as strong, or "skilled, or more energetic" (166). But in a truly ethical economic system the weaker worker is protected from himself as well as from forces he cannot control.

At this point in the essay the reversal begins to right itself. Still vibrating from his trip to Europe, London compares the scab to a British soldier who invades the land of the Boers (strikers). With *The People of the Abyss* and this set of three February 1903 essays—we will get to "The Class Struggle" next—London moves beyond his American parochialism. As he states a little later in the essay, "Civilization may be expressed to-day in terms of trade-unionism" (129). Not only is the scab like an imperial invader, he or she is also "not so generous after all." The scab exists because workers do not own their own machines. That is, the owners choose who gets to work, thus enforcing competition between laborers. In fact, "the machine, which never loafs and malingers . . . is the ideally perfect scab" (108). The scab-machine cannot have an ethics of generosity, and the "sentimental connotation of scab" holds true after all: he or she is a "Judas." The under-standable, ethical, no-fault conduct of the scab is rendered ungenerous and harmful by capitalistic forces outside of his or her control.

Now we meet up with our old friend John Graham Brooks, and now London puts him squarely on the side of those who are corrupting what would be, in a socialist economic universe, a morally upstanding economic system. Brooks's fear, as London said in his review of *Social Unrest*, is of the masses. Add to that, says London in "The Scab," the more intense fear of socialism taking over state and federal legislatures, "an aggressive political socialism" (116). And why must we fear this political takeover? What do the socialists want that would simply destroy America forever? London puts Brooks's blunt assessment at the heart of his essay: if socialism gains the upper hand in the democratic legislative system, it "will become a turbulent political force bent upon using every weapon of taxation against the rich" (116–17). We have moved from the individual status of a single scab versus a single worker, trying to break each other's head, to collective agency. The moral landscape has not changed. "Neither side is swayed by moral considerations more than skin-deep. . . . The only honest morality displayed by either side is white-hot indignation at the iniquities of the other side" (117–18). In fact, both sides are even more similar than thought at first glance: they both engage in violence and deny their violent means; they both pursue control of state apparatuses of legislation and enforcement; they both appeal to public opinion to win their case. But, even further, they both scab on themselves: "No scab capitalist strives to give more for less for any other reason than that he hopes, by undercutting a competitor and driving that competitor out of the market, to get that market and its profits for himself."[20] And that is the real reason trusts and unions exist: to protect themselves from each other.

In fact, trusts and unions come together to form an even larger entity—the nation—which then scabs on other nations. "At the present moment all Europe is appalled by that colossal scab, the United States" (126). London sees how capitalism desires to go global. Just as unions fight trusts, and a striker throws a brick at a scab, so too will nations form unions to fight other unions of nations in a world war: "The way for Europe to protect herself is to quit bickering among her parts and to form a union against the scab. And if the union is formed, armies and navies may be expected to be brought into play" (126–27). Thus, he forecast the major struggles of the coming twentieth century: "It would seem that England, fronted by the hostile Continental Union and flanked by the great American scab, has nothing left but to join with the scab and play the historic labor role of armed Pinkerton." London's emphasis on the economics of international diplomacy allows him to successfully predict the future.

The danger of taking the Olympian point of view of the merits and demerits of both sides is to stalemate the situation. A true socialist propagandist, as London well knew, takes sides and ignores wrongs perpetrated by the unions. This socialist, however, is in favor of neither unions nor trusts. "The union laborers of the United States have nothing of which to boast, while, according to their trade-union ethics, they have a great deal of which to be ashamed" (140). In fact, London manipulates one of his sources for the essay so that it seems that a die-hard trade unionist like Henry Casson, who dedicated *Organized Self-Help* to the American Federation of Labor, actually argues against the moral purity of trade unionism. Casson writes, and London marked the passage, "Not even the richest millionaire can stand alone against the Wall Street communism of wealth that seeks to conquer the commerce of the world. About two years ago a New York financier, rated at $20,000,000, withdrew from the Sugar trust, in which he had made his money, and struck out on his own account. He antagonized the great Railroad trust and several others, and the result was that his millions melted away like snow in June. He was bankrupted so thoroughly that he was obliged to turn over to his creditors his home, his chickens and his gold watch."[21] London repeats the story, his narrative instinct attracted to the telling details of chickens and a gold watch, but he inserts the trade unions into the story, aligning them with the trusts by cleverly renaming the Sugar Trust as the Sugar Union: "Mr. Casson tells of a New York capitalist who withdrew from the Sugar Union several years ago and became a scab. He was worth something like twenty millions of dollars. But the Sugar Union standing shoulder to shoulder with the Railroad Union and several other unions, beat him to his knees till he cried 'Enough.' So frightfully did they beat him that he was obliged to turn over to his creditors his home, his chickens, and his gold watch. In point of fact, he was as thoroughly bludgeoned by the Federation of Capitalist Unions as ever scab workman was bludgeoned by a labor union" (124–25). Casson, two paragraphs previous to his anecdote of the wayward capitalist, had insisted on the point that "the 'scab' capitalist is driven out of business by the trust, and the 'scab' workingman is driven out of employment by the union."[22] But he also insists, unlike London, that "the trade union tends to elevate and enrich the nation, while the trust tends to destroy it."[23] London would have none of that. Just as the words *union* and *trust* were interchangeable, so, too, were the organizations.

Also, if everyone (and every nation) is a scab, then London must direct the spotlight on himself, just to be objective about it. The arts do not escape his notice, but only the employer, not the employee: "When a publisher offers an author better royalties than other publishers have been paying him, he is scabbing on those other publishers." The interesting question, then, is whether a content producer can be a scab. A reporter can be, but London probably would argue that because he is a salaried individual, then he is a scab. The only exempt class are those born to wealth: British royalty and "the irresponsible rich." So authors do not fall into any category because they exist outside the economic system. They try to set their prices for their work (say, ten cents a word), but if they are offered less, then they must take it, a concession that does not meet London's definition of *scab*— taking less for more—because by taking less they do not either guarantee acceptance or displace another author's work. An author cannot undersell because his product does not compete directly with another. An individual's imaginative power may be wanted or not wanted in the marketplace, but when it is wanted it is not wanted to the exclusion of others, even if the others produce inferior work. There is a public demand for both high and low art. London, at all costs, needs to reserve a space within capitalism where bohemians can operate even antagonistically to capitalism. That seems to explain London's silent self-exemption from his otherwise rigorous and thorough analysis.

Weirdly, though, George Brett worried that the essay "The Scab" might work as a kind of scab itself in the first months of its publication history. Charles Kerr and Company (probably in the person of A. M. Simons) reprinted it as a five-cent pamphlet, and Brett worried that it would affect the sales of *War of the Classes*. Given London's definition of a scab—"*one who gives more value for the same price than another*"—it doesn't quite qualify, and London successfully argued that a cheap pamphlet would sell to those who did not buy a $1.50 book. But, still, he felt guilty in giving Kerr the rights to the essay, so he apologized to Brett.[24]

Although *Cosmopolitan* had rejected "The Scab," it was, again, the first outlet he turned to for his next essay, completed just a week later. "The Class Struggle" was rejected by *Cosmopolitan* and *Atlantic Monthly* and three other magazines before the *Independent* accepted it and paid him forty dollars. The *Atlantic Monthly*, on the other hand, had paid him $100 for "The Scab" after the *Independent* had rejected it. The mainstream magazines could not handle the more incendiary "The Class Struggle," while the *Independent* apparently thought "The Scab" too much of a departure from their own reformist principles. Hamilton Holt, the editor, had written to London earlier in the year about serializing *The People of the Abyss*. Although he could not print more than one or two chapters (which did not happen; London took Gaylord Wilshire up on his offer to publish more), he told London, "The next time you come to New York, I wish you would drop in and see me. From all I can gather, you are something of a social reformer after my own type." He wasn't, but, still, he was appealing to a broad spectrum of progressives.

Holt was a liberal reformer, a firm believer in democracy who nevertheless converted to "a mild socialistic program."[25] He sympathized with many points of view and published writers, like London, with whom he disagreed; one had to read the magazine's editorials to understand what exactly Holt believed in. When he endorsed Morris Hillquit, a socialist candidate for Congress, he wrote that he himself was "more of an individualist than a Socialist, but I do not see how we are ever to have any individualism in persons until we have socialization of goods and the means of production and distribution."[26] Six years later he borrowed seventy-seven thousand dollars from Andrew Carnegie and other industrialists to buy the *Independent* from his uncle. Still, he was open-minded and told London that "he could 'truthfully say that ["The Class Struggle"] was the best & clearest exposition of the industrial situation & tendencies he had ever seen.'"[27]

Holt prefaced the publication of the essay with this notice, reminiscent of the notice in the *Atlantic Monthly* for "How I Became a Socialist": "Mr. London is the author of 'The Call of the Wild' and a number of stories of the Klondike region which have placed him among the most popular of American writers. He is more than a literary man, however, being a student at first hand of social problems, as his latest book, 'The People of the Abyss,' will show. He is a Socialist. The following article is the best statement we have yet seen, from the radical standpoint, of the industrial and social conflict of classes." Editors and the public were getting a handle on London's unique authorial output.

"The Class Struggle" continues London's blending of politics and morality, of socialism and a generalized, nondenominational Christian ethics. First and foremost, though, the essay, just in its title, is confrontational, rebellious. In the last one hundred years the phrase "class struggle" has lost its controversial aspect, but in the early 1900s to assert that there was a conflict between classes or even that there were classes at all was, for some conservative and even some liberal thinkers, tantamount to admitting to a failure of democracy. Classes, so they argued, cannot exist in the U.S. because all are created equal and all have equal opportunity. "Struggle" was taken as a polite substitute for "warfare," and, as we have seen in Brooks's work, it was crucial to the political status quo to maintain a peaceful domestic equilibrium.

Thus "The Class Struggle" is the first essay in his collection *War of the Classes*, an even more provocative title. He first proposed the book collection—as yet untitled—on 15 August 1903. In a letter to Brett, he wrote, "[I] have a number of sociological and economic essays, all of them right up-to-date in their facts and conditions, and written in a popular style. In fact, they are sufficient to make a book of from forty-five to fifty thousand words. I am wondering if such a book would be available." London engaged in his usual self-promotion to Brett; the need of it felt greater perhaps because this book was another uncontracted surprise to his publisher. To accompany his anxiety about having it accepted for publication, he promoted the hell out of it: "They are studies which I have made in the course of attempting to grip hold of this gigantic, complex civilization of ours. And I am attempting to grip hold of it in order to exploit it in fiction, in what, if I succeed, will be the biggest work I shall ever do. It is a great field, and it is really and practically virgin."[28] Brett, bless his heart, was immediately enthusiastic and told London,

> I have long had in mind the possibility of some fiction master taking up the sociological facts of our existence to-day and putting them in fiction into a book which would be practically the greatest novel of its time. It is, however, absolutely essential that this novel, when it is written, shall have the human interest also and I commend to you for consideration in this connection the motif which is behind the character

of Valjean in "Les Miserables" as the most possible and most interesting from the standpoint of the character from which to take up industrial and sociological problems.[29]

How interesting, though, that London tried to persuade Brett to publish a collection of essays because they were a necessary precursor to a big work of fiction. It seems that London was thinking about writing *The Iron Heel* (the novel that was ultimately published in 1908) even as early as 1903.

Brett's readers, however, were decidedly unimpressed with the whole project, first entitled *The Salt of the Earth*.[30] The proposed collection of essays struck G. R. Carpenter of Columbia University as "merely youthful harangues, in which he makes the most of his undigested information. The unpublished essays—on the tramp and the scab, for instance—are a little more sound; but I do not believe it would be good for him, his cause, or yours, to have such loose and fluent and rash articles printed in book form by publishers of the first reputation."[31] The other reader of the volume was none other than Hamilton Wright Mabie, who seconded Carpenter: "Mr. London's essays in *Salt of the Earth* do not seem to me to have the constructive quality of his fiction nor the vigor and precision of style. The articles are not related; the chapter on Ghent's and Brooks's books is plainly interpolated and largely made up of quotations; the other chapters present conditions rather than remedies and seem to me too liberally sprinkled with generalizations and not sufficiently buttressed by facts. The book leads nowhere. There are some striking ideas and phrases in it; among the best of them the characterization of the tramp; but I do not think the book would justify itself."[32] Needless to say, Brett acted against the advice of both and published the book in 1905. He was, however, concerned about the quantity and timing of London's book publications, and when he accepted *War of the Classes* in October, he told London they should sit down together and discuss his plans for the next couple of years: "I think it would be advisable for us to talk over the whole matter of your publishing interests for the future with you and as I shall, in all probability, come out to San Francisco early in January next to look after some special matters that we have in hand out there. I have wondered as to whether you would be willing to leave this question of the time of publication of this book open until then."[33] London agreed, and they met in San Francisco in January just before London left for Japan and Korea.

London begins "The Class Struggle" with a summation of this situation: "Out of their constitutional optimism, and because a class struggle is an abhorred and dangerous thing, the great American people are unanimous in asserting that there is no class struggle" and that classes do not even exist in the U.S.[34] Then he clarifies: he doesn't mean the American people themselves, he means—as if you didn't know already, wink wink—"the press, the pulpit, and the university" (4-5). Let us not be hoodwinked, London says, and face facts. Trusts exist and unions exist, and though they may scab on each other and among themselves, as he wrote in "The Scab," they are nonetheless unequal entities. We might thus say that London wrote this essay to demonstrate his complete alliance with the workingman, in case anyone had misconstrued his intentions in "The Scab," thinking that because he was anti-trade union he must be anti-workingman. Even if the worker engages in questionable ethics and behavior, London's sympathies remain with him or her and with the desire to rise above one's class. Unfortunately, that desire is no longer obtainable. As he states in "The Class Struggle," historically, the American proletariat has been able to change class. "They were able to do this because an undeveloped country with an expanding frontier gave equality of opportunity to all" (7). But now, as Frederick Jackson Turner proclaimed, the frontier is closed and with it the easy class mobility of the nineteenth century. "Farthest West has been reached, and an immense volume of surplus capital roams for investment and nips in the bud the patient efforts of the embryo capitalist to rise through slow increment from small beginnings" (8-9).[35] The trusts have closed off opportunity. As we saw in London's earliest socialist writings, he advocated socialism because all men were not created equal and that in a democracy all did not have the same opportunities or rights. Socialism, not democracy, would restore equality.

But London wasn't about to become a spokesperson for the unions, for he felt they engaged in dissimulation. They refused to admit that they were engaged in class warfare and actually were advocates of this bedrock principle of socialism. He uses a series of unwitting quotations from Samuel Gompers (American Federation of Labor) and Henry White (United Garment Workers) to prove otherwise, for London championed the socialist strategy of "boring from within," and he clipped any number of newspaper stories that heralded the socialists' success in turning unions away from Gompers's and White's leadership. Because they advocate unlimited warfare against the capitalists, and capitalists do the same, London points out in "The Class Struggle," they all practice laissez-faire economics: "everybody for himself and devil take the hindmost."[36] It's not so much a question of mutual destruction but rather of following the wrong philosophy: "group individualism," that is, a group acting in only its own best interests (19). "But the facts of the class struggle are deeper" than that, says London (19), and the principal fact is the change in consciousness of the worker. Formerly a seemingly independent worker, now he or she is self-aware, "conscious," of being of a class, and class consciousness makes class warfare all the more inevitable. Driven from within, instead of being imposed from without, class identification hardens the division between capitalist and worker. London isn't arguing against class consciousness or class struggle. Again, he has taken the Olympian viewpoint. These are the facts, he says. And when socialists aren't allowed to be union members and militia members at the same time, when socialists now have unprecedented voting power, when socialists "have behind them a most imposing philosophic and scientific literature . . . [with which] they literally swamp the working classes in a vast sea of tracts and pamphlets," when socialists are more "indefatigable" than any "political party, . . . church organization or mission effort," then "they work for [the cause] with a religious zeal, and would die for it with a willingness similar to that of the Christian martyrs" (25, 26). According to London, class consciousness was a preexistent condition (whether people admitted to it or not), and it led to class warfare that would result in classlessness. All these facts contribute to a perpetual war and zealousness that London does in fact find necessary but abhorrent.

He especially focused on the question of membership in the National Guard and devotes three pages to this topic; in reviews of his essay and its oral version it generated the most comment because if unions forbade its members to be national guardsmen then not only did it imply radical socialism but also implied a freedom to riot and so seemed the most dangerous platform plank of socialistic unions. He copied nearly verbatim two sentences from an unsigned editorial in the *Socialist Spirit*: "The Illinois state federation of labor, at a convention held recently at East St. Louis, passed without a dissenting vote a resolution declaring that membership in military organizations is a violation of labor union obligations, and requested all union men to withdraw from the militia. President Alert Young of the federation declared that the militia is a menace not only to unions, but to all workers throughout the country" (23).[37] In this same editorial, the author cites a recent event in New Orleans, which London also copied word for word for his essay: "During the recent New Orleans street car strike, a whole company of militia, called out to protect non-union men, resigned in a body." This editorial cites the interesting moment during a recent coal strike in which the national guard "fraternized with the strikers" and "were in such pronounced sympathy with the strikers as to be useless as a guard" (22). London does not take a stand on the issue. Rather, he collects these instances to prove his point: that class warfare exists in America despite the self-interested denial by the capitalist class.

The number of newspaper and magazine clippings London collected to write this essay is well over one hundred. From *Advance* (1901), he cribbed the following: "The action of the Amalgamated Sheet Metal Worker's Association, says the 'Social Democratic Herald,' in incorporating in its constitution an amendment excluding from membership in its organization 'any person a member of the regular army or of the State militia or naval reserve,' has aroused a discussion involving wide issues." From the *Appeal to Reason*, he quoted its reprint of portions of D. M. Parry's pamphlet excoriating unions and promoting a unified front among capitalists.[38] From an editorial in *Literary Digest*, he copied almost word for word, "Mr. John Mulholland, of Toledo, Ohio, president of the International Association of Allied Metal Mechanics, recently stated that he did not want the members to join the militia. The Local Trades Assembly of Syracuse, New York, also recently passed a resolution, by a unanimous vote, requiring union men who are members of the National Guard to resign under pain of expulsion from the unions."[39] He took nearly verbatim a sentence from another article in *Literary Digest*: "*The Social-Democratic Herald* (Socialist, Milwaukee) advises the trade-unionists, in view of this decision, to stop trying to fight capital with money, which they lack, and begin fighting with the ballot, which is their strongest weapon."[40] He got his figure of one thousand strikes a year from a clipping also from *Literary Digest*.[41] From *Outlook* he paraphrased and copied the case of William Potter.[42] For the National Economic League's statement of purpose and the men who signed it, London quoted from *Wilshire's Magazine*.[43] He took his long quotation from Henry White from White's essay "Is Industrial Peace at Hand?" in the *Independent*.[44]

Two interesting facts are to be garnered from this litany of sources: while London was busy writing *The Call of the Wild* and plotting *The Sea-Wolf* he was actively gathering data for and conceptualizing his socialist essays of early 1903 that would form a large part of *War of the Classes*; second, most of his sources are from December 1902 to February 1903, meaning that in a very short time he gathered enough evidence to support his arguments. Sometimes London bothered to cite his sources, sometimes not. Sometimes he paraphrased, sometimes he plagiarized. Sometimes he neglected to date his clippings or even include the periodical title. We have to remember that his was not modern-day academic writing, complete with footnotes. To protect himself from accusations of intellectual theft or misquotation, he put all of them in a big scrapbook entitled "Trade Unionism," thus creating with his file system a kind of material footnoting.[45]

He couples the essay's facts to the new strategy of socialists infiltrating trade unions. Previously the socialists had alienated trade unions with their rhetoric and their principle of not collaborating with capitalists through trade unionism. Now, says London, "the socialists, fanatics and dreamers though they may well be, betray a foresight and insight, and a genius for organization, which put to shame the class with which they are openly at war" (29). "To-day the great labor unions are honeycombed with socialists, 'boring from within.'" (30). Unions simply want higher wages and better working conditions. Socialists want a new economic system. To get that system "they intend to destroy present-day society, which they contend is run in the interest of another class, and from the materials to construct a new society, which will be run in their interest" (47). London's intent behind his presentation of facts, and his insistence on the undeniability of the class struggle, is to hurry along the process. Let the fight begin, says London, so we can sooner know who will win. Thus, the essay doesn't end with his own sociopolitical program or even his outright endorsement of one or all or none of the parts of the socialist program. It simply ends with a question: "It is no longer a question of whether or not there is a class struggle. The question now is, what will be the outcome of the class struggle" (49).

In private, London could not imagine an end to the class struggle. Notes for a series of novels reads, "Why not write a series of novels, class struggles in various ages—beginning with rude tribes, early civilizations, middle ages, modern (Iron Heel), or another—& then, far in future—struggle of art classes."[46] What he means by "art classes" is rather difficult to glean (perhaps he is thinking that, in the future, when socialism has won, class difference would be defined by the kind of art and play that people would produce), but the concept of the class struggle now became one more organizing principle for London to understand all of human history. London once told Cloudesley Johns that "it's the Anglo-Saxon people against the world, and economics at the foundation of the whole business; but said economics only a manifestation of the blood differentiations which has come down from the hoary past."[47] Maybe, but a week later he told Johns that "nations do not fall before military prowess. Bad economics or killing competition is what kills them."[48] We would expect to see a racial component in that statement, but it is missing. Two years later, in his 1903 essays, biology and race concerns move to the background. Economics is the basis of human relations, and the class struggle is "at the foundation of the whole business."

Between 1901 and 1905, London collected newspaper articles and pamphlets and made notes for an essay to be called "The Disappearing Class." "Open up thus," he wrote and then typed a sentence from *The Communist Manifesto*: "The history of society is the history of class struggle."[49] The notes cite Brooks's *Social Unrest* once and Ghent's *Our Benevolent Feudalism* twice. Both pamphlets and a number of the articles are from spring 1903, indicating that he was deep into the drafting of the essay and that it would serve as a companion to "The Tramp," "The Scab," and "The Class Struggle." The disappearing class was the middle class, best exemplified by the small farmer. His essay notes continue: "Show the old contention of the German socialists, that the middle class would actually disappear (See Brook's 'Socials Unrest', chapter entitled, Revolution to Reform) and show change this contention has undergone, but be careful about it for fear of socialist criticism. As an independent class, sharing in the bi-partition of the revenues, it is disappearing. Make this point clear and definite."

What may initially sound like a repudiation of the socialist argument, following Marx, that large-scale farming, like large-scale industry, would replace the petty bourgeois farmer and so lead to collectivization is actually in agreement with it. Brooks argued that events in Germany and Belgium— two countries with which he was intimate—had shown the errors in traditional Marxian analysis. London affirms this ("show change this contention has undergone") and warns himself to "be careful" or else his socialist readers will misunderstand his intention. That is, German socialists may have experienced a change of thinking due to changes in European conditions, and it may even be true about American farming. But London nonetheless holds true to the more general point, that is, that the middle class no longer shares in revenues, even in agriculture, and that it grows more and more dependent on the upper class. This much is "clear and definite." As London wrote in his review of *Social Unrest*, Brooks "is not above feeling grave and well-contained satisfaction wherever the socialist doctrinaire has been contradicted by men attempting to practice cooperation in the midst of the competitive system, as in Belgium."[50] Notwithstanding Brooks's first-hand observations, with the disappearance of the middle class, the United States and other countries are faced with the volatile and untenable separation and antagonism of two classes, the wealthy and the poor.

In his unpublished short story "Two Children of Israel," London creates a young, working-class Jewish couple named Jacob and Leah. Jacob has a friend named Joseph Liebenbaum who takes Jacob to his first socialist meeting. During the meeting anarchists argue against socialists, and all varieties of socialists argue among themselves. "Jaky looked for a heated reply from the [anarchist]; but that worthy was deep in discussion with an intelligent greasy looking Servian, a member of the conservative school of philosophic anarchism—a cult distinct from that of ordinary anarchism. Jaky sought a fresh source of interest. Joseph Liebenbaum had come to a hitch with his friend regarding the political attitude of organized labor, and each was growing red in the face. At the upper end of the table, a collectivist and a communist were at outs. Near them, a stray nationalist had collided with a single-taxer." Breaking through the pandemonium, an unknown speaker tells the crowd that though they all have seemingly irreconcilable differences they are actually united by two things: "class consciousness and the recognition of the solidarity of labor." Jaky has no idea what those things are, and the speaker enlightens him: "First, the toilers must become class-conscious; when they have attained that condition the way is clear. They will have come to see that the interests of all labor are the same, that the attitude should be the same. Then will the racial disagreements and the wars of the nations disappear."[51] I don't believe that London thought that war would ever end; he distanced himself from utopian thought. But "The Class Struggle" and writing like this story fragment and his notes on "the disappearing class" indicate that, at the very least, racial concerns took a secondary position when he considered the reformation of American political and economic society. All men were not equal—and sometimes for London the racial component of that inequality was strong—but socialism could create equal opportunity and allow the strong, out of altruism, to help the weak. As he wrote to Johns in 1899, "the race with the highest altruism will endure," and by "altruism" he meant "sentiment," "charity," and "mercy."[52]

These qualities, whether of a race or of a political-economic society, form a generalized Judeo-Christian ethic. Even the class struggle is more than just mere competition for the control of the economic basis of society. As I have noted, in all four of his 1903 socialist essays, London links the profession of socialism to the profession of religious faith—and the deaths of socialists fighting for the cause to the deaths of Christian martyrs—so it should come as no surprise that at the same time that London was writing these essays (as well as all the other kinds of work he was sending out for publication), he was working on his novel about Jesus.[53]

THE SOCIALISM OF JESUS

Although documentation exists of London's first awareness of socialist doctrine, there is no similar documentation of London's first awareness of Christian ethics or even how he came to study the Bible in a serious fashion; he wasn't raised in a church-going, Bible-reading household.[54] One cannot answer conclusively whether London began by developing Christian or analogical Christian beliefs and then turned to a commitment to socialism or whether he overlaid his socialism with Christian rhetoric. I tend toward the latter view, a common-enough rhetorical development among American socialists.

In 1899 London wrote to Cloudesley Johns that he wanted to write his own fictional account of the life of Jesus. He had just finished writing his essay "What Communities Lose under the Competitive System," his entry in a *Cosmopolitan* essay contest. To remind ourselves, he argues that capitalism is amoral and "soulless" and that values like altruism and philanthropy, when practiced by capitalists, are hypocritical, all themes that are repeated in his 1903 essays. It was therefore a logical and progressive step in his thinking that led London from his *Cosmopolitan* essay to his first notes on what he referred to as his "Christ novel." London collected material on and made notes for his Christ novel from 1899 to 1913, but with varying intensity. His interests heightened during three distinct periods: 1899–1903; 1903–7; and 1911–13. Of all his unfinished projects, the Christ novel is the one that held his attention for the longest period of time.

Several themes emerge in these notes, rising and falling as time passes: London was alternately attracted by the figure of Jesus as socialist leader or as the archetype of peace; he struggled over the question of who was responsible for the death of Jesus; he was especially interested in juxtaposing a representative figure from a Nordic culture with a woman from the Semitic culture; he debated with himself on how to portray the Romans; and, most importantly, he worked at understanding the Christian and Jewish religions, trying to forge a spiritual belief for himself.

In developing his "Christ novel," London began with a Nordic hero, a character whom he called "the Goth." London planned for this hero to tell the story of the last days of Jesus of Nazareth as he himself had witnessed them. It is possible that London had been inspired to write this story by conversations he had had with Anna Strunsky, whom he had met in December 1899, a friendship that may also have inspired the story of Jacob and Leah in "Two Children of Israel." Strunsky challenged London to think creatively and historically, and London's imagination was such that he could picture himself a modern-day Viking and Strunsky as a woman with spiritual ties to a Jewish woman associated with Pilate's court at the time of Jesus.

At a very early point in the development of the idea for this story, London considered enclosing the Goth's life within a frame similar to one he eventually used in *The Iron Heel*: that of introducing the work through the character of a historian who tells the reader that he has worked out the true story of Jesus. Apparently, this historian was also to discover the manuscript of the Goth's story, a manuscript that enabled him to "explode" the myths of the Bible and other accounts. The novel was to be divided into "five movements" so that London could, if he had the opportunity, rework it into dramatic form and have it put on stage.[55] London abandoned this idea and continued plotting a more conventional novel.

He settled on the idea of the Goth's story being written down in Hebrew by a Jewish woman, whom the Goth loves, because he cannot read or write. Once again we have a story about authors. The Goth has an excellent memory and is "strong on natural figures"—meaning, it seems, that Nature was his source for poetic language: "When the Goth describes Christ—a spiritual look like that which comes upon the scalds when transported by singing, only more effeminate, more delicate, more refined."[56] He is practical, militaristic, and "a good trencher man." London stressed his power of storytelling, and he wrote out a bit of dialogue between the Goth and the Jewish woman to illustrate this power: "For, when I have spoken of the things I have seen in strange lands, (describes Rome and Caesar, etc.) often has she said: 'The power of vision is yours. Your words are colors and columns and rare fabrics, and gems, and great figures and sculptured lions and sphynxes, and as you speak, I see. Your eyes are wide apart and made for seeing. It is your eyes that have led you over the world, seeing, always seeing.' And I made answer: 'Then did they lead me to you, and they see you now, as they saw you that first day, when I rode through the streets of Jerusalem, on my way to Pilate's Court.'"[57] For London, the eyes were the organs of the imaginative power of an author, and he uses a similar description for his most developed author figure, Martin Eden.

In the opening scene, the Goth was to arrive in Jerusalem. The two lovers were to meet immediately. He would tell her about his boyhood and how he became a Roman soldier. They were also scheduled to discuss at great length the differences between their religions. At one point, London calls her the Goth's wife, but there is no hint of how their marriage was to be engineered. She, in turn, was to be an equally strong individual. "She was looked upon by the Jews as a wanton, because of her free life. They would have destroyed her, had not she received the protection of Rome. So they cursed her and defamed her. Her initiative, independence, and philosophical mind was repellent to them, did not coincide with their ideal of woman at all. . . . Have some palace scene, where Jewess confutes some of the Jewish sectaries."[58] London is translating the socialist principle of gender equality into characterization.

The other cross-cultural encounter that London focused on was that among the Romans, the Jews, and the Goth. The character of Pilate stands prominently in the notes as a stern and aloof bureaucrat. London pictured him as a man trapped into ordering Jesus's execution by the high priest, whom he detests; yet he has no feelings one way or another toward Jesus. "Let him be the personification of the iron heel of Rome. The whole thing to him an incident. What was one man's life to him? A stray street preacher, a fanatic." Once London had defined the Romans' attitude toward the Jews, he then outlined for himself how he, as author, should treat the Jews: "Outside of Goth and Roman disgust for the Jews, give the Jews a strong place in the book, because of their industry, their spirituality, and their militant past. Let their present be fearfully dissentious and quarrelsome," not unlike the socialists in "Two Children of Israel." London planned for dialogues on religion between a Jew and Pilate. Pilate was to advocate polytheism, "but the Jew says this falls into being absurdly imaginative and confusing, dividing perception from right conduct which is indivisible." London was treating Jerusalem and its people in no way differently from the way he would treat London and San Francisco, emphasizing their racial, religious, and political diversification. "Accentuate, always," he reminded himself, "the might of Rome, overshadowing the ancient world." The Romans were capitalists, the Jews, socialists.

The Goth, then, was meant to be the person who, so to speak, would eventually write "How I Became a Socialist." The plot was to turn, not just around the love affair of a Jew and a Norseman, but also around the Goth's encounter with the risen body of Jesus. In order to show the Goth's pre-Ascension attitude, London placed him at several scenes in which he could exhibit his indifference to the near riots over Jesus's presence in Jerusalem. He was to be present at Jesus's trial before Pontius Pilate. He is represented as being merely a loyal soldier to Pilate and irritated at the mob and their clamoring. At one point he suggests to Pilate that the mob should be cleared, as if the Jews were strikers and he was the militia for the twentieth-century industrialists; Pilate rejects this suggestion because it would disrupt his policy of appeasement. The Goth was also to be the commander present at the crucifixion who "orders the spear thrust into his side by the soldier, much in the same spirit any animal out of its misery." (At this point in his notes, London reminded himself: "Warning.—No lolly-gagging about the crucifixion—a matter of small moment to all concerned; sparse, brutish, natural.") The Goth was to meet, or at least hear of, Mary Magdalen before and after her conversion so that he could be psychologically prepared for his own possible conversion. London meant to build the story to the climax of Pilate ordering the Goth to steal the body of Jesus from his grave. The Goth presumably returns to Pilate and in conversation with him "describes it all, and lo, there was no body. 'I know not whether he did truly rise, or whether the Jewish priests stole the body and cast it to dishonor. Of this there has been talk. As I say, I know not; but I do truly believe that he did rise from the dead, etc.'"[59] Yet in the same set of notes, London could not quite bring himself to affirm the Goth's conversion: "After Goth is converted (if he is converted),—somewhere, shortly and to the point, in his blunt way, he argues it out. Could any blame rest upon Pilate. Was not Christ the fulfillment of the Prophecy of old-time? Before Pilate was conceived? Was it not intended from the foundations of the world, that Christ should be crucified? If Pilate had done otherwise than he did, and saved Christ, would prophecy been fulfilled? Was Pilate greater than God that he should alter God's decrees? Could he set aside and make null and void the prophecies of God?" Thus, a central dilemma for both the Goth and London from the beginning was the question of whether one could derive transcendent meaning from an encounter with an apparent supranatural event. And could this event be analogical to a political conversion?[60]

From 1903 to 1907 London was less concerned with twentieth-century Christian interpretations of Jesus and more interested in how twentieth-century socialists viewed the story of Jesus. He began to explore how Jesus could be seen as a social rather than a religious figure. His notes for the Christ novel written during this period show what sources he was drawing on for material not only for the still-to-be-written novel but also for his general ideas about Christianity and socialism. The more deeply he became involved in socialist writings, the further the idea of writing a novel about Jesus receded. He had found within socialism an outlet for his spiritual feelings.

London accepted, but only provisionally, doctrinaire socialism's reading of the history of Christianity. When he entertained the idea of turning Jesus into a modern-day labor leader, he may have first relied on Allan Ricker's article "The Political Economy of Jesus," published in January 1904, and thus something he would have read after he had returned from Korea. Ricker's thesis was that Jesus "spoke for the working class," that the first three hundred years of Christianity remained true to that message, and then "it was absorbed by the ruling power, and its whole purpose and scope made to reflect the interests of the ruling class" (5). Thus London used this pamphlet for both his Christ novel and for an essay he planned entitled "The Persistence of the Established"; at the top of the Ricker pamphlet he wrote, "File afterward with Christ novel," meaning after he was done using it for the "Persistence" essay. London may have first heard of Ernest Renan's *The Life of Jesus* from Ricker, who cites it in his article as the only life of Jesus "worth the reading." He marked a paragraph that pronounced Jesus "a dangerous labor agitator" and then wrote in the margin, "Develop that he was a labor agitator, and for that as well feared. Make a sweet, true character of Jesus." Later in the same article, next to a paragraph about tensions between "the Roman plutocracy" and the "unions," in which he says, "the proletarian or working class population vastly exceeded the master class . . . and they were very closely knit together in their unions," he wrote, "Pilate saw this."[61] Seeing this perhaps motivated Pilate, thought London, to crucify Jesus. Jesus died for the sins of the capitalists.

He read and marked the following passage in a 1906 article entitled "Economics of Jesus": "His [Jesus's] cleansing of the temple near the close of His career, which was one of the chief causes of his crucifixion, was an additional approval of the Mosaic principle of commercial equality and the climax of His condemnation of Mammon worship."[62] London toyed with the idea that the Romans were solely responsible for the execution of Jesus. If Jesus were a revolutionary leading an insurrection against the Roman state, then the Romans must be portrayed as the killers. One article London clipped for his "Christ novel" file was entitled "Jewish Innocence of the Death of Jesus."[63] The article summarizes a speech delivered in Congress by Allan L. McDermott who was prompted to offer his own exoneration of the Jews by the threat in Russia of the massacre of Jews. London became convinced that the Jewish people were not responsible for Jesus's execution, but he did not become convinced that the Romans were simply an early version of the American oligarchy. On this point and on the issue of the true nature of Jesus, London could not allow his radical socialism to determine his understanding of Christian history. He had to retain if not the divinity of Jesus at least his spirituality.

In this he was in accord with his longtime friend and adviser Frederick Irons Bamford, who was a Social Gospeler. When George D. Herron, "the intellectual leader of social Christianity" during the 1890s, toured California on a lecture trip, Bamford met and talked with him at length. Herron was among the first American social theorists to yoke Christian and Marxist rhetoric. "It was George D. Herron," writes Ira Kipnis, "who made the first real attempt to resolve the contradictions between Christianity and Marxian socialism. . . . He held that God worked through 'economic fact and development.' . . . The working class socialist philosophy of history alone gives the account of life and labor out of which a new religious synthesis can be wove." According to Herron, "the sources of life which [Marxist socialism] discloses are identical with the spiritual forces which Jesus revealed."[64] Though they agreed on essentials, one senses that Herron was too radical for Bamford's taste. Bamford felt more comfortable with the liberal proponents of the Social Gospel, such as Walter Rauschenbusch, who advocated ethics over theology but who did not openly call for revolution and who did not believe in the inevitability of class warfare.

Bamford was also a proponent of British socialism as advanced by Ruskin, Morris, Carlyle, and Arnold. In 1898 he organized the Ruskin Club, a sometimes informal, sometimes formal gathering of socialist intellectuals who engaged in spirited and vital discussions. Jessie Peixotto—the first woman to receive a doctorate from the University of California–Berkeley and who then became a professor of economics there, author of *The French Revolution and Modern French Socialism*, and the wife of Alexander Peixotto (artist and illustrator of works by London)—recalled that "Mr. Bamford called himself Secretary and he ran everything. He formed the Club and he made all the arrangements for the speakers. They were members often like Jack London, Austin Lewis, George Sterling. . . . The rest were a lot of young men—ministers, lawyers, professionals in general, largely from Oakland."[65] Besides those named, A. A. Denison (an editor at the *Oakland Enquirer*), Herman Whitaker (short-story writer and close friend of London's), Senator R. A. Dague of Alameda, several ministers, and others were members. Visitors included J. Stitt Wilson of Chicago, who lectured in 1901; Robert Royce (no relation to Josiah Royce), who was Austin Lewis's law partner; Edward F. Adams (a conservative editorial writer for the *San Francisco Chronicle*); Gelett Burgess; and the heads of various trade unions and churches as well as businessmen, engineers, and newspaper editors. At the first "Ladies Night" (6 December 1901), Bessie London was one of three informal hosts, and Anna Strunsky, Roscoe Eames, Ninetta Eames, and Edward Payne attended; Strunsky and Peixotto debated the merits of conservatism, and London, Lewis, Mollie Bloom, and H. G. Walker led the discussion.[66] Obviously, when London presented his ideas on central socioeconomic topics, they were rigorously tested and debated. The club disbanded in 1907.

Given that London was a revolutionary socialist, though a close friend of Bamford's, something that Peixotto may not have known, she said,

> I don't know why Jack joined. He spoke fairly often and was on the whole against the Club. Most of the members were clearly Fabians. They did not believe in Marxism. As you know, that is the distinction between Fabians and Marxists. Jack thought he was a Marxist, but there were days when he certainly wasn't. I have always thought

that he never understood Marxism in the least. I don't know if he was invited to be a charter member. I don't think so. All the Ruskin Club members that I know thought of him as a brilliant person with a theory of his own. He was very young at that time. He always wore soft white silk shirts and looked trim and neat. He was very merry and very good company but he had no sense of humor as Gelett Burgess had and no solemn habits of mind and speech as Frank Norris had. I should say that the Club was too solemn for him but I may be wrong in that.[67]

Jack would have thought they all took themselves too seriously and were seriously misguided in their political beliefs. He had read at least a part of *Das Capital* and all of the *Communist Manifesto* and so understood and approved that much of Marx and Engels.[68]

London joined the Ruskin Club in 1898, and he resigned his active membership in 1905 because of his move out of Oakland to Glen Ellen, though he did speak to the club in January 1907, just before his departure on the *Snark*. He joined as a favor to Bamford, but also because he thrived on intellectual stimulation and debate. He loved his intellectual opponents as much as he did his allies. At the same time that he followed Bamford's advice to read Ruskin and Morris, he was writing articles and delivering speeches that advanced a more radical socialism. In 1901 he led the meeting on the topic of revolutionary socialism versus trade unionism, and afterward the group agreed, contra London, that "the ultimate result of trade unionism in this country would be similar to what it had been in New Zealand and in England to compel the workingman into the consciousness of a common cause and to seek through political action to secure conditions which shall further their interests."[69] Joan London identifies London's and Bamford's basic conflict as that between a proletariat socialist and a "protestant evangelical Socialist."[70] They differed openly on two points. In 1905 London declared to Bamford that "what the Ruskin Club wants is life (intellectual dynamic life), and then it rejects life when it is offered."[71] A year later, they differed over London's organization of the Intercollegiate Socialist Society, a minor argument over tactics. Joan London's analysis of their differences seems to me to be correct: while Bamford saw the churches as taking a primary role in the reformation of American society and its economic system, London believed that the impetus could only be provided by the enlightened proletariat.

For Christmas 1907 he received another gift from Fred Bamford: a New Testament Bible.[72] The editor of this particular Bible, using the King James version as his base, arranged the gospels and letters chronologically by date of appearance so that the reader may "approach the New Testament in the same way as did the Christians of the earliest age of the Church."[73] Two marginal notes that London made show that he read this Bible with his Christ novel in mind. In the prologue, the editor summarizes the life of Jesus. Opposite the description of Peter's denial of Jesus, London wrote: "Hero sees and hears this."[74] The other note is similar. Opposite Mark 15.7–10, the description of Pilate offering Barabbas to the crowd, London wrote: "Have the Goth instrumental in catching Barabbas—& make Barabbas strong character—Also, as characters, the two thieves." This note's significance is two-fold. First, it shows that London planned for the Goth to participate in other matters than the crucifixion of Jesus. Second, because Barabbas was an insurrectionary, London clearly intended to make the political struggles of the time the context in which he would tell the story of the Goth and Jesus.

In some general way, Bamford and London could find common ground when it came to the intersection of socialism and Christianity. Though London was too radical to be called a Social Gospeler, he did agree with its major tenets. Bamford sent him a copy of Walter Rauschenbusch's *Christianity and the Social Crisis* shortly after it was published in 1907. London probably read the entire book, but he marked passages only in the introduction and in the chapter entitled "The Social Aims of Jesus." In a note to himself in his "Christ Novel" file, London reminded himself to return to Rauschenbusch for "splendid, most splendid, historical data on Jesus."[75] Rauschenbusch reaffirmed London's idea that Jesus's teaching had a major political impact. He marked Rauschenbusch's opinion that Jesus's use of the phrase "kingdom of God" "unfettered the political hopes of the crowd; it drew down on him the suspicion of the government; it actually led to his death."[76] But he also marked the passage in which Rauschenbusch shows that Jesus denied himself a political messiahship and any involvement in political and potential violent revolution against the state.[77] This is apparently the message that Bamford wanted to convey to London.

What appealed most to London about Rauschenbusch's exegesis was its illustrations of how Jesus lived above the law. Rauschenbusch portrays Jesus not as a socialist but as a social being who sought to unite the classes by teaching higher religious and social values than those current in his time. London was attracted to the idea that Jesus's teachings could not be made to fit into any particular political program, but rather that they could be used as part of a comprehensive program for overhauling American society. In general terms, two things appealed most to London about Rauschenbusch. One was his millennialism. The other was his belief that churches must be concerned with social reform. Yet they differed significantly in their orientations. While Rauschenbusch approached social reform from the church, London remained outside the church, hoping that it would be reformed as well. Just as the Social Gospelers were attracted to socialism, so was Bamford interested in recruiting London. But the two movements, as well as the two individuals, could not join forces. London could appropriate some of the ideas of the Social Gospel movement, but he could never belong to the movement.

In 1911 London once again turned his thoughts to his Christ novel. He had returned from his *Snark* voyage, he had begun in earnest his ranch and farm improvements, and he was in the process of writing two series of short stories, *A Son of the Sun* and *Smoke Bellew*, as well as an assortment of other short pieces. Sometime in 1911 London spelled himself from the heavy task of writing short stories and sketched notes for a series of novels that would in effect tell the whole history of the human race: "NOVEL. Why not a series of past and future novels? No. 1,—BEFORE ADAM; No. 2—CHRIST NOVEL; No. 3,—THE MIDDLE AGES; No. 4, some great proletarian-bourgeoise conflict story of the present; No. 5, THE IRON HEEL; No. 6,—THE FAR FUTURE, the perfected and perishing human race."[78] This note represents the first indication that London planned to place his story of Jesus in relation to other historical events. It would no longer be just another retelling of the story, whether cast in socialist rhetoric or not. Further, this note indicates that London felt that his novels were too narrow in scope. He was thinking in cosmic terms. He had always been searching for a synthetic philosophy ever since he had had his eyes opened by Herbert Spencer. Like many other intellectuals and writers of the time, he had had his sense of time expanded to infinity in both directions by the truth of evolution and the hope of socialism. Now he saw the possibility of fictionalizing all of human history, including his own prophecies of what humanity would be like when the sun began to burn out.

Also during this final period of working on the "Christ Novel" London arrived at a personally satisfactory though indeterminate meaning for Jesus. The most influential source for London was Ernest Renan's *The Life of Jesus*. It is a work of history, not theology. As a historian, Renan attempted to trace the development of Jesus as a man, the slow evolution of his thought and sense of mission, the reaction of the ruling parties—both Roman and Jewish—and the interior processes of the people who believed in the miracles of Jesus. Renan himself did not believe in the miracles, although he did assert that he was a religious man. Compared to some German biblical exegetists, he was conservative in his judgments of authorship and the historicity of the Gospels. He believed in the divinity of Jesus, not with the aid of dogma but through a personal encounter with and redefinition of the man Jesus.

All these qualities of Renan's appealed to London. Having dismissed Jesus-as-socialist—a position Renan shared—London could neither deny Jesus's importance nor affirm his stature as God. So he read Renan's book avidly, marking the margins and using the end papers for notes for the Christ novel. He was not so much interested in writing a novel about Jesus but about the men and women who came into contact with him. In other words, he was interested in how people had created a Christ out of Jesus of Nazareth. He typically left alone any chapter dealing with an explication of Jesus's message; however, any passage that explained how the Jews and Romans understood and reacted to Jesus received his utmost attention.

London's notes indicate that he concentrated on developing Pilate's character, and to some extent, the Jewish woman, but that he had the Goth's character firmly in mind. He summed up the Goth's final attitude toward Jesus in a brief note: "Hero marks strange charm of Jesus—even over himself." "Charm" is a key word for Renan; he uses it to explain Jesus's power over the multitudes and apostles. As Renan explains it, "Jesus owed these numerous conquests to an infinite charm of person and of speech. One penetrating word, one glance falling upon a simple conscience which was only waiting to be aroused, made such a one an ardent disciple."[79] To London, the word "charm" helped to explain a materialist's attraction to an apparently spiritual reality. It is for this contribution that London owed a greater debt to Renan than to any other source that he used. He gathered, perhaps, equal amounts of historical data from other sources; other sources even helped him to construct a framework of ideas about Jesus and Christianity. But Renan was responsible for a greater impact. Although it seems that London remained in doubt concerning the true nature of Jesus, he found in Renan a satisfactory explanation of Jesus's power and influence. He could suspend belief and remain in awe and wonder.

What this discussion of London's fictionalization of Jesus's life ultimately tells us is that his search for a true understanding of Jesus paralleled and at times blended with his participation in American socialism. Furthermore, whereas he could attach Christian rhetoric to his discussions of American capitalism and to his fictional creations of socialists such as Ernest Everhard, he could not attach socialistic rhetoric to his portrayal of Jesus. He decided that the message of Jesus transcended politics and held a deeper meaning. He did not believe in salvation through Jesus. But he did believe that worldly salvation could be achieved in the future through economic and social justice as long as *justice* included in its definition principles advocated by Jesus. It was ethics, not soteriology, that interested him, and socialism— especially if it condoned the violence between scabs and workers—seemed hollow without it. Charmian London quoted in her biography a letter from London to Stephen French in which he said: "I don't know whether Jesus Christ was a myth or not; but taking him just as I find him, just as I read him, I have two heroes—one is Jesus Christ, the other Abraham Lincoln."[80] According to a note by Charmian, London chose an introductory quotation for the Christ novel, though he never used it: "There is only one thing more wonderful than the reality of Christ, and that is, Christ never existing, that the imagination of man should have created him."[81] If the spirit of the imagination haunts Jack London the author, then the spirit of Jesus haunts the materialism of Jack London the socialist.

3   JACK LONDON'S PLACE IN AMERICAN LITERATURE

I wondered at the strength of it, and the horror of it. I could hardly sleep, it
so haunted me. I believed all the time it was you who was kidnapped and
you who were suffering untold agonies, day and night.
—Charles Warren Stoddard, letter to Jack London, on reading *The Sea-Wolf*

CLUBBING THE IMAGINATION

From a major though uncompleted writing project like the Christ novel, we learn more about London's composition process: how he combined multiple sources, composed multiple kinds of notes, used books as an impetus for rough drafts, and adhered to his own injunction to form a philosophy that will infuse one's fiction writing. Further, we now see how this process for a vast, eventually invisible work (a kind of ghost manuscript) is kept hidden if we pay attention only to the history of his writing process for material for publication. We marvel at the volume of London's published work without realizing how much lies hidden behind it. It would be an exaggeration to say that for every work he published he wrote parts or nearly wholes of works that never made it into final form. But the central lesson of his Christ novel, as far as we are considering London as a working author, is that his published works tell only part of the story of his authorial practice and accomplishments. He left a lot on the cutting room floor.

He would not, of course, mention this to beginning writers. It was a part of his secret life as an author. Neither would he mention how little money writing essays about writing earned him nor how it was wise to ignore a signed contract with a major international publisher in order to indulge one's own creative urge. Now we turn to the other essays he wrote in the ten weeks between finishing *The Call of the Wild*—his novel about the imagination—and beginning *The Sea-Wolf*—his novel about modeling authorship. For his early 1903 essays on writing and publishing—"Getting into Print," "Stranger Than Fiction," and "The Terrible and Tragic"—he earned a grand total of fifty dollars. To write one uncontracted essay and receive five dollars for it, as he did with "Getting into Print," would indicate a carefree attitude toward want. To write three in a row indicates a need greater than financial security. When he says in "Getting into Print" "I shall always be content to receive the minimum rate," we need to take him at his word, even if he learned how to drive the price of his stories up. Of course he would take more money, but money was not the point.

He wrote these essays while he was also completing his 1903 socialist essays and as he prepared himself to write *The Sea-Wolf*. They form a kind of hinge between *The Call of the Wild* and *The Sea-Wolf*. The first of the essays looks back to the former novel as it addresses the question of inspiration; the second and third look forward to the latter as they discuss reality versus romance, Poe, tragedy, and the horror story; in fact, since London came up with the plot and characters for *The Sea-Wolf* in January 1903, he was thinking about the novel as he wrote these essays.[1] They each have their own thematic concerns, but in general they act as a bridge between the novel that he was not contracted to write and the one he was. The essays are either implicitly or explicitly concerned with commercialism and art, and so we look to London's writings about writing to try to understand why he wrote what he wrote. Reading between the lines of his fictional output to discover the answer to this question is always a risky business, so we hope to find them answered straightforwardly in his writing essays. We will fail. Not only did he hide his true methodology and compositional process from his readers, his friends, and his publishers and editors, he also hid the true story of his beginnings as an author and how he maintained a living as a writer. His life was stranger than fiction. By the logic of his own argument in "Stranger Than Fiction," as we will see, he could not tell it straight. But the story of his life was the human document behind his writing, whether the genre was short story, novel, play, or nonfiction essay.

On 12 February 1903, after he had completed the review of Ghent's and Brooks's books and three stories for *Tales of the Fish Patrol*, but before he wrote three other socialist essays, he wrote "Getting into Print," originally titled "How I Placed My First Manuscript" or "How It Was Done."[2] We recall a similar piece he wrote at the end of 1901 entitled "Again the Literary Aspirant." Unlike "Again the Literary Aspirant," in which London railed against the paradox of magazines accepting only established writers (thus, how do beginners get established if they can't get published?), "Getting into Print" lays out concrete steps "to compass the paradox." Now he had a contract with Macmillan and had completed a second, successful novel for which he had just sold the serial rights to the *Saturday Evening Post*. One might think that he would write a celebratory, happy essay. Instead, the bitterness and frustration of "Again the Literary Aspirant" gives way to mythologizing and poor mouthing. He knew he had arrived and he knew he was in a position to tell beginners how to succeed, but he was a secretive, distrustful author. Not everything he says in this essay is untrue—just the story of his career, which he imagines runs only from the spring of 1897 to February 1899. Like the 1899 letter to Houghton Mifflin written as public relations material for the publication of *A Son of the Wolf*, this 1903 essay, though briefer, is equally misleading. London writes, not only did he have no money when he first "went up against the magazines," but also he knew nothing about publishing. Again, here is the no-mentor-but-myself model of authorship that he tried to convince his audience was true. "I lived in California, far from the great publishing centers," converting what was always a source of pride for him—and a nonnegotiable marker of authorial identity—into a liability.[3]

Part of the strategy of poor mouthing in an advice essay, though, is to persuade the beginning writer that if someone as handicapped as London could succeed then any beginner could do the same. You just don't have to start out the same way because he is now telling his "secrets." Yet his secrets are untrustworthy too. "Avoid the unhappy ending, the harsh, the brutal, the tragic, the horrible—if you care to see in print the things you write." These adjectives prompted the content of his next two essays on writing, especially "The Terrible and Tragic." But they also lead him to unwittingly create a new paradox. He appends to that sentence a parenthetical: "In this connection, don't do as I do, but do as I say."[4] In other words, you should keep your day job, write fiction, don't write poetry, write jokes if you are funny (like Mark Twain), practice writing in a notebook, read to learn how to write, eat well, and work hard.[5] But if London succeeded by writing about "the tragic" and "the horrible," then, a beginner might adduce, why should he or she follow any of the advice? The one kernel of advice London seems to be offering is don't follow the rules, mine or anyone else's.

A further instance of London writing advice contrary to his own practice appears in a brief set of notes called "Ideas for Literary Essays, or Essays on Literature. Maybe on literary topics":

The short story, high as an art form, poorly remunerative. Eight or ten a year, but no more if he keeps it up.

Difficulty of writing, compared with novel-writing. No padding. Every word must count. And here's the rub, for he's paid by the word. He is paid for length, not strength. . . .

Publishers shy at collections of short stories. They make practically nothing themselves, the short-story writer makes practically nothing, and there is as much chance of being struck twice by lightning, as there is of such a collection making a hit.[6]

How could anyone take such advice seriously, true as it may be, when it was written by someone who had written eighty-four stories in four years? He had published three collections by 1903. The most obvious contradiction, though, concerns novel writing. If writing novels is so much easier than short stories, and earns more, then one would think that London would have started out writing novels and would have no anxiety about doing so. Also, where is the concern he has for earning money on a regular basis so that he can have the time to write novels without worrying about income? Where is any mention of advances, of his strategy of publishing work in serials and in book form? No, London did not mean to reveal himself in these essays about writing and publishing.

Nevertheless, London did work hard and did mean that beginners should, too, yet here he even leaves himself open for multiple interpretations. On the one hand, he tells us, work hard. Get paid what you deserve. That seems to be the message of his story of encountering the publishing machine. On the other hand, that same story leads him to a different conclusion: "Let other men, thought I, receive the maximum rate, whatever marvelous sum it may be. As for myself, I shall always be content to receive the minimum rate. And, once I get started, I shall do no more than three thousand words a day, five days only in the week. This will give me plenty of recreation, while I shall be earning six hundred dollars a month without overstocking the market." Surprisingly, London espouses his bohemian economics, but he does not put it into rule form, which would go something like this: Play as often as you work. Earn just enough to keep body and soul together. If the market will pay more, then take it. Once again, especially in regard to that final directive to not flood the market, he could have appended the injunction to do as I say, not as I do. At this point in his career, readers would have known just how much he was publishing. And in the next couple of months, they would see three new works appear almost simultaneously, flooding the market.

There is a rotundity to what he means by *work*. To work doesn't only mean, as his story of his career seems to indicate, to write constantly, to send material out constantly. "Oh, I was prolific," he says, but he doesn't mean that he wasn't goofing off, flying kites, admiring the poppies in his bohemian Piedmont property. To work also means to "work for a philosophy of life," to "find out about this earth, this universe; this force and matter, and the spirit that glimmers up through force and matter from the maggot to Godhead."[7] This is the facet of the complete meaning of *work* that he chose to emphasize for beginners. It wasn't enough to write all the time, to keep a notebook, to organize yourself in your home writing office. You had to work for a higher purpose.

Now we can see another dimension to studying the process by which he almost wrote his Christ novel: Jesus was an intellectual vehicle—something to think with—to lead to a better understanding of "the spirit" that existed in conjunction with "force and matter." To understand Jesus was fundamental to his philosophy of life, and his philosophy of life did not include the imperative to work so hard that you became a mere machine. The point was to never have to work like a machine again, or like a work beast. To arrive at a better understanding of the nature of spirit was to help achieve a balance between work and play.

How does one get into print, then? London's imagined audience—probably working class like himself, with some amount of education, and a fondness for magazine writing—could easily track the advice that London lays out. After all, he spelled out his key words in capitals: "GOOD HEALTH; WORK; and a PHILOSOPHY OF LIFE. I may add, nay, must add, a fourth—SINCERITY [whatever that is, for he hasn't even used the word until this last minute, let alone define it]."[8] But for those who were brought up short by the injunction "don't do as I do, but do as I say," and for those paying attention to his career, there were troubling contradictions that pointed to a different path to getting into print: don't work too hard, leave time to enjoy life, write tragedies with brutal characters and horrible events, don't worry about what you eat or drink or smoke, try to get published in the elite magazines, get to know people—editors, newspaper reporters, other writers—who are involved in the publishing business. That's how London did it. By giving advice that he did not follow, he indicates how ambivalent, how puzzled, how disturbed, how haunted he was by his own imagination, his own shining spirit.

The traditional way to analyze "Getting into Print" is to focus on London's description of the submission and rejection process as a kind of machine—"the process seemed like the working of some soulless machine"—and then link it to a similar description in *Martin Eden*.[9] London employs the machine metaphor, however, only to describe impersonal rejections, and he leaves out all the personal rejection letters he received, letters that offered encouragement and good advice and notice that the editor would like to read something else by him. When he gets accepted—another element in his career that he hides from his readers—the machine is magically replaced by human beings like Bridge, Brett, McClure, Walker, and others. That is, he would never use the machine metaphor to describe his relations with the number of editors and publishers who took a genuine and personal interest in both his writing and his career. In this way, he also minimizes the importance of his acceptance by the *Overland Monthly* and exaggerates the importance of the *Black Cat*, something he did in his introduction to H. D. Umbstaetter's *The Red Hot Dollar, and Other Stories* and in other places. London fictionalizes his almost simultaneous acceptances from the *Black Cat* and *Overland Monthly* to create the illusion that writing for money was the only motivation he or any other author followed. This is, after all, what he imagined his audience wanted. To get into print meant to earn a living writing, and thus he valorizes *Black Cat* and denigrates the *Overland Monthly*.[10] Again, he was hiding something important, and this time it was the fact of his imagination and its never-ending imperative to write first and consider the marketplace second.

The most important trick he pulled in "Getting into Print" is to deny the importance of inspiration. On the one hand, he tells his reader to investigate the presence of "the spirit" in all things. On the other hand, in probably his most famous piece of advice to beginners, he says, "Don't loaf and invite inspiration; light out after it with a club, and if you don't get it you will nonetheless get something that looks remarkably like it." On the one hand, the immaterial animating force of all things should be sought after and understood. On the other, the immaterial animating force of an author's being should be beaten into submission. What did he mean by this latter directive? Why shouldn't one come to terms with one's inner spirit instead of beating it with a club?

That vivid image of something being beaten with a club indicates a thematic connection between *The Call of the Wild* and "Getting into Print." Consider this scene from the novel, and imagine Jack holding the club:

> And Buck was truly a red-eyed devil, as he drew himself together for the spring. . . . In mid air, just as his jaws were about to close on the man, he received a shock that checked his body and brought his teeth together with an agonizing clip. . . . He had never been struck by a club in his life. . . . He was beaten (he knew that); but he was not broken. He saw, once for all, that he stood no chance against a man with a club. . . . That club was a revelation. . . . . A man with a club was a law-giver, a master to be obeyed, though not necessarily conciliated.

Just as beating things with clubs bleeds over from *The Call of the Wild* and into "Getting into Print," so the concerns of "Getting into Print" are foreshadowed in *Call*. In other words he was using language from *The Call of the Wild* in his essay to describe the process of writing because *The Call of the Wild* is about the process of writing. This means that Buck is a figure for the creative imagination that must be beaten into domestication—it must be tamed—and do something useful like pull a sled. After being trained to earn money it can then be trusted (somewhat) and let free. Remember, in London's Klondike fiction he often makes the analogy between the men and dogs breaking trail in the snow and the black lines of writing on a white page. Buck, as the figure of the imagination, leads the hobo-miner-author across the page.

Buck starts out on a porch, doing nothing, producing nothing, just fat and happy and loveable. But once men start chasing him with a club he becomes "a red-eyed devil." Initially he doesn't do what they want him to do. Buck's transformation is often portrayed as a movement from domestication to primitiveness, and we can color code this transformation. He goes from red to white, from the red-eyed devil to the ghost-dog. Beaten into obedience, controlled enough to give London story after story, novel after novel, his imagination nonetheless breaks free in the end like Buck, more powerful, multiplying on its own in the wild. It creates without the seeming intervention of the artist. The artist can only sit back and watch it take control. Or the artist has died in a Barthian sense, like John Thorton, while the imagination lives on. Thorton enacts the death of the author. The imagination is eternal, and the author disappears while writing.

In "Getting into Print," London doesn't use the word *imagination*. He uses the word *inspiration*. Are they synonyms? London's writings on the subject aren't very helpful, and we shouldn't be surprised by that because he spent so much time denying its existence. So let's turn to an author, a romantic poet, who did theorize about the imagination, who also valorized John Milton, and whose career is marked by the same interplay of reading and writing as London's: Samuel Taylor Coleridge. In *The Road to Xanadu*, John Lowes's classic study of the workings of Coleridge's imagination— especially in how his reading directly informed his composition process— and how he produced the two poems "Kubla Khan" and "Rime of the Ancient Mariner," Lowes refers to Coleridge's "shaping spirit of the *imagination*" and "the informing *spirit* which broods over chaos to draw it . . . into 'the precincts of light,'" that last phrase coming from Milton's *Paradise Lost*. Here, then, is the very literary, very typical way of portraying the imagina- tion. "Sing, O heavenly Muse," writes Milton, in a work that London knew well and that he brought with him as a kind of lantern into the darkness that was the Klondike. In book three of *Paradise Lost*, Milton prays that the "Celestial Light" "shine inward, and the mind through all her powers / Irradiate, there plant eyes, all mist from thence / Purge and disperse, that I may see and tell / Of things invisible to mortal sight." That is, an element of the unseen world will give the poet the tools (the eyes) to see what can- not be seen by humans and then, as well, the voice to tell of these things. For Milton, the Muse is a heavenly light.

Lowes notes that, according to Coleridge, after we take into account the individuality of an artist "there [is] a precious residuum which is peculiar to no individual, but which inheres in the nature of the imaginative fac- ulty itself" (32). This is what he would call the primary imagination. The secondary imagination is quotidian. Everyone has an imagination. As par- ents, we tell our kids, "use your imagination." And that's a kind of work-a- day understanding of the imagination. But not all of us can write *Paradise Lost* or *Mutiny of the Elsinore*. According to Coleridge and Lowes, an image, something we read, goes into the deep well of memory or, as Henry James— another writer who, like Coleridge, was perfectly happy with his own creative talent—put it in the preface to *The American*, "the deep well of unconscious cerebration." It undergoes "strange transformation there." "It has merged insensibly, in hues and outline, with others of the myriad denizens of that mysterious deep, and what we think we have remembered we have actually, in large degree, unconsciously created" (56–57). So the imagination and the memory are inextricably tied together, and they work either in the unconscious or side by side with the unconscious. Of course, what does it mean to say that memory is in the unconscious? Bits of reading go into the deep well of memory. There they sit together, fusing, "and when the flash of inspiration at last [comes]—that leap of association which, like the angel in the Gospel, stirred to momentary potency the waters of the pool—it was neither" the one image or the other or one plus one but something entirely new. This describes the memory and the unconscious working together and then animated by "the flash of inspiration."

Here inspiration is not synonymous with the imagination. The imagination works as a combination of memory and the unconscious. Everyone has imagination, and everyone has inspiration, at least from time to time. But there is something else. According to Coleridge, it takes "genius" to make such fusions noteworthy. As Lowes cites Coleridge, "genius" is an "enhanced and almost incredible facility with which . . . the fragments . . . fuse and assimilate and coalesce" (59–60). First, conscious intellectual activity drops stuff into the well (the poet takes notes in a notebook); then these bits of reading matter, of observations of life, sit there and the imagination works on them; and then "it is conscious energy [genius], now of another and loftier type, which later drags the deeps for their submerged measure and moulds the bewildering chaos into unity." This is the process of the secondary imagination. So for Coleridge, inspiration and imagination are not synonyms necessarily. Sometimes he uses them interchangeably, but when he is being precise he separates them denotatively by their operation through time. That is, imagination is always present. Inspiration happens in a moment.

Is this how London understood the process of creativity? In an important way, it doesn't matter. Both terms signify something internal, something of the mind or soul or unconscious or the barely conscious. Both work together to produce art. Like Coleridge, London drew inspiration from reading. He pinned newspaper articles to sheets of paper and then typed notes for possible short stories based on what the newspaper article said. So if inspiration and/or imagination are being chased by a club, what in the creative process is holding the club? The genius of the individual author, would be Coleridge's answer, that "conscious energy . . . of [a] loftier type, which . . . moulds the bewildering chaos into unity." London would agree. In "Getting into Print," the man with the club is very much a rational, though hypersensitive being, with great eyes, with great vision. The artist molds chaos into unity. "'The imagination,' said Coleridge . . . '*sees all things in one*.'"[11]

But in *The Call of the Wild* we can't call the man in the red sweater a hypersensitive being, with great eyes, with great vision, can we? In a sense we can. The man in the red sweater who beats Buck into submission is simply one of many of London's Anglo-Saxon zone conquerors, men who take charge not just of their own lives but of all the world. They are brutal, but they have the vision necessary to try to conquer the world through violence. They turn the imagination into a Satanic red-eyed devil, but, by god, that devil pulls the sled. The man in the red sweater is the kind of author who simply wants to make a living. A hack.

So in his essay "Getting into Print" London seems to be saying that if you want to write fiction your imagination or inspiration will end up as something tamed, domesticated, but nonetheless devilish, something that might turn on you at any moment. But who wants to be a writer with a red hellish animal living inside you? Wouldn't we rather have a white ghost-dog of an imagination roaming freely, producing little puppies of stories out in the wild? Notice that the title of the essay is "Getting into Print," not "Once You Have Gotten into Print." For London, unlike Coleridge and Milton, the process of becoming a writer involves not only a transformation of the writer as he or she becomes more learned about the world but also a transformation of the faculty of the imagination. This is the ultimate meaning of "don't loaf and invite inspiration; light out after it with a club." To get into print, to start out, you must tame your imagination, train it, make it do what you want it to do, assert control. But at some point, and this is the unstated claim in the essay, you'll discover that great art evolves beyond that relationship between artists and imagination. At some point you have to put the club down and see where your imagination takes you. You have to let it run wild. I believe that London put the club down in the fall of 1902 when he began to write *The Call of the Wild*.

Thus, in January 1903, filled with doubt about his newly completed novel, about his relationship to his publisher, about his contractual status as an author, about his very place in American literature, he picked up the club again and wrote "Getting into Print." As I said, on the surface, he advised the beginner to take a club to inspiration and write about the happy stuff of life. His own way was the harder path to take, and he advised against it. For himself and also for the few of his audience who wanted more than just a regular run of stories in the magazines, he knew that to let your imagination wander freely, to write about ghosts and the tragic and the horrible, was the way to greatness.

Jack London could not help writing about ghosts and the terrible and the tragic because that was how he understood and described his relationship to his creative powers. For Coleridge and Milton, the imagination was a holy thing, a gift from God. Not to use it would be an unholy act. For London, it was a devil and a ghost. It either ripped you to shreds or left you half dead in the wilderness, pen in hand, as it howled its own song of the wild. For the professed man from Missouri, the man who insisted time and time again that if you couldn't see something, touch something, then it didn't exist, the imagination and/or inspiration are metaphysical in nature and therefore are open to question, to doubt. When you are perfectly at ease with your creative talent you mold chaos into unity. When you are upset or haunted by your imagination, you beat inspiration with a club.

"Getting into Print," while looking backward to *The Call of the Wild*, also looks forward to the next two essays, as well as to the Miltonic, satanic figure of Wolf Larsen. As I mentioned, "Getting into Print" ends with a keyword— "sincerity"—that is perhaps London's most fundamental nonnegotiable identity marker, and yet he leaves it there, on the printed page, unexplained. He thus had to write an essay about *sincerity*, which became "Stranger Than Fiction." Paired with Oscar Wilde's essay "The Decay of Lying" and London's *The Road*, we see how he created the figure of the hobo-author and how sincerity became such a crucial concept. Sincerity became the touchstone to solving the problem of how to be true to an imagination that requires the unbelievable facts of life in order to produce high art. Sincerity is the connection between artist and audience, the pledge of trust between the two.

In "Stranger Than Fiction," London emphasizes what the artist must do (or isn't able to do, in his case) in order to gain that trust. But there is a second element to the equation—what the audience must do—and that is the point of his story about the editor and the hobo, who was based on Frank Strawn-Hamilton. (And we might recall that sincerity is best explained in London's collection of hobo stories, especially in *The Road*.) The moral of the story is that editors and audiences would be much better off if they simply made a leap of faith and believed the story as written.[12] The seemingly true is more vital than the actual true fact. One can be honest without being faithful to the facts.

Sincerity is an affect, not a methodology, so it is impossible to describe it scientifically or explain how to put it to good effect. It is beyond rule making. *Be sincere* is not an injunction that can be followed or should even be stated, and so London doesn't. He writes around it. Sincerity is a quality of transparency (ironic for an author who does so much to hide the material writing processes he engages in) and naturalness. Ease and fluidity are other qualities that overlap with sincerity. Being real in the sense of rejecting the fake, the fanciful, the mercenary is required. To write simply for money or to allow one's primary imagination to guide one is to be insincere. Sincerity guarantees interest—*McClure Magazine*'s key word for quality fiction—and that leads to absorption. To be interesting is to transfer one's enthusiasm to another. Once that happens, the author and the reader are joined in affect; they are reading the same words and garnering the same feelings. The reader, in order for this process to work, must forget himself or herself, and once that egoless state is achieved he or she thus becomes absorbed in other lives.

Just as Coleridge posited two orders of the imagination, so, too, does London, though in a skeletal and underdeveloped fashion. One is associated with sincerity, and one is associated with its opposite. At one point in "Stranger Than Fiction" he says that "whenever I evolved out of my sheer inner consciousness some boyish adventure, it received the most flattering approval of the editors."[13] One might think that the "inner consciousness" is the topos of the imagination, and it is, but it is also the topos of fancy, a degraded form of imagination. That's what the word "sheer" indicates. The true imagination works with facts and with what one reads. It turns reality into fiction. Fancy is airy nothingness, as London might say. It appeals to editors because it usually leads to what is imminently saleable, the happy ending, the optimistic, romantic view of life. The true imagination begins from the tragedy of life. When London next says that "whenever my inner consciousness was not in working order, and I fell back on the facts of my life, wrote adventures I had actually gone through, things I had done with my own hands and head," he is deliberately masking the action of the imagination required to write those adventures, just to make the point that editors could not believe a (relatively) faithful account of unbelievable moments and characters in life: the woman behind Frona Welse, a tramp like Frank Strawn-Hamilton, a "pastoral experience" that involved his family. London pretends that reality can be transcribed. He knows it cannot. That is why he continued to write stories based on facts he had observed or on events that he read about in the newspapers.

The true imagination creates stories that are unbelievable based on facts. Because they are based on facts, London thinks the stories should be automatically believed—not necessarily accepted, but at the very least believed. He's shocked to learn that some readers (editors) don't believe him. The essay brings this shocking news to light: sometimes facts are not believable and thus the stories based on them seem untrue. But the artifice of this diatribe is obvious. A good story does not have to be grounded in believable fact. And more often than not London wrote stories based on believable fact, so his injunction at the end of the essay—"the man who writes fiction had better leave fact alone"—rings false and validates his own continued use of documentary material to ground his fiction.

We cannot overlook the humor of the essay, though, the tongue-in-cheek treatment he gives the topic. From start to finish, he treats his serious keywords "real," "true," "belief," "fact," even "inner consciousness" with a light hand and with an awareness of how meaning can reverse itself in different contexts. This lightness or affability connects so easily with the reader that we know from the start that he is being sincere. And since he is being sincere, when he says at the end that he prefaced the essay with "a solemn affirmation of its [the essay's] truthfulness" and is "confident that it will be believed by no one" because "it is too real," we immediately cry out, oh no, we believe you, even if the editors' actions seem preposterous.

Sincerity is the essence of what he called impassioned realism. Fiction needs imagination. Fiction needs absorption. The anthropologist William Dall protested against London's depiction of Native Americans because he thought they "are not only absolutely unlike the Yukon Indians, but they are unlike any Indians whatsoever." London countered by saying that Dall would have him load his stories with too many facts. What he had done in writing fiction was a matter of "artistic selection," something that a scientist like Dall would not understand. London at this point calls himself "an emotional materialist" who practices "idealized realism."[14] The materialist in him wanted to write factual stories. If that were possible, then all his stories would be theatrical. But the emotional, idealizing realist knows this is not possible. More often than not, London's stories failed for editors, audience, and reviewers when he made the facts visible. The stories failed because he had not used enough fictive cloth to cover the facts. They were too true in a literal sense. There was too much Dall-like realism and not enough Londonian idealization. He seems to make idealization into a dirty word because the imagination, "his inner consciousness," is so troubling. So he calls it unreliable and fake and untrue. But it's actually the thing that makes him a successful writer. And deep down he knows it. There is a thin line between fact that seems unbelievable, and thus did not happen, and the lying that fiction does. That is, fiction creates situations that did not happen, which is similar to the fact that is so outrageous that it could not have happened. So the successful fiction writer will use fact to make it seem like fiction. "Fact, to be true, must imitate Fiction," says the emotional materialist.

Three days later, in "The Terrible and Tragic," an essay not about how to write but what to write, he again tells his audience to avoid the terrible and the tragic, the ghosts, the material that made Edgar Allan Poe famous. One might hear an echo even of "The Pit and the Pendulum" in London's title. In "The Terrible and Tragic" London laments the absence of a publication that aims solely to publish high art, not yellow magazinism, that is, not material published to fit the expectations of editors and their readers. London points out that readers claim they do not want to read stories based on fear and with unhappy endings, but they cannot help themselves from reading them anyway. The best example of how this seeming hypocrisy is exposed is the work of Poe, whose publication history is "a paradoxical tangle. Editors did not like to publish his stories nor people to read them, yet they were read universally (and discussed and remembered), and went the round of the foreign newspapers." The situation, says London, remains the same in 1903: "No self-respecting editor with an eye to the subscription-list can be bribed or bullied into admitting a terrible or tragic story into his magazine; while the reading public, when it does chance upon such stories in one way or another, and it manages to chance upon them somehow, says it does not care for them." The point is that the audience, ashamed of its fear and not admitting to liking horror, should admit to the fear and the liking of horror because the terrible and tragic, as evidenced by Poe, lasts longer than "sweet and wholesome, optimistic" stories, which, we learned from his previous essays on writing, are written from the fancy, not the true artistic imagination.[15] Poe didn't make any money, says Jack, but he cleaved to greatness and sits among the giants, which is the final line of "Getting into Print": "With [sincerity] you may cleave to greatness and sit among the giants."

Not only is London addressing horror but he also is tackling, we now see, the larger question of what gets into the literary canon and what does not. In a roundabout fashion, London is facing up to Brett's injunction to write for a permanent place in the history of American literature. Poe, Ambrose Bierce, and the others serve as models for story writing, but they also stand in anxious relationship to their audiences.[16] In short, London's anxieties about his own status—now and in the future—is transferred to those authors of horror who came before him and serve as his mentors. He repeats the concern of "Stranger Than Fiction" that the best writing is not accepted (for whatever reason), that it is misunderstood and judged, not on its own merits, but on the supposed blindness and prejudices of the reading public. We, of course, remember his characterization of that audience in "Again the Literary Aspirant": "The uncultured mass cannot become cultured in a twinkling of an eye. . . . They ["our villains and clouts and clowns"], with their dimes and quarters in their hands, and their free and equal thumbs turned up or down, determine what shall live for today and for this month." How can they be trusted when they say they hate horror but buy it anyway? If only there were a magazine that published "stories that are bids for place and permanence rather than for the largest circulation."[17] If only he could write independently of market concerns.

At some point in 1903, London envisioned a collection of essays to be entitled "Hints on Writing: Confessions of a Magazine Writer." It was to include "On the Writer's Philosophy of Life," "Editorial Crimes," "The Question of a Name," "Phenomena of Literary Evolution," "First Aid to Rising Authors," and "Getting into Print." When he made this list, apparently "Stranger Than Fiction" had not yet been accepted. If he had included the latter, the volume would have totaled 14,500 words, large enough for book publication, though why he chose not to pursue the project is unknown. He never brought it up with Brett.

Between 1900 and 1903, he collected a number of newspaper articles by authors who had written similar essays about authorship. He typed up some notes, one set of which focused on the unpredictability of reviewers. One essay would focus on "those who monkey with the text. Though it must be granted that they oft-times monkey to betterment of the text—yet nevertheless they have no such right." It was as clear a statement as could be made of the inviolability of an author's right to control his text, akin to being able to write against market demands, against the power of reviewers to dictate what counted for quality, against the editors who set limits to an author's range of content and style. At one point he thought that he would model them after the "best possible literary essays such as Stevenson's."[18] In fact, London may owe his formulation of "idealized realism" and the requirement to avoid photographic realism to Stevenson's essay "A Note on Realism." Stevenson declared, "All representative art, which can be said to live, is both realistic and ideal." "Photographic exactitude" for both Stevenson and London was not more truthful than idealism and abstraction. In Stevenson's first line, we hear London's final line of "Getting into Print": "Style is the invariable mark of any master; and for the student who does not aspire so high as to be *numbered with the giants*, it is still the one quality in which he may improve himself at will."[19] These principles, plus the characterization of the literary canon as a group of "giants," indicates London's indebtedness to Stevenson. No wonder that of the two grave sites of authors that London visited in his lifetime, one was Stevenson. The other was Poe.

London was now mentally and emotionally prepared to write a novel of horror and tragedy that would vie for a place next to Poe. Brett wasn't urging him to write a horror story; he wanted a sea story, and he wanted it badly. London too wanted to finally write adult sea fiction, and he saw, after writing "The Terrible and Tragic," that he could combine the two genres and perhaps achieve the greatness that Brett was promising. That was his intention, and it is the first time that he approached a work of art with canonicity in mind. In a sense, then, and recalling his statement to Brett in the winter of 1902 that he felt he was beginning a new period in his career, London was (again) starting out as an author.

The conjunction of beginning a career and embarking upon a new work of art are not all that dissimilar. Edward Said, in his early work of criticism titled *Beginnings: Intention and Method*, argues that the beginning of a text and the beginning of a career should be considered in the same way. That is, for both, "the beginning is the first step in the intentional production of meaning."[20] For a text, that statement is obvious. For a career, it is not. We tend to define a writer's career after it is over, as if the author had no role in its meaning. Rarely do we look at what intentions the author had. London, like other first-rate writers, composed works, one following the next in a progression that he hoped would define the kind of writer he wanted to be. If a career is a conglomeration of texts, then an author's intention in how those individual texts relate to each other needs to be considered.

London told the public—through his essays on authorship and through interviews—that his career's meaning was one of independence, of solitary effort. This is the myth of the mentorless author. In "Getting into Print," London wants to convince us that he started from nowhere, knowing nothing. He made the same point in a 1903 interview with Fannie Hamilton, which was reprinted widely because of the success of *The Call of the Wild*. In her prologue to the interview, Hamilton re-creates the story London wanted promulgated: "Untrained and inexperienced, far from the great publishing centers, with no one to give him advice, and knowing no one who had ever written anything or tried to publish anything, he sat down and wrote in order to gain an experience of his own. Authorship on its own account made little appeal to him. The attraction lay in the supposed rewards of literature. Mr. London says he developed whatever mental power he had, to meet an economic situation."[21] He tells Hamilton, writing "is only work—just like any other business" (280–81). Having a career as an author was simply a job. By attributing his success to a simple desire to earn a living, he doesn't have to address the question of imagination. He wanted to keep that question and all the doubts it engendered to himself.

So London, in telling these stories of his authorial career, is creating a particular kind of myth. He is writing an origin story, like that of Noah's ark, or Adam and Eve. As a story, we see the similarity between his published work and his accounts of his life as an author. They have the same intention, the same methodology. He kept going back to the beginning of his career, refining the story to make himself more and more independent of other writers' careers. As Said says, "Beginning is *making* or *producing difference*; but . . . difference which is the result of combining the already-familiar with the fertile novelty of human work in language." In other words, "Beginning is basically an activity which ultimately implies return and repetition rather than simple linear accomplishment" (xiii). As with the story of his authorial career, so, too, with his texts. To begin a work of fiction or nonfiction, he drew upon the work of others—through plagiarism, through paraphrase, through inspiration—or he drew upon his own work. To begin meant to return to a previous accomplishment and then move forward. To deny this process of return, to turn his life story and his compositional process into a straightforward, telic endeavor, was to hide all the complications of his interior, writing life, especially the mortal combat he waged with his imagination. The true meaning of his career is one he never told.

He writes horror stories and tragedy because, as Arthur Conan Doyle put it in *A Study in Scarlet*, "where there is no imagination, there is no horror." Or we might find the same thought in Goethe who describes genius as partly constituted by "the Daemonic."[22] Or, as we shall see, we find that Hamilton Wright Mabie theorizes the daemonic as necessarily constitutive of the imagination. Buck is that demon of genius, the satanic avenging angel who restores order through procreation in the chaos that is the white, formless wilderness. Is it so surprising, then, that in his next novel he creates another demon genius who seems to share the same species as Buck? Again, embarking on a new beginning is, as Said says, a matter of circularity and repetition, not telic linear movement. In the world of Jack London, where there is repetition and return, there is ghostliness.

After telling his audience in the *Editor* that they should do as he says, not what he does, and after telling his audience in the *Critic* that there is good reason not to write tragedy or horror, he next writes a novel about a Poe scholar—that is, someone intimately familiar with Poe whose interior intellectual life then gets replicated in the exterior—who is tortured as badly as any character in Poe. The novel certainly did earn London a permanent place in American literature, but it also became a novel that cemented his reputation as a violent naturalist and proponent of radical individualism. He spent years trying to undo the damage this book did to the connections he saw so plainly among his socialist essays, his writing essays, *The Call of the Wild*, and *The Sea-Wolf*. Still, he was only twenty-seven. If he had been a baseball player he would have been just entering his prime.

THE LEOPARD MAN AND THE SEA WOLF

The last work he completed before beginning *The Sea-Wolf* was a short story entitled "The Leopard Man's Story"; later collected in *Moon-Face, and Other Stories*, it was not intended for *The Faith of Men, and Other Stories*, the collection he was just one story away from completing. It's a skit more than a short story, a recollection of two anecdotes that Jack had probably heard while circulating among circus performers, sniffing out possible feature stories for the *Examiner*. He had turned his attention away from the Klondike, and he was in a feisty mood, warming up for his full-length horror novel with a horror short story. He sent this tale to the *Black Cat* on 15 March, two days after finishing "The Class Struggle," and Umbstaetter rejected it. *Frank Leslie's Monthly* picked it up immediately, paid twenty-five dollars, and published it in August 1903, thus having a short story by the author of *The Call of the Wild* at the same time that the novel came out. Leslie's timing could not have been better.

Two things characterize the Leopard Man: first, his affect, which is melancholy bordering on no affect at all, a lassitude that renders him almost paralyzed when he isn't performing in the circus by appearing in a cage of man-killing leopards. Given that London had just completed several essays about labor and capital, he can't help ending the very first paragraph by stating that "his employers rewarded him on a scale commensurate with the thrills he produced."[23] So his affect is not caused by oppressive working conditions.

The second characteristic is his reluctance to tell the narrator his life story. The narrator appears to be a reporter sent by his paper to interview this man of daring-do, but the Leopard Man wouldn't or couldn't tell his story because "he appeared to lack imagination." He had no devil-dog living inside him, apparently, until his memory woke it, in good Coleridgean fashion, and he told the story, not of himself, but of two lion tamers each of whom have their heads bitten off by lions. As the title of the story says, he is an author figure. The first story is a warmup, an exhibition of "patience" by a man who "hated" the lion tamer. "Now, that's what I call patience," said the Leopard Man, "and it's my style" (897). Of course it is. He barely likes to talk, let alone act, and there's something creepy about the way he admires the patience of a man waiting years to see a nemesis get eaten.

But then the Leopard Man tells a slightly more complicated story of a hot-headed circus performer named De Ville (London had interviewed Peter de Ville for the *Examiner* in October 1901) who manages to get a lion to bite off the head of a man *he* hates. Again, the Leopard Man tells the story with such a coolness that now we begin to wonder about his sanity or even his humanity. In fact, we realize that his moniker indicates a monstrous conflation of feline and human, and his affect is a symptom of that monstrousness. In the face of such cruelty, violence, and treachery the Leopard

Man acts as if it is all so, so ordinary. His inability to see the "romance in his gorgeous career" (896), his striking inability to tell his own story, and his excitement at the thought of telling stories about headless men, whose decapitated trunks would be spouting quarts of arterial blood in the sawdust of the circus, should warn us that this reluctant author figure is a perversion, a freak of nature, half man, half cat. He foreshadows Humphrey Van Weyden's description of Wolf Larsen: "The jungle and the wilderness lurked in the uplift and downput of his feet. He was cat-footed, and lithe, and strong, always strong. I likened him to some great tiger. . . . The piercing glitter that arose at times in his eyes was the same piercing glitter I had observed in the eyes of caged leopards."[24] Or, more tellingly, in the scene in which Larsen attacks one of Death Larsen's crew, Hump says, "It was the leopard and the lion. . . . Wolf Larsen was the leopard" (231). "The Leopard Man" may be a light tale, but it served its purpose of warming up London for the main event, the writing of *The Sea-Wolf*. The Leopard Man's diffidence becomes, in exaggerated form, Wolf Larsen's unmoral nature.

BEGINNING *THE SEA-WOLF*

With *The Sea-Wolf*, London dispensed with the light-hearted tone of "The Leopard Man" and the theatricality of the essays and returned to the serious and absorptive mode of *The Call of the Wild*. He did not start until 10 April, having to correct proof for both *The Kempton-Wace Letters* and *The People of the Abyss*, as well as for *The Call of the Wild*. When he had sent off the proofs of the latter, he began *The Sea-Wolf*.

He did not know immediately what other ingredients—other, that is, than horror and data from sea travel—needed to be in the stew that was to make a canonical text. He knew what made for a good sea story. He had read Richard Dana, Frank Norris's *Moran of the Lady Letty*, Robert Louis Stevenson's *Captain's Courageous*, and other stories, but there is no evidence that any of these had a direct influence on the writing of *The Sea-Wolf*. He also may have read Joseph Conrad's *Tales of Unrest* in the late summer or fall of 1903, while he was still writing *The Sea-Wolf*; after interviewing him for *The Reader*, Fannie Hamilton sent London a collection of Conrad's stories, and London replied, "Now is my Conrad complete. I have glanced at the first tale, & been compelled to choose between it & my day's work, and have nobly put it down until bed-time."[25] Presumably, he fell asleep with Conrad.

There appears to be no direct connection between another of Conrad's works—*Youth*—and *The Sea-Wolf*, but London read it while writing his own novel and read it out loud to Cloudesley Johns while he was visiting London in the spring of 1903: "He read to me Joseph Conrad's 'Youth,' in boyish delight in sharing with kindred spirits his own joy of life."[26] (Do not fail to hear yet another meaning of the word *spirit* in this sentence; London's friends knew of London's investment in and characterization of the imagination as a spirit.) What London found in that story that might have been transferred to *The Sea-Wolf* was an affective discourse, elusive to capture and vague in meaning, but nonetheless strong in sensibility. It would be centered on the disjunction between Marlow's recollection of his youthful emotions in having his first adult responsibility aboard a ship and his current emotional life that sees, not a ship of great opportunity, but a leaky and dangerous craft, not a land of romantic adventure, but the East as it really is: strange ships at anchor, a cursing white captain, and a wall of staring "brown, bronze, yellow faces."[27] He does retain a vision of the East that came to him on that first voyage, which includes the "first sigh of the East" of "a puff faint and tepid and laden with strange odours of blossoms, of aromatic wood."[28] But it is all mixed together now with the sense that after all the time spent on the sea and in far-off lands all that remains is "only a moment; a moment of strength, of romance, of glamour—of youth!" How to communicate to his own readers that strength of naïve youth that London, too, must have felt on board the *Sophie Sutherland* as well as the subsequent loss of illusion he knew in 1903 (at the ripe old age of twenty-seven) was the task that enthused him to such a degree that he "exclaimed" to Johns before he began reading *Youth* out loud, "Listen to *this!*"[29]

There may have been other texts he drew upon, but, as he told Julian Hawthorne in 1905, "the local color of 'The Sea Wolf' was gained by some years of personal experience in the forecastle. The character of the redoubtable pirate, while true enough to life as regarded his brutal and sinister aspect, was imaginative upon the intellectual and philosophical side," meaning that he invented a captain who read so widely.[30] He did not have a plot in mind; later, he would describe the book this way: "This is a novel, not of plot, but of incident and development."[31] When he was well into the writing, he revealed specific incidents in an interview with a University of California student: "'I am working on a new book,' he said. 'Oh, it's going to be a sea story. The Pacific's the place, and the thing starts out with the wreck of the San Francisco ferry, then there's a wreck of one of the China Mail steamers and a wreck. . . . It has to be completed by the first of December, and I have been working several months."[32] Five months to be exact, and he didn't finish it until January 1904. There is incident and locale, but no plot. For this kind of novel, he needed strong characters. He started from what he knew: an author figure, oblivious to the danger of fog (an odd sort of echo of the Leopard Man), absorbed in his own life and the texts that are central to it. He is a critic and scholar of Poe, this Humphrey Van Weyden. The centrality of authorship and Poe in Van Weyden's life connects him to the next ingredient: a ship called the *Ghost*. London returns to the ship by the same name in *Cruise of* The Dazzler, both being modeled after the *Sophie Sutherland*, the sealing ship he sailed on in 1893.[33]

He also began with a different sort of half man, half animal. It's a wolf named Larsen, the antagonist to the Poe scholar, as if one of Poe's characters had come to life; we might even say he has come back from the dead. The final ingredient was the romantic interest, which by necessity should be absent in a story about the crew of a sailing vessel, and London knew that. In fact, Hump tells us what London knows about genre: "I had read sea-romances in my time, wherein figured, as a matter of course, the lone woman in the midst of a shipload of men." But those romance writers had not discovered "the deeper significance of such a situation. . . . [which] required no more than that the woman should be Maud Brewster," that is, someone exceptional (212). Because London imagined that a novel in the permanent place in literature had to be read by the many, the many demanded a romance. Accordingly, he contradicted or undermined the traditional sea story and, on his own terms, he created an "exceptional" love interest. His own terms were that she be another author figure, someone who recalls the force and multiplicity of Frona Welse and Hester Stebbins. It's as if he were saying to the clowns and the clouts that this is obviously a ploy to win your readership, but you won't even recognize it as such. And they didn't. Frona excited the crowd to such a degree that they called her a monster. But not one contemporary reviewer felt the same way about "a delicate, ethereal creature, swaying and willowy. . . . a bit of Dresden china" (212) who becomes a seal-clubbing, independently minded author named Maud Brewster. The reviewers and most readers ignored the fact that the novel was about her transformation as much as it was about Hump's or Larsen's death. For the many, Maud Brewster was merely conventional, and an afterthought.

London imagined Maud's transformation to be equal to Hump's. Before he began, London said in a letter to Brett, "My idea is to take a cultured, refined, super-civilized man and woman, (whom the subtleties of artificial, civilized life have blinded to the real facts of life), and throw them into a primitive sea-environment where all is stress & struggle and life expresses itself, simply, in terms of food & shelter."[34] The novel is about the contest of wills, a contest between those who live principally in alliance with the ethereal imagination and those who are grounded in Nature, in life. As we saw in "Stranger Than Fiction," Wilde says Nature imitates Art. London reformulated that decree: "The creative imagination is more veracious than the voice of life."[35] This is why Hump and Maud, the advocates for the imagination and bonded by a love that London takes very seriously, must win over Larsen, "the voice of life." It is Stevenson's idealism versus realism. That is, Maud Brewster joins with Hump as true authors to fight against Wolf Larsen who has captured the *Ghost*, that is, the imagination. He is like the man in the red sweater, beating the imagination with a club, thinking he is taming it but only making it more wild and violent. Maud and Hump need to seize the imagination from him so that they may write again. The plot of *The Sea-Wolf* is how true authorship seizes control. That is, the stories of the imagination must be allowed to trump the stories of facts. If Larsen were to write, he would be an antiromanticist, the author who relies on facts alone. He would be like Herbert Wace or Dall, ignorant of the writer's need to select and infuse facts with "the feels." Or, to put it another way, he is the voice of the white logic that is London's antagonist in *John Barleycorn*. London may be undermining the form of romance, but he takes that form's epistemology seriously.

Therefore, we have a new addition to the creation of the model for an author. To the hobo, the miner, the newspaperman, the artisan, and the romantic genius we add the sailor. We saw hints of this conception developing in his earliest sea stories. Going to sea meant wanting to write novels. Martin Eden is the fully realized figure of the sailor-author, but Hump and Maud are nearly as well developed. In the lazy hours of the dog watch, sailors would gather on deck to smoke and tell stories; they are natural storytellers, as Conrad's Marlow attests (as well as Richard Dana in *Two Years before the Mast*, and Albert Sonnichsen in *Deep Sea Vagabonds*). It is exactly that setting that begins *Heart of Darkness*, a beginning that is really an elaboration of the beginning of *Youth*. London must have noticed this methodological similarity between Conrad and himself. He felt his own creative impulses vindicated and encouraged by it, energized by Conrad to shoot for the glory of writing an important work of art.

There's something else besides the imperative to tell stories that sailors have in common, Sonnichsen notes in *Deep Sea Vagabonds*, and it is "the love of change, the spirit of unrest" (44).[36] Life on land is too predictable for them, no matter how enticing the family or the occupation. In a passage marked by London, Sonnichsen repeats the story of a fellow sailor who had tried to give up the life, and he became a lawyer, married "a good woman," and settled down. "But I couldn't stick it out. I wasn't happy a moment during all that time. A longing, undefinable yet horrible, seemed to consume my very vitals. I can't describe it any better than as the horror of knowing what will happen to-morrow and the day after" (41). Again, there is no imagination without horror, and sailors tell stories because they mimic their need to live a life whose ending is a surprise and a delight.

The uncertainty that London felt in how to write a canonical text finds expression in the very first line. That is, *The Sea-Wolf* begins with a confusion of how to begin: "I scarcely know where to begin, though I sometimes facetiously place the cause of it all to Charley Furuseth's credit." We can return to what he means by "cause" and "it," but first we need to look at what else he could mean by "to begin." Now that we see that he will be reporting on the substitution of one life's trajectory for another (in the traditional understanding of the novel, the sissy Humphrey becomes the man Hump), and knowing that he is an author figure, we see (again) that Said's observation about the beginning of a text and the beginning of a career are inextricable. We also see how much both are linguistic constructs. The beginning of Hump's career is what he says it is. Hump doesn't begin with or even consider the fog's role in the ferry crash; for an idealist like Humphrey, natural fact has nothing to do with the true nature of beginnings. If Hump were a critic in the twenty-first century he would have read and agreed with Said who said a beginning is "a necessary fiction."[37] Hump's facetiousness is part of his linguistic construction of the true nature of the beginning of his new career and his text (called *The Sea-Wolf*). Though Humphrey says he is being facetious when he offers that his new career began with Furuseth insisting he come visit, he doesn't offer a reasonable alternative, and he continues to be facetious for the rest of the paragraph, as if it were true—and it probably is, at least for Furuseth—that someone would read Nietzsche and Schopenhauer to relax. That is, after making a stab at explanation, he leaves it open-ended, inviting us to fill in this rather large blank.

Do we dare try? After it (whatever it is) is all over, when we reach the end of the text, we the reader might locate the beginning of it somewhere other than with Charley Furuseth.[38] Logically, Furuseth had nothing to do with Hump falling into the water, and so the usual interpretation is that the vagaries and chance happenings in Nature began Hump's new life and career, and this would be the way that someone like Wolf Larsen would construct the beginning.

Larsen would have found support in Said's *Beginnings*, which inadvertently is now even more relevant to the study of Jack London. Said, citing authors important to Larsen, points out how many central thinkers during London's period—Darwin, Nietzsche, Marx, Freud—were concerned with beginnings, including works such as *The Origin of Species* and *Birth of Tragedy*, works of course that London was fluent in, though London had read, at least, *A Genealogy of Morals*, and probably not *Birth of Tragedy* by April 1903. "What is interesting here," concludes Said, "is a transformation that takes place in the conception of beginnings, and this transformation is congruent with the change taking place throughout the creative disciplines. Satisfying the appetite for beginnings now requires, not beginning as event, but beginning as either *type* or *force*—for example, the unconscious, Dionysus, class and capital, or natural selection."[39] The vagaries of Nature fall into the category of a force that creates a beginning, though its impersonal nature puts into question the importance of intention and separates it out from the beginnings initiated by human agency. Mother Nature had no idea that Hump would write a book after she dumped him in the water.

But if we want to be faithful to Hump, the beginning is not to be located with fog or Furuseth; it must be something antecedent to the fall and to his visit to Mill Valley. How far back do we have to go in Humphrey's personal history? What is to stop us from going so deep in history that we end up with Milton, asserting that the beginning of human history starts with Satan in the garden? But perhaps that is exactly where London does mean to take us, facetiously, yet with deep seriousness. The text of *The Sea-Wolf*, then, is like an ouroboros. It begins with Adam in the Garden, who meets Satan; Eve comes out of nowhere, and the first parents leave the Garden to wander the earth together on a ship called the *(Un)holy Spirit-Ghost*. London's conception of a contemporary American canonical author was Poe, but the author to whom he ultimately compared himself was Milton. No wonder his self-criticism generated so much anxiety.

There is another dimension to a beginning that involves Milton. Playing off of Said's discussion of *Paradise Lost* and beginnings, we start with the obvious: *Paradise Lost* is about a beginning for humanity (one of many possible). It is about the beginning of man's fallen nature. Wolf Larsen, as a Miltonic Satan, then acts as a supervisor of Hump's newly fallen nature. He is Satan-like, not so much because he is evil, but because in a Miltonic sense he governs fallen life. This beginning erases completely what came before. Baptized in the waters of the bay, Humphrey begins a new life without the freedom he once had. Humphrey Van Weyden lived life as he had wanted, which, from Larsen's point of view, was a death in life. Once he falls overboard, all that changes. He is no longer free in the way he was. On board the *Ghost*, he is and he isn't a prisoner. He has liberties given to him by the captain. But they are severely circumscribed. It is a new world in which Hump finds himself. As Said says about both *Paradise Lost* and William Wordsworth's *The Prelude* (another British poet who appears in London's work, both by name and influence, and whom London was reading in 1900–1901), "Each poet uses his poem to begin to *put* man in the world, to situate him. Thus in each case man at the outset faces . . . a highly conditioned set of circumstances in which his existence . . . is properly inaugurated" (44).[40] Hump even has to transmit his new knowledge of beginnings to Maud. On one of her first days on board, he tells her, "All your experience of men and things is worthless here. You must begin over again" (209). When we understand both the beginning of the novel and the beginning of Hump's life in this way, we then understand why we want Hump to have fallen off the ferry and into the dangerous life of Wolf Larsen, contrary to what at first seems right. (It seems unfair at first that he suffers so much at the whim of Nature.) We understand why we get caught up in contradictory feelings about what is best for Hump. He should and should not have to suffer.

We also begin to understand why Wolf Larsen is such an attractive figure. As Maud says at the end of *The Sea-Wolf*, "Good-bye, Lucifer, proud spirit" (365). We root for him to teach Hump via "the voice of life" what the terrible and tragic nature of Poe really is—not seen as an intellectual, but as a sailor-author figure. Hump, in his prelapsarian state, is not a real author; he is merely a critic. In the end, despite becoming a sailor, we are unsure that he has become a real author, though we are sure he has become a better critic. But critics and authors operate within a different order of the imagination according to London. When Wolf Larsen becomes the ghost that is his ship's namesake, Van Weyden and Brewster have a telling conversation. "His life flickered out," says Van Weyden, realizing that Larsen had died overnight. But Maud says, contradicting him, "But he still lives." That is, the author, not the critic sees the ghost. She identifies and accommodates the ghostly imagination. That is why she calls him "proud spirit." She accepts Hump's pronouncement that "he had too great strength," and she adds, "But now it no longer shackles him. He is a free spirit." Hump agrees: "He is a free spirit surely," but it is unclear whether he understands that word *spirit* in the same way that Brewster does. And it is unclear whether he is simply agreeing with her in order to put the whole matter to rest.

THE RETURN OF THE BRICKLAYER

We do know where London stands on the matter of the ghostly imagination and the full meaning of *spirit*, and now we have to take a small detour to look at the figure of the bricklayer, who first appears in "Story of a Typhoon off the Coast of Japan," London's very first published work. Starting out as a seemingly inconsequential character, the bricklayer becomes absolutely essential to understanding the workings of London's imagination, and we will see how he is tied into not only several of London's accounts of the sea but also, and climactically, to *The Call of the Wild*. Few other characters in London's oeuvre appear as many times as he does; it is also striking that London uses him in fictional and nonfictional genres. From "Story of a Typhoon" to *The Mercy of the Sea* to *The Sea-Wolf* to "That Dead Men Rise Up Never," the bricklayer appears again and again like the ghost that he becomes.[41]

In "Story of a Typhoon off the Coast of Japan," the bricklayer lies dying in his bunk while the rest of the crew keep the ship running during the terrific storm. His death at the end of the storm serves as a convenient moment with which to conclude the tale. Beyond that, he has very little importance. In his next incarnation, though, the bricklayer becomes the central character of *The Mercy of the Sea*, yet another fictional reconstruction of London's seal-hunting voyage in 1893; early in his notes London instructs himself, "Work up the wonder-sail before the north-east trade, (look up High School Aegis sketch)."[42] This is a reference to the end of "A Run Across," which was written at the same time as "Story of a Typhoon." London wrote notes for *Mercy* sometime in late 1902 and abandoned the idea (for a number of years) in January 1903. London's first lines of these notes sum up the theme and plot: "(Very first line of very first chapter: 'The sea has no mercy—and enlarge concisely.) [the sea] Taking the Bricklayer, in all its heartlessness and end." That is, the narrative arc would follow a clumsy, ill-suited novice sailor for the duration of a sealing voyage in the north Pacific. After outlining the early events—a strong gale, the routines of the crew—that mark the bricklayer as a man apart from the rest of the crew ("his utter inability to understand the men or the life"), London has him slowly die from some unspecified cause: "Last hours, these people all busy with life, and he busy with death. . . . Last hours, growing weakness, storms, snow, etc." He becomes "a ghost in the midst of it all." His burial, link to ghostliness, his separateness from the crew, his participation in a sealing voyage: all these story elements overlap with Larsen. Thus the bricklayer, like the Leopard Man, serves as a trial run for the creation of Wolf Larsen. But there is one more similarity. The bricklayer's death and burial at sea sound very much like a first attempt at what later would become Larsen's own burial: "Canvas wrapping holds air, parsimonious captain, coal in bag—not heavy enough. Schooner hove to, man slid over off hatch-combing to leeward." In *The Sea-Wolf* Van Weyden "lifted the end of the hatch-cover, and the canvas-shrouded body slipped feet first into the sea. The weight of iron dragged it down." Perhaps every burial at sea is the same, but London wrote three versions of the same scene, and each of these three end with the end of a storm.

And then he wrote a fourth. In August 1909, two months after he had begun *Burning Daylight*, London turned to writing his final account of this 1893 voyage, "That Dead Men Rise Up Never." He had returned from the *Snark* trip the previous month, and it is likely that the extended sea voyage prompted him to revisit his first one. The notes for *Mercy* may overlap here and there with *The Sea-Wolf*, but they seem more like a rough draft for "Dead Men." The essay is strictly autobiographical, a snapshot of a moment in the life of famous author Jack London or perhaps, more simply, as a snapshot in the life of a common sailor. For it begins and maintains the feeling of a story told in the forecastle among fellow sailors, smoking and taking in the night, as if they were all characters in a Conrad novel. Marlowe, I mean London, begins with a nineteenth-century circuitous construction: "The month in which my seventeenth birthday arrived, I signed on before the mast on the *Sophie Sutherland*, a three-top-mast schooner bound on a seven-months' seal-hunting cruise to the coast of Japan."[43] The autobiography, though, takes on a different aspect, functioning as a baseline for how a new salt-water sailor should act: work hard, complain little, fight against personal abuse. For London doesn't want to tell his own story all the way through. He wants to present the picture of a novice who did not behave properly. This, again, is the bricklayer. In the notes to *Mercy*, we read, "When Sailing master sends him aloft and he flattens out, trembling, under the cross-trees. Could not frighten him higher." In "Dead Men," "Bullied by captain and mate, he was one day forced aloft. He managed to get underneath the cross-tree, and there he froze to the ratlines. Two sailors had to go after him to help him down." To the bricklayer, "the compass must have been a profound and awful whirligig. . . . He never did come to know whether ropes should be coiled from left to right or from right to left. It was mentally impossible for him to learn the easy muscular trick of throwing his weight on a rope in pulling and hauling." The *Mercy* bricklayer had similar problems stemming from ignorance and sloth: "He couldn't learn to skin seals. . . . He couldn't steer; he couldn't row, and couldn't learn." Like the bricklayer in "Story," and in *Mercy*, and like Larsen in *The Sea-Wolf*, this incarnation also mysteriously became "a dying man" and dies in a storm. "Make strong," London reminds himself in notes to *Mercy*, "the smallness of the space in which twelve men, eat, sleep, fight, gamble, etc, etc," and in "Dead Men" London tells us the bricklayer "died, in a small space crowded by twelve men." When he dies "he died hating us and hated by us." In *Mercy*, it is the same: "Captain hates him, hunters hate him, crew hate him, cook hates him, and so cabin boy."

Up to this point, we as readers find "That Dead Men Rise Up Never" rather absorbing, though seemingly without a point. A little short of the halfway mark, however, we read this surprising claim: "And now I come to the most startling moment of my life." For a man who has adventured on five continents (North America, South America, Australia, Asia, and Europe), this statement immediately grabs our interest. We expect to read of a moment in his life of a colossal challenge met with grace and perhaps even success. But it turns out that when London writes "my life" he means his authorial career. For "the startling moment" is his first encounter with the embodiment of his imagination, the ghost of the dead bricklayer. This bricklayer is not canvas wrapped, but, like the *Mercy* incarnation, the crew "laid him on a hatch-cover for'ard of the main-hatch on the port side. A gunnysack half-full [thanks to the cheap captain] of galley coal, was fastened to his feet." Like the service for Wolf Larsen, one of the crew reads the lines "'And the body shall be cast into the sea.' We elevated one end of the hatch-cover, and the Bricklayer plunged outboard and was gone." Contrary to custom and still hating the man, the crew in "Dead Men" throw his clothes and belongings overboard. As the *Mercy* notes read, "Casting clothes overboard instead of holding auction."

Then we are on new ground. No other telling of the *Sophie Sutherland* voyage contains the following scene. The lead-up to "the most startling moment" continues as London tells us that he decides to take the vacated bunk to show the superstitious crew that he is braver than they. They insist no sailor has ever taken a dead man's bunk and lived to the end of the voyage. They "told stories of awful deaths and grewsome ghosts that secretly shivered the hearts of all of us." We are back on the good ship *Black Cat*, captained by Edgar Allan Poe. At midnight, London is called for watch, and though he insists he is unafraid and remembers Swinburne, who said "that dead men rise up never," still, "my mind pondered on the tales of the ghosts of dead men I had heard, and I speculated on the spirit world." The sailor-authors had transferred their ghostly imaginations to London, the auditor/reader.[44] He now allows for doubt: "My conclusion was that if the spirits of the dead still roamed the world they carried the goodness or the malignancy of the earth-life with them." Of course, at that moment, he sees a ghost: "There, in the dim light, where we had flung the dead man overboard, I had seen a faint and wavering form. . . . Never before nor since, have I had such a shock." Of course not. One can only have one beginning as an author, though one may return to it like a ghost. This fact is ultimately what ties together all four portrayals of the bricklayer. London tells this story in any number of ways because it is the story of his beginning as an author, "the most startling moment of his life." Further, it is startling because it is transformative in the extreme. After he sees the ghost he is "panic-stricken." Out of the panic comes a crisis of identity. He loses his old self. In language that he employed in *Before Adam* and repeated almost verbatim in *The Star Rover*, he says, "I, as I, had ceased to exist. Through me were vibrating the fiber-instincts of ten thousand generations of super-stitious forebears who had been afraid of the dark and the things of the dark. I was not I. I was, in truth, those ten thousand forebears. I was the race, the whole human race, in its superstitious infancy." Later in the tor-tured hour of the dog watch (we will hear of a different ghostly dog at the end), when he sees the ghost for a third time, he advances toward it with a knife. "Step by step, nearer and nearer, the effort to control myself grew more severe. The struggle was between my will, my identity, my very self, on the one hand, and on the other, the ten thousand ancestors who were twisted into the fibers of me and whose ghostly voices were whispering of the dark and the fear of the dark that had been theirs in the time when the world was dark and full of terror." This startling moment is about returning to the beginning of being human and then coming back to consciousness as a new man, a man who has now seen a ghost. "This thing, whatever it was, I must face alone. I must work it out myself," says the author who claimed to have no mentor but himself.

"That Dead Men Rise Up Never" never resolves the question of the reality of ghosts. Just when London becomes convinced that ghosts are not real, he says he might after all learn that "dead men did rise up." We remember one of his earliest tales—"Who Believes in Ghosts!"—a declarative title followed by the name of the person who does, Jack London. Even after he offers a scientific explanation for the apparition, he tells us, "This was my first ghost." You would think that he was no longer susceptible to seeing ghosts. But no, he still is, later in life, in the Klondike, of course, the land of the ghostly white silence. Almost casually, in an offhand manner, he ends the essay by telling us that he has seen one other ghost in his life. The brick-layer "was my first ghost. Once again have I seen a ghost. It proved to be a Newfoundland dog." Is anyone in doubt that its name was Buck?

From 1893 to 1903, the bricklayer became so inflated with meaning that he could no longer be sustained, and his story had to be set aside. Some-one more occupationally important had to match the ambition and accom-plishment, both physically and mentally, of the main character of London's first sea novel. Thus, the common laborer becomes a captain, though they signify many of the same things. In one iteration certain characteristics get more emphasis than others. In *The Sea-Wolf* and "Dead Men," the horror of beastliness gets emphasized, and we lose sight of the differences between the common sailor and the captain. In "Dead Men," we learn that "the

Bricklayer was one of those horrible and monstrous things that one must see in order to be convinced that they exist. I will only say that he was a beast, and that we treated him like a beast." It's as if the bricklayer isn't simply a ghost of himself but is the ghost of Wolf Larsen. Again we hear the essays about writing that London composed in preparation for *The Sea-Wolf*. And we hear it, too, in both *Mercy* and "Dead Men." Both texts share a similar epigraph, a tie-in to "Stranger Than Fiction" appearing yet again. *Mercy* will be "a fairly truthful narrative of things that happened." "That Dead Men Rise Up Never" concludes with a warning sign, an echo of the sign that begins *Huckleberry Finn*: "To the Editor: This is not a fiction. It is a true page out of my life."

Once London has repeated the tale one last time, he had been exposed so often to the ghostly imagination that he could to some extent forgive its tortuous presence. London's attitude toward the bricklayer in "That Dead Men Rise Up Never" is calm and philosophical, neither praising him as a "proud spirit" nor hating him as a disruptive, violent force. After he calls him a beast and a monster (he might have simply called him a wolfman), London writes, "It is only by looking back through the years that I realize how heartless we were to him. He was without sin. He could not, by the very nature of things, have been anything else than he was." This is the expression of an author coming to terms with that wild wolf of an imagination that lives within him. We will return to this time in London's life where he is more at ease with his interior life as an author, but for now we can see that the writing of the bricklayer's life, including how London incorporated him into Wolf Larsen, was a process of coming to terms with his ghostly imagination.

AFRAID TO BEGIN

Hump (and London) don't know where to begin *The Sea-Wolf* because they have seen a ghost (or maybe it was just the *Ghost*) and still are not sure if it was real and if anyone will believe them. It may be a life-and-death matter, but it is a mark of London's artistry that some of the same wry humor with which London infuses "That Dead Men Rise Up Never" appears at the beginning of *The Sea-Wolf*, and it works as a kind of defense mechanism. As he says in the essay, either the apparition was a ghost or a joke. Of course the "real" explanation explodes that binary; science explains the ghostly presence. But London never stops calling reality ghostly, and the scientific explanation always seems slightly inadequate, and the whole situation needs humor to take away the fright.

The joke in *The Sea-Wolf* is that if Hump had been more persuaded by Furuseth of the value of the bohemian life, then he would never have had to be born again.[45] Once again, in London's work we see him create the illusion of a necessary binary by withholding or suppressing a third way; in this case, the bohemian, which transcends the binary of fact and romance. To blame a San Francisco bohemian for Van Weyden's fate is to deflect attention away from the anxiety of not knowing, in the final analysis, how anything, let alone a novel or a career, actually begins. We need to find the right words to do so, and that means an author is indebted to his imagination.

In the beginning paragraph, not only does Humphrey identify himself as an author, but he also sees a man reading his newly published essay on Poe in the *Atlantic Monthly*. *The Call of the Wild* began with a dog who does not read newspapers but who might read other media (perhaps literary criticism). *The Sea-Wolf* begins with a figure reading (again London begins with something familiar only to then elaborate on a theme), who foreshadows the great reader and critic himself, Wolf Larsen. This anonymous reader prompts two thoughts about reading novels. First, because he is reading criticism, we realize that the novel we hold in our hands will be open to criticism too. That is, the question of what is a good novel hovers above the text and gets incorporated into the text with the presence of author figures, readers, and the figure of the imagination.

But the stakes are even higher than that, as we have seen. London doesn't want to write merely a good novel. He wants to write a canonical one, trying to live up to the standard that Brett had set for him. Ambrose Bierce, in his famous comments about the novel, recognizes London's ambition: "But the great thing—and it is among the greatest of things—is that tremendous creation, Wolf Larsen. If that is not a permanent addition to literature, it is at least a permanent figure in the memory of the reader."[46] This desire manifests itself in the beginning paragraphs of the novel. We recall that "the stout gentleman" who is reading the *Atlantic Monthly* is reading Humphrey's "analysis of Poe's place in American literature." Hamilton Wright Mabie, editor of the *Outlook* and close friend of Brett, wrote an essay for the *Atlantic Monthly* (published in 1899) entitled "Poe's Place in American Literature."[47] In 1901 Mabie helped Brett verify London's identity and to locate London's whereabouts so that Brett could persuade him to become a Macmillan author. Brett's essay on the rise of the American canon, published in the *Outlook* in December 1903, fits nicely with Mabie's 1899 essay, and one can imagine the two friends discussing how their publishing ventures would elevate their relatively new country's status in world literature. Mabie also wrote very favorable reviews of *The Son of the Wolf* and *The God of His Fathers, and Other Stories*, so the two publishers were in agreement about London's achievements and potential.

In his essay on Poe, Mabie strums a chord about the artist's relation to his imagination that would have pleased London to a great degree. Discussing American canonical authors from William Bradford and Jonathan Edwards to Benjamin Franklin, Charles Brockden Brown, and Poe, he writes,

> In Brown's romances . . . there is, above all, the daemonic element, that elusive, incalculable, mysterious element in the soul of the artist, which is present in all art; and which, when it dominates the artist, forms those fascinating, mysterious personalities, from Aristophanes to Poe, who make us feel the futility of all easy endeavors to formulate the laws of art, or to explain with assurance the relations of genius to inheritance, environment, education, and temperament.[48]

Not only does Mabie's hidden presence in London's novel send a coded message to Brett that his new wild western author is adhering to his directive to write at the highest standards—standards that Brett would agree with, coming as they do from his good friend Mabie—but Mabie has confirmed for London what London has feared all along: the demon within is absolutely necessary for the creation of high art. The next step is to confront that demon, dominate it without beating it with a club, and win it over, knowing all along that the war will never end. The battle ends with the end of a book or story, but then the war begins again with the next book or story. The demon is a ghost, and a ghost never dies.

The next step—meeting Wolf Larsen—points to indeterminacy as well. In fact, like the fog that seems to permeate the entire novel, indeterminacy holds sway not just over the structure of the novel but also over some of the characters and their actions. Van Weyden and Brewster are queer; Van Weyden fluidly moves between gender identities. In the triangle of desire, we often lose sight of gender, especially of socially constructed ideas of gender. Also, Van Weyden, who is both a man named Humphrey and a man named Hump, vacillates between the two incarnations of himself.

The castration of his name by Larsen—an act that London thinks typical of book reviewers—signals both the creation of a new man and the retention of much of the old self. He remains a literary figure, and one senses he could easily write about Poe again, this time with more engagement—absorption—in the horror that Poe can instigate.

But when we look at the monstrousness of Wolf Larsen we enter a new realm of ideas. As I have said, he is like the Leopard Man or like Buck: are they men, or are they beasts? "You are a sort of monster," says Hump during their first discussion of ethics, when he compares him to a snake, tiger, and shark. "Now you know me," Larsen says. "Other men call me 'Wolf'" (82). One reviewer affirms Larsen's affinity to circus freaks: "'The Sea Wolf' rests upon the character of Wolf Larsen, a character so extraordinarily compounded as to attract attention as inevitably as the two-headed man of the side-show."[49] Larsen, though, is a monster gifted with great self-awareness; he knows he is a monster. Hump has insight (or in-sight, or inner sight, or, in other words, imagination), but it is limited (he is, after all, not a fiction writer but an academic). In fact, over two hundred pages of his first-person narration pass by before we are startled to learn, along with himself, that he understands himself to be a monster as well. While he fights with Larsen, he is so preoccupied with the life-and-death struggle that he doesn't stop to consider why Larsen is so attracted to him. That is, Larsen may say that he takes Humphrey on board to make a sailor and a man out of him, but what he doesn't say, but knows on the cellular level, is that he recognizes his younger self in Hump—a monster in the making. Like recognizes like, except Hump has no idea. To this he is blind. His complete self-realization is only possible when Maud Brewster comes aboard, and he remembers reading her work. "My *memory* flashed back to that first thin little volume on my desk, and I *saw* before me, as though in the concrete, the row of thin little volumes on my library shelf. How I had welcomed each of them! . . . They had voiced a kindred intellect and spirit, and as such I had received them into a camaraderie of the mind; but now their place was in my heart" (215).

This is a highly significant moment. Memory, vision, imagination, artistry, and reading are all bound together. What follows is self-realization and love: "My heart? A revulsion of feeling came over me. I seemed to stand outside myself and to look at myself incredulously." He is repulsed by what he now realizes he is: a monster. What's even more amazing, in a way, is that he had been told by Charley Furuseth, bohemian artist and representative of the suppressed third way of authorship, throughout their relationship that he is "'the cold-blooded fish,' the 'emotionless monster,' the 'analytical demon'" (215). He was a monster, half man, half book. Where Larsen was violent and terrible, Hump was pacific and pitiable. Where Larsen was sensual and attractive to men and women both, poor Hump is nearly asexual. "Furuseth was right; I was abnormal, an 'emotionless monster,' a strange bookish creature, capable of pleasuring in sensations only of the mind. And though I had been surrounded by women all my days, my appreciation of them had been aesthetic and nothing more" (216). As Hump says before Brewster comes aboard, the crew "are a company of celibates. . . . It would appear that they are a half-brute, half-human species, a race apart, wherein there is no such thing as sex" (129). They have "no balance in their lives. Their masculinity, which in itself is of the brute has been overdeveloped. The other spiritual side of their natures has been dwarfed—atrophied, in fact" (129). He is, of course, right but completely unaware of the irony of this. He sees in them what he refuses to see in himself. Once he does, he becomes a true man, not the macho male Larsen is and wants him to be, but a wholly realized, complete human.

His inability to recognize his own monstrousness is not the only thing to which he is blind. Maud Brewster enters as a highly accomplished author, but, as it turns out, Van Weyden's review of her poetry was as monstrous as Larsen's take on Van Weyden's work and, more telling, as critics of Jack London's. When Brewster identifies Van Weyden, she remembers his review and objects that he had called her "the American Mrs. Meynell!" (198). She doesn't disagree with the truth of the statement, but she adds, "I was hurt." London has transferred his own unease at being called the American Kipling to his fictional counterpart. For indeed she is another feminine embodiment of London's ideal author, a replay of Hester from *The Kempton-Wace Letters* as well as Frona Welse from *A Daughter of the Snows*.[50] She, too, has been robbed of her name by the critics. Van Weyden defends himself: "'We can measure the unknown only by the known,' I replied, in my finest academic manner. 'As a critic I was compelled to place you. You have now become a yardstick yourself.'" Both London and Brewster know what little consolation this is. In an unsigned article in the San Francisco-based *Town Talk*, which London clipped and saved, he read, "Jimmy Hopper will be sorry that his publisher advertised him as 'doing for the Philippines' what our own Jack London 'has done for the Klondike,' just as Jack is sorry that his publisher once said that he was 'doing for the Klondike what Rudyard Kipling has done for India.'" Van Weyden simply has no idea how facile and pompous he really is. But Brewster knows, and she turns the discussion to him, appealing to his vanity.[51]

The yoking of two diverse elements doesn't necessarily generate horror, but, as Arnold I. Davidson has written, when we examine horror and monsters together (as London encourages us to do), two things happen. We are forced to reexamine the relationship between "between the orders of morality and of nature," and we begin to look at the indeterminate boundary between the animal and the human, forcing us to be more exact in our definitions of both categories.[52] In *The Sea-Wolf*, London, by bringing together monsters and horror—or, as he called it earlier, "the terrible and tragic"—is encouraging us to rethink what he means by *human*. In the end, horror reaches its terminal point of usefulness. London wants us to think through horror and leave it behind, not embrace it and hold on to it. To be human is to retain the hope of achieving a unified self and transcendence. But to get there one must go through hell and meet the devil.

Therefore, it is not incidental to London's narrative that the question of Larsen's monstrosity arises while they are discussing ethics and morals. In chapter 8, Larsen plays cards with Thomas Mugridge, who had earlier stolen $185 from Van Weyden. The captain wins that exact amount, and Van Weyden claims it is his and should be given back to him. In Van Weyden's mind, it is unnatural—monstrous—that one should steal money and feel no guilt. Worse, since what happens on the level of individual interaction characterizes the larger social sphere, Van Weyden finds that Larsen's monstrosity determines the ship's social relations. Lucifer rules in hell. Might is right and there are no morals.

This is monstrousness and animality at its worse. The hyphen in the word *sea-wolf* ties two disparate characteristics together. It signifies an improbability that is supposedly nonetheless true. There walks on earth a thing, a living thing, that is both of the land and of the sea. Without the hyphen, it could be a ship's name. *Sea* would become a modifier, removing the landedness from *wolf*, rendering it metaphorical. But with the hyphen he becomes a monster, a combination of two things that do not belong together.

But there's another facet of the indeterminacy of his monstrosity besides his bestial nature. Hump says in the same scene, "Sometimes I think Wolf Larsen mad, or half-mad at least, what of his strange moods and vagaries.

At other times I take him for a great man, a genius who has never arrived." We hear an echo of Conrad's Kurtz in that characterization, if indeed London had read *The Heart of Darkness*. This clichéd notion of a genius being a madman, or a madman being a genius, points us to the humanness of the monster. Just as we relish the idea of a tough man teaching Van Weyden how to live in the world, so, too, do we become captured by the logic of the mad genius individualist.

It is this unlikely combination of the land creature who lives on the ocean that inspires the prerequisite attraction and repulsion necessary for the horrible state of monstrosity. One cannot take one's eyes off the thing that combines in unlikely fashion two disparate elements. Suddenly we sense the importance of eyes and vision in the novel. Eyes and vision are absolutely central to London's conception of the imagination and its processes. Brewster communicates largely through her eyes, indicating a direct control of the imagination, and Wolf Larsen's blindness signifies his loss of control over the imagination and foretells the couple's departure from his zone of influence. Borrowing again from *Paradise Lost*, London owed a great deal to Milton's brief formulation of the power of the imagination as "the Cell / of Fancie my internal sight" (8.460–61). And now more than ever we need to turn to the passage from *Martin Eden* that describes Eden's gift (curse) of imagination: "He, by some wonder of vision, saw beyond the farthest outpost of empiricism, where was no language for narration." The links among Eden (the place), the imagination, and the satanic critic (who promises fame but delivers debasement) is quite evident in *The Sea-Wolf*. Hump needs Larsen. He could not have seen himself properly without looking into the mirror that was Larsen. It taught him what it means to be more fully human, and he salutes him for that.

But Larsen the critic can accomplish only that, and like Satan he can return to hell triumphant yet ultimately defeated by his limitations. Maud and Hump "hand in hand with wandring steps and slow, / Through Eden took thir solitarie way" (12.648-49). They move beyond the teachings of their critic and deepest reader, and now in charge of the imagination they can create even greater art. Together, they foretell the birth of their children, much like Buck's progeny in *The Call of the Wild*. By choosing this conventional form of an ending, London asserts that the imagination needs the artist as much as the artist needs the imagination. Without the artist, the imagination is free but wild in the chaos of nature. With the control of the artist, in whatever form he wishes, the imagination through the medium of art can bring salvation to humanity.

The reader-critic deals with facts, and Larsen is irrefutable. But the artist sees the place where there are no words; he only feels the emotions, the romance of the matter, and thus deals with truths more grand. We recall the improbability of the giant mosquitoes that opens London's essay "Stranger Than Fiction," and another link between his writing essays and *The Sea-Wolf* is established.

More than just a simple chronological chain of events, though, these essays and this novel illustrate how London is working out the connections among the monstrous, belief, horror, and aesthetics. That is, this emphasis on the monstrous, on the confusion of animality and humanity, has, in addition to the questions of humanity and morals, an aesthetic dimension: what makes for good art? Sticking with sea stories, we remember London's opinion of *Moby-Dick* as art run riot, an orgy of creation. It is "beautiful" work, like the "beautiful exaggerations" of *Typee*, but not like *Two Years before the Mast*, the work of an artist who possessed an "untroubled vision," who was not "hag-ridden by imagination."[53] Melville and London may have shared a similar troubled relationship to the imagination, but London sought for the kind of control that he found in Conrad's stories. They show the artist dominant over the daemonic force of the imagination. Hump and Maud, like Melville, are attracted to the daemonic, and salute it. They acknowledge its facticity and necessary function, but to allow the monstrous to have control over the imagination is a fatal aesthetic mistake. Further, after flirting with "abnormal" sexual relations—Hump with Larsen (the man), Larsen (the animal) with Maud—the novel restores traditional heterosexual coupling as the desired sexual relation because London all along believes that the highest art is conceived in "normal" social relationships. At the same time that he believes it is perfectly natural to be attracted to those of the same sex and to be aroused by animality, he in fact believes it is a mistake to give in to those desires, in the same way that it is an artistic mistake to give in to the impulse to create an orgiastic work like *Moby-Dick*.

In the confrontation between Hump and Larsen we see the confrontation between an author and his audience. The "stout gentleman" on the ferry—named the *Martinez* after London's friend Xavier Martinez, the bohemian artist?—becomes Wolf Larsen, the reader-critic who has seized control of the imagination and feels entitled to tell the artist how to write a great novel.

Though Wolf doesn't write himself, he does possess the eyes of "the true artist," which are "wide apart," a description London uses for Martin Eden (*Sea-Wolf*, chapter 3; *Martin Eden*, chapter 1), thus cementing the likeness between Hump and Larsen triangulated by London with Eden. All of them possess an extraordinary visual acuity: Larsen and only Larsen sees Hump in the water after the ferry crash, and with Eden "nothing in [his] field of vision escaped." Larsen then is very much a part of the artistic community. This confrontation between author and audience gives the novel its theatricality. It isn't so much a novel of ideas as it dramatizes through dialogue the ideas he has been writing about in his previous essays. In a sense, Hump's transfer between ships is a movement of an author between two publishing worlds with two different audiences. Like London, he moves from the *Atlantic Monthly* or its supposed counterpart in the West, the *Overland Monthly*, to the *Black Cat*. In another way this beginning of the novel represents the beginning of London's career.

In fact, in yet another way London was returning to his first writings when he began *The Sea-Wolf*. "A Thousand Deaths," for which he received the first payment that matched his expectations of his worth as a writer and that appeared in the *Black Cat*, can be considered a first draft of the beginning of *The Sea-Wolf*. The narrator in this story also falls into the San Francisco Bay to be rescued by an authority figure (his father) who tortures him unmercifully, but in the name of science, until the narrator figures out how to kill him. In "Who Believes in Ghosts!" and "The Rejuvenation of Major Rathbone" one also sees the theme of rebirth. Although we may never know for sure, apart from Sonnichsen's book, it seems there are no sources for *The Sea-Wolf* because he already had tried out his ideas in early work.

Wolf is a reader and a monster. How do these two concepts come together? I have argued that the transference of emotion between author and reader mediated by the printed text forms a bond between the two, and further, that just as the author is haunted by his imagination so the reader becomes haunted by whatever of that imagination gets mediated by the text. Different readers retain different amounts or qualities of that imagination. With Wolf, his reading causes his imagination in turn to be fired to a maniacal degree, fevered and out of control. He is like the false author who is dominated by the feverish imagination, which ultimately blinds him and forces him to lose control. And it is this imagination-out-of-step-with-reality that characterizes him as a monster.

That is also how London saw critics. They were readers who imagined themselves the supreme reader, God, who knew what the imagination was and what it was supposed to do. Before 1904 and the publication of *The Sea-Wolf*, he had very little to say about critical reviews. In a rare instance, at the top of one negative, misinformed review of *The Call of the Wild* that he pasted into his scrapbook, he wrote, as if for the benefit of twenty-first-century scholars, "A reactionary publication which has it in for me because of my socialism and because I once saw fit to teach its editor a little etiquette and literary ethics."[54] But now, given his new investment in writing an important novel that would, he hoped, grant him a status apart from the public perception of him as another Kipling—that is, a novel that would grant him a name of his own—he was infuriated by bad reviews. This anger is not your typical authorial self-pity at being misunderstood. It is rooted in Brett's expectation that London will be considered a first-rank American author, an expectation, as I have said, that London wanted to meet. To become famous without the attending glory—or without unanimous approbation—will have great ramifications for the rest of his career. The crisis of being famous began here and culminates in the writing of *Martin Eden*, whose first title, *Success*, takes on a new meaning.

We've seen already how Brewster embodies London's anger at critics. In two separate sets of notes for essays he ultimately did not write, he excoriated those who had found fault with *The Sea-Wolf*. He was fair to reviewers who were fair to his work (even if critical), but for those whose prejudices stood in the way of their literary judgments, he could be brutal. In a paragraph of undated notes, London makes a list of things that reviewers have dismissed in his writing as improbable, unbelievable, and therefore inferior:

> the climb up the cliff; [a reference to the short story "Up the Slide"]; the seamanship of The Sea-Wolf; and finally, Love. I've got the reputation of a primordial beast, and they won't have it otherwise. I put in love-notes, touches, feels, out of my own experience. (Into Sea-Wolf). I was in love at the time, and lo, the critics had expected me to have my hero make love with a club, and drag my heroine off by the hair of her head and up into a tree. Because I didn't, they branded my love as sentimental bosh and nonsense. And yet I flatter myself that I can make love as well as the next fellow, and not quite so ridiculously as the average critic.[55]

It's hard not to focus solely on that juicy bit of biographical material—"I was in love at the time" with Charmian Kittredge—and so see London as Hump, protective of Charmian (Maud) in the face of the threat by critics (Larsen). But this isn't the whole or even most interesting part of the story. The idea that critics have turned him into one of his "primordial" characters strikes us as unfair, unflattering, and ultimately demeaning—until we read a second set of notes, whose title—"The Little Chattering Daws of Men"—makes the monstrousness of critics explicit. He also makes explicit his own wildness and why critics might get a "mistaken" impression of him:

"THE LITTLE CHATTERING DAWS OF MEN."

A la reviews of "Sea Wolf"——make it four or five thousand words long. Be serious, honest; tell what is true of it; that it is truth. Hell-ships coming into port every day. Also, instance Niedenheimer, the Chicago prototype of the Wolf Larsen character.

And give the psychology of the little chattering daws.——what kind of mind they have,——the rule of the dead——bourgeois, etc.

Some, (a few), whom I know personally, who rant in print against my stuff, talk about "healthy; manly, wholesome books" in contrast——and who privily clasp sin to them in the perfumed gloom.

A wolf-dog down here, a long street, meeting poodles and pugs—— their ludicrous non-understanding——describe Brown. He comes of the wild and the vastness, etc., and so I, telling my tale. Men who have never seen rougher life than tennis flannels and seaside resorts, telling me what is possible or not possible upon the great sea——also Youth's Companion story, "Up the Slide."

Also, the review of "The Sea Wolf" by man who knew the sea and its sorrows. Look up in clipping-book.

What they have to say about my "Sea-Wolf" love-making. Their love-making, far sillier. Let each of them go into his own experience, the fond foolishness, immortal asinity, then rise like God to laugh at the particular silliness of the kind of love in "The Sea Wolf." (Enlarge)[56]

We can easily follow London's divisions according to topics. First, there is the question of believability, especially of Wolf Larsen. Any number of reviews refused to believe that such a character could exist. He was monstrous, not because he was pictured as half man, half beast, but because he combined violence and learning in such extreme degrees. No man, the critics argued, could be so violent who had read so much. It seemed impossible to those who believed in the humanizing power of literature and philosophy that they could serve the purposes of the demonic individualist.

Within this topic, we find a subtopic of interest concerning London's conception of himself: the surprising self-identification with his dog Brown Wolf or Brown, and here we return to the question of London's own primordial nature. And yet the surprise quickly dissipates as we remember, not so much that he signed his letters to his friends "Wolf" or that he created a bookplate with the drawing of a wolf's head or that he called his dream house Wolf House, but that he created a chain of signification from wolf-dog Buck to the ghostly imagination to the ghost ship the *Ghost* back to a character named Wolf. Wolves and the imagination and the author were all intimately connected, and this is what he meant when he wrote, "He comes of the wild and the vastness, etc., and so I, telling my tale." The wolf-dog-imagination has given sight to the tale teller that ordinary men—the clouts, the clowns, the poodles, and pugs—do not have.

And of course these ordinary men, the bourgeois, the flannel-shirted tennis players, the inhabitants of Clubland, men like Humphrey Van Weyden, assume to be God and to tell the imaginative artist "what is possible or not possible upon the great sea," or even in the Klondike, as in his story "Up the Slide." He had been kind to these critics in "Stranger Than Fiction," but now he saw them as monsters who were worse than Larsen because they didn't dare adventure. More than that, they were insincere; they criticized love-making without admitting how invested in romance they really were. They criticized supposed immoral violent behavior without fessing up to their own peccadillos. One reviewer, someone who had known the sea, wrote an honest review of *The Sea-Wolf*; London had saved it in his "clipping-book." That was someone he could respect.

Attached to these notes was a paragraph from the San Francisco publication the *Argonaut*. In a section called "Epigrammatist," London marked "The nineteenth-century dislike of Realism is the rage of Caliban at seeing his own face in the glass." He then wrote "Oscar Wilde" next to it and "Chattering Daws." Harkening back yet again to what he had written in "Stranger Than Fiction," London was trying to turn the tables on the unbelieving public. They, not the realist author who writes with sincerity about things seemingly impossible, are the true savages. They are the antimoderns, and the artist, as Wilde has insisted, will lead them out of their darkness. There is a hint of Wilde's essay *The Soul of Man under Socialism* in *The Sea-Wolf*. As John Sutherland has noted, when we read the title of Van Weyden's projected essay, "The Necessity for Freedom: A Plea for the Artist," we are led to believe that he is under the influence of Wilde.[57]

Wilde and London (and apparently Van Weyden as well) believed that only the artist could reveal the structural deficiencies of capitalism that lead to poverty. Wilde, venturing away from politics and toward the general role of the artist in society, wrote, in *The Soul of Man under Socialism*, "A work of art is the unique result of a unique temperament. Its beauty comes from the fact that the author is what he is. It has nothing to do with the fact that other people want what they want."[58] London highlighted the passage and then, I believe, wrote his note about the rage of Caliban (17). "Indeed," wrote Wilde, "the moment that an artist takes notice of what other people want, and tries to supply the demand, he ceases to be an artist, and becomes a dull or an amusing craftsman, an honest or a dishonest craftsman" (17). And, of course, London highlighted this passage as well. Wilde had two takes on individualism: one was political and one was aesthetic. He joined them together. When he wrote that "art is the most intense mode of Individualism that the world has known" (17) because the artist can only create real art from his sense of being a unique individual, London agreed; see, said London to the chattering daws, you have no idea what it is to be me, to be the wolf howling with the muse's song. But when Wilde argued that "socialism itself will be of value simply because it will lead to Individualism," London disagreed. His marginal note reads, "socialism, scientific & up to date, does not endorse this" (13).

In fact, the marginal note is appended specifically to Wilde's discussion of socialism, marriage, love, and Jesus, and for a moment we can return to Jesus in the theater of socialism. Wilde claims that "socialism annihilates family life. . . . With the abolition of private property, marriage in its present form must disappear" (13). No, says London, adjustments to the marriage contract will need to be made, but its disappearance is not necessitated by the advent of socialism. This is a flaw in Wilde's philosophy of individualism, and we can see in Van Weyden's condemnation of the nonmarital state of the crew and its captain London's prejudice for heterosexual marriage. Wilde saw marriage as "legal restraint," whereas London believed right-thinking couples would not use marriage as a form of either bondage or prostitution. Wilde argues that "Jesus knew" that "individualism . . . converts the abolition of legal restraint into a form of freedom that will help the full development of personality and make the love of man and woman more wonderful, more beautiful, and more ennobling" (13). "And so," concludes Wilde, "he who would lead a Christ-like life is he who is perfectly and absolutely himself" (13). Perhaps, thought London, but, as we saw in the previous chapter, he had not yet worked out all the complications involved in twining the philosophy of Jesus with the socialist program. Wilde's conflation of Jesus's thought, individualism, and socialism seemed too easy.

For *The Sea-Wolf*, on another level of thought, London used Wilde, not so much as a basis for Van Weyden's thought as he did for Larsen's. Larsen is the individualist that Wilde celebrates, and Van Weyden is the altruist whom Wilde—and London—deplores. Van Weyden would advocate altruistic behavior toward the poor—that is, charity—but not the revolutionary principles so necessary to restructure society according to socialist doctrine. Wilde wrote, and London underlined this sentence, "Disobedience, in the eyes of any one who has read history, is man's original virtue"; and this epigrammatic statement seems Nietzschean in its rebelliousness against convention.

One might read *The Sea-Wolf* as a narrative in tune with "How I Became a Socialist," especially given that both were written as London was grappling with the Nietzschean concept of the blond beast. In the latter, London says that as a blond-beastly hobo he was a man, doing a man's work. When he discards his identification with the blond beast his Nietzschean concept of manhood disintegrates as well to be replaced by something new, the New Manhood, say, that risks effeminacy in order to be politically correct (in the Marxist sense). Hump as London was thrown from his comfortable bed into prison (or prison ship) and confronted with the extremity of the individualist philosophy. The double irony here is that Nietzsche, the advocate for anticonventionality, adheres to a very conventional idea of manhood, while, London, so often mistaken as a conventional man's man, overthrows—in superman fashion—the conventional concept of manhood. So, yes, it is a tale of coming to manhood, but it is a manhood that London doesn't endorse, that is, Larsen's brand of manhood. It is more a story of becoming a man in the sense that a man is able to think on his own and to become a socialist. But Hump fails in this regard.

Besides Wilde and Nietzsche, there are other literary echoes.[59] What a great twist upon the Miltonic pronouncement that *Paradise Lost* would be about "Man's first disobedience and the fruit of that forbidden tree." Of course, Larsen is not a socialist—he and Lucifer are anarchists, says Brewster, and we know how little London sided with them, despite his admiration and affiliation.[60] And when Wilde advocates individualism as a form of rebellion, Larsen can agree without giving up control of his capitalistic enterprise, the *Ghost*. And, at the same time, he can argue against altruistic behavior and confound the liberal Van Weyden. Larsen would understand the strength of the strong that defines London's revolutionary principles, and they both estimate Van Weyden's liberality as weakness. Let the strong on both sides of the political economy fence fight it out, hammer and tongs, say Larsen and London. May the best economic philosophy win.

Given London's distaste for the "chattering daws" and the multiple ways he attacked them, we might think that the reviews of *The Sea-Wolf* were devastating. Quite the opposite is true. To begin with, he must have been gratified by at least four reviews that picked up on the indirect telling of a socialist parable, one negative and three either laudatory or neutral and fair. Another displayed the reviewer's well-informed knowledge of London the author:

> Mr. Jack London is familiar to us in various aspects. One is that of the writer of socialistic articles for the *Atlantic*, another is that of the widely intelligent and keenly sympathetic sociological student, putting his first-hand observations into form in his masterly *People of the Abyss*; the third, and perhaps best-known phase of his work appears in *The Call of the Wild*, an understanding interpretation of the dog nature, together with a wonderful picture of life as it is in the far North. But through all these runs the one key-note of dissatisfaction with the present social order.

As with a number of others, this perspicacious reader noted the lack of plot in the novel but finds fault neither with that lack nor with the seeming implausibility of "the story." Instead, he or she singles out the political message of the book: The reviewer nicely captures both the political elements of the book as well as how Van Weyden's transformation isn't simply about gender politics, but is about the class struggle as well.[61] That reading is affirmed in the only review in a socialist publication that I found: "Wolf

Larsen is made the incarnation of our present competitive system. With gigantic constructive or destructive power, bestial materialism, utilizing all the scientific and literary knowledge of modern society, but only for the purpose of individual personal gain, he stands as the apotheosis of the individualistic capitalism of today."[62] These lines restate not only the political valence of Larsen's ideas but how Wilde's concept of individualism is simply neither complex nor comprehensive enough.

All the reviews, even the politically minded, spoke of the brutality and violence in the book. But just as with the violence, as many reviewers praised the love interest as deplored it. The number of reviews is overwhelming, so a sample of the positive and negative is called for. One review, at the top of which London wrote "Return" (meaning that he had sent this to someone and was asking him or her to return it so he or Charmian could paste it into his scrapbook), first summed up the criticism that the serial publication of the novel generated: "The most various criticisms have been passed upon it: some seem to have thought the story great; some perniciously immoral; some have simply choked on 'the brutality,' and refused to read further." Then, the reviewer excoriated the last half of the novel, condemning Maud and Humphrey as too "virtuous." "As usual, Mr. London's work is weak where women are concerned." Does this reviewer recommend the book to his or her readers? Absolutely! "As a whole, 'The Sea-Wolf' is a remarkable achievement. It is the strongest book London has yet given us."[63]

A similar review stated, "No one would have missed the love episode, and we would have had a shorter, but finer, achievement. . . . There is so much that is good in 'The Sea Wolf' that we could forgive the author almost anything."[64] Others were not so generous, and they "choked on" the brutality and the romance.[65] But a number found the romance singularly appealing, whether believable or not. For example, the *Christian Register (Boston)* found that Maud's "presence makes the strife [between Wolf and Hump] still more eager and momentous," like a novel by Clark Russell. "Of course in the end the right man wins, and 'They live happily ever afterward.' But how it all comes about makes a story which for those who like Jack London at all will be interesting and exciting as few stories are."[66] London knew Russell's work and its unreality and could not have been pleased to be compared to him, however much the reviewer meant it as a compliment. In Sonnichsen's *Deep Sea Vagabonds*, one of the sailors sums Russell up in way that London would have agreed with: "Clark Russell is not a favourite among the people of whom he writes. . . . [As one of Sonnichsen's shipmates said] 'He might be able to write a good text-book on ship-work, but when he writes novels he paints sea life about as true as dime novels illustrate life in the West—it's all cutlasses and boarding pikes with him."[67] Whether London was able to avoid or exploit the romantic claptrap of authors like Russell is another matter; I believe he was.

It's as if the reviewers couldn't help but place the book within the pantheon of American literature despite their divided attitudes—both among and within themselves. They could locate what was wrong with the book—an unbelievable main character, a conventional love story, a lack of plot, a mismatch of realism and romance, a too-violent kind of realism—but they could not define what made it great, though they were absolutely convinced it was. One reviewer tried to list its positive qualities and called it "wonderful in conception, in suspension of interest, in characterization, in presentation of unique situations and extraordinary men," and yet lacking in a "vital spark of genius, or humanity." Why? Because the violence was unbelievable, and this reviewer further refines this idea, in a way that is central for our own understanding of the connections between the novel and London's authorship essays:

> A critic once found fault with the theme of a story which a writer had presented to him. "Your plot is absurdly improbable," he said. "But," contended the author, "it is a true story. I know that it really happened." "That is of no importance," decided the critic, "it is not a fictional probability. It is reporting then, not literature." It might be safe to assume that a story is probable as long as the author can succeed in convincing the readers. There are some scenes in "The Sea Wolf" where Mr. London fails to do this, although it cannot be denied that he has made Wolf Larsen startlingly real.

In fact, the reviewer concludes, "'The Sea Wolf,' with its great vistas of the sea and the wildness of the storms of elements and passions, has a wonderful power, *haunting the memory* even after it has been finished. And a book which can accomplish this in these busy times of ours is assuredly out of the common."[68] So quick to call the story and characters unbelievable, the reviewer nonetheless finds herself "haunted" by *The Sea-Wolf*, and thus London's ultimate goal as a writer is achieved: to transfer his own sense of hauntedness as an author to his reader. The ghost within seems so improbable, and yet so real.

The critics may have objected to the monstrousness of conjoining two disparate fictional genres, but London would argue that such monsters, like the monster that is Wolf Larsen, is too real to be ignored. In any case, while he was reading the hundreds of reviews and pasting them in his scrapbook, he submitted to an interview with Julian Hawthorne, a brave and forgiving act because Hawthorne had skewered him two years previously for creating the monstrous female Frona Welse. Brewster, London said, "was in the story for the purpose of giving artistic balance; but Mr. London remarked that critics had censured him for bringing her in at all." No kidding. But this censure had now taken its toll, and London "spoke of the story with no enthusiasm, and seemed to feel more satisfaction in his 'People of the Abyss,' which was a plain record of actual investigation." *The People of the Abyss* had, of course, received its share of criticism, but now he was not only worn down by the critics but he was also feeling disenchanted by the creative process.

> When I [that is, Julian Hawthorne] wanted to know whether he derived no pleasure from the act of creative imagination, he said no; but afterward explained that, while the mere conception might be agreeable, the drudgery of writing the thing down took the good taste out of the mouth. Besides, looking at the product subsequently, in the cold day light—in the reaction from the creative glow—it was apt to look like poor stuff, which one was sorry to have fathered. It was best to let it alone, if one could afford to do so, and get out of this fleeting existence something real, personal, positive. But if one could not afford to take this attitude, then let him write his stuff as well as he could, sell it in the most favorable market, and forget it.[69]

Not only had London been deeply engaged in absorptive fiction for several months in 1902 and all of 1903, a kind of writing that forced him to confront the ghost of the imagination, a battle he could never win; not only had he had to suffer through the reviews of *The Sea-Wolf* for almost all of 1904; he had found *The Sea-Wolf*, unlike *The Call of the Wild*, to be a difficult and demanding project to complete. No wonder he was downplaying the attractions and fulfillments of writing.

As I said before, London began the novel on 10 April 1903, almost a month after he completed "The Leopard Man," two weeks after reading proofs of *The People of the Abyss* and *The Kempton-Wace Letters*, and the same day he finished reading proof of *The Call of the Wild*. As he told Brett on that day, "With these proof sheets [of *The Call of the Wild*], my desk is at last clean. I have already worked out plot, characters, details, etc., of it [the sea novel], and shall start in now on the actual writing of the Book." In January he had had the rudiments of the story, which means that while he was writing *The Call of the Wild* he was formulating *The Sea-Wolf* (tellingly, *The Call of the Wild* was at one point going to be called *The Wolf*).[70] In January, he had told Brett, "The superficial reader [the clowns and clouts] will get the love story and adventure; while the deeper reader will get all this, plus the bigger thing lying underneath," a thing he called *mastery*. As he pitched it to Brett, it was a case of civilization losing itself yet somehow mastering "a primitive sea-environment where . . . life expresses itself." What I have called the fight over control of the imagination, he calls "mastery" of "life," that is, "the voice of life" expressed by Larsen. He assured Brett that "I am not rushing it, and I intend to take plenty of time over it."[71] Brett replied, "I am glad to hear about the sea story and shall look forward to it with great pleasure."[72] But because he was so anxious to finally get a sea story from London, he couldn't restrain himself three weeks later after London had told him that he was going to take the money from *Call* and "engage cabin passage in a sailing vessel for the South Seas, take a typewriter, plenty of paper and ink, and the plot for my sea story along, and thus get the sea atmosphere on which I have during the last several years gone stale."[73] Brett replied enthusiastically, "I have felt very great hopes for the sea story and your plan of working it seems to me to be a desirable one. So few sea stories are appearing—and none of these, I may say, good for anything—that a really good sea story at the present time would, without question, achieve a very remarkable success."[74] No matter that London decided instead to buy the *Spray* and stay close to home, reading his old sea stories, Conrad, Sonnichsen, and others. Brett was thrilled.

And the thrill of anticipation continued after London signed the new contract for *The Call of the Wild*. That made Brett happy, but he was happier contemplating the future sea book, whose success he thought would be practically guaranteed both by the "subject" and by the imagined success of *The Call of the Wild*: "As I told you before I am going to try and do my best to sell this book and to push it in a way that will affect favourably the sale of all your forthcoming books, and I am most anxious that you shall follow it up with the sea story about which we have so often spoken. You have done this, 'The Call of the Wild,' in so original and clever a fashion that I am certain of your achieving an equal if not greater success in dealing with a subject which is so much more commercially possible, as the sea story is. I hope by the time this sea story is done that you will have a considerable audience and that we may be able to revise our publishing agreement to our mutual advantage by its success."[75] It is worth repeating: from a commercial standpoint, Brett was not entirely confident that *The Call of the Wild* would sell well, but he had absolute confidence in the salability of *The Sea-Wolf*.

By 29 May London had thirty thousand words done, which means he was writing closer to four thousand words a week since the beginning of April.[76] He was writing on board the *Spray*; he told Anna Strunsky "have just come in from a trip, during which I blew my sails into ribbons."[77] His joy is palpable, joy from writing a sea novel while sailing on his own first real boat.

On 2 July he told Johns that he was writing fifteen hundred words a day, seven days a week, which is both an exaggeration and a fact. By 24 July he told Brett he was halfway done, which means that he had written only seventeen thousand words in seven weeks, so he wasn't working at that frenetic pace for very much of the time. Or, to be even more exacting, he told Brett on 10 August that he had mailed the first half of the novel and that it would be between ninety thousand and one hundred thousand words long. If we take the larger number, that means he completed only twenty thousand words in ten weeks.[78]

A newspaper reporter set the idyllic Sonoma County scene in which London wrote his sea novel in the summer: "California poets and authors realize that the native muse has geographical preferences that cannot be lightly overlooked. There is no doubt that the muse is kindliest when her lovers court her in the little nooks nestling in the elbow of Sonoma Creek just below Glen Ellen. For it was here, in the old Osbourn home sitting snugly on a wooded hill, that Robert Louis Stevenson wrote some of his best tales. Here, too, Jack London wrote the book [*The Sea-Wolf*] that clinched his fame; and Sterling, latest of California poets, found the inspiration here for his 'Testimony of the Suns.'" The reporter doesn't use the word *bohemian*, but she might as well have, and it's clear that London was trying to maintain continuity between the bohemian house in Piedmont and the bohemian property in Sonoma County:

'Twas here [years back] that a sister experiment of the Brooke farm was tried. Like Emerson's dream of a demesne for mental aristocrats, the colony soon scattered, but their influence is still keenly felt.[79] Mrs. Ninetta Eames, the well known magazine writer [who interviewed London for the *Overland Monthly* in 1900 and was Charmian's aunt], has kept their memory green on her beautiful place known as 'Wake Robin Lodge,' and here every year a little coterie of writers and artists come to shake off the grime of the city and get close to nature in one of her prettiest moods.

How like Hump's bohemian friend Charley Furuseth.

The reporter stands amazed at London's workstation:

The spot that is reserved for Jack London's sanctuary is a rustic bit down by the brim of Sonoma Creek. Under a leafy roof of overhanging boughs stands the table where he writes. A wire clothes line stretched between the trees over the table is used for Mr. London's literary washing. Jack London's methods are as original as the man himself. When he gets ready to write a story or book that has been shaping in his mind, he sifts out all the notes pertinent to the tale, and with wire clothes pins fastens them on the line. To see these rag tags and bob-ends of paper flittering on the breeze, the passer-by would not fancy that they contained the data of months of hard work. When London hurried to Japan, he had to part a story he was writing in the middle, and he left out a line full of this literary wash which someone else fortunately took in before the rain had a chance to blur the invaluable notes.[80]

Since London was completing only *The Sea-Wolf* at the time he left for Japan, and he was living in Oakland at the time, it's unlikely that the reporter got this right; perhaps, when he left Glen Ellen in July he had left his notes on the clothes lines. Although he enjoyed writing outside, in Glen Ellen he had to; his quarters were a one-room shack, barely big enough to hold a single bed. In any case, the contrast between his bohemian lifestyle and the horror of *The Sea-Wolf* could not be greater. It's as if the beauty of his surroundings kept him from sinking too deep into the blood and gore of his tale. However, by far the greatest amount of the novel was composed on board the *Spray* or at Atherton's house.

London, in a significant departure from his usual practice, did not handle the serial rights for *The Sea-Wolf*.[81] Brett had been promoting London's work to Richard Watson Gilder, editor of the *Century Magazine*, "for some time past and finally got him to consider this book" without London's knowledge.[82] In August, Brett wrote to London, telling him that Gilder had expressed interest and that he wants to know what London is charging. "I am getting a minimum rate of three cents a word from the best magazines, where my best work goes. This is what I received from the *Call of the Wild*. In case the novel should prove available for the *Century*, I do not know whether Mr. Gilder would buy it for a lump sum, or pay a rate per word for the quantity he published."[83] So, swamped by his new, demanding novel and his personal affairs, London allowed Brett to take over. He also did so probably because he was departing from his usual method of composition as well. Rather than keep the book to himself until he had completed it, he revealed its half-finished state to Brett, who then seized the opportunity, as a means to promote the novel, to talk it up among his friends in New York, including Gilder. London would need another four months to complete it, but Brett was so confident in the novel's excellence that he negotiated with Gilder for a month to accept it for serial publication; on 5 September, Gilder called Brett to say he would take it, and Brett immediately wrote to London with the good news.[84] It was most likely a choice that London would not have made, especially given his recent interaction with the Gilders.

Richard Gilder's wife, Jeannette Leonard Gilder, was editor of the *Critic*. In December 1902, she had rejected "The Golden Poppy," saying that it was "delightful, but 'The Critic' is not a story paper. . . . Once in a green moon I have dropped into fiction, though you say that yours is a 'true narrative,' but not often."[85] She probably would have ignored the sign London posted at the end of the manuscript of "That Dead Men Rise Up Never," too, yet, in what may be the most ironic acceptance London ever received, she paid him twenty dollars for "Stranger Than Fiction." In September 1902, the associate editor of the *Century*, Robert U. Johnson, rejected "The One Thousand Dozen," saying, "This is a capital piece of work this Klondike story of yours, but it falls outside our range by the unrelieved tragedy of it. We hope you'll try us sometime with a cheerful tale."[86] In June he, too, had rejected "The Golden Poppy," and up to the publication of *The Sea-Wolf*, the *Century* had not published a single essay or story by London; they would later publish four stories, including "All Gold Canyon" and the second version of "To Build a Fire." To London, the outlet just wasn't high on his list of places to submit, and he rarely sent them anything; it was never his first choice. It's entirely likely that both Jeannette Gilder's and Johnson's letters, among letters like it, reinforced London's motivation to write "The Terrible and Tragic" and "Stranger Than Fiction."

But Brett looked to the *Century* as a place to help establish London's permanent reputation; after all, Gilder had serialized, among other significant works of American literature, *The Bostonians* and *The Rise of Silas Lapham* and edited selections of Mark Twain's *Huckleberry Finn*. He was inordinately proud of the latter—he even reminded Brett of it in a letter about serializing *The Sea-Wolf*—even though Twain had been reluctant to give it to him and then only a small amount already set in type of the book version.[87] No matter. Brett could forgive Gilder his egotism if he were willing to help promote London. Gilder admired *The Call of the Wild* and told Brett in late August that he wanted to publish the new sea novel, but he had two objections: one was "the dead level of almost sickening brutality in the first draft of the first half of the story."[88] London would not have been surprised by this judgment, though he may have been surprised by how the *Century* first advertised their new author's novel: "The story is told by a young man who is picked up after the wreck of a ferry-boat in San Francisco bay, and is taken forcibly on a sealing voyage under a captain who is a strange mixture of brutality and self-culture, and who is thought to be one of the most striking and original characters in modern fiction."[89] The magazine had figured out how to make the most of the violence.

Gilder's second objection seemed harder to meet but was actually easier, and because Gilder phrases it in such a charming way it is worth quoting in full. Remember, at this point Gilder has only seen the completed first half and a synopsis of the second, all of which Brett had passed on to him having received it from London:

> More troublesome is the question of the last half. There is nothing out of the way in the synopsis sent: In fact, the book as a whole [is] elementally interesting and ideally attractive—evidently it is the outcome of much living and thinking. Yet— . . . a woman—a lonely and presumably lovely woman. How is this to be managed, in a way to

[not] shock magazine readers—i.e. the American prudes. Here I will tell a story—dramatically.

Scene, London—Latter part of the XIX Century

Enter Thomas Hardy and Rev. G.

Thomas Hardy: I would like to write about things more freely—about servant girls in families for instance—but the public won't stand it. As for you Americans, you're awful prudes: My book is being *cut*, in several publications in America now.

———Rev. G: Yes, Mr. Hardy, I don't know but that prudishness is an American vice. But considering the rotten condition of the French theatre and modern literature, in great part—and the scandalous, disgusting goings on in a group of writers and others in London lately, I for one am willing to pay the price of prudishness for belonging to the decentest people on the face of God's Earth.

This probably has no application to the subject—but only to my own phrase of "prude." Yet—I want to be reassured as to the last half. What "ideals" are to triumph? Those of Kempton or those of Wace. I truly think that my precaution is needless—yet it is a rule we have to adhere to.

Gilder was nothing if not consistent; in an 1887 essay he expressed his prudery in almost exactly the same terms: "There are many who believe that America has the purest society in the world. Is not this purity worth paying for with a little prudery?"[90] As recent editors of *Huckleberry Finn* point out, "The *Century* was most concerned with offending the sensibilities of its readers by allowing profanity, libel, irreverence towards religion, sexual suggestiveness, immorality, or vulgarity."[91] According to one study of the magazine, "The strongest of taboos barred the frank treatment of sex. Gilder's . . . staff was even more vigilantly prudish. . . . Johnson was famous for his sensitivity to offensive passages."[92] One can draw a direct connection between the kind of realism Gilder preferred and his editorial practices. He upheld nineteenth-century genteel values. But, to go further, he had no sympathy for photographic realism, something London practiced in conjunction with his impassioned realism, a form of realism that Gilder and Johnson could tolerate to some extent.

That London could take sex offstage only meant that he felt it should not be photographed; he told his friend Cloudesley Johns, "I wonder how you will like the *Sea Wolf.* I'll bet you'll wonder how the *Century* dares to publish it."[93] He felt readers could see that scene for themselves if he gave them enough to go on, and so, without compromise, he could adhere to Gilder's injunction to profess the ideals of Dane Kempton, not Herbert Wace. Gilder seems to have prompted London to look at the romance in terms of his previous novel. In his "amplification" of the synopsis, London, in words that recall *The Call of the Wild,* tells Gilder, "Up to this point Humphrey Van Weyden has been singing another man's song, the keen and chilly song of materialism; from this point and to the end he will sing his own song, the warm and glowing song of love triumphant. The love that triumphs will be the passionate, romantic love of Dane Kempton (and I flatter myself that I shall be able to write it, and yet keep it in accord with the harsh physical environment of sea and storm and hardship)."[94] Kempton and the new Hump are "idealists."

Wace can be seen as precursor to Wolf Larsen in that both celebrate scientific rationalism and unsentimental poetry, a philosophy too modern for Gilder's taste and too affiliated with Zola and Hardy (whom London is reading and crying over in 1900).[95] Gilder likewise decried "the rotten condition of the French theatre and modern literature." Wace is the antibohemian critic, the advocate for a Machine Age, proletariat literature. He is thus attractive to a poet like Hester, just as Larsen is attractive to Brewster, but ultimately the lack of romanticism tilts the poets to Van Weyden and Kempton. And because London himself advocated the blending of passion and realism, what we can call the human document, he had no quarrel with Gilder and Johnson's editorial practice. London told Brett that he could assure Gilder that "the characters themselves will not permit of anything offensive. . . . I exploit brutality with my eyes open, preferring to do it through the first half and to save the second half for some thing better. . . . I am absolutely confident myself, that the American prudes will not be shocked by the last half of the book."[96] They could, after all, find common ground.[97]

After Gilder assured himself about his "needless" "precaution," he asked Brett for "a full synopsis" or, better, the rest of the completed novel. If he received the final draft of the first installment in a month or two, that is, by the end of September or October, he could begin running the novel in January 1904. He offered four thousand dollars for the whole shebang, and Brett conveyed the terms to his author, but with a very sensible warning: "Personally I should like to see the thing in the *Century* but if to put it there means the spoiling of it; or if to put it there means to hurry the book unduly so that it will not be up to the magnificent conception of it I shall be very sorry indeed."[98] Here is yet another example of Brett looking out not just for London's best interests but for his elevation to American literature's highest valuation. Within a week London mailed "an amplification of the synopsis of the sea novel," assured Brett that he had no problem with Gilder's editorial policy, and once again reiterated his own desire to take his time. But he also clarified the status of the draft that he had already mailed: "Mr. Gilder speaks of rough drafts. I do not make any. I compose very slowly, in long hand, and each day type what I have written. My main revision is done each day in the course of typewriting the manuscript. This manuscript is the final one, and as much time is spent on it as is spent by many a man in making two or three rough drafts." That is, what you have is what I want, though Gilder "has my full permission to blue pencil all he wishes."[99] He could even call it *The Triumph of the Spirit*. But the final, authorized version would be the text as published by Macmillan.

London hadn't written a word on the novel for the entire month of August, writing instead two short stories—"The Banks of the Sacramento" and "Love of Life"—and attending to his personal affairs. He started again on 1 September and promised to have the final first installment by 4 October and the novel finished in three months.[100] Yet again he departed from his usual practice. In September, he asked Brett for the first half of the manuscript back so that "a couple of friends [could] look over, suggest, and criticize."[101] The friends were Charmian and Sterling. It seems, because he had started and then stopped, that he had either lost the thread of the novel as a whole and needed to go back over it, or he had had a crisis of confidence and needed some outside advice and encouragement, or both. He also asked Cloudesley Johns to look over the first half; it was too late for advice on the serial version, but he wanted it for "all the book and the remainder of the serial publication."[102] Johns did so by 7 October, and London told him he would send more. In fact, Johns decided to come north, and by the beginning of November they were sailing, writing, and playing together on the *Spray*.[103] On 9 November, London wrote to Brett, telling him that it would be done the second week of December.[104] That was another optimistic estimation; this novel had its own timeline, and London could not rush it even as he tried to. This novel had to be written slowly. Johns left, and London returned to Oakland on 20 December. In the next eighteen days he wrote the final chapter—approximately three thousand words—and on 7 January 1904 he mailed the completed sea novel to Brett.[105]

But the writing project that had begun in a sense with "Stranger Than Fiction" could not be completed, it seems, until its author had treated the same old subject one last time. An "'old sea dog'" had read chapter 38 of *The Sea-Wolf* in manuscript for the *Century* and complained about the implausibility of two people restepping a mast of a sealing schooner. London wrote back to Johnson with an explanation; "I consulted, in rigging my schooner at the very start, the shipyard men. They gave me the figures, length, weights, powers of windlasses, etc."[106] The "old sea dog" was L. Frank Tooker. When he looked back on his career at the magazine, he bemoaned the fact that "its attempts to rise on the wings of a popular author's previous success . . . [had] been singularly unfortunate," and his long list of examples concludes with *The Sea-Wolf*. In a chapter entitled "The Business of Catching Larks," which he thought described Gilder and Johnson's editorial policy, Tooker takes London to task for violating those "sacred things," "truth and plausibility." Did he object to Larsen being a violent man schooled in philosophy? No. Did he object to the sudden appearance and subsequent centrality of a female character who just so happened to be familiar to and familiar with Humphrey Van Weyden? Not at all. He, who had written sea stories and poetry, felt compelled to tell Johnson and Gilder that it was impossible for two people to raise and set the masts of the *Ghost*. Despite London's retort, Tooker edited the text so that "certain modifications were made [in the dimensions of the *Ghost* and its spars and sails] that at least glossed the most obvious faults. They were not enough to obliterate them completely, but they made them less conspicuous, and London voiced no objection."[107] Of course not. London would make sure the original dimensions would remain in the Macmillan text.[108]

But the issue of the ship's masts was but a small detail in the larger picture of the novel's violation of Tooker's laws of truth and plausibility. How could Van Weyden, wrote Tooker in an exasperated tone, "be so wholly ignorant of practical things that on his first day aboard he threw ashes over the rail to windward and could not even peel potatoes, yet in a few short weeks of desultory and haphazard toil attain so extraordinary a degree of mechanical genius that, after sailing an open boat for many days through dangerous gales and high seas with perfect safety, he restepped the ridiculously tall masts of the schooner from which he had escaped—which had fortuitously come his way to the same desolate coast . . . rerigged the schooner, bent her sails, and alone with the heroine proudly set sail for Japan." It was "farcical. . . . It took the reader's lack of intelligence for granted." But Gilder and Johnson, so blinded by the success of *The Call of the Wild*, ignored these so-called factual lunacies. "And there you were," moaned Tooker. "Facts were immaterial in fiction; the illusion was everything, and the editors were willing to submit the case to a hundred thousand readers or more to prove their contention. . . . My contention that the illusion should be felt by those who had a practical knowledge of the facts upon which it was based, otherwise it was indefensible, had no standing."[109] Poor Tooker. The scourge of the editorial office of the *Century* had lost another battle in editorial taste and philosophy.

Tooker spoke for those whom London fought against all his career—the unbelievers, the discounters, those who refused to be absorbed into the reading of the work. Luckily London never had to read Tooker's memoir, but he did read the reviewers and made the mistake of thinking that they were the arbiters of the American literary canon. Up until *The Sea-Wolf*, he had seen the justice of the criticisms. But now, with Brett's injunction to aim for a "permanent place," he began to take such criticisms more seriously and more personally. He found that they frustrated his and Brett's new ambition, and they played on his insecurities about being a novel writer. Brett, for his part, admired the novel greatly. Back in August, upon receiving the first draft of the first half, he wrote to London, "I have read the half of the story which you sent me and it is certainly magnificent. Of course, one cannot tell how well it will fit in with the last half, but if the last half is as good in its way as this first half the book is a masterpiece and will enhance your reputation greatly."[110] When, in January 1904, he had read the whole manuscript, he effused: "I have had the pleasure of reading 'The Sea Wolf' and I may at once say that it has been a real pleasure to me and that I have thought it a very remarkable piece of work indeed, an advance over any work of yours that have seen and, indeed, I might add, of any American work of the same general sort that I have ever come across."[111] London's publisher had thus placed London in the canon of American literature. He neither expressed repulsion nor doubted the novel's veracity or sincerity. He would have told London to ignore the "chattering daws." Certainly London's abrupt departure to Japan and Korea to cover the Russo-Japanese War conveniently allowed London to ignore the vein of indeterminacy he had opened and to suppress his doubts and anxieties about what the novel may accomplish for him; he received Brett's affirmation, his certificate of inclusion in American letters, only when he was ready to come back, in June 1904. With what he hoped was a successful, status-affirming novel completed, he took off across the Pacific, strangely duplicating the voyage he had taken in 1893 and that he had in some sense re-created in *The Sea-Wolf*. This time, however, he was accompanied, not by sealers or critics, but by war correspondents, author figures who were in a way just as monstrous as those critics. In fact, they called themselves the Vultures.

THEATER OF WAR, THEATER AT HOME

Before London left for Korea, before he had even finished the first half of *The Sea-Wolf,* he chose to work for William Randolph Hearst's *San Francisco Examiner,* a maneuver he had made a number of times in the past: in 1901, to cover the Jeffries-Ruhlin fight and to conduct two interviews; in the summer of 1902, to write a series on a shooting contest and a number of miscellaneous feature articles; and, in November 1902, to report on the new mining building at the University of California–Berkeley. In June 1903, on the day his first wife, Bessie, and their two daughters left Oakland to summer in Sonoma County, he contracted with the *Examiner* to write an essay on the case of Edgar Sonne. He planned to make this the first of a number of pieces for the newspaper, but circumstances—both personal and professional—led him away from that plan. *The Sea-Wolf,* after all, exerted quite a gravitational pull.[1]

Edgar Sonne, whose "case," said the newspaper, is important "to every thoughtful person concerned with good citizenship," "presents a problem peculiarly difficult to solve." Sonne, "an unclean bit of wreckage," in the tabloid discourse of the *Examiner,* was a boy criminal. Eleven years old, he broke into a house, was arrested, and then was caught twice stealing money from his mother. He was placed in the Boys and Girls Aid Society home, from which he had already escaped once. "To set him free," posited the newspaper, "is to give full rein to his misguided instincts. To confine him in any penal institution is to destroy any possibility of making a self-respecting man of him." London, the paper said, was peculiarly suited to discuss this issue because of his work in the London East End and because of his thorough knowledge of American lowlife. So the reader, set up by Hearst's *Examiner*'s usual emphasis on "individual frailties, sex and crime, economic failures . . . and strange and mysterious happenings," was prepared for and hoping for the worst.[2]

London borrows from the paper's sensational rhetoric: Can "the stuff of his life . . . be cleansed" or was "the stuff of his life . . . too malformed and rotten"? Employing this binary of character and social policy, London used society's desire for sensational reporting against itself. London's vocabulary—"degenerate," "criminal"—is also informed by his recent reading in Enrico Ferri's *Criminal Sociology*, a book in which he took notes and applied them to Edgar's case before he wrote this newspaper article. For example, he wrote in the back of the book, "Question raised—is he, or is he not, a free agent. Is he a born criminal, or is he a criminal by contracted habits? A criminal he must be, for responsibility to society enters in. He is guilty of crimes against society, and society must protect itself. p. 30— apply this especially to the *boy*. . . . Responsibility—either keep Edgar in prison, let him go & indemnify individuals for the depredations he commits, or cure him."[3] Thus, he writes, "His record prepared me for the regular type of born criminal or degenerate, but my disappointment was agreeable when I found he was just an ordinary looking-boy." One feels that the article could have stopped there, with the reader thinking, oh, well then, never mind. But London has larger fish to fry than reader expectations: "Rottenness and irregularity of the teeth, an abnormally shaped roof of the mouth, and certain other peculiarities were all that might be classed as stigmata of degeneracy, but which, in themselves alone, signified no more than the notable teeth of our strenuous president." Because Hearst would not declare his own presidential candidacy for another six months, readers could not tell that poking fun at the president was a political tactic that both London and Hearst endorsed. After all, "apart from Eugene Debs . . . no candidate for office had a record of support for labor as straightforward and consistent as Hearst's."[4] London was burying his socialism just below the surface. Still, the paper wanted the boy in jail, and London was having none of it. Having found the fault of his criminal behavior in his mother's violent treatment of her son as well as with a "society . . . that permitted this disease to go unattended," he turned at the end to H. W. Lewis, superintendent of the Boys and Girls Aid Society for the final answer: "Edgar Sonne's youthful errors and society's mature errors may be retrieved together, but how much better it would have been, had society caught Edgar Sonne when he was younger." As London said, in an article that has become a classic of his protective nature toward the young and vulnerable, the poor and oppressed, "If society arrogates to itself the punishment of youthful offenders, then it must take upon itself the responsibility for the making of youthful offenders." It was never a simple question of laying blame. Jails and doctors, punishment and rehabilitation must work together.[5] It's a philosophical position he held consistently from this point on—from reading Ferri and writing about the case of Edgar Sonne, to portraying Jim Hall the escaped convict in *White Fang*, to advocating the end of capital punishment in *The Star Rover*.

Instead of continuing with newspaper work and in the theatrical vein, which he would have done had he stayed the summer in the city, he joined his wife and daughters on the Wake Robin Lodge property and began again to write *The Sea-Wolf*. When he had reached the halfway point (or what he estimated to be the halfway point), he took a break and wrote "The Banks of the Sacramento," a contribution tailored for the *Youth's Companion*, a companion to his sea stories for young people. Two weeks later, without having returned to the novel, and now back in the city, he wrote "Love of Life." He still owed George Brett *The Faith of Men, and Other Stories*, which lacked a mere one story for completion, but that story would have to wait till the next month.

He was intent on writing a story, also set in the Klondike, that relied on several supposedly factual accounts, and thanks to a complaint lodged with *McClure's*, who published "Love of Life," we know something about London's composition process for this story. The complainant asked *McClure's* why there was such a similarity between London's story and "Lost in the Land of the Midnight Sun," an article *McClure's* had published in late 1901. After McClure asked him to respond publicly, London wrote that, first, "it is a common practice of authors to draw material for their stories, from the newspapers." It is so common "that it is recommended by all the instructors in the art of the short story, to read the newspapers and magazines in order to get material," and we know that London read the *Editor* and learned this writerly tactic. By now we are well versed in the relationship between literature and newspaper writing as London understood it. "Here are facts of life," said London, "reported in journalistic style, waiting to be made into literature." So, yes, he had read Augustus Bridle and J. K. McDonald's essay about "the actual sufferings of a man with a sprained ankle in the country of the Coppermine River." But he also relied on "another narrative of suffering . . . a newspaper account of a lost and wandering prospector near Nome, Alaska." He also borrowed from Adolphus Greely's *Three Years of Arctic Service*. "On top of all this," as if explaining that writing a story was simply a matter of following a recipe, "I drew upon all my own personal experience of hardship and suffering and starvation, and upon the whole fund of knowledge I had of the hardship and suffering and starvation of hundreds and thousands of other men."[6] London incorporated several telling details from the *McClure's* essay, which are interesting only because they are misleading. London was not accused of plagiarizing, did not plagiarize, and did not lack for story ideas; if he had been, he would have used Bridle and McDonald's explanation for why the two men separate—bad blood and revenge. To use printed material was a way to fill out the original conception, it is the document to ground the human, and it isolated him from charges of an overheated imagination. When another complainant raised the issue of how, in the story, a minnow could move from one pool of water to another, London could answer: "For a moment I was quite flabbergasted" by what appeared to be a factual inaccuracy in the story; but "then I remembered that the episode actually happened."[7] He had read about it in one of his sources.

"Love of Life" begins with a poetic summation of the relationship between London as an author and the field that initially made him successful: "This out of all will remain— / They have lived and have tossed: / So much of the game will be gain, / Though the gold of the dice has been lost." This quatrain from Hamlin Garland's "The Gold-Seekers," more importantly, tells indirectly of that devilish wellspring of the imagination, the devil's dice box. Gold, the writing game, chance: the (un)holy triumvirate of London's writing career. He needed to return to his spectral Mount Olympus to write a new Klondike short story, something he hadn't done since February.

After absorbing the positive, life-affirming message from Garland, we wake up from our complacency and suspect an irony resides in the lines and in the title of the story. "Love," far from being a celebratory verb, signifies the irrational power of organisms to sustain themselves. "Love of Life" is about the fear that arises when life feels fatally threatened and the way it creates a prison in the open country: "He pulled himself together and went on, afraid now in a new way. . . . There were the wolves. Back and forth across the desolation drifted their howls, weaving the very air into a fabric of menace that was so tangible that he found himself, arms in the air, pressing it back from him as it might be the walls of a wind-blown tent." He is imprisoned as much by his biological imperative to carry on as he is by the heartless environment.

To our dismay, we realize we are in league with the imprisoning conditions of his existence. Like the scientists at the end of the story who rescue the poor miner (or like Wolf Larsen), we can only describe life—it is "persistent," it is "blind, unconscious"—we cannot empathize with it (938). As our nameless protagonist in "Love of Life" stumbles through the story (as helpless as Humphrey Van Weyden, who, like the protagonist, gains strength only when he boards a ship), we are never given any reason to hope for him, to care for him, to care whether he lives or dies. Here is the significance of London ignoring the bad blood that apparently existed between Bridle and McDonald's hero and his companion; London ignored that plot device because he did not want the reader to sympathize with the miner. The reader becomes like the "complacent awfulness" that surrounds him. "He fought with his fear," and we observe his fight dispassionately (924). He divests himself of more and more gold—the reason he is out there in the first place—and we think he might have a better chance of surviving if he travels without that weight. But, then again, he might die of starvation no matter how heavy his pack. It's really all the same to us. Live, die, gold, no gold—London has given us so little about his character that we are rendered as dispassionate as the White Silence. This is the art of the inspired author reworking, combining, and fusing together the reading material in his Coleridgean well that is his imagination.

Further, given that so little actually happens, and that what happens is repeated over and over—the days are the same, the nameless wanderer goes in and out of hallucination, in and out of painful hunger—we are thrown upon the force of London's prose. Our attention is focused, not on the events being depicted, but on how they are depicted. "He contemplated the bones, clean-picked and polished, pink with the cell-life in them which had not yet died" (933). As if tired out by plotting a novel, London stripped this new short story down to the barest of essentials—a story that worked only if the prose itself was beautiful—just as his main character is stripped down to "the life in him, unwilling to die." The man without even a name lives because that mysterious metaphysical thing called life has not expired. So, too, does a writer write words because that mysterious metaphysical thing called the imagination does not quit. "He saw nothing save visions" (933). It drives our hobo-miner-author forward to the sea, as we gain pleasure only in the telling of the story. This is the best of absorptive fiction.

He sent it to *Cosmopolitan*, where John Brisbane Walker thought that the image of a man biting through the throat of a sick wolf was too strong for his audience: "I have held 'The Love of Life' for a second reading. It's a magnificent piece of work but so ghastly that I fear to give it to men and women already piled with sorrows. Let me have something of the brighter side of life."[8] He rejected it, as he probably would have rejected *The Sea-Wolf* and its "brutality." But McClure loved *The Sea-Wolf.* Writing out of the blue— since late 1901, when he and London had fallen out over *Children of the Frost,* McClure and London had exchanged mail only twice, both times to discuss rejected essays—McClure exclaimed in January 1904, "You are doing greater work every time. 'The Sea Wolf' is masterly! Where are those stories you were to send us for the magazine? When are we to have your books again?"[9] The letter may have come unprompted by London, but McClure was following his usual pattern. As he had done with "An Odyssey of the North," he praised London's latest fictional work and asked for some for his own company. No matter that London harbored a grudge from how he had been treated. McClure knew London was bigger than that, and he was right. London responded immediately by sending him "Love of Life." McClure took it, paid top dollar (six cents a word, double what London had earned earlier that year), and credited four hundred dollars against London's debt to the magazine. Now London was appearing both in *Century* and in *Century*'s chief rival, and though London was never going to leave Brett for McClure, they were back on friendly terms. McClure even offered to pay him the four hundred dollars directly: "The main thing, and much more important than all of this, is that I want another story from you. 'The Love of Life' is a corker!"[10] London asked for the money and then corrected their accounting by pointing out (a) that he was owed four hundred twenty-five dollars for "Love of Life" and that (b) he had never been paid his hundred dollars for "The Question of the Maximum," a sore point from the past (McClure had accepted but never published the essay). The publisher said he couldn't remember what had happened with that essay but that "if you say so it is all right."[11] He sent London a check for four hundred dollars and credited his account one hundred twenty-five. McClure was back on the trail with London.

Replenished by his visit to his spectral Mount Olympus, he then wrote two more Klondike stories, the first of which, "Too Much Gold," would finally complete *The Faith of Men, and Other Stories.* When he wrote the first sentence it was as if London were anticipating the objections to the plausibility of "Love of Life." As we saw in the last chapter, so much of what he was writing in this period was concerned with strange truths and horror that we shouldn't be surprised by it: "This being a story—and a truer one than it may appear—of a mining country, it is quite to be expected that it will be a hard-luck story."[12] "Hard-luck" can be a mere rationalization for ignorance, and this story trades in ironic humor, another way London spelled himself from the unrelenting terribleness of stories like *The Sea-Wolf* and "Love of Life." But underneath the humor of this story lies a serious socialist point about the nature of contract and how it may facilitate exploitation, even among members of the same class; in fact, W. J. Ghent in his *Mass and Class* uses this story as an example of bad ethical behavior.[13]

"Too Much Gold" fits nicely into the collection *The Faith of Men*. On the surface, the collection might seem a series of light-hearted tales. But the humor, when it is present, always points to the seriousness of the white man's exploitation of the land and other peoples—including other white people—in the name of economics, greed, and domination.

The cover of *The Faith of Men* is similar to that of *The Sea-Wolf*, both of which were departures from the other covers. That is, they are more illustrative than interpretative. *The Sea-Wolf* simply shows Wolf Larsen shaking his fist while sailing his boat, not so much at anyone in particular as everyone and everything, including God. *The Faith of Men* presents a pine bough, fecund with pinecones. It is a representation of the Klondike as a tame, domesticated place. But unlike the cover of *The Sea-Wolf*, this new cover draws the reader into the stories under false pretenses. The Northland is never not going to be the ghostland.

The final short story London wrote in 1903, and the last one he would write for nearly a year, was "Negore, the Coward." Prepared by the irony of London's previous titles, we automatically think that Negore's "cowardice" will be defined as such by white society. And we would be wrong. This story, strictly speaking a Klondike tale, takes place among a Native American tribe, warring with whites, in the middle of the nineteenth century, during "the old days of the Russian occupancy of Alaska." Despite the change in time period, this story still marshals ghostliness, greed, and terror. It would not have been out of place in *Children of the Frost*. It is a straightforward tale: Negore, who has been wrongly labeled a coward by his people, proves his courage in the ultimate fight against the Russians and in death wins the heart of his beloved, a happy ending in London's fictional universe. It also forecasts London's trip to Korea in three months, and surely he would remember his fictional account of the brutality of Russian settlers in the Northland as he observed the war. In "Negore, the Coward," the Russians put out the eyes of Kinoos, the father of Negore's betrothed. They hunt and kill as many Native Americans as possible. As Negore says, "I heard the talk of the shamans and chiefs that the Russians had brought strange sicknesses upon the people, and killed our men, and stolen our women, and that the land must be made clean."[14] Not alone were the Anglo-Saxons ravenous brutes: The Russians and accompanying mercenaries from Finland and eastern Asia were "foragers and destroyers from the far lands beyond the Sea of Bering, who blasted the new and unknown world with fire and sword and clutched greedily for its wealth of fur and hide" (960).[15] Gold wasn't the only thing white men could have too much of. Any sympathy London may have shown the Russians in Korea in 1904 was tempered by the memory of what he wrote in this story.

In the mind of Charmian London, this story held a special place, though she was not quite sure how to define its centrality in London's work. In 1912, as she and Jack sailed around the Horn on the *Dirigo*, she wrote a long letter to Anna Strunsky, filled with news about their activities on board ship. But she also wanted to talk to Anna about Jack's writing career and what she thought of his work in the last eight or nine years—that is, since she had come into his life—especially *Burning Daylight*. "Nothing could exceed a few of his first stories," she wrote, "but there's a something else now—a broader, easier, more mature bigness *in the main*. Some women rail at Jack for weakness in this work since he married a second time—you know the sort. . . . Do you remember *Negore the Coward*? In that story is the *first* touch of what I hope, and feel, has helped Jack to fullness in his work—an expanding in his maturity."[16] By "maturity" Charmian probably meant a new sense of love and the possibility of happiness between a married couple, such as he and she were experiencing. A short story could have a happy ending, however painfully attained it might be. But perhaps she was also pointing to something that existed apart from his mastery of genre, of the form of the novel and the short story. Call it a maturation in worldview, an expansiveness in outlook, a desire to become a world author, not merely a national one. It would be first tested in Korea where his career would take him next.

SPECTACLE IN KOREA

It is important to stress the Russian presence in "Negore, the Coward" because we often think of London having never encountered Russian imperialism before he went to Korea in January 1904. Once in Korea, although he was denied access to the Russian army, he had several encounters with Russian prisoners of war. In Wiju, London took over a dozen photographs of Russian prisoners—on a balcony of a house; standing or sitting in the street; and dozens sitting and standing outside a house.[17] These weren't the first Russians he encountered. In Kuel-ian-ching, after the battle of the Yalu River, he looked through a window of a house and saw Russian prisoners. He turns this moment into something deeply personal, one of those moments central to his body of twenty-two dispatches from the East and so a good entry point into this work. In one of the most absorptive moments in his reporting, he profoundly identifies with the prisoners and then sees himself as a racial outsider.

> Into the windows of a large Chinese house I saw many Japanese soldiers curiously peering. Reining up my horse at a window, I, too, curiously peered. And the sight I saw was as a blow in the face to me. On my mind it had all the effect of the sharp impact of a man's fist. There was a man, a white man, with blue eyes, looking at me. He was dirty and unkempt. He had been through a fierce battle. But his eyes were bluer than mine and his skin was as white. And there were other white men in there with him—many white men. I caught myself gasping. A choking sensation was in my throat. These men were my kind. I found myself suddenly and sharply aware that I was an alien amongst these brown men who peered through the window with me. And I felt myself strangely at one with those other men behind the window—felt that my place was there inside with them in their captivity, rather than outside in freedom amongst aliens.[18]

This moment is fraught with identity politics. But it is also a moment of self-discovery or, perhaps, self-rediscovery. Staring at white men through a window is so much like looking into a mirror that we have to examine the totality—a kind of two-mindedness—of what London thought he was seeing. He cannot identify with the Japanese with whom he looks at the Russians because they are racially different, but he does not want to identify with the captured whites because they are imprisoned.

London never identified with the Japanese and Koreans, but he had grown comfortable around them; their association was frictionless and seemingly "natural." Before he encounters the Russians, he has made his peace with living, working, and traveling with the Japanese army. "I had been traveling for months with Asiatic soldiers. The faces were Asiatic faces. The skins were yellow and brown. I had become used to a people which was not of my kind. My mind had settled down to accepting without question that the men who fought had eyes and cheek bones and skins different from the eyes and cheek bones and skins of my kind. It was all a matter of course, the natural order of things" ("Russians Fight Japanese"). London means that it's "natural" for different races to live together, even if one is "superior" to the other. Then he sees the Russians and suddenly "the natural order of things" is replaced by a different "natural order": racial hierarchy. He is jolted out of his acceptance of being among "alien" people, the Japanese. The biosocial order asserts itself. He cannot ignore how he had been comfortable among those not of his "kind." But his own experiential construction of identity—a white man among the Japanese and Koreans—is at odds with his biosocial construction of reality. That is why his body rebels at the sight in the mirror. He doesn't see himself, completely. He sees himself as a doubled, contradictory signifier.

Further, part of his self-construction of identity is his bohemian nature. It allows him to get along with "alien" races, and it puts him somewhat at odds with mainstream culture. So he knows how in theory he should be, and he questions that identity, though biology trumps bohemianism as well as politics. He has also rejected his originary class identity, willfully moving from proletariat to the upper class. But the alienation that results forces him at times to take refuge in the biological fact of his racial identity, which is a stable, socially accepted identity. He may be bohemian, a social outcast, and nouveau riche, but he is just as white as the bourgeoisie. His two-mindedness is therefore a conflict between his self-construction of identity and a social construction of identity all of which maps onto two different orderings of races, one experiential, one biological.

When he sees the Russian prisoners, he has just witnessed the battle of the Yalu River where the Japanese forces had conducted a frontal assault and lost a thousand men. London finds this act barbaric, an "Asiatic" mode of sacrifice. Two subheads for this particular story emphasize the supposed racial differences between East and West: "Japanese Sacrifice Human Life in Order to Make Evident That They Are Worthy to Face White Men in Conflict. Make Unnecessary Frontal Attack." London and the Hearst newspaper headline writers see this sacrifice as both unnecessary and determined, both foreign and familiar. On the one hand, the Japanese did not act "white" in making the attack because "the Asiatic does not value life as we do." On the other hand, they acted as equals to or even superior to the "whites"; after all, they soundly defeated the Russians in the battle. London resolves this ambivalence by claiming "that a white commander . . . would not find justification for [this sacrifice of troops] in the eyes of his people at home" ("Russians Fight Japanese").

He sees the Russian prisoners, has his moment of internal conflict, and then meets with a Japanese military liaison at headquarters who discusses the victory in English and in terms London would have used: "Your people did not think we could beat the white. We have now beaten the white." The word "white" triggers "a vision" in London's mind of something he had just seen on the road back from the battle, after having seen the Russian prisoners. It is of the foot and leg of a dead Russian soldier piled on top of other dead bodies on a moving cart. The Japanese military liaison has effectively planted the idea in London's mind that that dead body could have been London's, just as the sight of Russian prisoners prompted him to think that but for the grace of God he could have been a white prisoner of the "yellow and brown" ("Russians Fight Japanese").

In a masterful stroke of storytelling rhetoric, he repeats slightly altered versions of his description of the foot three times in the final five paragraphs. The first description is the originary one: "It moved up and down with the jogging, two-wheeled cart, beating ceaseless and monotonous time as it drew away in the distance." Further down the road he sees a Japanese soldier wearing Russian boots that triggers a truncated version of the originary description: "the white foot beating time on the jogging Pekin cart." Finally, after the Japanese liaison officer briefs him, the phrase becomes "the white foot beating time on the Pekin cart." Each time London repeats the phrase he pares it down to its essentials, and the final time is the final sentence of the piece. The repetition serves to keep in his reader's mind the fact that the "white" lost. The use of that word "white" by the Japanese authority makes it clear that the Japanese were "white" enough to win, though not "white" enough to value life. The combination of fact and rhetoric create an ambivalent space—a two-mindedness—in London's head. He sees himself in the Russians, but he also sees a whiteness that is not him: not just the superior "whiteness" of the victorious Japanese, but also the whiteness of the Russians killing the Native Americans in the Klondike, just like every other "white" peoples, and the whiteness of the Russians who were inferior in battle to the Japanese. The sight of the white foot is of course a reminder of how powerful the Japanese are. But the foot's jiggling up and down is finally a symbol of his unease in the world, an unresolved conflict between who he thinks he is and whom he is seen as. He is both the subject and object of racial identity construction.

Layered with his biosocial identity formation is his identity as an author and correspondent. Before London sees the Russian prisoners, he rides through the battleground. "I passed the Japanese dead and wounded on the road and found myself thrilling gently to the horrors of war" ("Russians Fight Japanese"). We cannot miss the lack of compassion London exhibits toward the dead and battered soldiers, but there is something else at work in London's thinking here. Seeing the horrific results of a battle is what he had traveled so far to see. This is his quintessential moment of war corresponding. Later, in his final dispatch, he will complain that he didn't get to experience "thrills," the life-and-death moments that war correspondents under fire seem always to get to experience.[19] He only "gently" thrilled to the sight of the dead because he himself had not been threatened with death. He was close, but, it turns out, he never got close enough to become the kind of foreign correspondent that he so desperately wanted to be. He did not imagine himself to be just another Frederick Palmer or Edwin Emerson, professional foreign news correspondents. Like other newspaper writing, his war correspondence not only reported on facts but also used those facts to expound on larger sociocultural issues. Reporting on the war was not the end result but a means to access and report on the effect of extreme experiences on himself and others. It is part and parcel with his identity as a thrill-seeking bohemian.

There is one final turn of this screw of identity construction. Traveling on horseback, he is back on the road. Though it is not an American highway or railroad or a sea lane, nonetheless he is back being the traveling author, the hobo-author. He entitled one dispatch "Up the Peking Road."[20] To see prisoners, no matter what their color, is to bring back the threat of being imprisoned again. That is why he emphasizes the "captivity" of the Russians and the "freedom" of the Japanese. He would rather be free with those not of his kind than imprisoned with those of his kind. Again, this threat of imprisonment—this reminder of what had happened to the hobo-author in 1894—causes his body to sicken. To be both white and free doesn't guarantee liberty, and, being of two minds, he would rather be with those not of his own kind and free than imprisoned with white people.

Analyzing these ways that two-mindedness governs London's reaction to the multifaceted experience in Korea and Japan gives us a chance to avoid the supposed dichotomies that has governed previous understandings of this moment in his authorial career. We have tended to think that he had to choose between the Japanese and the Russians when he covered the Russo-Japanese War. Also, if we thought his reporting was only about imperialism and economics, then we tended to dismiss the racial content. There are other simplifications we need to avoid. Typically, we think of this six-month period as significant for London as an author, and rightly so, but usually that analysis takes place as if he had never been a reporter before, or had never been abroad, or had never critically examined the relationship between fact and fiction, between newspaper reporting and literature. When London left on 7 January 1904 for Japan and the war, he knew he was going to create a series of human documents, material that some future novelist—such as himself—might employ in his or her own fiction. He even bought a new camera for $67.50, and, though it may be surprising for someone whose work seems to value direct experience over book knowledge, he bought forty-five dollars' worth of new books to read on the ss *Siberia*, which, to varying degrees, he used as notepads for his collection of background material on the war.[21] He brought along several bound notebooks to serve as diaries, several pads of paper to use for notetaking in the field, and several pads of onionskin paper for writing out his "stories" in longhand; for example, he brought a little red address book in which he kept track of expenses in Korea and Japan, addresses, details like metric conversions of distance, and how big was a regiment, and how many tools and what kind do certain companies and regiments carry.[22] All these material supports are exactly the same ones he used when he wrote fiction. So we will look at the rest of his reporting to see how this journey further developed not only his ideas about race, imperialism, and economics, but also newspaper writing and, more generally, about theatricality and authorship.

Let's first take a step back and look at the global context of the war, which will illustrate how London could not simply take one side or the other. Russia and Japan's antagonisms dated back to their first armed conflict in 1804 and then intensified during the first Sino-Japanese War in 1894, when China was supported by Russia, Germany, and France; Japan had taken Port Arthur and the Liaodang Peninsula but was forced by the Western powers to relinquish it. Thus Russia was able to fortify Port Arthur and use it as a year-round port. Japan, being as imperialistic as Russia and shamed by its own concessions, was intent on reestablishing at least part of Manchuria and the Korean Peninsula within their sphere of influence. Korea had been leaning more and more toward Russia, especially after the Japanese assassinated their queen in 1895 and invaded the country a year later to instigate a general revolt. Russia, for their part, needed Korea to ensure a safe trade and military route between their two ports at Vladivostok and Post Arthur. Russia and the United States both wanted Russia and Japan to share equally in economic and military rights in Korea (no one wanted Korea to be an independent state), but Japan, having signed a nonaggression pact with Britain (and with the perceived covert support of the U.S.), was confident in battling Russia for hegemony over the peninsula.[23] In late July 1903, Japan presented its first demands to Russia, and the negotiations continued until 8 February, when Japan attacked the Russian fleet in Port Arthur and war was declared. Historically speaking, this is important to us now because Japan's victory threatened the U.S.'s own imperialistic advances in the Pacific and led to "the start of a 'cold war' between them, which culminated eventually in the Japanese attack on Pearl Harbor and the war in the Pacific."[24]

In 1903–4, however, the U.S. held a very different position. The United States was officially neutral and eventually helped negotiate the end of the war but also provided military advisers (including Douglas MacArthur and his father, Arthur) who marched with the Japanese army into Manchuria, and London even took a photograph of two of them, Colonel Crowder and Captain Marsh.[25] London and many other Americans "were also critical of Russian expansion in the Far East, of the cruelties of Russian despotism, and of the persecution of Jews, especially after the Kishinev Pogrom of 1903 when 50 Jews were massacred by a mob without government interference."[26] In fact, the *San Francisco Call* reported that the Russians had expelled all Jews from Port Arthur shortly before the war began and then, two days later, on the front page, that a representative of American Jewish organizations would meet with State Department officials and with President Theodore Roosevelt about steps to take to prevent the rumored upcoming massacre of Jews on the Russian new year (7 January) and "the whole subject of the status of the Jews in Russia."[27] London himself spoke out against the pogroms in an interview in late 1905: "These race prejudice riots in Russia have always been directly traceable to the government," and he supported a socialist overthrow of that government.[28] In a public lecture after his time in the East, he asserted that he and all the correspondents he traveled with were pro-Japanese before they arrived but turned against them because of their "abiding hatred of the white man."[29]

By at least December 1903, London was becoming conversant with the daily news of the anticipated war between Russia and Japan. He clipped an editorial from the antisocialist, racist, anti-Asian *Argonaut*, from October 1903, on the developing conflict. The *San Francisco Call* reported in early December on the front page that the "Far Eastern Crisis Nears Settlement," and nearly every day that month the front page carried news—almost always illustrated by photographs of the chief participants—of the on-again off-again negotiations as well as the continuing war preparations—both political and military—of Japan and Russia.[30] "Russia's Reply to Japan Rejected by the Council of the Elder Statesmen" read the headline on 18 December, and it was forecasted that Japan would soon send troops into Korea.[31] Finally, in what must have been the moment London and newspaper editors were waiting for before committing themselves to the expense of sending reporters overseas, the *Call* announced on 29 December that "Russia's Answer to Japan's Final Note Is a Refusal: Both Nations Contract for War Supplies in America." Two days later London signed his contract with the *Examiner*.

We don't know exactly how London ended up as a reporter for the Hearst papers, but it is likely that he approached Hearst and others as he finally saw the end of *The Sea-Wolf* coming, just as he saw the war developing. London claimed to Cloudesley Johns that he had chosen Hearst from among *Collier's*, *Harper's*, and the *New York Herald*.[32] On 31 December 1903, the day he signed his contract with Hearst, Robert Collier, editor of *Collier's Weekly*, wrote to Roosevelt asking him to write a letter of support for Frederick Palmer to the secretary of state, and he mentions that Palmer is one of three reporters that he is sending, the other two being Richard Harding Davis and Jack London; when London signed with Hearst, Collier replaced him with Edwin Emerson.[33] Presumably, after he had gotten an offer from Collier, he sent a wire to Hearst, asking for the job, and Hearst gave it to him on more favorable terms than he had received from Collier and others.

Hearst signed him without caring if London succeeded as a war correspondent. As he told Emerson, "I have just received a telegram from Jack London in San Francisco that he is ready to go to the front, and I have wired him to go ahead. I don't know what kind of war correspondent he will make, but whatever he writes is bound to catch on, so I don't care."[34] Hearst and London may have been more simpatico than either imagined. In a series of directives to his editors, Hearst wrote, "Try to be conspicuously accurate in everything, pictures as well as text. Truth is not only stranger than fiction, it is much more interesting."[35] Hearst was one of the first newspaper publishers to emphasize the newsworthiness of photography, even to the extent of creating a new post: picture editor. The combination of truth, text, photography, fiction, and interest/absorption would have resonated deeply with London.

The Hearst contract specified that he leave 7 January 1903 on the ss *Siberia*. War had not yet been declared, so the contract stipulated that if there were no war London would receive $500 a month plus expenses. If war were declared, he would get an extra $250. According to London's own calculations, he earned a total of $4,312.50 (for five and three-quarters months) or $111,276 in today's dollars.[36] (Richard Harding Davis, on the other hand, was earning $4,000 a month from *Collier's Weekly*.)[37] He would be reporting in case of war for a minimum of three months and then for however long Hearst thought prudent and necessary. He was allowed to take and publish photographs *"as he shall consider useful,"* and he had the right to publish his material in a book. The contract did not specify how many articles he should write in case of war (six, if war did *not* materialize, of two thousand to three thousand words), but it did specify that he "is *to diligently seek and forward, by the usual methods of conveyance, such information concerning the war and allied topics as may be appropriate for publication.*"[38] London stayed roughly three and a half months, from 18 March to May 25, in the theater of operations. (He was still physically present at the end of May, but he had applied for a pass to Tokyo, signaling that he was done.) He was gone from the U.S. from 7 January to 30 June, almost six months, and he completed twenty-two articles plus the essay "The Yellow Peril."

London's initial intention for covering the war—apart from enlarging the scope of his authorial identity—was similar to what he had accomplished with *The People of the Abyss*. "*People of the Abyss*," London had told Brett a year previous, "is simply the book of a correspondent writing from the field of industrial war. . . . It is a narrative of things as they are."[39] He would focus on the economic causes of a military war. We remember his essay "The Impossibility of War" (written February 1900) in which he argued that prolonged war would induce famines on the home front, leading to popular rebellion if sustained too long. Economics, he argued in that essay, not military prowess, would determine the outcomes of war. On 20 December 1903 London must have seen the report in the *San Francisco Call* that Russia was having trouble securing international loans for war preparations.[40] London would later predict, in 1904, that Japan could not win the war; they had borrowed money at 6 percent.

But his actual reporting slights the importance of economics. Every once in a while, he turns an economic eye and his political-economy-mindedness to the war zone. He sees immediately the class differences in Korea and how "the master class, which is the official class" (meaning, the class of officials, not workers) robs the poor of wages and reimbursement for food procured by the Japanese through the managerial class. "The Korean official can give the Occident cards and spades when it comes to misappropriation of funds. The Oriental term for this is 'squeeze.' Centuries of practice have reduced it to a science, and in Korea there are but two classes—the squeezers and the squeezees. The common people, of course, as all the world over, are the 'squeezees.'"[41] London even vociferously lobbies a corrupt Korean magistrate on behalf of the people of Sunan to return money he had unjustly taken. London does so, however, as much out of solidarity with the Korean working class as he does to not lose face as a so-called powerful white man and because he was "decidedly bored by my own society" while cooped up in Sunan, awaiting permission to continue north to cover the war.[42]

A combination of two factors led to his lack of reporting on the economics of war. First, his bibliography on the war and the countries involved shows he did not have enough background material to draw from, unlike the case of *The People of the Abyss*. Second, he was hindered in his reporting by the Japanese military. When he returned home, he told Brett that "I doubt that my stuff will make a book."[43] He was so disappointed that he reiterated his failure three days later, scapegoating the entire Japanese army for the failure: "Am now turning back to the States, quite disgusted with the whole situation so far as it concerns a correspondent getting material. Our treatment has been ridiculously childish, and we have not been allowed to see anything. There won't be any war-book so far as I am concerned."[44] In December 1904, he tried to market a shortened version of one of his dispatches, which was focused on economics and entitled "Korean

Money"; but it was an odd mix of travelogue, economic analysis, and self-deprecating humor, and it did not sell.⁴⁵ Later, he would make lists of Japanese names, for inclusion in possible stories, he wrote out a brief set of notes for a short story tentatively entitled "The Jap," and he used the death of a Russian he had observed at the battle of the Yalu River as material for a possible article called "How We Die." And, of course, he used some of his experiences and notes on reading for the Adam Strang episode in *The Star Rover*.⁴⁶ But he never completed a story, or a book, or a treatise on economics and warfare: just dispatches from a distant front and photographs of the poor, tormented people of Korea who seemed voiceless in this matter of nationhood.⁴⁷

In the end, his reporting and his photography forsook politics and an analysis of the world's class struggle in favor of an analysis of war based on biology and race. Since his photographs form an integral part of reporting, we can turn to them first and treat them not merely as appendages to his dispatches but as dispatches themselves.

We might think that his first preference was for action photographs of warfare and its immediate effects, but he never took a photograph of a dead soldier, a la Matthew Brady. He took photographs of various scenes of war—not of battles but of the logistics of warfare and of the impact of the war on civilians. And he took numerous portraits of ordinary Koreans. It is this latter category that has drawn the most critical attention. To us, his photographs of Koreans give voice to the stateless, but that was not necessarily his intention. To begin with, we have to look at the context in which he took his photos, that is, the sociocultural, as opposed to the militaristic, context. London ignores or fails to notice that his photographs of everyday Koreans and their lives are an ironic imitation of what he calls the Koreans' second most "salient characteristic" ("after inefficiency"): "curiosity" or *koo-kyung*, a Korean word that means "plays, lectures, sermons, horse-shows, menageries, excursions, picnics." As he waited in Sunan to advance further with the army, he lived in a house on the main drag, Pekin Road. Here, every afternoon, he "set up my photograph gallery," both mirroring and adding to the *koo-kyung*; just as the Koreans stare at him, turning him into a character in their plays, so London stares at the Koreans through his camera and creates an American *koo-kyung*.⁴⁸ In this way he is both disrupting the Korean gaze and documenting the people's outward appearance. After all, his staged portraits are of Koreans staring into the camera, and so London manages both to capture and disarm the power gained from their objective observation of foreigners.

Many of his portraits were set up by Manyoungi, his new Korean servant: "Manyoungi has quite entered into the spirit of my photography and fares forth enthusiastically to capture any specimen I desire" (77). That word "specimen" indicates a lack of empathy; he captures the people like pinning a butterfly. Some subjects did not know what the camera was and feared it as a "terrible instrument of death" ("Hermit Kingdom"). If London had any chance to actually bond with the people, he had to do it through the camera lens, forsaking one-on-one contact. Why would he not want to engage directly with them? In addition to them being "inferior," perhaps, to him, they seemed like ghosts. London writes that Manyoungi had "entered into the spirit of my photography," and surely "entered into the spirit" means "joining me in my enthusiasm." It may be an exaggeration to say that one can read that sentence to mean that he is photographing spirits. However, to begin with, London's activities as both a writer and photographer mirror the Korean population's supposed central characteristic of curiosity and observation, though he never explicitly identifies with the Korean populace. He only observes them observing him observing them, silently, of course, all dressed in white like ghosts, in their near-deserted villages, impassive. When he begins to discuss Korean dogs, he can't help but compare them to Klondike dogs. Then, in the very next paragraph, Korean civilians, because they are all dressed in white, become like "ghosts" walking in the mostly deserted countryside, as if the White Silence were present. In a dispatch entitled "Japanese in Invisible War. . . . It Might Have Been Battle of Ghosts," he writes of the battle at the Yalu River, "This was the battle—a river bed, a continuous and irregular sound of rifle firing over a front of miles, a few black moving specks. That was all. No Russians were to be seen. With all the hubbub of shooting no smoke arose. No shot was seen to be fired. The black specks disappeared in the willows. . . . It might be a war of ghosts for all that eye or field-glass could discern."[49] Because the Japanese military kept a tight rein on correspondents, they weren't allowed to see what they wanted to see, thus creating a kind of ghostliness around the entire theater of operations. The very subject of his work, the war, is a ghost; there one minute, and gone the next. Watching people watching him, photographing Koreans, trying to report on war news: The Korean experience for London is like looking into a mirror, a medium for entry into the subconscious, where he is struggling with questions like racial identity and authorial construction. It's as if he is engaged in spirit photography to reveal his true self to himself.

Some of his so-called portraits are simple voyeurism. He took photos of the naked asses of Korean laborers, the exposed breasts of Korean women, and even several photos of children showing exposed penises.[50] He took many photographs of street scenes, but even these two categories of photographs achieve the general effect of disrupting the centrality of the Korean gaze by interposing his own view of the matter. Sometimes this interruption is imperialistic and racist, sometimes it is private and experiential. In the final analysis, though, London is after documentation, the facts of the matter. His photographic work wants to be anthropologic, not artistic or spiritual or even polemical. He is not illustrating the down-and-outers of Korea, as he did in London with the people of the abyss. He has no political objective or program in mind. His character studies simply document life on the Peking Road outside his house or people he saw on the streets of Korean and Japanese towns and villages. Most of his photos were not meant for publication, and only one (entitled "Sunset on the Yalu") was taken for the beautiful effects of the scene. London may have carefully framed and composed his scenes, but they weren't taken for artistic reasons. His portraits weren't Arnold Genthian in nature, and neither were his landscapes like Ansel Adams's. They are like Edward S. Curtis's portraits of "the noble savage." He was not interested in advancing the art of photography. When he wasn't consciously taking shots for the newspaper, he took them for private reasons, as an aide-mémoire to form a stockpile of documentation in case he ever wanted to write about these experiences in the future.

For example, his extemporaneous portraits of captured Russian soldiers might have provided him with visual documentation for a story he outlined after his return, imagined as part of a series called *How We Die*: "four or five *subjective* studies of men dying—emphasizing the withdrawing into themselves, their own thoughts, etc." London typed out a full page of notes on "a Russian soldier, killed on the Yalu, Japs are crossing to East and flanking Russian Left—Russians are drawing in, along river to Kulien Ching." When London wrote this is unknown; the typewriter he used indicates a time before the *Snark* voyage. The story is deeply sympathetic to the Russian as it portrays him trying to escape Japanese artillery fire.[51] His camera was a prosthetic not just for seeing in a different way but for writing in a different way. And if the subjects are unwilling and scared of "the glittering mechanism [the camera] that they mistake for some terrible instrument of death" ("Hermit Kingdom"), then he welcomed that added drama, and subconsciously he knew it to be yet another manifestation of the irrational ghost world of Korea. So London relates that men cry and scream and beg not to be hurt all the while he and Manyoungi hold them in place to keep the subjects in focus ("Hermit Kingdom").[52]

There is a verbal dimension to his photography. A number of headlines for his dispatches proclaimed not just that his photos were firsts from the front but that his words were "word-pictures." They might be a "vivid glimpse" or "graphic story" or "typical Incidents by Way of Illustration" or even "vivid pen pictures," all as equally compelling as the photographs, if not slightly less so. It's a kind of middle-brow ut pictura poesis. Of course London would not have failed to notice the poverty and hardships of his subjects. But like the photos in *The People of the Abyss* (and, for that matter, his photos for his voyage on the *Snark*), they illustrate a tension in his authorial conception: that between his identification with his subject and his distancing of himself from that subject. We must never forget that London, in the process of becoming an author in 1893–94, saw authorship as a way to save himself from prison or death. If we locate an authorial presence in Adam Strang, the American sailor who lives in Korea in his 1915 novel *The Star Rover*, we see how complicated this relationship between traveler-writer and resident really is.

Now we can turn to his written word. In a number of other rhetorical ways, London reprised his role of hobo-author even before he began his formal work as a war correspondent. In fact, there is no indication that he wanted to be considered first and foremost a newspaper war correspondent; certainly he would not have been considered as such by his companions on board the ss *Siberia*: Frederick Palmer, James Hare, Robert L. Dunn, and other veteran reporters (Palmer, for example, had already covered the Greco-Turkish War, the war in the Philippines, and the Boxer Rebellion, though he and London shared similar experiences in the Klondike in 1897–98).[53] I'm sure they never "bucked a game run by the Chinese firemen of the *Siberia*," an activity reminiscent of London's time in steerage crossing the Atlantic a little over a year previous and a game a hobo would have felt comfortable playing.[54] London went where the working men went, and only by breaking his ankle on board between Hawaii and

Japan was he prevented from associating more with the Chinese firemen and other common laborers and allowing them to win their money back.

Even in his dispatches from Korea he downplays his identity as a war correspondent. In "Fighting at Long Range Described," he tells us that in the artillery duel over the Yalu River, "a tactical advantage may have been gained by the Japanese, which strengthened their strategic movement. Now, what is a strategic movement?" he asks, and we have a moment, typical in London's theatrical writing, of addressing and instructing his readership. But this is not, as London knows, what a war correspondent does; he would already know what "a strategic movement" is and presume that the reader does too. In the next paragraph, London makes clear the distance between who he is and who, say, F. A. McKenzie is: "This is modern warfare to the mind of this layman."[55] He is a mere "layman," not interested in becoming professionally conversant about the technical aspects of warfare. In his penultimate dispatch, he confesses that he had come to the war hoping to enter life-and-death situations: "I knew that the mortality of war correspondents was said to be greater, in proportion to numbers, than the mortality of soldiers. . . . [I wanted to be] where life was keen and immortal moments were being lived. In brief, I came to war expecting to get thrills."[56] No clearer statement of the bohemian tyro could be made. He did not want to be a war correspondent. He wanted to be placed in situations that were allowed only to war correspondents and soldiers. He wanted to fight a war without having to shoot a rifle or stab with a bayonet.

Within a week of his arrival in Japan, London was arrested for photographing people in the fortified city of Moji. It speaks to his inexperience, and newspapers either cited that fact or imagined he had gotten arrested for publicity purposes. For London, however, it brought back memories of being arrested for vagrancy on the road in America. He took three photos before he was stopped by a "middle-aged Japanese man," who then led the unsuspecting London into a police station: "The middle-aged Japanese was what the American hobo calls a 'fly cop.'"[57] Further, under questioning by the police, he is completely cooperative, that is, until they made it apparent that they thought it suspicious he had been wandering around, like a spy: "their conclusion from my week's wandering was that I had no fixed place of abode." He deliberately converts spying into hoboing in order to make this point about his mental state: "I began to shy. The last time the state of my existence had been so designated it had been followed by a thirty-day imprisonment in a vagrant's cell!" ("Jail in Japan"). Surely the punishment for being a Russian spy would have been greater than that. London fictionalizes this account (of course he didn't have a permanent home in Japan) just in order to tell us that he was a certain kind of author.

This is not the only moment of converting fact into fiction, and because the correspondents could not get close to the action, to warfare's killing, this war had the air of the unreality of theater. Frederick Palmer says about the day of the attack across the Yalu River: "There was to be a charge and the time for it was almost as exactly set as that for the rising of a theatre curtain" (68). London, who had for years now combined news reporting with fictional techniques, easily exploited this atmosphere. For no apparent reason, he does not use the real names of the two correspondents who accompanied him north on the Peking Road, F. A. McKenzie and Robert L. Dunn, for his first nine dispatches, calling them instead "McLeod" and "Jones," as if they were characters in a play. Then, without explanation, he begins to use their real names.

But this is not absorptive fiction, so ghosts and its other techniques lurk in the background. His model is not the Klondike story but rather his 1902 feature work for the *Examiner*. His writing is strictly narrative, using the first-person voice, a folksy kind of voice, alternating among humor, naivete, and irritation. For example, when he tells us about the Korean pony he bought (as if we really care what sort of animals he has), he explains that though short and small as a large dog the horse could carry an enormous weight. He considers it as a replacement for his own stallion: "If something happens [to it]. Jones's [that is, Dunn's] principal objection to this is that both my feet will drag on the ground, and I half believe him. To-morrow I shall mount it and find out for myself. Perhaps I may be able to tuck my feet up a little."[58] This is how a fiction writer closes a story, with a little self-deprecating humor about a minor incident. He never assumes the voice or style or organizing principles of the veteran war correspondent. There is rarely a lead, and little reporting. He often uses dialogue to further the action of the "story." He sets scenes as if he were writing a short story: "The morning of April 30th was hazy. The sun shone dimly, and the distant valleys and canyons seemed filled with the smoke of some vast conflagration. But this cleared away with the growing day and the valley of the Yalu lay before us."[59] He is intimately involved in all that he sees and wants to bring the reader along with him as he experiences every little thing. He is our guide in the theater of war, pointing out people, places, and things of interest—even down to the details of what Japanese soldiers carry—so that we, too, can feel we are present at the scene. Although it isn't stressed, there is an air of you-won't-believe-this to his writing. Once again fact is stranger than fiction, though he fictionalizes fact to make it more believable.

When London is arrested in Japan his true authorial identity leaks out. On the road in 1894, he had been a hobo-author pretending not to be an author. In the Klondike, he had been a hobo-author trying to be a miner, not an author. In England, he had been a hobo-author again pretending not to be an author. In Japan and Korea, he was the hobo-author who was (sometimes) masquerading as a war correspondent, not an author. In each field of authorship, his sense of what constitutes an author undergoes various permutations without damage or compromise of his fundamental, nonnegotiable understanding of himself as a writer. He is trying out different models of authorship. But now that he was famous, the outside world would not let him forget that he was a novelist and short-story writer, and this socially constructing identity formation was an obstacle to his own interior attempts to further remake his ideas about authorship. It was a new tension in his career, and he would have to face it and overcome it for the rest of his life.

According to a report on London's arrest in Hearst's *New York American*, "Mr. London had a hearing before the Japanese Military Commission, and pleaded that he was unaware of the stringent rules guarding the coast fortifications at the present time before war had been declared, and professed his willingness to abide by all regulations in the future and do no act which could be construed as an offense against the courtesy of the military commanders." At the same time, however, he insisted that "he was acting entirely within his rights as a war correspondent in taking a few snapshots of the Japanese fortifications from the outside." The affair concluded with London being freed from prison and having his camera returned, with the help of Minister Lloyd Griscom, the highest ranking American diplomat in Japan.[60] Clearly, he did not care what the rules were. There were no restrictions on the hobo-author, and as long as he acted from that premise, he got into trouble.

One of the regulations of the Japanese army for foreign correspondents included the injunction to "look and behave decently."[61] London deliberately dressed as he always had, regardless of how, previous to his time in

Japan and Korea, the American press and others had castigated him. For example, in the fall of 1903, when he applied for admission to the Bohemian Club, a newspaper columnist opined that he should not be admitted, not because of his impending divorce but because of the kind of shirts he wore.

JACK LONDON'S SHIRT

I hear that Jack London just squeezed through in his election for membership in the Bohemian Club. The new novelist is as unconventional in his dress as in his literary style, and never parts company with his negligee shirt.

Another whisper comes to me that London's flannel shirt was only used as a cloak for the real opposition to him, and that his recent divorce suit was a more potent cause. I do not believe that anybody can find much in that divorce suit to enlarge the halo around the head of the rising author of "The Call of the Wild," but the world long ago made up its mind that Bohemians, whether of the literary or the stage variety are not amenable to the same rules of moral criticism as people who trudge in the other highways of life. Perhaps the negligee shirt at full-dress affairs and the divorce suit combined were the cause of London's narrow escape from being blackballed. Anyhow, he pulled through.[62]

In the following paragraph from a New York paper, the writer brings together London's dressing habits, his status as a writer and newspaper correspondent, and his divorce, as if they all informed each other to help create the most complete picture of the man, Jack London. The account begins with the assessment that *The Faith of Men, and Other Stories* was evidence that

the man who wrote "The Call of the Wild" had begun to seek popularity rather than fame. Then he decided to go to the Far East as a war correspondent, and it was a good decision. It was a pleasant thing to be a war correspondent when you know how to tell what you see and know how to see what to tell. But before he left he dressed himself in a sombrero and a bright blue coat lined with red flannel. The coat had brass buttons all over it, and Mr. London's hair streamed from under his hat into the happy air like a beacon. It was not a businesslike coat, nor had Mr. London a reputable looking hat. His pictures (dressed in both coat and hat) were exposed upon the elevated railroad stations and at street corners before he went to the war. They were attractive, but they did not seem to suggest the author of "The Call of the Wild." News came from San Francisco yesterday that your writer had been sued for divorce. Mrs. London has recorded in her complaint objections to certain details of Mr. London's trip to the Orient. An action for divorce is not to be discussed before the trial—but that overcoat was inexcusable.[63]

Sometimes the press linked London's dress to a favorable take on his writing and the trouble other members of the press created around the issue of his actual identity. On the occasion of London giving a lecture on "Experiences of a War Correspondent in Japan and Corea" at the Home Club, the reporter says,

And what a unique figure Jack London is, as he steps before an audience. Nothing in the world will induce him to wear the conventional evening dress of the ordinary lecturer—and he looked quite as if he had walked from town a couple of miles over the hills. He is simply unconventional to the last degree. One remembers with a smile how the staid old Atlantic Monthly people wanted him to sign his name "John London," "John" being much more dignified than the informal "Jack." But he would have none of it, for if they didn't take "Jack" they needn't take the manuscript either, so they must needs be content with the signature, for Jack London is in a position to dictate to the publishers.[64]

Not surprisingly, then, in 1904 in Korea, a photograph by Hare of thirty-four correspondents shows a preponderance of military and pseudo-military attire, and a number of them look like Teddy Roosevelt the Rough Rider. London, in his most often reproduced image, looks like he did in London 1902, except in mittens.[65]

At least two other times he violated the unspoken rules of the war correspondent, and, like his apparel, these intentional violations speak to his conception of his authorial office overseas. The first occurred shortly after his arrest in Japan, showing that London was not intimidated by authority. London and Dunn were detained in Sunan, Korea, for a little over a week because they had traveled further than the Japanese military had allowed; they were escorted back to Seoul by the Japanese army. The second incident is reported variously but seems to come down to a punch thrown by London at a Korean servant. Frederick Palmer's account seems the most reasonable. "Soon after our arrival at the Yalu [London] knocked down one of our [Korean] servants for threatening him. This brought on a diplomatic crisis with the staff, which we solved by explaining that London was a most gifted writer, with a strong sense of the pioneer American's *bushido*, which responded with a blow of a fist to an insult."[66] That is, the Japanese command was upset that London had punched a Korean civilian, but once they heard London's justification they dropped the matter. London wasn't jailed, wasn't sent home because of the incident, and didn't need Davis's or Roosevelt's intervention, as some biographers have claimed.

The *American* of course had a vested interest in portraying London as favorably as possible. It even concluded the news report with the gratuitous observation that the entire event "goes to show the desire of Mr. London to get as near to the real thing as possible in acting as the representative of the 'AMERICAN.'" Either London had made a rookie mistake that could have been costly or, as the paper would have it, he would go to any length to get a story. From the point of view of the Hearst editors, however, as much fame that attached to London attached to the newspaper as well, and thus the newspaper mentions itself in connection with London at every possible moment. Many of the headlines for London's articles showcase London's fame—one article even carries his byline accompanied by the description, "special correspondent of 'The Examiner,' author of 'Call of the Wild,' 'God of His Fathers' and One of the Very Few War Correspondents Who Have Been Able to Press on with the First Japanese army and to Witness the War as It Is Fought."[67] When he returned home in June and published his final summation, the *San Francisco Examiner* deemphasized his role as correspondent, calling him its "special commissioner" "who added to his literary fame new laurels" as its representative.[68] This is the first time that his association with a publisher developed this double strand of fame. London had never felt so publicly needed. He realized that on a certain level, by playing in this larger theater of operations, it did not matter what he did, what he thought, what he wrote. His newspaper publisher could subsume his work under his status as a reportable object. Instead of being a theatrical writer he was becoming, somewhat against his will, a theatrical actor.[69]

Later, when he came home and collected his news clippings and pasted them into his scrapbooks (or asked Charmian to do it for him), he could see how his personal and professional affairs were imbricated in the press. Articles about London leaving for the East and about his taking photos of Japanese fortifications and of his release from jail appear among reviews of *The People of the Abyss, The Call of the Wild,* and of the first installments of *The Sea-Wolf,* as well as of his separation and divorce from Bessie; in fact, on the day of his return from Japan, while talking to reporters about his Korean experiences, he was served with papers concerning his divorce, a moment duly reported by those covering his talk.[70] His literary reputation got mixed together in the public's mind with his public performance as a correspondent and with his status as a private citizen.

Other newspapers besides the *American* were not collegial. One report circulated that "Jack London, the highly advertised war correspondent in the Stanley hat, has succeeded in being arrested the first day out. He seems to know how to sell stuff."[71] Again his attire signifies the kind of author he is. Another reporter combined London's inexperience with a loathing for his fiction: "Jack London, the infant phenomenon, has been jailed by the Jap. It is to be hoped they will burn some of his manuscripts."[72] A hometown newspaper, though, spun his inexperience in a favorable way: "Talk about luck! Here is Jack London on his first trip as a correspondent, and he manages to get locked up and more talked about than all the rest of them put together. It's good luck and well deserved."[73] It's not that his work had not been attacked in the same way before. The *Dawson Weekly News* wrote, when *Children of the Frost* had been published, that "in art the truest is not always the best. Jack London's stories of the Klondike, written in a comfortable Chicago office by a man who joined briefly in the stampede to the Klondike in '97, and who turned about and retired before reaching Dawson, are accepted on the outside as ideal realism, though the stories can hardly find readers here."[74] There's a certain amount of special pleading here, but the ratio of inaccuracies to the length of the report is so high as to indicate a need to aim at the famous. Another blurb linked his so-called poor writing to his war travels: "Jack London has gone to Tokio for a newspaper syndicate. After reading his recent potboilers [*The Faith of Men, and Other Stories*] I have more than once found myself wishing he would go to and stay at a place where pencil and paper are not. London was a bright writer, but of late has succumbed to what Louis Stevenson calls the 'damnation of the check book.' His easy writing is mighty hard reading."[75] These assessments and attacks are interesting not so much because they expose

London's inexperience—we would be aware of that even if we hadn't read these news clippings—but because they combine shameless pronouncements on both London's personal and professional lives, as if they cannot be extricated from each other, as if one actually contributes to the other; he writes saleable fiction so therefore he wears a Stanley hat—or is it the other way around?

Further, these articles are on the same continuum that was so pronounced in *The Sea-Wolf* reviews. He had become a target. His fame as a writer was changing in kind. From being a rising star in American literature, a rival to Kipling (or just another Kipling), he had arrived at a higher place of achievement that brought with it the invitation to fatal critique. Of course he was not the only one. Richard Harding Davis, John Fox Jr., and Frederick Palmer all were excoriated for their writings from Tokyo. They too were accused, not of being inexperienced, but of being inauthentic. Their reporting was suspected because their literary writings were assessed negatively, and the negativity came from the detection of their insincerity. Surely there is a certain amount of professional jealousy and territoriality. If you were a famous author who had chosen to report the news, watch out. Everything about you was fair game to anonymous staff writers who did not like being reminded of their anonymity and small pay.

In Korea, he could only be the kind of author he was, no matter how much he wanted to experience the life of the war correspondent. He was a newspaperman who happened to be at war. When London pleaded with Griscom to help get his camera back, he told him that the camera was an essential tool of the war correspondent, just like a plumber's tools.[76] We can safely assume that Richard Harding Davis, Frederick Palmer, and others did not see themselves as plumbers. Again, London's working-class mentality leaks into his conception of himself as an author.

But if he was separated from his compatriots by class, dress, and inexperience, he was joined to them in class terms within the context of Japanese society. As he jotted in one of his notebooks, "newspapermen are of very low caste," and what follows that remark is one of his worst racist rants: "The real Japanese, not the Japan of cherry blossom, or Fiji on teacups and fans—but the Japanese which is not civilized and the Japan which is Asiatic—which takes our science, but nothing else. Paradoxical—savages who strangely use our weapons—as if Indians should do the same. Their mental processes are different—courts in Japan—no justice."[77] He almost replicates the analogy he made in *The People of the Abyss*: the poor of the East End of London are as isolated and unknowing of modern life as the Inuit, and there, too, we saw London's class anxieties at work. He did not want to be a savage, and in Japan and Korea he did not think of himself as a member of the lowest class. London's antagonism toward the Japanese is couched in racial terms, but it is as if he is borrowing the rhetoric of racism to express his class anger. For he knew, and he knew it right away, that two fundamental differences existed between himself and the Japanese army and its leaders and between himself and Japanese politicians. One was racial, and he had tried in the nineties to work out these differences in biosocial terms in his writings in the *Aegis*. The other was new to him, and it was based in a class difference of the Japanese's construction. When he was arrested for using his camera, the police asked him his "rank," and "by rank was meant business, profession. 'Traveling to Chemulpo,' I said was my business; and when they looked puzzled I meekly added that I was only a correspondent" ("Jail in Japan"). Obviously he had learned his place in Japanese society shortly after arriving.

In the first pages of *The Theory of the Leisure Class*, Thorstein Veblen discusses the class structure of Japan based on occupations: "In such communities the distinction between classes is very rigourously observed; and the feature of most striking economic significance in these class differences is the distinction maintained between the employments proper to the several classes." Given that he discusses "barbarian" or "feudal" communities, Veblen's ranking of the warrior and priest classes as highest and second highest may have informed London's Northland fiction as well.[78]

London spells out his understanding of the "caste" system in an interview he gave once he returned from Korea and Japan: "The Japanese does not in the least understand the correspondent or the mental processes of a correspondent, which are a white man's mental processes. The Japanese is of a military race. His old caste distinctions placed the fighting man at the top; next comes the peasant after that the merchant, and beneath all the scribe. These caste distinctions are practically in force to day. A correspondent from the West is a man who must be informed by printed instructions that he must dress and behave decently."[79] Note how he quotes from the printed sheet of regulations correspondents were given by the Japanese military.

The one moment in which he embraces (almost literally) a Japanese man out of a sense of brotherhood is when a group of Japanese "pressmen" attempt to get his camera back from the authorities.[80] They, too, were plumbers, and when their spokesman told London of their efforts on his behalf, he says, in his very first dispatch, "I could have thrown my arms about him then and there—not for the camera, but for brotherhood, as he himself expressed it the next moment, because we were brothers in the craft. . . . We parted as brothers part, and without wishing him any ill-luck, I should like to help him out of a hole some day in the United States" ("Jail in Japan"). It's important to note that the anonymous "pressman," not London, is the one who initiated the talk of brotherhood. One can even read this moment as equivalent to saying, "Some of my best friends are Japanese." At the same time, he bonded with those of the lowest classes, however temporarily, and here was one who wanted to help not just to return his camera but to salve their mutual supposed inherent inferiority.

Still, racism is racism—begged, borrowed, or stolen—and there is no excuse—class anxiety, illness, inexperience, intense sense of isolation and otherness—for London to employ its rhetoric. His scientific, religious, and social explanations all highlight his need to proclaim his difference from every other race. In none of his published writings or notes that I have examined did he affirm an equality between whites and races of color. He didn't look for similarities, for those traits shared by all humans that make for true unity. The only similarities among races that he allowed were defined by class, and biology (as he understood it) trumped class. London was never far removed from his boyhood self who made fun of Chinese men in Oakland. If a Japanese "pressman" could identify with London, then London welcomed the bond; but if there was disagreement, London blamed the inability of races to think alike, to act in concert. His biological theories were as objectionable as his political theories were praiseworthy. His personal political and racial interactions were too fluid to be categorized as single-mindedness. He could take a personal kindness and make it into an expression of the Brotherhood of Man or, at least, a simulacrum of it. Or he could take a personal slight and make it the expression of a racial dynamic. He formed his racial and political theories independently of his own personal experience.

He incorporates this personal resentment into his conception of what it means to be a war correspondent. In fact, by incorporating so much of what he thinks and how he feels he validates the *Examiner*'s confluence of war news and news of the war correspondent, and this confluence transforms the correspondent into a modern-day personality, famous for being famous. This confusion of object and subject does not happen simply because there is so little to report, and it occurs for two different reasons. The newspaper is motivated commercially. Personalities sell. London's motivation is not commercial, it's personal. From the very beginning, London writes himself into his reports, as if he is trying to explain to himself what it is he is doing. Again, partly this is the voice of his inexperience, but it is also an expression of his authorial office. One of the most fascinating moments in his reports is his attempt to explain to the Moji police why he took the photographs he took. Instead of simply saying, "I took them because a war correspondent has to find details of everyday life to help explain what the war means to the common people," or, as logical, "I took them because I had suspended my role as a correspondent in favor of being a simple tourist and wanted photographic reminders of my time in Japan," he offers the enigmatic explanation "because I wanted to. . . . For my pleasure." Then he turns, theatrically, to us, and here he converts his resentment into something larger, personal but also philosophical:

> Pause a moment, gentler reader, and consider. What answer could you give to such a question concerning any act you have ever performed? Why do you do anything? Because you want to; because it is your pleasure. An answer to the question, 'Why do you perform an act for your pleasure?' would constitute an epitome of psychology. Such an answer would go down to the roots of being, for it involves impulse, volition, pain, pleasure, sensation, gray matter, nerve fibers, free will and determinism, and all the vast fields of speculation wherein man had floundered since the day he dropped down out of the trees and began to seek out the meaning of things. ("Jail in Japan")

To like something, in London's worldview, is to express a biological imperative. One cannot help but like what one likes. He is not evading or humoring the police (at least, not simply). He really is concerned about the foundational reasons that drive humans to pleasure; and being a hobo-author is only an insufficient description. The real reason is "to seek out the meaning of things." This is what humans do, and this is what he was doing in taking photographs. Further, in describing his photographic subjects to the police, London says that he described them so many times that "I have dreamed about them ever since, and I know I shall dream about them until I die"

(29). Linking dream states to photography and then, in the next paragraph, to the very beginnings of mankind ("the day he dropped down out of the trees") is a constant intellectual construct in London's thought and shaped his ideas about authorship.

The other war correspondents (that is, those who made it to Korea; we have to exempt men like John Fox and Richard Harding Davis who made no attempt to do so) had none of these concerns and in fact worked assiduously to keep themselves out of their reporting. This is a mark of their professionalism, something London felt unencumbered by because he did not see himself as a mere war correspondent. However, all of them dealt with racial difference and how it might inflect their reporting. Thanks to Frederick Palmer, David Fraser, Robert Dunn, and others, we get a view of London at work on the (Peking) road and can compare how they dealt with it in comparison to London.

Palmer, who best understands what the Japanese military thought of foreign correspondents, quotes "a secretary of legation in Tokyo": "The Japanese were absolutely prepared for this war and all possible contingencies save one. . . . They overlooked the coming of a small army of correspondents representing the public opinion of two great friendly nations [Britain and the U.S.]."[81] In his interview with Field Marshall Marquis Yamagata on the day of the declaration of war, Palmer asked how the military kept its secrets so well. Yamagata demurred, saying that even Japanese newspapers were "not yet enough advanced to be discreet."[82] Because London spent so much time with Palmer, even to the point of quoting him in one of his notebooks about how one could report war news accurately without being censored, he knew why the Japanese army imposed severe restrictions. The Japanese employed the tactics of stalling and restraint in order to keep their military affairs secret; it had nothing to with supposed differences between Eastern and Western ways of thinking. London's anger at the restrictions (fueled by compatriots like Dunn, who also should have known better) is partly the resentment of a fiercely competitive individual who felt the Japanese had bested him.[83] But in print he explained his "loss" in racist terms.

A reporter for an Oakland paper tried to be kind to London when he discussed various reactions to the Japanese strictures placed on correspondents; Richard H. Barry, the *Oakland Chronicle* reporter, is quoted saying the Japanese treated him very well and that after a while he was given access to the front and able to write and photograph everything except strict military secrets. The article's unnamed author says that London and Davis "left Japan imbued with the impression that the Japanese have a secret dislike and contempt for all white men. Perhaps this adverse opinion is due to temperament. At any rate, it is not the one held by Mr. Barry, who has had the advantage of a longer and wider acquaintance with the Japanese than that enjoyed—or born—by Messrs. London and Davis. Mr. Barry wore no literary honors on his sleeve, and seems to have recognized that military exigency cannot be subordinated to a desire to be obliging. Perhaps he did not assume that the Japanese were his social and mental inferiors, and by exhibiting a feeling of frank companionship, failed to create an atmosphere of antagonism."[84]

When we read London's dispatches in their chronological order, we are struck by the absence of racism early on. However, in his fourth report, his racist rhetoric bursts forth and continues till the end. He issues generalizations about Koreans, Japanese, and all "Asiatics." "For the Korean is nothing if not a coward, and his fear of bodily hurt is about equal to his inaction." "The Asiatic is heartless. The suffering of dumb brutes means nothing to him. . . . The Japanese may be the Britisher of the Orient, but he is still Asiatic. The suffering of beasts does not touch him."[85] In an encounter with a wronged Korean, he pronounces, "in his short life he had learned, what all Asiatics learn, that it [justice] is a characteristic belonging peculiarly to the white man, and that from the white man only is it obtainable" ("Moffett"). (We recall the brief notebook jotting he made, "courts in Japan—no justice" quoted earlier.) I mentioned, too, that he condemned the Japanese for conducting a frontal attack that no white general would have allowed. And then there is his concluding interview, back home at last, in which he characterizes the Japanese as "a precocious child" and asserts that "the Japanese does not in the least understand the correspondent or the mental processes of a correspondent, which are a white man's mental processes. . . . The Japanese cannot understand straight talk, white man's talk" ("End of Usefulness").[86] London simply will not allow the Japanese the privilege of exercising delaying tactics to preserve the secrecy of their military movements. Palmer probably talked to London until he was blue in the face, to no avail.

By mid-May, encamped in Feng-Wang-Cheng, north of the Yalu River, London is ready to write an essay of generalizations, uninhibited by any hint of race prejudice. Entitled "The Yellow Peril," the essay carries forward all that he had learned from his time in the Klondike observing ruthless whites decimating Native Americans and their culture through greed and corruption, and it replays themes from his earlier essay "The Salt of the Earth," especially in its concerns for racial superiority and warfare. What I am calling two-mindedness is evident in "The Salt of the Earth." On the one hand, he deplores racial injustices perpetrated against African Americans; on the other hand, the Anglo-Saxon oppression of them indicates only the "scientific" "truth" of evolution. Again, biology trumps politics; "the white light of science" trumps ethics.

For the most part "The Yellow Peril" is about the differences among the Koreans (still cowardly and inefficient), the Chinese (industrious, open to the new ideas of "the machine age"), and the Japanese ("a fighting race"). These are delineated to show who the West has to fear most, and the result is the combination of Japanese managers and Chinese workers: "The Chinese has been called the type of permanence, and well he has merited it, dozing as he has through the ages. And as truly was the Japanese the type of permanence up to a generation ago, when he suddenly awoke and startled the world with a rejuvenescence the like of which the world had never seen before. The ideas of the West were the leaven which quickened the Japanese; and the ideas of the West, transmitted by the Japanese mind into ideas Japanese, may well make the leaven powerful enough to quicken the Chinese."[87] Later we will see how this idea concerning the relationship between the Japanese and Chinese gets fictionalized in a 1907 story called "The Unparalleled Invasion."

This is the true "peril" that the West faces. But the peril is couched in terms of "race adventure," and, according to London, races wax and wane. Now the Anglo-Saxon reigns supreme, but, knowing that its tenure will end, London asks who then will take its place as the dominant race of the world (for it's always a competition for land and resources, and warfare is eternal).[88] "Why may not the yellow and the brown start out on an adventure as tremendous as our own and more strikingly unique?" Even though the Japanese can imitate and borrow Western science and technology, they are "imitating us only in things material. Things spiritual cannot be imitated." The West, that is, the Anglo-Saxon, may be a violent breed but "back of our own great race adventure, back of our robberies by sea and land, our lusts and violences and all the evil things we have done, there is a certain integrity, a sternness of conscience, a melancholy responsibility of life, a sympathy and comradeship and warm human feel, which is ours, indubitably ours, and which we cannot teach to the Oriental." A better description of the Malemute Kid could not be found. The Anglo-Saxon may have "strayed often and far from righteousness . . . the colossal fact of our history is that we have made the religion of Jesus Christ our religion. No matter how dark in error and deed, ours has been a history of spiritual struggle and endeavor. We are preeminently a religious race, which is another way of saying that we are a right-seeking race." Here, then, we have the London of the Klondike ("Yellow Peril").

We are prepared for the next thought, which should be something like this: the Japanese, or "Asiatic," is not a religious race, is not "right-seeking," and has no soul or heart; just remember how they treat animals. But it's not that simple. "Religion, as a battle for the right in our sense of right, as a yearning and a strife for spiritual good and purity, is unknown to the Japanese. Measured by what religion means to us, the Japanese is a race without religion. Yet it has a religion, and who shall say that it is not as great a religion as ours, not as efficacious?" He then quotes Inazo Nitobe: "To us the country is more than land and soil from which to mine gold or reap grain—it is the sacred abode of the gods, the spirits of our forefathers. . . . To us the Emperor is . . . the bodily representative of heaven on earth, blending in his person its power and its mercy." This is Shintoism as explained to the West by a Christianized Japanese who became a Quaker, a professor of agronomy, and a California resident while writing *Bushido, the Soul of Japan* (1901), an immensely popular book.[89] Further, according to Nitobe, "the tenets of Shintoism cover the two predominating features of the emotional life of our race—Patriotism and Loyalty."[90] London then takes this definition and turns it into a limitation. The Japanese may have a religion, but it is a religion that worships the emperor and therefore the state. So it is not a religion of the spirit. It is instead synonymous with patriotism. It's the same claim he makes in one of his dispatches: "The Japanese are so made that nothing short of annihilation can stop them. Patriotism is their religion and they die for their country as the martyrs of other people die for their gods." Thus, "the Asiatic does not value life as we do" ("Russians Fight Japanese"). The Japanese, according to London, know nothing of individualism. Hence, "he relates himself to the State as, amongst bees, the worker is related to the hive," which he exalts and glorifies ("Yellow Peril"). The Japanese are simply mindless bees.

Still, "The Yellow Peril" concludes, not with racist invective and a call to arms to prevent what he sees as the next race to rule the world (London was very susceptible to apocalyptic thinking), but rather with an accounting of his own racially limited way of thinking: "No great race adventure [and here he means the "Asiatic"] can go far nor endure long which has no deeper foundation than material success, no higher prompting than conquest for conquest's sake and mere race glorification. To go far and to endure, it must have behind it an ethical impulse, a sincerely conceived righteousness." So we the "gentler reader" might think that London is arguing that the "Asiatic" will fail because of his or her own limitations and thus the Anglo-Saxon has no reason to worry. But, no, he is arguing something different: "But it must be taken into consideration that the above postulate is itself a product of Western race-egotism, urged by our belief in our own righteousness and fostered by a faith in ourselves which may be as erroneous as are most fond race fancies" ("Yellow Peril"). The fact, says London, is that we anticipate the decline of the white race, but we don't know how the conflict between white and yellow and brown will develop, though we will know in the twentieth century. No matter. For the present, he sides with those of his own skin color because that is how he identifies racially. It is the same argument he will make when he covers the Jack Johnson–Jim Jeffries fight in 1910. The African American fighter may be superior but because London is white he roots for the white man. The Japanese and Chinese may have their own "sincerely conceived righteousness," but it is not "white," and therefore he will have none of it.

So, London came home from the East with his racism and race pride intact, expressed through his two-mindedness. Biology always trumps politics, and he was no further from a socialist dream of the Brotherhood of Man than he was in July 1904. Joan London has him yelling in a political meeting held in the fall, "What the devil! I am first of all a white man and only then a Socialist!"[91] Did he mean to say that the Koreans he reveals so touchingly (by accident?) in his photographs and the Japanese correspondents he called brother were inferior to the white man? Was his servant, Manyoungi, whom he brought back to the U.S., inferior? Yes, to put the answer bluntly. As he said in a letter to Bailey Millard in 1906 to convince him to buy articles about the *Snark* voyage, "Of course, I'll take a cook along, and a cabin boy; but these will be Asiatics, and will have no part in the sailorizing."[92] Were the differences between races so insurmountable that no political action could be taken to address worldwide capitalism? He would not go that far. He was capable of making concessions. In his assessment of the 1904 election, he reverses his racist outburst in that political meeting his daughter cites and declares that socialists in Japan are brothers to socialists in Russia who are brothers to those in America.[93] We do not know the context of his outburst about being a white man first (not that it would excuse it), but the context for his political analysis is clear: socialism could not win at the polling place (not that London believed in the long-term efficacy of electoral politics) unless socialists presented a united world-wide front. London's capacity to hold two contradictory thoughts at the same time—all Asians are heartless, some Asians I have met have heart; Asians do not think the way white people do, all Asians and whites belong to the Brotherhood of Man—does not diminish the unfortunate power of his racial essentializations. Socialist politics became utopian—a dreaded word for him—when confronted with the realities of race and biology. It's not that biology invalidated politics; one could still fight for the cause, and London never gave up trying. But biology limited what one could achieve politically, and the inequality of the races meant that the Brotherhood of Man was that much more difficult to achieve. To identify with the poor of all countries was to act as if they were equal in all respects. London always worked from the premise that all men and women are created unequally, and biology limited the ways in which that inequality could be addressed.

If London, as an Anglo-Saxon, was biologically determined to both love and detest his own race, then so, too, could an "Asiatic" hold contradictory thoughts simultaneously. In March, London wrote about a confrontation he had with a *yang-ban*, a nobleman and magistrate. London wanted to convince him to stop robbing the people of Sunan. As the conversation developed, London shifts our attention to Manyoungi, who is watching the proceedings: "In his head was the ferment of a new idea, the Western idea of the rights of man. In his head were mutiny and revolt. In his head, though dimly perhaps, were the ideas of Revolutionary France. In his head were hatred for the *yang-ban* class and defiance. But in the soul of him was the humility of generations, a thing not to be downed in a day by any idea of the head" ("Moffett"). In short, breeding bests class struggle. "I do verily believe," concludes London, about himself as well as about Manyoungi, "that his humble demeanor was as much reflex action as that of the new-born fly-catcher bursting its head through the shell and snapping its beak at the first passing insect" ("Moffett"). Both he and Manyoungi—and Manyoungi stands in for all "Asiatics"—were at last united in their likeness to the reflex actions of other animals. In this limited and ultimately unsatisfactory way, biology and politics could be united as well. The promise of "Negore, the Coward," which Charmian detected, would have to wait to be fully realized. London's experiences in Korea did little to change his worldview.

As an ironic coda, in 1907 London, as well as other correspondents, received a medal from the Japanese government for their excellence in covering the war. No record of London's reaction exists, though he did carry it with him for part of the *Snark* voyage.[94] He may have thought it would help smooth out any troubles he might encounter with the Japanese, a kind of talisman that showed how correspondents might not be such an inferior class after all.

CLASS WARFARE

After London returned home from Japan, he did not write a single word for publication for two and a half months. He then took ten days to write *The Game* in September. After that he wrote a newspaper account of the crucial November election, a short story that takes place in Korea ("A Nose for the King"), the introduction to *War of the Classes*, and a play based on his short story "The Scorn of Women." The short story is the only interruption in this sustained period of theatricality. Sport and politics and the aftereffects of the war reporting all reinforced London's desire to make his theatrical mode literal and try to write a play. After he completed *The Game*, his principal authorial activity for the rest of the fall and well into the winter of 1904–5 was composing and revising his play, arranging for actors, and considering various plans for production.

He was deep into his theatrical mode, unwilling to give it up to write absorptive fiction. A commercial reason may have motivated him as well. Brett felt, as he had in December 1902, that London was releasing too much material too quickly. London did not share that concern as long as he was alternating absorptive and theatrical writing. But publishing socialist essays at this point in London's career raised a related concern for Brett. When London asked Brett back in August 1903 if he were interested in publishing what eventually became *War of the Classes*, Brett replied that he was, but that he had a caveat. We should talk in person, he said, and they did, in the first week of January 1904, just before London left on the s s *Siberia*.

Brett gives us an idea of the major topic of discussion in his letter to London in 1903: "You have achieved a very considerable success with the publication of your 'Call of the Wild' and you are to publish, beginning in the January *Century*, a new novel, which will be free for book publication towards the end of 1904 [*The Sea-Wolf*], and your name will be very considerably before the public in connection with these two books for some time to come, and the whole matter is of such great importance from every point of view that" Brett wanted to meet in person and spell out all the possible ramifications, both short-term and long-term. The immediate matter was the timing of the publication of his socialist essays. The larger matter was two-fold and interconnected: How to maintain his image of a successful novelist and how to maintain the momentum of his sales. That is, Brett's fear—partly fueled by the negative reviews he had received from his readers for the manuscript of *War of the Classes*—began with the premise that London had become famous in 1903 as a novelist, a fiction writer. Brett anticipated that the fame of *The Call of the Wild* would help drive sales of his next novel, and it did. So, Brett did not want to dilute the brand, to put it in twenty-first-century terms. A collection of socialist essays, no matter how good, would take attention away from Jack London, Novelist. It might even damage his sales, for some buyers would not want to read anything written by a revolutionary. Obviously, Brett was ignoring the political content of these two novels in order to make his argument.

To make his case even stronger, he proposed an idea for a major novel. Two weeks after Brett and London met, he wrote to London in Korea: "I trust that you may have decided by this time to write that Indian race story of which I spoke to you. I have thought it over often since we talked of the matter and am more than ever persuaded that it is a possible book and involves the chance of a considerable success. It has occurred to me that your hero might have some such visions of the past as would enable him to dream of the crossing of the Behring Straits by the northern Chinese tribes, from which, it seems to me, the preponderance of evidence derives the origin of the American Indian."[95] London replied, "Yes, I have thought often, of that Indian race-story, but it's a stubborn thing, and the get-at-ableness of it has so far eluded me. It's a big thing—if it can be done, and if I can do it."[96] London never wrote this novel, but he did take notes on it, making it sound very much like the stories in *Children of the Frost*: "Point of view: At the time of the coming of the first settle[r]s; how the Indian lived;

how he hunted and what; how he lived and married (minor love interest); the eruption of the white settlers and how he was viewed and the Indian sentiments and feelings of him and whether the Indian at that time foresaw the extinction of his race; the love story between the white settler and the Indian girl (major love interest). The whole to be absolutely from the Indian standpoint except that possibly it may need to be spiritualized, not to say sentimentalized."[97] This note is cut from a full page of paper, suggesting there were more notes to the novel. The hints provided by Brett suggest that *Before Adam* grew out of some of London's ideas here.

London, however, had his mind set on publishing his socialist essays and objected to an indefinite publication date for *War of the Classes*. He felt that because many of the essays were based on contemporary newspaper articles and current sociological data they would soon be outdated. From Korea, stewing in Seoul after being sent back from Sunan and the front by the Japanese authorities, he wrote to Brett complaining that his publisher, when they had met in January, had probably read only the first essay, that is, "The Salt of the Earth." "If this is so, would you mind glancing at some of the later-written essays, 'The Scab,' 'The Class Struggle,' 'The Tramp,' etc., with the object of a change of conclusion regarding the expediency of not issuing as a book for an indefinitely long time to come. The later-written essays, to me, seem to have a timely importance. I'll abide by what you say, but just give a second thought to them."[98]

But Brett had already made up his mind and said so in a response to London's April letter, which London didn't get until he returned to the U.S.: "I read the whole of the essays in 'The Salt of the Earth' and enjoyed them a good deal personally, but my opinion as given to you in regard to their publication was deliberate and intentional and I should be sorry if you decide to put them out at this time. Of course we will do in the matter just as you wish but it seems to me that it would be a mistake to publish, especially in view of the early appearance of 'The Sea Wolf' in book form, which cannot fail, I think, to be very successful indeed."[99]

London backed off, allowing for Brett's experience in publishing to dictate matters, but only temporarily. In one of the most fascinating characterizations of his own authorial production, he wrote to Brett in November 1904, both wondering what had happened to the plans for publishing *War of the Classes* and prodding Brett to get the book out among the public: "Not to utterly forget the *Salt of the Earth*," wrote London, less than a week after the stunning success of Eugene Debs's third-party candidacy, "why couldn't that book be brought out this summer, after *Sea Wolf* has run its run?—That is, if it can be brought out without loss to you. You know I have a sneaking liking for it [hah! more than "sneaking," one should say], and I have waited pretty patiently while my favorite child was set aside for my mongrel fiction children."[100] We might want London to mean by "mongrel" something like a work of art that combines elements of fiction and non-fiction. But, no, London means it as an epithet. That he could call *The Sea-Wolf* "mongrel" shows how deep he was in his theatrical mode and how committed he was to socialism.

Brett caved, as we all know he would, but not without a final reminder, couched in his usual antiseptic publisher's idiom, of the possible negative impact of publishing socialist essays. You must make it up-to-date, he said, "because its publication will have a considerable effect on the future popularity of your other work. I myself read the 'Salt of the Earth' with a great deal of interest and pleasure but I conceive that, its appeal being to a somewhat different audience than the usual book audience, that it might act detrimentally on the book audience if we are not careful to make it just as good as it can be." He even warned London that cheap editions of Ghent's *Benevolent Feudalism* and Brooks's *Social Unrest* had failed miserably and had cost the company money, so a cheap edition of *The People of the Abyss* that London had proposed would not be feasible.[101]

The result of their meeting and correspondence was, first, the delay of *War of the Classes* until 1905 (but only till the spring), second, London holding back on production, and, third, a nearly anonymous book cover for *War of the Classes*: a dark maroon color (suggesting revolution, but perhaps not a violent one) and a blank front—no title, no name; the spine alone carries the title and London's last name. London thus made concessions to his publisher. At this height of his popularity, Brett told him that "you have the public very much at your feet and can command practically one of the best audiences that this country affords to any novel writer of this day or generation."[102] Brett once again asserts that London has earned a high place in American literature. Nonetheless, London saw no reason not to risk that popularity and even that high place in the American canon, if it meant publishing essays he believed in. Money was a concern, but, again, it was not a constitutive component of his authorial identity. As if an afterthought, he responded to Brett's assessment of his popularity by only noting that "as my earning capacity increases, my output diminishes. With all the top-notch magazines offering me from 8 to 10 cents per word, I am writing nothing for them."[103] Here is yet another clear signal of an artist following the demands of his interior life.

War of the Classes went through a number of title changes, from *Salt of the Earth* to *The Struggle of the Classes* to its final appellation, and two changes to its initial table of contents. At first, London wanted to include "The Salt of the Earth," his 1901 essay about war and race. But once Brett had accepted the volume for publication and determined to have it come out in spring 1905, London pulled the lead essay—it really didn't have anything to do with class warfare and he may have felt, especially after writing "The Yellow Peril," that it wasn't as up-to-date as the others—and retitled the collection after what he thought was its strongest essay, "The Class Struggle," though he told Brett "if you, or any of your people, should hit upon a better title, I should be glad for the opportunity to consider it."[104] Brett himself decided he liked the title *The Class Struggle* best of all, but somebody somewhere decided to make it parallel with nearly all of London's titles and used the genitive construction *War of the Classes*.[105]

When London submitted his preface, written 12 January 1905, he also submitted a new table of contents, which showed he had decided to pull "What Communities Lose by the Competitive System" as well; it, too, had only been tangentially related to the major theme of the class struggle; and, besides, when Upton Sinclair read the book manuscript he said, "[I] think you're off on the end of Wanted new law—but then you don't care what I think."[106] But he did care and he pulled the essay. By the end of December, in accord with Brett's plans for bringing the book out in the first half of 1905, he was ready to update and revise the essays and to add a preface.[107]

We should complete the analysis of the preface to *War of the Classes* even though we have jumped ahead of the composition of *The Game* and other, shorter works. The preface, the first published work written after "Big Socialist Vote Is Fraught with Meaning" and before a major essay, "Revolution" (which I will turn to in the next chapter), shows how much some of the issues of the previous year still lingered. It begins, "When I was a youngster I was looked upon as a weird sort of creature," a kind of monster, but not because he was a leopard or wolf man (he would be signing his letters "Wolf" in a few months), but because he was a socialist. And not because he himself had decided on this characterization but because the press had constructed his own monstrosity for him: "Reporters from local papers interviewed me, and the interviews, when published, were pathological studies of a strange and abnormal specimen of man."

The preface does not present the book as a whole, summing up the arguments and justifying each essay's inclusion. London had decided to let the essays speak for themselves. Instead, he told of his experience of having the two major political parties co-opt his and other revolutionary socialists' ideas. The history of socialism in America up to 1905, according to London, was one of defanging. This process was another characteristic of the class struggle. Socialism, according to the bourgeois, was tolerable when it was "a sweet and beautiful utopian dream." Many of its ideas were regarded as impossible, and those that weren't were "stolen" (like municipal ownership of utilities), and so "the workingmen had been made happy with full dinner-pails." It is a commonplace today to remark on the tameness of turn-of-the-century socialism and how issues like child welfare and the eight-hour work week were considered radical then, but tame now; London knew it and called it what it was: capitalism's effort to save itself by incorporating what it needed to survive from that which threatened its existence; Ghent called it benevolent feudalism. It was all about suppressing class warfare.

But, as London notes at the turning point in his preface, echoing his most recent socialist essay ("Big Socialist Vote Is Fraught with Meaning"), the November 1904 election reignited class warfare. Far from being tamed, asserts London, "Socialism is a menace. It is its purpose to wipe out, root and branch, all capitalistic institutions of present-day society. It is distinctly revolutionary, and in scope and depth is vastly more tremendous than any revolution that has ever occurred in the history of the world." The bourgeois regard class warfare as a "terrible and hateful thing," but socialism, reinvigorated, "is a world-wide class struggle between the propertyless workers and the propertied masters of workers." When London describes socialism as "a menace, vague and formless," he echoes his very first essay on socialism ("What Socialism Is") as well as his foundational text for his political philosophy, *The Communist Manifesto*. Socialism, like communism, is a specter that haunts America. London the haunted author knew a thing or two about ghosts, and it was a relief to him to be able to place the ghost outside himself. This is a fundamental characteristic of all his theatrical writing.

London takes on the old canard that socialists with money cannot be socialists. This is a condescending characterization of the moneyed classes: "They told me that my views were biased by my empty pockets, and that some day, when I had gathered to me a few dollars, my views would be wholly different—in short, that my views would be their views." London regarded his wealth as a rebuke to the capitalists in two ways: socialism allowed for working-class wealth, and he used his money in the service of others, not as a means to propagate wealth untethered to labor.

He revised his manuscript in a number of ways, but the most interesting change comes in the final, impassioned sentence. In the manuscript, he wrote first:

> The capitalist must learn . . . that socialism deals with what is, not with what ought to be; and that the material with which it deals is the "clay of the common road," the warm human, fallible and frail, sordid and petty, absurd and contradictory, even grotesque, and yet, withal, shot through with flashes and glimmerings of something finer and god-like, with here and there sweetnesses of service and unselfishness, desires for goodness, capacities for renunciation and sacrifice, the wonder of love, and at times and with conscience, stern and awful, at times blazingly imperious, demanding the right—the right, nothing more nor less than the right.[108]

Later, he crossed out "the wonder of love." He believed man was capable of love, but perhaps it struck him as too personal, that is, devoid of political charge.

THE (WRITING) GAME

Back in December 1902, when London and Brett had signed their two-year contract, London was intent on giving Brett six volumes: a collection of Klondike stories, *Tales of the Fish Patrol*, *The Kempton-Wace Letters*, *The People of the Abyss*, *The Flight of the Duchess*, and *The Mercy of the Sea*. Because *The Sea-Wolf* fulfilled the contract in the place of *Mercy* and he had abandoned *Flight of the Duchess*, London owed Brett only one book for the time period 1903-4. *The Game* became that book, though Brett made it clear that any new novel had to appear in 1905.

When London asked Brett, in July 1904, for an increase in his monthly advances to $250, he prompted Brett to revisit the current contract with the intention of renewing it for another year. Brett noted that London's books' earnings were short of his advances so far by $2,000, so he proposed that he keep Heinemann's payments to London. He also wanted, besides the sixth book called for by the 1902 contract, a volume of short stories or something like it in case *Tales of the Fish Patrol* could not come out because they were still being serialized by *Youth's Companion*. It took very little negotiating, then, for the 1902 contract to be renewed. As Brett wrote, "I am, of course, at all times most anxious to meet your wishes to the fullest possible extent."[109] London would never lose his favored author status.

In October 1904, Brett began making plans for Macmillan's spring list and asked if London would have a novel for the spring.[110] London replied, "No, I'm pretty sure I'll have no spring book." Then he added, diffidently, "In the three months since my return, I have written nothing at all, with the sole exception of story enclosed herewith—which I hope may interest you as an attempt to do the ring."[111] At this point he considered *The Game* a rather longish short story.[112] Brett was interested; unfortunately, because his initial response is missing its first page we do not know what he said, exactly. In the next few days, however, he wrote again, saying, "You will see that I have been thinking a good deal about the story since I read it and have been more and more impressed with its power and vividness." He suggested a way to enlarge it: turn it into a series of stories featuring Joe Fleming the boxer because "I feel sorry that it is too short to be published alone in book form. . . . If it were collected with some others on the same subject I should expect it to attract a good deal of attention, and while perhaps it could not have any very wide sale with the ordinary book public it would still pay for itself and might, outside of the ordinary book public, do very well indeed."[113] London demurred, saying that "I've been thinking it over, your suggestions, and I don't think I'd care to tackle a series of stories on the ring. Besides, it would be impossible to run this same character through the different stories; for he has his beginning and end right here in this one story."[114] Brett immediately replied that, yes, of course, he dies, but the series should not feature him as the hero "because his ending is not only tragic but very mournful under the circumstances, and the public likes, as I think I have told you before, to have its endings cheerful wherever it is possible to do so. [See your own essay "The Terrible and Tragic in Fiction," Jack] Such a character . . . might very readily furnish a string of very good stories as a part of his career, and it might not perhaps be necessary from the artistic standpoint to kill him off at the end, but to make him retire from the ring."[115] Brett knew London didn't want to enlarge the book this way; from London's point of view, the book began from a point that made his death at the end inevitable.

But Brett thought that London, if he just had time to consider the proposition, might decide to delay publication until he had worked out a satisfactory way to extend the story. So Brett once more pushed him to expand the novella, this time abandoning the idea of a series of stories and advocating the addition of three thousand to four thousand words.[116] London had mixed feelings about this new tack: "It's the hardest kind of work to do that adding, but I believe I can do it—simply recast the first portion of it, keeping a grip in accord with the last portion, which cannot be added to."[117] Brett now felt that London could be pushed further, so he made his offer: add three thousand to four thousand words, we'll illustrate it heavily, and then "sell it to the public outside of the ordinary reading public, i.e., the large number of people who are interested in sports of all kind but who do not ordinarily read books at all. If we succeed in getting this audience for the volume it would, I think, interest your public for your other books considerably."[118] London would subsequently argue that the book could appeal to everyone—"It is one of my best efforts. It is the unusual thing. Has novelty and all that. Also, it is all things to all people. Those who stand for prizefighting, will like it. Those who dislike prizefighting, will find it an endictment [sic] of prizefighting. Those who know nothing of prizefighting will be curious, etc. etc. Also, it has good healthy sentiment, love, etc."[119] And in acceding to Brett's desire for more words in virtual exchange for signing a royalty contract, he argued that it was "the best short thing I have done. The motif is tremendous, the subject vastly more interesting to the average man and woman than they or you would think, while the novelty of it—well, it's pretty novel for a literary effort, that is all."[120] Brett stayed mum about London's estimations. He was happy enough to have London commit to enlarging it by twelve hundred words after submitting the manuscript and then, in page proof, by another thousand words.[121]

And, in the end, Brett won out on serial publication. At first, London wanted McClure to take on *The Game*. McClure was interested in it, but only as a small book. "It is all so magnificently real," he told London. It is so real that it is more "faithful" to reality than a cinematic representation, "and you do get wonderful physical effects with your writing!" Here is the cinema of attractions, a realism so striking that its power to shock affects the viewer's very body. This is the first time that London's work is compared to the movies, and in the next decade the comparison will become a cliché. McClure's assessment, however, is a continuation of his insistence on photographic realism. So McClure thought the novella "a remarkable piece of work," but, much to London's frustration, McClure said, "I think you know why we cannot publish it in the magazine."[122] It is not too short for a book, but it is too long for the magazine. So McClure pushed yet again for a book, and again London replied with silence.[123]

Metropolitan Magazine felt no compunction. With London's revised manuscript in hand, the editor told Brett he wanted to divide it between two issues after all. Brett thought it a good plan because to run it in one issue would harm book sales. London, however, insisted otherwise: "It would be absolute ruin to it to divide it. You see, it is a thing without plot, and must be read in one sitting."[124] There were limitations, in London's mind, to a magazine's treatment of his text. Brett, after London pronounced his opposition to breaking the serial into two parts, told London that though they were "diametrically opposed" he could nonetheless see how London's position wouldn't hurt his own. "In the long run," Brett wrote, reinforcing London's own plan for combining serial and book publication, "an author is judged almost entirely on his reputation, not by the things which he publishes serially in magazines—which, after all, are read and most of them forgotten a month after they come out—but by his published books, which being in a permanent and easily accessible form, really tell towards his standing in the world of letters and before the public."[125] The publisher knew how to give way in order to ultimately win, and win he did, though only because London decided to lengthen the story.

Brett lost out on a different issue: payments. He initially offered London a lump-sum payment of $1,500, but London, citing his dissatisfaction over possible lost royalties for *The Call of the Wild* asked for an agreement based on royalties, which Brett gave him. London's was not an unreasonable complaint, but it didn't take into account the money Macmillan earned as a result and Brett's subsequent willingness not only to publish everything London wrote—they could afford the gamble—but also his general attitude of giving London whatever he wanted, including huge advances and loans. Further, as Brett pointed out, it would have been too costly to bring out *Call*, short as it was, with no illustrations, under a royalty agreement.

Illustrating *Call* had doubled its production costs. Brett explained to London that the "quantity price" for a novel that sold for $1.50 (as all London's novels did) was seventy-six or seventy-seven cents. The publisher had royalty, manufacturing, and marketing costs for each novel (besides salaries and overhead); the manufacturing cost for *The Game* was twenty-eight cents per copy. Brett was being incredibly straightforward and honest with London, a not so common attribute of relationships between publishers and authors. London appreciated the transparency greatly.[126]

Even with London's additions, the text still wasn't book length. Because Macmillan could use the magazine's illustrations as part of the agreement to serialize it, Brett decided he could hire a second illustrator and not increase the production cost too much more.[127] His idea was to use "decorative illustrations to fill out the pages and full page decoration and illustration to make up the bulk. In this way I think I shall be able to make of the story about 180 pages and if you can add a few words, as I suggested, in the proof anywhere it will, of course, aid me materially."[128] The book combines the work of London, Henry Hutt (hired by *Metropolitan*), and T. C. Lawrence (hired by Macmillan). So London went from half-heartedly hoping that Brett would have some interest in it to complying with his publisher's wishes to expand it considerably. Again, it wasn't about the money; it was about seeing it appear on its own in book form.

Neither London's prediction that everyone would be interested in *The Game* nor Brett's prediction that sports lovers would buy it proved to be true. At the beginning of 1907, the sales were so dismal that Brett asked London permission to sell off their overstock of four thousand copies at fifteen cents a copy. The binding alone of each copy cost thirteen cents, so Brett was taking a financial hit of some magnitude. "It seemed to me," said Brett, "that the book had human interest of a very decided kind, and I expected that it would be very widely read by the younger men." But, he admitted, his experiment in publishing had failed: "It appears that the younger man who would be likely to read a book of this kind does not, as a matter of fact, read books at all, but confines his reading to the newspapers and periodicals."[129] London agreed, and Brett dumped *The Game.*

WRITING *THE GAME*

Sometime in 1904, London jotted down the outline for this story in a date book he kept irregularly: "Prize fight story Young girl (maybe pretty candy-store girl) in love with sailmaker fighter who taking care of mother & younger children & buying home for them, needed the money—$5 to $50 purses—Lovemaking pure & innocent She's going to see the last fight—her marriage—they had bought housekeeping goods that day—peephole arranged from dressing room—opponent big, & black, & beastly, Her own man, fair, beautiful, clean cut face, fair hair—fight all from her point of view—as she sees it the terrible yells of the audience—& when he goes down, count of ten, award fight—Carried into her dressing room, the doctors—'He will never fight again.'"[130] Instead of an African American fighter, London's protagonist ends up fighting a white man. And then there is the matter of the ending. Not only will his protagonist never fight again, but at some point London decided he must die.

The Game is, among other things, about gaming and its various manifestations. This point may seem obvious, but boxing is not the only game the story is about. In fact, the idea of gaming is bohemian by nature; gaming is play, and we recall how London kept boxing gloves in his bohemian bungalow in Piedmont, as well as kites and fencing swords. He traveled with boxing gloves on the *Snark* and boxed not only with Charmian but also with Ernest Darling, in Tahiti. In a 1903 letter to Charmian Kittredge, he linked kites and boxing as attributes of a life lived "placidly and complacently." This is another typically complicated statement from London. He loved kite flying and boxing, but he could denigrate them as illusions to keep oneself happy in the face of the knowledge of deeper, more meaningful realities. The complete passage is as follows: "I have experienced the greater frankness," he told Charmian,

> with a man or two, and a woman or two, and the occasions have been great joy-givers, as they have also been great sorrow-givers. I do not wish they had never happened, but I recoil unconsciously from their happening again. It is so much easier to live placidly and complacently. Of course, to live placidly and complacently is not to live at all, but still between prize fights and kites and one thing and another I manage to fool my inner self pretty well. Poor inner self. I wonder if it will atrophy, dry up some day and blow away.[131]

He was constantly debating with himself the value of bohemian pursuits, and though his concern about lying to himself is deeply felt, so, too, could be his celebration of the supposed placid and complacent life of kite flying and boxing. When he discussed Shaw and pessimism and life's illusions with Blanche Partington in 1904, he wrote that he found so much of life amusing, and

> were it not amusing, it would give me the hurt of tragedy. I know the amusement is illusion, but I insist upon the illusion; I must insist if I would continue to live. It is my last big illusion, the straw of the drowning man. For the same reason I cherish other illusions. The urge of the red blood in me toward woman is the urge of Dame Nature toward progeny. But I work off the red blood in me in other sense-delights, (heaving on ropes, diving from springboards, skylarking, and whatnot), in such moments of sense-delight I firmly believe that I am realizing and vindicating the life that is in me—illusion, of course illusion, but if you should tell me when at the summit of such delights that it was illusion, I should be offended and irritated and recoil from you (as you and other women recoil from Shaw), as something unhealthy that made not toward life and surviving.[132]

Here, in the middle of his so-called long sickness, he avows the "illusion" of play that sustains life. Bohemianism combined in complicated ways the playfulness of life and the seriousness of death.

An interviewer once said about him in 1905, "Bohemian in his tastes, careless as to dress, the author of the 'Sea Wolf' is a man who would attract attention anywhere and in any gathering."[133] He often called writing "the game," as he did in an interview with Emanuel Haldeman-Julius in 1913, an appellation that both captures the ease and difficulty of bohemian employment. Its difficulty was intimately tied to psychological depression. At times London could grow quite vehement in his momentary distaste for the authorial life. As he said to Emanuel Haldeman-Julius, "I assure you that I do not write because I love the game. I loathe it. I cannot find words to express my disgust."[134] London was not thrilled with this interview, given Julius's supercilious attitude; Julius concluded the interview by asserting that he knew the source of London's "pessimism": "I feel positive that your liver is out of order." Given Julius's disparagement of people like Bernarr Macfadden and Horace Fletcher, Julius was simply poking fun at the older London's seriousness. But London regarded his "pessimism" as a personal flaw and not to be trifled with. As he once told Blanche Partington, "I should like to tell you about the 'disgust' phase of my nature. I do not brag about it, I am not proud of it, but I recognize it as a fundamental of my nature, and I have known it ever since I first knew anything about myself as a little boy."[135] When he worried about the state of his interior self and grew depressed, he took it out on his principal occupation. The ghost within rose to ascendency.

Ultimately, however, he thought of writing as a game because of the intense enjoyment it provided. In an early letter to Anna Strunsky, he linked through simile the ambition to publish in good magazines to kite flying: "Let me tell you," he said to Anna, "that anything you write would be accepted by the *Overland*, and further, that I wish you to fly your kite far higher than that."[136] Anna herself would generalize London's idea of play so that it became a metaphor for a life well lived: "His was not a vulgar quest for riches. In his book 'The Game' he explains the psychology of the prize fighter to whom the ring is symbolic of the play and the purpose of life itself. To become inordinately rich through the efforts of his pen was his way of 'playing the game.' It appealed to his sense of humor and his sense of the dramatic to house members of the I.W.W., comrades of the road or Mexican revolutionaries in a palace. The best was none too good for them or for any man. Not only had the abyss not been able to swallow him up; the abyss had risen with him."[137] Not incidentally, this essay appears in a bohemian newspaper, which also featured articles entitled "Sex Mores in the Village," "24 Hours after You're Broke," and "King of the London Bohemians." After his death, London had moved not only into the history of American socialism and American letters but also into the history of American bohemianism.

In 1914 he would call the military battles in Mexico "The Red Game of War," further enlarging upon his ideas of what could be called a game. But now, in 1904, gaming was an attractive combination of entertainment for entertainment's sake, luck, thrill, and potential tragedy. Even the writing of it was bohemian in intent. In the same letter that he informed Brett that he was "hard up" and needed money to buy land and a home for his daughters and pay onerous legal fees for his divorce, he told Brett that even though the magazines were offering more than ever, he had written a novel independent of financial need: "*The Game* is not a magazine story—I don't expect to find a magazine that will dare touch it."[138] It partakes too much of the terrible and tragic.

Even, or especially, tragedy—the fearsome, unacknowledged desire for an unhappy ending—lurks in the background of the life of a bohemian. The bohemian lifestyle, so often portrayed as happy-go-lucky, lazy, and carefree is in reality an incredibly difficult path to follow. Deliberately divorcing oneself as much as possible not only from money but also from mainstream culture, bohemians struggle on a daily basis. The central question of what one does with oneself during the day if one does not have a routine—a routine job, a routine marriage, a routinized life—becomes, for most people an incredibly difficult question to answer. When the day is unstructured and each day requires invention, the value and stress on the imagination accelerates. At the same time, as a compensation for the immense reliance on the interior life, the physicality of life becomes emphasized as bohemians celebrate the body that social norms (especially at the turn of the century) want to keep hidden.

The game of boxing perfectly mirrors this in a couple of ways. Women were not allowed to attend boxing matches not only because they were violent but also because they were erotic. As London puts it in *The Game*, when Genevieve sees Joe disrobe in the ring, "her face was burning with shame at sight of the beautiful nakedness of her lover. . . . The leap of something within her and the stir of her being toward him must be sinful. But it was delicious sin, and she did not deny her eyes. In vain Mrs. Grundy admonished her. The pagan in her, original sin, and all nature urged her on" (111). London thought Charmian was game, so the word also means that readiness, that willingness to participate in bohemian life. To build one's body for the sport of throwing and receiving punches is to delight in one's physical capacity, an emphasis on the body's pleasure that deeply infuses bohemian thought. To become an athlete is simply taking to the extreme the act of lying nude on a beach.

If London did not consciously pitch his descriptions of the male body for both the female and the male gaze, he found out after Charles Warren Stoddard let him know his opinion of the descriptions of Fleming's nudity. Stoddard, who by 1905 was a fairly regular correspondent, wrote to him after staying up late at night to read this latest novel from his "son":

> The story seems to me wonderfully well told. It is throbbing with life. I don't know any where else—this side of my glorious Walt Whitman—any thing quite so splendidly viril [*sic*] and the pages describing the appearance of Joe Fleming in the ring, stripped to the natural buff. It is the apotheosis of the flesh and of sexual love; you enable and purify the newd [*sic*]—it is born noble and pure—and

make it so beautiful in itself that an honest reader feels ashamed to wear clothes.

How dear old Walt would have gloried in you! The photo you enclosed is a joy. You look as fit as a young Greek god. What Joe says about his being clean is as wholesome as the sweetest Gospil [*sic*] ever writ. I believe in this Gospel according to Jack—I glory in it![139]

We will see further connections among bohemianism, Whitman, and turn-of-the-century political life, but for now we see how Stoddard's response to *The Game* puts the traditional understanding of the novel on its head.

Of course violence is also fundamental to boxing, and it would be a mistake to say that violent behavior is unknown in the bohemian world. But violence is not what London celebrates about boxing. It is incidental to the real thing. And the real thing is performance, graceful movement and intelligent design and execution under deathly pressure as Hemingway (or Freddie Mercury) would say. Thus the cover of *The Game* features a ghostly figure not unlike Atropos, one of the three Fates, who, eye-balling a lifeline, is ready to snip it with scissors.

London, who violently objected to Hutt's illustrations for *Metropolitan*—"it seems to me that they would ruin the sale of any book ever written. . . . They are preposterous"—loved Lawrence's work, which included the cover.[140] "The running illustrations," wrote London to Brett, "of the text by Mr. Lawrence, including the Love and Death motives, are splendidly sympathetic in themselves, and also tremendously illuminative of the text." The deathly, spectral quality of the story is picked up from the cover in the final of three initial illustrations just before the text begins. We see the figures of a happy couple dancing with cupid in between, and then we notice above them a pair of skeleton hands holding strings that manipulate the family as if they were puppets. Love and Death are also on stage, and box, eternally.

The novel is puppet theater, though it is a play almost entirely without dialogue, especially in the fight chapters. Boxing, being a bohemian event, is also an art event, a staged theatrical event. The fight is portrayed as an event seen by two audiences: the audience of men ringside and the audience of one woman looking through a peephole, as if she were Jack London behind the curtain to avoid public scrutiny. *The Game*, then, is also a theatrical novel about the theatricality of fame. The beginning scene—so completely novel for readers of Jack London's fiction who expect to be brought into a cabin in the north, or on the trail, or on a ship—is fraught with fame. Joe the boxer not only garners "open-mouthed awe" from the elevator boy and the neighborhood kids but also from the owner of the carpet store in which the story begins.[141] We are in an odd geographic, psychological, and commercial space—not quite the elemental space of the trail or sealing ship (which the boxing ring is allied with) and not quite an interior space of Clubland (where a number of London stories from 1897 and earlier took place). As with Joe, fame has dislocated London from his usual fictive haunts and taken him to a place where he and his main character are not completely comfortable. True, Joe's uncomfortableness stems mostly from a source other than his fame (which we will return to), but Joe, at twenty, is portrayed as an innocent, a young man unused to everything of life except the moments he lives in the ring. He may not be adept at handling his public, but as a fighter that skill will come (would come, that is, if he hadn't been killed in the ring). As Helen Dare, a reporter for the *San Francisco Call* put it in an article she wrote about James Britt—an article that London cut out and pasted in his copy of *The Game*—"The fighter, I gather, has his public to consider and conciliate, to win to him, just as much as has the actress who prepares a gown and manner and private character for the especial discovery of the interviewer who purveys her to the reading world and the fighter in consequence says not what he has to say, but what he thinks he ought to say."[142] In all facets of his life, then, the boxer must be an actor, and we've seen how uncomfortable London was in being a public figure; success without fame was his goal.

In fact, *The Game* is about a boxer who is on his way to abandoning the fame and money of the boxing life. In the novella's opening scene, Joe is buying carpets for a new house for his new bride, who insists he give up fighting. This is the major conflict of the novella: Joe "saw only the antagonism between the concrete, flesh-and-blood Genevieve and the great, abstract, living Game. Each resented the other, each claimed him; he was torn with the strife, and yet drifted helpless on the currents of their contention" (29-30). Later, during the fight that forms the central event of the novel, Genevieve admits to herself that the Game is mysterious to her: "The Game had not unveiled to her. The lure of it was beyond her. It was greater mystery than ever. She could not comprehend its power. What delight could there be for Joe in that brutal surging and straining of bodies, those fierce clutches, fiercer blows, and terrible hurts? Surely, she, Genevieve, offered more than that—rest, and content, and sweet, calm joy" (150–52). But just as the Game itself is a mystery so, too, is the part of Joe that belongs to the Game. As London sums it up at the end, "She was stunned by the awful facts of this Game she did not understand—the grip it laid on men's souls, its irony and faithlessness, its risks and hazards and fierce insurgences of the blood, making woman pitiful, not the be-all and end-all of man, but his toy and his pastime; to woman his mothering and care-taking, his moods and his moments, but to the Game his days and nights of striving, the tribute of his head and hand, his most patient toil and wildest effort, all the strain and the stress of his being—to the Game, his heart's desire" (179–80). This Joe has a face she doesn't recognize. It seems to be made of steel: "She had thought she knew him, all of him, and held him in the hollow of her hand; but this she did not know—this face of steel, this mouth of steel, these eyes of steel flashing the light and glitter of steel" (165). As London had written in 1901 about the Jeffries-Ruhlin fight, Joe was a denizen of the Machine Age.

Joe is not an author figure. He "lacked speech-expression. He expressed himself with his hands, at his work, and with his body and the play of his muscles in the squared ring" (18). Genevieve is not an author figure either—despite her similarity to London, hiding behind the wall/curtain and watching his actors act—and London takes pains to explain why: "Her vocabulary was limited, and she knew little of the worth of words" (54). Still, Joe is subjected to a number of significant pressures and displays a number of qualities that London would designate as authorial. He works with his hands and gets paid per performance. The pressure of family is the same, especially remembering the pressure exerted in late 1898 on London when he was on the verge of giving up his writing career to support his family as a mail carrier. There is "the chance of a lucky punch" or strike in both occupations. "Lost of chance," says Joe at one point (91). Perhaps most importantly, boxing is theater, a literary occupation. Boxing has its acts, its main characters and subordinates, its opening scenes that set the stage for the later action and then the denouement and climax. Comedy, if the fight isn't close (*the fight was laughable* is a common idiom) and tragedy, if someone dies. And, of course, there is the newly found fame.

In the beginning scene, when we read Joe and Genevieve's reticent and embarrassed response to the carpet store proprietor's self-insertion into their plans for a fresh, clean living space (upon hearing of their plans "he rolled his eyes ecstatically for a moment, and then beamed upon them with a fatherly air" [34–35]), we feel the return of the pre–Russo-Japanese War Jack London. He explains their response as a class response. If they had been middle class, their blushing would have been "prudery," "but which in them was the modesty and reticence found in individuals of the working class when they strive after clean living and morality" (35). We applaud the class distinction at the same time that we wonder if before the carpet episode they lived an unclean, immoral life. Carpets, of course, cannot cover up what ultimately leads to death. Genevieve Pritchard changes the course of Joe Fleming's life not just from the proletariat to the middle class, from bohemianism to mainstream culture, but from life to death. She is the unwitting catalyst of the tragedy of Joe Fleming.

There are a number of connections between the story and two newspaper reports London wrote about boxing matches, both featuring James Britt, who seems the model for Joe. London reported on the first Britt-Nelson fight in which Britt won the lightweight title in 1904, and this fight—with its bloody violence—may have given London "the feels" he needed to write *The Game*.[143] As I noted above, London pasted his own report for the *San Francisco Examiner* (10 September 1905) on the second Britt-Nelson fight in his copy of *The Game*, partly because the fight was so similar to what he had described in that novella, confirming the authenticity of his work.

Britt, the intelligent one, lost to "the beast," Oscar "Battling" Nelson. Joe boxes against John Ponta, who "was too decided an atavism to draw the crowd's admiration. . . . He was an animal, lacking in intelligence and spirit, a menace and a thing of fear, as the tiger and the snake are menaces and things of fear, better behind the bars of a cage than running free in the open" (119). (We are reminded of the battle between the intelligence of Humphrey Van Weyden and the bestiality of the Leopard Man–Wolf Man, Wolf Larsen.) In London's account of the 1905 fight, which is another of his newspaper contributions that strains against convention and then bursts out in essayistic analysis, he quickly disposes of the news in the short lead paragraph (Britt got beat) so that he can turn to why Britt lost.[144] To understand why, London tells us, we need to know what the phrase *abysmal brute* means. It's as if London really doesn't care who had won or how. Only the characters and the drama count. "Let me explain," says our guide—and we should keep in mind that in 1910 London will write another boxing novella entitled *The Abysmal Brute*—"by abysmal brute I mean the basic life that resides deeper than the brain and the intellect in living things. It is itself the very staff of life—movement; and it is saturated with a blind and illimitable desire to exist. The desire it expresses by movement." We are reminded of a number of characters in the Klondike stories—for example, the recent "Love of Life"—reduced from civilized human beings to almost unidentifiable masses of protoplasm whose will to live keeps them in motion. It is the state that predates the atavistic, the primitive. "It came into the world first. It is lower down on the ladder of evolution than is intelligence. It comes first, before the intellect. The intellect rests upon it; and when the intellect goes it still remains—the abysmal brute." It doesn't define just humanity. "We see it in a horse, tied by too short a rope, frantic, dragging backward and hanging itself. We see it in the bull, bellowing and blindly charging a red shirtwaist; in the strange cat, restrained in our hands, curving its hindquarters in and with its hind legs scratching long, ripping slashes."[145] His imaginative power providing telling details, London crosses the boundary between newspaper reporting and fiction, between essay and newspaper reporting, and between essay and fiction.

How we get from a momentary event like a boxing match held in September 1905 in Colma, California, to the eternal moment of a cat or a bull or a horse fighting an elemental battle is testimony to London's conception of what a newspaper article could do and what a newspaper was for. London's readers want a lesson on what constitutes and defines a human being. It is necessary knowledge for understanding what happens in a boxing ring. So when London says, "the best man won—according to the rules of the game," we know now that *the game* means something bigger, grander than mere boxing. Game is life at its limit meaning. There are other games as well, and the article ends on that note. After detailing the blows during each round, London concludes, "All hail to both of them! They play the clean game of life. And I, for one, would rather be either of them this day at Colma than a man who took no exercise with his body to-day but instead waxed physically gross in the course of gathering to himself a few dollars in the commercial game." That is, let us celebrate the bohemian life, which is vastly superior to the game of simply earning money.

The publishing history of *The Game* ends with the return of James Britt. London, so interested in reviews after the debacle of *The Sea-Wolf*, now went on the offensive. In a letter to the editor of the *New York Saturday Times*, he excoriated their reviewer who—once again—called his story false to life. No wonder London saved his Colma report. After recalling the review of *The Sea-Wolf* by someone who supposedly knew all about the sea yet criticized London for inaccurate details about sailoring, London told the editor that "I doubt this reviewer has had as much experience in such matters as I have. I doubt if he knows what it is to be knocked out, or to knock out another man. I have had these experiences, and it was out of these experiences, plus a fairly intimate knowledge of prize-fighting in general, that I wrote *The Game*." And then London insisted that the event in question—could someone be hit with such force that they would be thrown backward onto the canvas, crushing his skull and dying?—was something that actually happened "in the very club described in my book. . . . Incidentally, this young fighter worked in a sail-loft and took remarkably good care of his mother, brother and sisters." We'll never know if London is telling the truth. But to cinch his argument he cites Jimmy Britt. In a moment that is remarkably like Woody Allen pulling Marshall McLuhan from behind the scenes to support his opinion against some pontificating douchebag in a queue for a movie in *Annie Hall*, London quotes "a letter from Jimmy Britt, light-weight champion of the world, in which he tells me that he particularly enjoyed *The Game*, 'on account of its trueness to life.'"[146] Later, Britt, in an informal conversation with a *San Francisco Examiner* reporter, pointed to something about London's talent, not only as a fight reporter, but as an author in general. He said, "That fellow Jack London is all right. He can 'see' a fight." The interviewer repeated the remark to London and added, "For real realism that word 'see' just fills the bill." London agreed wholeheartedly: "Real writing is the power of sight, of 'seeing' the thing." About this same time, he told Brett, apropos a proposal from the French writer Georges Dupuy to translate the Klondike story collections, "I call him an artist, and by the word I mean not 'painter' but 'temperament.' He *sees*."[147] As London wrote about the poet Russ Brissenden in *Martin Eden*, "He, by some wonder of vision, saw beyond the farthest outpost of empiricism, where was no language for narration."[148] During the next summer, London will take "the power of sight" beyond realism.

But Britt's validation doesn't end there. Sometime in August 1905 Britt called London on the phone to tell him that he was going to review the book for the *San Francisco Examiner*. The connection was bad, so London sent him a note: "Dear Britt: There is nothing so conducive to the popularity of a book as good, healthy criticism. Be honest and say what you think about it—good, bad or indifferent. Take a full-arm swing at its deficiencies.

Review it critically. I assure you I will not be offended. If you don't think it is lifelike, say so." Britt reviewed the book favorably and noted especially the lines that had caused so much doubt in the *Times*'s reviewer: "Here is a paragraph of the beginning of the end. 'The whole back of his skull. Never saw anything like it in my life.' To me those are the most intensely realistic lines of the book."[149] As London had called it, and Macmillan had said in its spring catalogue for new fiction, "The Game: A Transcript from Real Life," London had created a human document, and Jimmy Britt had authenticated it.[150] This is the beginning of the confluence of three streams of intellectual conceptualizations—what is fiction, what is sight, and what is photography—that blend into the grandest question of all: What is the best medium of artistic representation?

At some indeterminate time, London wrote out notes for an impassioned essay derived from his prizefight reporting. Entitled, presumably tentatively, "Britt," the notes excoriate those who decry prizefighting for its violence but who condone industrial and military violence. Deaths in the ring, points out the enraged author, number far fewer than those in factories and in war. Among the hypocrites, London counts his usual triad of guilty parties: plutocrats, religious leaders, and academics. They celebrate the mind over the body. They grow fat from lack of exercise, so they cannot appreciate the multiple values of boxing. They are cowardly in two ways. They refuse to learn the game, and they play the devious game of commerce. "Cowardly to ignore the flesh," writes London. "These men . . . who sit around at desks and chase the dollar with tremendous exercise of craft, deceit, and guile—and ride in cars, etc. and who consult doctors for their miserable bodies' sakes—who hold up hands at the thought of a prizefight—and who complacently sit down and gorge themselves on roast beef, rare and red, and pursuit of dollar, will not protect the machines in their factories—and permit said machines to mangle, batter, and destroy out of all humanness thousands of workmen every year."[151] The notes form an intellectual background for all of London's prizefighting stories and show how the word *game* has multiple meanings that celebrate the body over the mind, that expose the hypocrisy of capitalism, and that warn the working-class heroes of the ring that even the glory of their sport can betray them.

After he finished *The Game*, on 29 September 1904, he continued in a modified theatrical mode and wrote "A Nose for the King," the only short story he wrote that is set in Korea; a Korean, he said, told him this story when he was overseas.[152] He elaborated in a note to himself that may or not have been sent as a cover letter to the *Black Cat*: "A Nose for a King" "is not strictly the product of my own imagination. The germ of the story, the nose-idea itself, I got from a Korean nobleman in Korea. The shaping of it into a story, the working out of the idea, etc., is mine. I was arrested by the Japanese soldiers in the village of Sunan, in Northern Korea; and while held in the village a number of days, killed time by visiting and interviewing the Korean provincial officials who had not fled. They in turn visited me, and on one such return visit, swapping yarns through my Korean-Japanese interpreter, the nose-idea, in crude form, was given to me. I made a note of it at the time and labeled it 'A Black Cat Story.'" Yet a page from his Korean notebook reads, "Short Story—humorous—about the man with the nose—see on[e] of my Korean books, probably the one by a missionary."[153] It's possible that he alludes to the book on Korea as a possible background source, but it may be that this unknown book actually has the nose story in it. Whether he heard it or read it, the "germ" is the document behind the story. The "germ" is the inspiration. The rest—"the shaping," "the working out"—is the work of the imagination. In any case, besides giving us a blow-by-blow account of the progression of a story idea, London reveals the working of the imagination. Interestingly, he doesn't credit himself for being the sort of human that hears/reads a story and decides to write about it. No, the inspiration belongs to someone else. He just happened to rework it. I suspect this dichotomy speaks to an uneasiness with his imagination.

Because he wrote it for a *Black Cat* story competition, he was not motivated to return to this genre for its own sake; in fact, he wouldn't write another short story for seven months, so the competition and his loyalty to *Black Cat* must have fueled his desire, but only so far. The manuscript, typescript, and magazine publication all exist and show how thoughtful his revisions were even for a story he wasn't wholeheartedly invested in. He revised in three different stages: once while writing in pen, once again in manuscript but with a pencil, and then a final time as he typed it. He called it "a skit, written, typed, and sent off in one day," downplaying yet again the effort he put into constructing and revising a story, displaying sprezzatura, the typical bohemian attitude of studied nonchalance toward artistic creation. He had a title problem, first choosing "The Nose" and then allowing *Black Cat* to change it to "A Nose for the King." Unlike "Moon-Face," a mostly theatrical skit (though much more horrifying) that he had submitted to a similar contest and lost, "A Nose for the King" won third prize and $350, a sum consistent with his earnings.

There are absorptive qualities to this story. Yi Chin Ho is a condemned man—that is, a ghost—who tells a fabulous tale for lots of money to escape death. He is a liar who sells a picture on a piece of paper to someone for a vast sum of money. So he is a false author figure, a corrupt politician who redeems his crime by paying the money back that he had stolen, but does it by robbing an innocent man by selling him fake art. The story is told with key repetitive phrases—"a wart," "much-to-be-respected"—that infuse the story with lightness and humor that follows from the dark humor of cutting off someone's nose to save someone else's face. And it is a story of a story of a story. Still, it is in the end a sketch that has staged scenes, very little plot, and a preponderance of dialogue that drives the action forward.

GEORGE BERNARD SHAW IN THE KLONDIKE

Having written a short story that shares many similarities with a play, he was ready to write a play taken from one of his short stories and so enter the literal theatrical mode for the first time in his career. The years 1904–6 represent his most intense involvement with theater, if only because he was now learning that particular game. There are other important reasons to look closely at London's obscure, understudied plays. First, he never quit trying to write a successful play. After he failed to have *The Scorn of Women* dramatized, London wrote another play—*A Wicked Woman*—in the summer of 1906. These two plays represent the beginning of a long vein of playwriting that continues into the next decade not only with traditional theatrical forms but also with his support for those who wanted to turn his stories into movies. This support reached an apotheosis when he collaborated with Charles Goddard and George Sterling to write a version of Goddard's *Hearts of Three*. It was the final, full-length work that London completed before his death. He called it his "moving-picture novel," an attempt to categorize a new blend of genres; instead of first writing a short story and then rewriting it for the stage, as he did with *Scorn of Women* and *A Wicked Woman*, he started from a mix of generic forms—novel plus movie script—to yield an experimental artform.

As in the years previous to the fall of 1904, his theatrical mode of writing insulated him from the life-and-death demands of the absorptive mode, expanded his concept of himself as an author (can a short-story writer be a novelist, be a newspaper writer, be a playwright?), and, now, protected himself from the turmoil of being a public figure. Uncomfortable with being an actor on the public stage, he wanted to work behind the curtain.

In the past, he had hovered about the edges of the theater world, immersing himself in reading plays, and George Bernard Shaw (as well as Henrik Ibsen) was a particular favorite. "I have read all of Shaw's plays and carefully studied them," he told an interviewer in 1905. "To me he is one of the biggest men alive, an intellectual giant." In fact, discussing Shaw's work led him to make one of his most profound statements about his own art. "You can't go into the subject of art anywhere without being brought right up against the theory of socialism. . . . You have got to get right down to the root of a subject and you will find socialism the basis of art."[154] Not surprisingly, then, he wrote a brief set of notes at about this time for something he called "Marlowe—Play.": "Bring in an Inventor, and Inventor's daughter. Have Inventor's machine throw out a lot of men. Also, how he was robbed by the Capitalist. An act in Capitalist's house, showing tenderness and refinement and the views they hold on Charity, Discontent of Workers; Reform must spring from the individual, thrift, drink, etc., etc. Criticism of Capitalists by their servants. Very brief. A contrast—Capitalists father refusing $50 for widow of killed workingman (careless), and then giving his own daughter thousands for some little gewgaw she wants to buy."[155] The Machine Age not only features speed and efficiency and new possibilities for prose style but also the elimination of jobs and the alienation of the workforce from the creation of goods and services.

While he was plotting and then writing *The Game*, his close friend and on-again, off-again lover Blanche Partington (the theater critic for the *San Francisco Call*) encouraged him to write a play. Shaw's work was always forefront. She wanted him to go with her to see Shaw's *Candida* ("I [am] just wild to see *Candida*," he said in return), which was playing in San Francisco, and he declared, for the first time, "Gee! I'd like to write half a dozen *real* plays, even if they were unactable and were never acted."[156] Blanche was not the first one to pester him about play writing. He told Blanche that his sister-in-law Corinne Maddern "is very anxious to get me interested in the stage. . . . She likes to be able to introduce me to theatrical people, believing, no doubt, that it helps her standing with them—and she has a daughter and ambition for that daughter."[157] Once he had completed *The Game*, he told Charmian that he was "beginning again to consider tackling a play."[158] On the same day, 4 October 1904, he told Blanche that since Mansfield and Ethel Barrymore were "still after me," "I'm beginning to warm to the idea, and if I get the chance should like to try my hand at a couple of curtain-raisers—perhaps as a beginning. Gee! I'd like to turn out a good play just once!"[159] Having reached a plateau of success with novel writing, he hoped to experiment with his writing talent and to enlarge his authorial office.

He chose "The Scorn of Women" as the basis for his new play, he said, because "it is not a short story," but a skit.[160] It's difficult to understand his characterization, since it is false. "The Leopard Man" is a skit. "A Nose for the King" is a skit. "The Scorn of Women" is a deeply realized story, reliant most of all on the careful depiction of character. Unlike London's skits, this story is driven by a strong narrative voice, not dialogue. And when the climactic moment arrives, not Flossie's arrival, but rather Freda Maloof's confrontation with Mrs. Eppingwell, the moment is impossible to render otherwise than in narrative: "It was another flashing, eternal second, during which these two women regarded each other. The one, eyes blazing, meteoric. . . . The other, calm-eyed."[161] The gaze of the women into each other's eyes establishes and confirms their equality, and no amount of dialogue could carry this scene with the same power.

He had trouble with this scene. Sometime in the fall, he read Stewart Edward White's *The Silent Places*, a Klondike novel. On the endpapers, he carefully wrote out revisions for the second act and the all-important confrontation between Freda and Mrs. Eppingwell. He wrote a full page of dialogue between the two, including Freda's pretension to snare Vanderlip; she tells Eppingwell that she always already wants men, any man: "Men, just men." But what follows that line in a parenthetical note to himself indicates the late composition of these notes: "Better, this as it stands is a bit too gross." Here in the back of White's book he reached a state of tasteful indirection to convey Freda's all-important sensuality. The dialogue he wrote in the back of White's book appears in the final version.[162]

To better understand London's textual representation of authorship in the play, the most significant change between story and play is the addition of the comical Dave Harney. In a moment that is meant as comedy but in reality is deadly serious for our consideration of London's constellation of ideas, Harney buys a newspaper from the mail carrier, newly arrived in the Klondike store. All the Klondike denizens are starved, not just for real food, but for news, and suddenly with his purchase Harney has a monopoly on it, which he will trade only for sugar. London thus works into his play the theatrical connections between newspaper writing and playwriting. Perhaps the most important structural change between story and play is the added emphasis on the theme of the defeat of hypermasculinity. Because London needs to extend the time it takes to delay Vanderlip's departure to the water hole so that Flossie can arrive in time to meet him, London chooses to create a long scene involving Vanderlip's near raping of Maloof. That Maloof defeats him with a strength superior to masculine muscular culture shows how indebted London was, thematically, to Ibsen and Shaw.

In order to get his play performed, he needed to convince an actress (he knew no actors) to promote it, and "The Scorn of Women" features two strong women characters, perfect for the women in theater with whom he was becoming acquainted. This may have been the real reason he chose "The Scorn of Women" for the basis of his play. As London worked on the play, word got out to the papers. The first reports were that Ethel Barrymore was interested in acting in it. In a chatty item, the reporter tells of a conversation with Barrymore, who had met London recently, was "much taken with him," and thought he and Joseph Conrad were "the only two persons who are writing big things now." The talk turned to the play, and the reporter asked her to describe her role: "Mr. London knows almost nothing about the stage. I mean, nothing about the technique of the stage. He asked me many funny questions about exits and entrances. He will be compelled to study a good deal before he writes the play, but he will do it; and I am very sure that the piece will be well worth while when he has completed it."[163]

To learn about "exits and entrances" he turned again to Shaw, and in the fall of 1904 he, Charmian, and Blanche Partington were reading and discussing (separately) *Widowers' Houses* and *Man and Superman*; he even gave an edition of the latter to Partington.[164] In October he told Brett, "I don't imagine I'll tackle a long effort until the beginning of the year. I expect to potter around the next couple of months writing several short stories, and trying my hand at a play—not a serious big effort of a play, though I'd like some time to write a really big play."[165] On 3 November he had finished the first act and on 25 November he was finished with the second.[166] He was calling it *The Way of Women* and on 29 November gave the first act to Charmian to read.[167] By 2 December he was into the third act—on this day he gave Partington the second act to read, from whom he took notes—

and by 5 December he was done.[168] "Not a big effort," he told Strunsky. "Wouldn't dare a big effort. An experiment, merely.—Lots of horseplay, etc., and every character, even Sitka Charlie, is belittled."[169] The experiment took two forms. First, he was experimenting with a new genre. Second, he experimented with theatrical conventions. He had written a play with no leading man and two leading women. Try as he might to hide his pleasure in completing the work, nonetheless he began to actively pursue women who might be interested in starring in it and help get it produced.

In late December 1904, he went to see Mary Shaw in G. B. Shaw's *Mrs. Warren's Profession* in San Francisco and then had dinner with her. "Liked her better than any actress ever met," he told Cloudesley Johns.[170] Mary Shaw, whose career was ruined by those who disagreed with her socialist politics, took on controversial, overtly feminist roles, including that of Mrs. Warren in Shaw's play, for which she was arrested in New York City, along with the producer, under the Comstock antiobscenity laws. In fact, when London was interviewed in Chicago shortly after his marriage to Charmian Kittredge in 1905, the first question the interviewer asked was his opinion of her arrest and the censorship of a play about prostitution. "It seems to me," said London, "it was the most ill-advised action I have ever heard of. Instead of compelling the producer to withdraw the play, it should be produced in every city of the country, and its effect would be beneficial."[171] In a confluence that only cements further the connections between boxing and the theater, Shaw gave his play its title because "the tremendously effective scene . . . in which [Mrs. Warren] justifies herself, is only a paraphrase of a scene in a novel of my own, *Cashel Byron's Profession* (hence the title, *Mrs. Warren's Profession*), in which a prize-fighter shows how he was driven into the ring exactly as Mrs. Warren was driven on the streets."[172] When an interviewer asked London if he would write "a modern 'Cashel Byron' for Jimmy Britt," he knew exactly what he was talking about—after all, the plot for *Cashel Byron's Profession* is similar to London's own work on boxing—but he dodged the question of Shavian influence and said, instead, "I've never seen Britt act."[173] For London, when boxing is play, it is bohemian. For both London and Shaw, when boxing is income generating, it represents, like prostitution, capitalistic exploitation of the worker. The theater thus gave London access to cutting-edge artists who were unafraid to promote causes he agreed with.

Although Mary Shaw proved uninterested, London thought Blanche Bates might be. She was starring in a play in San Francisco, and London went to see it and her, twice, in January. His attention to her was so pronounced, at least to some observers, that the newspapers took it as the beginnings of a romance and then an engagement. But there may have been a different (or merely an additional) reason. London sent Bates the first draft, and she panned it. "First and foremost," she wrote,

> no actor's word amounts to much really—regarding a play—but, from my point of view and the one criticism I make is—that the thread is too slender to hang a three act play on. In reading, of course, the manuscript has the grip that all good stories have—But it is fine *reading*— not fine acting possibilities—that grips. . . . Make [Captain Eppingwell] the leading male character—Vanderlip is impossible as that—there must be a manly, interesting hero-chap—no matter what messes he is in—he must not be made ridiculous.[174]

London ignored her suggestions. He wrote to Charmian, "Blanche Bates, in suggestion of making a struggle between Freda and Mrs. E. for Capt. E, violates the eternal art canon of *unity*. It is *another* story. I violated all the conventional art-canons, but not one eternal art canon. I wrote a play without a hero, without a villain, without a love motif, and with two leading ladies."[175] But in the end he knew that what he had gained from unconventionality he had lost in coherence. In early January, he told a reporter that his play was still in its first draft and that "of course I shall rewrite it entirely—probably several times."[176] He then spent February and March revising the play with Charmian's help; he added quite a bit of dialogue in the first act. In late February, he explained a plot device to her that she had found objectionable, and he did not change that. Sometime in February, he completed the draft and expected Charmian to simply type it up and mail it to James Pinker, his British agent, and to Minnie Maddern Fiske, his wife's cousin and successful actor, who had expressed interest in reading it. But Charmian had more questions and suggestions. In late March they worked on it together; her diary for 22 March 1905 says, "Most of day at Mate's. Working hard on Scorn of Women. Finished corrections and criticisms etc." And then on 23 March, she writes, "Finished sorting and doing up play"; her typescript includes instructions to the director of the play, which were not included in the published version.[177] He was now ready for feedback from the third and final actor to look it over.

Minnie Maddern Fiske, forty years old, was a successful actor and married to Harrison Grey Fiske, her agent and manager of a theater in New York City they operated together for six years. She was also Bessie Maddern London's first cousin. Initially, Minnie liked the play and passed it on to her husband.[178] Due to various delays and the distance between coasts, she wasn't able to send Fiske's comments until July. The Fiskes now saw insurmountable problems: too much depended on Freda; the play lacked a male lead; and the plot was not strong enough. Minnie did see something noteworthy in the play: "It seems to me to be more of a revelation of Klondike life and Klondike types than a play in the technical sense. It occurred to me that it might be well if the play were called 'A Night in Dawson,' and undoubtedly something unique and deeply interesting could be evolved in the way of a new sort of play,—that is to say, a play that was a photograph of an average 12 hours in Klondike life."[179] Undoubtedly, the Fiskes were correct in their analysis, but this final comment points to something else. She called it "a photograph," meaning that its realism was that of the supposed one-to-one correspondence between object and photographic representation. The realism appealed to her, and she was the only of London's readers to understand that he was aiming for "a new sort of play." But she didn't understand that the lack of a hero, the lack of a plot, and the emphasis on Freda were all intentional.

By the time London received these comments, he had moved on from theater. His response is grateful and respectful, but he stood his ground. He knew he had failed: "I am afraid that in this, my first effort, I too bunglingly expressed my idea; what I did try to write was a play that departed frankly from stage-conventions, and cut itself off sharply from stage tradition." It was a play about women and how they cooperate and live according to altruistic, that is, socialistic principles. He knew the play didn't work technically, but he remained committed to writing his kind of play. Having thoroughly imbibed the work of Ibsen and Shaw, he told Minnie that "big dramatic art . . . cannot very well rest on the stereotyped-traditional-conventional."[180]

In May he had told Brett that he was waiting for comments from Fiske, and Brett responded with a slight note of awe at London's multidimensional artistic talent.[181] While they waited he got some positive feedback from another source, Ada Lee Bascom Marsden, to whom he had sent the play while she was writing a play based on "The Great Interrogation"; she was a well-known playwright (*A Bowery Girl* and *Three Men in a Flat*): "It [is] a remarkable play for a first effort. It has atmosphere, and it is a novelty . . . potent factors." She thought Maloof, Harney, Sitka Charley, and "The Scotch Woman are finely drawn characters," but she mistook Vanderlip as a hero, and for that role "I do not think it would appeal to an audience." The only suggestion she made was to bring in Flossie a bit earlier to establish Freda's fine character sooner. Freda was the principal attraction, and Bascom thought the play would be a hit.[182]

It wasn't until mid-1906 that London felt it was time to publish *Scorn of Women* in book form. He sent the manuscript without warning to Brett, with a note saying he still hoped it might be produced: "I am dickering around with these very unsatisfactory actor-folk, and when it is staged, having already published a small first edition, it might then be good policy to bring out a second edition."[183] It must have come as a surprise to the publisher to hear of London's plan—they had been corresponding regularly for the past several months about what should be published and when, and London had not mentioned the play—but Brett instantly agreed to the idea of "a small first edition." It had to have a very limited print run because, first, theater managers do not like to put on plays when they have already been published in book form. Second, "there is not very much demand for plays printed as books, although usually a good play will manage to sell an edition of a thousand copies in the course of time even if it is not acted. Of course the situation is somewhat different if the play should be put on the stage and should become really popular, in which case it has some small sale but never anything really to boast of in the way of numbers."[184] They both knew, without saying it, that this play was not going to be popular. London replied that he saw the wisdom of Brett's analysis and told him to hold off, but London's patience lasted only two months.[185] By September, Brett told him the play had been sent to the printer to generate first and second page proofs, and they agreed to have the play come out in November. Its blank cover, lack of illustrations, and small print run guaranteed its nearly invisible appearance in the marketplace.[186]

When he had felt satiated by the theater, he again turned to Shaw to explain his turn back to fiction. Explaining to an interviewer who had asked him when he would write another play, he said, "I'm up to my neck now on a novel. . . . Then I've got to lecture. I've got lots of work to do. A year of other work must intervene before I can come back to playwriting. And as Shaw has said, I hope to 'come fresh from life instead of stale from the stage'" ("Jack London, Dramatist"). Not that he had exhausted his theatrical impulse entirely, but he had grown tired of the theater world's conventions and had redirected his creative energies to genres he knew best.

The theater world, however, began to see the inherent theatricality of his work, and he started getting offers to dramatize his stories; *The Sea-Wolf* and *The Game* drew particular attention. Bascom wrote a one-act play based on London's short story "The Great Interrogation." As reviewed by London's friend Blanche Partington, the play appealed because of London's strength in drawing character and writing dialogue, but the "stagecraft is poor; production is somewhat too literary and needs touches of playwright." Partington is under the impression that London wrote the play, but Bascom was solely responsible for its construction.[187] The playbill, however, lists the authors as London and Bascom. Both of them attended the premiere and spoke to the audience afterward. London, "in his customary revolutionary garb," gave all credit to Bascom ("London's Play"). Bascom's sister actually wrote a thank-you note to London "for your graceful speech in my sister's behalf."[188] Yet, a few days later, in the office of the *San Francisco Examiner*, London told an interviewer, "I'll tell you just how it came about. I wanted to learn how to write Past, Present and Future all at one time. I wanted to develop those in dialogue, while the story ran on—not the dialogue of playwriting, but of short story writing. Now you know it's darn easy to stop your story and revert to the Past, or speculate on the Future—you simply stop your story and tell it in the third person. But I wanted to keep things moving, and just for practice, you might say, I wrote the little story of 'The Great Interrogation,' which is practically the same as the play Mrs. Bascom and I have made from it." Later in the same interview, when the interviewer commented that the play was convincingly real and "seemed mightily to convince a theatreful of soft city dwellers," London commented, "I had collaboration in that. The good old popular conventions were not all omitted. In fact, I've written only one play without collaboration," that being *The Scorn of Women*.[189] These comments suggest he helped write the play, but in a letter to Bascom he writes, "In the matter of the dramatization of my story, 'The Great Interrogation' it is understood that my name shall appear as collaborator and the proceeds from royalties of the play shall be divided equally between us. You have my permission to arrange for the production of the piece."[190] When London signed his contract with Bascom, he did not retain dramatic rights, something he would have done if he had considered himself a coauthor. I think London, in the interview, is simply alluding to his contribution as the original author of the plot and characters. Bascom is the one who put it together as a play. In fact, a few days after meeting with London, Bascom wrote that "you have the material, I have served a long apprentice-ship in stage-craft, and if you will we may effect a money making combination. . . . If you will furnish the story, I will put it in dramatic form, and I am confident I can market it to our mutual advantage."[191] By May 1905 she was finished.[192]

In 1906, an agent named Helen McCaffry enticed London to collaborate with playwright (and, later, screenwriter) Harriet Ford on a play set in the Klondike.[193] Even *Scorn of Women* continued to generate some amount of interest; Minnie Maddern Fiske's husband, Harrison Grey Fiske, wrote to London in the fall of 1905 to tell him that he had discussed its possible production with a theatrical agent, Alice Kauser, and if he was willing to send the manuscript to her she might be able to get it staged. London, after striking out with a different agent, Elizabeth Marbury, in 1906, did indeed turn matters over to Kauser, though ultimately to no avail.[194]

For now, though, he felt it was time to turn his back to his audience, turning inward to reignite his relationship to the ghost within, and produce a deeply absorptive novel. In fact, in early December he had completed notes for its "*motif.*" He was going to begin with the ghost-dog in the wild and then bring him home: "evolution, instead of devolution; civilization instead of decivilization." He did not have a title yet, but it would emphatically not be called "Call of the Tame." It was not a "sequel," but a "companion."[195] It would be called *White Fang,* and soon London discovered that the ghost of the imagination adapted very well to a domesticated environment without losing any of its terrifying aspects.

5   REVOLUTION, EVOLUTION, AND THE SCENE OF WRITING

Jack London was now so famous that in December 1904, Robert Collier, of *Collier's Magazine*—he who had hired Richard Harding Davis at four thousand dollars a month to cover the Russo-Japanese War—wanted London to take a year "to loaf" and write "a free, spirited picture of human life; what men are working for, and why; from one end of America to another." Collier imagined a writer who could combine "Walt Whitman's largeness, something of Kipling's observant eye, something of Stevenson's humour and charm, something of Frank Norris' epic feeling. You are the only living writer who combines these qualities." Only a month after the election of 1904, when Eugene Debs moved into third place among the presidential candidates, charging London with new energy to become one of the most vocal critics of American capitalism, a leading magazine editor asked London to be the "American writer to tell the American people about America."[1] Not only was London famous, he had become, at least potentially, the representative writer of the American people.

Loafing and writing across the continent was something London did in 1894 as a hobo. It still appealed to him, but he was realizing the diminishing returns from this authorial construct. When London pitched *War of the Classes* to George Brett in 1903 he said that these essays would form a sociological study of "this gigantic, complex civilization of ours. And I am attempting to grip hold of it in order to exploit it in fiction, in what, if I succeed, will be the biggest work I shall ever do."[2] He was receptive to Collier's proposal, but he wanted to comment on life in America not so much from the perspective of the hobo-participant, as he did in *The People of the Abyss* and his hobo stories and essays, but from an outsider's position who still had intimate knowledge of the streets. He made tentative notes about the project, entitling it "The American Abyss," and he imagined it would be a series of articles eventually collected in book form. It would focus first on

Chicago—"write up a barrel-house in Chicago"—and New York City—"a chapter on a flesh-&-blood prostitute. Take her around some, learn her life, causes, philosophy of life, generalizations on life, upon the things I take her to, etc." The one exception to his desire to stay above the scene was an idea to write about prisons. He wanted to "find out some hell-hole of a prison & have myself arrested & sent to it. A splendid chapter, to say nothing of newspaper articles."[3] He wanted to advocate for prison reform, but from the inside out. This experientially informed subject-position was similar to the position of the hobo-author, but it was more limited in scope. At the same time, it had a focus that indicated a larger concept of authorial identity than the hobo-author.

After weighing his options and carefully considering the new directions his ideas about being an author were taking him, he turned Collier's very lucrative offer down. Collier, despite the attractiveness of his plan, hit three sour notes with London. First, Collier's deal threatened to tie London to a single magazine for too long. He wasn't ready to be exclusive with his serializations. Second, Collier wanted exclusive book rights; London knew he might be able to bargain with Collier on this point, but he was not interested in bargaining, as we will see in his similar interaction with Caspar Whitney, the editor of *Outing*, who published *White Fang* despite his failed effort to get book rights. The third was Collier's reluctance for London to write overtly radical socialist essays: "Yours is not an academic socialism, I know, and I believe there are men and women everywhere whose wrongs have never had a voice, for whom you are peculiarly qualified to speak. Not that the note of rebellion need predominate, but that it might be made incidental to a sort of patriotic propaganda." "Patriotic propaganda" sounded just like "Fourth of July oratory," something London detested. To write while suppressing his political beliefs ran contrary to London's maturing sense of his authorial office. Although still very much a bohemian author, attracted to the life of travel, adventure, and writing, he was more and more intent on becoming a public scourge of American capitalism. He needed the appropriate public venue to do this, and Collier could not provide it.

THE TURNING POINT

Revolution was in the air. In the presidential election of 1900, the socialists and Eugene Debs placed fourth, behind even the Prohibition Party. In 1904 they placed third, gaining almost 3 percent of the popular vote while the Prohibition Party did not earn 1 percent. The socialists had quintupled their vote total in a short span of time. The enthusiastic and rapidly growing response of American voters to the socialist cause electrified London and other socialists. This event prompted a turning point in his political writing, exemplified by three pieces he wrote in the winter of 1904-5: "Great Socialist Vote Explained" for the *San Francisco Examiner*, the preface to *War of the Classes*, and perhaps his most famous essay, and certainly his most infamous lecture (based on the essay), "Revolution." The preface acts as a hinge between the *Examiner* piece and "Revolution." All three share ideas, phrases, tone, and rhetoric. In personal terms, this election brightened his life and gave him hope for the future of his country. London, after he wrote *Martin Eden*, declared that, unlike his main character, who commits suicide, the people had saved him; that is, his belief in the common man's ability to rise up against the master class seemed affirmed. He is, I believe, remembering the effects of the 1904 election, which elevated his mood considerably. If indeed London was depressed during this time, his depression was not as long or as intense as he portrayed it to others.

On the face of it, the blues seemed as far from his door as possible. In the fall and early winter of 1904, excited about his new ventures into the theater and playwrighting, ecstatic over Eugene Debs's vote totals in the 1904 election, and busy loving both Blanche Partington and his soon-to-be-bride Charmian Kittredge (and there may have been others), he nonetheless claimed he was losing interest in life. Of course his very public breakup with Bessie Maddern London (especially for someone who sought so hard to protect his inner life from public scrutiny) the minute he returned from Japan was upsetting, even depressing. He called it his "long sickness," but it certainly didn't hinder either his creativity or his production. Two months later, in fact, he seems to have regained a fair amount of emotional balance. In a 30 August letter, London tells his paramour Partington that Shaw knew the difference between living with life-sustaining illusions and living with naïve optimism. Explaining to Blanche why she, as a woman, was irritated by Shaw, he wrote,

> Why shouldn't Shaw irritate you? Truth is usually the most irritating thing in life. . . . As a man, had I a few of the commoner illusions left to me, I'd be intensely obtuse to Shaw, or intensely irritated by him. . . . All the optimism in me (which is the life germane) would rise up in

revolt. Only the life survives that finds life good, and life can be found good only through illusion. . . . But you may ask me, therefore, how I manage to continue living, having lost the commoner illusions? And I answer, by replacing them by a single illusion, by an attitude of non-seriousness, by watching the serious worms write most seriously and by being amused thereby.

Not only does this passage remind us of his brief depressed state of mind in December 1898 but also of his debate between the white logic and the optimist in *John Barleycorn*. In other words, if indeed he were depressed during 1904–5, it was no different from other times. We recall his essay "Pessimism, Optimism, and Patriotism," from 1895, in which he aligned a pessimistic outlook on life with the working class. London was a born pessimist, who tended to the extremes of joyousness and self-pity. His was a life that routinely and quite naturally moved from depression to joy, over and over, year after year.

It's easy, though, to be seduced by London's grandiose rhetoric; of course, when he is depressed it isn't mere depression. No, it must be "a long sickness," and it must be just like Nietzsche's. London may even have used the term as an excuse to Charmian to explain why he didn't want to settle down with a single woman. Charmian knew that London's "long sickness" was, in addition to all its other connotations, a euphemism for delay in attaching himself to her permanently. In her catalogue of books read in 1904–5, she writes about four works of Nietzsche (*A Genealogy of Morals, The Antichrist, The Case of Wagner,* and *Thus Spake Zarathustra*), "How he helped and comforted me, thru' *his* [that is, Nietzsche's] 'Long Sickness' to understand the Long Sickness of one I loved, and who helped me all thru' *my* Long Sickness of body and mind. Dear Nietzsche!"[4] Of course one might read this as the gratitude of someone who had to witness the severe depression, however temporary, of a lover. But to me, it reads more plausibly as the hopeful gratitude of a person who might see her unrequited love turned into mutual affection. When London told Blanche Partington that he regarded his pessimism as a character flaw, not something he was proud of, it's as if he knew he had done Charmian wrong.

There certainly is no hint of this depression in his writings of this period. "Revolution" is the culmination of the thought processes begun with "Great Socialist Vote Explained" and continued with the preface to *War of the*

Classes. I should say that all three essays are intellectually founded on the political essays he wrote in 1903, "The Class Struggle" in particular. London renewed his enthusiasm for the cause after the election because electoral politics had proven more efficacious than he had thought it ever would. It had laid the groundwork for the real revolution. Previously, he had thought elections, at worst, were a distraction and a detour from the real work of revolutionaries. Now he saw it as the first step. In "Great Socialist Vote Explained," one of his clearest statements of what concrete steps socialists would take to institute the new regime, he wrote,

> The working-class, socialist revolt is a revolt against the capitalist class. The Socialist party aims to capture the political machinery of society. With the political machinery in its hands, which will also give it the control of the police, the army, the navy and the courts, its plan is to confiscate, with or without remuneration, all the possessions of the capitalist class which are used in the production and distribution of the necessaries and luxuries of life. By this it means to apply the law of eminent domain to the land and to extend the law of eminent domain till it embraces the mines, the factories, the railroads and the ocean carriers.

This, then, is the goal "of the American citizens who have raised the red banner of revolt." Class struggle, London saw, could be conducted, at least initially, through the electoral process. His conclusion illuminates his change of tactics. Tired of the pointless violence of strikes, he writes, "It is not a strife of lockout and blacklist, strike and boycott, employers' associations and labor unions, strike-breakers and broken heads, armed Pinkertons and injunctions, policemen's clubs and machine guns. It is a peaceable and orderly revolt at the ballot box, under democratic conditions, where the majority rules."[5] He was also characterizing the socialist movement as a law-abiding movement to broaden its appeal. In "Revolution," however, he made his complete feelings about the electoral process known. If voting worked, fine. But "if the law of the land does not permit [the socialists' peaceable destruction of society "at the ballot-box"], and if they have force meted out to them, they resort to force themselves. They meet violence with violence. Their hands are strong, and they are unafraid."[6] Note the emphasis on hands, for hands will become a synecdoche for both union power and union weakness in *The Iron Heel* and *The Valley of the Moon*. Sometimes, even in *The Iron Heel* and *The Valley of the Moon*, hands signify atavistic tendencies. In "To Build a Fire," the loss of the use of hands leads to death. Atavistic strength, however, is not incompatible with modern progressive and revolutionary acts to change society.

An editorial in the *San Francisco Call* foretold the future. If William Randolph Hearst (who labeled London in a sidebar accompanying his essay as "one of the world's greatest authorities on socialism"), Jack London, William Jennings Bryan, and the entire Democratic Party were to combine under the banner of socialism, then America would not be merely a classless society. It would become a private-property-less society. "That is the purpose of Socialism."[7] London himself had quoted similar editorials in his preface to *War of the Classes*. "The Democratic Party of the Constitution is dead. The Social-Democratic Party of continental Europe, preaching discontent and class hatred, assailing law, property, and personal rights, and insinuating confiscation and plunder, is here." Hysteria and fear among the ruling classes were palpable, and London was intent on exploiting it all. Like an attack dog, he went for the throat. His political speeches during his 1905–6 lecture tour enraged thousands.

For London the rise of socialism wasn't just a matter of national politics. It was a true international movement. As he said in the preface to *War of the Classes*, socialism "presents a new spectacle to the astonished world—*that of an organized, international, revolutionary movement.*" In his analysis of the election, London quoted a 1904 statement from Japanese socialists to Russian socialists enjoining them to repudiate the "imperialist" war between their states. "For us Socialists, there are no boundaries, race, country or nationality." In "Revolution," he quoted the same statement to make the same point, and he further elaborates: Socialism "passes over geographical lines, transcends race prejudice, and has even proved itself mightier than the Fourth-of-July spread-eagle Americanism of our forefathers" (5). In "Great Socialist Vote Explained" he cites the formation of socialist groups in Cuba at the end of the Spanish-American War, and the same sentence appears almost verbatim in "Revolution." Revolution was an international event, there were seven million socialists worldwide to make it happen, and in his new major essay he took pains to list the numbers of socialists in a dozen foreign countries. As Joan London said, "Although Jack [after his time in Korea and Japan] did not alter his opinion of the Japanese, he soon confined open expression of his dislike to friends, and in public utterance made an effort to keep his socialistic perspective."[8]

In "Revolution," he also repeated his emphasis in "Great Socialist Vote Explained" on the transmission of socialist thought through print. Contrasting populism's temporary success with socialism's years-long rising popularity, London grounds that popularity in the education of the masses through circulars, newspapers, pamphlets, and magazines written and produced by socialists. In "Revolution" he briefly reiterates this point: "This revolution is unlike all other revolutions in many respects. . . . It has also a literature a myriad times more imposing, scientific, and scholarly than the literature of any previous revolution" (4-5). Here we see the originary thought that led to his participation in the Intercollegiate Socialist Society in 1905-7. We tend to forget that London's massive outpouring of socialist writing was only part of an even more massive international print culture of socialist thought. As a result, the propagation of socialism was an educational program as much as it was a political movement, and London established himself as a leading professor. As Jason Martinek says in his recent study, "If American socialists in the Progressive Era had a central axiom, it was 'Workers of the World, Read!' Indeed, for turn-of-the-twentieth-century socialists, reading was a radical act. . . . The printed word, they believed, was 'mental dynamite.'"[9] Literacy rates had risen in America at the turn of the century to coincide with the so-called golden age of magazine publishing; it was the last historical moment that books and other printed matter had little competition from other media. In a telling analysis, London contrasts the failure of populism and the People's Party with the rising success of socialism and finds that the print-based educational program of the latter gave it the substance and staying power that populism lacked. "Behind the Socialist movement in the United States is a most imposing philosophic and scientific literature. It owns illustrated magazines and reviews high in quality, dignity, and restraint; it possesses hundreds of weekly papers which circulate throughout the land, single papers which have subscribers by the hundreds of thousands, and it literally swamps the working classes in a vast sea of tracts and pamphlets" ("Vote Explained"). For London, just as writing had its absorptive and theatrical qualities, so, too, did reading. When one wrote in a theatrical mode, one hoped to instigate action in the reader. The reader then took this imperative and became an actor in the political theater. Later in the twentieth century, the Black Power movement would discover these same truths, and, not surprisingly, both movements were largely working class in origin.

London emphasizes the transmission of ideology through print for another reason. Newspaper editors are "parasites themselves on the capitalist class by moulding public opinion." Unwilling to indict all editors—he was after all routinely given a public platform in Hearst's *San Francisco Examiner*—London nonetheless moans about "a loss of pride in his species"—not the human species but rather the species of newspaper-women and men. But even the clear-eyed, sympathetic editor is "ruled by stomach-incentive, is usually afraid to say what he thinks about" socialism and the class struggle (36, 37).

London made a connection between the speech "Revolution" and *The People of the Abyss*. When he delivered the speech at the University of California–Berkeley, he said, "When I was in London writing my book 'The People of the Abyss,' I went down to Kent with a London cockney to pick hops." He then cites his friend's poverty and that of England's and Europe's struggling poor as causes for the increase in socialism's membership.[10] Not surprisingly, London repeats two tactics in "Revolution" from *The People of the Abyss*. First, in the latter he compared the lives of the London poor to those of First Peoples and found that modern capitalism, despite its machinery and modernity, had failed to provide basic necessities that "primitive" peoples took for granted. The same was true in America, though now, instead of using Native Americans as his example, he turned to "the caveman," a harbinger of his novel *Before Adam*. "The caveman" becomes the ally of the socialist: "Why is it that millions of modern men live more miserably than lived the caveman? This is the question the revolutionist asks" (26).

The second tactic is to catalogue a number of newspaper articles about the despair of the poor, the stories of suicides and starvation. Having considered writing an essay about the poor of New York City, back in 1902–3, and thinking back on his recent note taking for "The American Abyss," he now was able to use his old research to great effect. "In the city of New York 50,000 children go hungry to school," he writes, and so, for the sake of the children, we must have revolutionary socialism (26). Capitalism kills kids! Another newspaper article he used cried out "Mother Strangles Two Babies," the story of Mary Mead and how poverty drove her to kill two of her three children.[11] After one hundred years of newspaper stories about domestic tragedies even worse than the Meads', facts about the poor and starving have lost their shock value. But, for London, that interpellation of

newspaper articles with "Revolution" gives his fervid rhetoric an empirical grounding, a hallmark of his way of constructing a human document.

The final point to make about "Revolution" is its advocacy for a bohemian economics that would ground a bohemian lifestyle. True to all bohemians, London wanted all people to partake, if they so wished, of an easier,
softer way of life. As he says in the essay, capitalists aren't to be deplored
because of their wealth. Being a rich man himself, that would be hypocritical. No, the awfulness of capitalism is the mismanagement of the distribution of wealth, a theme he promoted in "What Communities Lose by
the Competitive System." American society needs to be reorganized along
economically altruistic lines for the country to regain its soul. America,
in its post–Industrial Revolution state, has everything it needs to feed its
entire populace. This is the Machine Age, but unfortunately we have let
the machines master us. The soulless machines have created a soulless
economy. "With the natural resources of the world, the machinery already
invented, a rational organization of production and distribution, and an
equally rational elimination of waste, the able-bodied workers would not
have to labor more than two or three hours per day to feed everybody, to
clothe everybody, house everybody, educate everybody, and give a fair
measure of little luxuries to everybody. . . . Not only would matter be mastered, but the machine would be mastered" (27–28).

The goal is not simply to revise the production and distribution of wealth.
That is the means to the real end. The real end is honest leisure time and
luxury. The goal is to work, not twelve or ten or even seven and a half hours
a day. Bohemian Jack wants everyone to enjoy life to its fullest, and you
can't enjoy life if you are working more than two or three hours a day. "In
such a day incentive would be finer and nobler than the incentive of to-
day, which is the incentive of the stomach [in his earlier essay he called this
competitive economics]. . . . On the contrary [people] would be impelled to
action as a child in a spelling match is impelled to action, as boys and girls
at games, as scientists formulating law, as inventors applying law, as artists
and sculptors painting canvases and shaping clay, as poets and statesmen
serving humanity by singing and by statecraft [note the conjunction of poet
and statesman, which is a way of saying the absorptive and the theatrical]"
(28). Spelling bees, games, scientific discovery, art: all become the same
because all are created in a time of genuine leisure. The Brotherhood of
Man is an admirable utopian dream, but London adds to it the dream of

"the spiritual, intellectual, and artistic uplift" caused by right economics leading to honest, moral leisure time (28).

London's economic ideas are very similar to those of John Maynard Keynes; both imagined the etiology of the history of economies as a world of less work, more culture. In general, then, "Revolution" derives directly from the preface to *War of the Classes* and "Great Socialist Vote Explained," and, further back, from his work from 1902-3—*The People of the Abyss*, "The Class Struggle," "The Scab," and of his reviews of Brooks's and Ghent's work—and even further back from his first expositions on populism, pessimism, and public ownership of utilities. It grounds socialism on the power of print culture. In short, "Revolution" represents the culmination and distillation of his socialist thought. If there is one essay from which radiates all the intellectual influences on and future implications of London's socialist thought, it is "Revolution." Consider, as we will, how London made use of it while writing *The Iron Heel* in 1906. For these reasons, it took the place for the most part of "The Class Struggle," "The Tramp," and "The Scab" when he chose to give a speech.

But he also placed it at the top of his speeches queue because he had now decided to distance himself from those who were antagonists to the cause. Thus, it completely alienated him from middle and upper classes in the Bay Area who had embraced him as a great writer and, they thought, a part-time tame socialist. He reveled in the alienation. Johns went with him to deliver "Revolution" in Stockton, California, in 1905. He reports, "Jack was chuckling . . . knowing that most of the comrades in Stockton were polite parlor socialists who would be startled by his insistence upon the class character of the socialist movement."[12] After giving the speech, he berated the audience, viciously: "You are drones that cluster around the capitalistic honey-vats. You are ignoramuses. Your fatuous self-sufficiency blinds you to the revolution that is surely, surely coming, and which will as surely wipe you and your silk-lined, puffed up leisure off the face of the map."[13] Note that one can read this prediction as a violent overthrow not just of an economic system but of Veblenian "leisure" engendered by wealth.

Just as capitalist economics needs to be replaced by bohemian economics, capitalist leisure activities ("silk-lined, puffed up") should also be replaced by bohemian, healthy pursuits. Capitalist *leisure*, as Thorstein Veblen defined it, "does not connote indolence or quiescence. What it connotes is non-productive consumption of time. Time is consumed nonproductively (1) from a sense of the unworthiness of productive work, and (2) as an evidence of pecuniary ability to afford a life of idleness."[14] For a bohemian such as London, real leisure time results from a decrease in the hours per day everyone has to work. It is also equivalent to loafing and is evidence of the impecuniously enforced lack of productive time. That is, since money is of no consequence neither is it necessary to use leisure time to show the public one can afford not to work. Nor is it necessary, says Veblen, to obtain "some tangible, lasting results of the leisure so spent." (44). A leisured gentleman (or capitalist) does not value labor, especially "industrial employment" (45); therefore, he needs to exhibit the results of leisure time to display both his antipathy to labor and his ability to avoid it. These results take the form of "quasi-scholarly or quasi-artistic accomplishments" and range from the raising and racing of dogs to the learning of Latin and Greek (45). London and other bohemians escape the life of labor without denigrating it, which is why London's emphasis on its bodily and soulful harm is so important. (If labor with one's hands weren't so dangerous then it would be entirely appropriate for all, even children.) And, needless to say, the tangible results of the bohemian life of leisure are true art and true scholarship.

Unlike "What Communities Lose by the Competitive System," "Revolution" dispenses with polite rhetoric. The goals are the same; only the tactics have changed. With fame comes frankness. He told his friend Frederick Bamford that his presentation of "Revolution" at University of California–Berkeley, "was not to modify [by which he must mean reform] but to make it a stinging blow, right between the eyes [like a boxer's punch to the face], and shake their mental processes up a bit, even if I incurred the risk of being called a long-haired anarchist."[15] London has stopped being polite, and this affected the publication history of "Revolution." He first submitted the essay to *Cosmopolitan*, presumably because they had published and awarded first prize to "What Communities Lose by the Competitive System." But five years had passed, and John Brisben Walker, now assisted by his son, balked at the radicality of "Revolution." They offered London one hundred dollars and immediate publication, but London turned their offer down because the price was too low. Both Walkers were friendly in their apologies for not taking the manuscript at a higher price.[16] With the magazine's finances in decline, the Walkers practiced their kindnesses with London because they did value him as a fiction writer and needed to keep a popular author like London in their stable. But Walker Sr. "had become so involved in automobile manufacturing and allied activities" that he decided to sell the magazine to William Randolph Hearst in 1905.[17] Bailey Millard, former literary editor at Hearst's *San Francisco Examiner* and a friend of London's, became the editor and quickly asked London for a contribution to the series "What Life Means to Me." London was becoming a Hearst author in more ways than one.

London would deny this, however. In his cover letter for "Revolution" to *Collier's*, London lied to Collier about his experience with *Cosmopolitan*, saying that "Walker was going to publish it in *Cosmopolitan*, but that we disagreed about rates [true], and before we could settle said disagreement, the *Cosmopolitan* passed into the hands of Hearst. And you can depend upon it that the article was too strong meat for any of Hearst's publications."[18] Actually, as Walker had explained to London, he was willing to publish the essay even though it was too radical for his audience's taste, but they just couldn't pay London's price. That was in April. Hearst didn't buy *Cosmopolitan* and replace Walker until the end of the summer. Hearst had published "Great Socialist Vote Explained," so Hearst could certainly have stomached "Revolution." London, however, did not want to be labeled as anyone's writer, let alone Hearst's.

After the rejection by *Cosmopolitan*, London tried *McClure's* and then *Atlantic Monthly*. He changed the way he pitched the essay, downplaying his passion and his conviction that the future would be revolutionary socialism. In 1905, faced with the prospect of having his seminal essay on socialism rejected by every magazine, he played up the essay's empiricism: "It is an essay composed of facts. There is not one bit of prophecy in it. . . . The Revolutionists exist. . . . You will note that I do not say their doctrines are *right*. I merely state what their doctrines are, in the process of describing things that exist."[19] True, "the Revolutionists" did exist and in larger numbers than ever before. But to conclude the essay with "the revolution is a fact. . . . The revolution is here, now. Stop it who can" does not aspire to the same concreteness. That is, one might argue that, given the fact that Debs didn't win a single electoral vote, the revolution had not yet arrived. To announce its arrival, though, does not have to be "prophecy." We might call it jeremiad.

McClure, too, balked at the prophetic mode in which it was seemingly written. McClure, who had rejected every piece of nonfiction London had sent him since October 1901, was kind, but only because he wanted fiction. "Yes," he began his rejection letter, using an affirmation of London's position and of his own agreement with the point of the essay, "'Revolution' does deal with a very live thing; and yet, though I can sympathize with your views, we cannot, editorially, agree that the facts you prophesy are so imminent. What is more, it has become a sort of unwritten law that McClure's shall, in general, deal with facts rather than with prophecies."[20] London answered him forcefully, though his letter is lost. McClure wrote back, "You take my breath away! Perhaps you are right; perhaps it is all in the point of view, and mine is not right yet?"[21] McClure might concede any point just to get another story out of London.

Like McClure, Bliss Perry at the *Atlantic* certainly was not snowed by London's attempt to appear objective, and he was perceptive enough to see how much of a Hearst writer London had become in terms of tone and audience appeal: "This article does not seem to us adapted for use in the Atlantic. Our objection to it is based, not at all upon the ideas that are expressed, but upon the fact that it does not seem to us that you have chosen the right style of talk for an Atlantic audience. Forgive me for saying that many passages of the paper read precisely like editorials in one of the Hearst newspapers."[22] When London denied he was a Hearst writer, he did so to avoid the charge of sensationalism, even though his subject matter lent itself to that mode of representation. Debased theatricality becomes sensationalism, a mode of writing that London's facticity countered successfully.

London next tried *Everybody's*, and John O'Hara Cosgrave wrote a very friendly rejection: "Ten thousand apologies for having kept this so long, but it became a subject of controversy. A variety of people had to read it; the young and ardent spirits demanded it; some of the elders hesitated. The result was still older people had to be consulted. Age can generally be depended upon to err on the side of conservatism, and the consequence is that I return your manuscript with regret. It's a bully good piece of writing, and while I personally do not feel your case the case for revolution, it's capitally urged."[23] "Capitally urged," not cogently argued. Clearly, his immense fame as a fiction writer could not carry over into success with his political essays. Finally, in August 1905, he sent it to *Collier's Weekly* with practically the same just-the-facts-ma'am cover letter he used to the *Atlantic*. Collier gave him five hundred dollars for the essay. Not only was the remuneration noteworthily high, but the mere fact that *Collier's* took it was shocking. "Just had a talk with your Randolph Walker," wrote Gaylord Wilshire to London a month later, "and he was astonished that Collier's should have taken such a hot article."[24] Even more shocking to London was Collier's initial reluctance and then eventual reneging on their promise to publish the essay. At first Collier accepted the essay with the same reservations Walker had; it would damage their subscription role: "I want to print your 'firebrand' as a piece of literature, even though a few hundred thousand of our capitalist readers *will* stop their subscription. How much do you want for it? Don't penalize me too heavily for having the nerve to print it. Yours, for 'Revolution'—not for revolution."[25] London should have guessed what the outcome would be. They actually went so far as to set it in type and mail proofs to London, who corrected them and sent them back in October.[26] Then they held on to it until March 1906 when Norman Hapgood, the editor, told London that it had lost its impact because of "his lectures and speeches" on tour.[27] Hapgood wanted his money back when he returned the manuscript in 1908, but London refused.

Everybody in the New York publishing world found out that Collier's had gotten cold feet. A year after it was accepted, James Randolph Walker, now working for the *Times Magazine* in New York City, asked if "Revolution" were still available.[28] Also in 1906 Upton Sinclair asked London if he could get it back from Collier's since it had become apparent they were not going to do anything with it, and he wanted to publish it in his new magazine.[29] London retained faith up till 1909, though he told Bamford as early as December 1905 that he feared Collier's would renege. It had happened with McClure's and "The Question of the Maximum."[30] McClure had used the excuse that the data of the essay had become dated, but that was only after it had languished in the editorial office. As with Collier's, it was a case of an editor having the brain but not the heart to publish an essay that would offend readers. London said as much to James Randolph Walker in August 1906 when Walker wanted to publish "Revolution" in his new magazine: "I don't [know] what's the matter, but between you and me I imagine they have got cold feet. . . . If you get around to using it, you have my full consent to disavow all responsibility for it, and belief in the content of it, just as long as you publish it."[31] In the next month, he asked Collier, "Why, oh why, don't you publish 'Revolution'? You can disavow all responsibility for it and attack it editorially in any way you please." He told Collier again at length that it was simply "a statement of fact," but Collier would neither respond nor budge.[32]

In 1908 "Revolution" appeared overseas in *Contemporary Review*, thanks to James Pinker, London's agent. London received twelve pounds.[33] And then in 1909, after paying London fifty dollars, Charles Kerr published it in the *International Socialist Review*.[34] As Mary Marcy explained to London when she asked for a story for their upcoming 1909 Christmas number, "The Review circulation has jumped from a circulation of about 2,000 to nearly 20,000—within the past fourteen months. It is now beginning to pay for itself and we intend, as its circulation continues to grow, to make it ever better until it shall in time be the ideal magazine—of, by and FOR the PROLETARIAT."[35] After years of donating material to the cause—which he would not stop doing—he finally got paid for revolution.

At the end of yet another dramatic reading of "Revolution," London gave his audience a hint of what his next work would be. "Jack London, the distinguished author, lectured in Shattuck Hall last evening on 'Revolution,'" said the University of California–Berkeley newspaper. "Owing, no doubt, to the speaker rather than the subject of the address, which was strictly Socialistic, the hall was well filled. . . . [London said,] 'I think that some day I shall prepare a lecture on "the Persistence of the Established," for it is the established that stands, and the socialistic, or revolutionary movement is established and will stand to the end.'"[36] At the very beginning of "Revolution," London wrote, "These are numbers [of socialists] which dwarf the grand armies of Napoleon and Xerxes. But they are numbers not of conquest and maintenance of the established order, but of conquest and revolution." That phrase "the established order" easily morphs into "the persistence of the established," and for London, *established* has a triple connotation. Not only does it refer to the capitalists who perpetuate themselves through greed, corruption, and violent oppression of the working class, but it also signifies all conventions—political, social, and cultural—that London tirelessly attacked in nonfiction and fiction, in content and form; in *Martin Eden* he uses the phrase to describe editorial blindness to new styles. In its third meaning, as his comment suggests, *established* does not have to mean "totalitarian" or "oppressive." An established socialist order indicates an eternity of form too. The tension between antagonistic established political orders would have been the principal preoccupation of the essay, a tension that becomes open warfare in *The Iron Heel*. Although London's notes for this projected essay and public comments seem to indicate that he foresaw a future of competing eternal forms of socioeconomic order, revolution—a real possibility in 1904, and a less convincing outcome for London just two years later—or its violent suppression would determine the supremacy of either capitalism or socialism.

"Persistence of the Established" is alternatively titled in his notes "Rule of the Dead" and "Stability of the Established." The title "Rule of the Dead" seems to have originated in a quotation from Anatole France that London considered using as an epigraph: "If the will of those who are no more is to be imposed on those who still are, it is the dead who live, and the live men who become the dead ones."[37] As poetic as *dead* is (and as resonant with his constant preoccupation with ghosts and the permeable boundary between the dead and the living), it doesn't allow for the multiple connotations of *established* and thus London chose the latter for his title.

It is important to reiterate the multiple significances of London's unpublished work. Besides being another example of how he conducted research for his nonfiction, his work on "Persistence of the Established" is simultaneous with the composition of several short stories and *White Fang*. His ability to work in three genres and in multiple fields of interest frustrates standard definitions of what sort of author London was.

To write his essay, London collected over sixty magazine and newspaper articles as well as four pamphlets, then wrote out by hand and typed up nearly twenty pages of notes. A central book-length text for London was Lincoln Steffens's *The Shame of the Cities*, which had been published in March 1904. "The most celebrated critic of American politics during the first decade of the twentieth century," Steffens, born and raised in San Francisco and a graduate of University of California–Berkeley, was no stranger to London; he had written several reports on manuscripts London had submitted to *McClure's*, so even though today he is known simply as a muckraker, Steffens was, to London, a sympathetic colleague and fellow Californian, though they were widely separated by class.[38] Further, Steffens believed in and fought for an undifferentiated common good, a generalized public that was united in its opposition to political malpractice. London, on the other hand, was under no illusion about the fragmentation and competing interests of "the people." Still, not surprisingly, when London wanted evidence of how corrupt politicians maintained their status quo, he read and then copied out two long passages from *The Shame of the Cities*. Steffens

insisted in his introduction that "this is not a book. It is a collection of articles. . . . Done as journalism, they are journalism still. . . . They were written
with a purpose . . . to sound for the civic pride of an apparently shameless
citizenship." London agreed. This was journalism at its most impassioned,
written with sincerity and integrity. In search of empirical evidence of how
capitalism required boodling and other forms of illegal practices to maintain itself, London hit a vein of gold in Steffens's nonfiction.

But urban corruption was just one facet of the larger intentions he wanted
to realize in "Persistence of the Established." One of the essays he collected
was by James Brisben Walker, who in 1905, now safely detached from a
subscriber-driven publication, began publishing a five-cent newsletter
entitled the *Twentieth Century*. It was dedicated to "solve [the] problem
of distribution in a scientific way." That is, now that "the production of
wealth" has been solved, America must "take steps in the advancement
of a scientific distribution—toward the destruction of the present competitive system which results in such 'monstrous opulence—monstrous
poverty.'"[39] London, of course, had been advocating a restructuring of the
distribution of goods and service since he published his own essay on the
topic in Walker's *Cosmopolitan*.

Now, having completed *The People of the Abyss*, "The Class Struggle,"
"Revolution," and other essays, he had formulated socioeconomic ideas
beyond those that Walker was advocating. As London had discussed in
earlier essays, the control of public opinion was essential to those who
maintained the economic status quo. A number of clippings he filed away
under the rubric "Persistence of the Established" discuss the new "science"
of lobbying and corporate public relations. It was shocking to American
progressives to learn, for example, that Elihu Root, former secretary of war,
had been hired by the tobacco trust. One of London's clippings listed ten
ex-members of the cabinet who "are now running Wall Street" as bankers,
lawyers, and New York City's chief of police. A long article in the *Pandex*
detailed the ways that the coal, railroad, and insurance companies had created "press bureaus."[40] It all seems like old business to twenty-first-century
citizens inured to backroom dealings and confident that federal conflict-
of-interest laws prevent gross corruption. At the turn of the last century,
however, such linkages were startlingly novel and prompted deep concern
in the socialist world. As one clipping reasoned, "And the people expect
relief from trust exploitation by electing democrats and republicans! As

well expect liberty by supporting friends of the king. The trusts never select Socialists, because they recognize in them enemies, not friends."[41] The year 1906 saw the first of David Graham Phillips's series of groundbreaking articles in *Cosmopolitan* (written with the aid of the magazine's new owner, William Randolph Hearst), entitled *The Treason of the Senate*.[42] Even earlier, in 1905, London had clipped an article from *Literary Digest* detailing Senator Chauncey M. Depew's illegal financial dealings with Equitable Life Assurance Society.[43]

London created a subcategory entitled "Moulding public opinion" and filed several articles concerned with the manipulation of the media by the ruling class. As always, London was supremely interested in the rhetoric of revolution. In an article in *Russian Review*, for example, London underlined these lines about the czar's published proclamations in its state-controlled press—"The *Moskovskiya Viedomosti* . . . receives also financial support from the personal purse of the Tzar and the grand dukes"—and then wrote next to it, "nor are subsidies unknown with our American Press." In an editorial from the *Independent*, London marked the following opening paragraph: "The newspapers that are retained by the 'money power' are of two easily distinguishable classes, namely, the reputable and the disreputable. The reputable sheets devote any amount of space to the exposure of every kind of wrong-doing except that which is indulged in by their own patrons. . . . The disreputable sheets defend not only the financial misdemeanants, but also the political bosses and machines."[44] London's focus on the media is a natural outgrowth of his discussion of the new socialist media as a counterbalance to the capitalist press in "The Class Struggle" and "Revolution." As another clipping notes, Jay Gould, Cyrus Field, Pierpont Morgan, and other industrialists all held controlling interests in newspapers.[45] London read Henry George's *The Menace of Privilege* in 1905 and noted especially one of George's larger points, which coincided with the intent of "Persistence": "To protect and extend the favors that are its life, Privilege further endeavors . . . to influence public opinion through purchase or intimidation of the press and through gifts to the university and the pulpit."[46] George Brett had sent this book to London, who replied while just beginning his lecture tour in late 1905: "I have just glanced at the Preface of Henry George's book which you so kindly sent me, and I know that I shall enjoy reading it, agreeing with his destructive criticism while disagreeing with his constructive theorizing."[47] London did not agree with George's remedies, but he did find George eloquent on the corruption and degradation of the American republic since the eighteenth century.

London compiled a related series of clippings, not just on the oligarchs' ownership of the media, but on their attempts to influence editorial decisions through withholding advertisements. *Collier's* published an editorial in July 1905 that republished a "threat" in the trade magazine *Canner and Dried Fruit Packer*: "The business of canners, preservers, and manufacturers of food products is being greatly injured by various journals throughout the country, such as *Collier's*, the *Woman's Home Companion*, the *New York World*, the *Chicago Chronicle, Physical Culture Publication*, and others. . . . If every packer in the industry will take this matter to heart and cut out his advertisements, we think that some of these journals will wake up to the fact that they have taken a wrong stand in the matter." *Collier's* put it baldly: "In other words, if we tell the people that certain manufacturers feed them poison, the manufacturers at large are to coerce us with the money argument."[48] *Collier's* continued its attack on the food and health industries with a series on patent medicines by Samuel Hopkins Adams, noting at one point that one F. A. Cheney, who manufactured Hall's Catarrh Cure, devised advertising contracts with media outlets that automatically terminated if any legislation were passed that harmed his industry; the implication was that the media would work against such legislation to preserve its advertising revenue.[49] It is not coincidence that the publications named were major outlets for London's work. Also of interest is how easily progressive ideas about food as advocated by people like Bernarr Macfadden in his physical-culture publications were easily portrayed as radical politics when they ran counter to corporate food production values.

Industrialists, corrupt senators, and other politicians, as well as self-serving publishers and editors, weren't the only ones who comprised "the established." A number of articles detail the corruption and hypocrisy of religious leaders. As Eugene Debs once said, "Tread on the toes of capitalism and the church emits a squeal," a "proletarian pointer" published in the *Worker* that London clipped and labeled "Persistence." In his copy of *Wayland's Monthly* for January 1904, London marked a paragraph in Allan Ricker's article "The Political Economy of Jesus" about the saints and the development of canon law and wrote in the margin, "Persistence—show the paganization of the church, and its passing into the hands of the economic masters."[50] Walter Rauschenbusch pointed out that the class struggle manifested itself of necessity within congregations and made itself known every Saturday and Sunday: "When the Christian business man is presented as a model Christian, working people are coming to look with suspicion on these samples of our Christianity." Why should churches be surprised, then, to see their working-class members seek out alternatives to established religion when they "are now developing the principle and practice of solidarity, which promises to be one of the most potent ethical forces of the future, and which is essentially more Christian than the covetousness and selfishness which we regard as the indispensable basis of commerce."[51] Rauschenbusch and London diverged on many points, but London's point in "Persistence" is to create a large-enough tent of discontents to overwhelm the capitalists.

Colleges and universities that fired outspoken professors like Thorstein Veblen colluded with the plutes. One note in its entirety reads, "The mushy thought of the Established——and yet it endures. Contrast Prof. Veblen, etc., etc., who was fired out of Chicago University [often derided in the socialist press as the Standard Oil University of Chicago] because his thought is not 'dead' thought; because he will not be ruled by the 'dead,' because he is in revolt against the rule of the dead, because he is dynamic rather than static." Having read Veblen's *The Theory of Business Enterprise*, London copied out a passage on the media's role in "how the established persist. . . . The majority of 'dead' individuals who enable the established to persist." According to Veblen, in a quotation London contemplated using at the very beginning of the essay, "The first duty of an editor is to gauge the sentiments of his readers, and then tell them what they like to believe. By this means he maintains or increases the circulation," and nothing he does contravenes the desires and ideology of his advertisers.[52]

Even though London honored some professors for their outspokenness and not simply for their political ideology (after all, Veblen was no socialist), for the most part he castigated the academic profession for being in the service of the capitalists. In an article in *Wayland's Monthly*, George D. Herron wrote in a passage that London marked, "The distinctive characteristic of a class civilization is its fear of free inquiry. The owners of the world dread nothing so much as a search into the sources of their ownership and its authority. . . . Hence it follows that the teaching class, whether it be religious or academic, literary or journalistic, depending as it does upon proprietary interests for economic sustenance, is inevitably a courtier or retainer class; it must teach those things pleasing to its masters."[53] Andrew Carnegie announced in 1905 that he would set aside $10 million worth of U.S. Steel Corporation bonds "to pension aged college professors," a plan that socialists derided as an attempt to buy the academy's allegiance. Again, these essays and clippings will provide London background material for *The Iron Heel*, but London would employ many future fictional characters as professors, and their nature is tainted, explicitly or implicitly, in each story by these socialist attacks on the academy that London compiled from 1905.

To London's eye, it was an easy connection to make between university life and industrial life given the general rubric of "the established." He typed out the comments of a collar-starcher from Troy, New York, about her current strike against the factory owner; she noted how ministers and merchants secretly support the strike but "are afraid to offend the manufacturers, whose patronage is worth more than that of the workers."[54] London then wrote in pencil next to the quotation, "In connection with Carnegie and Rockefeller gifts. It is all well enough to disclaim in impassioned rhetoric that all this is untrue; but every sober one of us realizes that human nature is inclined to justify that by which it benefits." Contrary to such natural conservativism, London proposed his own equally "impassioned rhetoric" in order to convince "the stick-in-the-muds" that they would indeed benefit from change. Indeed, it was a battle of rhetoric. For this reason, London read Arthur Schopenhauer's *The Art of Controversy* and took notes from it for the essay. "Every man feels how thoughtless it is to sanction a law unjust to himself," Schopenhauer wrote and London copied. How to show the absurdity of conservativism was his aim.

So to become a member of the established one did not have to be a politician, religious or political leader, or industrialist. One could simply be resistant to change. London compiled a number of instances of such refusal in the face of technological improvement. In other words, to refuse to become modern was to become one of the undead who frustrated the betterment of the people. London wrote a long note about how advances in anesthesiology were held up by religious close-mindedness: "Many contended that pain was ordained by the Creator, and that to seek to annul pain was blasphemy for by such act one doubted the goodness and wisdom of God." London even copied out a short passage from Jacob Riis's autobiography, *The Making of an American* (354) that told of his "pet scheme" to hire an optometrist for every public school "partly as a means of overcoming stupidity—half of what passes for that in the children is really the teacher's; the little ones are near-sighted; they cannot see the blackboard." Other instances of such short-sightedness included those who opposed the Suez Canal, the transatlantic cable, the Louisiana Purchase, Lewis and Clark's expedition, and Alexander McKenzie's explorations west of the Rockies. Discuss, London said to himself, "the way the stick-in-the-muds boggled at Columbus, at every inventor and discoverer."[55] Seen in this light, London's own adventures and travels become a kind of ethical imperative to broaden one's mind, not in a trivial touristy sense, but in a deeper way that allows for new ideas, change, even revolution. To stay at home, to stop moving, is to become deader and deader. "Unable to shake off the rule of the dead," London jotted down, "to perceive the new thing, to be dynamic rather than static, etc." To crystallize is death, and one's worldview has to be challenged by the simple act of travel. Travel was a necessary adjunct to all of his writing because it stimulated and radicalized thought.

The personal entered into the essay, not for its own sake, but to make the larger point about why the established are able to persist. "Reverence for the Constitution," he noted, "invoke Constitution, and any nefarious act on part of capitalists goes through. . . . . Does one look with reverence and awe upon a city statute? No difference between it and the Constitution— similar instruments, however." Still smarting about being misquoted in the papers after he gave "Revolution," he told the story:

> Once a man in Colorado named Sherman Bell, a man employed by a capitalist Government to break a labor strike, said, "To hell with the constitution!" But the writer [meaning London himself], quoting this as being said in Colorado, was bitterly assailed in the capitalistic press as an anarchist. . . . Result: the speech and its doctrines were discredited along with the writer, while the established persisted strenuously as ever, and with a basis of reason in the minds of those who helped it persist.[56]

The point is that just as intellectual conservativism reinforces the established so, too, does patriotism. "Patriotism a powerful force for persistence," he wrote. "The workingmen who vote for the capitalist parties—enlarge." London connected this observation to something he had marked in Steffens's *The Shame of the Cities*: "The commercial spirit is the spirit of profit, not patriotism; of credit, not honor; of individual gain, not national prosperity;

of trade and dickering, not principle."[57] Although London could feel patriotic—we remember his avowed love of America when he returned home from Europe in 1902 and Korea in 1904—he nonetheless exposed the way true patriotic feeling could be warped. He would even go so far as to say, as it was said in the fifties, that too many believed that what was good for GM, Rockefeller, Carnegie, and others was good for America. For that reason, America had to be remade, and not merely reformed.

One final note should be made about London's intentions for this essay before we move out of the theatrical realm—and we have been in that realm since January 1904—and into the absorptive. That is, as much as London grounded this essay in the empiricism provided by Steffens and others, he wanted to infuse that objectivity with passion. So when he defined his fiction as "impassioned realism" or himself as an "emotional materialist," we should not forget that he could easily have defined his nonfiction in the same way. The keynote for all the material he gathered is contained in four lines of poetry from William Watson's "For England": "Timorous, hesitant voice, how utterly vile I hold you! / Voice without wrath, without truth—empty of hate as of love! / Different notes from these, O watchman, blow to the midnight! / Loud, in a deep-lulled land, trumpeter, sound an alarm!"[58] Wake up! Wake up! cried London the watchman to his slumbering, dead-to-the-world fellow citizens. The capitalists have come like a thief in the night and are stealing your country right from under you. The meek shall not inherit the earth, after all. My use of biblical references is not willful. When London typed out these lines, he titled it, "A Laodicean." We can trace a continuity not only from London's 1904–5 essays to the work he did throughout 1905 and into 1906 on "Persistence of the Established," but also from his earliest work on Jesus, socialism, and the Christ novel he never wrote. London's theater of socialism never closed.

THE RETURN OF WHITENESS

We do not know why London abandoned "Persistence of the Established"; perhaps he did so because in his attempt to be all-encompassing he had finally become too general, too vague. Perhaps the terms *persistence, established, the dead* carried too little specificity. Perhaps London wanted to collect even more data to make the essay even more encyclopedic, and then, as other matters like the writing of fiction and the building of the *Snark* took over, "Persistence" faded into the background until he tackled "the established" in *The Iron Heel*, in August 1906, using a different genre of writing and so making the essay redundant. It certainly never lost relevancy, but London returned to straight fiction, and two months after he had completed "Revolution," he began a new short story. It had been six months since he had last written one—"A Nose for the King"—and a year and a half since he had written a short story based on his experiences in the Klondike. Saturated by his time spent in the realm of the theatrical, he was ready to turn inward.

He wouldn't stay long. The imperative of socialism was too strong at the present. But he did produce six incredibly strong works of fiction between April 1905 and October 1905: "The Sun-Dog Trail," "The White Man's Way," "The Unexpected," "All Gold Canyon," "Planchette," and *White Fang*. It rivals his fictional output in three previous, distinct periods—spring 1897, fall/winter 1898-99, and the winter of 1902-3—and it signals his new financial strength in the story marketplace. He had received a larger than usual sum of three hundred fifty dollars for "A Nose for the King" in 1904, a staggering sum for such a slight story, and this indicates the beginning of the influence of his fame on his pay rate. But for "The Sun-Dog Trail," a short story of real substance and consequence, he received, for him, a record-breaking amount, five hundred dollars; we remember that he had received six hundred dollars for *The Game*, which was almost twice as long. From now on, London regularly—though not always—received no less than five hundred dollars per story; that's fourteen thousand in 2018 dollars.

The first words of fiction that London wrote in 1905 were "Sitka Charley," the opening words of "The Sun-Dog Trail." Sitka Charley was, as Blanche Bates had told London, the most fully realized character in his play *The Scorn of Women*, and so he stands as a bridge between London's theatrical and absorptive modes of writing. Start with someone familiar, thought London, as he returned to fiction, and though he might have chosen the Malemute Kid (a white man who became like a Native American), he chose instead Sitka Charley (a Native American who became like a white man). He had already appeared in London's first Klondike short story that got published, "The Men of Forty-Mile" (if only by name), and then in "The Wisdom of the Trail," "The Scorn of Women," "At Rainbow's End" (again, by name only), and "The Grit of Women." In the latter, Sitka Charley walks a sun-dog trail with Passuk, the woman who demonstrates the grit of women: "[I]n the day the sun-dogs mocked us till we saw many suns, and all the air flashed and sparkled, and the snow was diamond dust."[59]

Sitka Charley, one of the great author figures from northern Londonland, brings us back not only to all the snowy scenes and frost-bitten characters of *A Son of the Wolf, The God of His Fathers, and Other Stories*, and *Children of the Frost*, but also to authors, readers, writing, and the ghostly imagination. The title itself tells us that this is going to be a ghost story; sun dogs are a kind of ghost of the real sun, a mimicking of the sun that indicates that this story will be about ghosts, the tricks of the eye, and the relationship between reality and artistic representation. London begins his return to writing fiction with a story about writing and understanding fiction. "The Sun-Dog Trail" is the title of the story London wrote, but it is also the title of the story (or is it a painting?) that Sitka Charley tells (or paints?). Remembering Sitka Charley the storyteller, we are reminded of our own identities as readers. We are ready to sit down beside the fire and listen.

The Malemute Kid would have served these same functions, but Sitka Charley has a capacity to reflect on life and death that the Kid does not. Both are author figures, but Sitka Charley has spent more time in deep absorptive time and space, and as a result, in both "Grit of Women" and "The Sun-Dog Trail," he wonders about the great questions of existence. In the former, he confronts his audience with an irony: "Death is kind. It is only Life, and the things of Life that hurt. Yet we love Life, and we hate Death. It is very strange" (468). The story closes with Sitka Charley looking out of the tent upon a sky filled again with sun dogs, and we, the readers, like Charley's audience, think the kind of thoughts about life, death, and the ghostly life of in-between that only a deep absorption can summon.

In "The Sun-Dog Trail," he once more picks up that thread of deep thought. While on the interminable trail, he says, "We are like sleep-walkers, and we walk in dreams until we fall down. . . . Sometimes, when I am walking in dreams this way, I have strange thoughts. Why does Sitka Charley live? I ask myself. Why does Sitka Charley work hard and go hungry, and have all this pain?" For money is the "foolish answer," and after this trip he never again works for money, "but for a happiness that no man can give, or buy, or sell" (981-82). Malemute Kid may have been the master ethicist of the land where there were no laws, but Sitka Charley allows London to delve more fully into questions that go beyond the Kid's capacity. Sitka Charley is the bohemian author extraordinaire. Though it is difficult to imagine Sitka

Charley flying kites in the Klondike, his voice is the voice of London in "Getting into Print," London's great proclamation of the bohemian artistic life.

London also chooses Sitka Charley over someone like Malemute Kid to consider race, and racial consciousness forms the backbone to the story and works in tandem with considerations of authorial consciousness. Sitka Charley is born Native American, and he can never be anything but nonwhite—biology trumps culture as well as politics—but he can be accepted as white by whites, especially if he speaks the language of whites. "He had never learned to read or write, but his vocabulary was remarkable," and rhetoric, so important to London to understand politics, was fundamental to understanding race. Sitka Charley's mastery of English and of "the white man's point of view, the white man's attitude toward things" was "remarkable." But this story is about how a Native American understands the white artistic process better than the white narrator, who is a painter, but could just as well be a writer. The story tells us that there is something about artistic creation that is more easily accessible to those with a "primitive" frame of mind than to those who are "civilized."

The very first sentence of "The Sun-Dog Trail" reads, "Sitka Charley smoked his pipe and gazed thoughtfully at the *Police Gazette* illustration on the wall" (969). London closes the gap of five years between "Grit of Women" and "The Sun-Dog Trail" with the single image of a man looking. Vision unites the two. But rather than looking out at nature so that his audience can look within, Sitka Charley, in the new story, beckons us to look with him at his object of fascination. He is in a classic pose of absorption—quiet, smoking, at rest. In the next sentence we are confirmed in our role. The narrator tells us that he, too, has been both looking at Sitka Charley looking and at the illustration. He and we want to know what Sitka Charley is thinking, and here Sitka Charley's "whiteness" makes a difference in the story, beyond making him attractive to a white audience. Sitka Charley thinks all white men understand paintings or illustrations, and so he, too, wants this understanding. What we don't realize until the end is that he has his own way of understanding pictures and is merely measuring his intelligence against a white understanding.

The picture is of one man shooting another man, and Sitka Charley begins the discussion by saying, "I do not understand" (969). The narrator describes the action of the painting but knows he has failed to enlighten Sitka Charley; he was "aware of a distinct bepuzzlement of my own" both because he doesn't understand why Sitka Charley doesn't understand and because he has an initial inkling that he himself can't grasp the picture's meaning, and thus he says he was also "aware" "of failure to explain" (970). Sitka Charley counters with a "why" and the narrator is stumped. "That picture is all end," says Sitka Charley, "It has not beginning." Again the narrator feebly explains, "It is life," to which Sitka Charley says, "Life has beginning" (970). But the debate isn't simply about realism versus romanticism, about how artistic selection distances art from life. It is about the inherent mystery of life and art. Sitka Charley knows the mystery of life, but he learns that art copies from life but without being able to impart any meaning separate from what one sees in life. He thought that whites painted pictures to explain life. At the end of the story, he knows that what whites paint (and write) only describes life.

He does learn something new about painting. At first he thinks that painting is not true to life because "something happen in life. In picture nothing happen" (971). He tells the narrator that a painting cannot be true to life no matter how artful the rendering of detail because it represents a moment frozen in time, which is not possible in reality. A painting cannot show "the beginning" or the "end" of the action portrayed; presumably, according to London, a movie audience of Native Americans would instantly understand what was going on, and this is not as trivial as it may seem. In fewer than ten years London would equate movies with dreaming. According to London, because Native Americans are by nature closer to the original race of mankind, and because dreaming is the access point to the primitive stages of man, Native Americans would intuitively know how to read movies. And, as we shall see, it is their proximity to primitive race consciousness that allows them to understand art in a way unavailable to the overcivilized whites.

But the narrator, because of his "Western race-egotism"—and now we see how London has been, from the first paragraph, developing an intellectual thread from the conclusion of "The Yellow Peril"—thinks he is teaching Sitka Charley how to read a picture.[60] London also transforms a powerful moment from one of his war dispatches. After the narrator realizes that Sitka Charley *can* perform a close reading of a painting, he tells Sitka Charley that a painting is like a moment in time, composed and framed by a human instead of something natural, like a window that frames a moment of sight into a cabin. "You see a cabin. The window is lighted. You look through the window for one second, or for two seconds, you see something. . . . You saw something without beginning or end. Nothing happened. Yet it was a bit of life you saw. You remember it afterward. It is like a picture in your memory. The window is the frame of the picture" (971). Now Sitka Charley understands. He had not understood the function of memory in making art. He understands that whites think of art as life robbed of movement. The narrator emphasizes the one-to-one correspondence between life and art. "Pictures are bits of life." Because of this truism, the narrator understands art, and once Sitka Charley affirms the truism, "Yet is it a true thing. I have seen it. It is life," the narrator thinks he has transferred to Charley the pictorial wisdom of the white man. But when Sitka Charley agrees that the picture is life, he is not talking about the correspondence between signifier and signified. He suddenly understands that the mystery of life can be contained within a painting too.

Each time Charley draws on his pipe, his meditative state signals a new turn in the story. Now that he understands what white people mean by art, he is going to try to educate the narrator, though of course the narrator has no idea of Charley's intention. And now we get the story/painting that Sitka Charley calls "The Sun-Dog Trail." First, we remember that the narrator told us that Sitka Charley "had remarkable powers of visualization. . . . He saw life in pictures, felt life in pictures, generalized life in pictures" (971). This facility also reminds us of that favorite phrase of newspapermen and women, "the word-picture." We are back discussing ut pictura poesis. Although Sitka Charley tells the narrator that he is going to relate a story that he wants the narrator to paint, that is not the real purpose of the story, for the question of how to paint the story never surfaces again. The purpose is to teach the narrator that painting may be like life, but it is like life only because it, too, is a mystery.

He tells a story—a ghost story, of course, because it takes place in the North—a story of how he, a woman, and a man travel the sun-dog trail for months. The hardship turns them into "wandering ghosts" (978). "We sleep like dead people, and in the morning get up like dead people out of their graves and go on along the trail" (981). Breaking trail, unlike in "The Devil's Dice Box" and "The Odyssey of the North," does not end with gold, writing, and chance. It begins with the living, who are then converted into the undead, who then may or may not become human again. This lack of terminus, however deadly, is a decided turn in London's fiction. Even in "Grit of Women" there was a purpose, a goal, if only to tell someone of the dire straits in which the men of Forty-Mile had found themselves. They may or may not be rescued, but at least Sitka Charley carried the message. Even in "Love of Life" there was a goal: to escape the North. Here, though, in "The Sun-Dog Trail," on the same kind of trail, there is no gold to be found, no message to be carried; to reinforce this point, London has Sitka Charley give up his job as a mail carrier and become simply a highly paid guide for the Joneses. But he is a guide to a random point in the snowy wasteland, a point determined only by where the object of the Joneses' wrath happens to fall, unable to continue any further.

The story concludes with an image that parallels the image we began with: the shooting of a man. The narrator and Charley have exchanged subject-positions. At the beginning of the story it was Charley who asked why one man killed another. Now, at the end of both representations of "The Sun-Dog Trail," it is the narrator left helpless in the front of artistic representation. "But why did they kill the man?" he asks. Charley lights his pipe, and we get the conclusion. Charley has knowingly told a story that will repeat the *Police Gazette* illustration in order to turn the tables. Knowing the utter cluelessness of the narrator, his story demonstrates that the two parallel trains of thinking will never meet. The painter doesn't realize it, but Charley knows not only the mystery of life but also that the white man thinks there is no mystery. Condescendingly, the narrator says, "You have painted many pictures in the telling." And when the narrator says, "It was a piece of life," as if that answered everything, Sitka Charley mimics the narrator, knowing it explains nothing and knowing that unlike himself, the narrator has learned nothing on this day in a cabin in the North.

The cabin is a miniature art museum, its walls hung with paintings of all sorts. It has an analog in the discussion about art. When the narrator tries to explain painting to Sitka Charley, he tells him to imagine seeing a man writing a letter in a cabin. The arts of painting and writing are thus constantly blurred together in the story just as they were in the popular imagination of the time and the constant reference to word-pictures in the press. What was crucial for London was not only the ability of words to generate pictures in the mind or the ability of painting to generate words in the viewer's mouth, but also the epistemology of representation. That is, what knowledge do we gain from artistic representation and how best can we access that knowledge? The emphasis on race in "The Sun-Dog Trail" and the final resolution in which Sitka Charley ends up wiser than the white narrator tell us that, for London, civilization masks the mystery of life. By *civilization* London includes the technics of art. Art, then, is civilization's creation of a prosthetic for natural vision. Art may be beautiful, but it blocks the immediate and more truthful vision of the natural eye. The eye sees that there is mystery behind the veil. It sees that there is a spiritual side of life. As Sitka Charley learns, we may paint a picture or write a story, we may even create a moving picture with a story that is a string of "many pictures in the telling," but no art object brings us closer to the ultimate meaning of life that we so often seek. "The Sun-Dog Trail" shows London at a new stage in writing. His author figures are still privileged characters, but now they realize that they must be in touch with the primitive, through dreaming, to access pictures. In a year, he will have his author figure in *Before Adam* begin his story with "Pictures! Pictures! Pictures!" In two years, Martin Eden will begin his novel with his own confrontation of a painting, which baffles him as much as the *Police Gazette* illustration baffles Sitka Charley.

The racial thematic continues, though along a different vector, in the next story he wrote, "The White Man's Way." Instead of art, the principal concern is legal justice. Just as Sitka Charley functions in part to show a white audience how its aesthetics are overcivilized and thus suspect, so old Ebbit and his wife, Zilla, show a white audience that its sense of jurisprudence is culturally determined. Two Native Americans, one of whom is their youngest son, each commit what seems to be the same crime—the murder of a white man—but one is allowed to live and the other, their son, is hung. It's not that the white legal system is so complicated that outsiders like Ebbit and Zilla cannot understand it. It's that to an outsider there is no difference between killing in self-defense and killing without motive. They see the white legal system as inconsistent and mysterious. Whites, on the other hand, do not understand the Native American legal system, but—and here is yet another example from London of white-race egotism—they do not call it mysterious. They call it primitive and denigrate it for being so.

The narrator of "The White Man's Way," to his credit, is merely baffled by Ebbit and Zilla's sense of justice. He offers no comment after Ebbit tells him of the death of their second son and asks for explanations for other legal cases that the couple tells them. Their first son was killed in a canoeing accident in territory governed by whites. According to Indian law, those who govern a territory with "bad water" must pay a penalty to the family of the killed. But the whites do not understand this law and refuse to pay. According to Indian law, if a dog steals food from you, you may beat the dog; if a man steals from you, the man must die. "But if you kill the man, why do you not kill the dog?" asks the white narrator, and while Zilla sneers at his ignorance, Ebbit calls it "the way of the white man." Ebbit explains that men need dogs to pull sleds, so they are not killed (989).

The uniqueness in London's thought is not that he is arguing for the superiority of either system of justice. The uniqueness resides in his two-mindedness. One system works for one culture, one system works for the other. To mix the two is fatal. He'll stick with the white way because he is white, but he won't silence or denigrate the other. In a page of notes for a possible story, London began, "How an Indian could not understand the innermost traits of the white man, and how he paid for it with his life." This nameless Native American had watched whites pay outrageous prices for goods and services "on the Chilcoot Trail," and so, when a band of whites decided to form "a relief expedition" and save a "starving tribe of Indians" miles away, he tried to charge them for driving the dogs; they wanted him to do it for free, as they were doing it for free. "But he is obdurate, for he had learned from white men how to hold out for a bargain." He "had caught the commercial spirit, but not the altruistic nor the racial." So they hang him. That is, he became a capitalist without realizing that some white men are socialists. "He did not understand whites; nor did whites understand him" is London's final note.[61] The point is that London believed Native Americans could neither assimilate nor survive on their own terms.

The Native American legal system cannot possibly govern the life of the Machine Age, but the white way—so ignorant and undesirous to understand—is equally incapable of producing a fair result within Native American culture. The most laughable instance is that of the story of Mobits, who steals flour from a white man. The penalty, according to white law, is to put him in jail for theft instead of killing him. But the tribe has no word for jail nor any comprehension of it. Jail, for them, is simply "a house" and "good grub." Mobits wants to stay in jail because his life is far worse outside of it. The narrator again has no comment. He sees this white absurdity, just as he sees the absurdity of a Native American killing a botanist in order to be taken by the whites to California. The narrator, who becomes a storyteller after being the audience for Ebbit's storytelling, is the perfect listener and thus instructs us in how to listen to the Other. The Native American Other, like the "Asiatic," is foreign and primitive compared to Machine Age whites, but within their otherness lies value, a value that can expose the injustices of the white race. Still, even in the face of its ignorance and the inability to understand, one cannot resist the white race. It is too powerful. Ultimately, the narrator can afford to be calm, kind, and understanding. He need not respond to the stories of Mobits's theft or of Bidarshik's hanging because he knows he is witnessing the end of the power of a race of people.

"The White Man's Way" took five days to write; it weighed in at 5,300 words, while his other stories of the spring of 1905 averaged around 8,000 words. Still, he received $530 for the story from the *New York Tribune*, ten cents a word. He had first sent it to *Century*, but the prudish Robert Johnson—whom we last heard from when *Century* serialized *The Sea-Wolf*—rejected it. Always on the lookout for the offensive incident or scandalous description, Johnson sounds disappointed not to find anything salacious and had to retreat to aesthetics: "There is nothing about this sketch, 'The White Man's Way,' to object to except that it is not a story, but a transcript of experience. . . . Give us a piece of real fiction, with beginning, middle, and end, and some of your own rare and individual charm."[62] He wanted a conventional narrative, and London agreed with him that it wasn't conventional; he hadn't intended it to be. To Johnson, the story wasn't objectionable—"I can remember that my reason for sending it to you was that it was not bluggy nor horrible, and that you had stipulated that you did not want any bluggyness nor horribleness"—and it wasn't a conventional narrative—"'The White Man's Way' is certainly not a short story with beginning, middle and ending."[63] The unstated claim is that Johnson and Gilder are not recognizing a different sort of, though equally artistic, form. In this way London becomes Sitka Charley to Johnson's narrator of "The Sun-Dog Trail."

A less secure author might have taken offense at this narrow-mindedness, but London let it go. In his reply, he simply stuck it to him for money. He pointed out that *Collier's* had offered him a thousand dollars an article to partake in Robert Collier's scheme to journey across America, that *Outing* had just paid him ten cents a word for *White Fang*, and that he and Richard Gilder had discussed payment and that they had tentatively agreed on eight cents a word—but that was before the Collier and *Outing* offers. The magnanimous London pointed out that "in the meantime my rate has been going up, though I have not been selling anything. This, as you will readily understand, is due to conditions outside of me, and to which I not only gracefully but gratefully yield." So because we all have to obey the invisible hand of the market and because *Century* wants exclusive serial publication rights—that is, forbidding even English serial publication—London tells Johnson that he should give him ten cents a word and he would give *Century* exclusive rights.[64]

Johnson was irritated by this letter in two ways. He detected some sense of unfounded confidence in artistry in London's tone, and he felt it warranted a lecture from someone who was older and vastly more experienced. "In general, my dear Mr. London," said Johnson from his lofty perch at the eastern publishing establishment, "I hope I may be permitted to say to you that the present commercial situation of the short-story writers seems to me to be unfortunate for them in the fact that it makes an extraordinary temptation to them to put out episodical work or character sketches in place of well-knit, dramatic work conceived with proportion and a continuity and variety of action." Of course, "The White Man's Way" is neither an episodical story nor a character sketch, but Johnson couldn't see it for what it was. "American short stories," Johnson continued, "are generating into mere glimpses of life instead of artistic compositions, and I am afraid that the public is getting tired of the kind. You have published so little heretofore"—shocking! London had published four collections of short stories and six novels, all with major East Coast publishers—"that the way is clear for you to make every piece of your work tell in this respect, and, as, ever since reading `The Call of the Wild' I have been an admirer of yours and deeply interested in your work, I hope you will pardon this bit of homily from one who has been thirty-two years at the business of editing and, moreover, has a pride in our American fiction."[65] It's not surprising that he did not mention the objectionable *The Sea-Wolf*, but the condescending tone is uncalled for. London, who did not need to be reminded of "a pride" in American literature, took the high road. Three weeks later, he sent them "a real short story"—"All Gold Canyon," which Johnson promptly accepted. After London sent back the page proofs in August, Johnson sent him a check for five hundred dollars, less than seven cents a word. Johnson closed the letter with the stipulation that in the future they will pay him ten cents a word: "We think this ought not to apply to a story the rate for which was arranged in advance. Is this not right?" London only shrugged. If they wanted to shortchange him, he had many other editors who would pay his top rate. Johnson told him, "We do not attempt to compete with the tremendous special prices which one occasionally gets for spectacular work in other quarters. We hope that the reputation of The Century and its loyalty to its contributors in presenting their work to the public, will to a certain extent compensate to authors for the difference which occasionally is found between our prices and those of others."[66] London, an expert poor-mouther himself, easily recognized it in others.

While Johnson was lecturing London on the aesthetics and economics of short-story publishing, London took two weeks to complete "The Unexpected," another Klondike trail story, and sent it to his old friends at *McClure's*; McClure had been begging London for either a serial or a single story, McClure insisting that his magazine was the only place for London's work. He took it and paid ten cents a word for the first five thousand words and then five cents a word beyond that; since London still owed them $476 from the advances he had received back in 1901, this story more than squared his account.[67]

"The Unexpected" begins with a line that might have been addressed directly to Johnson, a commentary on his literary expectations. "It is a simple matter to see the obvious, to do the expected." Leave it to London, though, to tie formulaic fiction to human behavior and evolution. "When the unexpected does happen, however, and when it is of sufficiently grave import, the unfit perish. . . . When they come to the end of their own groove, they die." London, the always experimenting author, never content with a formula, describes himself as an author in the next paragraph: "On the other hand, there are those that make toward survival, the fit individuals who escape from the rule of the obvious and expected and adjust their lives to no matter what strange grooves they may stray into, or into which they may be forced."[68] Like his report on the Britt-Nelson fight, he begins far afield with his reader, taking him or her in an unexpected intellectual direction that will explain the point of the story. The reader simply has to trust him.

It turns out that the reader has no reason to worry. The story works in a traditional, expected way, working against the point of the story. That is, if a short-story writer stays in his or her groove, then, by the evolutionary law stated at the beginning, that writer shall die. To write this story is to work one's way toward suicide. Further, to write this kind of story, to meet the expectations of editors like Robert Underwood Johnson, is not prostitution but suicide. That would be the case if it weren't for the unexpected that crops up in the telling of the story. The plot demands a turn, and since the story is supposedly about the surprising yet utterly predictable duplicity and greed of humans, we are shocked, surprised, but then, in hindsight, reassured both by Dennin's treachery and the conventionality of the story's turn. No, what is unexpected, shocking, and surprising, and therefore most artful and alive in the story, is how Edith Nelson decides to hang Dennin. "It came to her that the law was nothing more than the judgment and the will of any group of people." Her "original sociological researches" counter "the legacy of her race, the law that was of her blood and that had been trained into her." If hanging Dennin was counter to white man's law, then whose law, what race's law, was it? We know from "The White Man's Way" that Native American law says that murder is punishable by death: no jail, no trial, just death. How like that system is the miners' meeting system that Hans tells Edith about. "All the men of a locality came together and made the law and executed the law" (1011). The two conceptions of law go together then: the idea that law is socially constructed and that Native American law, like miners' law, is as valid as traditional white society's law, which demands all the accouterments of a fair trial. That, then, is the real unexpected. And it is doubly unexpected, coming as it is clothed in the structure of a conventional short story.

Originally entitled "The Legacy of Law," and then "The Heritage of Law," and then "The Great Unexpected," the story ends in manuscript, like its thematic predecessor "The White Man's Way," with a footnote attesting to its basis in fact, which was then cut in the final version: "The above is a true story. Michael Dennin was hanged at Latuya Bay by Mrs. Nelson in 1900."[69] A year later, in August 1906, London probably regretted the excision. The story appeared that month and drew a letter to the editor from disbelieving Alaskans in the *Seattle Post-Intelligencer*. London, of course, immediately wrote a letter to the editor and took his usual tack: if a story appears in a newspaper, it is supposed to be true, so don't blame me if it turns out to be false. "Turn loose and lambaste your fellow-newspaper-men who are responsible for this."[70] It actually was true and confirmed by the Seattle newspaper. Once again, London was frustrated by a pointless concern over the factual basis for his work.

One murder over gold leads to another—one treacherous act after another—and it makes no difference if we are in the ghostland of the North or a seeming Edenic valley in California. His first title for "All Gold Canyon" was "Sudden Death." That would stress the murder in the pocket mine. Then he changed it to "The Pocket Hunter," the murderer himself. Then he changed it to "All Gold Canyon," the place that the pocket miner murders. There is no law in this story, only crime: crime of one man against another, crime of one man against nature, and the crime of capitalism against humanity. For this is a parable of what happens to the natural world if capitalism is left unchecked.

The gorgeous setting rendered in beautiful prose at the beginning of the story previews the idyllic atmosphere in which White Fang finds himself at the end of his story, so we know that his civilized state is not guaranteed to be a happy one if we have read "All Gold Canyon." London constructs the green Eden in the short story, not to promote California as a paradise but for two other, related reasons. First, it is in sharp contrast to the white hell of the northern landscape. Second, the contrast is undermined by the viciousness that occurs in the little canyon. It turns out that if this canyon—this beautiful, untouched natural paradise—can be infiltrated and destroyed, then there is no place on earth safe from man's—specifically the Anglo-Saxon man's—rapaciousness. It isn't mere greed and carelessness of the pocket miner, however, that destroys the canyon. It's a particular kind of greed, that of the "commercial spirit," the lust for yellow metal that has caused so much pain, suffering, and death in the North. And now London shows how that capitalistic death-dealing desire for money destroys all it touches in the South. There is no escape, except through socialism, and there is no socialism in the deeply pessimistic "All Gold Canyon."[71]

Five days before he had begun "All Gold Canyon," London wrote a review of Leroy Scott's *The Walking Delegate*, and this break in writing short stories signals his turn to the Southland in his next three works: "All Gold Canyon," "Planchette," and *White Fang*. An important theme in "All Gold Canyon" is first sounded in this review, so we should take it up before going back to the short story. *The Walking Delegate* is a novel about a fight over leadership of the Ironworkers' Union in New York City, loosely based on recent events in New York City involving the walking delegate for the Ironworkers' Union, Sam Parks, and their 1903 strike. Parks was subsequently arrested on charges of extortion, and he died in Sing Sing prison in 1904. As London says in his review, "It is a study of Sam Parks, the notorious labor leader whose corrupt dealings threw much of odium upon the trade union movement and at the same time gladdened the hearts of all capitalists with the exception of those capitalists who were compelled to share with Sam Parks their profits and to share with him likewise in his corruption." Scott joined the Ironworker's Union to gather information for the novel. He lived with his friend William English Walling in the famous University Settlement—a private institution, like the Hull House, dedicated to helping immigrants transition into American life—in New York City from 1902 to 1904, and later became friends with Anna Strunsky as well. To a large extent this book came out of the hopes triggered by Bloody Sunday in St. Petersburg and the defeat of the czar in the Russo-Japanese War. This was the year of such fever-pitched enthusiasm for the coming revolution that Walling, Strunsky, and her sister Rose all lived and worked for the revolution in St. Petersburg. For his part, London stayed home and continued to promote the cause, and so this review is a piece with his own newfound enthusiasm that began with the 1904 election and continued in 1905 with his national lecture tour.

The novel and its author may have been recommended to London by Strunsky by way of Walling, or perhaps by Walling himself. As London called it, it is "a human document," a straightforward, unromantic view of union leaders, bosses, and the ways they become corrupted. He marked a passage that appealed to him particularly because it might be the characterization of someone he himself had created: "She was not conscious that she had in a measure that rare endowment—the clear vision which perceived the things of life in their true relation and at their true value, plus the instinct to act upon that vision."[72] "Clear vision," for Scott and London, means an ability to see through artifice—the false constructions of social reality—to the heart of a matter; in these moments, there is no relativism, only the truth. The hero of the tale, Tom Keating, has a similar background to London's: "Though he had left school at thirteen to begin work, he had attended night school for a number of years, had belonged to a club whose chief aim was debating, had read a number of solid books and had done a great deal of thinking for himself. As a result of his reading, thinking and observation he had come into some large ideas concerning the future of the working class" (102). There the similarity ends. London consistently objected to the reform measures advocated by lefties like Scott, but he sympathized with Tom Keating, the trade unionist, and his creator, and in the name of socialist solidarity, London reviewed the book favorably.

Of course there were other, political elements that attracted London, most prominent being those he noted in the back of his copy of the novel and then rewrote and included in his review. The treachery of Foley, Baxter, and others informs most of London's notes. "Begin with graft and rot-tenness everywhere in business life. Then—production for profit instead of service—a sample. Then—the old sinning and the new. The old prim-itive struggle for existence, and the new struggle for existence." Not only are these notes tinged with evolutionary thought but also they are high-lighting the continuity among the short stories he was writing at this point and this review. Betrayal and treachery, treachery and betrayal. When we read "The Unexpected" as a story of the cooperative commonwealth gone bad because of lack of internal protection and law, we see its similarities to London's review of *The Walking Delegate*. When the commercial spirit, not altruism, governs social groups, murder and corruption are natural results. They are natural because, according to London, the fight between labor and capital over wages and profits is exactly the same as the fight between two primitive men fighting over meat: "Primitive man fought over the division of the meat of some slaughtered animal. Modern man fights over the divi-sion of an abstraction (dollars and cents), which, in turn, represents meat."

The theme continues into "All Gold Canyon." There is something primitive to Bill the miner. "Thinking was in him a visible process," says the narrator. He is almost savage in appearance, and like any savage, there is an element of the child in him: in his eyes there was "much of the naivete and wonder of the child" (1019). He lives outside, and there is a fine line between the jungle of urban New York City and the jungle of "All Gold Canyon," a blurry boundary that London makes central to his review: "As is true of any jungle, in this commercial jungle there is a conflict of interests."[73] His notes in the back of Scott's novel read, similarly, "It is a transcript from life, from 20th Century life, from 20th Century life in New York City where the steel fabrics (skyscrapers) are reared into the sky to constitute themselves upstanding peaks, outjutting spurs, in the Jungle of Commercial empire—Then, next, the deeds of the Jungle." His focus on the natural geography of the canyon at the beginning of the story repeats his focus on the manmade geography of New York City. London had been reading chapters of Sinclair's *The Jun-gle*, so the simile of the jungle was fresh in his mind, but it had been a part of his vocabulary since at least *The People of the Abyss*. Bill, like the char-acters in *The Walking Delegate*, is a denizen of the jungle.

In his review, London writes, "In any human jungle there must be codes of ethics and violations of codes of ethics." The "particular and peculiar sin of the commercial jungle . . . is betrayal. Betrayal, or treachery, is the sin most commonly committed in business life of today." London makes the connection between Foley's betrayal and that which happens in both "The Unexpected" and "All Gold Canyon" very explicit: "It is secret, hidden, a snake-in-the-grass sort of act directed against one's fellows to the hurt of one's fellow, and it does not even rise to the dignity of the old-time ambuscade." Now that the analogy between urban and country jungles was reinforced with the mention of the classic Western stab-in-the-back, London decided to base a short story on just that act. If there is anything attractive about the action in "All Gold Canyon," then it is that the sneak attack isn't as bad as the kind of illegal, immoral machinations conducted by Foley. But that ain't saying much.

London had been reading Edward Ross's essay in the *Atlantic Monthly*, "New Varieties of Sin," but he was less concerned about convincing the public of the immorality of the new secularization of sin and how to expose the moral decrepitude of capitalism than celebrating the lost art of public ruthlessness. When Ross says, "The shedder of blood, the oppressor of the widow and the fatherless, long ago became odious, but latter-day treacheries fly no skull-and-crossbones flag at the masthead," London thinks, in his review of *The Walking Delegate*, not how to legislate laws to convict the new capitalist criminals, but of his favorite pirate: "Captain Kidd . . . was open and above board. He hoisted skull and cross-bones to the masthead, and took openly and without treachery" (10).[74] London quotes Ross, "The little finger of Chicane has come to be thicker than the loins of Violence" (11). He thinks not of how awful the modern-day pirates are but how Kidd's murdering was ethically superior to capitalism's treachery. "All this is because commercial society is based upon production for profit. If society were based upon production for service, betrayal and treachery would cease to be. But that is another story," a story that a reformer like Ross cannot tell (12). The review ends on a pessimistic note: "'Graft' is the modern slang for what was once the most terrible of sins, namely, treachery and betrayal" (35). Not murder, not rape, but "treachery and betrayal" are the greatest sins, and the Machine Age—and now *machine* includes political machinery—is defined by this most horrible of sins.

In a long letter to the Central Labor Council of Alameda County, California, written in August 1905, London continued this train of thought: "All machinations of the men-of-graft-and-grab-and-the-dollar are futile. Strength lies in comradeship and brotherhood, not in a throat-cutting struggle where every man's hand is against every man." He was writing to praise "the workmen of Alameda County" for "sending a share of their hard-earned wages three thousand miles across the continent to help the need of a lot of striking laundry girls in Troy," New York. These are the girls whose case was reported in a newspaper article that London clipped and included in his file on the "Persistence of the Established." We might recall that in 1899 London had disavowed the Brotherhood of Man. "Socialism is not an ideal system, devised by man for the happiness of all life," he wrote to Johns. "It is devised for the happiness of certain kindred races. It is devised so as to give more strength to these certain kindred favored races so that they may survive and inherit the earth to the extinction of the lesser, weaker races. The very men who advocate socialism, may tell you of the brotherhood of all men, and I know they are sincere; but that does not alter the law—they are simply instruments, working blindly for the betterment of these certain kindred races, and working detriment to the inferior races they would call brothers."[75]

Earlier he had written, "Yes; the time for Utopias and dreamers is past. Co-operative colonies etc., are at the best impossible," giving the background for what he means by "ideal."[76] That was back in 1899, and once again we can see how the election of 1904 changed either his thinking or the way he presented himself publicly. At the very least he now had concrete, empirical evidence of the selflessness of the working class and trade unions. This epistolary document also represents not only a continuation of his socialist thinking from the early winter of 1905, and a presentiment of his speaking tour and engagement with the American public in the winter of 1905–1906, but also an incorporation of the idea of spirit from his fiction early in the year, including *White Fang*. In his letter to the Alameda Labor Council, he wrote, "I am with you in the brotherhood of the spirit, as all you boys, in a similar brotherhood of the spirit, are with our laundry girls in Troy, New York." Spirit, then, is anticapitalist. We remember that the women workers had said that their church had told them to end their strike and to obey their "masters." London scoffs at the religion of capitalism and promotes a different spiritual higher power. "And not only does brotherhood give organized labor more fighting strength, but it gives it, as well, the strength of righteousness. The holiest reason that men can find for drawing together into any kind of an organization is *brotherhood*."[77] It's as if Saint Paul had written an epistle to striking Greek or Roman workers.

The letter ends, of course, with his signature, but even this is a departure from previous practice. He signs the letter, not "yours for the revolution," as was typical for him, but rather "yours in the brotherhood of man," echoing the voice of the narrator of *The Iron Heel*. His thinking about the coming brotherhood, the "ideal," had changed. Instead of never happening, it would definitely and ultimately take place in the future. It may be the far-off future, but nonetheless it would happen. I think this new element—the spirit of altruism that defines the working class—signals a sincere reappraisal of his earlier take on the Brotherhood of Man. Spirit represents a higher law than politics, a worthy competitor to biology.

What remained constant, however, was London's loathing of capitalism and capitalists. To return to "All Gold Canyon," Bill's murder of his attacker may be justified as self-defense, but his defacement of the landscape and the treachery of his attacker are not. When we watch Bill the miner and his nameless attacker struggle in the pit, we can see Bill and his attacker as capitalists who pollute the cooperative commonwealth. The canyon is, on the face of it, a place of great beauty, but it is more than that. It is "somnolent with the easement and content of prosperity, undisturbed by rumors of far wars" (1018). That word *prosperity*, seemingly so out of place—how can a natural landscape be prosperous?—is our clue to its connection to the urban jungle, but in contrast. The canyon can only be prosperous when its riches (the gold) are left undisturbed. The canyon embodies the successful cooperative commonwealth. If the jungle is a city, then the canyon can be that place where humans have achieved both economic and social balance, a place like the cabin in "The Unexpected," before the murder occurs. Edith and Hans are to Bill as Michael Dennin is to the nameless attacker. Thus, when Bill takes the gold, he robs the canyon of its prosperity, its peace. The gold gone, the jungle may overgrow the eternal scarring caused by Bill, hiding the ravaging he effected, but nothing can replace the gold.

A final note on "All Gold Canyon." The presence, departure, and return of "the spirit of the place" (1017) suggest an absorptive tale, and indeed Bill is an absorptive figure, so focused as he is on finding gold. Bill, however, is a false author figure. When he is absent, the spirit—a "wraith"—resides in the place. When he comes, the spirit disappears. The ghostly imagination won't have anything to do with him or his kind. Need it be said? London did not write for money alone. The most Bill can imagine in the way of art is a degraded hymn (perhaps of London's own composition) that insists we look "untoe them sweet hills of grace" and "fling yo' sin-pack on d' groun'" (1019). The irony is clear. By dismissing (throwing his "sin-pack") the capitalist sin of raping the landscape, "the sweet hills of grace," he is able to get rich. The inverted V of his mining symbolizes the upside-down nature of his creative effort. Only Bill could call such a beautiful place "All Gold Canyon," an appellation that misses its natural beauty and claims as its essence the hidden, human-valued treasure.

THE GREEN ABYSS

Bill, Edith, Hans, and even Tom Keating (who betrays "the right and the truth" in order to save the union, as London says in his review of *The Walking Delegate*) all are elastic enough to survive the unexpected event, the surprising turn that not only tests one's fitness to survive in the (urban) jungle but also marks the narrative's downhill movement to climax.[78] In the next and final story before *White Fang*, "Planchette," we are still in the Southland and in a natural environment that, like the canyon, has the potential to be a self-sustaining cooperative commonwealth. Much of the beginning of the story—apart from the mystery of Chris's inability to marry Lute—depends on London's rendering of the beauty of Sonoma Valley. "Have you ever heard of the secret pasture?" asks Lute, after another of London's sustained word-pictures exalts the countryside, and we think of the hidden canyon that Bill destroys. Just before Chris falls to his death, London again ceases the action to describe the natural beauty of the landscape: "It was an abyss of green beauty and shady depths, pierced by vagrant shafts of the sun and mottled here and there by the sun's broader blazes. The sound of rushing water ascended on the windless air, and there was a hum of mountain bees" (1069). It is gorgeous. But, like Alfred Hitchcock, London had discovered (first in "All Gold Canyon") how the terrible and tragic can come in the daylight. That word *abyss* should trigger our readerly anxiety, for nothing good happens in an abyss in London's work, even if it is green.

Sonoma Valley is another All Gold Canyon, and the unexpected happens just at the moment the narrator tells us to look at the beauty on the surface and not the evil beneath it. But now the question is not about whether the characters can adapt to a change in circumstances, but rather what the underlying cause of that change might be. London has moved out of the world of evolution into the world of psychology. Right away we are taken into the psychological realm. Chris Dunbar has a secret that he can't share with Lute Story, but it is so momentous that it prevents him from marrying her. While we are contemplating what such a secret might be, Chris's horse mysteriously goes mad, trying to kill him in an act of betrayal (a thematic residue from London's previous three pieces of writing), and only after great effort do both he and Lute regain control of the horse. The next day, Chris's horse commits suicide, trying to take Chris with him. These events are left unexplained—as is Chris's secret—when the story takes another turn, this time to a scene of writing. Gathered about a planchette, guided by Mrs. Grantly (a spiritualist), the group watches Chris perform some automatic writing, which ties together the three seemingly disparate plot lines: Chris's secret, the horse's murderous behavior, and the writing of the planchette. The ghosts of Lute's father and mother seize control of the planchette, and their messages reveal an ethereal marital spat: the father wants to kill Chris because of his secret and the mother wants Lute to love Chris no matter what. The father wins and takes control of yet another horse who manages to commit suicide and kill Chris in one grand jump into a rocky, green abyss. Lute is left alone on the trail at the end of the story, paralyzed by the death of her love.[79]

The story seems at first another *Black Cat* story, one of London's favorite genres. It is the most obvious genre to get him and us close to the ghostliness of his imagination without revealing that this is exactly what he is doing; he wants to protect the deeper, more personal questions about the nature of his imagination. But there is something more at work here. The rhetoric used by Lute and Chris in discussing the horses' betrayal—"obsession," "healthy-minded," "normal"—and the scene of automatic writing suggest that London was newly exploring psychological literature and the ways it may inform his creation of characters and, more importantly, how he may come to understand his own psychological workings as an author in a new way. As Chris tells Lute, "We are playing with the subjective forces of our own being, with phenomena which science has not yet explained, that is all. Psychology is so young a science. *The subconscious has just been discovered*, one might say. It is all mystery as yet; the laws of it are yet to be formulated."[80] This is in answer to Lute's assertion, after their second scene with the planchette, that her father's "ghostly hands" will kill him. Through (automatic) writing we learn of his murderous intent. We are used to the self-reflexivity of London's writing about writing, but now it occurs on a deeper level.

At the suggestion that something possessed Dolly the horse to try to kill Dunbar, "they laughed together at the idea, for both were twentieth-century products, healthy-minded and normal, with souls that delighted in the butterfly-chase of ideals but that halted before the brink where superstition begins" (1047). They laugh again, and Chris says, elaborating on the word *obsession*, "an evil spirit. . . . But what evil have I done that I should be so punished?" (1047). This, of course, is the obvious question that the story asks. But if we read the story as another of London's attempts to grapple with his imagination, the question becomes something like, What have I done to deserve this continual torture meted out by my unconscious life? Why can't I not write? What invisible force directs me to this occupation? Am I possessed? Where is my will to stop? Is writing an obsession? Every now and then London had to revisit the source and methods of his creative imagination. What agency is it that guides my pen and creates things out of thin air that I was not aware of until I wrote them? What is that spirit? London broadcasts the self-reflexivity of the story by naming three of his characters Story: Lute, Robert, and Mildred. The name Lute Story not only references writing but also music. "Planchette" is about the artist and his art.

What kills Chris Dunbar is an undisclosed, and therefore psychoanalytically untreated guilty conscience. A different author would make its revelation the climax of the story. But London's narrative makes the actual act irrelevant. By not naming the actual cause of guilt, our focus is on the guilt itself. It is enough to know that Dunbar is guilty and has not expatiated his guilt. Or, if we read this in psychoanalytic terms, as the story suggests we do, the guilt Dunbar feels is a pathogenic secret, a secret that causes illness and even death. Henri Ellenberger in his *Discovery of the Unconscious* (a titled he could have taken from London) traces the practice of confession of a pathogenic secret from the Catholic Church to hypnosis. "There came a time when the knowledge of the pathogenic secret and its treatment fell into the hands of laymen," Ellenberger writes. "When this happened is not known, but it may have been among the early magnetists."[81] We are right back to the scene of automatic writing in "Planchette." Mrs. Grantley is, says Dunbar, "a weird little thing. . . . I'll wager she doesn't weigh ninety pounds, and most of that's magnetism" (1051). It's such an odd comment, that almost off-the-cuff remark about magnetism; after all, how can a person be composed of magnetism? The modern-day reader will dismiss it as an anachronism, but, placed in its proper context, the remark makes sense as an attribution of someone implicated in the history of psychoanalysis. Mrs. Grantley's task, after all, is to bring out the secret and help Dunbar—and the Storys—work through his psychic difficulty. The ultimate goal, of course, is to achieve a healthy, sexual relationship between Chris and Lute.

Not only is this story a mate to "All Gold Canyon" (and, more indirectly, with the review of *The Walking Delegate* and "The Unexpected" and "The Sun-Dog Trail") but it is also a precursor to two major works of fiction that London wrote in the next decade: *The Valley of the Moon* and *Little Lady of the Big House*. The former ends with the two main characters, Billy and Saxon, communing with nature and the "spirit of the place" and facing the dilemma of either living poorly in the country but maintaining their place's natural beauty or mining the property and so become wealthy. *The Little Lady of the Big House* ends not with the male character dying but rather with the "little lady" committing suicide rather than living with a man who, like Billy Roberts, has chosen to live by the lights of the commercial spirit. With hindsight, we are tempted to be glad to watch with Lute Story as Dunbar plunges to his death—not because he deserved to die, as her father thinks, but because his death has saved her from a life in the prison of a Dick Forrest–like Big House.

DISCOVERING THE UNCONSCIOUS

The ghost story and the history of psychoanalysis may seem far apart, but London's fictional writings show how close they are. We often characterize London as a Darwinian or as a social Darwinist, as if Darwin's ideas formed the only influential intellectual environment at the turn of the century. But London can be placed just as easily within the development of international psychology—besides, can we forget how much of a Darwinist Freud was?—and the evolution of his conception of the human psyche is informed by the evolution of psychologic thought in America.

London owned copies of Alfred Binet's *The Psychic Life of Micro-organisms* and *On the Double Consciousness*. Both were issued in translation as pamphlets in Paul Carus's Religion of Science Library series.[82] Although the former was published in 1903, indicating London's earliest interest in psychological research, the latter is of greater interest. Published in 1905, the same year he wrote "Planchette," it is very likely that this pamphlet inspired him to present Chris Dunbar's take on psychology—that there are two levels of the psyche, conscious and subconscious—and hence marks the beginning of London's investigations into the new science, which culminated in his reading of Freud's essays, Carl Jung's *Psychology of the Unconscious*, and the work of other authors like Otto Rank.

On Double Consciousness proceeds by a series of, basically, three steps in orderly fashion in harmony with Pierre Janet's dissociative psychology, which held that hysteria was "a permanent state of dual personality," a concept that was "not only the culmination of the first dynamic psychiatry, but . . . also the starting point of the new systems of dynamic psychiatry, notably those of Janet, Breuer, Freud, and Jung."[83] This duality grew out of "the study and practice of magnetism and hypnotism," which first developed the dipsychistic model of the mind. This doubling of the ego (understood in its pre-Freudian sense as simply the controlling element of the mind), for many psychologists, explained the existence of artistic inspiration and dreams as well as "mysticism and mediumistic manifestations."[84] Janet, Jung, and Freud all began from dipsychism, though the latter two developed more complicated, polypsychistic systems of the mind. If London had encountered these ideas—they are not present in Binet, and, apart from their apparent apparition in "Planchette," there is no evidence that I have found that he did so—he could easily define his art as something akin psychologically to his mother's occupation, but historically more advanced; that is, writing fiction may be akin to a medium's storytelling, but it is more advanced along psychology's historical continuum.

Binet's first step in *On Double Consciousness* is a brief history of "experimental psychology in France," which is, as Binet says, scattered at best, given the lack of international communication. But in France the focus is on "psychology affected by disease" (9). The principal question was whether an unconscious phenomenon "was a purely physiological phenomenon" or whether it emanated from within (3). The latter was the position taken by Théodule-Armand Ribot, who, according to Binet, though he rejected metaphysics, nevertheless "a certain metaphysical character attaches to [his] ideas" (3). Binet, for his part, stated that "we know *absolutely nothing* regarding the nature of unconscious phenomena," and this is the position Chris Dunbar takes as well. Hoping for a scientific, empirical understanding of unseen forces at work in conjunction with or emanating from the mind, Dunbar (and Binet) can only hope for further experimental evidence.

The next step is to assert and demonstrate the existence of a double personality, or double ego, or double consciousness; the terms for describing the psyche were very fluid at this time. As Binet says, "In truth, is not the idea extraordinary, that in hysterical individuals there should exist two distinct personalities, two egos united in the same person" (10–11). He discusses two methodologies for demonstrating the existence of the divided self: experiments done with those who suffer from partial hysterical paralysis who can nonetheless perform physical acts with the afflicted bodily part that are suggested to him or her by a doctor. Thus, if one part of the mind is controlling the paralysis, there is another part overriding the paralysis. The other methodology is automatic writing with a planchette (also performed by hysterical patients), and now London really became attuned to Binet's pamphlet. Binet cites William James's experiments with "normal individuals" whose results, says Binet, "closely resemble those obtained by myself with hysterical individuals." Thus the boundary between "normal" and "abnormal" is broken down; as Binet later stresses, "of course, the normal type has only an ideal existence" (20, 76). Thus people like Dunbar and the Storys can write messages transmitted to paper by a hidden or second consciousness. As Binet writes, experiments in America "consist in asking a person to place his hand upon a planchette that can serve for the purposes of writing and to remain immovable without thinking of anything. When the subject is nervous it will sometimes happen that the planchette becomes agitated and begins to write thoughts entirely foreign to the subject; the latter remains motionless and has no consciousness of anything" (26). We remember that after each session with the planchette, Dunbar is sleepy, his act almost an act of sleep writing, as if a dream were in control of his actions. We can see how London is creating analogies between spiritualism, dreamwork, and the creative imagination, except that he is most interested in pinning down the identity and location of that imagination. Is it outside himself, like a ghost (dog), or is it inside himself, like a possession? Or can the ghost live inside himself? Is it some sort of combination of the two? Much of London's absorptive fiction from this point on is written to answer these questions.

The third and final step for Binet is to test his theory of the double consciousness on nonhysterical patients. The tests are partially successful. He is able to determine that the mind can split its attention between two simultaneous motor skills, but he cannot conclude that each is "accompanied by [different] states of consciousness" (84). On the other hand, he has determined that "the rudiment of those states of double consciousness which we have studied first in the hysterical, may with a little attention be found in normal subjects" (83). In fact, he reveals that his experiments duplicate the successes of experimenting with automatic writing with "normal subjects. . . . Automatic writing is the best known of these facts of double consciousness" (83). That is, it provides the best evidence of a double consciousness, and this would be enough for London. The story's genre dictates that the second, hidden consciousness must be a ghost, but it is clear that London's ghost is both inside and outside Dunbar. He is inside, helping him write warning messages to himself (you will die, or "die," if you don't divulge your secret), and outside, pushing him off the cliff. Lute "sees" her father push him, but she does not "see" him help Dunbar write.

And yet the ghosts in this story are real. They kill. The mistake, London tells us, comes not from rejecting superstition, but in not believing in the unseen. Lute and Chris are correct in saying that there are no such things as witches, evil spirits, and the like. But they underestimate the unseen. The ghosts that medievalists believed in are actually inside us, residing right beside the imagination, which acts in league with it. Unadmitted crimes, the guilty conscience, haunt us. Lute doesn't see the ghost of her father kill Dunbar. Her imagination sees it, prepared as it is by her memory of her father's life. She is the author figure whose imagination, because it is ghostlike, is able to work in tandem with ghosts. That is, the imagination is becoming for London something that resides in the psychological world. He isn't sure what to call it, but in his effort to locate and define it, he is sure it is something that psychology can help him understand. "Planchette" represents London's turn from Poe to Freud.

As a story, "Planchette" marks a transition between the nineteenth-century terrible and tragic (we can't forget Poe's interest in mesmerism) and the twentieth-century beginnings of dynamic psychotherapy. Twice we hear in the story the voice of either Lute or Chris explaining to each other and to us that they are citizens of the twentieth century. They don't believe in medievalism, in superstition, in ghosts. The fact that they have to deny medievalism and superstition shows how close they are to nineteenth-century conceptions of the unseen. At the same time, their employment of a new psychological vocabulary shows how much they reside in the twentieth century.

For example, after the first incident with a horse, Lute and Chris agree that the horse's attack was "subjective," perhaps an "obsession," which, at this point in the history of psychology, could mean either "a compulsive interest" or "tormenting of a person from without by an evil spirit."[85] As Ellenberger writes, Catholics used *obsession* to mean a kind of possession called "lucid possession," as opposed to somnambulant possession wherein the subject is unaware of being possessed. An obsessed person, on the other hand, "remains constantly aware of his self, but feels 'a spirit within his own spirit,' struggles against it, but cannot prevent it from speaking at times." The possessing spirit is a kind of parasite that lives "in the soul." *Obsession*, writes Ellenberger, is "a word that has been adopted by psychiatry, though with another meaning."[86]

The story's deployment of twentieth-century psychological vocabulary, its self-reflexivity, and the centrality of the scenes with the planchette invite comparisons with Freud's "Note on the Mystic Writing Pad," written twenty years later. Both the mystic writing pad and the planchette are alternative technological means to write, and both are intimately connected to memory and the structure of the psyche. Both posit, to use Jacques Derrida's phrase, "a scene of writing."[87] That is, writing for both Freud and London is not simply an aid to memory but a gateway to understanding the relationship among various components of the perception-consciousness system. When, for example, Uncle Robert's writing is completed, the group decides that the message came from either "the subconscious mind" or his memory of some New Thought group, theosophists, or Christian Scientists. Dunbar opts for a combination of the two on the assumption that the subconscious mind contains short-term memories. Mrs. Grantly tells us that "a day or a year is all the same in the subconscious mind. . . . The subconscious mind never forgets" (1056). This is pure dipsychism. But what is most interesting about Grantly is that she does not favor one explanation over another. "I am not saying that this is due to the subconscious mind. I refuse to state to what I think it is due" (1056). You might think that the spiritualist would advocate for the role of the undead in sending these messages, but, like a good empiricist, she simply gathers information and evidence and tests various theories.

She does employ the rhetoric of spiritualism, encapsulated by the word *influences*. There are other competing rhetorics to describe what we use the word *imagination* as shorthand for, or, at the very least, whatever it is that moves the planchette. There is the rhetoric of New Thought, a constellation of ideas that influenced the writing of *The Star Rover*. There is the rhetoric of psychology, a "science" opposed in London's universe to the metaphysics of Christian Science and theosophy. There is the rhetoric of spiritualism, represented by Mrs. Grantly. And there is the religious or pseudo-religious rhetoric, with an emphasis on the word *soul*, used by Lute.

In the second paragraph, Lute—because for four years she has been wondering why Chris will not marry her—is characterized by a "determination that is reached through a long period of pleading. . . . In her case it had been pleading, not of speech, but of personality. Her lips had been ever mute, but her face and eyes, and the very attitude of her soul, had been for a long time eloquent with questioning" (1035). Chris's interactions with all people is marked by an "all-pervading caress. . . . It was largely unconscious on the man's part. He was only dimly aware of it. It was a part of him, the breath of his soul as it were, involuntary and unpremeditated" (1036). In fact, Lute describes herself at one point as "a prophet"; she characterizes Mr. Barton as a man who worships "fetishes and idols" (1062). Dunbar makes fun of her in biblical terms, as if borrowing her own source of rhetoric will be a more convincing way of showing her the fallacy of her beliefs (see 1062). Finally, after Lute describes Chris's warm-hearted nature, and he laughs about it shyly, she says, "When you are laughing at all that I have said, you, the feel of you, your soul,—call it what you will, it is you,—is calling for all the love that is in me" (1053). Here she wavers between the religious rhetoric that comes naturally to her and the psychoanalytic rhetoric employed by Dunbar, that is, "the feel of you," or, rather, the emotional life that gives one a sense of identity. The hint here is that the sense of "feel"— the ability to sense the emotional content of a person, of a situation, even of a landscape (which has a spirit)—is somehow akin to the imagination and may be located in the same region of the psyche, that is, somewhere in the subconscious.

Lute is, then, in the final analysis a twentieth-century woman. She senses that her religious rhetoric is insufficient to describe not only the empiricism of the planchette but also the possession of the three horses and the "sight" of the ghost killing Dunbar. None of the rhetorics except that of spiritualism holds sufficient power to explain these events. But we've seen how spiritualism and magnetism lead to psychoanalysis. As Ellenberger sums it up in *The Discovery of the Unconscious*, "No branch of knowledge has undergone so many metamorphoses as dynamic psychiatry: from primitive healing to magnetism, magnetism to hypnotism, hypnotism to psychoanalysis and the newer dynamic schools" (v). London is telling us that the new science's explanatory power is borrowing from spiritualism to explain the human psyche but that psychology will eventually take its place. The subconscious, when it is explained, will account for automatic writing and "possession." "I don't know all the mysteries of mind," says Dunbar, "but I believe such phenomena will all yield to scientific explanation in the not distant future." In the meantime, twentieth-century denizens like Lute will project their fears upon the psychic landscape and call them ghosts. As the narrator tells us, when she "placed her hand on the board she was conscious of a vague and nameless fear at this toying with the supernatural. . . . She could not shake off the instinctive fear that arose in her—man's inheritance from the wild and howling ages when his hairy, apelike prototype was afraid of the dark and personified the elements into things of fear" (1060). If fear of the unknown—called "the supernatural"—could be replaced by anthropological science's history of man, then ghosts could be replaced by the workings of the unconscious. As much as Lute loved Chris, if he could not marry her then she wished him dead, even if her mother counseled her against it. In London's work, it is typical that the wrath of the father is more powerful than the love of the mother.

London finished the story on 2 July, having begun *White Fang* while he was writing "Planchette." In early June, London wrote to Cloudesley Johns, who had asked him if he had started *White Fang*. No, said London, "am writing some short stories in order to get hold of some immediate cash," clearly an exaggeration since after "All Gold Canyon" (which he had just completed) he didn't write another short story except "Planchette" until late February 1906.[88] Charmian finished typing it on 1 July, and he mailed it to his first choice, *Collier's Weekly*, the next day. Collier rejected it, as did the next six outlets. One of those was McClure, who was so busy insisting that he needed a story from London that he was forgetting that he was rejecting nearly everything London sent him.

He couldn't get "Planchette" published because the mystery of Chris's unwillingness to marry Lute is never explained. "In this mystical tragedy sort of thing, it seems to me you ought to give the reader some clue to get prepared for it, and that's why I feel that what you reach here is both unexpected and insufficient," said McClure, and he certainly has a point.[89] To a modern reader who finds Chris's silence willful, McClure's opinion is reassuring. It was echoed by John Cosgrave and Gillman Hall at *Everybody's*.

They were desperate for something from London, but "we are very much disappointed that this manuscript of yours is a supernatural story. We shy at that type generally and we would much rather have something more characteristic of Jack London," said Hall. By "characteristic" he meant Klondike. But there were faults on the story's own terms, and Hall was principally concerned with how "Planchette" violated the norms of the genre. A ghost story should be mysterious, but "more elusive" than how London has presented events. "You have made your facts too specific," Hall wrote. Objecting to the Hitchcockian horror, Hall instructs London that the mystery should not have "the color of daylight." At the same time that "the accidents to Chris [are] too bare-faced and the last one almost without explanation," "the cause of the accidents . . . should have been a little more related to actual realism."

The story, that is, was too real when it should not have been, too obscure when it should have been real.

The second fault is that "the planchette game" takes the story out of "the supernatural realm into a line of some fakiness"; the general public at least thinks so and thus "impair[s] the serious purpose" of the story. The third fault is with Chris and Lute's relationship; why can't they marry? It's a question of plotting: "Some parts of the story are not worked out,— . . . you start a train of thought which in all rights the reader should know the ending of."[90] George Sterling, on the other hand, found the mystery compelling: "I congratulate you on not telling why Chris couldn't marry her; but it will make the average reader sore."[91] Perhaps it was to McClure's and *Everybody's* credit that they so ably foretold the average reader's likes and dislikes. London knew what they meant and what they wanted. His next story to McClure was "The Unexpected" and to Cosgrave, "Brown Wolf."

Its length argued against itself, too. At 16,147 words, "Planchette" is three thousand words longer than *The Game*. Finally, Bailey Millard, the editor who succeeded John Brisben Walker at *Cosmopolitan*, accepted it in early March 1906 as part of the financial package they put together for London's trip on the *Snark*; Millard was doing everything he could to make it appear London was sailing around the world as the correspondent for *Cosmopolitan*, and giving London ten cents a word for such a long story was part of the strategy.[92] They published it in two parts, June and July 1906. Knowing beforehand that Brett would not bring it out as a heavily illustrated novella— after the hassles involved with *The Game*, London had learned his lesson—

London did not bother to even bring the matter up with his book publisher except to tell him that he had devised a new collection of short stories to be called *Moon-Face, and Other Stories*. He hoped it would meet with Brett's approval as his new fall season book; Brett agreed, and it appeared in September 1906 and included "All Gold Canyon" as the spiritual companion to "Planchette."[93] *White Fang* appeared the very next month.

THE SPIRIT OF THE PLACE

"Planchette" illustrates the slow and imprecise movements in America from the Machine Age to the Psychoanalytic Age. It works, too, within London's career, as a transition from his pre-1905 stories to the stories of the future, beginning with *White Fang*. We can trace this transition linguistically. Neither accidentally nor incidentally, the phrase "the spirit of the place" first appears, explicitly, in "All Gold Canyon" and then implicitly in "Planchette." Lute's parents are the spirits of that place, Mrs. Grantly matches to the deer, and the two couples play the role of Bill the miner. But because the two couples come, to use London's terms, in the spirit of service and not capital they do not scare off the spirit. Bill as we remember is a false author figure because the spirit cannot abide in the same place as he. We can see how London's focus shifts slightly between "All Gold Canyon" and "Planchette." The two capitalists of the former become a fat "capitalist" sitting at the table. His name is Mr. Barton, and he is involved in "water-power-long-distance-electricity-transmitter, or something like that" (1052). Barton, with his water plans, sits on the sidelines as the two couples engage with the spirit of the place. Even when the principal action involves artistic activity, capitalism is always in the background.

Further, there is an interesting confluence of fiction and nonfiction in this character. A couple of months previous, London had been asked, as the socialist candidate for mayor of Oakland, what his position on ownership of the water supply was. His response was unequivocal: "The position of the Socialist Party then is to let the capitalist class and capitalist parties settle this bond question to suit themselves. It is none of the business of the working class. Municipal ownership under capitalism is not a part of the socialist programme. . . . In the language of Marx and Engels, 'We disdain to conceal our views and aims and boldly declare that our ends can be attained only by the complete overthrow of all existing economic conditions.'"[94] The quotation comes from London's favorite political text, *The*

Communist Manifesto. Barton's time would come though, thought London, when the specter of socialism would throw him off a cliff.

Barton also reminds us of the stories that have come before and of the relationship between a capitalist such as himself (and Bill, and all the others) and the imagination. There is none. As Chris says, Mr. Barton "doesn't look as though he could give an ox points on imagination" (1052). Thus, Bill, and Barton, and those who work for the commercial spirit are either antiauthors (Barton) or false authors (Bill). Either they have no imagination or operate according to the dictates of fancy. But the narrative vacuum that Barton leaves is filled by the spiritualist and the activity she leads that bridges the gap between the living and the dead (London "knows" there is such a gap because his imagination seems to flit back and forth between them) and serves as a representation of the act of writing. In other words, London is once again more focused on imaging his inner life. We anticipate the same sort of connection in *White Fang* between spirit and emotion, social critique and the imagination, and the primitive and the unconscious.

We are not disappointed. White Fang feels more than he thinks, and his connection to the unseen, both inside and out of his interior life, is strong. The unconscious is linked to the primitive stages of mankind because just as the unconscious determines the behavior of an individual so, too, does the primitive determine the behavior of the race, in London's terms. This isn't Haeckel's theory of recapitulation, but it is kin to it. The biologic stages of growth of an individual may not replicate the stages of humankind as a whole—Haeckel's recapitulation theory had been discredited, and London shows no evidence of believing in it—but London did seem to think that stages of the psychologic maturation of an individual matched to various races. The white race, of course, was the most adult of them all; African Americans, Native Americans, South Sea islanders, and others were like children. White Fang instinctively knows this. As London's narrator says, "To be sure, White Fang only felt these things. He was not conscious of them. Yet it is upon feeling, more often than thinking, that animals act; and every act White Fang now performed was based upon the feeling that the white men were the superior gods." What does he mean by "superior"?

> It was at Fort Yukon that White Fang saw his first white men. As compared with the Indians he had known, they were to him another race of beings, a race of superior gods. . . . It was a feeling, nothing more,

and yet none the less potent. . . . They possessed greater mastery over matter than the gods he had known, most powerful among which was Gray Beaver. And yet Gray Beaver was as a child-god among these white-skinned ones.[95]

This passage doesn't signal a change in London's thinking about Native Americans. They could act in a superior moral way to whites and still be childlike and less "powerful" than whites. The white "race" was more "powerful" because they were creators of the Machine Age, which had no room for teepee-living, nomadic, hunter-gathers of the North. The power lay not in inherent superiority of white skin but in the tools and buildings "white gods" had created. In an ironic reversal that London was aware of, the interior life of Native Americans was as adult as was the whites. Biology could not explain all things as he slowly educated himself in modern psychology. The primitive inhabited all races, and people like Sitka Charley and Gray Beaver had the complicated inner lives that separated them as much as possible from the primitive.

But the novel's principal focus is not so much on the unconscious as it is on facets of evolutionary theory and their connection to social critique. (He would shift the focus from evolution to psychology in his next novel, *Before Adam*.) In fact, the novel is London's first attempt to advocate for prison reform. That is the underlying motif. But let's backtrack and start at the beginning. In the famous first lines of *White Fang*, we learn that "the land itself was a desolation, lifeless, without movement, so lone and cold that the spirit of it was not even that of sadness." First we note that unlike the landscapes of "All Gold Canyon" and "Planchette," this one, despite its spirit, is a "lifeless" wasteland. As if we needed it, here is another clue of the ghostliness of what London means by spirit. Spirit is not the life force, the élan vital, in the Klondike wintery wasteland. It is entropy.

Compare it to how a contemporary, Stewart Edward White, conceives the silence. In *The Silent Places*, a novel London read as he prepared to write *White Fang*, the silence is indicative of "the old, inimical Presence," "the unknown Presence watching these men."[96] The spirit of the place in White's work, like London's, may do harm, it may not; it is entirely indifferent. It is not a religious god, but, unlike London's, it is a god nonetheless. In fact, at one point he describes it as "aloof, unheeding, buddhistic, brooding in nirvanic calm" (109). At first, the only ghosts in White's northern universe are the First Peoples who are such only because they move so quietly. However, at one point he does mention "the White Silence," and when winter comes he describes the main characters as ghosts traveling through the "winterland" and that now "it was the land of ghosts" (195). But this attribution is motivated only by the deaths of characters, not because of the deeper bond between landscape and the imagination and the act of writing that London constructs. White also differs from London in that his plot affirms the strength and necessity of capitalism. The plot of *The Silent Places* is the pursuit of two white men to capture a Native American who has reneged on a debt; to capture and punish him is to solidify capital's dominance in the Northland. And, in comparing White's racial understanding with London's, we hear London scoff at White's uncomplicated celebration of the Anglo-Saxon and the reduction of the First Peoples (and other minorities) to simple "savages." The final line of the novel, spoken by a young Anglo-Saxon woman after a main character sings a song about "good darkies," is a biblical quotation: "the greatness of my people," she says, and the novel becomes just another racist tract sanctioned by the misappropriation of Christianity (304).

Suddenly we are faced with the possibility that London is writing against someone who was influenced by London's early Klondike stories. Or, more simply, we see London reading himself through the lens of White's novel, a rather odd moment of self-reflection in the history of American literature. Sometimes London used his sources as traction to go in an opposite direction, as if competing with his fellow authors—and White was a buttoned-up, bourgeois writer like Richard Harding Davis—to convey the truth of the North. His sources, by their failed attempt to grasp the totality of London's work, proved to him that his work was genuine: effectively communicating the emotions of his stories, their originality, and their sincerity.

London's spirit of the place is also the Freudian death drive. As psychoanalysts Jean Laplanche and J.-B. Pontillis have written, "Freud sees the mark of the 'daemonic' in this phenomena—the mark, in other words, of an irrepressible force which is independent of the pleasure principle and apt to enter into opposition to it." "In fact what Freud was explicitly seeking to express by the term 'death instinct' was the most fundamental aspect of instinctual life: the return to an earlier state and, in the last reckoning, the return to the absolute repose of the inorganic."[97] It is linked to aggression, both as it is directed externally and internally. So the death instinct may be self-destruction, though it doesn't have to be. While we read *White Fang*, we should be aware of how London was managing these various concepts. Following "Planchette," London's interest in the unconscious was increasing, and he was beginning to place things in it that he had formerly thought were exterior to the human psyche. In this way the spirit and the death drive were becoming linked in his mind.

The concept of the death instinct or death drive isn't something London was familiar with; Freud didn't discuss it until *Beyond the Pleasure Principle* (1920). But the death drive may be the closest modern-day concept that we have to explicate by analogy what London was reaching for when he was calling the spirit of the place—of the Northland—the Wild or eternity. The death-dealing Buck knew it. He heard the call of the wild, and what he heard and what defines the affective nature of the landscape in *White Fang* is the same thing and acts as the bridge between the two works; it helps make *White Fang* less a "sequel" and more of a "companion," as London called it.[98] That London labels the three parts of the novel with some variation of *wild*—"The Wild," "Born of the Wild," and "The Gods of the Wild"—testifies to the centrality—or eternity—of the word.

The phrase *white fang* contains both the predominant descriptor of the landscape and a metonymic descriptor of the Wild: a ghostly fang, symbol of aggression and a death-dealing dog. It is another name for the spirit of the place. Instead of a novel about a dog who doesn't read, *White Fang* is about wolves who lead us to the realm of the instincts, of the unconscious. In the end, White Fang falls asleep, dreaming. London's next novel—*Before Adam*—is about what happens when you enter the realm of the unconscious and what you find there.

In case one might think I am exaggerating the importance of the spiritual realm in the novel, consider London's 1914 letter to the editor of the *Bookman*, who had just published a negative review of *The Valley of the Moon*, citing London's promotion of the animal and the primitive nature of humankind. The reviewer has a very limited view of "what he calls the Jack London School—a school which is lacking in spirituality," London wrote. "Ask him if he has ever read *White Fang*, and if he finds a deplorable lack of spirituality in that book."[99] So, to return: There are two manifestations of spirit at the beginning of *White Fang*. The first is the spirit of the place, "a laughter cold as the frost and partaking of the grimness of infallibility. It was the masterful and incommunicable wisdom of eternity laughing at the futility of the life and the effort of life. It was the Wild, the savage, frozen-hearted Northland Wild" (3). But spirit also takes the shape of ghosts in the landscape. These ghosts are dogs; they are "rimed with frost" and so as white as ghosts (3). There are also men, pulling a sled with a body in a casket. They too are covered in frost: "This gave them the seeming of ghostly masques, undertakers in a spectral world at the funeral of some ghost." The spirit of ghostland may laugh at their effort, but the ghost-dogs are pulling a ghost-sled guided by two ghost-men who are caring for a third ghost. "But under it all they were men," says the third-person narrator, and so we have the classic battle within London's psyche between the imagination conceived as life-giving and the imagination conceived as death-dealing. Not just the story of White Fang and his mother, but all stories come out of this ghostland.

They hear "a faint far cry. . . . It might have been a lost soul wailing" (6). It is of course the song of the wild, inspired by the call of the wild, sung by White Fang's mother. We have picked up where *Call of the Wild* left off. Buck may have been male, and White Fang's mother female, but the ratio of dog to wolf seems the same, and certainly their totemic relationship to the imagination is the same; later White Fang himself becomes Buck-like in his relation to the Wild and its call: "He could not immediately forego his wild heritage and his memories of the Wild. There were days when he crept to the edge of the forest and stood and listened to something calling him far and away" (132). White Fang's mother's affiliation with the ghostly imagination/spirit manifests itself in her physical description. Bill thinks she looks "almost cinnamon" in color, but the narrator makes sure we understand why he thinks so. Note first, in general, the emphasis on color, something London favored in his works before 1902. "The animal was certainly not cinnamon-colored. Its coat was the true wolf-coat. The dominant color was gray, and yet there was to it a faint reddish hue—a hue that was baffling, that appeared and disappeared, that was more like an illusion of the vision, now gray, distinctly gray, and again giving hints and glints of a vague redness of color not classifiable in terms of ordinary experience" (26–27).

We learn three things from the coloring of White Fang's mother. First is that Bill—is he supposed to be a younger version of Bill the miner in "All Gold Canyon"?—is both unreliable and confused, but naturally so. If White Fang were indeed cinnamon colored, then she wouldn't have been a wolf. So the narrator makes sure we know that Bill is confused. But then we learn that it is an honest mistake. White Fang's mother does look red, but it was a "baffling" color because it seemed an illusion; the red was there and then not there, like a ghost. And, like a ghost, the color is "not classifiable in terms of ordinary experience." If you had seen a ghost throw a horse and its rider off a cliff, then you would be able to classify the color. But normal human beings or, better, your typical scientific or empirically minded citizen, would not be able to tell you what color the wolf was because you need knowledge gained from extraordinary experience to be able to tell. You need to move beyond empiricism into the realm of the unconscious where the imagination and ghosts and ghost-dogs live. And now we see why he is named *white* fang. But the red that is there in his mother and then not there is the color of anger, of wrath, the Red Wrath so famously present in *The Star Rover* as that unconscious, primitive anger that motivates Darrell Standing to kill his colleague. Red is the color, then, of the primitive, which is also deep in the unconscious. We feel fear, like Bill and Henry, when we see the red-colored she-wolf rise out of the unconscious.

The story of the first three chapters is the story of two men gradually falling deeper and deeper into the unconscious; of course Henry goes all the way into death. But Bill stays alert for as long as he can until, robbed of sleep during the day, he finally keeps dozing off with the wolf pack just outside his fire. Then, "He came out of a doze that was half nightmare, to see the red-hued wolf before him." Is she real? Is he really awake? Or is this a dream image from the unconscious? Actually, it is a dream image from the unconscious that magically takes material form in his waking state, for in the ghostland the boundary between life and death, consciousness and unconsciousness is permeable. In the final scene London makes this permeability explicit: "He dreamed. It seemed to him that he was in Fort McGurry. . . . It seemed to him that the fort was besieged by wolves. They were howling at the very gates. . . . This howling now bothered him. His dream was merging into something else—he knew not what; but through it all, following him, persisted the howling. And then he awoke to find the howling real" (41). Of course this is a masterful description of what happens to us when we get so tired that we fall asleep with our last waking moment's reality infiltrating our dream state until our dream state becomes a representation of our waking reality until we actually do awake and find that our dream state was mirroring reality to such a degree that it was incorporating elements of conscious life around us. The point is the interchangeability of conscious and unconscious states. We dream and we think we are awake. We are awake and we think we are dreaming. To make this point, though, London emphasizes the primitive nature of this waking/dreaming state. We wouldn't notice the permeability unless we were under extreme duress and experiencing the fears that primitive man experienced: the fear of falling, the fear of being eaten alive by wild animals. That fear is the key to seeing how consciousness and unconsciousness can be the same. Or, rather, how the elements of the unconscious—the ghosts that reside there—can become as real as any fire that we might throw at starving wolves. That is the nature of the Wild, and thus the first section ends.

Part 2 is the love story of White Fang's mother and One Eye, the birthing of her brood, and the early life of White Fang. Now that we know White Fang's mother lives in both the conscious and the unconscious mind, what else might we learn about her and her son? Are they really both tame and wild, dog and wolf? Is there a permeability between these two states as well?

When London had written to Bamford in May 1905, he asked for information that would inform this section of the novel: "Can you find out for me the following: (1) when do wolves mate? (2) how long do they carry their young? (3) What time of the year do they bring forth their young?"[100] It seems Bamford sent him the entry for "wolf" from the *Encyclopaedia Americana*, which London typed up and then used to construct White Fang's biographical timeline; his notes detail when the wolf was conceived, born, when he "quit his mother," and how he lived for fifteen years, as well as his physical attributes, especially his coloring: "The gray wolf commonly sports reddish and blackish individuals. Maybe the mother of White Fang had a moderately red tinge; his father was the regular gray wolf. White Fang himself was gray, but with reddish tints and glints in full coat." White Fang's coloring is as London's signal to the reader that he is quite aware of the facts of the early life of wolves.

Part 2 is a simple narrative of the primitive's need for reproduction, the sex urge that is as basic as the hunger urge—the subject of the first part—though there is no hint of wolfish intercourse; White Fang seems to be immaculately conceived. Yet the presence of the unconscious, of memory, of experience makes itself known. Even a wolf can be influenced by the unconscious. "Of her own experience she had no memory of the thing happening; but in her instinct, which was the experience of all the mothers of wolves, there lurked a memory of fathers that had eaten their new-born and helpless progeny"

(68). Wolves have memory, experience, and inherited instincts. They perform conscious actions and instinctual actions that are similar to the actions humans perform from both instinct and the unconscious drives. There are significant similarities between the instinctual life of a wolf and the instinctual life of humans, but it's not the similarities as such that interest London. It's the way that he can explain the worlds of the conscious and the unconscious of humans through the examination of the simplified life of a wolf. As London says about White Fang, "The gray cub was not given to thinking—at least, to the kind of thinking customary of men. His brain worked in dim ways. Yet his conclusions were as sharp and distinct as those achieved by men. He had a method of accepting things, without questioning the why and wherefore" (81). Further, when he is out of the cave for the first time, London writes, "The cub was learning. His misty little mind had already made an unconscious classification. There were live things and things not alive" (90). The important thing for us is not what White Fang classified, but that he did this at all; and he did it using an unconscious process.

But there is more to the wolf unconscious. Beyond the process of thinking, there is the way wolves and men come to know fear and, presumably, all emotions: "Never, in his brief cave-life, had he encountered anything of which to be afraid. Yet fear was in him." How was that possible, you may ask? "It had come down to him from a remote ancestry through a thousand thousand lives. It was a heritage he had received directly from One eye and the she-wolf; but to them, in turn, it had been passed down through all the generations of wolves that had gone before" (84). Just as Darwin, Weismann, and other evolutionists had used primitive life forms to explain the natural laws that applied to humans as well, so London was using fictional animal constructs to explain the interior life of humans. His next novel, *Before Adam*, will take these comparisons and explanations even further.

If part 1 gave us the view of animal life from the point of view of humans, part 2 gives us the view of animal life from the point of view of an animal and thus a deeper understanding of evolution. One of the first things we learn about White Fang is that he "had bred true to the straight wolf-stock—in fact, he had bred true, physically, to old One Eye himself, with but a single exception, and that was that he had two eyes to his father's one" (76). To our modern intellect, this "exception" seems comic. Why would London feel the need to point out that the most striking physical characteristic of the father was not passed down to the son when we all know that his one-eyed blindness occurred during his life and was not a genetic deformity? Because London is making the point that he is not a neo-Lamarckian. We will return to this topic a little later, but for now it is important to point out how London incorporated the vast amount of reading he did in evolutionary theory into his fiction, sometimes in a very subtle way.

The principal law of evolution that White Fang learns, though, is "The aim of life was meat. Life lived on life. . . . The law was: EAT OR BE EATEN" (107). White Fang, when he thinks, thinks by classification—this object fits this pattern of activity and so belongs in this group; a rock is different from a bird because it doesn't move or peck his nose—and "out of this classification arose the law" (107). Much of what London writes about White Fang's mental processes strives to make a distinction between how wolves (and other animals) think and how humans think. So after this grand pronouncement about meat, life, and death, London's narrator says, "Had the cub thought in man-fashion, he might have epitomized life as a voracious appetite, and the world as a place wherein ranged a multitude of appetites, pursuing and being pursued, hunting and being hunted, eating and being eaten, all in blindness and confusion, with violence and disorder, a chaos of gluttony and slaughter, ruled over by chance, merciless, planless, endless" (108). This passage represents the best of London's writing, and not just in the rhythm and sound, in the choice of words and how they are used. It is a potential endorsement of evolutionary determinism and, at the same time, a potential disavowal. London has led us to believe that wolves think and do not think like humans. So, a wolf, if it could "look at things with wide vision" (and of course by now we are trained to see the connection between sight and thought, between sight and the imagination), it would see and understand the way a human does. But that doesn't mean that a human would come to the same conclusions about life, chance, and death; it just means that a wolf could draw general conclusions from empirical fact. So a wolf would come to the conclusion that life is a matter of blind chance, of eating and being eaten. And men who are wolves, like Wolf Larsen, who goes blind ("all in blindness and confusion"), would come to that conclusion as well. But presumably we nonwolves (or are you a wolf?) would come to some other conclusion, perhaps a more altruistic, socialist conclusion, for who wants a world that is governed by blind instinct and chance?

White Fang is very much about not thinking like a wolf, and the second part concludes, not with the ambivalence of the narrator's pronouncement on determinism and chance but rather on the affirmation of "easements and satisfactions." In a blatant forecast of the ending of the novel, the narrator tells us, right after the passage on determinism, that there were other "laws" besides the law of meat: "To have a full stomach, to doze lazily in the sunshine." And we will soon read, if we haven't already done so (some readers can't help but read the final lines of a story early on), the final line of the novel: "[H]e lay with half-shut, patient eyes, drowsing in the sun" (327). Here we see the law to live life to its fullest: "life is always happiest when it is expressing itself" (109). And life expresses itself when wolves sleep in the sun, when a wolf gets "remuneration in fill for his ardors and toils, while his ardors and toils were in themselves self-remuneration" (109). That is, when a wolf works hard, it gets paid. And payment comes also in the form of doing what it is made to do. There are two kinds of happiness, then, equally strong, equally good. And they lead to moments of relaxation, of laziness, of moments of bohemian life. The law of meat, if a wolf could "think in man-fashion," is superseded by the life of a bohemian. What's so fascinating about this discussion is that the narrator doesn't bring this up explicitly as he or she does when the matter is meat and chance and death. We might miss the fact that wolves aren't aware of this law in the way they are aware of the law of meat. This silence on the part of the narrator leads us to accept as fact that wolves are made for lazing about in the sun, like a bunch of bohemians. When White Fang partakes in the sun-drenched life, "he was very much alive, very happy, and very proud of himself." So life isn't only about meat. It's about enjoying your body when it is full of meat. And an author writes for money, though not for money's sake, but for the moments money can buy an author time in the sun, flying kites and picking daisies. So says the final lines of part 2 of *White Fang*.

Part 3 begins with White Fang's discovery of his dogness, a fundamental part of his identity that had been obscure to him but that awakens in him when he first encounters humans. His encounter is defined by two things. First, "the cub had never seen man, yet the instinct concerning man was his" (114). Now we realize we have been prepared for this by London's discussion of instinct and memory, when White Fang's mother bristled at One Eye's presence during the suckling period. "Not alone out of his own eyes, but out of the eyes of all his ancestors was the cub now looking upon man. . . . The spell of the cub's heritage was upon him, the fear and the respect born of the centuries of struggle and the accumulated experience of the generations" (114). (As an aside, this is language London uses in *The Star Rover* to describe Darrell Standing's past lives.) Like Buck, he attacks the Indians who first try to handle him (who thus give him the name White Fang), but when his mother reveals her dogness he, too, submits to the Indians. He may have bred true to his father, but in this first encounter with humans we know the answer to the question I asked earlier: yes, there is permeability between dog and wolf, and it is centered on the instinctual and biological level. Though his reaction to the power of humans may be likened to that of "the wonder and awe of man at sight of some celestial creature, on a mountain top, hurling thunderbolts from either hand at an astonished world" (121), he nonetheless has his mother's doggy instinct of submissiveness to humans, a willingness, in short, to be petted. In fact, this is the second other-worldly metaphor London employs to describe White Fang's reactions to the world, and both liken him to a person in strange circumstances. So, though London often makes explicit the point that wolves and dogs are not human, he links the two species through metaphor so that we may better understand not only canines but also *Homo sapiens*.

One chief difference between the species is their understanding of god or of the power greater themselves. For humans, London's narrator says, the "gods are of the unseen and the overguessed, vapors and mists of fancy eluding the garmenture of reality, wandering wraiths of desired goodness and power, intangible outcroppings of self into the realm of spirit" (130). For dogs, their gods are flesh-and-blood, club-wielding, fire-making humans, and this point is important to understand how White Fang becomes domesticated. Once he accepts the rule of gods, be they beastly like Beauty Smith or loving like Weedon Scott or indifferent like the masses of gods in San Francisco, he has separated himself from the Wild. But the characterization of humans' gods is extradiegetic, a pointed commentary on the intellectual fallacy of believers. Believers mistake real power for ghosts that are placed into the "realm of the spirit" by those who project themselves into false tales created by "fancy." At least for humans, the ghostland on earth is mirrored by the ghostland where the gods live. All this is another facet of what London means by the word *spirit*.

Interestingly, though, White Fang, when he runs away from the Indian camp, has an absorptive moment very much like any London author figure. His feet newly cold, "he curved his bushy tail around to cover them, and at the same time he saw a vision. There was nothing strange about it. Upon his inward sight was impressed a succession of memory-pictures" (51). Nothing strange about it, eh Jack? How do we actually know that wolves and dogs and wolf-dogs have humanlike memories? They do and they don't. When White Fang runs into his mother after he is a year old, she does not remember him. "A wolf-mother was not made to remember her cubs of a year or so before." He of course remembers her, yet in the face of her biological forgetfulness "all the old memories and associations died down again and passed into the grave from which they had been resurrected" (176). Again, memories and instincts, which live in the realm of the unconscious, a spirit realm, are like ghosts, and the unconscious is like a grave. Here is yet another clear instance of the permeability among species that speaks to the nonspecific nature of the unconscious. That is, all species have an unconscious, have memories, because all species have instincts.

Animals have instincts; people have drives. For London, they were the same. In this way London could link the unconscious of an animal to the unconscious of a human. These ideas form the (intentionally simplified) biopsychologic underpinning for the telos of *White Fang*. The telos of the novel is not, as London told Brett back in December 1904, the civilization of a dog. If that were the case, the novel would have ended on page 314, with the unspoken mating of Collie and White Fang; the chapter heading— "The Call of Kind"—even harkens back to *The Call of the Wild*, suggesting that here is the moment of true companionship to the earlier novel. But the novel doesn't end there. The novel has been building, we now realize, to the climactic moment when White Fang kills Jim Hall. Here we might well ask, What then was London's aim in showing the civilization of a dog? The point, in fact, was to advocate for prison reform. But only at the end do we realize that.

London had just gotten involved, for the very first time, in the case of a prisoner. His name was Joe King, a name that resonates in the name of the criminal in *White Fang*, Jim Hall. London contributed money for King's appeal of a conviction for murder. "I have promised $30.00 to pay printing of appeal to Supreme Court of Joe King," writes London to Johns in October 1905, six days before he completed the novel and so in the midst of writing the final chapters. King was "a poor devil in Co. jail with 50 yrs. sentence hanging over him and who is being railroaded."[101] Jim Hall, in *White Fang*, we learn, "was innocent of the crime for which he was sentenced. It was a case, in the parlance of thieves and police, of 'railroading.' Jim Hall was being 'railroaded' to prison for a crime he had not committed. Because of the two prior convictions against him, Judge Scott imposed upon him a sentence of fifty years" (318). London had found the perfect fictional covering for his new social advocacy. If a dog could become civilized and a productive member of society, then so could a seemingly "incorrigible" criminal (316).

All of *White Fang* moves to the incident with Jim Hall, that is, the moment when White Fang kills himself, or rather the beast within, as represented by Hall. His civilization isn't complete until he commits this murder in defense of his "love-master." To begin with, we recall how many times White Fang, up North, is likened to a prisoner. He is born inside a prisonlike environment, a cave with four walls. "His world was gloomy. . . . It was dim-lighted" (77). We remember that when he escapes his prison he suffers from agoraphobia. He feels like a man on Mars, just as a prisoner would feel who, having spent years behind bars, would recoil from the overstimulation of the free world. Then we recall how Jim Hall is likened to White Fang. We recall how Hall killed a guard. He ripped his throat out with his teeth. Just as White Fang is like Jim Hall, so is Jim Hall like White Fang. At the beginning of the final chapter, we learn that Jim Hall "had been ill-made in the making. He had not been born right, and he had not been helped any by the moulding he had received at the hands of society. . . . He was a beast—a human beast, it is true, but nevertheless so terrible a beast that he can best be characterized as carnivorous" (315). This could serve as an accurate description of White Fang up North, especially in the custody of Beauty Smith. But even before his capture by Smith we learn that "his heredity was a life-stuff that may be likened to clay. It possessed many possibilities, was capable of being moulded into many different forms. Environment served to model the clay." And so, if White Fang had never gone back to the campfires of men, "the Wild would have moulded him into a true wolf" (177). And just as the environment had molded the wolf, so the environment had molded the man who had turned into a wolf.

This is the argument for prison reform. Fix the environment and apparently bad people will become good. Few of London's novels make so clear his injunction that socialism lies at the foundation of the creation of art. We think the art of *White Fang* is the love story of a dog and his master, when we should be looking instead at the instillation of love and altruism in a formerly savage being (wolf, prisoner, they are the same). Socialism, in this context, is a form of government that attempts to deal honestly with the savage nature of humankind. It is the only system of government that offers, like Weedon Scott petting White Fang, love and altruism to combat our instinctual savage nature. "It was the beginning of the end for White Fang—the ending of the old life and the reign of hate. A new and incomprehensibly fairer life was dawning. . . . On the part of White Fang it required nothing less than a revolution. He had to ignore the urges and promptings of instinct and reason, defy experience, give the lie to life itself" (255). Note that the biologic transformation of White Fang is called "a revolution." It's a revolution because his reaction to love goes against his instincts. And it's a socialist revolution because White Fang learns the meaning of altruistic behavior. The contrast between Beauty Smith's using White Fang to earn money and Weedon Scott's disuse of White Fang could not be more political.

Earlier I said that we expected to find in *White Fang* the same connections London drew among the emotions (or "feels"), the imagination, social critique, and the spirit in the stories written previous to the novel. What we perhaps didn't expect is to see how that constellation of ideas is also connected to his understanding of evolution, the most obvious area of the history of ideas that *White Fang* is related to.

First, we will want to follow London's connections among evolutionary theory, criminality, and primitivism, and we can go back to the fall of 1905 and the Jimmy Britt–Oscar Nelson fight. Boxing was a legitimate sport, of course, but it existed in a gray area between civilized life and criminality. When London wrote up his report on the Britt-Nelson fight, he infused it with thoughts about evolution that become more prominent in *White Fang*. The emotion of anger is the key to accessing our most primitive self. The primitive human's rage, says London in his boxing coverage, is like the horse "tied to too short a rope," like the bull incited by red, like the "strange cat, restrained in our hands"; it expresses not just the earliest of human emotions but the very character of life itself. Movement, anger: this is life. This thematic, so reminiscent of the Leopard Man and Wolf Larsen, ties together his 1905 writings. The impulse to commit crime is something that comes out of the mysterious unknown, or the unconscious. It's one of the instincts or drives. White Fang is a murderer. Jim Hall is a murderer. Hall doesn't get the chance that White Fang had, or that boxers have, so he stays a murderer till the very end. But White Fang ends up a mix of

Jimmy Britt—the finely constructed bourgeois—and Battling Nelson—the brutish proletariat.

Clay—or heredity—is crucial, of course. Jim Hall was "badly made." But even though London weighed nature and nurture together, *White Fang* is mostly about how environmental factors "mould" a living being. To understand London's thinking about the effects of nurture, we have to begin with the differences between Jean-Baptiste de Lamarck's theories of the inheritance of acquired characteristics and August Weismann's refutation of it. We'll then move quickly to eugenics and social reform, specifically prison reform and biological theories of criminality, and end up with the creation of Jim Hall. London's thought in this arena remained consistent throughout his career, as he taught himself more and more from biology and sociology.

By 1900, there were more neo-Lamarckians in the American scientific community than there were Darwinists.[102] They believed that evolution was caused primarily by a highly complex series of actions within, and reactions to, the environment. These actions included "habits and instincts, use and disuse of particular organs, the struggle for food, and other conditions of existence." The effort of organisms, characterized by use and disuse and influenced by environmental factors, concentrated "growth forces and produce[d] physical change," which were then inherited. Advanced traits were continually passed on until the "growth forces" dissipated.[103] Then the process of retardation began, and degraded characteristics were passed on until extinction. Thus a species recapitulates the life span of an individual, from youth to old age. This was Ernest Haeckel's theory of recapitulation.

London was initially exposed to Lamarckian biology through Haeckel and Herbert Spencer; yet London was not a neo-Lamarckian. Within months of reading Spencer's *First Principles*, he had turned to August Weismann's *Essays upon Heredity*.[104] By August 1899, he had realized how severely Weismann contradicted Spencer's Lamarckian biology. Cloudesley Johns responded negatively to London's suggestion that Weismann was correct in his biological "researches," and so began a flurry between the two correspondents about language and inheritance. London replied to Johns that "you have muddled 'acquired characters' with 'fixed characters,' it is these latter which are hereditary. Language is an acquired character; a Semitic nose a fixed character. The one is acquired in the lifetime of the individual, the other inherited from an ancestor."[105] Johns persisted, championing the inheritance of language. London replied:

A certain monarch once isolated some babes upon a tower, where they were fed, etc., but allowed no vocal intercourse with the world. It was an experiment. When they had grown up it was found that they were simply idiots. Beyond a few inarticulate sounds by which they expressed the primary passions, they did not speak. Beyond the necessary actions correlated with mere existence they were idiots. Having received no vocabulary from their kind they were unable to think. No man ever received one word from an ancestor by means of heredity.[106]

London's example of the monarch's experiment was taken from Weismann's essay "Retrogressive Development in Nature." Weismann uses this and similar examples as conclusive disproof of the inheritance of acquired characteristics. In his next letter, London pressed his point home:

Of a surety, if a cerebral structure of an ancestor which renders him an idiot or a Kleptomaniac is transmitted to you, you will resemble him in that, to a greater or less degree as excited or mollified by environment. So with color blindness, for instance, or a thousand and one other similar things. But a vocabulary does not come under this head at all, except that the cerebral formation inherited may be limited as regards memory or quantity of words.[107]

According to London, then, morphology, not environment, accounts for kleptomania, idiocy, and an innocuous variation like color blindness. These are fixed characters, capable of being passed on from generation to generation, modified only to a small degree by environmental factors. A "cerebral formation" is inherited, not through the process of acceleration or degeneration, but through the operation of Weismann's immortal germ cell. London does not say that if one or both of one's parents were idiots, then the progeny will automatically be idiots; he is merely making clear to Johns that one does not "acquire" idiocy, as one does acquire language, during one's lifetime. In *White Fang*, then, White Fang's wolfishness and his dogness—especially his loyalty—are elemental biological traits passed on in a Weismannian sense. Jim Hall's tendency toward bad behavior is also Weismannian, though, as with White Fang's elemental characteristics, it can be influenced dramatically by environment.

London, as we have seen, was not inclined to participate in mainstream reform movements. He would, if he had the chance, vote against capital punishment, and at the beginning of 1915, he accepted an invitation from M. B. Kovenal to become a member of the advisory board of the Anti-Capital Punishment Society of America. But he believed that the root of the problem of the maltreatment of prisoners lay deeper than mere reform: "Prisons are merely a symptom. When you try to reform prisons you reform symptoms. Meanwhile the disease remains. What we ought to do is to tackle the disease. . . . A lot of philanthropic effort of the present time is mere waste."[108] London's preference for the revolutionary restructuring of society, based on what he understood as sound biological principles, led him to believe in a radical reorganization of the prison system. If the question were how to eliminate crime in the future, London promoted as one option the efficacy of sterilization. If the question were how prisoners should be treated in the present, London answered that drastic reform was necessary. In an interview in 1915, he states,

> I would turn prisons into hospitals. My basic belief is one of pure
> determinism. Each person moves along a line of least resistance. . . . If
> I break our so-called laws, I can't help it. I do it because I'm sick. There
> is something wrong with me. I'm a sick man. And I need doctors. I
> need all the skilled science of the twentieth century to investigate and
> see, and try if anything can be done for me to keep from doing what is
> hurtful to the whole body of my fellow-creatures. The whole of scien-
> tific criminology is with me in this. It's only the fools who are not.[109]

He wasn't of course a strict "determinist," or else how could he imagine altruistic behavior or the beneficial effects of the environment? Criminality is a disease that, although incurable, must be treated for the protection of society. But, according to London, the current methods are inhumane. To kill or beat a criminal (or a dog) does not recognize the inevitability of a criminal's (or dog's) actions. New methods, based on a biological understanding of the causes of crime, must be instituted.

One important source of London's ideas on criminal reform was Enrico Ferri's *Criminal Sociology*, the only book on criminology in his library in which he took notes, and a book he read in preparation for writing about the case of Edgar Sonne. His choice of this work and his notes indicate how, once he had formulated an understanding of the biological foundation of a particular social problem, he then moved beyond biology to sociology.

Ferri, along with Cesare Lombroso and others, formed the positive, as opposed to the classical, school of criminal studies. They rejected a legal understanding of crime and turned instead to a study of the criminal as a person. In general, they were determinists who sought to replace punishment with proposals to both treat the criminal and protect society. The historian Clarence Ray Jeffrey has noted that

> the Positive School has dominated American criminological thinking. . . . As a result of this orientation, criminology has been dominated by an interest in the individual offender: his personality, body build, intelligence, family background, the neighborhood from which he comes, or the groups to which he belongs. The basic assumption since Lombroso's time is that an explanation of human behavior is an explanation of crime.[110]

Ferri states that in order to understand the causes of crime, one must analyze both anthropological and psychological data. Relying on the work of Lombroso and others, he first affirms "the undeniable fact of the hereditary transmission of tendencies to crime, as well as of predisposition to insanity, to suicide, and to other forms of degeneration." Second, he affirms the inheritance of psychological abnormalities—"moral insensibility and want of foresight"—which are equated with "that ill-balanced impulsiveness which characterizes children and savages" and which account for a criminal's "defective resistance to criminal tendencies and temptations." Although Ferri's understanding of heredity is Lamarckian, and not Weismannian, London could still accept his general conclusion. It is the operation of both physical and psychical forces that account for crime, states Ferri; neither heredity nor environment is alone sufficient to explain its occurrence.

The most important consequence of such a conclusion was that Ferri was able to both affirm and deny the existence of a criminal type. Ferri said that the criminal type, as defined by Lombroso, exists, but accounts for only 40 to 50 percent of the criminal population. Ferri, in a passage London marked, then refined the classification of criminals into five categories: "criminal madmen, born criminals, criminals by contracted habits, occasional criminals, and criminals of passion."[111] As London read Ferri's elaboration of these categories, he marked the passages explaining "born criminals" and "criminals by contracted habits." When Ferri states that "no doubt the idea of a born criminal is a direct challenge to the traditional belief that the conduct of every man is the outcome of his free will, or at most of his lack of education rather than of his original physio-psychical constitution" (29), London was prompted to write in the back of the book: "Question raised: is he, or is he not, a free agent? Is he a born criminal, or is he a criminal by contracted habits? A criminal he must be, for responsibility to society enters in. He is guilty of crimes against society, and society must protect itself."[112] It is interesting that London questioned the idea of whether "he" (in this case, Edgar Sonne) might be a criminal at all. He then decides that criminals are such in relation to their effect on society.

On the next page, Ferri explains his third class of criminals "whom, after my prison experience, I have called criminals by contracted habit. These are they who, not presenting the anthropological characteristics of the born criminals, or presenting them but slightly, commit their first crime most commonly in youth, or even in childhood—almost invariably a crime against property, and far more through moral weakness, induced by circumstances and a corrupting environment, than through inborn and active tendencies" (30). London marked this passage, and then wrote: "apply this especially to the boy." Edgar Sonne would not be pictured as a "born criminal" but rather as a criminal created by his environment, countering the expectations of the bloodthirsty public, as London sensed the *Examiner*'s audience to be. Further along in Ferri, London noted, "attitude of the state. Responsibility—either keep Edgar in prison, let him go & indemnify individuals for the depredations he commits, or cure him.—Does society concern itself sufficiently with the curing of criminals." London next marked the passage in which Ferri editorializes, "The death penalty is an easy panacea, but it is far from being capable of solving a problem so complex as that of serious crime." And finally London marked where Ferri quotes Quetelet, saying, "Moral diseases are like physical diseases: they are contagious, or epidemic, or hereditary" (251).

Ferri guided London to the position that criminality can be both hereditary and environmental and reinforced London's position against capital punishment. He also gave London the justification to think of curing crime in the same way we might cure a disease.[113] Crime, then, must be understood in biosociological terms in order for true and effective reform to take hold.

We have seen that London was not a strict hereditarian. In a letter to Margaret More (the girlfriend of Donald Lowrie, an ex-con who figures prominently in the creation of *The Star Rover*), London declared flatly, "It happens that I do not believe in crime, nor in sin."[114] At an undetermined point in his career, he outlined a short story that would have as its motif, "Environment makes criminals." In that scenario, he planned for the wife of a "habitual criminal" to give birth to a child who will become a criminal as well because, one assumes, a criminal father will teach his children criminality, intentionally or not.

Now it is time to return to *White Fang*, where he plotted his deliberate and characteristic course between two opposites, acknowledging the importance of both heredity and environment. We remember that White Fang "grew stronger, heavier, and more compact, while his character was developing along the lines laid down by his heredity and his environment. His heredity was a life-stuff that may be likened to clay. It possessed many possibilities, was capable of being moulded into many different forms. Environment served to model the clay, to give it a particular form." And we remember that what was true of the dog was true of Jim Hall:

> He was a ferocious man. He had been ill-made in the making. He had not been born right, and he had not been helped any by the moulding he had received at the hands of society. . . . The more fiercely he fought, the more harshly society handled him, and the only effect of harshness was to make him fiercer. Strait-jackets, starvation, and beatings and clubbings were the wrong treatment for Jim Hall; but it was the treatment he had received from the time he was a little pulpy boy in a San Francisco slum—soft clay in the hands of society and ready to be formed into something. (315-16)

Edgar Sonne becomes Jim Hall. The latter is congenitally defective ("not been born right"), and his environment has only encouraged and stimulated his defectiveness, prodding him into criminal behavior.

Thus London believed that despite a person's inherited tendency to commit a crime, society had an obligation to create a humane environment that would discourage such tendencies. This was London's program for the present. For the future, if society were indeed serious in its efforts to better the human stock, then a eugenics program was the most efficacious. He maintained a double vision regarding the nature-nurture controversy, and specifically the problem of crime. He advocated an abolishment of capital punishment, the total reformation of the penal system, and the sterilization of criminals. He, on the one hand, believed that criminal tendencies were inherited. On the other hand, he believed in the efficacy of medical treatment for prisoners. Finally, we can see how, in *The Star Rover*, he regarded with great respect the innate qualities of a habitual criminal such as Jacob Oppenheimer or a murderer such as Darrell Standing. Their biological inheritance and environmental conditions do not render them blameless, but, as London understood the problem, the causes of crime required society to own up to its part in the creation of "degenerates" and so treat criminals in a humane, not bestial manner.

London may have concluded his fictional rendition of prisoners in *The Star Rover*, but at some point he worked up notes for a novel in which Jim Hall would be the central character. London outlined how complex the formation of a criminal could be: "Develop the life of the convict in last chapter of 'White Fang.' Begin with childhood, boyhood, give nature, its potencies, the potencies that were blotted out by environment, & the potencies that were realized by pestilential environment—work up the whole thing, in detail, from infancy to frightful wild-beast climax." Jim Hall would become White Fang.[115]

When White Fang realizes his full evolutionary potential, that is, when a favorable environment conspires with heredity in a beneficial way, it means he suppresses his natural instincts. It means he separates his consciousness from the unconscious. "He had learned control and poise, and he knew the law. He achieved a staidness, and calmness, and philosophic tolerance. He no longer lived in a hostile environment. . . . Life was soft and easy. It flowed along smoothly, and neither fear nor foe lurked by the way" (307). He could, in fact, mate and produce offspring, and it isn't too much of a stretch to see how those puppies are metaphors for books birthed by an author. We recall the links between Buck and White Fang. Both are conveyors of the call of the wild and thus intimate with author figures, if not actual author figures themselves. Buck did not read the newspapers, but he might have written for the newspapers. Not surprisingly we get a similar conceit in *White Fang*. When Jim Hall escapes San Quentin, "the newspapers were read at Sierra Vista [the Weedon ranch], not so much with interest as with anxiety. . . . Of all this White Fang knew nothing" (318–19). Again, we have a dog-wolf who doesn't read the newspapers, but perhaps writes for them, producing little puppylike stories.

White Fang's affinities with ghosts and ghostliness don't end with his life in the Northland. When White Fang first duels with Collie, he knocks her over and begins to run. "And all the time White Fang slid smoothly away from her, silently, without effort, gliding like a ghost over the ground" (285). The ghost-dog in the South may be civilized, evolved, and capable of producing art, but he is still a ghost, the medium for the imagination. Up North, White Fang's dog partners were terrified of his ghostliness, the wild that lived in him: "Much of the Wild had been lost [in the dogs], so that to them the Wild was the unknown, the terrible, the ever menacing and ever warring. But to him, in appearance and action and impulse, still clung the Wild. He symbolized it, was its personification" (190). His dogness may have won out, but the wild was still there. That is, London was realizing that when he separated himself too far and for too long from his originary, savage life, with its direct connection to the unconscious, he felt alienated from some necessary part of himself, the part that made him an author. Fortunately, he could see, as he developed these ideas about biopsychology, that the ghostly unconscious could still rise up, and that it should. Writing was becoming not so much a torment and a grappling with some mysterious unknown, unseen force within himself, but a way to become a whole person, a way to end the alienation of the unconscious. In some way, *White Fang* is about London's growing acceptance of the ghost within.

CASPAR THE FRIENDLY EDITOR

The composition of *White Fang* occurred within the context of London's newly heightened fame. He was also writing fiction with a new imperative. His contractual security with George Brett and the Macmillan Company forestalled any concerns about book publication; Brett, amazingly enough, had even consented to publish *Scorn of Women*. Having temporarily finished his long flirtation with the theater world, London returned to his more accomplished vocation and began writing stories that he wanted to represent his best work. Experimentation in one genre helped maintain expertise in another. His artistic accomplishments coupled with his fame now produced a surprising turn of events: In early 1905, he sold the serial rights for *White Fang* to Caspar Whitney and *Outing* before he had even begun it.[116]

On 4 December 1904, he told Brett about his new novel idea. London now trusted Brett completely.[117] It's possible that London was prompted to write *White Fang* by a newspaper article that he clipped and saved in his scrapbook the day before. "The Call of the Tame: An Antithesis," by Flora Haines Loughead, is both a book review of *Call* and a report about a real dog named Bones, born in the North and brought back to San Jose.[118] "I'm dropping you a line hot with the idea," wrote London. "I have the idea for the next book I shall write—along the first part of next year. Not a sequel to *Call of the Wild*. But a companion to *Call of the Wild*. I'm going to reverse the process. Instead of the devolution or decivilization of a dog, I'm going to give the evolution, the civilization of a dog.—development of domesticity, faithfulness, love, morality, and all the amenities and virtues. And it will be a *proper* companion-book—in the same style, grasp, concrete way. Have already mapped part of it out. A complete antithesis to the *Call of the Wild*."[119] One might think London was piggybacking on the success of *The Call of the Wild*, but that supposition runs counter to his conception of his authorial self. London began a story neither because he knew it would sell nor because he had read a single source, like Loughead's review; he always had a combination of aesthetic, political, and intellectual reasons to begin a work, and he always relied on several sources. Even if he did get the idea from Loughead to write a story about a wolf-dog who is "rescued" from the North, he tried out various ideas in essays and stories between December 1904 and July 1905. And he was reading other possible sources, like Stewart Edward White's *The Silent Places*. London wasn't going to follow Loughead's lead; he would transform her idea completely, as we will see, according to his return to the absorptive state and his principal concern about the nature of his imagination. At most, Loughead gave him the direction his plot should take, which, given London's propensity to revisit plots from previous stories, would probably have occurred to him sooner or later.

Weirdly, nine years later, London wrote a fan, thanking him for liking *The Call of the Wild*. In the very next sentence, he wrote, "Now I am wondering if you have ever read my Call of the Tame—the tale of a wolf-dog of the Northland who drifted south to California and came into the domestic fold. The name of the book is WHITE FANG."[120] London (deliberately?) misreads his novel three different ways: it is not the call of the tame; White Fang does not "drift" south; and he "came into the domestic fold" in the North while living in Weedon Scott's cabin.

In the same week that he told Brett about his new idea, he also wrote to Charmian with the same message, but he sent her his preliminary notes (which don't seem to have survived, but which he described as "the *motif* for my very next book").[121] The *motif* or theme at least initially was the ethics of evolution and how Darwin forecast the evolutionary basis for human cooperation.

As he told Brett, he had no intention of starting *White Fang* right away. He thought he would begin writing in February while on board the *Spray* with Cloudesley Johns, a kind of duplication of his writing scene for *The Sea-Wolf*, but he abandoned the effort and wrote "Revolution" instead.[122] After the trip was over and he had written two short stories, he learned from Whitney that they wouldn't publish the novel until spring 1906. Still, he thought he would try to begin the novel again. He asked his friend, the librarian Frederick Bamford, for material on wolves—their mating and cub-rearing practices.[123] But three days later, when he got the information Bamford had sent him, he decided to set it aside again, blaming *Outing*'s publication schedule for his procrastination.[124] Instead, he wrote his review of *The Walking Delegate*, "All Gold Canyon," and "Planchette." These stories stand on their own, of course, but they were also trial runs for the novel.

We can establish that London first had the idea for the novel in December 1904, told Brett and Charmian about it, sold the rights, let the book gestate seven months, and began writing on 27 June 1905—at least that's the date he told Brett, and the date stamp he had begun to use to mark the page he had finished writing for the day says 27 June, as does Charmian's diary.[125] In his sales notebook he says he started on 1 July.[126] On the first page of the manuscript, he wrote, "Begun July 2/05."[127] The difference in dates is insignificant. What is significant is that once he began writing, he did not interrupt himself until he was nearly through, on 10 October. In September he wrote his article on the Britt-Nelson fight, and on 7 October he completed his review of the book *The Long Day*. He was completely engrossed by his novel, and the numerous word-jammed manuscript pages that are filled with uncorrected sentences show how focused he was.

When Brett first heard the idea, he had to convince himself that it was good: "Since receiving your letter of the 5th about your companion volume to 'The Call of the Wild' I have been thinking over the project carefully and have worked myself into a pretty enthusiastic point of view in regard to it." He then explained his initial dismay: "Sequels or continuations of successful books so seldom reach anything like the audience of the originals, but as I think the matter over I come to be persuaded that the new book if equally well done and if done with that grasp that characterizes the other story has an even greater possibility of appeal to a wide public." What changed Brett's mind? He realized that, given London's emphasis on "faithfulness, love, morality, & all the amenities," the book would have a happy ending. Brett felt *The Call of the Wild* had not sold as well as it had might because, as he told London in the same letter, "many were deterred somewhat by the natural course of events in the earlier novel." He instructed London, "Let me suggest in connection with this story that you do not mention it as a sequel or even as a companion to the earlier book but instead let people suppose that you are doing an entirely new thing."[128] London may have had the requisite knowledge of the marketplace to avoid promoting his book as a sequel and so emphasized how *White Fang* would be a "companion," but Brett was having none of the distinction, another illustration of how London wasn't actually considering the commercial potential of the book; that is, Brett was telling London that it wasn't enough to make the distinction between sequel and companion as far as sales went. A commercially minded author would have seen that. Instead, full of vigor after the socialist victory in November, London was concerned principally with using a dog to illustrate, not the dystopic, anarchic world of Buck, escaping the brute workplace of the capitalistic mining world of the North, but the service-oriented morality of a socialist life in the South. If this meant that the book would end happily, so much the better, though that happy ending is qualified by White Fang's murder of Jim Hall and the revelation that Hall was wrongly accused and falsely imprisoned. A strictly happy ending wouldn't include an indictment of America's penal institution.

After Brett's discussion of the business end of writing the novel, London began to think of its sales potential. "Yes, your idea about companion story to *Call of Wild* is precisely my idea. There must be no hint of any relation between the two." As long as Brett was enthusiastic about the novel, London was happy to talk turkey. "Even in title I had decided there should be not the slightest resemblance. I have figured on naming book after dog— *White Fang*, for instance, or something like that. Now I believe that that very title, *White Fang*, has splendid commercial value."[129] But he wasn't going to bend the *motif* to fit audience expectations.

The writing went well, intense days of high and uninterrupted production. By 3 July, he had six thousand words completed, a little under one thousand words a day. In mid-September he told his longtime friend Mabel Applegarth that "I don't know whether I'll be able to finish *White Fang* before I start East, which is in early October."[130] He did. He finished on 10 October and mailed the manuscript to Brett the next day. "Hope you will like it. You will find there is not much resemblance between it and *The Call of the Wild*, and I don't think anybody will dare to assert that I have humanized the dog."[131] No one complained. But when Brett read it—he now dispensed with outside readers—he had a few suggestions after his initial sugar coating: "What a fine, strong, artistic story *White Fang* is, and how the reading of it impresses you with its truth!" His hope—expressed in July that "it should be the most successful novel of modern times"—was realized.[132] "It seems to me, I may say, the strongest piece of work of its length that you have done, not only in part but as a whole"—an important comment because some have found it to be a loosely connected and rather unsuccessful joining of several short stories. But "there are a few pages just before the end where it might, I think, be strengthened, i.e., in the pages devoted to White Fang's earlier life in the Santa Clara Valley. These pages just here halt a little, in my opinion, and it may be that in finally revising the story before its appearance in book form that you will, if you agree with me now that I have called your attention to the matter, change it slightly."[133] He left the nature of the changes to London, who ignored the suggestion. He was on his lecture tour, and when he received Brett's letter he was in Iowa with Charmian, just days away from getting married. He merely expressed his gratitude that Brett liked the story and that though he thought it a "bigger book" than *The Call of the Wild*, he didn't expect it to sell as well.[134] Brett respectfully disagreed. Although he took this opportunity to remind London of the risk that serialization could diminish book sales (he cited Owen Wister's newest book as an instance of this, estimating that magazine sales had cut his book sales by half), nonetheless he predicted that he could sell fifty thousand copies in the first print run and twice that within a year.[135] By August 1906 he could say that they were receiving a high number of advance orders.[136] And on 4 November he exulted that it had sold thirty-five thousand copies already.[137] Yet later that month a slight note of caution entered his commentary on its sale: "The sale of the book has not started up much since the first orders of which I told you, but it could hardly be expected to do so soon." He stressed how much advertising they were giving the book and how his salespeople were emphasizing it.[138] By the next month, however, his disappointment was forthright; it had only sold forty thousand copies.[139] Still, at the end of the year he was celebratory. London had just written, telling him how happy he was with the reviews. "I courted fate in the first place when I dared to write a companion-piece to *The Call of the Wild*. But God was with me! For at any rate I have escaped the fate I courted."[140] Brett agreed: "You did an extremely dangerous thing in writing 'White Fang' and I cannot be too thankful that the story turned out, as it did, so great a success and so great an advance, as I believe it to be, over the previous work."[141] Though sales did not reach the levels either had hoped, still, the book did well enough.

Perhaps Brett had been right after all. Perhaps serial publication adversely affected book sales. Caspar Whitney, the editor of *Outing*, certainly felt that way, but his insistence on obtaining both serial and book rights wrecked any future relationship he might have had with London. London's experience with *Outing* was trying, even though, in the middle of the process, Brett had encouraged London by saying, in his typically elliptical, formal prose, "I should make no doubt you would find it very easy to arrange to your pleasure [the novel's serialization] there being so many magazine editors at present who are keen to obtain material from your pen."[142] They were, and Whitney was willing to pay top dollar, but unlike Brett, Whitney could not accede to an author's will.

After London sold the rights to *Outing*, he told Brett that "they had been trying like the devil to get the book."[143] The process actually had started with a bang back in the summer of 1903. Whitney wrote to London out of the blue, saying, "I have just finished reading the Call of the Wild; it's a corker, the best of its kind I have ever read. I wish we had had it in Outing. Each one of the chapters is practically a short story and we could have run it easily. I hope we will have something from you one of these days."[144] Whitney was an interesting character. He interrupted his participation in the negotiations for *White Fang* and took off for the Amazon Jungle and a two-thousand-mile trip. Previously he had covered the war in Cuba and traveled twenty-eight hundred miles through the Barren Grounds.[145] He was offered the editorship of *Outing* in 1900 and cofounded the Explorers Club in 1904. And at the end of London's life, he was busy reporting from Europe on World War I while his wife was running a Belgian relief program in London.[146]

His Northland and Amazon trips were sponsored by his magazine, as he put it in an editorial, "not only because [*Outing*] stands for the adventurous American, the man in whom remains, undying, the old-time pioneer spirit, but because as well it believes it is doing a valuable public service in exploring new parts of what is getting to be an old country, in carefully mapping out districts that have been practically unknown, and in furnishing accurate knowledge of the people and the animals and the vegetation that live in them."[147] He sounds like his good friend Theodore Roosevelt. Frank Luther Mott calls the ten years Whitney ran the magazine "the highest point of excellence in its history," both in terms of content and design; and its circulation reached one hundred thousand in 1905 and stayed there for five years.[148] Whitney and London were a great match; as the editor said while they ran London's novel, "*White Fang* is another great story, not only because Jack London has the gift of story-telling, but also because he has lived and suffered all that he so intimately describes."[149]He certainly suffered while dealing with Whitney. The next time London heard from the globe-trotting, death-defying editor was January 1905, just before he left for the Amazon. Having heard about *The Game*, Whitney sent a one-line telegram: "Want serial rights your Story The Game your figure writing."[150] He then followed it up aggressively with a letter. "You know I have always told you that your stories belong in OUTING. You are our kind of people, and our readers are your kind of people. I understand you are at work on another story, and I would like to get the serial rights for that also, In fact, OUTING wants to tie up with you, and wants to get hold of the serial and book rights of the next story you have after the one that you are at present engaged on, and the book rights for which I suppose you have disposed of."[151] Of course London had already settled on *Metropolitan* as his serial outlet for *The Game*, but when he received Whitney's letter he was ready to give *White Fang* to them. In fact, a month later Whitney wrote again after hearing about London's proposed around-the-world expedition. "Is the three months' cruise to be for material gathering? If so, let me have it. In a word, what I want is to get your next serial and book." Acquiring both serial and book rights didn't strike Whitney as a problem. The larger goal was "making the Outing Publishing CO the house of America for virile fiction and books of travel, adventure and of outdoor and kindred subjects."[152] London had to make it clear to Whitney that he had a contract with Macmillan. As he told Brett, "I am having difficulty in selling *White Fang* serially. The leading magazines are willing to give me 10 cts a word for serial rights, and Harpers offer that much for American serial rights alone;—but all of them append the proposition that they are to publish the book. So in each case, so far, it is all off."[153] Brett suggested he send it to *Everybody's*, with whom he had discussed the matter that week, and maybe that discussion forced Whitney's hand.[154] London didn't have time to write to Cosgrave at *Everybody's* before the irrepressible Whitney made his next offer. Whitney pushed, but he was willing to compromise: "Are you so committed to the Macmillan's that there is no offer from us for the book rights that you will entertain? If we are out of it on the book rights entirely, we, of course, will be glad to have the serial rights alone, but why couldn't we make you more money if we had both, and why wouldn't that suit you better?"[155] Because London wasn't in it for the money, pure and simple.

Then Whitney left for the Amazon and turned things over to James Knapp Reeve, a familiar name to London. Reeve had been the editor of the *Editor* and author of *Five Hundred Places to Sell a Manuscript*, a book London touted as crucial to his initial success in the marketplace. Reeve confirmed their desire to have the serial rights alone, and he reiterated their payment of ten cents a word. All he needed was the length of the story and the date he would get it.[156] London told him he hadn't started to write the story, so *Outing* would not be able to publish it in the early summer as they had hoped, and then he conveyed the happy news to Brett. Whitney returned, took over the correspondence from Reeve, and immediately set in on acquiring London's next book: "I am very happy to know that Mr. Reeve had closed with you for 'White Fang' and I hope this is the beginning of several others. The next one you must let us publish in book form as well as serial."[157] London had no intention of abandoning Macmillan and simply did not respond to Whitney's entreaty.

But Whitney did not let up. In May, after London told him that he was about to begin writing, Whitney said, "Let me take this opportunity in saying that I am mighty glad that we have this story from you and remember that we want your next one, book rights as well as serial." Why did Whitney think London would eventually give in? "We will show you a thing or two in advertising," enthused Whitney, "and giving you extensive sales."[158] He promised his book publishing company would spend $50,000 in advertising for a list of six books: "This is probably the largest advertising appropriation of any publishing house in America, and that used to push six books will be more satisfactory to authors than if it were used to push twenty-five or thirty."[159] Money, sales, and exclusivity would be London's if he said yes.

Although London continued to say no to Whitney's unending, aggressive requests for both the book rights to *White Fang* and to what would be *The Cruise of the* Snark, Whitney finally revealed why he had been so insistent. London had sent him a new short story, "Finis," in November 1906. Whitney loved it, but he wanted to make it the first in a series called something like "The Tragedies of the North or Wilderness Travel, or whatever you may call it."[160] London thought it a great idea, and though he was finishing up *The Iron Heel*, he thought he could write the series as soon as he completed it, around the middle of December. Whitney demurred, returned the manuscript, and pronounced why he had been heavily pursuing book rights. "I am obliged to return you FINIS, because I am not going to buy any more good stuff unless I can get with it the book rights. . . . It is a surprising thing to me that most authors do not realize that it is only a question of time when serial and book rights must go together; otherwise, the plum is not good enough for the magazine no matter how rare and juicy it may be."[161] London sent this letter to Brett and wanted to know Brett's opinion about Whitney's new venture into book publishing and his prediction that book and serial rights would soon be sold together. Brett didn't think much of Whitney's book publishing company and predicted (correctly) that it wouldn't last long. He also told London not to worry about Whitney's absence from the serial market because "such matter as you write must always be . . . in first rate demand."[162] Interestingly, though, both Brett and Whitney wanted the same thing. They both wanted to control an author's entire output, Whitney by contracting all rights, and Brett by eliminating serial publication all together. On this matter, Brett was silent, and London did not pursue it.

For his part, London respectfully reiterated his loyalty to Brett—and the need for loyalty—and bemoaned the fact that he and Whitney could not agree about serialization sans book publishing rights.[163] Whitney responded, "You are quite right in being loyal to your publisher; I do not want you to break faith with him. It is simply a business proposition. . . . No series of stories at ten cents the word from any author is good enough if we do not get with it the book rights also."[164] And that was that. London never heard from the stridently masculine, Rooseveltian editor again. But Whitney may have planted the idea of a connected series of stories in London's mind, for, instead of *The Tragedies of the North*, London wrote *The Road*. The trail, the road, the path of a ship on the ocean: they all blur together in London's mind, representing the same thing: both the object of his writing and the scene of his writing.

THE JACK LONDON SHOW
GOES ON THE ROAD

FEEDING THE SOCIALIST

n December 1904, while he mulled over the offer from Robert Collier, who was lobbying him strenuously, London was asked to engage in "platform work," sponsored by "the largest and oldest lecture bureau in the world," the Slayton Lyceum Bureau. This request appealed to his evolving sense of authorship in a way that Collier's did not. He was quietly but determinedly intent on shedding the image of the hobo-author in favor of something new, something less contentious in the national press, something more strongly politically inflected, and the bureau's plan came at an opportune time. Collier's offer to pay for London's trip around America as a hobo-observer-writer became, in London's hands, a trip around America as a famous lecturer-author.

He was an experienced public speaker. Ever since he had completed his essay "The Question of the Maximum" in late 1899 and given it as a lecture to the Ruskin Club and at other socialist events, he was courted by a wide array of organizations. In September or October 1903, London was approached by an unknown party to give a brief lecture tour: "I am considering a proposition to go East in [January] & deliver ten lectures. The trip, as outlined, will take about a month, and will be a vacation to me, also will be educational, and in a small way may have advertising value," he told George Brett.[1] A month or so later he decided against it.[2] In 1904 he spoke constantly, using "The Class Struggle" and "The Scab" as his texts. Public speaking wasn't always a political act; he had also presented accounts of his adventures and had read aloud from his fiction. But socialist ideals demanded an audience, and he was always ready to proselytize.

He learned to speak in public as a socialist soap boxer in the spring or summer of 1895; he was nineteen and wanted to engage an audience directly, theatrically. According to one of his contemporaries, his first speech "was too fiery for those conservative times and people were incensed and wanted action taken to prevent a repetition of similar agitation. Mayor Chapman [of Oakland] said it did not amount to anything as the property [the park around Chabot Observatory, now Lafayette Square] was given to the city for lecture purposes, and thus the matter was left for the time."[3] That summer, he followed the lead of men who had first taught him the principles of socialism, men like Frank Strawn-Hamilton, Max Schwind, and Jim Whitaker. Three months into his friendship with Cloudesley Johns, when London first discussed socialism with him he linked it to the question of who were the best speakers in the Bay Area, not which books he relied on for knowledge about socialism.[4]

At the same time, and this is absolutely crucial for understanding London's self-education, most of the sociopolitical literature he read contained debates with and criticism of other authors. So, for example, when he read Laurence Gronlund's *The Co-Operative Commonwealth*, he had to absorb Gronlund's critique of Herbert Spencer. When he read biological monographs, he had to absorb, say, August Weismann's critique of Lamarck. London's reading was at all times active and dialectical.

Socialism, public speaking, and food distribution were intertwined in the Bay Area at this time. This third element of a social triad should not come as a surprise. Even before Upton Sinclair's *The Jungle* energized not only the general public but also the government to institute clean food legislation and a broader awareness of corporate malfeasance, the idea of proper health combined with small farming and distribution techniques bonded with turn-of-the-century collectivist sympathies. No other country was like America in its embrace of the utopian possibilities of socialism, and the formation of numerous cooperative communities—usually established in rural areas—led to basic reconsiderations of land use, farming techniques, food distribution, and diet. The result was a burgeoning cooperative food movement that took expression in the formation of rural communes and urban grocery stores. Not all of them were utopian. Ever since the National Grange in the 1870s and the Farmers' Alliance in the next decade, "workers and their unions . . . were closely allied with organizations of farmers." What separated these organizations from the utopian colonies was the former's affiliation with political parties.[5] Despite this key difference, it is significant to place the formation of utopian colonies within the larger context of intentional cooperative communities.

Socialists, largely working outside of political parties, fought against food trusts and the incorporation of farming, especially in a largely rural state like California. "Farm labor was replacing farm family as the basic mode of agricultural production," and farm laborers attracted the socialist movement.[6] Several examples of this confluence of socialism and rural communal living show how closely London was associated with it. George Speed, one of London's earliest and closest friends in the Bay Area socialist movement, got his start in the Kaweah Colony in Tulare County, California; this colony was initiated by Burnette Haskell on the ideas contained in Laurence Gronlund's *Co-operative Commonwealth* and on his experiences as an organizer of the International Workingmen's Association in San Francisco.[7] As we shall see, Upton Sinclair followed a similar path.

Probably the most famous socialist who was also deeply involved in utopian community building was Job Harriman. Directly influenced by Edward Payne and the Altrurians, he founded Llano del Rio, located in the Antelope Valley outside of Los Angeles. This was in 1910, after losing the Los Angeles mayoral election because the McNamara brothers confessed to the Ink Alley bombing, a cause célèbre in the socialist world. If Los Angeles couldn't become a cooperative commonwealth, then Harriman hoped to accomplish similar goals on a smaller scale. And to a large degree, he and his fellow colonists succeeded at Llano because of their agricultural endeavors.

In the summer of 1895, London met Whitaker, Strawn-Hamilton, Schwind, and others in City Hall Park or Chabot Park, or it could have been at Becker's Hall, a Socialist Labor Party (SLP) hangout located above Fred Becker's Grand Central Market, a grocery store at 908 Washington Street in Oakland; London joined the SLP in 1896.[8] Whitaker worked at a different grocery story, a cooperative owned by Halvor Hauch located at 31 Telegraph Avenue. Hauch was Danish, born in 1860. He emigrated to California in 1889 and died in 1920. He was so popular that Oakland's flags flew at half-mast on the day of his death. He became the president of the California State Retail Grocers Association and had three kids. He was a close friend of Frederick Bamford and J. Stitt Wilson, the future socialist mayor of Berkeley. He was an active member of the Ruskin Club.

London knew him outside the Ruskin Club as well. His close friend Jim Whitaker had a job delivering laundry supplies to various laundries in the East Bay. One day in 1895, Whitaker fell into conversation with Hauch about socialism, and, shortly after, Hauch hired him to manage the store. Hauch took him to a meeting of the SLP, and then Whitaker met London. They probably met in City Hall Park, while Jack listened to the political arguments. Whitaker took him to the Socialist Labor Party meeting and that's when London probably met Hauch as well. At the very least, London met Hauch whenever he, London, went to the grocery store to meet up with Whitaker. These friendships survived contentious discussion about socialist philosophy and tactics, and they all remained friends until London's death. For example, in 1906, when London gave a talk in front of the Ruskin Club about his recent lecture tour, Hauch introduced him, saying, "We value him as the true man, the loyal comrade, and we honor him for his fidelity to the great cause to which he has devoted his life," even though Hauch, Bamford, and the rest of the club disagreed with London's revolutionary politics.[9] In 1913 London wrote to a friend from his ranch in Glen Ellen: "Can't begin to tell you how sorry Charmian and I are at the fact that you are unable to visit us. J. Stitt Wilson, Professor Bamford, and Mr. Hauch, a bunch of real socialists, are here day after to-morrow for a several days' stay."[10]

There was a third grocery store in the Bay Area tied to reform politics. It was set up by Edward Payne, future husband of Charmian London's aunt, Ninetta Wiley. Payne had arrived in Berkeley in the early 1890s as the first Unitarian minister in town. Formally a Congregationalist, he had resigned from that sect and worked with Dwight Moody in Chicago's poor neighborhoods, and he generally ministered to down-and-outers wherever he was. In Berkeley he allied himself with the Christian Socialists. In 1893, when London first began to write, Payne and others formed the Altrurian Society. Named after William Dean Howells's novel *A Traveler from Altruria*, the group—including Payne and a small number of married couples and single men—met in Oakland and formed a cooperative colony—a commune—and named it Altruria. The communards bought 185 acres of land, six miles outside of Santa Rosa, and moved there in October. Payne, because he had his congregation still in Berkeley, stayed in the Bay Area, but helped form subordinate groups or councils that sought to practice their socialist principles in the ways that they could.

One council was formed in San Francisco, and in February 1895 Job Harriman took over the running of their cooperative grocery store; he, too, was a Christian Socialist and a close friend of Payne's. Later he became Eugene Debs's vice presidential running mate. In 1897 London called Harriman "the best popular socialist speaker on the Coast."[11] Just as London was beginning his speaking career, in June 1895, the Oakland Council of Altruria founded the Altruria Co-operative Union, a combination grocery store, bakery, and laundry located at 1110 Market Street. In about a year it was successful enough to take over the management of the San Francisco store. Jeremiah Roberts and his wife owned and operated it and negotiated with Henry Gibson to establish a bakery and, with C. O. Frenzel, to establish a laundry as part of their co-op.[12] The Altrurians disbanded after a year and a half.

We remember that London's 1899 story "Two Children of Israel" focuses on a socialist meeting in a room above a grocery store, a scene that he reworked for *Martin Eden*. London's beginnings as a public speaker, as a socialist, and as a fiction writer are intertwined and fed off of each other. Of course, he was first a writer, having published his first work of art in 1893, but he never gave up lecturing, and his later ranching and farming activities were rooted in these first experiences in Oakland's world of politics and food. Given London's familiarity with cooperative efforts in the food industry, it's not hard to imagine that his Beauty Ranch in Sonoma County, not that far from the site of the Altrurian commune, and especially his willingness to house and employ many workers, were an attempt to replicate these earlier endeavors that mixed food and politics. Even as late as 1906, he and Charmian "rode to Altruria and put up at [Burke's] Sanatarium."[13] In 1895, though, he was more focused on socialist ideas and public speaking. His socialist friends taught him how to speak from a soapbox or from the stairs of a public building to an impromptu crowd. What London wrote in "Getting into Print" applies equally well to public speaking: you have to have a philosophy of life, and socialism gave him the intellectual grounding for both his speaking and his writing careers.

But they didn't teach him how to promote himself; that, he learned on his own. With the help of his friend and fellow high school student A. Walter Tate—they were both in the Henry Clay Debating Society—he was able to get his name, personal story, and ideas into the newspapers. London wrote his first socialist essay, "What Socialism Is," in the fall or early winter of 1895, and then got Tate to write a profile of him. Together, the two newspaper articles appeared in the *San Francisco Chronicle*. Tate's profile was titled "Jack Loudon [*sic*], Socialist: The Adventurous Career of an Oakland Boy Who Traversed the Continent on a Breakbeam and Shipped as a Stowaway." Besides London's boyish identity, Tate emphasized his public speaking appearances. Tate wrote, "I first met him in a debating society. . . . Since then I have often seen him surrounded by a group of men, giving his ideas on" socialism. London intuitively knew the value of publicity and self-promotion.[14] Two months after the appearance of these twin pieces, advertising both the person and the ideas of Jack London, the *San Francisco Chronicle* reported that London was "holding forth nightly to the crowds that throng City Hall Park. There are other speakers there in plenty, but London always gets the biggest crowd and the most respectful attention."[15] It is possible that Tate and London dreamed up the identity of boy socialist to increase his visibility on the political scene.

Outdoors and improvisatory, soapboxing was prep work for lecturing. Lecturing in a hired hall in front of paying customers was the next evolutionary step. Also, writing essays like "The Question of the Maximum" and, later, "Revolution" fulfilled his mission of reaching both a listening and reading public. The theatrical nature of his essays easily translated into the theatrical public presentation of those same ideas, and we will see how he used speechifying as a way to test out drafts of his essays. Thus the idea of a national lecture tour grew organically out of his years' worth of experience in public speaking, out of his desire to test out ideas for essays, and out of a desire to become a nationally known spokesperson for the Left. Collier's offer simply could not fulfill all these desires, but Slayton could.

The Slayton Lyceum Lecture Bureau trafficked in both nostalgia and modernity. The word *lyceum* would have resonated with members of Jack London's public who recalled pre–Civil War organizations like the Star Lecture Course. Lyceums were both a place and a committee that sponsored the lectures. They were wildly popular from around 1830 to 1860. According to Edward Everett Hale, the public lecture became a secular form of the weekday sermon that English Puritan clergy sought to deliver outside of their home areas and that Bishop Laud and the English religious establishment suppressed. "High among the causes which sent Winthrop's colony to Massachusetts was the passion of such men as he to hear lectures on week-days."[16] The lyceum committee would choose a lecturer on behalf of the general public. A lecture was supposed to be "serious and moral . . . an oratorical form deliberately and carefully separated from all partisan and sectarian discourse."[17] The committee organized public lecture series for both the spread of general knowledge and the chance for the general public to meet and hear prominent Americans like Lloyd Garrison, James Russell Lowell, James Bigelow, and Ralph Waldo Emerson; as Hale wrote, "[Graham] Phillips, [Theodore] Parker, Ward Beecher, and even Garrison, would have been little known outside a small circle around their respective homes but for this lecturing practice."[18] This was the golden age of the lyceum. As Emerson said, "There is now a 'lyceum,' so called, in almost every town in New England." And Starr King was "the author of [a] lyceum chestnut. Some one asked him what his honorarium was for each lecture. 'F. A. M. E.,' said he—'Fifty And My Expenses.'"[19]

The lecture might be a one-off, it might be one in a series delivered by the same speaker, or it might be part of a course of lectures on a single topic. The speakers had typically gone to college and belonged to debating societies. The audience, in turn, expected something knowledgeable if not wise. Often the committee would be associated with a Young Men's Association or Young Men's Christian Association, and the committee and its audience "were aspiring and ambitious," people who saw life as "a process of individual self-creation." Thus, "knowledge had to be organized and dispensed, less in rigid, prepackaged patterns than in ways that let people pick and choose what they wanted, when they wanted it."[20] If Hale had exaggerated in his claim that the lyceum system was indicative of the Puritans' desire for freedom of expression, at the end of the golden age many concurred with Hale's foremost idea that there was something "peculiarly American" about the lyceum system. G. W. Curtis, a popular prewar lecturer wrote in 1887, "The lyceum of the last generation is gone, but it is not surprising that those who recall . . . its golden prime should cherish a kindly and regretful feeling for an institution which was so peculiarly American, and which served so well the true American spirit and American life."[21]

There were many factors that led to the dissipation of the lyceum system. The Civil War played havoc with the concept of a unified American life, and even before 1861 abolitionists were transforming the lyceum lecture course into a platform for a particular (righteous) cause. Many elements of the old system survived into the twentieth century, especially the economy of fame, the delivery of knowledge, income, and the association with YMCAs. But partisanship had usurped the objective presentation of ideas; and, more generally, the change in the constitution of the American public sphere—given the turn-of-the-century increase in magazine readership and other forms of popular entertainment—necessitated a new emphasis on "the circulation of sensation and capital" instead of "the circulation and discussion of ideas."[22] And so by 1906 it was not out of the ordinary to have London deliver public polemics on socialism.

H. L. Slayton founded his lecture bureau in Chicago in 1874, while he practiced law in the city. In the next year he was successful enough to give up his law practice, and in seven years he had seven assistants in the office, managing over six hundred musical concerts and over two thousand lectures.[23] By 1888 it was capitalized at the tune of $10,000 (roughly a quarter of a million dollars in 2016). The process of booking speakers was straightforward. After the speaker was signed, the company would contact its freelancers across the country or the representative of the venue. Acting as representatives of the bureau, they would set up the lectures and supervise the actual event. Sometimes Slayton or Charles Wagner (secretary of the bureau) would handle the individual initial negotiations themselves with the venues, but they always managed the contracts, billing, and reimbursements for the speakers.

After London's return from Korea in 1904, he had become less interested in living and observing life on the road and more interested in the public advocacy of socialist principles, especially because he felt the nation was moving toward a socialist majority rule after the 1904 election. He wanted to speed that process as much as possible; and reprising his role as a hobo-author would not invest him with an effective status. A public lecture forum, he thought, would be more effective than publishing essays in *Collier's*. Thus, we are witnessing a maturation of his authorial persona; eventually, the construct of hobo-author, so fundamental to his authorial identity, would become the construct of sailor-author. Both incorporated the fundamental characteristic of vagabondage or mobility, but the former construct became too limiting for him because it limited his international appeal and his rising fame. So he turned Collier down, said yes to Slayton, and then a month later wrote the essay that he easily turned into his most famous lecture—"Revolution." On 18 October 1905, two days after he completed *White Fang*, he left for the East on the lecture tour. He left his concerns about the imagination, ghosts, and the spirit sleeping on a California porch and took his theatrical work on the road with a new sense of his national role as an American author.

Fame, like a black lagoon, creates its own creatures. H. H. Fuller worked for Blanchard and Venter, a West Coast lecture management firm, in 1904, and their address appears in London's copy of James Knapp Reeves's *500 Places to Sell a Manuscript*, a book London used as a kind of address book for business correspondence. Later Fuller would end up in Hemingway country in northwest Michigan as the superintendent of schools for the town of East Jordan and still later would become a sales rep for an educational publishing firm. Fuller wanted to set up a lecture series for London in order to make money for himself. He knew he couldn't pull it off alone, so he approached Slayton with the idea; perhaps his own firm wasn't interested. At the same time, though, he cold-called London at his house, falsely representing himself as an employee of Slayton, and proposed a deal: if London agreed to pay him a commission on each lecture, then he would get Slayton to give him the best possible terms, meaning that he wanted to represent both London and Slayton. London agreed (and wrote Fuller's address into his address book), but said later that he just played along, amazed by Fuller's willingness to work against Slayton's best interests. Of course Fuller recounted the initial days of setting up the tour in late 1904 differently: "Slayton would probably not have taken you on had you not had the game of talk from me," he wrote to London. "I was closeted with Wagner of that bureau for some time. Slayton [himself] was called in. They wanted to know especially if you could talk. I told them I had heard you and knew. Wagner was interested all the time but the old gentleman, Mr. Slayton, was leery. He was a friend of mine and took my word for something."[24] He did, and Charles Wagner wrote to London after the meeting, telling him that Fuller had lobbied on his behalf and that he, Wagner, was prepared to make an offer. London wrote back, wondering what Fuller's role in the negotiations was, and Wagner told him that "Mr. Fuller was not making you a proposition for this Bureau, for he has no authority whatever to do that."[25] Once London sorted out the relationships—and regretted that he had ever been nice to Fuller—and signed a highly remunerative contract with Slayton, Fuller disappeared, and London never heard from him again—until the spring of 1906 when Fuller insisted London owed him money. Now a school superintendent, but still hard up for money, he begged for $200 from London. When that plea didn't work, he convinced a lawyer to demand money from London and threaten a lawsuit based on the supposed oral agreement they had made. London refused to bite. He was used to what fame brought.[26]

Besides generating the occasional dishonest entrepreneur, fame warped the public's perception of the author. For the Slayton Lyceum Bureau, London was simply entertainment; in today's vocabulary, in which production values outweigh content, he was merely the talent, the content provider. In 1905 the word most often used was not *entertainment* but rather *attraction*. In the bureau's flier entitled "Jack London: Author and Lecturer," used to promote his tour, the first line read, "The Slayton Lyceum Bureau takes great pleasure in presenting Jack London to the public as a platform attraction."[27] Wagner sought to convince London to do the tour because it would be good publicity—one can never be too famous, he told London twice in their correspondence—and publicity leads to higher royalties.[28] But for the bureau the key was entertainment value. Not only was Wagner concerned about whether he could "talk," that is, be articulate and charming, but Wagner also needed talent that was attractive—enough to draw large audiences. He produced a four-page pamphlet that recounts London's biography as London told it to Fannie K. Hamilton in 1903. There are also two paragraphs describing London's physical appearance, with an emphasis on his boyish charm, good looks, and "a square firm-set chin."[29] No neurasthenic he.

In a profile of London as a public speaker, P. S. Williams also noted his lady-killer smile. More generally, he defined what was possibly the clearest distinction between the pre–Civil War function of the lyceum circuit and the more modern form it had taken by 1905: "This is a day of advertising and the best lyceum attraction is first a man of famous achievement—secondly, he may be, but often is not, a lecturer." Writing in the *Overland Monthly* a year after the tour and after interviewing London about his experiences, Williams added, "The Slayton Lyceum Lecture Bureau of Chicago, ingeniously persuaded him that people who bought his books were entitled to see him. So London generally prefaced his talks with an explanation that he appeared before audiences rather for inspection as a wild animal than as an entertainer."[30] London repeated this observation about his role as a lecturer to a reporter in Iowa after a week of lecturing: "I can make more money at home, and be at home with my swimming and boxing and fencing, and be where I can write, for writing is my work," he said. But his audience has "been good about buying my books. Possibly there is a debt there," and so lecturing was a way of being loyal to his readers; for the same reason, throughout his career he answered every letter he received. But the larger issue was the presentation of the author: "As I understand it my stunt is to get up there and let people see me. My talk is . . . to give me something to do while I am there. It is like a wild animal in a menagerie, or the man who killed three women in a church tower."[31] Without delving into London's psychological makeup too deeply, it is worthwhile to point out that London, perhaps subconsciously, is identifying himself with a predominant character in his fiction; from Wolf Larsen to Jim Hall to Darrell Standing, he created the wild animal murderer, animated by a red, primitive rage that was inherited from prehistoric humankind, a rage embodied by the atavistic Red-Eye in the next novel he would write, *Before Adam*. He consciously had identified with Brown Wolf as beings who both came from the wild. This is a popular kind of fictional character and thus should be a popular persona to adopt on stage. By acknowledging the audience's disinterest in what he actually said, he could take advantage of the separation between exhibition and content. It gave him license not only to dress as he felt but to speak freely. One night he could attack capitalism. The next night he could, as he did in Des Moines, give "a sort of psychological and moralizing ramble from the time he was 4 years old down to the time of the new yacht he is building."[32] It didn't really matter as long as a typical audience member could say, after the speech, "Ain't he like his picture? . . . And what a beautiful face!"[33]

Being on display as "a wild animal" or murderer meant he could be controversial, and he stirred up the public both by getting divorced and remarried in a matter of days and by professing radical views. One might think that such behavior would negatively impact his draw. After all, how much of a draw would a divorced, hard-core revolutionary be at the YMCA or athenaeum club in a small town, the typical audience for a Slayton Lyceum Bureau attraction? Wasn't he too controversial? Even the small matter of being photographed while smoking was questionable. When the bureau was putting together a brochure to advertise the lecture series, they asked for a photograph of the author without a cigarette: "The negligee pictures [a negligee was an informal shirt, the kind London wears in the photo on the cover of this volume] are excellent, and we would use them if it were not for the cigarette, but we believe that would detract from their value with some of our very 'Y.M.C.A.'ky' college people." Yet even his shirt drew condemnatory comments from, for example, the Des Moines Women's Club.[34] Was the audience repressing a sexual desire? In the *Boston Post*, readers learned that "the author's dress bespoke his democratic ideas. . . . His shirt was bosomless, silken and topped with a limp, almost invisible collar, from which hung a white necktie."[35] Did women or men swoon at this description? Is there the same implication in a Los Angeles paper in which the reporter recounts meeting Cloudesley Johns, his mother, and his grandmother? "Cloudesley is a bosom friend of Jack London's whose peculiar negligee dressing he affects."[36] The repetition of *bosom* is quite curious indeed. I hear an echo of Whitman in all this sartorial description.

It is unclear whether Slayton and Wagner knew exactly what London would speak on—and thus how controversial he might be—when they first approached him. In his first letter to London, Wagner wrote, in order to convince London to hire them to manage the tour, "We have managed Thompson-Seton, Hamlin Garland, Lorado Taft, W. D. Howells and other men in the literary world."[37] These were not political men with complicated personal lives. Apparently, Wagner just assumed that London would read from his fictional work or talk about his adventures as a Klondiker and war correspondent. They made financial arrangements without discussing the actual content of the lectures. Later in 1905, when the bureau printed its advertising brochure, it included a list of talk titles that might be offered: "Experiences," which might include "Tramp, Klondiker, Correspondent"; "The Class Struggle"; and "Readings from *the Call of the Wild*, and Short Stories." "The Class Struggle" might be revolutionary in nature, but it would have been hard to say definitively from the title. Even though he had finished "Revolution" in February, it was not listed as a possible talk.[38]

But controversy could work in both the bureau's and the attraction's favor, and surely when people came to see the "wild animal," they wanted to be titillated or even mildly frightened, and thus entertained. Like the readers of Poe and some of London's stories, they may not have known to what degree they were attracted to the terrible and the tragic. However, when controversy erupted, the bureau stood by its man. Nobody at the bureau could have predicted that London would marry Charmian Kittredge early in his tour. It was a "sensational marriage," according to P. S. Williams, and "Mr. London was not approved in some of the more Puritanical communities."[39] Even if he hadn't gotten married for his second time, both his fiction and his politics excited protest. After receiving a letter of protest from a preacher, the secretary of the home office (and no relation to the creature from the black lagoon), Fuller, told him that "if the reverend gentleman had read London's books he should have discovered that there was a brutal streak in the author's nature and been prepared for it."[40]

But it was his attacks on the wealthy that generated the most controversy. He knew it would happen. After all he had delivered "Revolution" in Stockton in order to draw an adamantine line between himself and the bourgeois in his own neighborhood. In Oberlin, Ohio, he gave a lecture on socialism that went over well, but the same talk later in front of a "select audience in New York . . . an organization of substantial and able men" caused a near riot in the meeting room of the club. Said London, "Well, before I got through they were all up in arms, and the chairman was the fiercest of all. They hotly challenged my statements and fired questions at me that were hair raisers."[41] The event might have been the inspiration for Ernest Everhard's verbal attacks on the members of the Philomath Club in *The Iron Heel.*

Two off-the-cuff comments repeated during his tour created especial controversy. He quoted Judge Advocate Major Thomas McClelland saying "to hell with the Constitution" to people who objected to the army's attempt to suppress socialists in the labor war in Colorado. Some members of the press attributed the saying to London himself, thus branding him as a dangerous anti-American. He had also remarked that bomb-throwing radicals in Russia were his comrades. London consciously gave the country reason to suspect his intentions and wonder how he conceived of the relation between violence and politics. The point is not so much that the audience was appalled and vocally oppositional. It's that London deliberately provoked them, deliberately generated controversy and thus more attention to the socialist cause.

But the larger, more theoretical point to make is about the dramatic nature of London's endeavor. By focusing on that word *attraction,* we can easily see how lecturing is similar to the cinema, another medium of attraction. London's appearance on stage at the podium is a precursor to his cinematic representation in the next decade. His lecture tour occurred during the transitional period between what Tom Gunning famously called the early period of cinematic representation, or "the cinema of attractions," and the next period when narrative and fictional genres dominated. London's tour shares all the features of the cinema of attractions without the obvious intervention of film technology. His tour and the films made before 1906–7 can be characterized in the same way: "Theatrical display dominates over narrative absorption, emphasizing the direct stimulation of shock or surprise at the expense of unfolding a story or creating a diegetic universe. . . .

The cinema of attractions moves outward towards an acknowledged spectator rather than inward towards the character-based situations essential to classical narrative."[42] Gunning has said that "the reference to Fried [by using the terms *absorption* and theatricality] was deliberate and was essential for me thinking through the issue."[43] He repeats the terms when he explains the source of his term *attraction*. Coming from Sergei Eisenstein, "An attraction aggressively subjected the spectator to 'sensual or psychological impact.' According to Eisenstein, theatre should consist of a montage of such attractions, creating a relation to the spectator entirely different from his absorption in 'illusory depictions.'"[44] The technology of the lecture tour could not create a montage, but the effects of both the tour and the cinema were the same. It's worth forecasting how films of London's works—produced after 1910—followed the general trend of cinematic expression laid out by Gunning—less theatrical, more absorptive—as London turned his attention away from the theatrical presentation of his ideas. After 1910, he wrote only a few essays. In 1905–6, however, London's speaking tour indeed was a temporary abandonment of the mode of absorption for the mode of theatricality.

Wagner called him a "one season novelty."[45] Although controversy was good for business, it must have been ulcer-inducing to manage a flame-thrower rhetorician like London. Whether he could have reprised his tour or not is less important than that word *novelty*, a word closely associated with *attraction*. London's lecture tour was not meant to be an educational night for those who bought tickets; he was no Ralph Waldo Emerson or James Russell Lowell. Unlike the Chautauqua movement, the Slayton Lyceum Bureau wanted its stars to entertain its audience, and London proceeded to both entertain and to shock.[46] His direct challenge to his audiences was not appropriate to the older form of the educational lecture, but it was indeed a cousin to the cinema of attractions.

As a significant attraction, London could earn the bureau's top rate. London grossed approximately $3,270 on his tour (something like $87,000 in 2015), but another, perhaps more significant exchange took place in the nonmaterial real.[47] We recall that, in 1899, as a beginning author, in exchange for publicity managed by the *Overland Monthly*, London took a low rate per story. He did the same with Brett and *The Call of the Wild*. Now, as a famous public figure, he could insist on the highest rate and still get maximum publicity. London earned advertising and visibility as a public figure as well as the position of the foremost scold of the plutocrats in exchange for the attraction of his personality and presence. He sold the latter for the former, and it could not help but affect not only his career and sense of being an American author but also his writing.

London's contract with Slayton, dated 23 January 1905, stipulates that he perform twenty-five times in the first five weeks (starting from sometime between 15 October and 5 November) for which he would receive seventy-five dollars a night plus hotel and traveling (mostly train fare) expenses for himself and his "servant" (as the contract had it), Che Manyoungi, who worked as London's body man from 1904 to 1907.[48] If he lectured more than twenty-five times, he would receive one hundred dollars per lecture. He himself would collect the money, subtract his fee and expenses, and mail the remainder to Slayton.[49] At some point he apparently renegotiated his fee. According to Slayton's itinerary sent to London, his fees were determined in advance and varied from locale to locale: his first lecture, in Matoon, Illinois, netted him $125; on 5 November, in Toledo, he earned $200; in Grand Forks, he earned $150 on 3 February 1906, the final stop.[50]

By March 1905, Slayton was advertising London in its newly conceived the *Slayton Courier*, a monthly newssheet about their attractions. There on the front page, without a cigarette, stares the sensitive-looking young author. The puff piece is simply a reprint of part of a 1903 interview by Fannie K. Hamilton, and no mention is made of socialism, only his recent fame with *The Call of the Wild*.[51] Individual venues also touted the author as part of their lecture series for the 1905–6 season, which might include a violinist, a "churchman," and a "humorist." Northwestern University's YMCA advertised London as a "Novelist and Socialist, Friend of the 'Under Dog.'"[52]

The tour was physically demanding, though it did, of course, have its great moments. Charmian wrote in her diary that at times these were the happiest days of her life (she hadn't yet sailed on the *Snark*). After all, they got married in Chicago on 19 November, honeymooned for weeks in Maine and Jamaica (where they met and dined with Ella Wheeler Wilcox), and received accolades and attention all over the country. At the same time, though Charmian enthused on her wedding day that "Jack [is] adorable—my perfect bridegroom and lover, at last," she added, "Night made hideous by reporters!"[53] Near the end, in January 1906, she wrote, "Sweet nights on trains! These are happy days of understanding and love. 'In the land of love,' Mate says."[54] Being in the spotlight night after night added to the stress of a grueling schedule. Beginning on 22 October in Kansas City, London traveled back and forth through the Midwest, then the East, then back to Chicago to get married, and then back to the East, ending up at Bowdoin College on 7 December. A sympathizer sent him some advice from his mother, who had heard him speak: "You looked somewhat worn with the fatigue of it all and spirits such as yours are all too rare in their sweet simplicity and utter lack of self-consciousness, so please spare yourself by talking to the crowd for only an hour at a time, and let us keep our Friend on the planet where he is so much needed for as long a time as possible."[55]

After his lecture at Bowdoin, he ceased lecturing temporarily for Slayton, and the intensity of his socialist message increased. His itinerary for Slayton specified engagements in October and November of 1905, the one date in December, and February 1906. His contract stipulated that he "agrees not to accept engagements from any other Bureau or Management during the life of this contract, and to protect our mutual interests as far as public engagements are concerned."[56] So while he suspended his work for Slayton (having given at least twenty-five lectures, he was allowed contractually to do this), he was free to lecture during the rest of December and January on behalf of the newly formed Intercollegiate Socialist Society (ISS) and other political organizations.[57] The intensification of his public support of socialist principles was partly a natural byproduct of the new locales; instead of delivering "Revolution" at the People's Institute of Elyria, Ohio, or at YMCAS, he spoke in front of thousands at Harvard and Yale Universities, the Grand Palace and Carnegie Hall in New York City, and the University of Chicago. He appeared at Harvard University on behalf of the ISS where fifteen hundred people heard him speak for two hours, giving his speech "Revolution." His new friend George Galvin, with whom he had corresponded and now met for the first time, organized three other lectures: at Tremont Hall (where he also gave "Revolution"), Unity Hall, and Faneuil Hall.

George Galvin, a doctor at and general manager of the Emergency and General Hospital in Boston, wrote to London in December 1906, asking if he would like to speak at several locations around the city, the proceeds going to London and the ISS, and, "if any thing is left over our local to receive something."[58] Galvin had written to London in June on a different matter, asking him for his opinion of his latest article in *Arena*, "Our Legal Machinery and Its Victims."[59] Galvin was an ardent supporter of London's; he once claimed that "his name was on my lips every day of my life. Yes, every hour of my life, for patients always received more socialism and industrial unionism from me than medicine, and I quoted Jack."[60] He wrote this in a letter to console Charmian after Jack's death, but if he exaggerates he is excused. When London was in prison in 1894, he was "forcibly vaccinated by a young medical student, who wanted experience." Eleven years later, having read Galvin's article, he wrote back, photographs were exchanged and they became friends. Galvin informed London that he was on excellent terms with all the professional news hounds in Boston and that he would get a favorable reception. He also told London to supply "a skeleton" of his speech to the press because "that is the only way we get anything."[61] Galvin was a good friend of Upton Sinclair's as well and familiar with an editor at *Black Cat*, William Lincoln Balch. Balch claimed in a letter to London that it was he who had accepted "A Thousand Deaths" for publication after changing the title and editing the story.[62]

The letter was occasioned by London's unannounced visit to the editorial office of *Black Cat*, where London talked to Balch's wife. Balch's narrative of that moment of acceptance confirms London's account in "Getting into Print"; the magazine asked permission to cut the story in half, which London agreed to, though London doesn't mention the change in title. He also does not mention that Balch doubted London's identity: "I took [Jack London] for a pseudonym. I supposed you to be some young Englishman—a younger son in hard luck in this country—and had been nicknamed 'London Jack.'" Here yet again is another editor who was convinced that Jack London did not exist and more proof that London was interested not so much in making a name for himself but in establishing his name as his own, something the lecture tour accomplished in spades.

The London party left the U.S. for a honeymoon in Jamaica on 27 December, but the lecture tour wasn't over. In fact, on 19 January 1906, around four thousand people heard him speak at New York City's Grand Central Palace (sponsored by the ISS), and large crowds heard him at Carnegie Hall (a benefit for the *Socialist Call*), the Educational Alliance (for the Socialist Literary Society), and at Yale University (ISS).[63] The talk at Carnegie Hall was so successful that an audience member wrote the following day that "it made me rejoice to hear your good words and to see a man among American artists who alone dares to proclaim a high unselfish purpose. You are showing that here, as abroad, literature is not necessarily a name for impotence."[64] Finally, he headed back west and gave three talks in Chicago: at the University of Chicago (originally scheduled to be held in Kent Hall, the event was moved to Mandel Hall because of the size of the crowd), the West Side Auditorium (a benefit for the Socialist Party), and the County Normal Training School. He received no payment for his talks in Boston, New York, New Haven, and Chicago.

Now leaving the urban centers of socialism, he resumed his itinerary for Slayton, if only for two occasions. After speaking in St. Paul, Minnesota, he gave his final talk at the University of North Dakota–Grand Forks on 3 February. Slayton got him to the Rockies, and then London paid for his own way home. (There would not have been many venues to choose from between Grand Forks and Oakland.) Slayton had tried to set up two lectures in Southern California, but he couldn't get the two venues to coordinate the dates.[65] Any number of biographies cite illness as a reason London ended his tour when he did; he even wrote to Johns in Los Angeles telling him that he was sick. But Charmian London's diary paints a very different picture; she makes no mention of illness—and whenever he or she was sick she discussed it—and instead writes about how much fun they had on the train from North Dakota to Oakland, playing cards, reading Turgenev, and socializing with the others on board.[66] It was just simpler to tell Johns that he was sick than it was to explain the various logistical problems of setting up the Southern California lectures.

London, thus, had given forty-four talks in fourteen weeks, averaging one every other day for over three months. He had put his socialism on stage, a one-man show featuring the best in accusatory, inflammatory, anticapitalistic rhetoric. He took a month's break and then, at Oakland's Dietz Opera House, in March, he delivered a new speech, "The Rising Tide of Revolution." Following his earlier practice, he converted part of it into the essay "Something Rotten in Idaho," about the wrongful imprisonment of Charles Moyer, Big Bill Haywood, and George Pettibone.[67]

A digression is called for here: The master of ceremonies for that evening in Oakland was William McDevitt, who later would write a somewhat accurate firsthand account of his experience working with London. He says, in general, "Jack was averse to any more 'money-for-himself' lectures, and so he very gladly offered as a *part* of his contribution to the cause of socialism in California his readings or lectures." McDevitt was a committed, active socialist and was one of those arrested in the infamous April riot at Lotta's Fountain after the Moyer-Haywood protest meeting at Woodward's Pavilion.[68] He is entirely on point about London's lack of profit motive. London thought it was ethically wrong to take money for the cause from people who could ill afford it. His ethic joins Left politics and bohemian economics. In any case, once he returned from the East, the earthquake of April 1906 put an end to his local lecturing until December.

The tour was both arduous and financially beneficial, but there was a third consequence. It gave London the opportunity to become a part of the national socialist movement by meeting both the nameless members and the well-known leaders of a number of factions, as well as prominent opponents to the newly burgeoning leftist movement. Considering how London was educated in socialist ideology—informally and by western-ers like himself—we shouldn't forget how much of an outsider London was to the national Socialist Party. Men like Morris Hillquit, Victor Berger, A. M. Simons, and John Spargo—all members of the National Executive Committee (NEC)—ran the political apparatus, hoping to keep both the union leadership—especially those of the Industrial Workers of the World (IWW)—and the bourgeoisie out of their campaigns. To them, London, because of his proletariat credentials, his life in the West (which kept him from attending, for example, X Club meetings or the two Noroton Confer-ences where he might have solidified friendships with the eastern Socialist Party establishment), his rise to national prominence apart from the efforts of the Socialist Party leadership, and his longstanding involvement in both the movement and the party made him a special case, someone who could help the leadership without being a part of it.[69] After hearing him speak in Chicago, Simons wrote,

> The Socialists of Chicago are all enthusiastic over the results of your work here and any time you want to come back they will get the Audi-torium for you. . . . I don't suppose you have any left over manuscript that you could deign to bestow on the International Socialist Review. A few years ago it was still possible for us to get the best manuscripts because the magazines would not take them, but nowadays since Socialism has become popular we find ourselves in the presence of some powerful competitors. However I am still hoping that you will work up a reputation that will make it too dangerous for capitalists to use quite all your stuff so that we may get a little something.[70]

The right kind of controversy was good, especially in the highly competitive field of socialist publishing, an irony that must have struck London forcefully, he being the author of "What Communities Lose by the Competitive System." Some months later, London sent Simons his article on the Moyer-Haywood trial, though only after Arthur Brisbane at Hearst's *San Francisco Examiner* had silently refused it.[71] Earlier, in 1902, John Spargo, another centrist and NEC member, asked London for a contribution for the series "How I Became a Socialist," a request with which London complied. London's political fame overlapped with but also grew apart from with his fame as a story writer. Sometimes his fiction-writing readers were alienated by his politics, but as socialism gained more and more prestige, that alienation diminished. And London's tour helped grant socialism more legitimacy nationwide.

Publicly he stayed above the political machinations of the NEC as well as the squabbling in party meetings. When his friend William Walling wrote to him in 1909 that Simons was trying to steer the Socialist Party toward an accommodation with the American Federation of Labor, he was vehement in his support of Walling's position: "If the socialist movement in the United States goes in for opportunism then it's Hurray for the Oligarchy and the Iron Heel."[72] London's friend Ernest Untermann, in correspondence with Joan London while she was writing her biography, concluded, "He saw the socialist leaders who received the most publicity and backing from the membership were mediocre politicians with little or no respect for the scientific foundation of socialism."[73] Like Walling, London was more interested in "the movement and not . . . the party. The two are not identical."[74] In 1910 Walling assessed the Socialist Party in negative terms: "I should say that the organization already contains, along with some radicals and revolutionaries, some of the most conservative and reactionary people I have ever met—who have entered it for private or business purposes and to take advantage of the popularity of the idea."[75] Walling, an outsider like London, captured one of the principal reasons London resigned from the Socialist Party six years later.

"The spectacle of an avowed socialist, one of the most conspicuous in the country, standing upon the platform of Woolsey Hall and boldly advocating his doctrines of Revolution was a sight for Gods and men." So ran the overheated rhetoric of Alexander Irvine, the chair of the Connecticut Socialist Party. In attendance, besides "the majority in the hall" who "were

from the city, and included many Germans, Russians, Italians and Jews"—
that is, members of the largest immigrant groups at that time, newcomers to
U.S. citizenship—were "several hundred men from the University," including Arthur Twining Haley, the first lay president of Yale and antisocialist,
and Professor William Graham Sumner, a well-known social Darwinist.
Irvine, who had set up the Yale talk, was enraptured by London, even if
the latter men were not.[76] Upton Sinclair, Mother Jones, J. G. Phelps Stokes,
Oscar Lovell Triggs, Jane Addams, Jessica Binford, Parker Sercombe, A. M.
Simons, Robert Hunter, and other prominent figures met London for the
first time during the tour, and his message and charisma worked to cement
relationships that continued for the rest of his life.

Just one example: Surely one of the great moments of the tour, equal to
the chaotic, clamorous, and well-known reception he received at Yale University, occurred in New York City. After delivering "Revolution" at Grand
Central Palace, Mother Jones dramatically walked from the back of the hall
to the stage and emphatically embraced London before the multitudes.[77]
They had corresponded in late 1905 about writing a review of *The Long
Day*. Earlier in Boston, at Faneuil Hall, she had given an introductory talk,
and London's speech had supported and reinforced Jones's work on poverty and child labor. He was quoted in the paper as saying, "Mother' Jones
says to me that she has worked alongside children 6 and 7 years old, that
the whistle blew for them at 4:30 am; that they drank back coffee and ate
bread dipped in bacon grease for breakfast; that they went to work at 5:30
and worked till noon, and then worked from 12:30 till 7 pm. She has seen
them killed; she has seen their hands torn off by machinery. . . . She has
seen them killed, but the capitalists would rather listen to their agents, who
report 'all's well,' than hear of the story of suffering from Mother Jones."[78] In
a later letter, she told him that as she toured the South, "I wish I was near
you to get you to give the frightful tragedy of child life in the slave pens of
Capitalism a good write up."[79] Not surprisingly, London wrote his most
famous short story about child labor, "The Apostate," two months after he
returned home, and *The Iron Heel* takes up the cause as well.

"REVOLUTION"

He gave several talks on the road, the most significant being "Revolution."
I've discussed this essay in the previous chapter, but not its evolution as a
text and, more importantly, its relation to texts he wrote before and after it.

"Revolution" most likely started out as a speech; in fact, in its first incarnation he tested out material that he then rejected for the final version after several public airings. On 20 January 1905, a week after he had given "The Class Struggle" in Normal Hall and nearly two months before he completed the final version of "Revolution," he delivered the speech for the first time at the University of California; a transcript was printed in the *Socialist Voice* and reprinted in *People's Paper*, a Santa Barbara socialist newspaper.[80] In this version of the speech, the beginning is nearly the same as the published essay by Macmillan—"Yesterday morning I received a letter from a man in Arizona"—but there is no other overlap. He mentions George Sterling's reasons for joining the Socialist Party, speaking at the Ruskin Club on "Why Am I a Socialist": "He said, 'Socialism is the only clean, noble and live thing in the world today worth fighting for.'" He quotes "a statement from the celebrated English scholar Frederick W. Harrison," confirming London's major premise that "modern society [is] hardly an advance on slavery or serfdom." This work and his deployment of it repeats his methodology from *The People of the Abyss*; though he didn't use Harrison's work in *People*, it could have easily made its way there. Either London had read it for *People* and could not find a place for it, or he continued his research into the causes of English poverty after he returned. Either way, he fits it into "Revolution" right after he directly cites his experience in the East End: "When I was in London writing my book, 'The People of the Abyss,' I went down to Kent with a London cockney to pick hops. One night, when going to bed, I stripped. My chum looked in wonder at my brawny body glowing with health, and then at his own scrawny body, white and lifeless. He said, holding out his arms and legs: 'They are so because I hadn't enough to eat when I was a boy.'" London then turns to a quotation from Robert Hunter's new book *Poverty*, a sociological analysis of American poverty; this quotation and statistics about poverty in New York that he incorporated in the final draft of "Revolution" are the only published results of his desire to write an American *People of the Abyss*.

But a further link, and even more telling, exists among *The People of the Abyss*, this first draft of "Revolution," and the next novel that London wrote, *Before Adam*. London closed *People* with a seemingly fanciful comparison between the Inuit and the East Enders. Their primary characteristic for London is their near isolation from modern society, as if they lived in a prehistoric time: "They are a very primitive people, manifesting but mere glimmering adumbrations of that tremendous artifice, Civilization." The extent of their technological progress is bow, arrow, fire, and half-underground shelter. In the first draft of "Revolution," he makes the analogy between the Inuit and prehistoric man explicit; he writes, "About three years ago I went into the Klondike. I saw there a body of Indians called the Innuits. There is an immense difference in time between them and us. They are still in the Bone Age." (Since this is a transcription of a speech, it's possible that London said "Stone Age," not "Bone Age"; the latter, however inaccurate, is still charmingly poetic, and I will continue to use it if only half in fun.) Using his firsthand experience in the Klondike in "Revolution" shows how wedded he still was to using his time in the East End to buttress his arguments for revolutionary change.

He next gave it as a speech in front of the Unitarian Club in San Jose on 25 January and to the Ruskin Club in Oakland on 27 January. The news report for the former indicates it was very similar to the University of California speech.[81] London was still referring to the Inuit, and he continued to quote from Hunter. But at some point in the month between his address to the University of California students and the completion of the essay he replaced the Inuit with "the caveman" as his example of how the so-called sophistication of capitalism has caused a previously unknown poverty to the human race. The first trace of this change that I've found is in the version he gave in Stockton, at the Critics Club, on 26 February. Again the first paragraph is approximately the same as the text in "Revolution" and in *People's Paper*, but departs from the latter and overlaps to a significant degree the former, meaning he was delivering what he came to regard as the final draft.[82] In fact, on the day he was to give the speech, he wrote to Charmian that he was bringing the handwritten text to her for typing. Yet he must have felt, after the typing or perhaps after the rough reception that he had received in Stockton, that it still needed some work because he waited till 13 March to mail it. The night before, he had delivered it at the Dewey Theatre in Oakland as a kind of campaign speech for his unsuccessful run for mayor of Oakland.[83] The point—besides the important one that this text of one his most famous essays and speeches went through a number of drafts and significant changes—is that London, by changing his example of the Inuit to that of the cave dweller, was probing even further back into human history for justification for revolutionary change. The example of the cave dweller, so much more abstract than the Inuit, becomes an example of how primitive capitalism can be. The Inuit stopped working as an example, I imagine, because they had adapted to modern Western society and its economic system and thus lost some of their credentials as primitives. But the cave dwellers, who managed to live comfortably without the profit motive, are a perfect example not only of a human community that lived in cooperative fashion but also as a shaming device for London's contemporary plutocrats. Even cave dwellers are better off than those exploited by the capitalists. London jettisoned his autobiographical narrative that partially structured his first draft of "Revolution" in favor of a more abstract set of data and examples that could appeal to a wider audience, not just those interested in the comings and goings of an individual American author. The fact that a few audience members objected to the example because cave dwellers, they felt, must have gone through periods of want or even starvation (missing London's point that cave dwellers were never habitually deprived of food because of resource mismanagement) may have prompted London to do further study in the Bone Age and write a fictional narrative about denizens of that time.[84]

Several newspaper transcriptions of the speech before and during his lecture tour show that the text of "Revolution" continued to change.[85] Each version differs from the others, principally by showing how London extemporized, giving emphasis on one point one day, another point on another day, deleting passages and adding new material, making "Revolution" a fluid text, adaptable to changing audiences and circumstances. Though London regarded the printed text of the essay in the Macmillan collection *Revolution, and Other Essays* as his final word on the matter, all these texts should be considered together as a single work.

Shortly after he had mailed off the essay, one report of the speech given in April 1905 says that "the speaker gradually forsook his topic for a long time in order to quote various statistics and facts regarding the condition of labor and capital in this country to-day. He referred to the reports of the United States Government on these issues and cited many incidents showing how child labor is being used by capitalists for their own gain, even though thousands of lives are sacrificed."[86] Neither the *Socialist Voice* nor the *People's Paper*'s versions contain references to U.S. labor statistics, but the finished essay does. It seems he had a basic text for his speech but that he could dip into the completed essay manuscript and pull out material as he saw fit.

On tour he constantly added material to incorporate either feedback he had received or news items he had just read. According to one account, he spoke extemporaneously before he delivered "Revolution." First he mentioned that as a poor kid "he had looked up to the society that was above his head, as to a class in which all men were well fed, well clothed and spoke a beautiful language," his point being that it was an illusion. This point led somehow to his comment about university students, that they were "clean and noble, but not alive. But life is alive, and we who are live creatures and alive should deal with it with passion." German and Russian students had passion, but not American students, and obviously he equated passion with a belief in socialism.

"Another side step from the lecture," wrote the Boston reporter, "came when Mr. London explained how by the 'siren song of Socialism' many laborers were being constantly won over to Socialism." As an example, he gave this story of Eugene Debs's conversion from labor rights activist to socialist leader: "We [meaning socialists] send men, whenever there is a strike, to organize the strike, talk to their meetings, but along with that we sing the song. When the strike fails they come over. An example of this is Debs. He organized the great Chicago strike. He looked the field all over, planned his campaign as he would a battle. He was right. If they had done as he expected he would have won, but they got an injunction against him, and he went to jail without trial. We sent a man to the jail and he did some thinking and came over." Another "side step" cited by the reporter is something London had included in the essay version of the speech: the case of Mary Mead who had strangled her children so that they would not starve.[87]

Two recent events steered his attention away from the topic of revolution, the first applying more to the general topic of socialism: his meeting with Boston businessman Thomas Lawson; while Lawson affirmed "some" of "the principles of socialism," London countered with the challenge that Lawson was, in the last analysis and at best, a pseudo-socialist. "He believes he can achieve [Socialist ideals] through financial methods [not revolutionary ones]. . . . I believe that in his faith in money Mr. Lawson is showing the natural characteristics of his class." It was an informal, sociable meeting, but at least one Boston paper portrayed it as a meeting of childlike dreamers.[88]

This led to another recent interpolation that was, strictly speaking, off the topic of the coming socialist revolution, though he also made mention of it in the essay form of "Revolution." London claimed a number of times, both in interviews and in off-the-cuff remarks at his speeches, that "the newspapers do not give the Socialists a square deal; they will not give me a square deal in the morning."[89] In the essay version of "Revolution," he qualified the generalization, a qualification I quoted in the previous chapter but bears repeating: "Parasites themselves on the capitalist class, serving the capitalist class by moulding public opinion [the newspaper editors] cluster drunkenly about the honey-vats. Of course, this is true only of the large majority of American editors."[90] He knew that his audience and readers would know which newspapers were conservative and guilty of antisocialism and which were not. When asked by a reporter about "the surprise his Socialistic arguments created, he fell back upon the inaccuracy of newspapers, the 'hidden hand of malice in the kid glove of capital.'" And when he was back home and asked to reflect on the outrages he had caused, especially with his supposed support of the inflammatory statement "to hell with the Constitution," he said, "Yes, another case of being the victim of reporters' readjustment of facts. Oh, no! I am not trying to demonstrate that reporters are natural born liars—and yet—Why, do you know while I was in Chicago I had two reporters struggle with my immortal soul for hours trying to get me to say that I am a believer in free love—which I am not a bit."[91] At the same time that he wanted to be truly represented, he accepted the fictionalizing impulses of newspaper reporters. Later, he would pledge allegiance to his fellow inksters. At the end of the tour, he would affirm the positive contributions to the American cultural and political scene made by reporters and newspapers in general. He was not about to disown his authorial upbringing.

EXPERIENCE VERSUS ADVENTURE

"Revolution" was not the only talk he gave; he gave three others, and he also drew material from "What Life Means to Me" to preface "Revolution." One was based on his 1903 essay "How I Became a Socialist," and it appears he only gave it in Boston, probably because he gave five lectures in and around that town and didn't want to repeat himself every night.[92]

The second one was an autobiographical talk called "Experiences," which he gave—among other places—in Lake Geneva, Wisconsin, near the beginning of the tour, Orange, New Jersey, near the middle, and in St. Paul near the end of the tour. It began with the Klondike: "Packing," he said, was "my first experience." It's an odd choice of words and an odd choice of events. *Experience* isn't quite the same word or concept as *adventure*, though they can be taken as synonyms. In his writings, he would abandon *experience* in favor of *adventure*, a more capacious term and one that he had used before, though incidentally, in "How I Became a Socialist," when he talks about being locked up in Erie County Penitentiary for "adventuring in *blond-beastly* fashion."[93] *Experience* denotes personal events; *adventure* denotes a more abstract realm. *Experience* seems to denote real-life struggle as opposed to the romance one might find in or mistake for *adventure*. *Experience* says, "These things actually happened." *Adventure* says, "Something like these things happened, but this story tells a more complete truth." *Adventure* is *experience* infused with feeling, passion. It is impassioned realism.

But London hadn't quite formulated this concept of adventure yet, which happens during the writing of *The Cruise of the* Snark, *Martin Eden*, and *Adventure*. So in this lecture he continued to talk about his Klondike experiences. There was "sleeping out in cold weather, going after moose, the ice, cold effects, whiskey as paper-weight, playing cards in cabin, feet cold face sweaty." He turned away from struggle and survival and referenced the unbelievable mosquitoes who appear in "Stranger Than Fiction" and then used material from "Housekeeping in the Klondike." If he followed the order of his notes, his lecture turned from the Klondike to hoboing, hinting at the links between the miner-author and the hobo-author. The third element of experience was his conversion to socialism: "Experiences—tell how I passed coal for the Oakland, San Leandro & Haywards Electric Railway— preface this with: 'People sometimes wonder why I am a Socialist. 'Of my experiences I will relate on only—couple of more whys, perhaps; Buffalo experience. Vivid picture of passing coal, half drunk on 'GARONNE'—be sure to group these different experiences."[94] His fourth experience was that in war, and so he repeated his stories of being a war correspondent in Japan and Korea.[95] He wasn't going to let a night pass without lecturing on socialist principles or on his own formation as a socialist. "To group these different experiences" was to show his growth as a socialist. All his experiences served to form his Left ideology.

The third lecture is a bit of a mystery. His notes for the lecture are labeled "Notes of Fanueil Hall Lecture," and he may have given it only once, at Faneuil Hall in Boston on 26 December; I have not found any record of him giving this lecture before or after, though it seems to repeat some points he made in "Revolution," and he in fact called it "Revolution" in his diary. But his own notes for the lecture show it differed significantly from "Revolution," and perhaps he changed his mind at the last minute and composed the notes on the day of the lecture. It seems principally an immediate, ad hoc response to criticisms he had been receiving on tour. *Boston Globe* noted the difference between his previous talk at Tremont Hall, where "he lectured from a manuscript to a scant 200 people . . . [an] earnest, dogmatic, scheming talker." At Faneuil Hall, "he was the incarnate, burning spirit of protest against present conditions; the fanatic, if no better name be found, who sees in his remedy for social wrong an absolute panacea. . . . He was apt, strong and convincing; his audience sat spellbound for two hours— and it isn't every socialist, nor every writer either, who can hold a Boston crowd for two hours, let alone keep them warm that length of time." It seems to have been one of his most successful talks. The reporter was especially struck by the audience. "The audience itself was most significant. It was not the mere mob of discontent, the people of the abyss, who came to hear their wrongs pitied and have their sores licked. There were 2000 of them. . . . there were artists from the Back Bay, students from Harvard and Technology, young politicians and lawyers, doctors, substantial business men of the city, and, of course, a large body of men and women who work for their living." There was "an astounding number of women." They were orderly, attentive, and responsive—and "for the most part they were well dressed." Even his audiences were judged by the clothes they wore.

In his notes London divided the lecture into several topics, usually beginning each section with a quotation from a letter he had recently received. His notes start with "Destructive criticism See letter. What the trouble is all about. Division of the joint-product. Quote Harrison 224 World market Hard times." This first letter came from a graduate student who had heard his talk at Harvard: "In your indictment," he wrote to London, "you made no attempt to offer a remedy for existing conditions. This will not go with thoughtful audiences." Thinking of his earlier essays against the single tax, in favor of public ownership of utilities, and so on, London replied to his audience in Faneuil Hall,

> We do have a remedy. My attitude here has been that of destructive criticism. We have constructive criticism, but I devoted myself to the other side because—it's the psychology of the thing. You know about

magazine advertising; you must construct, if you wish to succeed, advertisements that will attract attention and awaken interest. I have talked in the constructive way; easily, sweetly, passively—and aroused almost nobody. I prefer here to strike between the eyes, to make the indictment and to ask the capitalistic class to answer it. They never have and they never will.

According to the reporter's paraphrase, London then "explained that the whole trouble in society today lies in the division of wealth which is the joint production of capital and labor." The reference to Harrison is of course to Frederick Harrison, whom he quoted in the first draft of "Revolution."

The next section begins with another response to recent criticism: "Boston journal—on every man getting a job. The surplus labor army. State the indictment. (Factories in England.) Engineer (like sailors and Consul) and Mother Jones. Ruling class isolates itself." The *Boston Journal* had taken him to task for extemporaneously claiming at Tremont Temple that the lack of jobs in the area explained the continued existence of the poor: "It makes my blood boil," said London, "to hear some man who never knew what it was to go hungry or want work say: 'Any man can get work if he wants it.' It is the most damnable lie ever uttered." A reporter went looking for work advertised in the want ads and found many positions; London failed to acknowledge that "many of the jobs as mechanics and along the water front were full-time."[96] London countered in the speech that these were actually only part-time jobs: "A Boston paper sent out a staff artist and a reporter to get work—just before Christmas. I'd like to see them holding the fine jobs they found just now." And part-time labor wasn't a problem for the cities exclusively. "Under the old system of agriculture," said London, picking up on a theme he explored in *The People of the Abyss* and then would try to rectify on his own ranch in the next decade, "men stayed on the soil all the year round. But now, with improved machinery, we have driven a great portion of the people to the cities because the soil cannot support them. They tell of the Kansas cry for men, thousands of men, in harvest time. But harvest time does not last long, and those men who went to Kansas to get in the harvest couldn't stay there now for their bare board. When men were needed to build the New York subway, there was no trouble in finding 40,000 laborers; did all those men quit jobs to work on the subway?" Despite the accuracy of his "indictment," the ruling class refuses to acknowledge it because "it is part of the policy of the capitalist class not to know how much misery is being endured, to go away and not to live with the laboring class." Nothing has changed in the last 110 years, as wealth continues to maintain a physical distance as wide as the income disparity that defined the Gilded Age.

The reference to the "Engineer and Mother Jones" led up to a big laugh from the audience. London told them of a "fire protective engineer" who had written to him "that he has been all through the factories in the south, and that there is no such child misery as I mention." He then cited his conversation with Mother Jones that I quoted earlier. The audience at this point must have been rapt, silent, horrified. "Yet who listens to 'Mother' Jones? They would rather listen to the engineer; he is the agent of the capitalist, and he makes a report that all's well in the world and God's still in heaven." At this point the audience broke into laughter. London held them in the palm of his hand.

"Many grant all that I say," his notes read at this point, "but then bring Malthus against me." The reporter was not impressed with London's explanation of Malthusian law ("Mr. London stated the law of Malthus rather badly"), but London managed to get his point across. In his notes he broke it down with three bullet points: "(1) Law is not biologically true (2) Grant it, are not yet pressing against means of subsistence (3) Grant that we are—the inevitable 'Malthus be damned.' And finally, it can't be worse. We'll manage more rationally." His elaboration of these points was nicely captured by the reporter: "In the first place," the reporter paraphrased, "the law of Malthus does not apply, for the higher the organism develops, the less prolific it is. The codfish must lay 1,000,000 eggs to produce one codfish, but not so the human." Then he let London speak for himself: "The very lives of the men who quote this gives them the lie. All the stork hears on 5th Avenue is 'shoo! shoo!'" The rich, who apparently are a "higher" organism than the poor, do not reproduce as much as the poor. Why? Because "life under difficult conditions tends to be more prolific. The man in the sweat shop craves happiness, though he cannot play golf or go to the theatre when his work is done. So he goes in for drink, and he goes in for children. The children, of course, he doesn't want; they're the accidents." And the crowd laughed uproariously. Sex and socialism were an unbeatable combination.

Then he turned to his second point: "Again, even if the Malthusian doctrine is true, there is no need for the means of subsistence to be insufficient for a geometrically increasing population. Labor-saving devices will take care of that. Again, granted that we are actually in danger of pressing against the means of subsistence, remember what the New York laborers told Cunniffe, who explained to them the error of their ways. 'Malthus be d—d,' they said. 'We're not interested in future perfection of the human race, we want plenty, and we want it now.'" M. G. Cunniff (London misspelled his name) was a British labor leader who couldn't convince British workers to limit their birthrate voluntarily in the face of the implacable Malthusian law; London here is taking a piece from his essay "The Class Struggle." He then continued: "Finally—I deny, by the way, that the law of Malthus applies to society to day." To focus on that law is to avoid the betterment of society. Even if the law is true, socialism cannot be denied; as he said in Chicago later that month: "Evolution brings revolution."[97] "Suppose," London argues, "the workingmen get all the joint product of labor and capital, will things be any worse? If we press on the means of subsistence, we can press more mercifully than is done now. If that day should come, can't you imagine a simpler, more merciful method of getting rid of surplus humans than running them through the mills and taking 10 or 12 years to destroy them?" Although he hadn't yet discovered eugenics, London's support of that controversial program was based on the premise that enforced sterilization and selective human breeding would defeat the inevitable collapse of civilization if Malthus's law held true (and in the next few years he would change his mind about the inevitability of the Malthusian doctrine). A eugenics program managed by socialists was the most humane way to forestall the human tragedy of mass starvation, if it ever came to that.

He closed the speech on an optimistic note. His notes read, "Men must first become good. New birth. Come in out of the rain. . . . Incentive. Love to excel. Ambition. Patriotism. Ethics. Religion. Love." The reporter paraphrased the conclusion, perhaps exhausted from taking notes for two hours: "The speaker ended his long talk with a picture of the ideal condition, claiming that socialism is not an appeal to laziness, and that even then two hours' work a day is all that is necessary to live, everybody will still be busy from sleep to sleep, because the incentives of the love to excel, ambition pure and simple, religion and love—which he explained by a picture of the poor young man who saves and scrapes to get enough to marry on—will still exist." What an odd autobiographical allusion that was!

Although the reporter barely alluded to it, this conclusion was motivated by London's response to another letter he had received, this time from Frank Coburn, a Boston socialist, in response to remarks he had made in "Revolution" delivered at Tremont Hall. At the top of the letter, Coburn had clipped a newspaper paragraph: "In conclusion London declared that if the social status could be reconstructed on an equal basis, it would be necessary for every man to work but 3 hrs. each day in order to have all the people live in comfort and happiness." To this, Coburn told London, "Increased economic efficiency is what Socialism stands for, and as you raise the standard of personal efficiency, involving physical improvement of the human stock, you will so greatly increase the sum total of legitimate human desires that the race will have to keep on working right up to its fatigue point to purchase the things it needs. . . . Three hours, indeed! What we want to pray for is for the strength . . . to work . . . eight hours, ten hours, twelve hours. Don't let's appeal with our Socialism to the lazy, the incompetent. Let's make it a gospel of the efficient." London marked the last few sentences and wrote in the margin of the letter, "We'll work all our waking moments, and most of our work will be play."[98] He closed the lecture by quoting the letter and presumably ended with his proclamation of bohemian economics: work should be play! As he had written in *The People of the Abyss*, in the chapter entitled "Inefficiency," "It must be understood that efficiency is not determined by the workers themselves but is determined by the demand for labor." Further, "inefficients are being constantly and wantonly created by the forces of industrial society." Those who advocated the "gospel of efficiency" were actually acting in concert with capitalism. London was willing to risk inefficiency for bohemian concerns like comfort, play, and art. The "voice of life" had to be shouted down by the voice of the imagination.

Constant attention from the press, attacks on his moral character and political beliefs, and the nightmares of the logistics of a lecture tour all combined to convince London "that this has been his first, last and only lecture tour," as Williams concluded his essay.[99] And yet he refused neither to refrain from speaking to reporters nor to seclude himself. Sometimes a mainstream newspaper would applaud his efforts, and he answered in kind. When London extemporaneously claimed in a talk in Chicago that women in that city worked in sweatshops for ninety cents a week, people were appalled, and several newspapers sought to refute his assertion. "The action of the *Chicago American*," he told a reporter in late January, after he had left the East Coast, "is in such sharp contrast with the manner of certain other papers that I am glad to acknowledge it. . . . I knew what I said was true, but I did not possess the names or addresses of the victims I championed. Now I know where they live, and I can get some information at first hand, for which I thank the American."[100] When he was interviewed in St. Paul, just after leaving Chicago, he was even more effusive in his praise for reporters. "Proceeding to room 208 [in the Ryan Hotel] the reporter found Mr. London seated in a big chair smoking a cigarette, with Mrs. London curled up comfortably on the bed reading to him from a book. The door was opened by a Japanese valet." In this cozy domestic scene, a routine set after so many days on the road, perhaps prefiguring their imagined circumstances on board the *Snark*, London talked of his experiences in Korea and tramping, of literature, of his future plans for sailing around the world, and of reporters, the latter topic following directly from the penultimate one: "My object in building this craft is to give me all the time I want abroad and make me free of steamboats and the beaten path of travel, which is the curse of the age—the route of the tourist. What I want to do is to study industrial conditions in every great city in the world. That is my object in setting out on this journey." This point may surprise London scholars and enthusiasts, who have routinely supposed that London traveled to the South Seas for the sake of experience, for the sake of egotism, for the sake of doing what he wanted (his infamous pronouncement "I Like"), for the simple act of escape. No, there is a direct connection—in more ways than one—between his lecture tour and his *Snark* trip. His authorial role on that trip, as he made clear to the St. Paul reporter, was to be an internationally known newspaperman-sociologist: "The thing these days is to get at the facts. The men who are doing this are the newspaper men. They are the only men today who know things as they are. There is no dust in their eyes and they are holding up the truth to many people who do not wish to look it in the eyes."[101]

Still, he never drifted too far from his assessment of the majority of newspapers and their complicity with capitalists. Summing up the press coverage of his trip for a hometown reporter, he addressed the controversy of his marriage, the banning of his books in Connecticut, his opposition to anarchism, and the controversial statement "to hell with the Constitution" ("I quoted Sherman Bell, leader of the troops in the Colorado labor war").[102] Given the general treatment of his views by the press and their collusion with the enemies of socialism, London was naturally harsh about reporters at times. When journalists forget their role as sociologists, then they succumb to fancy and lie to serve the dominant ideology. On the other hand, he and a handful of reporters could maintain scientific objectivity and then place the facts at the service of reform politics.

In the privacy of his study back home he made notes for a lecture on his lecture trip, capturing the bifurcated view he had of the press. He wanted to be humorous as well as serious. The tour was succeeding until "the miserable associated press misreport" about his divorce and marriage: "work in the free-love-detail reporters of Chicago." He wanted to exaggerate his supposed economic losses "because of the editorials men wrote—quote from all of them the most outrageous ones." His final note recounts "my surprise at sensation because in Havana I met K.C. reporter, who told me his disappointment at the mildness of my lecture." He never did complete this lecture, but it led him to a logical next step: to incorporate the insight that "the ten-cent exposure magazines . . . are catering to the bourgeoisie against the plutocrats."[103] This note was for his projected essay "Persistence of the Established." We see how this insight informs the chapter "The Machine Breakers" in *The Iron Heel*, where Ernest Everhard urges the bourgeois business owners to side with the proletariat before they get destroyed by the oligarchs.

Perhaps the most significant lesson he took from his lecture tour was that being a national journalist-sociologist-author was not enough. He had the ambition to apply what he had learned on tour to a larger, hugely ambitious project of becoming the international commentator on the evils of industrial capitalism and so become a spokesperson for the world's poor. The same intent that drove him to go to the East End in London drove him to go around the world in a boat.

JACK LONDON HELPS FOUND THE SDS

The speech at Yale, as well as those at Harvard University, the University of Michigan, and the University of Chicago (and perhaps others as well; there are no full records) were organized and promoted on an ad hoc basis on behalf of the newly formed Intercollegiate Socialist Society. Because the iss came into existence as London was touring and because the iss existed only as a loose collection of study groups, it is a mistake to say that he toured under the auspices of the iss. There was a group of officers nominally in charge of the organization, but they did not plan, arrange, or supervise lectures in the first several years of the ISS's existence. Local groups took care of their own lecture series with one exception. Shortly after London was elected president, George Strobell—a Christian Socialist, a successful jewelry maker, and a friend of Upton Sinclair—told London that he was organizing the Harvard Union, the University of Chicago, and a New York City talk because none had yet taken charge of "the speaker's committee." George Strobell also told London that Thomas Wentworth Higginson "moved around like a young man when he heard you were coming" and insisted that London arrange a meeting with him; I do not think this took place. He also gave him George Galvin's address and facilitated their meeting.[104]

The ISS is a microcosm of what happened to American socialism in the twentieth century, both in terms of its membership and its organizational trajectory. Its formation also afforded an opportunity for London, Upton Sinclair, Jane Addams, and other prominent radicals to meet. London was not the only one who was moved to action by the 1904 election, and Sinclair was inspired to undertake a national pedagogical mission by Debs's success. In December 1904, having completed his research for *The Jungle*, Sinclair conceived of a socialist organization that would "awaken an interest in Socialism among the educated men and women of the country," an idea similar to the teach-ins and independent study groups formed on campuses in the sixties by students who found their college courses irrelevant in the face of contemporary political change.[105] This is not a fanciful comparison. The ISS changed its name in the early twenties to the League for Industrial Democracy (LID); in 1933 it became the Student League for Industrial Democracy (SLID); and then in 1960 it changed its name to the Students for a Democratic Society (SDS). Mark Rudd, who led the successful student strike at Columbia University in 1968, wrote in his memoir about his moment of radicalization during a meeting of Columbia's Independent Committee on Vietnam (ICV): The members of the ICV "took themselves so seriously you'd think this was a debate of the workers' soviet of revolutionary Petrograd in 1917. But they were also mesmerizing, articulate, and burning with conviction. By comparison, my professors seemed tame and bloodless. In my European history class, revolution was something that had happened in 1789 in France. But these zealous radicals in the ICV were talking about the class nature of the American system and about revolution happening right now."[106]

It's as if he borrowed his rhetoric directly from Sinclair: "Since the professors refused to teach the students about modern life," wrote Sinclair in his autobiography, "it was up to the students to teach themselves; so I sent a circular letter [in 1904] to all the college socialists I knew of and invited them to organize."[107] He also sent it to London the revolutionary, Leonard D. Abbott (the editor, anarchist, and public intellectual), Charlotte Perkins Gilman (novelist and activist), J. G. Phelps Stokes (settlement advocate), William English Walling (London's friend and husband of Anna Strunsky Walling), Clarence Darrow (well-known attorney who had defended Eugene Debs in 1894), Oscar Lovell Triggs (magazine publisher/editor, reformer, and tireless proponent of the Arts and Crafts movement), Benjamin O. Flower (editor of the *Arena* and a progressive, not a socialist), and Thomas Wentworth Higginson (the famous abolitionist, women's rights advocate, and editor of Emily Dickenson's poetry), who all agreed to support the idea, and to William Lloyd Garrison, Julian Hawthorne, Thorstein Veblen, John R. Commons, Richard T. Ely, and George Rice Carpenter who refused, for one reason or another. Veblen thought it wouldn't succeed because a previous attempt at the University of Chicago had failed. Hawthorne thought college undergraduates were too immature to assimilate the ideas of socialism. Commons and Ely, both professors at the University of Wisconsin, declined on the grounds that they could not "endorse the socialist philosophy." Carpenter, who had been George Brett's outside reader for all of London's submissions, including *War of the Classes*, said he was in sympathy with the movement but that "the time is [not] propitious."[108]

Sinclair also wrote to Fred Bamford. The Ruskin Club—as well as W. J. Ghent's X Club in New York City, the Social Reform Club, and other informal discussion/lecture groups—may have been an inspiration for Sinclair to form the ISS. Bamford, however, disagreed with a basic premise for the group: to recruit men and women from the entire spectrum of socialist thought. To invite men like Edwin Markham, William Dean Howells, and Clarence Darrow, said Bamford in his reply to Sinclair, was a mistake. Sounding as revolutionary as London, he wrote, "No militant body can be built up by such men . . . . We want men tingling all over with the glory and greatness of our cause."[109] Bamford, it turns out, was prescient.

In June 1905 Sinclair sent a slightly revised version of the call to organize, this time signed by London, Stokes, Higginson, Gilman, Darrow, Triggs, Flower, Walling, Abbott, and Sinclair. This was a powerful group of public intellectuals who represented a broad range of socialist thought. There were other differences as well besides intellectual ones. Only Abbott, London, and Sinclair paid dues to the Socialist Party, only Abbott was not native born, Gilman was the only woman, and London was the only proletariat by birth. Their diversity (it could have been greater; more women and minorities should have been included) helped cinch the argument that this organization was aiming for an objective appreciation of a new political movement.[110] The call asked simply for people to send their names to M. R. Holbrook, who was the temporary secretary and the current secretary of the Collectivist Society.[111] It was published in socialist and mainstream papers, and over two hundred letters were received.

It also triggered some backlash in the press. In a June 1905 article in the *National Civic Federation Review*, the editor, Ralph Easley, denounced the proposal. He used long quotations from "The Class Struggle" to illustrate "the virulence of Socialism" and cited London's speech at the University of California and his quotation from Hunter's *Poverty* to show how overheated rhetoric makes socialism look "ridiculous" and perverts the youth of America.[112]

Oscar Triggs responded to this article in the first issue of his new magazine, *Triggs's Magazine* (begun after he had left *To-Morrow*) and sent it to London. Triggs's response is significant for a number of reasons. First, he and Parker Sercombe, a fellow Chicago reformer, are pivotal figures in the study of London's thought because they all combined the political and the aesthetic and promoted an Arts and Crafts ideal. A former teacher at the University of Chicago—an institution that seemed to always be lurking on the periphery during this period of London's activism—Triggs had helped publish Carl Sandburg's 1906 profile of London in Sercombe's *To-Morrow Magazine*.[113] Now, his 1905 response to Easley's attack on the ISS made him London's ally, and the latter read his article avidly. Triggs laid the foundation for his response by comparing scientific experimentation to social experimentation. "The speculative thinker in sociology is branded as an enemy of the human race. . . . Anarchy and socialism are alike derided. . . . To deny the System [the System! how sixties of Triggs to say this] is to be an infidel. . . . In view of the freedom permitted the investigator in science and other fields, does it not seem unreasonable and unscientific to oppose social experimentation?" Quoting from Sinclair's June 1905 call for the organization of the ISS, Triggs simply cannot believe Easley's resistance: "It is amazing that anyone should take alarm at so simple a proposal." He quoted from Easley's personal attack on J. G. Phelps Stokes—"some man of wealth whose capital has come to him through inheritance or marriage, and whose vanity is tickled by being called a 'millionaire socialist,' devoting his wealth to the uplifting of the down-trodden masses." Stokes had responded to Easley in print, too, and Triggs quoted him: "I simply agree with the basic principles of socialism and believe there *is so much that is good in the doctrine that we wish* to bring them to the attention of educated men and women throughout the country. The movement is purely educational." London underlined the italicized words in this quotation, rejoicing in Stokes's grit.

In the next paragraph, where Triggs quoted from Thomas Higginson's rejoinder to a critical notice in *Harper's Weekly*, London also marked these words: "As Theodore Parker used to say, 'I am not particular with whom I unite in a good action.' As to the object in view it is clearly enough stated in the call itself; the movement does not aim to produce socialists, but to create students of socialism.'" Easley attacked Higginson, too, calling him a "pulpitless clergy[man]," naïve about the objectives of the ISS. Higginson had famously proclaimed in his letter to *Harper's*, "Those who seriously criticize [the ISS] must be classed, I fear, with those medieval grammarians who wrote of an adversary, 'May God confound thee for thy theory of irregular verbs.'"[114] Easley, feeling that his very sense of being an American was being challenged, retorted, "Mr. Higginson can no longer plead ignorance of the facts as an excuse for his surprising association with an organization whose purposes and whose origin are utterly at variance with his distinguished record as an American soldier and patriot." At this initiatory moment, in the summer of 1905, still overjoyed by their success at the polls in 1904, socialists across the spectrum were united.

Triggs closes his essay with a mild-mannered though radical statement, one that echoes Sinclair's take on American higher education and forecasts Mark Rudd's assessment in the sixties: "For my part I would sign a similar call for the study of anarchism, or of any other social theory. *College students are apathetic—too much so—if not actually reactionary. . . .* College professors are eminently 'safe and sane' and can be depended upon to check the spread of any revolutionary contagion. At college one learns to divorce thought from action. It might be deemed dangerous for workingmen to think, but college-men not at all. They may be wise as serpents but they are harmless as doves."[115] So spake the ex-University of Chicago professor.

Again, London underlined the words I italicized; note how similar they are to Tom Hayden's description of writing the 1962 Port Huron Statement, the foundational document for Students for a Democratic Society: "We were rebelling against the experience of apathy, not against a single specific oppression. . . . Apathy, we came to suspect, was what the administrators and power technicians actually desired. Apathy was not our fault, not an accident, but rather the result of social engineering by those who ran the institutions that taught us. . . . It was for this reason that our rhetoric emphasized 'ordinary people' developing 'out of apathy' (the term was C. Wright Mills's) in order to 'make history.'"[116] Hayden, Triggs, and London all had firsthand knowledge of the failure of higher academia to motivate its students to even think about changing society.

Triggs in fact wrote a second essay in his first issue, this time focusing on the failure of academia to educate the young. It is the source for the infamous "observation" by Paul Shorey, the chair of the Department of Greek at the University of Chicago, that the "university ideal" (Shorey was a Platonist) was "the passionless pursuit of passionless knowledge."[117] Triggs cited London's early draft of the "Revolution" speech (its Berkeley incarnation) and called for students to put aside their indifference to national political matters and "take sides. Sooner or later you must choose whom you shall serve. . . . Even as you read this you exclaim: 'Take what side! What issue!?' It is as I expected, you do not know what I am talking about." They do not know what he is talking about because the education that ISS was offering was missing from their college curriculum. They were still under the influence of institutionally manufactured apathy. "Professor Shorey of the University of Chicago is responsible for a new definition of the University Ideal. In speaking at the dedication of Lincoln Center he called this wonderful something we have all seen but never understood: 'the passionless pursuit of passionless intelligence.' Triggs then easily glided into a quotation from London's early draft of "Revolution": "Jack London said recently to the students of the University of California: 'As I look over the universities of my land to-day, I see the students asleep, asleep in the face of the awful facts of poverty I have given you, asleep in the greatest revolution that has come to the world. . . . Awake to its call.'" Did they awake to the call? asks Triggs. No, but "sooner or later you men and women of the universities, this apathy must be overcome. . . . Soon the issue will be joined as sharply as that of slavery in the past or as that of temperance in the present."[118] We can see why the abolitionist Higginson was courted to support the ISS. For these socialists, racial equality was the same as economic equality. Within a couple of weeks of receiving these articles from Triggs, London wrote "Intercollegiate Socialist Society," his own attack on American college students, an essay I will turn to shortly.

In the summer of 1905, while Easley, Higginson, and Stokes were debating the merits of Sinclair's initial plans for the ISS, Sinclair and Strobell saw that there was an overwhelmingly positive response to their plan. Thus they issued a third call. Besides repeating the paragraphs of the second flier, it included "a proposed plan of organization." Devoid of definitions of socialism and of any political platform, this initiatory statement outlined who could be a member—high school and college students, their instructors, and anyone interested enough to apply for membership to the executive committee—what officers would be elected by the membership, and how they shall be elected. It also asked everyone who was interested to meet at Peck's restaurant in New York City at 2:00 p.m. on 12 September 1905. The event was reported in the papers. "Socialist Club Names Jack London President," but that seemingly objective headline quickly gave way to conservative bias. "The name of the society seemed to cause a considerable amount of trouble, for there were ninety-eight kinds of socialists present. Sinclair defined socialism as 'anything the papers don't like.' Then the clock stopped. This was regarded as a favorable omen. Some member shut the windows so the intense spirit should not escape and overwhelm the passersby." After detailing who was elected to office, the reporter couldn't resist a final jab: "and the treasurer [is] Mr. Lovejoy, who 'is not used to handling large funds.'"[119] Ah, the Gilded Age reporter's wit! After the meeting and on the same day, Strobell sent London a letter informing him of his appointment as temporary president of the ISS; Sinclair became vice president, Owen Lovejoy, a college student, was treasurer, and the executive committee comprised George Strobell, J. G. Phelps Stokes, Mrs. Darwin J. Meserole (a wealthy wife of a banker and stockbroker), John Willis Cooke, and Henry Laidler, a student at Wesleyan who stayed with the organization for fifty-five years.[120]

London accepted the offer to preside over this eclectic group of socialists. In Boston, while he was on tour, he was asked why the society and its study of sociology and socialism was formed, and he replied, "Why am I interested in sociology? Because I was one of the poor people and I have been oppressed by the capitalists. Banded effort can balance things, individual effort never. I believe that every college should have clubs to study sociology. Let the thing appeal to the reason of the college man and if he thinks best then he can reject it. At least let him study the question. I believe that heredity and environment determine all that a man's life shall be, and one can change the balance, perhaps, by having a clean, pure healthy environment."[121] How large looms the "perhaps" for the author in the midst of an intellectual transition. London was modifying and enlarging his concept of the relations of environment, heredity, and politics. Edgar Sonne and Jim Hall were criminals made by society in equal measure to any possible heredity factors. In fact, this moment may well be the first time in a public utterance that London explicitly allowed for the effects of one's environment to help shape a person's being. He couldn't do it without equivocation because he hadn't disavowed his biological determinism. Still, under the influence of a broad range of socialists who all agreed in the necessity of changing one's environment for the better, London couldn't help but support the dominant Left ideology to help forge an alliance with all manner of socialists.

There is an interesting set of undated notes for an essay or debate that he entitled "Round Table" that removes the hesitant "perhaps." "The whole thing to show," writes Jack to himself, "that while heredity gives potentialities, environment realizes or crushes these potentialities. import of this to socialism." Nothing else in these notes, however, pertains to this "whole thing." One page (out of five) comments on the importance of labeling his time as the Machine Age: "We have mastered machinery? Yet machinery has mastered us. None of us can escape it. It has made the modern metropolis, the sweat-shop and the slums. It determines our art, our ethics, our very lives."[122]

London's estimation of the importance of environment must have been modified by his reading of Edwin Seligman's *The Economic Interpretation of History*. He marked more pages in the chapter "Freedom and Necessity" than in any other, although this chapter is devoted more to criticisms of Marx's theory than with its exposition. The first criticism Seligman deals with is economic fatalism or determinism, which he discounts. London marked the passages that quote Thomas Huxley on free will—"Nobody doubts that, at any rate within certain limits, you can do as you like. But what determines your likings and dislikings?"—and, more to our immediate point, the controversy between Weismann and the neo-Lamarckians—"Neither Weismannists nor Neo-Lamarckians deny the obvious fact of the influence of present environments on the individual as such."[123] Genetics is crucial and determinative, London was realizing, but, just as Seligman pointed out about the importance of economics, it cannot account for all human behavior and the amelioration of social ills. In one more passage that London marked, Seligman writes, "In the present industrial system the offer on the part of any one employer to double the customary wages of his workmen will have no appreciable effect upon the general relations of labor and capital."[124]

Motivated by Triggs's two essays as well as by his election as president to the ISS, London decided to write an essay about the new society. He completed it on the train from San Francisco to Chicago at the beginning of his tour, and it was the first writing he did after he completed *White Fang*. Calling it "Intercollegiate Socialist Society" but published under the title "The Rise of Socialism" in the *Syracuse Herald*, he outlines the reasons necessary for the ISS's formation. In fact, the first sentence of this essay forecasted his shift of emphasis away from the biological determinism that he had expounded upon to the Boston interviewer: "Socialism to become operative must be expressed politically." It's as if he had decided that socialism had passed the test of biology and now needed to be promoted politically. His one note for the essay lays out its organization: "Potentia. In introduction, show how backward the American university—compared with European universities, etc.—radicals very few, etc. and then the response. [illegible word] awakening."[125]

London starts with the international situation, both historically (the French Revolution) and the current situation in Russia (especially the aftermath of Bloody Sunday). Then he moves to one of his foundational political-philosophy principles: "The history of society has been that of a class struggle." Once the working class has succeeded to power, then "cliques," not "classes" will continue to "struggle"; he could not foresee the end of differences among the socialists, but they would be united in certain basic ideas. In a sentence that at once foretells the future of socialism in America, his future novel (both in the sense of having yet been written and of taking place in the future) called *The Iron Heel*, and his own hopes for mankind, he wrote, "It may be several centuries before the bread and butter question is settled, but then the only contention will be over questions of beauty, of art, and subjects which the working people have not time now to think about." London may have been heavily involved in politics, but he never lost sight of his principal occupation nor of his desire for all to share in the bohemian life. If we all could experience work as play, as a nice change, instead of being engaged in forced work, then the people could be attuned to the highest "considerations" known to mankind.

Then he moves from the international political realm to the state of affairs in universities internationally, if only to show how backward and dangerous to progressive thought the American university is: "The radicalism of the German university is too well known to be elaborated upon. In Germany a man may be an announced and pronounced Socialist and yet retain his professional chair. In the United States, on the other hand, the announcement of a professor's conversion to socialism is promptly followed by his dismissal." Sounding very much like a member of the SDS, he offered a challenge to American university students: "Nor have the American students been a whit more radical than their universities. A student riot in behalf of an instructor dismissed because of his political opinion has never occurred. Nor have the American students ever been known to riot because of their own radical political opinions, nor in sympathy with a strike of organized labor." Given London's ten-year dissatisfaction with the university system—beginning with his enrollment at the University of California for a semester and his continued encounters with university men and women who did not think for themselves and did not show the least sympathy with the working class or for revolutionary socialism—it's not surprising that he attacked complacent students. Clearly, London saw the ISS as an institutional means to continue his disparagement of higher education. Thus, we can see his participation in the ISS on the same continuum as his inclusion of professorial characters—from Freddie Drummond to Darrel Standing—in his fiction.

He continued his attack on students, borrowing heavily from Triggs: "Not that the American students are meek and spiritless. They riot and rush and rough it as readily as any students in the world. But they have had no call to express political and social dissatisfactions. They have not been vexed by political and social dissatisfactions. In such matters they have been quite satisfied. They have been conservative—very, very conservative." They needed the kind of education that only an organization like the ISS could provide. Why? Because of

> the "university ideal." This ideal has been well formulated by Professor Shorey of the University of Chicago. He calls the university ideal "the passionless pursuit of passionless intelligence." According to this, warm human life has been no concern of the university. The university has not interested itself in the clay of the common road, but has kept its eyes fixed aloft on passionless intelligence—remote and dim and cold as the stars. And from this far gaze, the university has desisted only long enough, at times, to look disapproval at the occasional professor who has begun passionately to reason about life and society and the meaning of it all.

Here is the first time London uses the phrase "the passionless pursuit of passionless intelligence," a phrase that became an effective shorthand during his lecture tour for all things wrong with the university system.

The working class had passion. They lived on the street. They could not afford to be objective. University students were swaddled in the American idealistic democratic conception of freedom and democracy. The working class knew this idealism was a political illusion foisted on the young through their education to convince them that there was no need to struggle, that inequality simply did not exist. "It was not the university that discovered" that "liberty and equality were passing away," and so it was up to the working class to form an organization like the ISS to reeducate the youth of America. Even before the election of 1904, which London again cited as his touchtone for activism, "there were Socialist party clubs and Socialist study clubs in half a dozen colleges." Thus, "the time was ripe for arousing the university and a call was sent out." He then included the June 1905 three-paragraph flier, asking for interested people to respond by mail and cited part of Higginson's response to *Harper's*, which Triggs had included in his article, that must have rung especially significant to someone who had not been shy about the influence of Herbert Spencer: "'The movement is based on the obvious fact that we are more and more surrounded by institutions, such as free schools, free text books, free libraries, free bridges, free water supplied, free lecture course, even free universities, which were all called socialistic when first proposed, and which so able a man as Herbert Spencer denounced as socialism to his dying day.'" No wonder the individualist Martin Eden is a follower of Spencer.

Given the resistance to socialism's multifaceted program, London asserted that "the Intercollegiate Socialist Society is militant and expresses itself in no uncertain terms." He cites an ISS call to students that premised the call for militancy on "the silence of our colleges and universities concerning the international movement (of socialism). . . . There can be no chance save in the active and persistent efforts by those of the student body who have come to understand the demand of the people for economic freedom and self-government." Students will have to fight for their economic and intellectual rights because the ISS "will not be met as a dove of peace by the universities themselves."

Just look at the reaction of the editor of the *National Civic Federation Review*, wrote London. Easley says, "He has received 'a multitude of letters from university and college presidents and professors and ministers of the gospel,' who have thanked him for disclosing the real aim of the Intercollegiate Socialist Society."[126] Easley and his cohort exist, as they explicitly state, to combat "the rising tide of socialism. . . . When the tide of socialism rises in spite of the passionless silence of the apathetic university it is time for the students themselves to learn the nature of socialism." The ISS will not only encourage the young to study socialism but it will also help reform the university system and infuse it with the passion that animates the working class. The enemies of socialism were on the attack, and London understood his tour, his support for the ISS, and his socialist publications as a pedagogic enterprise and a revolutionary accelerant.

Given London and Triggs's common interest in the Arts and Crafts movement (an aesthetic manifestation of their socialism), it's not surprising to see Triggs's paragraphs prominently used in a 1906 pamphlet advertising the ISS.[127] Other items in the pamphlet include the initial call to join the society, a list of officers, a reprint of Higginson's letter to *Harper's*, and its articles of incorporation. The latter concerned its "objects and plans" (to provide printed matter for the study of socialism by university, college, and high school students) and qualifications for membership (any student "above the rank of grammar school" as well as anyone "interested in the work of the Society, elected to sustaining membership by the Executive Committee, who pays $20 or more a year to the propaganda fund of the Society").

The ISS's recommended reading list was divided into six sections: (1) Theoretical Socialism (elementary), (2) Theoretical Socialism (advanced), (3) Current American Problems, (4) Fiction, (5) Popular Pamphlets, and (6) Socialist Periodicals.[128] When London published "What Life Means to Me" in *Cosmopolitan*, Sinclair told him it would be perfect for the ISS.[129]

About six months after the first public announcement of the society's formation, a progress report was released to the public, signed by Strobell, London, and Sinclair, but also by Morris Hillquit and Robert Hunter. The former was a cofounder of the Socialist Party of America, and the latter was active in the settlement movement and managed the University Settlement House in New York where William English Walling and Leroy Scott, author of *The Walking Delegate*, had lived. As I said, he had written *Poverty*, cited by London on his lecture tour and by Easley in his defamatory essay in the *National Civic Federation Review*.

The progress report stated that the organization now had forty dues-paying members, though over a thousand people had expressed interest in helping the ISS. The ISS had study chapters or reading groups at Wesleyan (the first to form), Michigan (the group that changed into the SDS in the sixties), Yale, Harvard, Columbia, Bryn Mawr, and the University of Chicago. Other campuses had expressed sincere interest, speakers were lined up, authors were committed to write essays, and volunteers were ready to distribute literature, but the ISS lacked the personnel to print and mail ISS material. So the progress report was really an appeal to the membership to fund a full-time secretary, and the signatories to the appeal—London, Sinclair, Hillquit, Hunter, and Strobell—pledged their contributions in the hopes that others would follow.[130]

The appeals helped. In the first year, the ISS had $284.37.[131] By May 1907, when London gave up his presidency and Stokes took over, membership totaled 82 and the bank account was up to $400. Four years later, the membership was 720 and the account contained over $4,000.[132] In 1911 the ISS hosted a speech by Victor Berger, newly elected as the first socialist congressional representative, at Carnegie Hall, drawing a large crowd.[133] In 1913, a year in which the *Intercollegiate Socialist* (edited by Laidler) listed fifty-seven college chapters on its masthead, William English Walling, who by then was on the executive committee of the ISS, spoke in Chicago to 350 members.[134] In 1916 it reached its peak number of chapters, seventy-one, and two years later it had declined to thirty-nine chapters.[135] As it turned out, Owen Lovejoy, the treasurer, did not have to handle huge sums after all, but the membership numbers became significant.

The student study groups, besides arranging speakers to visit their campuses, submitted essays to newspapers. For example, in 1907, the University of California group published "Words That Will Become Obsolete" in the *Socialist Voice*; Arthur George of the Berkeley group had sent it to London who passed it on to the *Socialist Voice*. It began, tongue in cheek, "We, the Simplified Language Committee of the Intercollegiate Socialist Society, recommend after careful deliberation, that the following three hundred words, with their roots, derivatives and related forms, be, as rapidly as possible [relegated to] academic obscurity, or entirely abolished. In order that this may be accomplished, we recommend that all habits . . . and practices, that have caused their introduction into the language, be, by every possible means, done away with, and that new laws, standards and methods be sought, that shall, by their logical operation, render the use of these words obsolete." Included in the three hundred were *adultery, alien, assassin, anarchy, beggar, proletariat, profanity, polygamy, war, whore, working class, unmanly, syphilis, vagabond,* and *oligarchy.* In case readers might accuse the group of being destructive, not constructive, it created "an additional list of three hundred words, to represent the type of language that we desire to have preserved and brought into more general usage, reflecting the growth of those laws, standards and methods of social activity, which are indifferently known as democratic, republican or socialist, replacing the anarchistic language and ideals that now prevail." These words included *candid, belief, benevolence, best, better, brave, business, busy, faith, fame, family, federal, capital* (*productive property*), *celebrity, cash, literature, love,* and *loyalty.*[136] The emphasis on the linguistic nature of politics greatly appealed to the committee's advocate.

Even though a number of college students pledged to begin ISS clubs— including those at Harvard, Wesleyan College, and the University of Chicago; London had the power not only to antagonize his political opponents but to inspire the young—the ISS never sustained its national significance, at least until it changed its name in the 1960s.[137] The itinerant nature of undergraduates as well as to their on-again, off-again interest was reported in the *Socialist Voice* of Oakland: "It will undoubtedly be of gratification to the comrades generally to learn that the 'Social Progress Club' at the University of California has at last settled down to business. Since the inception of our club, a year ago, little of practical value has been accomplished; of late, however, we have decided to carry on a more active educational and propaganda campaign which, I feel sure, can but result in great good. Arrangements are now on foot for a series of lectures to be held on the campus. We hope to keep the ball started by Jack London, rolling."[138] Whether that ball rolled or not is unknown. Henry Ralston, the undergraduate at Yale who signed London's name to his own essay "Things Alive," published in Yale's alumni magazine, is another example of undergraduate dilettantism; after helping to form an ISS chapter at Yale, he graduated and eventually became a real estate agent in Florida. But this dilettantism is merely another form of the enthusiasm for socialism that took over the country after 1905. As Hillquit said, "Socialism became popular, almost a fad."[139] Hillquit, however, did not admit to its decline and portrayed the ISS as a move from "idea and symbol" in its first years to a "career of growth and expansion under the joint direction of Harry W. Laidler and Norman Thomas" after World War I.[140]

But American students were handicapped by a number of factors. They lived in "a play-world or imitation of the larger life outside their institution" (unlike their European counterparts) and susceptible to an inexperience "bordering on helplessness." And they were also faced with the large question of which socialism to commit to. The society's avowed purpose was to simply study all aspects of socialism, but with moderates like Hillquit and Stokes running the show—Hillquit was president for ten years—the society was guaranteed to remain aloof from any form of revolutionary socialism. Some eastern chapters did participate in the 1912 IWW strike at the Lawrence textile mills, and Walling praised the IWW at a time when Haywood's membership on the National Executive Committee of the Socialist Party was threatened. Walling, while a member of the ISS executive committee, also helped found the NAACP (W. E. B. Dubois lectured under the auspices of the ISS) in the face of opposition from men like Victor Berger; in fact, Hillquit resigned from the ISS when Walling accused him of being pro-German at the beginning of World War I. In 1918 Stokes resigned because of Hillquit's and others' pacifism. The war, which triggered the opposition between those who believed in the international solidarity of the proletariat opposed to capitalist wars and those who resisted German hegemony, split the ISS apart. To be specific, "the controversial 1917 St. Louis Declaration of the Socialist Party of America divided its executive committee on the issue of support of American entry into World War I, and the conscription of college students into the military and the passage of the Espionage Act of 1918 drastically reduced its membership and activities," wrote Karnoutsos. "The Society never fully recovered from these blows," she concludes.[141]

To some extent, then, the ISS stalled in its growth and influence for the same reasons that a nationwide socialist political party never accomplished more than electing a single congressional representative to office: it tried to encompass too many conflicting ideologies within socialism. As I hinted at previously, Stokes was asked to give the introduction to London's speech at the Grand Palace. Soon after London spoke in New York City, Stokes, the man whom Upton Sinclair described as "timid and sensitive, and does not believe in class hatred," gave a speech that the newspapers headlined "J. G. P. Stokes on Socialism: Takes Issue with Jack London."[142] Stokes declared, "There is a great deal of misunderstanding and error which prevails in criticisms of Socialists by capitalists and vice versa. For instance, at the Grand Central Palace, in New York, the other night, your friend and mine, Jack London, made this remark to his audience: 'Every capitalist is your enemy and every workingman is your friend' I know what Jack London meant by that. Let us see if his statement is correct, if it is logical." He found it was illogical because London profited from capitalists like his own editors and publishers. Stokes wasn't quibbling over semantics. He wanted London to be more precise, more thoughtful, not incendiary.[143]

London's rhetoric was proving divisive. Others within the ISS had similar reactions. Laidler told Sinclair that he disapproved of London's choice of "Revolution" for his New York City appearance under the auspices of the ISS.[144] Mabel C. Willard, a socialist and dedicated member of the ISS, told Sinclair that after London's New York City speech friends of hers who were sympathetic to the cause had been "shocked back into conservatism. To them, Mr. London seemed a 'revolutionist, an unsafe leader of the youth of the country.'"[145] Further, as I mentioned before, Higginson, who had agreed to be on the board, did not attend the meeting at Peck's restaurant and cancelled his appearance at one of London's East Coast lectures, and it is fair to speculate that he did so because he differed so fundamentally from London's revolutionary message.

London did not respond in public either to Stokes's pronouncement or to Higginson's apparent cowardice, and his term as president was meant to be temporary, but it does seem fair to say that he distanced himself rather quickly from the ISS when he realized that active socialists of whatever ideology would not predominate in the society. He did write back to Bamford after his friend criticized him for becoming involved in the ISS. "It seems to me as clear as day that the socialists of the ISS will have to withdraw eventually and found their own clubs," wrote Bamford, because, as he told another friend, "only men who have the fire can communicate it."[146] But London countered that the socialists who joined the ISS would eventually turn it into a socialist organization, boring from within in the way that London hoped socialists would capture the trade unions. For now, however, he was being realistic about the political status of college students; not only were they not socialist, they did not know what socialism was, so socialist college clubs could not be formed. Only clubs that studied socialism would germinate. How odd to see London being more cautious, more patient than Bamford. Though Bamford was afraid that their disagreement would damage their friendship, London assured him it would not.[147] As it turned out, Bamford was correct. The ISS did not become a training camp for young socialists, and it seems London anticipated this.

THE IMPORTANCE OF UPTON SINCLAIR

As deeply invested as London was in the tour, he was equally concerned about maintaining his writing schedule. He neither wanted to give up commitments he had made in late 1905 nor forego possible inspirations for new projects while traveling. Just before he left on his fame tour, he wrote to Bamford, explaining why he could not visit him any time soon. He felt his new writing commitments were overwhelming. He was a week from finishing *White Fang*. "I have agreed to review *The Long Day* for the *Examiner*. . . . I have agreed to write an article on the Intercollegiate Socialist Society, for an international News Syndicate [the Potentia syndicate]. I have agreed to write a 500-word article on Upton Sinclair's *The Jungle* for the Trust Edition of *The Appeal to Reason*; and an additional review of *The Jungle* for either the Hearst Newspapers or the New York *Independent*."[148] Partly he wanted to convey how busy he was—and thus, like a modern-day academic, how high his status was—and partly he wanted to convey his commitment to the cause. "In addition I am burdened with correspondence from the Socialists all over the country, asking me to lecture, because they understand that I am going on this lecture-tour." He said as well that he had not yet prepared the lectures he would give, though surely by this point he knew he would give some version of "Revolution."

Further, he was begging for some amount of control over his life. Just as he had told Collier that he couldn't write for his magazine because he didn't want to be tied down to a single writing project, he had told Charles Wagner, secretary of the Slayton Lyceum Bureau, that he didn't want to do the lecture tour if it interfered with his writing. Wagner had tried to reassure him: "A lecture trip need not necessarily interfere with your writing. You could lay aside one or two months, say November and December, 1905, and let us fill up that time for you, and you can devote the rest of the time to literary work."[149] He let himself be persuaded, but just as he was leaving, he felt his writing schedule was being dictated by others. Looking ahead, we can see his eventual departure for the South Seas as not only an attempt to become an international proponent for socialism but also an emphatic no to demands to give more as an author than he was prepared to do. For all his sincere protestations about the centrality of politics in his working life, he was first and foremost an author.

In the fall of 1905 London finished *White Fang* and reported on the second Britt-Nelson fight nearly simultaneously, infusing the same themes in each of the two seemingly disparate genres. That moment when he decided to write about the civilizing of a dog seems to have excited a deeper concern about the savage, or primitive, a concern that would ramify at least through the writing of *Adventure*. We might even see the next novel after that one, *Burning Daylight*, as the culmination of his extensive treatment of the savage, for the hero is a kind of White Fang brought out of the North and "civilized" by capitalism.

Besides the thematic of the binary of savagery/civilization, his representation of the Brotherhood of Man took central place in his writing. Just as he was finishing *White Fang*, London also wrote a review of Dorothy Richardson's *The Long Day*, an act of solidarity with women workers in New York City. As he told Bamford, "the writer is a socialist woman, and the book is about the working girls of New York."[150] Mother Jones had written to him in September, asking him if he would "kindly review a book written by a young girl who has been up against the rocks of Capitalism."[151] She alluded to the work she had been doing with the laundry workers in Troy, New York, and part of the reason London wrote the review was to be included in "the brotherhood of man." If the socialists of Alameda County could send money, then he could invest the power of his name and position as one of the foremost American authors in the cause of exploited workers in, as

Mother Jones said, "the slave pens of Capitalism." London then wrote to Jack Barrett of the *San Francisco Examiner* to ask if they would be interested, and Barrett said yes.

The Long Day, which grew out of Richardson's newspaper reporting on labor conditions for women in New York City, was "one of the most prominent examples of the extensive 'working-girl' literature published at the turn of the century. The first-person story of a young Pennsylvania schoolteacher forced by circumstances to seek work in the factories of New York, *The Long Day* created a sensation when it was published."[152] Undoubtedly, London's review helped prolong that sensation. "Here is a true book," he began. "It is a human document." We remember that by this pairing of antimonies—the human and the document—he voices his central definition of literature: "impassioned realism." The theatrical must be infused with the absorptive. In this case, the document speaks of how capitalism has rendered the human into a beast. Just as boxers lose their physical beauty so, too, do women workers face the reality of how physical labor destroys "that beautiful body. . . . How will she retain the color of in her cheeks? . . . How will she keep her springy step? . . . the resilience of her muscles?" If his discourse sounds "sexualized," it is because he fears that capitalistic manual labor will destroy the reproductive function of women: "Last but not least, how will she keep the strength in her loins, from which, strong or weak, must come the next generation of women and men?"[153] Of course men, too, suffer from the threat of being rendered impotent by such work.

This review is invested, though lightly, with the dichotomy of savage versus civilized. "In the ancient world, where men ran naked, killed with their hands and drank blood from their enemies' skulls, one worked for oneself." Only London could imagine the political economy of the Bone Age. The point is that the means of production in civilized America are owned, not by the naked individual, but by the capitalists and "before the hungry individual can go to work he must get permission from the owner of a machine." The Machine Age is defined not only by the degradation of the worker, not only by the separation of labor and value, not only by the huge income gap between the proletariat and the plutocrat, but by the age's mismanagement of basic necessities. Either one starves or one works and in so doing destroys one's body. "Here is work to be done by every human creature that takes pride in the fact that he is human and not a beast."[154] To be a beast would be to ignore the pain and suffering of women like those whose desperate work lives are recounted in Richardson's book. But workers whose jobs degrade them aren't the only potential (work) beasts. Anybody, says our advocate for the weak and disadvantaged, could end up as such.

Both Richardson and Mother Jones greatly appreciated the review. After London had sent Richardson a copy of the review and a letter, Richardson wrote, "I hardly know how to express my gratitude and appreciation for your more than splendid review of The Long Day." He had asked her if she were a socialist, and she was enthusiastic in her affirmative response; she was in fact close friends with Eugene Debs, and she told London that in the not-too-distant past she had been more radical than now: "I used to be with the revolutionists a great deal, and there is nothing, of course, like the personal element in keeping alive the spirit of this, as with all other faiths."[155] Like so many socialists, including London, becoming a socialist was akin to a baptism. "I owe you a debt of gratitude for the magnificent review you gave my friend's book. I need not say to you how fully both she and I appreciate it," wrote Mother Jones, adding that she hoped to meet him during his lecture tour.[156] Not only did they meet in dramatic fashion at Fanueil Hall and the Grand Central Palace, but London, Charmian, Richardson, and Gaylord and Mary Wilshire spent an afternoon together in New York. Socialism and authorship blended together on the tour. There were other literary gatherings, with, at various times, Edwin Markham, Elsa Barker, and Charles G. D. Roberts. And one can only imagine what Carl Sandburg and London would have shared had they met in Chicago instead of missing each other by a matter of days.[157] These gatherings of painters, photographers, novelists, and essayists represented a different sort of brotherhood. It was a community of artists, as strong or stronger as his political communities.

He continues the thematic of the Brotherhood of Man in his next artwork, "What Life Means to Me." Bailey Millard, the relatively new and energetic editor of *Cosmopolitan*, dreamt up this series, and, besides London, the contributors included John Burroughs, Edwin Markham, Julia Ward Howe, Upton Sinclair, and others. London was indebted to Millard. As had many New York editors, Millard had come east from San Francisco, having worked at every major Bay Area newspaper as well as all the minor ones, with one or two exceptions.[158] When he worked at the *San Francisco Examiner*, he had accepted London's short story "Uri Bram's God." Three years later, London thanked him for publishing some of his feature stories and asked if Millard might give him an opportunity to review some books. It seems that Millard had provided him the opportunity to write regularly for the *Examiner* in the summer of 1902, and they knew each other well enough for London to close out his letter on a personal note, saying he identified with Millard and his unsuitability for working in a newspaper office nine to five, his love of good literature, and his need for the "fresh open life."[159]

So Millard thought of London first for his new series for the *Cosmopolitan*. He wrote to London in early November 1905; Jack had been lecturing for nearly a month by the time he got the proposal: "We are trying to secure from each of a half-dozen or more prominent writers and men of affairs an expression of his philosophy of life, in which a strong biographical note shall be heard. This expression is to be given in a three thousand word article, which shall sum up the writer's experience of life, tell what he stands for and what he would like to accomplish or see done in the world."[160] When Millard received London's response, he told the author that there had been a shift in the series' purpose: "From the tone of your note in reply to my request for the article on your philosophy of life, I should take it that you understand this to cover the history of your experience, rather than your views in relation to a citizen's object of existence. Our title for the article has been changed to 'What Life Means to Me,' and I shall be obliged if you keep this in view when writing."[161] It's a subtle shift, but it seems to indicate a desire on the magazine's part to receive an apolitical essay, something that would not include London's "views in relation to a citizen's object of existence." No matter. For London, there was no hiding the significance of his political conversion, and, in any case, he received the second letter after he had completed the essay.

Luckily, Millard seemed happy enough with the essay. The magazine announced the series in February 1906 after having received London's copy: "What life means to the thinking man of eminence is a subject in which there is much curious and much valid interest. Take the man of large affairs, take the philosopher or the famous novelist. We read him and read of him, but how little do we know of his private view of life?" Not much, apparently. "Among those to respond to our invitation for literature of this sort was that forceful writer, Jack London," continued the editorial announcement, "whose views are so eloquent and refreshing that they will be the first to be printed in this noteworthy series."

It wasn't the first time Millard had asked London for his opinion on a hot topic of the day. In the same issue as the editorial announcement, the magazine ran a piece by Frederick Upham Adams, who had asked ten prominent American men to comment on the general question, "Are Great Fortunes Great Dangers?" Adams asked a series of more specific questions concerning public ownership of utilities, taxation, and inherited wealth. London's answers were the most radical and unforgiving in their socialism. To the question, "The wealth of several of our American capitalists is now conservatively estimated at from $100,000,000 to $500,000,000. Can a man render to his country or to mankind a service which will entitle him to so great a reward?" London said, "No; the sum of the remuneration to all our patriots and statesmen from the beginning of our history is not so large." To the question, "Does the possession of a billion of dollars in the hands of an individual constitute a menace to the republic?" London replied, "Yes; a menace as colossal as the sum of dollars." "If it shall become desirable to legislate to lessen the disparity between those of vast wealth and those of moderate or small holdings," imagined Adams in a more naïve time, "what measures would you recommend? How about an income tax? How about an inheritance tax?" London answered with his most challenging program: "I should recommend the application of the law of eminent domain to the land, and the making and applying of a similar law to the machinery. The result would be the collective ownership of all land and all machinery and then there would be no disparity of wealth. The income of every able-bodied individual would then be the income earned by his toil and not earned by his possessions." And, to the questions, "Do you favor the municipal own-ership of street railways, gas plants and similar utilities? Do you favor or oppose the government ownership of railways?" London was emphatic: "I favor municipal ownership of all municipal utilities; state ownership of all state utilities; national ownership of all national utilities." It was rare for London to offer constructive criticism of the current economic system, and this series of statements may be his most concise and accessible.[162]

His contribution to "What Life Means to Me" conveyed the same political-economic message, but in personal terms. If we divide up the title in three parts, we see that he formed the essay from a combination of genres: the self-help essay, similar to his imagined "Hints to a Beginner" series ("What Life"); the autobiographical conversion tale of the uninitiated, unthinking, uncaring citizen of America baptized by the fire of social responsibility and thus the making of the socialist heart and brain ("Means"); and the monu-mental, theatrical statement of one's presence in the public imaginary ("to

Me"). The title resonates with "How I Became a Socialist" for three reasons. First, they were written at the invitation of magazine editors to establish a series. Second, they share the same combination of genres. Third, the meaning that he finds in life is the reason he became a socialist.

"What Life Means to Me," however, subsumes the other essay. Written on the train to Kansas City in November 1905, it provided London with the opportunity to think systemically about his life so far—the centrality of socialism, to be sure, but more than that. Five years later, responding to a minister's sermon that attacked *Martin Eden*—and thus Jack London, if you followed the minister's lead in reading the novel as pure autobiography— because he had no faith, London responded with a paragraph from "What Life Means to Me." "Let me here quote some of my faith," he told Reverend Charles Brown in a letter to the *San Francisco Examiner*:

> I look forward to a time when man shall progress upon something worthier and higher than his stomach, when there will be a finer incentive to impel men to action than the incentive of to-day, which is the incentive of the stomach. I retain my belief in the nobility and excellence of the human. I believe that spiritual sweetness and unself- ishness will conquest the gross gluttony of to-day. And last of all, my faith is in the working class. As some Frenchman has said, "The stair- way of time is ever echoing with the wooden shoe going up, the pol- ished boot descending."[163]

We'll explore the connection between that last sentence and *The Iron Heel*, but for now the connection between the two is clear; in November 1905 he hadn't had the idea for writing that specific novel, but he had the ambition for writing some kind of socialist novel. This essay also looks forward to his lecture tour and deals with the anxiety of facing a possibly unreceptive national audience. In fact, while reading the essay one gets the impression that it was written after the tour was complete—"I stayed in hotels and clubs and homes and Pullmans and steamer chairs with captains of industry, and marveled at how little traveled they were in the realm of intellect"—but he is actually recounting incidents and feelings he had while lecturing in the Bay Area and during the first few weeks of his tour.[164]

The essay is structured in three parts, each part marked by a variation on the first sentence: "I was born in the working-class."[165] In the first part, he posits his childhood poverty as a "bottom"; it's not exactly an abyss, but it was something to climb out of. The essay's original subtitle was "The Confession of a Climber."[166] Not surprisingly, then, the image of a ladder—a socioeconomic ladder—predominates as he decides to earn as much money as possible to escape poverty and achieve "all that was fine and noble and gracious" (392). He does this by becoming first a newspaper boy, second an oyster pirate, and third a worker at various unskilled jobs. Exploitation matters little to him because "it was all in the game." But "too much work sickened me," he says, and that's what drove him to become a tramp: not resentment toward the employer who had hired him to replace two men, not the hard labor that he was engaged in, but rather an excess of work. This is not the story of Johnny in "The Apostate." It's an odd, incomplete, and vague statement of a major change in his life, especially since it marks the end of the first third of the essay. Rather than decide to work more intelligently, to take a different, less onerous job, he decided against all work: "I did not wish ever to see work again. I fled from work. I became a tramp." So without a real explanation, London tells us he is perfectly content to abandon the socioeconomic ladder and became accustomed to "bloody sweats in slums and prisons" (394).

The second part begins, "I had been born in the working-class, and I was now, at the age of eighteen, beneath the point at which I had started." Now he was in "the pit, the abyss, the human cesspool." To escape the abyss, one needs, not a ladder, but knowledge. At this point he dispenses with the abyss/ladder metaphor and turns to a second governing metaphor: the house. In eight months this metaphor would become literal in his essay "The House Beautiful." Here, in "What Life Means to Me," he imagines all the classes of society defined by where they might live in a house. The proletariat lives in the basement, the rich on the parlor floor, and the brain merchant in the attic, where the good bohemians live. "It was true, the diet there was slim," he wrote, "but the air at least was pure" (528). In the attic he found out he was a socialist. That is, he had been converted without knowing it, and only after he read intellectually did he realize what his philosophy of life really was. It was a combination of revolutionary socialism and an intense "warm faith in the human, glowing idealism, sweetnesses of unselfishness, renunciation and martyrdom. . . . Here life was clean, noble, and alive." But, and here the similarity to *Martin Eden* is pronounced, he becomes disillusioned because, after being admitted to the parlor floor—"as a brain merchant I was a success" (528)—he did not find life being lived. In lines forecasting extemporaneous remarks he would make on his tour, he writes, "I had expected to find men who were clean, noble, and alive. . . . It is true, I found many that were clean and noble; but with rare exceptions, they were not *alive*." And then he repeats what he had just written in his essay for the ISS: "In this connection I may especially mention the professors I met, the men who live up to that decadent university ideal, 'the passionless pursuit of passionless intelligence'" (529).

Suffering from disillusion with the materialism and corruption of the successful, our narrator begins his third section: "So I went back to the working class, in which I had been born and where I belonged" (530). Birth is biology is fate. Not only was he fated to return to the working class, but the upper floors of the house are fated to fall. "Then we'll cleanse the cellar and build a new habitation for mankind, in which there will be no parlor floor, in which all the rooms will be bright and airy, and where the air that is breathed will be clean, noble and alive" (530). The very air we breathe will be socialism. This is exactly the rhetoric of "The House Beautiful" and, looking even further into the future, his and Charmian's intent for their ultimate living quarters, the Wolf House. The brain merchant–author imagined a stable, utopic dwelling in which the correct mode of life could be led, but the actual, flesh-and-blood author under sail would no sooner put down permanent roots in a house, no matter how perfect and grand in conception, than he would cease to write.

The essay is actually more interesting for what he left out than what he put in. Like his earlier essays about his beginnings as an author ("Getting into Print" and so on), "What Life Means to Me" is the tale of someone who raised himself. It is further codification of his mythology of self-creation, of the man who never had parents, siblings, or a mentor. Amazingly, he never once mentions that he learned to write and that he had become a successful author. He uses the euphemism "brain merchant" instead of *author*. He never once mentions that he is married and that love might be a fundamental concept of what makes life worth living for him. These absences are necessary to create a particular public image: the solitary genius. This conception of the author is more marketable than the image of a proletariat writer, true, but London is interested in making a different point. By calling himself a brain merchant, he means that he sells brain power, not a commodity like a book. The publisher sells books. The author uses his brain to write the book and thus sells his brain power. By constructing the publishing business in this fashion, he retains his position vis-à-vis the capitalists as a laborer, using not muscle but brains.

Perhaps reminded of his previous newspaper work by his invitation from Millard, but mostly because he could not leave the world of newspapers for very long, he next wrote a mildly amusing piece on an obscure religious sect in Boston. Some Hearst newspaper reporters took him to the Odd Fellows' Hall where he witnessed a ceremony of the Holy Jumpers, enthusiasts who combined strenuous physical exercise with prayer and meditation.[167] "As I looked at six happy-faced Holy Jumpers disporting themselves on the muddy pavement in front of the Odd Fellows' Building yesterday afternoon I could scarcely refrain from joining them. They looked so happy. Besides, I haven't been getting much exercise lately."[168] The light tone befits his admiration of those who find the essence of established religions worthwhile but are able to encapsulate it in a modern-day social practice: "To praise the Lord, and at the same time to send the blood surging through all the body, flushing away waste tissue and building up new tissue, is certainly killing two birds with one stone." But London saw more than the benefits of physical exertion and prayer. In one beautifully succinct sentence, London captures not only the inner meaning of the Holy Jumpers but also what he most sought after in his own adventuring: "Their happy hearts became articulate through the flesh." London sympathized with this direction in socioreligious thought, but he could never become more than a bemused supporter. Brother Ericson, who gave a sermon (and apparently stood still to deliver his talk), appealed "to the poor and lowly, to the tired and miserable and long-suffering. . . . In place of their misery and suffering he offered them gayety and laughter." He also offered an alternative to "the pomp and display of the churches [which] he called . . . 'steepled clubhouses.'" Although the article gave London a respite from the intensity of the socialist movement—which would in London's view create a more hospitable world for fringe movements like the Holy Jumpers than the established religions—the fight for economic, political, and social justice had to do more than offer laughter in the place of poverty and demanded a seriousness unknown to New Thought advocates.

London had hoped to write steadily while on tour, but he produced only three brief works: the essay on the ISS, "What Life Means to Me," and his newspaper article on the Holy Jumpers. It seems that Slayton and London were wrong to imagine that he could maintain his usual productive writing schedule while on tour. Yet we can see from the latter as well as from some of the comments he made to reporters that he was mulling over ideas for sustained fiction. Nearly five months had passed since he had finished *White Fang*, and he used his time away from his writing desk to mentally plot out his next sustained period of writing.

RETURN TO THE SOUTHLAND

Picking up where he had left off in October 1905, his very first work completed at home was a turn back to absorptive fiction about a Klondike dog; he completed "Brown Wolf" on 2 March 1906, a month after his return from the East.[169] It is often said in Jack London studies that, faced with the costs of his everyday life and the new financial demands of preparing for his and Charmian's trip around the world in a boat, London wrote what he wrote in 1906 and 1907 simply to pay the bills. This in fact is not true. When London returned from his tour, he took stock of his contractual obligations with George Brett and Macmillan, realized he needed to complete a book of stories, and promptly set out to do so. He was contractually obligated to write stories, and "Brown Wolf" was his first of two to complete what would become *Love of Life, and Other Stories*.

London made two sets of notes for this story, a definite departure from his practice; it seems likely that one set was written before the tour and another set after the tour as he thought harder about the story. In a July 1905 letter he told Brett that "in October I start East on this lecturing-trip, and during this lecturing-trip I have mapped out for myself to write a series of brief, nervous, strong, dramatic sketches."[170] In the first set of notes—written in words "brief, nervous, [and] strong"—entitled "Short Dog Story," he writes out the bare (dog) bones of a plot. Note how he leaves out plot details to first get at essentials:

> A Dog—great love—one master. Second master. After years, both masters together—& dog has to choose between. First master in Klondike, all hardship, & suffering, & toil—second master, in Southland, all soft things, comfortable. (How I win Brown.) The struggle in the dog. Tries to make both masters go off together. They agree to let him decide. Second master has a wife. A lick for her. His colossal perturbation & indecision. His whining & barking—his swift turns back and forth & between the two masters. Tucks head in wife's lap. First master goes off

down trail. Can see him go, farther & farther. Dog lies down with second master. True to their compact, man & wife do nothing. They sit, watching & waiting, with beating hearts. And in the end, dog bounds off & runs to overtake first master. End with man & wife, sitting a bit apart, in same position. They look at each other. The woman smiles, but the tears well into her eyes. Man's eyes frankly wet. Maybe end right here, probably so—unless something tremendously appropriate and culminative may be said by one or the other.[171]

In the second set of notes, he begins to fill in the details. First come the names. The second master, the resident of the Southland and married to Madge, is named, first, Jim, then Joe Irvine. By the time London had begun writing, though, he had already decided on Walt Irvine. Skiff Miller and Walt's wife, Madge, retain the names that he had decided on in these notes. Next he figures out that the two masters actually argue about the merits of each locale: "First master [Skiff Miller] contends that dog is happier in the Northland." The second masters love the dog so much because it was so hard to win his affection. Within this context, London lets the idea out that the figure for his imagination is "remote and alien." This contest of wills—the master/author wooing his muse, taming it—leads London to see how the narrative will take shape. "Maybe beginning of story," he writes next, "and of their walk. 'Where's Wolf?' wife asks. 'Running a rabbit. There he is. And no rabbit. Describe Wolf. Then: 'They loved the dog very much.'" I will discuss the master (author)/dog (muse) relationship later, but now we see how the word *notes* is a bit of a misnomer. As he wrote out these notes, whole phrases and sentences form a rough draft for the story.

More details follow: the first master, Skiff Miller, is looking for his sister, then Wolf appears, licks his hand to the astonishment of Walt and Madge, and "then the explanation begins." Now the narrative arc is firmly in his mind, and he sees the second master, Walt, getting angry, and Miller acting cool, who says (in a line London used verbatim in the story), "I reckon there's nothin' in sight to prevent me takin' 'm right here & now." In these notes, though, he imagined Miller making the "generous" offer of letting the dog decide between the two, not Madge. It's a subtle shift in narrative, but it is crucial in that Madge—obviously a Charmian London figure—provides a kind of moral compass for the men. In the story (and not in the notes), she tells Miller convincingly that "you consider only what you like.

You do with him as you would with a sack of potatoes or a bale of hay."[172] In both the notes and the story, Miller then voices a retrograde understanding of women: "I know the ways of women. . . . Their hearts is soft. When their hearts is touched they're likely to stack the cards, look at the bottom of the deck, an' lie like the devil—beggin' your pardon, ma'am. I'm only discoursin' about women in general," to which Madge sarcastically replies, "I don't know how to thank you" (194).[173] Never mind that London portrays both Miller and Walt as soft-hearted and "touched." It's Madge who sees the larger ethical picture. To commodify a living being, especially one capable of love for humans, is a sin. It leads to slavery. Future figures of Charmian in London's work will often function in the same way.

The published story begins with an author figure and a scene of recognition and identity, as if London were restarting his authorial career as a fiction writer. Walt Irvine, a poet, waits outside his house in Glen Ellen, California, as his wife, Madge, comes out, asking, "'Where's Wolf?'" and then calling out "'Wolf! Wolf! Here Wolf!'" Given that Jack's nickname was Wolf, that question, "Where's Wolf?" addressed to her husband, becomes a kind of query that hopes to discover what had happened to her writer-husband, the author she had known so well for years but that, after a long absence out East, seems to have disappeared (169). Walt assures her that he has not. "Mine is no futility of genius that can't sell gems to the magazines," Walt tells her, and then, as if he had just finished reading an essay by Jack London called "What Life Means to Me," he says, "I am no attic singer, no ballroom warbler. And why? Because I am practical. Mine is no squalor of song that cannot transmute itself, *with proper exchange value*, into a flower-crowned cottage, a sweet mountain-meadow, a grove of redwoods, an orchard of thirty-seven trees, one long row of black berries and two short rows of strawberries. . . . I am a beauty-merchant, a trader in song, and I pursue utility" (170). With the introduction of the Marxist term *exchange value*, we recognize the fullness of London's conception of his authorial office at this moment in his career. The tour had only reinforced and clarified his economic position as an author. He didn't write for money; he wrote to create beauty and to live in bohemian splendor. But beauty paid, and he wanted to be paid for it.

Thus he compares himself to Orpheus, a figure London would have known from Offenbach's *Orpheus in the Underworld*. But we sense a blustery, inflated tone, which Madge proceeds to puncture by calling him, not

Orpheus, but "a street-arab" (170). Neither one nor the other, Irvine is more like Edwin Markham than anyone else, a poet London had hung out with just two months previous—someone of genuine artistic talent who nonetheless succeeded in the magazine trade.

Brown Wolf is a beautiful object himself, and, coincident with London's evolving interest in the remote past and the remote future, he seems to have come either from the past (he is after all a living being whose savagery is like that of the animals of the Bone Age) or from the future (the narrator calls him as "remote and alien as a traveller from another planet"). In a book he most likely just finished, *The Universal Kinship*, by J. Howard Moore, London marked a passage that buttressed the evolutionary science of a dog's lifelong loyalty to a single owner.[174] Like Buck, Brown Wolf is affiliated with London's muse, being beautiful and timeless. The narrator offers no explanation for Irvine's obsession to capture him and to keep him. Irvine happens upon him by chance, captures him, and sees him leave again. When Brown Wolf first appeared on the ranch, like a down-and-out tramp, Walt and Madge fattened him up only to see him depart. This capture and escape happens again and again until "he accepted the inevitable" (1076). They decide he is a Klondike dog-wolf, and, like Buck, longs to run wild in the North. But like White Fang, he can also settle in Sonoma Valley, content to lead a semidomesticated life as Walt Irvine's familiar. He lies at Irvine's feet while he writes.

When Skiff Miller the Klondike mailman—an author figure in his own right—appears on the ranch, like Wolf, out of nowhere, a battle between the North and the South begins. Should Wolf be domesticated? is one way of putting the question. The larger question, however, is, dual. The first part has to do with biology: can he be domesticated? Isn't there something essential about the wolf-dog that makes it wild? The second part is London's metaphoric treatment of his relationship to his muse. We remember that while Wolf lay at Walt's feet, he was distracted almost to the point of paralysis: "Between petting and talking, [Walt lost] much time from his work" (178). Walt has a muse already, a southern muse that is poetic in nature and seems most able to inspire poetry about the beauty of their surroundings. Wolf, however, is a muse of the Northland for writers describing a world with barely a landscape at all, just whiteness.

The end of the story was forecast at the beginning. Wolf's continued attempts to escape Sonoma Valley are now climaxed. The North has come to him in the figure of Skiff Miller, and inevitably the two are reunited. Biology trumps the civilizing process, and we cannot escape our past. Miller will manage the letters of the English language with this muse by his side, and London thus reaffirms his commitment to writing about the Northland. The abyss of the "Devil's Dice Box" and "An Odyssey of the North" may not be his dominant source any longer, but it was his first conception of the source of his imagination. When White Fang came and stayed south, London's imagination found another topoi, another abyss from which stories arose.

In eighteen days he would begin another Klondike story to complete an eight-story collection. But first he had to fulfill a promise to Upton Sinclair to write a review of *The Jungle*, which had been published in the *Appeal to Reason* from February to November 1905 and then by Doubleday Page in February 1906. That London published three different commentaries on this book not only testifies to his sincere appreciation but also marks *The Jungle* as central to his political-literary philosophy. No other book and no other author during his career received so much public attention from him. Sinclair, in 1905, was not famous, he was twenty-seven, and he was broke and depressed. London, though only two years older, was now nationally famous and rich and eager to pull as many deserving unknown authors into the limelight with him as possible. This was another duty of the office of American author as London understood it.

First, in the July issue of *Appeal to Reason*, London's initial comment about the novel, solicited by Sinclair, appeared on the second page in a box above the installment for chapter 16: "The Jungle is going splendidly. I liked the opening but now I like it least of all. The way the story picks up and keeps picking up is tremendous. It has stirred me and made me sit right up time and again. There has been nothing done like it. You have my heartiest congratulations."[175] I mentioned earlier that London told Bamford in late 1905 that he had promised a five-hundred-word review for *Appeal to Reason*'s "Trust Edition" and a longer newspaper review, all this as a response to Sinclair's impassioned plea sent to London in September 1905: "Warren [Fred D., the managing editor of the *Appeal to Reason*] and I are agreed that two things are wanted. (1) He is preparing a Trust Edition—three or four million copies (fact). He will put an account of the book in this, and he wants a 500 word review of it from you. (2) An article about it to appear in the Independent the week the book is published (about Feb. 1) This can be easily arranged, as Holt asked me for an article about my work this very week. The article could be called 'A Proletarian Novel' or something like that, and discussed as a picturesque product of the War of the Classes."[176] London's notes for the shorter review seem written immediately upon receipt of this plea: "Jungle A Proletarian novel The Uncle Tom's Cabin of Wage Slavery."[177] The latter phrase opens the review: "Here it is at last! The book we have been waiting for these many years! The 'Uncle Tom's Cabin' of wage slavery! Comrade Sinclair's book 'The Jungle!' and what 'Uncle Tom's Cabin' did for black slaves, 'The Jungle' has a large chance to do for the wage-slaves of today." The review emphasizes its proletarian nature and the necessity for the proletariat to read and promote the book. The general public may laugh at the book or abuse it, he says, but "the most dangerous treatment it will receive is that of silence." "Comrades," he exhorts at the end, "it is up to you!"[178]

A little over three months later, on 6 March 1906, London wrote his extended, emotional, unadulterated, laudatory review that in time became a kind of manifesto for the socialist movement. Again likening the book to *Uncle Tom's Cabin*, London took his own advice and shouted his praise from the rooftops. He ignored the obvious weaknesses of the book and instead forecasted that "not only may it become one of the 'great sellers,' but it is very likely to become the greatest seller." He promoted it as a conversion story, which it is, not as a tract on food safety, which it became in the minds of most American readers. He explained why it had to take place in Chicago, an argument he would adhere to when he wrote *The Iron Heel* later in the same year: "He selected the greatest industrial city in the country . . . the most perfect specimen of jungle-civilization. . . . Chicago certainly is industrialism incarnate, the storm-center of the conflict between capital and labor, a city of street battles and blood." It is also obvious that his focus on the binary of civilization/jungle shows him still mulling over his next novel, *Before Adam*.

Short of calling the novel a human document, London insisted on its veracity in the face of the kind of criticism he routinely received: that the incidents seemed so extreme that they could not be true. He in fact references himself (rendered anonymously as "a public speaker" on tour in New York City) as someone who had cited statistics about wages in Chicago that newspapers had called lies.[179] He also references a discussion he had in Chicago with A. M. Simons, who had been Sinclair's guide in 1904 when he was doing research for *The Jungle*; Simons, whose pamphlet *Pack-*

ingtown had been influential for Sinclair, told both Sinclair and London about the accidental drowning of a child in a puddle. His review stresses how un-American America had become: "It depicts what our country really is, the home of oppression and injustice, a nightmare of misery, an inferno of suffering, a jungle wherein wild beasts eat and are eaten."

The narrative of Sinclair's main character, Jurgis Rudkus, fits right into London's own autobiography; early on, working in the jute mill and the electric company, London thought he could ascend the ladder he had just described in "What Life Means to Me" by working hard and harder. Thinking of his own experiences as a child laborer, London forecasts one of his next short stories, "The Apostate" when he quotes extensively from the chapter in which little Stanislovas works in a factory placing lard cans in reach of a machine for three dollars a week. Upton Sinclair, of course, would have read "What Life Means to Me" after it was published, but, influenced as he was by *The People of the Abyss* and other works by London, he includes his fellow socialist author in the narrative, calling him "a young author, who came from California, and had been a salmon-fisher, an oyster-pirate, a longshoreman, a sailor; who had tramped the country and been sent to jail, had lived in the Whitechapel slums, and been to the Klondike in search of gold. All these things he pictured in his books, and because he was a man of genius he forced the world to hear him. Now he was famous, but wherever he went he still preached the gospel of the poor."[180] London modestly does not mention this passage.

Nor does he directly reference Jurgis's conversion to socialism, the main intent of Sinclair's narrative. The point for Sinclair was not to convince the American people to pass stringent food purity laws but to horrify the public in order to convince them to become socialists. London does refer to the "over four hundred thousand men and women" who as socialists are promoting the book. And his review closes with a sarcastic direct address to capitalists: "Dear masters, would it not be wise to read for once the literature that all your working-class is reading?" In the end then, London and Sinclair, and "London" and Jurgis, emphasize the conversion power of literature and speechifying.[181] In 1906 even the "masters" read books; they just didn't read the right ones.

London had now successfully built up a reputation as an important book reviewer, but there are two reasons why we do not think of him participating in this traditional role of the literary man. One is that the books he chose to review principally involved socialism, not contemporary fiction. Two, his review of *The Jungle* was his final one. He would write blurbs, letters of encouragement, and introductions to books, but never another formal review. Partly, he was soon out of the country, reading only the books he deemed absolutely necessary for his future writing projects, and so he was also out of touch with those who might ask him to write reviews. Partly, he never really saw book reviewing as an integral part of his authorial office. It was too much like office work. He had larger aspirations, so at the height of his fame and influence he chose to no longer endorse or reject the writings of his contemporaries in this formal way.

GEORGE BRETT AND THE FUNCTION
OF CHARMIAN LONDON

George Brett and Jack London had last had a sustained correspondence when they conversed about *White Fang*. After that and all during the tour, their relationship maintained stasis. Brett had asked London in September 1905 if the author could coordinate his tour with Macmillan's advertising department, and London provided him with his itinerary (though I haven't found any evidence that the company actually tried to promote his work in conjunction with the tour).[182] But before this, in the summer of 1905, they had to work out some contractual items. Macmillan balanced their books in July and issued year-end royalty checks in November. London, in June, had asked Brett for an accounting and an advance on the year-end royalty because he needed a down payment for the Hill Ranch, the beginning of his project to piece several properties—when they came up for sale—to form what he called his Beauty Ranch. Brett agreed and sent him a check for $8,300 ($214,000 in 2016).[183]

Thus in July Brett continued and expanded the conversation. He raised the questions of the special term in their contract—that is, did London still want monthly payments as advances toward royalties?—of his actual royalty rate, and of what London owed Macmillan in terms of book production—a volume of short stories and a novel for 1906. London replied that he had three-quarters done on a book of short stories (he had just finished "Planchette," which would complete *Moon-Face, and Other Stories*) and that *White Fang* would stand as his yearly novel. Brett agreed and pinned his monthly payments to three hundred dollars a month. Brett also assured London that his royalty rate of 20 percent was higher than that of any other

American author; further, he suggested London might take less in order for Macmillan to have more money to promote the book. "The author gets on each book about three times to four times as much as the publisher, so that the amount of margin which is left for the working of a book, in case it needs large sums spent upon it, is insufficient."[184] London responded with a new idea: instead of 15 percent on the first five thousand copies and 20 percent on any sold over that, he would receive 15 percent on those that sell fewer than five thousand total, and 20 percent for those that sold more than five thousand. Brett reminded London that the initial costs of "plates, composition, typesetting, illustrations," and so forth justified the lower royalty rate for the first five thousand, but he was happy to make the change.[185] The new contract was signed in September.[186]

Sometime after arriving home, he made a list of Klondike stories that had been published but uncollected and saw he had 34,935 words for a new volume to follow *Moon-Face, and Other Stories*.[187] We have already seen how he completed "Brown Wolf" to fulfill his contractual obligation, but after he completed it, he hesitated to add it to the collection because it did not take place in the Klondike. Then he wrote a straightforward Klondike story called "A Day's Lodging," begun a day after finishing his review of *The Jungle* and decided to include both stories as well as "The Story of Keesh," a relatively ancient story completed in 1901. Thus he had one story from 1901, two from 1903 ("Love of Life" and "Negore, the Coward"), three from 1905 ("The Sun-Dog Trail," "The White Man's Way," and "The Unexpected"), and his two newest stories of 1906 to comprise *Love of Life, and Other Stories*.

"A Day's Lodging" (in another sign that he was just getting used to writing absorptive short stories, he did not have a title in mind when he started; on the final page of the story, he wrote a note to Charmian: "make title 'A Day's Lodging.'") is a reimagining of "The Scorn of Women." The marital problems of the Southland infect the Northland. "A Day's Lodging" begins with a passage of writing from something called "Narrative of Shorty"; Shorty may or may not be the same character who appears later in *Smoke Bellew*. His narrative reads as if it were testimony in a trial, putting us, the reader, in the position of jury. The question posed by Shorty is who started a stampede over "NOTHIN'" and why.[188] Could it be John Messner, who starts off the story with his dog team carrying on an unknown mission? We like Messner immediately because he, like Madge in "Brown Wolf," recognizes that it is unnatural to "break you to harness, curb all your natural proclivities, and make slave-beasts out of you" (47). We also are reminded of the cover of *The Call of the Wild*. For the past three years, London has stuck to his analogy between dog workers and human workers. His lecture tour only made him more inclined to make the analogy more explicit.

And, of course, he hasn't relented on portraying the North as ghostland: "The world slept, and it was like the sleep of death" (48). We expect talk of ghosts next, and we are not disappointed. When the doctor and Tess settle into the cabin, and he mentions her name, Messner "became suddenly alert. He looked at her quickly, while across his face shot a haunting expression, the ghost of some buried misery achieving swift resurrection" (54–55). Though "the ghost was laid again," momentarily, at least, Messner becomes ghostlike, overtaken by his past relationship with Tess. By depositing the bag of gold in the hole, he disposes of the ghost, at least temporarily.

The story is similar to London's model story of the source of his imagination. Like "The Devil's Dice Box" and "An Odyssey of the North," we have all the elements in place. A cabin with gold and writing—"the light in the cabin was dim, filtering through in a small window made of onion-skin writing paper" (1091)—and chance. A stroke of "luck" placed these three characters alone in a cabin. But the abyss is absent; in fact, London makes a point of placing the cabin on a rise above the river. And madness and death are absent; though Messner's temper flares, he has changed, says Tess, and he maintains his calm. "I don't get excited any more," he tells his wife (65). The Kilkenny cats have disappeared. The story, like "Brown Wolf," is thus not about the Northland and the imagination so much as it is about marriage and the Southland. But, still, like "Brown Wolf," it demonstrates a slow shift in London's thinking about the sources of his imagination. Married to a woman he loves—Charmian/Madge—and no longer married to Bess/Tess, he signals that his inspiration could be more dependent on love and the right woman than it is on ghosts and the fear of death. That was his hope, at least.

It seemed possible that changes in one's circumstances, most importantly in relationships, could impact significantly one's relationship to one's own creative interiority. After the lecture tour, women become more central to not only his creative vision but also to his understanding of how that vision comes to him. As independent and creative spirits—we think of Frona Welse and Maud Brewster—women have always been central, but now they become central because they are independent and creative and married to author figures. Graham Womble and John Messner are not author figures—though, presumably Messner was, given that he is a former English professor from the University of California—and that may be why, at the end, Tess curses not just Messner but also Womble. "You beasts! You beasts!" she cries at the end, unhappy with her treatment by the men, who, by their own admission are unethical in their trade of money for woman. "The woman, leaning against the bunk, raging and impotent, watched herself weighed out in yellow dust and nuggets in the scales" (74, 73). Though Messner at both the beginning and the end of the story treats his dogs humanely, he cannot be said to treat Tess the same way, no matter her own fault in running away with Womble. If Shorty's narrative has placed us in position of jury, we end up finding in favor of Tess.

For all their entanglement with the Northland, "Brown Wolf" and "A Day's Lodging" seem to signal London's real interest in staying in the Southland. His next two stories, now that *Love of Life, and Other Stories* was complete, take place wholly in California. They begin what he envisioned would be his next collection of short stories, but in fact that collection—*When God Laughs, and Other Stories*—stalled. He didn't complete its final story until 1909, and it wasn't published until 1911. For now, we can focus on this recent, inchoate shift in London's conception of the origin of his imagination and look closely at his final two stories before he began *Before Adam* and before the 1906 San Francisco earthquake and its profound impact on his thinking and writing.

I said that his next two stories seem to signal London's intention to abandon the Klondike, but "When God Laughs," being more theatrical than absorptive, feels as if it could take place in the North as well as the South. It features two men (they could almost be ex-miners returned from the North) in a cabin in a storm, discussing the philosophy of love. Typical of London's theatrical productions, the story is all dialogue, no setting. We know it takes place in California only because the characters make mention of it.

The text begins with an acknowledgement to Harry Cowell and a stanza from Charles Swinburne's long poem "Félise" about the death of love between a man and a woman. She may appeal to the gods to make him love her again, but "none shall move the most high gods, / who are most sad, being cruel."[189] Harry Cowell wrote an essay entitled "Rest: A Mood"; in 1904 London sent it to his friend Blanche Partington.[190] The essay, a light, meditative piece on death, fits nicely with the thematic of "When God

Laughs," as well as the previous two stories. One may think a dog really loves you, and then he runs off with a previous, more-loved master. One may think he loves and is loved in return, and then the woman runs off with another man. God laughs at your expectations. Whether the man leaves the woman, as in Swinburne's poem, or whether she leaves him, love cannot remain for long.

Other like-minded poetry suffuses the story: lines from William Sharp (Fiona Macleod), Alfred Austin, Curtis Hidden Page, and Mitchell Kennerly. All are marshaled by the two debaters in the story, Carquinez Monte and the unnamed narrator, who over wine argue about how to choose the proper lifestyle in the face of disappointment, decay, and death. Cowell closed his essay by writing, "Is this world weariness a method used by a gentle Providence to make us in love with the mysterious, veiled face of Death? I know not. As for me, I shall wait until it be dark before I make myself ready for sleep" (7). Here is London's own and often-repeated affirmation that he shall live his life and make use of his days in the face of their apparent uselessness and pointlessness.

In such a self-consciously literary story, we shouldn't be surprised that we come face-to-face with several author figures: the subjects of the extended discussion about love and death, Marvin Fiske and Ethel Baird, are sculptors, and the narrator's companion is a painter, Carquinez Monte, who is similar to London's friend Xavier Martinez, and who more likely than not once challenged London in the way that Monte does: "Think not that you have escaped by fleeing from the mad cities. You with your vine-clad hills, your sunsets and your sunrises, your homely fare and simple round of living! . . . The gods know how to deal with such as you. . . . You have elected surcease. Very well. You will become sated with surcease. You say you have escaped satiety! You have merely bartered it for senility. And senility is another name for satiety. It is satiety's masquerade. Bah!" (7–8). Arnold Genthe's one published memory of London and Martinez together is of them arguing: "Hot arguments on any subject which came into our minds were the order of the day, and I have a picture in my mind of Jack London sitting at one end of the table, intense and questioning, and Marty at the other, gesticulating with a chicken bone." Genthe remembers Martinez wearing an "inevitable red flowing tie."[191]

Martinez echoes Cowell, who writes that "the artist . . . [is] the most fortunate of men [because he or she] serves Beauty, most delightful of mistresses—and most exacting." Thus even the artist cannot find peace in surcease. "Neither by day nor by night may he rest him. There are no Sundays in his calendar. . . . This side of Death, what sleep, think you, is there for him?" Perhaps you think, as Harry did, concluding his roster of occupations that seem immune to constant toil and world weariness, that the bohemian or "aristocrat," as Cowell calls him, would be exempt.[192] No, Cowell and Monte want to make clear to London and the narrator that you can leave the city, move to the "arcadian homes and vineyards" of Sonoma Valley, but you cannot escape.[193]

Though in "When God Laughs" the narrator and Monte begin discussing the narrator's escape to the country, they equate his desire to live in the country with Fiske and Baird's marriage. To the narrator, they (and he) have finally achieved happiness. To Monte, who has the final word, both the narrator and the married couple are only deluding themselves. "We never win," he says at the end. "Sometimes we think we win. That is a little pleasantry of the gods" (24). When London says that God laughs, he means that Death laughs at our attempt to become immortal through love and art. Carquinez Monte comes to his conclusions because of his "white vision," a variant of the White Logic that structures a similar debate in *John Barleycorn*; Carquinez is also the name of the straits where London almost drowned in a drunken accident, an incident he relates in *John Barleycorn*. No wonder that "When God Laughs" begins with Carquinez feeling "the mellow warmth of the vine singing in his blood." His white vision comes from alcohol. There is an extraordinary line about Carquinez that is a mere aside to the story but that betrays London's deep understanding about the nature of alcohol. It comes at the end of his description of Carquinez's drinking habits: "It was worth while to get Carquinez to loosen up" (4).

The debate was the mustard seed of the story that London outlined in his notes. He lists his characters: the narrator was to be named Monte, then Manuel, Carquinez, and then he decided not to use the first name and then he decided the narrator would be someone else. The woman was Ethel Baird and the man, Marvin Fiske. But for the latter London's first choice was a surprising one: Martin Eden.[194] But there is no easy one-to-one correspondence between fiction and nonfiction. We are not dealing with autobiography, though London is using his own life as he used newspaper and magazine articles: a basis of fact to be played with.

Further, in the notes, Fiske is described as "a Dante, a la George," that is, George Sterling. In "A Wicked Woman," another character is based on Sterling—Ned Bashford—and we learn why George is nicknamed the Greek. Given that Fiske is Martin Eden is (and is not) Jack London (these are rough approximations) but also Dante and Sterling, and given that Carquinez "savored of the Greek," drinks hard, and is an artist, and given that George the Greek appears in "A Wicked Woman," and then also in *Martin Eden* as Brissenden, we see how much London was thinking of fictionalizing his and his friend's lives during this moment in his authorial career. A big shift in the autobiographical source material occurs, then, when he comes back from the South Seas and begins writing novels more often than not centered on figures loosely based on Charmian. Thus we can loosely characterize the shift as a movement from George to Charmian, a shift from doubting the value of monogamy to its acceptance despite its faults.

The notes for "When God Laughs" outline the vague setting: "First the narrator and the mountain bungalow. Then the beginning, or conversation leading up to man & woman. We discuss satiety. Told by the fire at midnight in mountain bungalow, a sou'easter storming and crashing. Once, in the tremendous gusts, a tree falls. Rattling of windows—sometimes whole house ashake aquiver." But, befitting the theatrical nature of the story, the rest of the notes contain dialogue. Even though one is tempted—and may be right to do so—to read the story of Marvin Fiske and Ethel Baird as stand-ins for Jack and Charmian, the notes indicate that London identified more with the unnamed narrator by using the first-person pronoun in samples of dialogue instead of the word *narrator*: "He: You remember her? I: A warm saint, holy as love and sweeter. He: That is she! You know! A warm saint, sweet-fleshed and woman—and yet, somehow—drenched through with that holiness as air with perfume." London notes that both Marvin's and Ethel's previous loves had died and that "rather than the French joy in the flesh" (London's euphemism for sex, of course, but also something more: a philosophical, bohemian love of all things sensual, of the pleasures of the body) "they had the Saxon soberness in the flesh," though this gets reversed in the story: "They were not cold wraiths," ghosts that is, even though both are artists. "They had no Saxon soberness in their blood. Temperamentally theirs was the French joy in the flesh. Everything is good—so long as it is not possessed. Satiety and possession are Death's horses; they run in span." Sex alleviates ghostliness.

But Monte has his moment of hesitation: "Who am I to delve into their soul-stuff?" he says. "I am but a frog, in the dank edge of a great darkness, gazing goggle-eyed at the mystery & wonder of their soul-flames. On my lips their love-philosophy is mangled." Nevertheless, delve he does. He has read the couple's letters. He has read Ethel's diary. He has watched them closely. "Before I understand their secret," he says, "I wonder & wonder. One day a book of verse—a page well used—book opened to it. 'Not yet, sometime [lines from Curtis Hidden Page's poem "Love's Waiting Time"].' They would keep love, the fickle sprite, the fore-runner of young life. It is illumination. I see with white vision their blameless souls, & I laughed, hee hee, for it is the blameless souls of children. They do not understand. They play with nature's fire. They laugh at God. They would stop the cosmic sap. They have invented a system which they bring to the gaming table of the universe and win out. Beware! God runs the bank. They cannot win." And so he discovered the secret of their love's seeming permanence: they never kissed, let alone had sex.

In this way, the way of the anchorite, they maintained the freshness of their desire and kept surcease and satiety at bay. Except that the gods, according to Carquinez, cannot stand for humans to be happy: "I watched. I said nothing. As the years pass—'ah ha,' I laughed to myself. 'They have outwitted God! They have shamed the flesh and blackened the face of the good earth-mother. How were they to know? They were artists, not biologists.'" And so, partly because of the biologic imperative to procreate and partly because the gods have their own logic, they took desire and love away, randomly, one night, and a week later Fiske died in an accident and Baird retreated to a convent. (In the notes, Fiske dies three months after the departure of Cupid and she dies as well, her diary going to Carquinez.) The narrator is angry at the close of the narrative, not convinced by the moral of the story. No matter. Carquinez has the last word. Carquinez may not win us over either. He is at the end described as "a veritable Mephistopheles in velvet jacket" (24).[195] If the devil makes the argument, then shouldn't we reject him and his arguments outright? Yet it is Carquinez who enunciates what must be the ultimate answer to the question of satiety. He says of the couple as he observed them trying to cheat the gods at their own game, "They would learn that their system was worthless and throw it away. They would be content with whatever happiness the gods gave them and not strive to wrest more away" (20). Like the best of London's theatrically minded stories, "When God Laughs" succeeds because it presents a world dominated by complicated, seemingly contradictory thought. If the gods are indeed cruel, then the devil can help us lead lives of at least temporarily attained happiness. One must continue to make art and love despite—or because of—the grinning noseless one.

We shouldn't be surprised that London had the devil of a time placing this story. It was the first one he gave to the agent Paul Reynolds under terms of a new partnership. Reynolds first took it to E. M. Ridgway of *Everybody's Magazine*, who had just accepted *Before Adam* and was starting a new, eponymous magazine. He was dying for a new short story from London, but not an "objectionable" one like "When God Laughs."[196] Reynolds took it to several others, but "your story 'When God Laughs' is going to be a very difficult story to handle," he told London, and asked if he would take a lower rate and object to selling to the *New York Herald* or some other newspaper. Also, he wanted to change the title to "Where the Gods Laugh" (or maybe he meant "When the Gods Laugh" because he consistently called the story "Where God Laughs"). "This would carry out your idea and would eliminate the atheistic or perhaps irreligious suggestion which the title at present conveys."[197] London put the kibosh on that suggestion, quickly. And then Reynolds proved his value: after nine magazines rejected the story, "I got The Smart Set to take it," even though they couldn't have the English rights; London had hired James Pinker, the English agent, to handle those for all his work. So Reynolds had to sell cheap, and London got two hundred dollars for the story, way below market value. But if he continued to write "objectionable" tales, implied Reynolds, he would continue to make less money. "Have you not got some other short stories that you would let me sell that I could get a big price for."[198]

The story was ill-suited for a general audience not just because of its "irreligious" title. It wore its radical politics on its chest, so to speak. Monte of course is not the devil, though alcohol-fueled cogitation may make him seem so. Rather, he's a politically active artist. It's no small detail in the story that Monte wears a red necktie: It "stood for the red flag (he had once lived with the socialists of Paris), and it symbolized the blood and brotherhood of man." Coupled with the detail that Messner's dogs in "A Day's Lodging" are like wage slaves and that Walt Irvine in "Brown Wolf" participates in the bohemian economic distribution system, these stories demonstrate that London's socialism was never far from the surface.

His politics boiled to the top in his next story, "The Apostate," even though it is one of his most intensely absorptive stories; it's as if his theatrical dimension had become embedded in his subconscious. The idea for a story about child labor had been circulating in his mind for, perhaps, years, but it crystallized when two new acquaintances encouraged him to do it. The first was Mother Jones, who attended his lecture at Fanueil Hall. He centered that talk on child labor and quoted from Jones and her own research into child labor and exploitation.

The second was F. Hayden Carruth, the literary editor of *Woman's Home Companion*. They had met in New York City during the tour, and, after London encouraged him to visit in California, Carruth arrived on the ranch the day after London did. Just before he had left for the West Coast, Carruth received a note from his assistant editor, Gertrude B. Lane, who later became famous as the editor of *Woman's Home Companion*: "If you don't get J.L. into line, there will be one who will believe that *no one* could have done it. We shall miss you while you're gone,—but don't hurry back if you bag the game."[199] They went horseback riding with Charmian, and Carruth asked London to do on-site research in the South and write up an essay or article on child labor in cotton mills. Charmian wrote in her diary, "Hayden Carruth came. Tragedy!!! Mate decided not to go."[200] In fact, London wrote out a list for Carruth of writing already contracted and plans already in process:

I have seven (7) months between March 1st and October 1st.
I am pledged to do the following:
One novel 4 months
Five short stories 1 month and 2 weeks
One play, 1 month and 2 weeks

TOTAL 7 months

I am also pledged to do the following, and how I
    am to squeeze it all in I do not know:
Several book-reviews,
Socialist articles,
"Persistence of the Established"——a 6,000 word article
Another play, in collaboration. I should have
    done my share four months ago.[201]

It was not an auspicious time for Carruth to make his pitch. Still, he did extract a promise from London of a single short story of indeterminate subject. It must have been a vague sort of promise. Carruth wrote to his wife, the day after his visit, "that he had failed although he had got London 'very much interested.'"[202] Based on that hint of interest Carruth wrote London immediately upon his return to remind London, "as you suggested," of the promise. To spur London's interest, he suggested "a child labor story." "Our people (I mean the owners of the 'W.H.C.')," Carruth wrote, "seem to be growing more enthusiastic on the child labor matter, and say that they will keep hammering away at it till something is accomplished if it takes five years." He wanted it in a month so that it could be properly illustrated "by as good an artist as we can find."[203] The very next day Carruth wrote again, insisting that "you *can* write a story which would be a wonderful help to the movement against the abuse, a movement in which personally I feel more interest than I ever felt in anything before."[204]

Carruth couldn't have known how prepared London was to write such a story, and he must have been overjoyed to receive London's prompt agreement to write it and to meet Carruth's deadline. "Of course I am pleased to know that the story is coming on," Carruth wrote back in an easy and confident tone, as if he and London already had a long-term relationship, "and that you are going to make it a child labor story. I am sure it will be something that will help the good work."[205] The story appeared in the September issue of *Woman's Home Companion* and effectively complemented the magazine's nonfiction attacks on child labor.

Another source for the idea of "The Apostate" was Upton Sinclair's *The Jungle*, in which Stanislas helps run a canning machine; Sinclair's book was so much on his mind that London had even suggested to Carruth that his magazine publish Sinclair, but Carruth begged off, saying that the editor, Arthur Vance, "somehow didn't seem to cotton to the Sinclair idea." (Carruth then mentioned that he had gotten John Spargo to contribute an essay to *Woman's Home Companion*, thus betraying his own mild progressiveness.) But there was another source or, better, a motivation or intent. In his notes for "The American Abyss," the American version of *The People of the Abyss*, he told himself to "take a gamin, who has never been out of the city, down to the country."[206] Although this is not quite the plot of "The Apostate," it certainly shows London thinking about not just the opposition between city and country but also the debilitating effects of extreme poverty on children. It connects directly to the data and narrative concerning child labor in textile mills that he developed for "Revolution"; in fact, one of his notes for "The Apostate" reads "Johnny—look up in Ruskin talk," an allusion to "Revolution," which he delivered to the Ruskin Club on 27 January 1905.[207] "The Apostate" then is a natural outgrowth of his reading of *The Jungle* and his reminiscences for "What Life Means to Me" and provides the capstone to his lecture tour.

There are at least two newspaper and magazine sources for brief episodes in the work life of the main child character, Johnny. London had already formed the idea of the story when he consulted an article from his files called "Turning Children into Dollars," by Juliet Wilbor Tompkins. Next to a paragraph describing the general and unbearable noise inside a twine factory, London wrote "description of his work first part of story." London didn't borrow any of the language from that paragraph, but he did from the next one he marked with the notation, "when the inspector came." Tompkins described a scene in a soap factory between a one-legged boy and an inspector who was hiding:

> And then a one-legged boy is discovered lurking behind some barrels. The inspector eyes him reproachfully; she has had that individual boy dismissed from three factories within the year. He is a wan and stunted little person, his body eloquent of his needs, his face dully obstinate. "Why, Antone! And you promised me faithfully that you would go to school," she [the inspector] exclaims. Antone bursts into tears. "Please, inspector, two babies died on us, and we're awful poor," he sobs.[208]

In "The Apostate" London renders the scene this way:

> The one-legged boy was not so fortunate. The sharp-eyed inspector hauled him out at arm's length from the bin truck. His lips were quivering, and his face had all the expression of one upon whom was fallen profound and irremediable disaster. The overseer looked astounded, as though for the first time he had laid eyes on the boy, while the superintendent's face expressed shock and displeasure. "I know him," the inspector said. "He's twelve years old. I've had him discharged from three factories inside the year. This makes the fourth." He turned to the one-legged boy. "You promised me, word and honor, that you'd

go to school." The one-legged boy burst into tears. "Please, Mr. Inspector, two babies died on us, and we're awful poor."

London marked and employed yet one more paragraph, this one describing a different sort of factory job:

[A boy] sat all day in a closet lighted by a gas jet, with a little stick in his hand, watching a great stream of cloth that poured down from above and passed over a hot roller that ironed its surface, his business being to guide the cloth if it showed a tendency to swerve to the right or the left from the roller. It was easy work—horribly, wickedly easy. Not a muscle of his body was getting proper development; his mind slept undisturbed as his eyes dully watched the cloth stream. A born poet might have worked out his greatness in that hot cell. . . . But this was just an ordinary, human boy, easily demoralized, easily persuaded to let all his faculties rot in return for about two dollars a week.[209]

In "The Apostate," Johnny, like Tompkins's nameless boy, might have had an active mental life, if not for the dulling routine:

When he was eight, he got work in another mill. His new job was marvelously easy. All he had to do was to sit down with a little stick in his hand and guide a stream of cloth that flowed past him. This stream of cloth came out of the maw of a machine, passed over a hot roller, and went on its way elsewhere. But he sat always in the one place, beyond the reach of daylight, a gas jet flaring over him, himself part of the mechanism.

He was very happy at that job, in spite of the moist heat, for he was still young and in possession of dreams and illusions. And wonderful dreams he dreamed as he watched the streaming cloth streaming endlessly by. But there was no exercise about the work, no call upon his mind, and he dreamed less and less, while his mind grew torpid and drowsy. Nevertheless, he earned two dollars a week.[210]

The namelessness of Tompkins's subject—of both the boy and the factory—and the way London retains it indicate the all-pervasiveness of the American debilitating factory system and the amoral quality of capitalism; if London had specified Johnny's locale, this national indictment would have lost its power. Further, note how London converts Tompkins's would-be "poet" into Johnny the dreamer. Dreams are synonymous with poetry, with writing. Johnny's artistic sensibilities are defeated by capitalism, a conclusion we will see active at the end of the story.

The second source is similar to the first and pertains to the next job Johnny managed to land. On 16 August 1905, Owen R. Lovejoy, the assistant secretary of the National Child Labor Committee, addressed the annual convention of the International Association of Factory Inspectors. An unknown socialist newspaper printed the speech, London clipped it, and circled a story Owen related:

> The proprietor of a successful glass house recently with pride brought me to a small boy who sat on a low stool tying glass stoppers into small bottles. He sat bent over his work, the bottles held between his knees and the bundle of string at his hip, his body thrown forward and his chest contracted, his thin arms flying with the swift and accurate motion of a perfect machine, as he hurried in his labor for ten hours a day. Three knots were made for each and his daily task was 300 dozen bottles. As a machine he is perfect, but as the precursor of a healthy man he is a failure. He has been reduced to a bundle of quivering nerves.[211]

Here is London's reworking of this pitiful story:

> He got work in a glass factory. The pay was better, and the work demanded skill. It was piece-work, and the more skillful he was, the bigger wages he earned. . . . It was simple work, the tying of glass stoppers into small bottles. At his waist he carried a bundle of twine. He held the bottles between his knees so that he might work with both hands. Thus, in a sitting position and bending over his own knees, his narrow shoulders grew humped and his chest was contracted for ten hours each day. This was not good for the lungs, but he tied three hundred dozen bottles a day. . . . This meant that he had attained machine-like perfection. All waste movements were eliminated. Every motion of his thin arms, every movement of a muscle in the thin fingers, was swift and accurate. He worked at high tension, and the result was that he grew nervous. At night his muscles twitched in his sleep, and in the daytime he could not relax and rest. He remained keyed up and his muscles continued to twitch. (48–50)

Here is a perfect example of London's use of newspaper reporting. He takes a near-photographic account and colors it with feeling, adding necessary detail and emotional effect. This is the process of impassioned realism. It serves as the proper narratological method to counter capitalism's Machine Age hegemonic discourse. Avis Everhard, in *The Iron Heel*, will adapt this same aesthetic for her manuscript.

"The Apostate" begins with a prayer and then an injunction from little Johnny's mother: you don't work, you don't eat. Unconscious of her import, Johnny's mother is voicing a principle from Laurence Gronlund's influential tract on the fundamentals of American socialism, *The Co-Operative Commonwealth*, a book London relied on when he wrote his first essay on socialism, "What Socialism Is." Gronlund wrote, "Adam Smith observed that 'the produce of labour is the natural recompense of Labour'; and St. Paul declared that 'if a man will not work, neither shall he eat.' The New System—as our definition points out—will put these doctrines into practice."[212] But there is a tension in Gronlund's work between those who work and those who choose not to; for socialism will allow for the latter: "Our Commonwealth leaves everybody at perfect liberty to work as much or as little as he please, or not at all, but makes his consumption exactly commensurate with his performances."[213] Gronlund has no plan for those who do not work, but to escape from the wage-slavery system is not an effective means of protest; it only raises the status of an individual, not the class. But this seems to be what London advocates in this short story. The life of a boy is at least as important as the reformation of the economic system.

There is another, equally powerful valence to the beginning of the story, which has more to do with its fictional mode than with economics. Johnny's antagonism toward God is an important theme in the story. In his notes, London wrote, "Work up his Revolt against God. This early in story. . . . Head story with the child laborer's prayer." And when London first imagined Johnny going down the road, feeling bad, he wrote, "As he went down the road. Just tired. He thought of the roaring loom room. His revolt against God etc. was over. He had no bitterness."[214] When the reader reads the opening prayer he or she is actually praying; it's impossible to read a prayer without praying. It's a performative. Thus, as we enter into the state of prayer we become deeply and movingly absorbed. The prayer, the mother's injunction, and the title tell us not only that capitalism is a religion but that workers who rebel—the original title was "The Rebel"—are akin to that original rebellious angel, Milton's Satan.[215] Johnny works at a job in the jute mill, and the hyperrealistic details of his job come from London's firsthand knowledge. In this poor world of bread, coffee, cold pork, bobbins, and weaver's knots, only sleep, dreams, and the illusions borne from lack of knowledge of the larger world provide relief.

Relief, though, is temporary. Johnny is not capable of time travel, like the heroes of *Before Adam* and *The Star Rover*. In fact, trapped in the here and now, Johnny experiences time in a frighteningly monotonous way: "Nothing ever happened. There were no events to mark the march of time. Time did not march. It stood always still" (55). He had no future, and he had but a miniscule past. There is a moment in the narrative that we see London explicitly deny Johnny what other of his future characters will have: "There was one other memory of the past," in Johnny, his paltry memory consisting only a vague picture of a girl he once had a crush on, the lucky discovery of a quarter on the sidewalk, and eating prunes (once) and custard (twice) at home. This other memory was a "nightmare," a "race-memory of man that makes him fall in his sleep and that goes back to his arboreal ancestry" (54). In less than a week, London would write of his narrator in *Before Adam*, "Rarely were my dreams tinctured with happiness. . . . I was a city boy. . . . I . . . wandered in my sleep through interminable forests." Thus there is an exchange between these two works. Johnny, like any human, comes from an "arboreal" past. But without the fulsome memories of his past life that the narrator of *Before Adam* has, Johnny is denied his full humanity. His interior life is as poor as his exterior life. Johnny and his mother are not author figures, and their world has no imagination in it. Though there is an abyss—the "American Abyss"—and a cabin (the family's house is more like a shack or cabin), there is no writing and there is no gold. And there is certainly no luck. For an author so deeply invested in all facets of the imagination—its origin, its longevity, its care, its power—this loss of the imagination is the most tragic casualty of poverty. Johnny used to have "dreams and illusions," when he was eight. But now, no longer. He is twelve. God laughs indeed.

Now we see why he is fixated on a tree when he comes to the realization that escape from the machines and the oppressive present is actually possible. When he tells his mother that he is leaving to go "anywhere," "the tree across the street appeared with dazzling brightness on his inner vision" (63). With proper rest from his machine work, a kind of imaginative power returns to him. He now knows that he can do something besides work. It is the insight of all bohemia. Johnny isn't rescued by radicalization or political action. He is rescued by the imagination. Individual creative production counters mass production by machinelike people rendered identical, their particularities erased as they all become the same machine.

The larger point raised in the story is the true meaning of the Machine Age. We might take it to mean, as London sometimes did, that it denoted the technological advancement of his time. It signaled speed, efficiency, productivity, progress, all in the name of increased wealth. For London, however, the cost was greater than the reward. If a child should be born in a factory, be raised in a factory, work in a factory, and die in the factory, then this child is no different from a machine. Amelioration cannot come from child-labor laws, for it keeps bread winners out of families desperate for cash. Progressivism was not a choice. If socialism cannot replace capitalism (the theme of his next novel, *The Iron Heel*), escape to the country—that is, bohemianism, a complete transformation of one's life—is the solution. "The Apostate," with its hyperreal details and unrelenting narrative of the daily life of poverty is an absorptive story with a strong theatrical urge. It stands as one of London's most accomplished acts of blending his two principal modes of fiction writing.

His final five works between his return from his tour and 1 April 1906, when he began *Before Adam*, tell us much about his growth, position, and status as an author. "Brown Wolf" is a Klondike story that takes place in the South. "When God Laughs" takes place in the South though it feels as if it occurs in the North. This easy mix of locales speaks not only of London's position as a Pacific Rim writer but also of his national prominence. He had mastered all locales, though his return to the Klondike made that locale a kind of touchstone, a place to return to be replenished as an author. George Brett published *Love of Life, and Other Stories* in 1907, and it seemed an oddity, for by then the Kipling of the Klondike had shed, in his public's mind, both Kipling and the Klondike as authorial markers. Now, with the publication of *The People of the Abyss*, *The Sea-Wolf*, and *War of the Classes*, as well as his sensational appearance across the country in the name of socialism, books like *White Fang* and *Love of Life, and Other Stories* must have seemed atavisms. If London was aware of this, then his next novel was not simply about prehistoric humans but about writing stories that were, in a sense, biological predecessors to his newest work. The time of the Klondike was the modern-day Jack London's prehistory as an author.

RED ATAVISMS AND REVOLUTION

On 2 April 1906, three days after he completed "The Apostate," Jack London began *Before Adam*, only six months after completing *White Fang*. In the interregnum between these two novels he wrote five short stories, two book reviews, two essays, and two newspaper reports. His productivity—a superficial but popular method for testing the vitality and quality of an author's imagination—indicates no lack of story ideas, a concern raised later in the year by a national discussion (continued into this century in London studies) about the relation between *Before Adam* and an earlier novel on the same theme by Stanley Waterloo entitled *The Story of Ab*. Far from being out of ideas, exhausted, or sick from his lecture tour (or with life in general), London was as energetic and productive as he always had been. Travel, a necessary component of his authorship, stimulated, not retarded, his imaginative capability.

Another indication of the vitality of his imagination is the thematic content of his new novel. *Before Adam* moves forward along a line of inquiry into the new psychology that London had begun with, at least, "Planchette" and *White Fang*. If *White Fang* is a companion to *Call of the Wild*, then *Before Adam* is a companion to *White Fang*. The lecture tour was a kind of hiatus from the rigors of self-exploration made manifest in fiction. Not only is *Before Adam* a deeply absorptive novel, but it represents a more fully developed exploration into the nature of his imagination, building on ideas expressed in those two earlier works. Spiritualism, August Weismann and his concept of the "germ-plasm," and the intersection of psychology and evolutionary science all are topics that London picked up again in early 1906.

As with the gestation of previous novels, the idea for *Before Adam* developed over many years, though it is notoriously difficult to single out a moment in time when he saw the whole of any future piece of writing. There are clues in his notes for the novel and in his library, and they indicate that *Before Adam* built up slowly in his mind; unlike, say, the process for writing the Christ novel, this stop-and-start process actually bore fruit.

To begin, we need to return to the work of the German scientist August Weismann and visit London's earliest mention of writing a story based on Weismann's theories of heredity. In a letter to Cloudesley Johns from 1899, when he first read *Essays upon Heredity*, he said, "Funny, that 'freak story,' as you called it, by Grant Allen. I had but recently finished reading some four hundred and odd pages of Weissmann's [*sic*] theory of the germ-plasm, was deep in the study of those who had taken up the controversy of Weissmann [*sic*], and had been evolving a tale on memory something similar to Grant Allen's. You will notice he had founded his idea on Weissman too. Anticipated again."[1] "Memory," of course, doesn't mean an individual's recollection of a past person, place, or thing; London means to equate it with biological inheritance of traits. A cell remembers in order to reproduce a previous generation's characteristics. There are a number of Allen's stories in which such a conception of biological memory operates: In "A Child of the Phalanstery," a couple who marry in belief of "the progressive evolution of universal humanity" (shades of *The Kempton-Wace Letters*, a connection we will see is quite explicit in London's mind when writing *Before Adam*); in "Langalula," Christianity is revealed to be nothing more than veneer on a so-called savage; in "The Backslider" the focus is on the artificiality of religion in the face of a love "that had filled every heart in all [the main character's] ancestors for innumerable generations."[2] The hero is even an avid reader of Spencer. And then there's "The Churchwarden's Brother," featuring that favorite hereditary experimental subject, a set of twins. One is a murderer and ready to be hung, the other is equally bad but has maintained through sheer willpower social respectability until he goes off the rails, gets drunk, and tries to murder his wife and instead commits suicide; thus heredity wins out.

We do not know which story London and Johns are discussing. He did see a kindred authorial practice in Allen's work, that is, expanding or exaggerating scientific fact to fit a particular genre of fiction writing. Thus, no particular story proclaims obvious Weismannian influence, though that isn't really the point. The important point here isn't even that London was frustrated by discovering a progenitor of sorts for a story based on Weismann. The point is that as soon as he had finished reading Weismann, he was prompted to write a story based on his reading.

In Boston, during the lecture tour, we can tell he was mulling over a possible story about a civilized man becoming savage. His seriocomic newspaper story on the Holy Jumpers indicates indirectly that he was looking ahead to his next major writing project. In the article, he pointed out that "it is no new phenomenon, this religious excitement of theirs":

> The Voodoo priest and the Indian medicine man conducted similar performances when the world was very young, and man was just beginning to climb out of the trees and make fire. The Holy Jumpers attain a pitch of exaltation quite similar to that attained by the men who fasted in deserts, or by the dervishes who whirl their consciousness away. This same pitch is attained by the Hindoo sage who steadfastly contemplates his navel till all the world whirls around him, and he rises above time and space to meet God face to face, and from His lips learn the mystery of eternity. Holy Jumping, as Dr. Hudson would undoubtedly call it, is merely a process of self-hypnotism, whereby the conscious mind is lulled to sleep and the subconscious mind is awakened and put in charge (70–71).

There were still Voodoo priests and First Nation medicine men in 1906 of course, but London's point is that they should be considered as atavistic as the Holy Jumpers. To see modern-day worship and then see beyond the contemporary scene to locate its origins in so-called primitive practices, he reveals not only his intention to write a novel about prehistoric man and woman but also his mounting interest, almost obsession, with the prehistoric; it will feature in a significant amount of his fiction for the rest of his career.

The holy man who fasts in the desert appears in *The Star Rover* in a short narrative that seems out of place among the stories of Lady Om, Daniel Foss, and the others. But now we see its function. Beginning in 1905 and 1906, London was most concerned about eternal time: about eternities of the past and about eternities of the future. If the present is stasis, a time of no time, or the time of the death drive, as London thematizes it in "The Apostate," then he wants to find its cause in the remote past and represent its amelioration in the distant future. *Before Adam* is the beginning of his novelistic treatment of the past. *The Iron Heel*, composed later the same year, is the beginning of his novelistic treatment of the future. He will never abandon the present and his critique of it, but at the midpoint of his career he was looking backward and then forward as far as his inner eye could see in both directions. In a 1905 interview he said that he "wanted to learn how to write Present and Future all at one time."[3] His foray as a playwright was intimately connected to considerations of past, present, and future. As H. G. Wells wrote in *Mankind in the Making*, a book London read just before composing *The Iron Heel*, "from the idea of organic Evolution has ensued . . . that great expansion of our sense of time and causation." Further, time "has opened out from the little history of a few thousand years to a stupendous vista of ages."[4] London's author figures needed every ounce of their wide vision in order to take into account that vista.

It was one thing to watch Bostonians exercise themselves religiously and write that such exercise was analogous to ancient practices. It was more difficult to find a scientifically sound mechanism to fictively render the continuity between the sociobiology of that ancient world and twentieth-century America. One key was Thomson Hudson's popular *The Law of Psychic Phenomena*, the "Dr. Hudson" of the Holy Jumpers article. Located somewhere in the middle between serious scientific study and New Thought science of mind cure, Hudson's book can also be read as a precursor to Henri Ellenberger's history of dynamic psychiatry, *The Discovery of the Unconscious*, given its emphasis on topics such as the feud between the Nancy school of mesmerism and Charcot at the Salpêtrière Hospital.[5]

Hudson's history of mesmerism and hypnotism cites the major figures and their work accurately or, at least, in agreement with later historians like Beryl Satter.[6] I've somewhat simplified Hudson's detailed account of the battles among the mesmerists, Charcot's Paris school, and the Nancy school if only because London was not interested in their various antithetical claims. Hudson, however, sought to "bind the facts of psychological science into one harmonious whole" (91). One difference between the schools would have caught London's attention. According to Hudson, Charcot believed hypnotism worked only on "diseased," that is, "hysterical" persons, especially women. The Nancy school believed hypnotism worked on healthy, "normal" individuals. The latter hypothesis suited London best. One more side note should be made: consistent with Hudson's theoretical framework, ghosts are real in that they are a manifestation of the subjective mind (it has the power to move objects, hear voices, and create immaterial objects perceptible to the senses) but not proof of the return of the dead. (That is an unresolvable claim.) Spirit photography substantiates this claim about ghosts, despite the numerous cases of fraud. He links it to astral projection.

Hudson argued that a scientific study of the mind's operations—which would explain topics central to London's thinking like the link between poetry and madness, the operation of hypnotism, and the presence of ghosts—would also justify faith in Jesus. Hudson's science is a broad rendition, common to his era, of psychology, and it can be placed on the continuum that Ellenberger establishes between shamanism and modern-day psychiatric practice. By connecting mesmerism and spiritism, Hudson is consistent with his fellow American psychologists.[7] And to make himself even more obviously American, he grafted Christianity to psychology. To a large extent Hudson is interested in placing Christian faith on a scientific basis.

But in the midst of Hudson's general metaphysics and despite much self-delusion on the part of Hudson about the rigor of his objectivity, London would have found an emphasis on truly scientific study. According to Hudson, given two facets of the mind—the subjective and the objective—and given that faith is, a priori, a component of the subjective mind, we simply have to turn off the objective mind and access the subjective in order to have the faith that Jesus so obviously demonstrated was right and true. We can suspend objectivity through auto-suggestion or self-hypnotism.

He first establishes the validity of hypnotism as a medical procedure, differentiating it from Mesmer's experiments by a single attribute: whereas Mesmer "cured" people while they were awake, James Braid, one of the early key proponents of hypnotism, put them to sleep. It is a distinction Ellenberger marks as central in the progression from mesmerism to psychoanalysis. But in a conceptual move that Ellenberger does not discuss, Hudson then discovered that people could fall into hypnotic sleep without the influence of another and that this sleep could be obtained without suggestion.[8] Combining these "discoveries" produced self-hypnosis. Further, hypnotic sleep was the same as regular sleep. "The memory of the subjective mind is perfect," says Hudson (217), and so in sleep a "freak" of evolution like London's narrator could, scientifically, recall his past life as a Stone Age being.

One gathers from London's article that Hudson would have come to the opposite conclusion, namely, that religious faith is obtained through a trick of the mind called self-hypnotism. Thus, Hudson's book did not provide London with the scientific rationale for undercutting the metaphysical beliefs in the "Voodoo priest" and "Hondoo sage." London reworked Hudson to come to the conclusion that belief in a higher power, attained by intense physical exertion or not, was a fallacy produced by the mind hypnotizing itself. In a way, he uses Hudson's psychologic science of hypnotism against himself, that is, using science to undermine metaphysics. In *Before Adam*, however, the question of religious belief drops out, and London seizes on the psychical mechanism of self-hypnotism as a tool to access past lives. Psychological science thus acts as a gateway to the fictive rendering of the scientific truth of the narrative of evolution.

London was thoroughly grounded in Alfred Binet's psychological vocabulary, and *On Double Consciousness* is most likely London's authority for replacing Hudson's terminology of *subjective mind* and *objective mind* with the modern constructs of *conscious mind* and *unconscious mind*. But two concepts appear in Hudson's book that also play important roles in the frame story of *Before Adam*: the perfect memory of the unconscious and the release of the conscious/objective mind in sleep, thus creating access to the unconscious/subjective mind. These claims allowed London to create a narrator who puts himself in a hypnotic state in order to discover his past life as an early hominoid.

To capture that past world in a fictive frame, London turned to a number of other books, some of which we can identify because, for the first time, we have extensive preliminary notes—amounting in some cases to several pages of a rough draft—for a novel; either he departed from his usual practice or, more simply, these notes were preserved, perhaps because it is his first novel written while married to Charmian. Unlike other collections of notes, there are no newspaper or magazine clippings included among his handwritten notes. One book appears in his notes twice, which is more than any other source: *The Universal Kinship* by John Howard Moore, which he read during the first three weeks of writing *Before Adam*. It is useful for what I might call my sociological archaeology—the uncovering of friendship and intellectual networks that have been obscured by a focus on so-called great men and women. The circulation of this book among diverse cultural workers, especially in Chicago, exposes social and intellectual connections that otherwise might never have been discovered. Like the ruins of some temple of which we can only see the barest of outlines, these social connections become apparent only when we strip away extraneous notions like fame and canonicity and expose the similarities of reading and the exchange of ideas.

Moore, a Kansas farm boy, graduated from the University of Chicago, taught zoology at Crane Manual Training High School in Chicago and the

University of Chicago, married Clarence Darrow's sister Jennie, committed suicide in 1916 at the age of forty-four, and was perhaps best known for being a prominent vegetarian and author of *Better World Philosophy*. As the headline of his obituary notes, Moore was thoroughly disenchanted by the human race, a deeply held belief in man's wrong-headed stewardship of the earth that crops up repeatedly in *The Universal Kinship*.[9] Moore and his work recently have been taken up by animal rights activists, of which London may be seen as a precursor.[10]

Better World Philosophy as well as *The Universal Kinship* were published by Charles Kerr, a prominent Left publisher in Chicago and a firm very familiar to London (Kerr also published the *International Socialist Review*); both books were reprinted in 1908 by Parker Sercombe's Chicago publishing firm, To-Morrow Publishing Company, and Darrow was a regular contributor to Triggs and Sercombe's magazine. Kerr sent the latter book to London in March 1906 with a request for a blurb or review.[11] A socialist, Moore most likely circulated in the politically active circles of Sercombe, Darrow, Triggs, Sandburg, Addams, and others and probably was in the audience of London's Chicago lectures. In his letter to Kerr, which was published as a book review in Triggs's *To-Morrow*, London wrote, "I do not know of any book dealing with Evolution that I have read with such keen interest." He wrote notes for his letter to Kerr on the front matter of the book, suggesting that he had just finished reading it.[12]

For London, however, the main intent of the book—to promulgate Darwinism in order to assert the equality of all animals to humankind—was less interesting than its discussion of past and future time. Serious scientists like Weismann were acutely aware of how the study of evolution and heredity expanded scales of time and space; as Weismann concluded his *The Germ-Plasm*, "We are thus reminded afresh that we have to deal not only with the infinitely great, but also with the infinitely small; the idea of size is a purely relative one, and on either hand extends infinity."[13] Moore writes, while discussing evolution, "How hopelessly dependent we are upon the past, and how impossible it is to be really original! What the future will be depends upon what the present is, for the future will grow out of, and inherit, the present. What the present is depends upon what the past was, for the present has grown out of, and inherited, the past. And what the past was depends upon a remoter past from which it evolved, and so on. There is no end anywhere of dependence, either forward or backward. Every fact, from an idea to a sun, is *a contingent link in an eternal chain*" (85). Man's place in this chain is a small one, a fact Moore insists on to reduce the egotism of humankind and inspire a broader ethical consideration of the rights of animals. "*Man* is *not* the *end*, he is but an *incident*, of the infinite elaborations of Time and Space" (319). A commonplace observation, albeit suffused with scientific veracity, it nevertheless confirmed London's ongoing cogitation about story writing as part of that "eternal chain."

He took notes in Moore's book for *Before Adam* and for something he called his "Far future book" (which would soon get the title "A Farthest Distant"); for example, when Moore discusses "The Earth an Evolution," that is, the inevitable change, decline, and extinction of the sun and earth, London marked these pages for "Far future book" (30–35). At the same time, he used it to create certain details. In one note for *Before Adam*, he wrote, "Old Folk, appearance—see 'Kinship' p. 27." Another note reads, "p. 24 Kinship to show that they resembled microcephalous [*sic*] idiots—emphasize this idea." On page 24, he marked a quotation from Lester Ward in *Dynamic Sociology*, which ends, "The brain development [of "primitive man"] would perhaps be too low for the average of any existing tribe, and would correspond better with that of certain microcephalous [*sic*] idiots and cretins, of which the human race furnishes many examples." But the beginning of that same quotation may have furnished London with the idea to begin the novel with images: "'If before the appearance of man on the earth,' says Ward in his 'Dynamic Sociology,' 'an imaginary painter had visited it, and drawn a portrait embodying the thorax of the gibbon, the hands and feet of the gorilla, the form and skull of the chimpanzee, the brain development of the orang, and the countenance of *Semnopithecus*, giving to the whole of the average stature of all of these apes, the result would have been a being not far removed from our conception of the primitive man, and not widely different from the actual condition of certain low tribes of savages.'"[14] The "imaginary painter" easily becomes the former historical self who escapes from the germ plasm to paint the pictures of primitive life that so torment the narrator. A definitional claim later in the book may have reinforced the idea to begin with pictures: Moore defines the imagination as "the picturing power of the mind" (199, 257). London's conception of the imagination was more capacious, but it could accommodate this general formulation.

Moore's book may have laid the foundation for London's own inchoate, radical (at the time) ideas about the fair treatment of animals, ideas expressed in his stories featuring wolves, horses, leopards, dogs, and others, and thus London was well-situated intellectually to agree with Moore. Moore wrote his book out of the realization that man was not sui generis, that he had not had "a unique and miraculous origin" (4), that their commonality of evolution made animals equals to man in many unrecognized and actively denied ways. Man "is a pain-shunning, pleasure-seeking, death-dreading organism, differing in particulars, but not in kind, from the pain-shunning, pleasure-seeking, death-dreading organisms below and around him" (5). Moore's "splendid, virile English" and "masterly knowledge of the subject" endeared this book to London.

Other significant marginal markings by London concern the orangutan, the chimpanzee, the gorilla, and the gibbon—their physical characteristics, especially their hair and skeleton, and their resemblance to "the lowest races of human beings" (18–26). Racism infiltrates this text, and London does not remark upon it. But he made a point of separating his protagonist from any association with the so-called lower races. In the middle of the comparison between humans and apes, London wrote, "Big tooth a Gibbon" next to Moore's observation that "it is, at least, interesting that the orang and gibbon, who live in Asia and its islands, where the brachycephalic races of men supposedly arose, are themselves brachycephalic" (22). The gorilla, chimp, and black African humans, according to Moore, are all "dolichocephalic" (22). Still, the emphasis in both London and Moore is on the continuity between all apes and all humans, and when Moore writes, "Men and anthropoids live about the same number of years, both being toothless and wrinkled in old age," and "The hair on the upper arm and that on the forearm, in both anthropoids and men, point in opposite directions" (27), London double barred both, starred the latter passage in the margin, and wrote: "The one old one that looked like our gardener's grandfather. They were blood brothers in appearance—and no finer argument for the common origin" (27). This becomes, in chapter 15 of Before Adam, "Marrow-Bone was the only old member in the horde. Sometimes, on looking back upon him, when the vision of him is most clear, I note a striking resemblance between him and the father of my father's gardener" (194). In an earlier passage, Moore wrote, "In the manlike apes the large toe is opposable to the other four" (20), a characteristic Big Tooth singles out about his father. And Moore discusses atavisms briefly in an unmarked passage (46–47), unmarked probably because it was a concept London was already familiar with and didn't rely on Moore to create Red-Eye, the atavistic creature in *Before Adam*. In fact, in the long section entitled "Organic Evolution," London didn't bother marking a single line; he knew all this already.

The second section of *Universal Kinship* is a metaphysical claim that the "general similarity" of the nervous system of all vertebrates proves the similarity of their "mental constitution and experience" (111). "The jelly-fish and the philosopher are not mental aliens," a line London underlined (112). Thus Moore thought "physical evolution" substantiated "psychical evolution," another discredited material theory. One might think London skipped over this section, but, no, his interest in the psychical never flagged, and the pages of this section are as marked and underlined as the others. He picked and chose, and he must have smiled when Moore wrote, "A struggle for existence is constantly going on, even among the words and grammatical forms of every language. The better, shorter, easier forms are constantly gaining the ascendency, and the longer and more cumbrous expressions grow obsolete" (116–17). Later in the chapter, when discussing the "vestigial instincts" (134) of donkeys, quails, dogs, and other animals, Moore connects these "useless and absurd" (134) instincts to "the vestigial parts of language," that is, the silent letters of human language. For Moore, *vestigial* had to retain its material denotation and not become metaphoric, because he argued for the direct correspondence between physical and psychical evolution. London, for his part, marked the first passage on language because it coincided with his refutation of Herbert Spencer's *The Philosophy of Style* in "Phenomena of Literary Evolution." No matter that Spencer's theories of language seemed more in accordance with evolutionary theory, that is, that evolution moves toward complexity and heterogeneity. Moore, London, L. A. Sherman, and others saw the Machine Age demanding a speedier, homogeneous style, and because the Machine Age was so obviously an evolved form of human life, its prose style must also be a product of evolution. The Machine Age may be a more complex time, but for London (and Moore) the hallmark of their age was speed and force, not multiplicity.

A long part of Moore's discussion of "psychical evolution" deals with the evolution of civilized man from "savage" man, which affirmed what London had been writing since *The People of the Abyss* whenever he sought to deplore the supposed superiority of the modern-day capitalist to the more "primitive" civilizations like the Inuit or caveman. This is the beginning step in reading the "caveman" of "Revolution" and the Pleistocene-era peoples of *Before Adam* as harbingers of the twentieth-century socialist. In fact, we might trace the origin of *Before Adam* to that subtle shift from the First Peoples of *The People of the Abyss* to the "caveman" of "Revolution." It's also an antievolutionary stance, one might say, but it served London politically in a way that Moore was either unaware of or resistant to. That is, to say unequivocally that humankind was evolving emotionally and intellectually was impossible if the highest form of human social development was understood to be the cooperative commonwealth based on altruistic, not profit, motive.

Yet in a passage marked by London and then indexed by him in the back matter, Moore asserts that "altruism is older than the mountains, and selfishness hardened the living heart before the continents were lifted" (142). Moore's understanding of evolutionary theory is and is not teleological. The worm and the child and the primitive cannot think or feel the "higher emotions" (138); the twentieth-century human lives as the end product of both psychical and physical evolution. "The human soul is the blossom, not the beginning, of psychic evolution," says Moore in the same passage (142), and the corollary is that "non-human beings have souls," too, meaning that they possess "joys and sorrows, desires and capabilities, similar to our own" (146). At the same time, to counter the idea of the divine origin of humanity, Moore has to assert that what we feel and think is similar to what the Bone Age humans felt and thought. There is both continuity and progress: "How did Darwin's dog know his master on his master's return from a five-years' trip around the world?" says Moore (143), and London double marked this passage because it resonated so much with his own experience that he used it as a prompt to write "Brown Wolf."

To return to his thoughts about a novel of the Pleistocene: London next marked a passage on "the anthropoid races." Not surprisingly, if one has followed Moore even inattentively, "they have the same emotions and the same ways of expressing those emotions as human beings have" (147). What a relief for the novelist writing of a time that might seem too foreign to re-create, a time about which there is so little information. Here is the fact to underpin the fiction, the science to dispense with magical thinking.

The third and final section of *The Universal Kinship*, "The Ethical Kinship," is unannotated and carried little interest for London. Instead, he continued to draw on his science library and pulled Weismann's *Essays upon Heredity* from his shelf (or his memory) as he made notes for the novel. Weismann, like Moore, was a zoologist, but he also had expertise in botany, and his work still stands as an original contribution to evolutionary theory. He was friends with and corresponded with Charles Darwin, Herbert Spencer, Ernst Haeckel, and others even though he stood apart from them on key issues like the inheritance of acquired characteristics. But they all pursued the underlying causes of heredity, and all posited a cellular-level agent. Weismann's concept of the germ plasm competed with Charles Darwin's gemmules, Spencer's units, and Haeckel's plastidules or cell nucleus. And though "Haeckel was the first biologist to identify the nucleus as the repository of the hereditary substance," "Weismann's elaborated theory, inevitably insufficient, was a brilliantly conceived prototype of the modern conception of the cytological and molecular basis of development."[15] As historians of science like Robert J. Richards and Mark Francis redeem through careful archival analysis the work of early evolutionary theorists like Haeckel and Spencer, London's own engagement with their work becomes more sensible and laudatory. He even sent Haeckel a copy of *Before Adam*, who then replied by postcard: "Best thanks for your interesting book 'Before Adam.'"[16] Spencer, Haeckel, Weismann, and others were the initial proponents of "organic memory theory, which proposed that memory and heredity were essentially the same and that one inherited memories from ancestors along with their physical features." We know this theory to be at best incomplete, but, as historian of science Laura Otis writes, this "wrong" theory is fascinating because it took memory out of the metaphysical realm and made it material or "*knowable*."[17] London's intellectual pursuit of the nature and meaning of memory, convinced that it was somehow related to the imagination, follows exactly the history of the theory of organic memory that Otis outlines. From Darwin, Spencer, and Haeckel to Freud and Jung, European thinkers—so very influential in the United States—sought to answer the fundamental question of "how does the past live in us?"[18] For London, to answer this question meant he might find an answer to a central question of his authorial life: How do I live with these haunting memories inside me?

In several letters written in the summer of 1899, London told his friend Cloudesley Johns that he was reading and promoting Weismann's essays from *Essays upon Heredity and Kindred Biological Problems*. London may have turned to Weismann a few months after reading his former teacher David Starr Jordan's book *Foot-notes to Evolution*.[19] This book is the source of London's weakly committed-to position as a "materialistic monist," a philosophical identity he learned from both Jordan and Haeckel. "The idealists and all the rest of the metaphysicians have vainly struggled to win me," he told his friend Fannie Hamilton.[20] He was not an idealist, but out of his fear of being mistaken for one—especially after writing a modern-day ghost story like "Planchette"—he insisted on his materialistic philosophy, an overdetermined assertion if there ever was one.

He often paraphrased Jordan's aphoristic "The final test of truth is this: 'Can we make it work? Can we trust our lives to it?'"[21] Jordan set aside metaphysics as a serious field of inquiry. Citing William James's definition of metaphysics as "the persistent attempt to think clearly," Jordan asserts that science makes the same attempt but that metaphysics deals only with "fields where exact data are unattained or unattainable" and thus, foundationless, unreliable for truth claims. London used Jordan's scientific philosophy to protect himself from the obvious metaphysical presence of the imagination, insisting to the public that he had no room for doubt about ontological or phenomenological matters all the while suffering from that which could not be seen but that tortured his inner life. London's scientific materialism is but a failed bulwark against the metaphysical imagination. Could he trust his life to it? It was a question he had to answer daily, exhaustingly, and, exhausted by his continuous battle with his interior life, later in life he had to abandon the Jordanesque scientific realism.

But Jordan outlined the history and development of evolutionary theory in his work and provided London with a useful intellectual framework. Though Jordan discussed the debate between Haeckel and Weismann concerning the inheritance of acquired characteristics, he remained agnostic, waiting for further evidence. But London was convinced from the very beginning of the central contribution of Weismann's work: "He has struck a heavy blow to the accepted idea of acquired characters being inherited."[22] From London's point of view, Weismann's initial acknowledgement and then dismissal of Spencer's *Principles of Biology* must have proved a landmark in his thought, a move from the nineteenth to the twentieth century. This was intellectual advancement. Weismann, unlike Spencer, could be trusted as a scientific source. Like Hudson's discussion of self-hypnotism, Weismann's concept of the germ plasm provided him with a tool to enter the prehistoric world and provide continuity between it and the Machine Age.

In his letters to Johns, London, we saw, accurately described the import of Weismann's work. In his fiction, however, he deliberately turns Weismann into a neo-Lamarckian, as if he really did think that Allen's stories were Weismannian. Thus, in his notes for *Before Adam*, he writes, "Introduction Weismann's 'Continuity of the Germ-Plasm—immortality—containing the racial memory. a freak in me." In the introductory chapters of his novel, the narrator marshals Weismann to prove that he "in this one thing, [is] to be considered a freak. Not alone do I possess racial memory to an enormous extent, but I possess the memories of one particular and far-removed progenitor" (19–20). The claim that he can relive the life of a particular person from the middle Pleistocene is of course the doorway from science to fiction, but the narrator insists that Weismann, not he, is responsible. "Follow my reasoning," he says, but his first assertion is already on shaky ground: "An instinct is a racial memory. Very good. Then you and I and all of us receive these memories from our fathers and mothers, as they received them from their fathers and mothers. Therefore there must be a medium whereby these memories are transmitted from generation to generation. This medium is what Weismann terms the 'germ-plasm.' It carries the memories of the whole evolution of the race" (20). But nowhere does Weismann use the word *memory*, and nowhere does he assert that selfhood—however primitive—is inherited.[23] In fact, in "The Duration of Life," Weismann says that from generation to generation "that which persists, is not the individual itself—not the complex aggregate of cells which is conscious of itself—but an individuality which is outside its consciousness, and of a low order."[24] Weismann was concerned with ontogeny and the discovery of the mechanisms of heredity. In this way, we see *Before Adam* as science fiction, that is, as a fictional genre dependent on scientific fact for plot development and denouement. We can also see it as a precursor to science fiction in the sense of positing a future human environment, thus connecting it to the next novel London would write, *The Iron Heel*. For our discussion of the present novel, however, this deliberate misuse of Weismann is a way for London to turn the story into a tale based not only on evolutionary science but on psychology as well.

The mix of these two broad social scientific fields isn't idiosyncratic to London. We often think of narratives of prehistoric times as necessarily growing out of the fields of archaeology, anthropology, or sociology. We need to remember that men like Moore considered psychology an equally apt science to understand the evolution of human behavior and that it was only because it was in its infancy that we so poorly understood our barely erect ancestors.[25] We remember London's observations of the Holy Jumpers and how they provided him with a window into ancient religious observances. Just as London relied on evolutionary theory for the writing of *Before Adam*, he was equally interested in employing theories from comparative psychology. The former gave him access to prehistoric times and its description. The latter gave him a way to better understand the origins and nature of his own imagination.

Governeur Morris's 1904 novel *Pagan's Progress*—a title, like *Before Adam*, that alludes to the superfluity of Christianity in understanding the origins of humans—gave London an example of how to embed modern psychology in a prehistoric narrative. Morris imagines his cave people dreaming, but they dream "about the ancient ages when they had not been men; of long, cool leaps from tree to tree; of feet that had the grip of strong hands, and of the great fear that had driven them to become men—fear of the other beasts, fear of the night."[26] If emotion drove evolution, then psychology had to play a part in the recovery of what prehistoric man was and what his progenitors were. London would have found the main character in *The Pagan's Progress* interesting because he is an artist. No Man is called by that name because he would not hunt or make weapons. He draws pictures on bones, scratching out whole narratives and must live on charity.

There are two more sources London drew on that we need to discuss before we turn to the composition of the novel: one a textbook and one a novel. "'Anthropology' Language pp. 116–117." This citation in London's notes for *Before Adam* refers to Edward B. Tylor's *Anthropology*, a textbook to a relatively new field of academic endeavor by one who is sometimes called "a 'father of anthropology.'"[27] Tylor held the first chair in anthropology at Oxford University. Moore cites this work, though London may have found it on his own. London obviously was looking for scientific information to tell him how his characters may have communicated with each other, but the two pages he refers to—and which he marked in the margins—are basic information that a lay person could convey: humans commonly use hand gestures to convey meaning, and, not surprisingly, it was then believed, this is how "savages"—Native Americans, the indigenous peoples of Australia and Africa, and others less technically sophisticated than twentieth-century Western peoples—communicate exclusively. Sign or gestural language is not an artificial construct of our era but rather a timeless mode of expression, writes Tylor, and when it is combined with imitative or gesture sounds we have what Tylor calls "Natural Language." Natural Language is "the common language of all mankind, springing so directly from the human mind that it must have belonged to our race from the most remote ages and most primitive conditions in which man existed."[28] London could easily imagine it to have been in use in the Bone Age.

The second source, familiar to London scholars, is Stanley Waterloo's novel *The Story of Ab*. Although it neither appears in his notes nor is marked more than once in the margins of his copy, *The Story of Ab* provided London with a kind of limit case or perhaps experimental piece of writing against which he could measure his own work. London may have read it as early as 1899, and it gave him a jumping off point, a prompt.[29] It's a kind of literary companion who tells London how not to tell his story and thus points the way for his imagination to explore. It's a different sort of reading from what he was looking for in *Universal Kinship* and *The Germ-Plasm*, not a search for factual material or philosophical foundations or justifications, but rather an overture to a potential literary younger friend to establish a relationship that would be mutually beneficial. This supposition of mine partially explains the pique he displayed when he was accused by Waterloo of plagiarism. "I wrote *Before Adam* as a reply to the *Story of Ab*, because I considered the latter unscientific."[30] I don't think that statement is entirely accurate, and we can see how London is codifying his relationship to *The Story of Ab* to eliminate any ambiguity of his friendly relations to that text.

Initially, and while writing *Before Adam*, he felt a filial relationship to the novel that had preceded his (and the other prehistoric novel that he had read, Morris's *The Pagan's Progress*). London obviously borrowed certain plot devices from Waterloo: the killing of an attacking animal by humans hanging down from a tree (hyena in Waterloo, boar in London); the friendship and adventurous journey of two young males (Oak and Ab in Waterloo, Big-Tooth and Lop-Ear in London); and the layout of a habitation protected by fire (Waterloo) made into a habitation by people who knew how to make fire (London). In his notes he contemplated, "They got an elephant by frightening over a cliff," an event that would have been similar to one in *The Story of Ab*; Waterloo has his people frighten a mammoth over a cliff. The first knowledge of bows and arrows, the move from life in the trees to life in the caves, the domestication of dogs, the discovery of fire all are events that overlap between the two novels, as well as any history of the Paleolithic that the two authors would have read. London even borrowed the idea of including a map of the area where his people live, though Jack's is more detailed.

Still, this is hardly plagiarism. And when London wrote to a reporter from the *New York Times* about the case, he grasped the significant and defining difference between the two works: "I tried to reproduce the primitive world in an artistic form, which same Mr. Waterloo did not do. His whole story is full of meat, and interesting; yet, through the use of an awkward form, Mr. Waterloo failed to create the convincing illusion that is proper to any work of fiction."[31] It is the same objection he made to William H. Dall's criticism of his treatment of northern Native American life. That is, unlike Waterloo and Dall, London does not wear his science on his sleeve.

Waterloo professes to have relied on the most up-to-date, accurate information about life in the Stone Age, so great detail is spent on dress, meals, and other daily activities. But he is not interested in the evolutionary development of the mind and emotions, and so the psychological dimension, so predominant in *Before Adam*, is completely absent in *The Story of Ab*. Further, Waterloo routinely employs language from his age either to describe what plot developments take place ("the aristocracy of the time had gone to sleep" [25]) or to compare his age to the Stone Age ("there was no formal naming of a child in those days" [30]). In this way, Waterloo makes the cave people familiar, palatable, and understandable. So, again, unlike in *Before Adam*, the absorptive state of reading—what London calls the "illusion"—is interrupted continuously, as if Waterloo were periodically shining the light of 1897 into the eyes of a reader trying to become engrossed in the long past. One never really settles into the lives of his characters.

The one mark in London's copy of the novel is significant because it defines another major difference between his work and Waterloo's. There is a question mark in the margin in pencil next to these lines: "She was a female Esau of the time, just a great, good-hearted, strong and honest cave girl, of the subordinate and obedient class which began thousands of years before did history, one who recognized in the girl who stood beside her a stronger and dominating spirit, and who had been received as a trusted friend and willing assistant. . . . Her name was Moonface."[32] London's question mark is an exclamation of surprise, consternation, and disagreement: What? does he really mean to say that class structure existed then and that an "honest cave girl" necessarily would be a member of the Stone Age working class?! How repellent to London it would have been to have someone justifying the concept of class on evolutionary, not socioeconomic grounds. Waterloo's nineteenth-century concept of class was foreign to London's experience, intellectuality, and sensibility.

London may have borrowed one other plot feature from another writer, H. G. Wells. Wells, incidentally, was a friend of Grant Allen and Joseph Conrad and was familiar with the work of Edward Tylor, thus reminding us that London not only was exceptionally well read in the popular literature of both America and England (was there anyone of his generation better read?) but also was a virtual member of their circle, and they of his. Wells wrote a favorable review of *The Kempton-Wace Letters* for *Wilshire's Magazine*. In his letter to Waterloo, responding to the charge of plagiarism, London cites Wells, Andrew Lang, and Rudyard Kipling as three authors he, and, presumably Waterloo, was familiar with.[33] When George Sterling sent his friend his assessment of the manuscript shortly after it was written, he assumed London was as familiar with Wells as he was with Waterloo.[34] We don't know if Wells, Lang, and Kipling were indeed direct influences on *Before Adam*, but Wells's novella "A Story of the Stone Age" is interesting for three reasons. First, Wells is the only socialist who wrote prehistoric fiction before London. Second, the novella is the "junior companion" to "A Story of the Days to Come," a dystopic story; they were paired in the 1899 volume *Tales of Space and Time*. By pairing *Before Adam* and *The Iron Heel*, London may have been mimicking Wells. Third, in "A Story of the Stone Age," Wells imagines a fight between a progressive (Ugh-lomi) and an atavistic caveman (Uya) over a woman (Eudena), a fight that gets reenacted in *Before Adam* between Big-Tooth and Red-Eye over Swift One. Wells also emphasizes the importance of rivers as a mode not simply of travel but of evolutionary progress, he emphasizes the origin of fear in the darkness that hides carnivores, and he uses the term *squatting-place*, three thematic and rhetorical items present in *Before Adam*. Wells also imagines that his characters dream and that in their dreaming they can imagine things that then help them in their waking lives; thus does Ugh-lomi figure out how to create a stone axe. But there are many differences, including Wells's inexplicable decision to re-create the interior monologue of Andoo the cave bear and other animals, making the novella more of a Kiplingesque animal story or young-adult novel than any of its brethren.[35]

London boiled all his reading—except perhaps Waterloo—down to a few short paragraphs in the frame story. "For your convenience," the narrator says, addressing his audience directly, as if he were a mesmerist setting his audience's minds in the proper orientation—that is, susceptible to his suggestions—"since this is to be no sociological screed, I shall frame together the different events into a comprehensive story."[36] As a side note, we might expect a different word than *convenience*, something more like *entertainment*; but part of the mission of this author is to instruct his readers, though in a much more subtle fashion than Waterloo's. To explain how an author might know what early humans and their environment were like—even if it means perverting Weismann—allows London to combine the two sciences of heredity and psychology. This combination, which no other author creates, is London's major contribution to the genre of prehistoric fiction. Waterloo, Wells, and Morris all use the third-person point of view, and we feel the loss of absorption that we feel when reading *Before Adam*. It doesn't matter if the explanation is unconvincing. London isn't teaching a seminar; he is writing a novel. Thus when George Sterling read the manuscript and objected to the novel, saying that "your opening chapters are so far from convincing (I hate to use that *word* on you!) that I think you'd better have left out all explanations, and approached the theme as Wells or Waterloo did," he misses the point.[37] The explanations are there to tell us about the character of the narrator, not to teach us about heredity and evolution. Still, the opening chapters will make us think about the two sciences that London has combined, innovatively. Even in his most absorptive work there lurks an element of the theatrical. He also hides his radical politics in the story as well.

We know that this solicitous attitude of the narrator to the audience is one of London's earliest formulations. His originary notes for the story say,

> Maybe utilize this as a medium to tell a very ancient life—and love tale make it as primitive as possible—when man was in earliest stages— part ape—The narrator has inherited memory to an unusual degree— and remembers dreams after he wakes. Most primitive life, wooing, and tragedy. Sometimes one dream, sometimes another—but pieces together from the different dreams a fairly comprehensive story.
> And yet the whole thing vague while the parts are vividly concrete.

He argues his explanation of it by inherited memory—(instinct) to a remarkable degree. He tells it as a written narrative—writes it himself.[38]

We don't know what the "this" is in "maybe utilize this," for the notes were attached to a piece of writing—perhaps a book page, or a newspaper, or a magazine story—and now separated from it. But whatever "this" was, in his mind it would work as a "medium," a word that could direct us in two ways. First, *medium* might denote the form the story would take, a frame story. Second, it could denote a spirit medium, like his mother; Flora being the first storyteller he knew, he might have retained the dual concept of storyteller/medium that his mother embodied. It is noteworthy that for the first week of April (and the first week of the composition of the novel) Charmian read and corrected proof of "Planchette" (with Jack, I imagine, answering any questions), featuring the machinations of a spiritual medium. Charmian's aunt's husband, Edward Payne, a spiritualist, and London, argued about metaphysical subjects in the evenings of days during which London wrote *Before Adam*.[39]

Either way, the meaning is clear: the story is channeled, coming from the imagination through the medium (of text or person) and to the reader. Note the emphasis on the narrator as author. The narrator not only tells us of his previous life as a caveman. He not only frames that story with the psycho-scientific explanation "of the meaning of the things I know so well" (2). To do so he must choose among his dream visions, ordering them, editing them, and giving them the proper descriptive language in order to transform the "screaming incoherence" of a "vast phantasmagoria" into a coherent narrative.[40] We even have the first false poet, Big-Tooth's stepfather who is called the Chatterer. Here then we return to that familiar triumvirate of London's authorial construction: the author figure, the haunting imagination, and the reader entering the author's world as if a participant in one of Flora Wellman's séances. The roots of modern-day psychology that London found in works like Hudson's showed him how spiritism—however questionable it was as a methodology to expose human consciousness—existed on a continuum with a science he could put his faith in. London evokes the science of psychology in which he was learning, blurs it, and then uses it as a frame to make the narrative of adventure even more stark and appealing.

For adventure is a keynote of *Before Adam*, a word that we find in the unattributed, and therefore unusual, epigraph: "These are our ancestors, and their history is our history. Remember that as surely as we one day swung down out of the trees and walked upright, just as surely, on a far earlier day, did we crawl up out of the sea and achieve our first adventure on land." Who could its author be who so acutely forecasted the content of this new novel? Why, the author of the new novel himself! It is in fact a passage from *The Kempton-Wace Letters*, the epistolary discussion of the nature of love. Herbert Wace, the economics doctoral student, tells Kempton, the poet, that to understand the nature of love one must "follow me down and under the phenomena of love to things sexless and loveless."[41] One must begin at the very beginning and ask, with Herbert Spencer, What is life? Or, in Spencer's own words, "What distinguishes Life in general?"[42] Though we may laugh at Wace's sententiousness, he dares to define love in terms of the reproduction of "unicellular organisms. Such a creature is a tiny cell, capable of performing in itself all the functions of life." It is able, "as Herbert Spencer says . . . 'to adjust the inner relations with outer relations,' to correspond to its environment—in short, to live." From that single cell life moves to multicellular organisms until we get to "the jelly-like organism [that] develops a bony structure, muscles by which to move itself, and a nervous system." Wace breaks off his narrative of evolution—to say to Kempton, "Be not bored, Dane, and be not offended. These are our ancestors, and their history is our history," and so on with the rest of the epigraph.[43]

One might think that Spencer's influence on London continued from when he first read him to now, in 1906. But this narrative of evolution that Wace intones was a narrative told by more scientists and social scientists at this time than Spencer, and we have to remember that even in *The Kempton-Wace Letters* the name of Spencer and his definition of life (which significantly is not a part of the epigraph to *Before Adam*) tells us more about the character of Wace than it does the intellectual influences upon London. We saw him do this with Spencer's *The Philosophy of Style*, and we'll see him do it again in his next novel, *The Iron Heel*, and in *Martin Eden*. This was a pattern with London, to play with Spencer's name and quotations as if they were intellectual markers but without any real investment in the actual ideas; sometimes the play involves attributing the ideas of certain thinkers he has repudiated to fictional characters. Remember, it was already in 1899 that he had read Weismann and by now his political education was developed enough to see Spencer as a reactionary. The epigraph to *Before Adam* is thus meant as a reminder of the generic narrative of man's evolution from ocean to trees to savannah to city. To the careful (perhaps obsessive) reader of London it is a reminder that there is an intellectual continuity from his past works to his present; perhaps his audience had forgotten this, distracted as they had been by stories of the Northland, by *The Call of the Wild*, *The Sea-Wolf*, *The Game*, and *White Fang*—unless they had been affected by the presence of the primitive in all those works. Or if they had received the letter that Waterloo received after accusing London of plagiarism: "You say that you worked fifteen long years. How long do you think I have been working in my study of science? Read my *Kempton-Wace Letters*, my *Call of the Wild*, my *War of the Classes*, (especially these three)—read everything I've written, and you will find that I am firmly grounded—not in Stanley Waterloo—but in the same scientific writers that Stanley Waterloo is grounded in."[44]

The first words of the text proper are a repeated declarative that indicates a high level of mental anxiety: "Pictures! Pictures! Pictures! Often, before I learned, did I wonder whence came the multitudes of pictures that thronged my dreams."[45] We are beginning with an adventure of the mind. The narrator seems overwhelmed by these interior images, so much so that the repetition of the word *pictures* is a loud cry for help, an insistence that they stop. That London contemplated making that anxiety a never-ending constant in the life of his narrator is evidenced by the changes he made in the novel's manuscript. Initially, he wrote, "Often did I wonder whence came the multitudes of pictures that thronged my dreams." In fact, he goes on to say that "they tormented my childhood, making of my dreams a procession of nightmares and a little later convincing me that I was different from my kind, a creature unnatural and accursed."[46] Later in his frame narrative, he explains that evolution "gave sanity to the pranks of this atavistic brain of mine" (21). Clearly, here is a man in need of psychiatric assistance. The narrator wants us to understand that the inserted phrase "before I learned" indicates that he was educated in college about the true meaning of his experiences. As he says, he learned his psychological vocabulary as well as "the explanation of various strange mental states and experiences" (a learning process that sounds as much like therapy as college education).[47] But the emphasis on higher education seems overdetermined, covering what truly happened. He actually has had some kind of medical, psychiatric help. The novel, instead of being written from inside an asylum, is written after residence in one. The narrator's first chapters are written to convince his readers that he is not mad.[48]

Unless you believe in racial memory and in his use of evolutionary science to explain what happened to him. Given the patina of learning that he provides by citing Weismann, the reader certainly wants to believe that his experiences are the unique mental constructs of an atavistic brain. But that explanation seems far-fetched, and as I pointed out earlier, Weismann's work—nor any work by any evolutionary scientist—does not support the narrator's contention. That's why his explanation seems overdetermined. The narrator misapplies Weismann to cover his own psychiatric illness.

If one needs biographical assistance in accepting this reading, one need only consider the case of the Londons' close friend Frederick Bamford. He was struggling with depression and spending a fair amount of time in Burke's Sanitarium close to the ranch in 1905 and 1906. In February, before London began writing the novel, he encouraged his friend to come to the ranch and "rest."[49] Two days into writing the novel, London wrote to Bamford that "we are sorry to hear that you have been down again" and insisted he come to the ranch.[50] A month later he told Bamford what he had told himself a number of times: "The sweet country cannot but refresh you, after the wear and tear of the city."[51] Bamford visited the Londons on the ranch a number of times during the writing of *Before Adam*. In turn, in May, the Londons visited the sanitarium. Further, on the morning of the 1906 earthquake, the Londons first went from the ranch to the home for "the feeble-minded," located in Glen Ellen. Depression, anxiety, and mental illness in general were not just on London's mind but in his mirror. His novel's narrator, not surprisingly then, tells us in the very first chapter how the simple act of visiting a circus prompted a "semi-disassociation of personality" and he became so "nervous and overwrought" that he had to be taken home "sick with the invasion of my real life by that other life of my dreams."[52]

Insanity is a theme that runs through London's notes for the novel (and we will see it again in a note from around this time for a short story in a projected collection called *Created He Them*). On one page, he imagines that Red-Eye, the atavism, is insane or partially insane: "The villian [a word London misspelled throughout the notes]—Red-eyes—rims were red and the eyes blood shot—he had terrific spells of passion. Maybe less sane than they. Work the idea of partial insanity." "Less sane than they" implies that the group or Folk were completely sane, but not necessarily. In another note, he characterizes them as similar to the residents of an asylum: "Have adumbrations of the later councils of Indians. But they only chattered and cut up. All talked at once. No consecutiveness. (Remember insane asylum)—each filled with his own ideas or impulses Yet sociability and gregariousness were satisfied by these councils."[53] We remember his note from *Universal Kinship* and Moore's claim about the size of the skulls correlating with intelligence: the smaller the skull (microcephalus) the smaller the intelligence. In a note, he wrote, "Big Tooth They had larger heads than the Tree People, smaller heads than the Fire People," and we know from the text that the Tree People are the least developed, the Fire People the most developed. It's not such a small leap for London to go from lack of intelligence to insanity. Thus, London is employing the same mix of anthropology and psychology that he had read in Moore. His rough historical timeline concerning meetings of these three kinship groups seems to have three different stages: primitive (atavisms: bordering on or actually insane); premodern Native American gatherings (the Tree People, who were rational); and modern-day institutions (the Fire People, who were advanced enough to conduct conflict resolution and determine policy). Atavistic behavior, therefore, is less rational, more questionably sane than the psychological norm of the twentieth century. Given that the narrator describes himself as an atavism—more precisely and more troublingly, "a freak of heredity, an atavistic nightmare" (20)—we must again wonder how mentally balanced he really is.

Whether the narrator is (or was) insane—a ripe candidate for Mesmer or Charcot—he is certainly haunted by his dreams and by his imagination. Late in his narrative he explains where the human fear of the dark comes from: "As imagination grew it is likely that the fear of death increased until the Folk that were to come projected this fear into the dark and peopled it with spirits" (185-86). Again, London is drawing connections, drawn first in his earliest stories, among the imagination and fear and spirits, infusing it this time with evolutionary theory. Rather than postpone the mental trauma of dealing with the ghostly imagination by writing theatrical and political essays, he confronts it—as he did in *White Fang*, but this time trying to assuage his fear with intellectual effort. One can see his reading and preparation for writing this novel as a way to counteract the effects of the imagination, to rein it in and contain it with mental constructs other than those that produce spirits. As with his attempt in *White Fang*, his endeavor works, but only temporarily. He will never be able to domesticate his imagination.

By devising a time traveler as a guide to accompany us into the prehistoric age, London has no problem engaging the reader deeply in his novel's life and thus solving the problem that Waterloo could not. Then to turn that guide into an unreliable narrator—unreliable because he seems so mentally unstable—gives London the method to incorporate not only the latest evolutionary science but also the latest psychological research. London uses the new psychology both to popularize the idea of racial memory and the inheritance of basic human emotions like fear and also to help give form to the novel. It explains why *Before Adam* is a frame story. (His next novel, *The Iron Heel*, is also a frame story, and this time London's political ideology explains the need for the frame.) The narrative of Big-Tooth is the exemplum of the new theories London is teaching his readership.

London deploys two new terms: *projection* and *disassociation of personality*. The presence of these psychological terms in the novel, so familiar to us now in the twenty-first century, should surprise us. London's narrator uses *projection* nearly in its precise modern-day form, but in two, differing ways. First, he says, "My dream personality lived in the long ago, before ever man, as we know him, came to be; and my other and wake-day-personality projected itself, to the extent of the knowledge of man's existence, into the substance of my dreams" (12–13). Here he uses projection in a generic fashion, though the similarity between its definition here and filmic projection is interesting in light of the similarity between his visions and cinema.

But its second use is the psychological one. He uses it against those who would try to explain away his memories of the Bone Age. "The doubting Thomases of psychology" would say that it is all "due to overstudy and the subconscious projection of my knowledge of evolution into my dreams" (21). Yes, that is exactly what we would say in the face of the fantastic explanation the narrator offers instead. No one can become a caveman, no one can remember being a caveman, and it's really a matter of wish fulfillment. By mistaking his dream images of trees, snakes, blueberries, and other matter as his memories of himself as a long-dead person, he actually wishes to escape the stresses and mysteries of his own life. But of course our (mentally unbalanced) narrator disavows this explanation, even though he admits that he was the worst student in his college class—he was too busy with athletics and billiards, sure signs of him being a denizen of Clubland—and so shouldn't even be aware of these technical psychological terms. Is it too much to say that he was taught this term during his psychiatric care—what he calls college—and now refuses its applicability?

The second term he teaches us is *disassociation of personality*, but instead of following its precise meaning and so serving as an explanation for his fantasy of a previous life, he uses it in an entirely idiosyncratic way. He says that his second, split personality actually lived in the past. The narrator says that he is not reincarnated; that would be the spiritualist's explanation. Instead, he relies (mistakenly) on this psychological construct. True, the pictures that so torture him are driven by this personality split. He is actually two people, but the clue that he appropriates the term for his own uses is supplied early on. He tells us that although he usually becomes his earlier personality during his dream states, sometimes he becomes Big-Tooth in broad daylight; for example, as a child, he changes personalities at the circus in the face of the lion's challenge. We might say he suffers from multiple personality disorder and, again, dismiss him as insane or unbalanced. And, as I said before, I would argue this is correct. But to simply dismiss him (and thus cease reading the novel before the framed narrative actually begins) would be to miss out on the connections among psychology, anthropology, and heredity that London wants to instruct us in. Indirectly, London teaches us something about the social construction of mental illness. The illness itself is real enough, but its reception is socially constructed to serve different aims.

Still, our surprise and wonder at London's deployment of the term should not be inhibited. Not only do we not expect such a term to be used to define the presence of a previous prehistoric life accessible to the memory and articulation of a twentieth-century person, but also the term itself did not enter the English language until 1906, when Morton Prince's *Disassociation of Personality* was published.[54] Binet discussed dual personalities three years previous to Prince, and London most likely was still drawing on Binet, not Prince, while writing *Before Adam*; I have found no evidence that he owned Prince's book. Further, *projection* does not appear in either Binet or Prince as far as I can determine, and it appears to have been first used as a spiritualist term, meaning the transference of a strong person's will (the medium's) into a weaker person who reads the transference as the presence of a phantasm now residing within him. This is clearly not how London uses it. But the modern psychological use of it wasn't put into general circulation until Freud made use of it in his analysis of Schreber.[55]

Neither Binet nor Prince discuss the role of projection or disassociation or multiple personality in terms of the creative imagination. For London, however, the pictures that haunt our narrator and keep him in the borderlands between sanity and insanity are driven by, are the function of, his "disassociation of personality." If we believe that the narrator is actually suffering from multiple personality disorder, then London is using this new term to describe what happens to a creative artist when he creates characters. Not only does his imagination act like a ghost and haunt him. It also threatens to make him insane by splitting his self.

London tackled the nexus of spiritual possession and creativity in his very first third-person narrative, "Who Believes in Ghosts!" (retitled "The Ghostly Chess Game"). It was the first time he manifested his mental and spiritual discomfort with his imagination. The faculty that he had decided would lead him out of the slavery of manual labor seemed always to betray him, but in ways he did not understand and could not anticipate. And so he began his lifelong obsession with telling stories about stories, *Before Adam* being the latest and now most mature expression of his need to distance himself from that source of unease. In "Who Believe in Ghosts!" Damon, Pythias, and George, three friends in Clubland, tell ghost stories as exempla of spiritual possession. "In a vague sort of way," says the narrator, "he realized that he was undergoing a reincarnation. He felt himself to be rapidly evolving into some one else."[56] More than that, though, the story tells us of London's own fears of losing himself in the creation of (fictional) others.

The connection between the story and *Before Adam* is explicit, but reincarnation becomes the scientific inheritance of humans' need to bond together, a clear sign of the maturing of London's fiction. Thus, the reference to Damon and Pythias in chapter 7 of *Before Adam*, the main characters from the early short story, is a reference to them as exemplars of friendship. Lop-Ear and Big-Tooth eventually become Damon and Pythias because time is erased in the face of the eternal verities about human nature. Yet the logic of the narrator of *Before Adam* breaks down if his story does not include the same strong bond of friendship. The original Greek story now becomes a generalized account of the origin of human altruism or, as the narrator says, "a foreshadowing of the altruism and comradeship that have helped make man the mightiest of the animals" (91). It comes from that moment when one caveman felt empathy for his wounded friend and sacrificed his own safety for the welfare of another: "And there rises up before me all that was there foreshadowed, and I see visions of Damon and Pythias, of life-saving crews and Red Cross nurses, of martyrs and leaders of forlorn hopes, of Father Damien, and of the Christ himself, and of all the men of earth, mighty of stature, whose strength may trace back to the elemental loins of Lop-Ear and Big-tooth and other dim denizens of the Younger World" (91–92). If we can't trace each individual of the current human race back to a particular "denizen," but instead trace human characteristics back to our ape ancestors, then the narrator's story of living the life of one particular Bone Age dude fractures, and we are again left with the strong suspicion that the narrator is mentally fragile, if not insane, convinced that he is possessed by the dead figure from the Younger World.

So we can read *Before Adam* as either an early psychoanalytic case study in delusions of grandeur, or, given the seemingly casual reference to Damon and Pythias, it can be read as a kind of ghost story. In fact, when the narrator tells his story for the very first time—to his best friend at eight years old—the friend "laughed at me, and jeered, and told me tales of ghosts and of the dead that walk at night" (10). He mistook them for "feeble fancy," a failed attempt to create a convincing story. The narrator—and Jack—finds himself in Jack's familiar position of telling a story that is not believed, but is fiction so shouldn't be believed, but should be realistic enough in order to be believed enough to convey the truth of the narrator's emotions. The narrator is haunted—terrified—by his past, though it's not the past of himself but rather a scientifically proven past of all humans; he just happens to be special, like an author, and his ghosts become the story that he tells. The ghost is the imagination and the content of that imagination, just as Buck was the imagination and the content of that imagination. There is no more absorptive state than deep sleep.

In sleep and in the hypnotic state there is no sense of time. This is true of London's conception of racial memories. Time ceases to matter if we can in the span of a few hours jump back to the mid-Pleistocene. "There is one puzzling thing about these prehistoric memories of mine," says the narrator. "It is the vagueness of the time element" (38). His note on this matter is close to the text: "One puzzling thing—time is bad. Doesn't know whether one yr. or 5 yrs. have elapsed between this and that. Can only tell time by judging change in appearance of his fellows." We saw how time collapses when we think of Lop-Ear and Big-Tooth as reliving life as Damon and Pythias, the latter being scientific inheritors of human altruism. The same inconsequential nature of time happens with the appearance of ghosts too. What was past becomes present and forecasts the future, if only to be a memento mori. The lability of time brings together these seemingly disparate concepts, that of prehistoric lives and ghosts. It is the job of the author, so says London's narrator, to reinstall time so that a narrative can be written: "It was all a jumble. . . . It was not until I . . . had dreamed many thousand times . . . that I got the clew of time, and was able to piece together events and actions in their proper order. . . . I shall frame together the different events into a comprehensive story" (24). Our narrator-author is not only a time traveler but also a time master, one who manipulates time for his own linguistic purposes. But one cannot write a novel without first experiencing timelessness.

There is another mode of absorption and timelessness: the spiritualist's séance. Given London's constant public expression of antipathy toward all things metaphysical, given the more mature treatment of the thematics of Damon and Pythias, and given his research into the psycho-evolutionary sciences, we would expect London to disavow the séance, and in *Before Adam* he does so, but in a private, subtle way. One way he distanced himself from the very real debt he owed to his mother—the spiritual medium and first storyteller he knew—was to title his works with citations to every member of an immediate family—son, daughter, father—or a collective—people—but never mother. In *Before Adam*, however, the mother is a strong presence, a real departure from his previous works. In fact, the first line of his story proper is "I do not remember much of my mother," a somewhat odd thing for someone to say who has such a powerful memory that he can recall events from the Paleolithic (25). No matter. The first four-color illustration in the book (by the incomparable Charles Livingston Bull) is of his mother saving her baby boy from a wild boar. In the beginning was the mother. The mother is present and powerful, and again we note London's maturation as an author. He is now able to acknowledge her as a significant influence in his writerly life. But, and here is where the disavowal kicks in, she is "old-fashioned. She still clung to her trees." The more evolutionarily advanced anthropoid apes lived in caves, but Big-Tooth's mother "was suspicious and unprogressive." By chapter 5, she disappears from the narrative, an anachronism in the more progressive scientific life of her son.

The narrator can't help but use anachronistic terminology ("unprogressive") to describe the group's members. Just as he assigns names to some (though not to his mother! another way to distance himself from her) "for the sake of convenience" (42), so he employs twentieth-century language to elucidate the sociology and linguistics of his people. Because London's modern-day language is not that of a third-person narrator, like Waterloo's, it has a diegetic function. At the beginning of chapter 11 he says that the descriptions he gives are his, not his character. He is both inhabited by Big-Tooth and in turn inhabits him. "It is by the medium of my dreams that I, the modern man, look through the eyes of Big-Tooth and see." Big-Tooth doesn't have language. He spoke in sounds of which his group had fewer than fifty. London in fact devotes several pages to the "tools of speech" and its evolution (40). His notes are filled with entries like the following: "Choruses A-bang! A-bang!" "Ha-ah, ha-ah, ba-ah-ha!" "Eh wa! eh wa! eh wa hah!" which are repeated in the novel (184). It is one more indication that this is a novel about telling stories, about the imagination and how it expresses itself. In addition we come to understand something about the absorbed individual. While one dreams (or while one is in an absorptive state) one doesn't have language. One has pictures, images. The things the narrator sees exist for him apart from language. The narrator is actually translating what he hears and sees in his dreams into a language we can understand; part of this thematic is represented by the placement of numerous pen-and-ink drawings by Charles Bull in among the words, so images interrupt words, words flow around images, and so represent their interchangeability. The narrator's translations are words about pictures or word-pictures—or word-become-pictures in the reader's mind—a term we remember encountering for the first time when London published his very first story, "Story of a Typhoon," as an entry in the *San Francisco Call*'s contest for the best "word-pictures." We also remember Sitka Charley in "The Sun-Dog Trail." This isn't imagism. This is about how London (and others of his time) understood the nature of language. And these pictures in the brain aren't paintings. They are photographs.

Thus, there is another valence to this constellation of psychological disorder–creative imagination–evolutionary theory. When London says the narrator is remembering the life of his "particular and far-removed progenitor" (20) or is dreaming of his progenitor—Big-Tooth—he inhabits his body and sees out of his eyes. Logically, then, these pictures are actually a combination of still photographs and moving images. When he dreams he watches the movie of Big-Tooth's life. When he awakes, he sees the still photographs of that life. The point is that if one took *pictures* to mean paintings, one would miss three crucial elements of how London understood the operations of the mind—especially of the imagination: the realism of a dream image that rivals that of a photograph, the cinematic quality of dreams, and the ghostly quality of both. *Before Adam* is a textual precursor to London's involvement in early American cinematic efforts in the next decade. Just as, in this novel, he tries to distract his readers and himself from the ghostly quality of his imagination by defining it in scientific evolutionary terms, so later he will use the technology of film to try to achieve the same effect, and again to no avail. He cannot escape the ghostly nature of both the imagination and of photography and cinema.

We see, then, a progression of thought in his fiction as he deals with his relationship with his imagination and his interior life. In 1905, "Planchette" focused on spiritualism as a historical antecedent to psychiatry. *White Fang*, while employing modern psychological terms, emphasized evolutionary science. *Before Adam* returns to an emphasis on psychology while expounding in a more complex way his readings in two other sciences, in both heredity and anthropology. In his notes, he makes it clear that his narrator (while perhaps having undergone psychotherapy himself) analyzes himself as if he were a patient: "On looking back he weighs and analyzes emotions, motives, etc. In the actual event itself—just simple and often erratic impulses and emotions. he does a certain very inconsecutive and illogical thing in that early life. Looking back with his modern man's brain, he sees how inconsecutive and illogical the act was, and also the acts of all others."[57] In the novel itself, this note (as with all the notes he used, the wording is almost verbatim in the final text) comes late—at the beginning of chapter 11. London deliberately interrupts Big-Tooth's tale, jerking us back to a wakefulness within the absorptive state of reading. We never leave that state. But we experience a shift from dream to waking just as the narrator does. This happens to remind us that what we are holding is not a story told by a prehistoric humanoid but rather a translation of his images into words and of his actions into analysis: "It is I, the modern, who look back across the centuries and weigh and analyze the emotions and motives of Big-tooth, my other self" (137). Once done with this digression, he says, "And now to return to my tale," as if it were a suggestion from a hypnotist or psychoanalyst for the narrator (and us) to return to the dream state (139). The form of the novel is that of self-analysis. The narrator has discovered his unconscious and tries to make sense of it.

And then London adds another layer, that of the political.

Ernest Untermann, the translator of Karl Marx and others into English and friend to London, visited the ranch while London was writing *Before Adam*. Perhaps he gave him a copy of one of his latest translations, Wilhelm Bölsche's *The Evolution of Man*. It is not marked by London, but he would have been interested in it, for it was advertised by Charles Kerr as an affordable textbook on evolution for the laboring class. "Modern socialism is closely allied to the modern scientific theory of evolution," Kerr's blurb for the book read. "If laborers understand science, they become socialists, and the capitalists who control most publishing houses naturally do not want them to understand it."[58] Kerr's mission was pedagogic, and he believed that an educated working class in all intellectual fields would promote a socialist revolution; this of course was the purpose of the Intercollegiate Socialist Society as well.[59] But, more specifically, Kerr, Bölsche, Simons, Untermann, and other socialists believed that knowledge of evolution would counteract the power of the alliance between established religion and capitalism. Capitalism used traditional religion to keep the poor in place and thus frustrate class consciousness and revolution. That is why London rebelled against Waterloo's political conservatism. That is why he referred to *War of the Classes* when he cited proof of his education in preparation for writing *Before Adam*. That is why he chose the title *Before Adam* over the other possibilities he had in mind: "The First Lovers," "The Long Ago," "In the Youth of the Younger World," "The Younger World," "The First Love Tale."[60] It's not simply a tale of prehistoric man or of two early lovers. As important as John Milton was to London, this novel's time frame precedes Milton's poem and thus succeeds it in terms of man's intellectual development.

We can thus read *Before Adam* as coincident with Kerr's mission. However mad and unreliable Big-Tooth may be, his narrative of life in the prehistory of man is meant to be instructive in the ways that collective action succeeds where individual action fails. We've already seen how London subtly works into the friendship of Big-Tooth and Lop-Ear the origin of human altruism, the basis for the alternative to the capitalist competitive system. London's socialism expresses itself in other ways as well. The fight between the Fire People and Big-Tooth is about technology; more precisely it is about the evolution of the technology of warfare. It is about fire versus no fire, bows and arrows versus stone throwing. For London's readers, it might as well be about machine guns and cannons that London talked about in 1902 and the British empire versus the Boers. Also, the fight with Red-Eye is about warfare with atavisms, as if there would be no war if atavistic humans did not exist. But they do and we must fight them. When Red-Eye murders Crooked-Leg and takes the Singing One, the Folk "felt the prod of the gregarious instinct," which is the source of socialism, "the drawing together as though for united action, the impulse toward cooperation," but the impulse needs language to define it, and they did not have it yet (181). So Red-Eye the imperialist gets what he wants because there is no collective to oppose him. Warfare is an atavism. *Modern warfare* is, therefore, a contradiction in terms. If we were really modern we wouldn't be fighting. But evolution is uneven, and this is another lesson of *Before Adam*.

Collective action could not take place among tree dwellers. When "the more progressive members" (43–44) move into caves, we can date from that moment the possibility for socialism. For if everything else about human nature finds its origins in the Paleolithic, certainly forms of government do too. *Before Adam* is London's attempt to discover the root of his political identity.

The cave dwellers do initiate a kind of collective action, though it is not against a common enemy. After Red-Eye takes the Singing One, the Folk gather instinctively into a "hee-hee council." One of London's more idiosyncratic yet deeply pertinent notes for the novel reads, "The 'hee-hee' council, meaning the council of laughter 'Hee-hee' parties or gatherings, where they gather to laugh." In the novel these councils branch off in history in two directions: toward "the great national assemblies and international conventions of latter-day" (the most prominent in 1906 being national and international conventions of socialists) and, most importantly, "a unanimity of rhythm"—the gatherings were accompanied by Folk banging sticks on logs in time together—and thus the origin of music and speech: "whenever we were so drawn together we precipitated babel, out of which arose a unanimity of rhythm that contained within itself the essentials of art yet to come. It was art nascent." Thus he locates the source of a different form of authorial identity in this Younger World.

Art and play, as I have argued all along, are a crucial combination for the creation of bohemian culture, and London's Folk are nascent bohemians. London's notes for the novel are filled with references to play and laughter: "Most all that they learned was in the course of play"; "Once he found a gourd, the seed rattled, had lots of fun with it" (96). In the novel, whenever Big-Tooth and Lop-Ear escape the very real threat of death at the hands of Red-Eye (or punishment at the hands of the Chatterer), they laughed and laughed. When Big-Tooth begins to domesticate a dog, it is a crucial moment with which London emphasizes the "inconsequentiality" of their lives. These characters would rather play than provide themselves with more than adequate shelter, with more than adequate food. They enjoy life instinctually. They find humor in everything. They are made to have fun. To domesticate the dog, Big-Tooth plays with him, though it fails because Lop-Ear would rather eat the puppy. But their evolutionary progress is slow because "we played through life, even the adults, much in the same way that children play, and we played as none of the other animals played" (98). The function of art and play, besides being instinctual, was to induce "forgetfulness"—a sense of timelessness—in the face of helplessness or strife. "We danced and sang in the somber twilight of the primeval world, inducing forgetfulness, achieving unanimity, and working ourselves into sensuous frenzy" (184). Here is the origin of Dionysian rituals and those gatherings in which London himself took a part in Piedmont, Copa's Restaurant, the Bohemian Grove, Monterey, the Valley of the Moon, and other places. It all started with a political rage against the fascistic Red-Eye and "our rage against Red-Eye was soothed away by art" (183–84). Red-Eye, the atavism, whose genetic lineage does not lead to *Homo sapiens*, does not play. Humans are human, London says, because they would rather play than do anything else. This, too, is part of his political subtext. Humans have to learn not to be bohemian. They have to learn against their nature to be capitalists. Humans are naturally altruistic, not rapacious, greedy bastards.

Science, seen in this context, is actually a necessary evil. Evolution occurs because of threats to humankind, and playing is not an adequate response to those threats. But science counteracts the instinct to play. It turns life to seriousness. Whether it's learning about the germ plasm, or the definition and makeup of the unconscious, or the proper formation of society into governing units, science replaces the time humans would rather spend responding to their deepest need, which is to play, to create art.

Still, the end of the novel is a warning. No amount of art or individualistic behavior will save the Folk from a warlike fascist named Red-Eye. Freedom of expression cannot survive fascism. At first, London thought the novel deserved a happy ending, though someone—and that unlucky someone is Lop-Ear—of course has to die. That death would balance the survival and perpetuation of the genetic material in which the narrator's memories inhere: "The flight of Swift One and me through the vast marshes. The stragglers arriving in the caves by the sea. Are molested no more by the Fire People Death of Lop-Ear. The end." Then London changed his mind. After "People" he drew a line to an open space on his note paper, crossed out "The end," and wrote, "until toward the end, when Swift One and children and I go to S.E. in search of a safer place. Leave horde. Meet Tree People and Red-Eye, after skirting south of marsh and away from Coast—find a quiet place—End." Then he changed the ending again. London dreamt of an idyllic ending, what we might call a Valley of the Moon ending, a "quiet place" "away from the coast." Instead, Red-Eye takes over the Tree People and the final sentence is "He is Red-Eye, the atavism" (242). That is London's warning, which he duplicated in *The Iron Heel*.

The importance of the atavism is evident in Charmian's diary; whenever she notes that she has finished a day's worth of work on the novel, she calls it "the atavistic book."[61] Red-Eye is the end, and he is the beginning, the omega and the alpha. For London had already plotted out his next novel, and it forecasted the end of the modern-day Red-Eyes. In fact, before he started *Before Adam*, he told George Brett that his very next novel would be *The Iron Heel*, but then he chose to write *Before Adam*. We don't know why he suddenly changed his mind, but it may be that because the two novels were thematically linked in his mind—time stretched to eternity before, time stretched to eternity after—he decided to work chronologically. Maybe he saw *The Iron Heel* as the happy ending he could not write for *Before Adam*. He didn't see it happening in his own lifetime, though. Red-Eyes rule the world for many centuries, Big-Tooth is dead, and Swift One tells the tale.

COMPOSITION AND CHARMIAN

On 26 March 1906 London told Brett, "I think I shall write this summer a book to be entitled *The Iron Heel*." On 2 April, he began writing *Before Adam*. Neither his correspondence nor his manuscript material indicate why in the short span of five days he changed his mind; he even had a title for his novel of the future but not for his novel of the past. Perhaps because he projected the latter to be only thirty thousand words—about the length of *The Call of the Wild*—he thought he might first knock that off and then devote himself to a novel that would be more complicated and much longer. Ironically, once he reached the twenty-thousand-word mark in *Before Adam* he saw it would be ten thousand words longer than he had anticipated; this time the writing did get away from him, and the ghost within seemed as untamable as ever. He took his time. He allowed himself to be interrupted. Again, because London so often insisted that he wrote one thousand words a day, it's useful to see how much he did write per day. On 8 April he says he had the first two chapters done, about 3,800 words, about one thousand words a day since he had taken 6–7 April off to lecture at the Ruskin Club.[62] Then he spent 8 April writing his essay on the Moyer, Pettibone, and Haywood trial. He also had been assisting Charmian in reading page proof for *White Fang* and "Planchette." He sent off the newly determined table of contents of *Moon-Face, and Other Stories* to Brett. He resumed writing on the ninth, but more slowly now, and on 13 April he had finished only another two thousand words, or about four hundred words a day.

The next interruption, unplanned, came on 18 April at 5:14 in the morning. He could easily have been up by then, and his manuscript at approximately the seven-thousand-word mark has a note to himself, as if he had been ready to write, but was called away: "(remember being chased, cuffed, bitten—mother rushed in. family quarrels [no closing parentheses]," and then left his desk to see how bad the earthquake had been.[63] It's the only note of its kind in the manuscript and represents a notable departure from his usual practice, which was to write a note on a separate piece of paper and include it with the notes and drafts he had written before embarking on the actual writing of the novel; for example, before he began work on chapter 7, he wrote, "Must work in shortly—the tree People—who were apes—nothing more." Perhaps when he resumed writing on the twenty-first or twenty-second he wrote a single note, a kind of reassurance, which he contemplated using in *Before Adam* but never did: "There were more earthquakes in those days—more frequent and more terrible."[64] On the twenty-fourth, he wrote "Story of an Eye-Witness," his account of the earthquake, and on the next day he said he had thirteen thousand words of *Before Adam* completed. He had begun speeding up, writing two thousand words a day. He took a break after reaching the twenty-thousand mark on 2 May, slowing down to a thousand words a day. He and Charmian then rode horses throughout Sonoma County, from Glen Ellen to Fort Bragg and back south, arriving home on the fourteenth and beginning writing the next day. There was just one more interruption—a two-day trip to Oakland and San Francisco to see the dentist and take a three-hour car ride through San Francisco—and then he finished the novel on 7 June, his final stint being twenty-one thousand words in twenty-five days. He wrote 41,230 words in 73 days, about 560 words a day.

Before Adam was the first novel he wrote while married to Charmian, and for the first time she collaborated on the writing. On page 10 of chapter 14, we read the sentence, "Red-Eye seized her by the hair and dragged her toward his cave." Charmian, on her own, added "of the head" just after "hair," and that change stayed in the final version. Also, in chapter 17, she changed the word "smashed" to "broken" in the sentence "His old bones must have been sadly smashed." And in the same chapter she added "in their faces" to the sentence "They fled silently and swiftly, and with alarm in their faces." In the final chapter's second paragraph, she changed "snakes" to "serpents" in the sentence "Large trees are about us, and from their branches hang gray filaments of moss, while great creepers, like monstrous serpents, curl around the trunks and writhe in tangles through the air." These are small textual changes, but they represent a momentous change in her and her spouse's professional relationship. Before this moment she never suggested additions or deletions to the manuscript. It may be somewhat of an exaggeration, but it seems possible that with the presence of Charmian's hand in his manuscript for the first time, London was inspired to create his first female narrator, Avis Everhard of *The Iron Heel.*

Charmian had another task to perform related to the novel's composition. When London wrote his last words of his novel of prehistory and psychiatric illness, Charmian scheduled every minute of his day "to circumvent the blues he had once forewarned he might be subject to upon the day of completing a long manuscript." Thus, "there was little or no depression."[65] The act of writing was an aporia. It triggered the presence of the ghostly imagination that in turn created an anxiety and depression that only more writing could alleviate. As with the Folk in *Before Adam*, art was a salve, but only temporarily. Art is always a life-and-death matter for Jack London, and as David Starr Jordon wrote in *Foot-notes to Evolution*, "the test of sanity is its liveableness, for insanity is death."[66] But now we see how London used writing as a kind of therapy, as a hedge against going insane, being driven mad by the ghost within.

As he had done with *Moon-Face, and Other Stories* and *Love of Life, and Other Stories* in 1906, London sent the completed typescript of *Before Adam* to George Sterling for commentary. Perhaps their literary friendship was founded on a similar distrust of and torment by the imagination; Sterling once described his muse as "the Fiend."[67] Sterling was honest, if prone to his usual romantic hyperbole, in his assessments of Jack's writing, and London could trust him. In May, after reading Edwin Markham's essay on the California earthquake, Sterling told London, "You make most of your contemporaries seem like men of paste. They can never be fit penmates nor pen-adversaries to you."[68] He thought "What Life Means to Me" "a fine thing. . . . If only I could deserve to write anything half as good!" He was immediately engrossed by *Tales of the Fish Patrol* and read it in one sitting.[69] But he thought *Before Adam* "punk."[70] This even though London had described it to him as "a skit, ridiculously true, preposterously real."[71]

Sterling did manage one compliment: "I must admit that the story possesses to a considerable degree the element that's *never* lacking from your work, and that is *interest*."[72] We remember that "interest"—a vague but compelling term—was the hallmark of *McClure's Magazine*'s aesthetic, and London had mastered it. Interest, besides denoting freshness and excitement, was in essence another word for absorption, and Sterling had been hooked and drawn in deeply despite what he felt to be the novel's preposterousness. Later, Sterling reported that their mutual writer-friends Jimmy Hopper and Jim Whitaker liked *Before Adam* more than *The Call of the Wild*, and Bamford loved it. Sterling commented, "I'm sorry for them. I concede its scientific value; but you can give so greater literary value. I don't want crab-apples, however good, from a pippin tree."[73] Porter Garnett, however, found ten scientific errors in the first chapter, said Sterling later, so the bohemians of the bay were divided on the book's value.

George Brett also had reservations, though he had faith in his western author now that he had written *White Fang*, a "masterpiece."[74] He was confident in recommending the yet-to-be-completed *Before Adam* to E. M. Ridgway, editor of *Everybody's Magazine* via Paul Reynolds, the agent. Reynolds had told Brett that Ridgway was looking for a thirty-to-forty-thousand-word serial from London, and the possibility struck London as an answer to his most vexing problem in his current publishing relations. Just five days after returning to Glen Ellen from his lecture tour—an indication that the matter was foremost in his mind—he had written to Brett that because "magazines [are] practically all owned by book-publishers" he was not getting the best price for serialization. Negotiating with Robert Collier, S. S. McClure, and Caspar Whitney had been arduous. McClure, especially, tried every trick to bring London back to his magazine and thus to his book firm. (The latter was failing and would be absorbed by Doubleday, Page, and Company in 1908.)[75] He had held up the publication of "Love of Life" to get another story. When London told him in early March 1905 that "there are no more short stories," he asked for the first look on anything longer. "I shall always feel that McClure's is the proper place for your work," he argued, without realizing what kind of competition Collier and Whitney represented.[76] McClure, when he heard that London would be visiting New York City during his lecture tour, even told London that "from now on I am going to be in the office myself most of the time," hoping that London wouldn't notice the qualifier "most of the time"; they actually did meet, though, in January 1906, and then McClure complained that they hadn't talked long enough "about your future work."[77] When he heard that *Outing* had been given first look at *White Fang*, he insisted on getting first look at the next long piece of writing, which turned out to be *Before Adam*. London complied, and thus began a bit of trouble.

While in the midst of writing *Before Adam*, London pitched his novel to McClure, emphasizing its "interesting" qualities. It is "the most primitive thing every written, and I think I am doing it in a lively and interesting fashion. There is a love-motif! a hero! a villain! rivalry!"[78] McClure was initially enthusiastic, writing that a mid-Pleistocene plot "would, I should think, be a theme you could handle with wonderful power."[79] And then he asked for the book publication, too, if he accepted the manuscript for a serial. And, repeating an exchange that had occurred a number of times from 1901 to 1906, when London sent the manuscript, McClure demurred, thus making London's dealings with magazine–book publishers even more frustrating. London's fame, as he had always suspected, was never enough to guarantee acceptance, and magazine publishers could never be happy without book publication.

Brett, always the careful thinker, agreed and disagreed with London's analysis about serial publication. London had analyzed the situation correctly but left out a determinant factor: his fame. "With your fame," Brett coolly surmised, "there ought not to be, I think, the slightest difficulty in selling your serial rights at good prices for you at any time." He sensed London's chief unspoken complaint—that he was devoting too much time and energy to the matter—and offered to take over.[80] He didn't mean that he himself would sell the stories. He would bring Reynolds on board. Previously, Reynolds had worked with McClure to dispose of stories that Big Daddy did not want for his own magazine. From now on, though, Reynolds would be working directly with London, who didn't realize at first that this was the arrangement. He was just relieved that he didn't have to do it anymore and mentioned to Brett that selling serial rights to his projected output from the *Snark* voyage to both McClure and Whitney had foundered on the question of book rights. Thus, hearing that Brett and Reynolds had quickly secured the interest of a magazine for a book not yet completed was sweet.

But London had unintentionally complicated things by offering it in April to McClure first. In May Reynolds told Brett that he had given *Before Adam* to Ridgway, who offered either five thousand dollars or a kill fee of five hundred.[81] The magazine could afford it; in 1907 the circulation was over half a million and between 1908 and 1911 it led all general interest monthlies in the volume of advertising.[82] In fact they were doing so well that they solicited material from London for a new magazine called *Ridgway's*, a short-lived publication that London did not contribute to.[83] Reynolds, when he heard about the London-McClure discussion, blew a gasket because Ridgway's kill fee (and Reynolds's own 10 percent commission) was based on getting the "first look." "I am sorry you made this promise to McClure because while I can see where McClure gained, I do not see where you gain," Reynolds wrote to London. "You made a present to McClure of an option that was worth $500.00." To add more salt, a different magazine, said Reynolds, would pay a kill fee of one hundred dollars based on the reading of a synopsis. Let me handle your serialization offers, he practically begged, and either McClure will back away from your promise, or he will pay what others are willing to pay.[84] London stuck to his promise, which led Reynolds to propose a somewhat shady course of action: If McClure takes it—and Reynolds imagined that he would—then the deal is done. But if he refused it, then don't tell Ridgway that you have given McClure first look. We could not "honorably" take the $500 if Ridgway rejects it, but there is no need to tell Ridgway that McClure turned it down "as this always tends to prejudice a man."[85] Then

Ridgway contacted Reynolds for an update while McClure had the manu-script, forcing Reynolds to implement a modified plan without London's approval: "I told Mr. Dennison [Ridgway's assistant] of Everybody's . . . that you would have preferred to sell the story without previously submitting it," and that the first-look option was no longer available, but *Everybody's* would be able to read the manuscript if London chose to send it out. Reynolds laid out the ethics of the situation: "I think this satisfies all the demands. We do not tell lies, and yet we leave the matter open so that, if McClure declines the story, we can still submit it to Everybody's without their having known that McClure had declined it."[86] It seems fantastic that Ridgway wouldn't figure out that the first-look option had disappeared because Reynolds or London had given it to someone else. But Reynolds believed in telling only as much of the truth as was necessary to keep from lying. But it turned out for the best for Reynolds: McClure rejected the manuscript; London tele-graphed Reynolds to move the manuscript from McClure to Ridgway, and he did, giving Ridgway a week deadline.

In mid-July, Reynolds informed London that Ridgway accepted it for five thousand dollars. And then Ridgway found out about the McClure business—natch!—but Reynolds "told them what was the truth, that the story seemed to be an exceptionally good one and I did not want them prej-udiced against it by learning in the first place that McClure had declined it." And then he slammed McClure: "This is a fact to be remembered about McClure, by the way, that he sometimes talks a little too much!" Reynolds didn't think much of Daddy McClure. As far as getting money from them, "they're slower than cold molasses."[87] While McClure was still considering *Before Adam*, Reynolds told London, "The only reason that I suggest the possibility of their declining is that McClure seem to me to be looking for the perfect serial, and when they see any actual serial, they always seem to question whether it won't offend somebody among their precious readers."[88] London would have immediately remembered that McClure had accepted but never published his socialist essay "The Question of the Maximum," that McClure rushed to grab onto the latest thing, like London after he had been published in the *Atlantic Monthly*, but routinely let it go as he moved hurriedly onto the next latest thing. Nothing could have warmed London's heart more than to realize that other professionals would have agreed that having McClure terminate their contract in 1901 had been in his best interests. Reynolds, for his part, was eager to take on more work from London. Five hundred dollars was a hefty commission.

"I am glad you fellows liked *Before Adam*," wrote London to the other editor of *Everybody's*, John O'Hara Cosgrave, London's friend and correspondent from the early aughts, "the most conservative and conventional of editors," as London had once described him. "I've got a sneaking kindly place in my heart for that yarn."[89] "Sneaking," because he was not at all confident that it would do well. He told McClure much the same thing after he rejected it: "I have a sort of genial regard for that skit, myself, and it is so damnably, healthily innocent."[90] He was more frank with Brett; he was neither hopeful for its prospects nor willing to revise the book to make it more appealing to a wider audience. Once Brett had read it, his publisher wrote that it needed something more. For one thing, it lacked appeal to women readers. The "love-motif" simply never developed. In fact, the narrative's emphasis, when it came to love, fell on Red-Eye's brutalization of his spouses, not on the tepid romance between Big-Tooth and the Swift One. Because Brett remembered he had made the same objection in the past, he couched his criticism in a suggestion that London should incorporate somewhere in the novel the fear of rats and other rodents that men rarely if ever shared. He ventured, perhaps after discussing the matter with a university professor, that women had inherited this fear from the Bone Age because rats and mice threatened cave babies, something that cavemen would not care particularly about; he didn't need proof, but he did learn from Reynolds in June that a woman's magazine had turned down an opportunity to read the novel.[91]

But, more than its lack of appeal to women, the story lacked "a certain human connection between the story and present-day readers," an "everyday appeal to present-day readers not specially interested in the science or psychology of the situation."[92] The battles between Big-Tooth and Red-Eye and the Huck Finn–like raft and walking journey of Big-Tooth and Lop-Ear were not enough to interest readers, male or female. Still, as much as London agreed with Brett's assessment, he was not about to revise it. "Concerning what you say about the certain lack of human connection between the story and present-day readers, that I should be compelled practically to write another story, in order to establish that connection." And then to mask his minor annoyance that Brett could not accept the book for what it was, he switched gears and reminded Brett how difficult it had been to revise *The Game*. "It was a sort of nightmare to me," he said, linking perhaps unconsciously his own writing to the nightmares of his narrator in his new novel.[93] Brett knew when to cease offering advice and said nothing more about revising it.

London admitted that the "human connection between the story and present-day readers" was missing. He couldn't fix it because he had written it with a different goal in mind, and he was willing to accept the consequences. Perhaps, he told Brett in a rhetorical move that he hoped would placate his publisher, that "it might develop, after the grown-ups are done with it, into a sort of stand-by boys' book. I should imagine boys would delight in reading" a book without a strong love interest and adult scenes of action.[94] In fact, in 1915, he considered writing a series of stories based on Red-Eye and "the two young, primeval gentlemen," obviously focusing on the boyish adventures of these three, though it would be "a scientifically correct and philosophic and humorous treatment."[95] These characters could not be made into something they were not, that is, appealing to women readers. Instead, before he thought of doing that series, he would write *The Valley of the Moon*, which incorporated all those elements he had promised McClure, plus rats. Women loved it, and still do.

Before Adam was published in 1907 with a deceptively simple cover. It featured the title and author in red letters outlined in white. Given the metaphoric meaning of *red* in the novel, the color subliminally tells the reader that this is an "atavistic novel." Further, a series of three pairs of footprints track from the bottom of the spine to the top right corner of the front cover across the sand-colored binding. In one of his rare suggestions for improving a cover, London wrote to a Mr. Walton, who had sent him the "stamped cover" for the novel, "The color of the cover itself should be of the color of sand, thus completing the illusion of the footprints being actually made in sand,—prehistoric sand, if you please."[96] The feet clearly belong to a prehistoric person, part human, part ape. The effect is uncanny. The footprints are of ghosts, our ancestors from the Paleolithic. Because they look fresh, by seeing them we automatically become one of the people who left them, or one of the people who would see them during that period. Or we are put in the curious position of Robinson Crusoe, stranded on our island planet. We thought we were alone, but, no, someone from our past is still here. We want to find out who. We are immediately drawn into the novel without a conscious act of belief.

As if all that signification were not enough, there is in fact a political dimension to the footprints in the sand. We remember the epigram from "Revolution," lines from James Russell Lowell's long poem "A Glance behind the Curtain": "The present is enough for common souls. / Who never looking forward, are indeed mere clay / Wherein the footprints of their age / Are petrified forever." We see yet again London's preoccupation with infinite time stretching backward and forward. Revolutionaries, not "common souls," leave permanent footprints in the sands of history, and so we see who belongs to those footprints on the cover of *Before Adam*. As London told the critic Philo Buck, "Get up; wake up; kick in; do something. . . . A hundred thousand socialists are men who can get up and fight on their hind legs like me. Who do not criticize but who do."[97] Revolutionaries and authors are men and women of action. London's insistence on action is the socialist dream of taking apart society in order to put it back together correctly. To do that is to leave your footprint in the sand forever.

RED FLAG OF REVOLUTION

Red can be the color of atavism but also of revolution, both negative and positive aspects of rage. After a week of writing *Before Adam*, London paused to contribute to the national dialogue about the wrongful imprisonment and imminent trial of Charles Moyer (president of the Western Federation of Miners), Bill Haywood (secretary-treasurer), and George Pettibone. In early March Gaylord Wilshire asked London twice to contribute to a special issue he was doing on the three men.[98] Wilshire's timing was a little off. London had just completed his review of *The Jungle* and was now in absorptive mode, writing short stories, so he demurred. But days later, perhaps prompted by Wilshire, London gave a speech, entitled "The Rising Tide of Revolution," at Oakland's Dietz Opera House on the thirty-fifth anniversary of the beginning of the Paris Commune. He "dwelt upon" their arrest, even though he was so hung over that friends doubted he'd be able to speak.[99] A fellow Oakland socialist, Chris "The Dane" Bergenhammer, remembered that he, London, and other socialists drank beer and whiskey at the Pabst Café way past one in the morning. Then "a reporter from one of the papers came down as a waiter and wrote us up as anarchist and nihilist." London's friends put him on a streetcar. A few hours later he gave his speech.[100]

According to one report, "the most sensational features of the hour and a half discourse were his references to the Moyer and Haywood cases." The lead quotation included, "If they are found guilty on evidence no better than that which convicted the Haymarket martyrs, I believe it will take the whole United States army to carry out their execution." Socialists, said London, are the only organized group in America—including religious and other political groups—that have "declared against war," but they would fight for a just cause like that of the Boise Three.[101] Note the link between the Boise Three and the Haymarket "martyrs." London couldn't have known that half of Haywood's ashes would be buried next the monument to the Haymarket victims in Chicago (the other half was buried next to John Reed's under the wall of the Kremlin). He might have found out later—or felt so himself—that a number of socialists had hoped the three would be hanged; the cause, for some, required bloodletting and sacrifice. Some felt, too, that martyrdom, not acquittal, would have been a bigger victory against President Theodore Roosevelt, who supported the prosecution; there was always something akin to religious fanaticism in the early years of American socialism.[102]

In the first week of April, Jack Barrett of the *San Francisco Examiner*, London's principal contact at the paper, asked him to cover the trial in Idaho. London said no, but now, with a speech in hand, he was ready to write an essay. Another local event spurred him on. On 8 April, a protest meeting in Woodman's Pavilion (a popular boxing venue in San Francisco) in support of the three prisoners was followed by a famous riot at Lotta's Fountain instigated by policemen who tore down a red banner above the crowd, which included William McDevitt, and were then themselves attacked by the crowd.[103] London, who had been invited to speak at Woodman's, instead wrote the essay.[104]

The text of "Something Rotten in the State of Idaho" is not the first publication that showed his interest in the case. He had been thinking about the fearsome threesome ever since they had been arrested. (Big Bill was considered second only to Eugene Debs as the most dangerous lefty in America.) The case plays a prominent role in "Revolution." Built from the speech at Dietz Opera House, the essay itself begins with a similar rhetorical device as *The Call of the Wild*. He leads the reader in a false direction, intentionally. Moyer, Haywood, and Pettibone "are guilty, and they should be swiftly and immediately executed. It is to be regretted that no severe and more painful punishment than hanging awaits them." It's a rewrite of a straightforward proposition he made in his speech at the opera house: "I say, and I know that I voice the sentiment of every socialist and labor unionist [but not anarchist] in the United States, if these men are guilty of these murders they deserve nothing better than hanging, for in that case they have played into the hands of the enemy; in that case they committed rash acts that no leaders of the working class should commit."[105] Of course he can confidently voice the harsh justice of the socialist because he knows without a doubt that the three are not guilty, that their arrest and transportation from Colorado to Idaho was a federal offense, and that they will be acquitted. Writing the essay for the mainstream press, London wanted principally to repeat the facts of their arrest and incarceration so that the general public could see behind the façade created by the mine associations in conjunction with the capitalist press.

It was too radical for Barrett, who never published the essay. London and various people at two Hearst papers—the *San Francisco Examiner* and the *New York Evening Journal*, including Barrett and Arthur Brisbane at the New York paper—argued with London about payment both for this essay and for his review of *The Jungle*, which they had published in a "garbled version."[106] London insisted that Barret had asked for both texts and thus should be paid even if they weren't used. London had an unequivocal letter from Barrett asking for the review.[107] As for the Moyer-Haywood-Pettibone article, London wrote to the business manager of the *Examiner*, W. S. Bogart, that "this article I had written by request. It had been ordered through Mr. Barrett by the NEW YORK JOURNAL. And Mr. Barrett told me that he would see I got paid for it."[108] W. S. Bogart responded saying that, no, the review had been written and published as a favor to Sinclair and that the Idaho article was simply offered and rejected.[109] London's version seems the most plausible, and like *Cosmopolitan* with "Revolution," the Hearst organization simply got cold feet and tried to cover them.

Several months later, Barrett asked London to take on an investigative reporting job for the paper; there was a strike among sailors, and Barrett wanted London to sign onto a ship sailing between Eureka and San Francisco as a scab. He also promised that if London would just come to his office they would be able "settle up the matter of the Steunenberg killing and the review of The Jungle."[110] Neither happened. London wasn't sore with Barrett, and he forgave Brisbane by saying, in 1909, "DAMN the $200.00! After having settled the question of principle [in the end none of the newspaper writers contradicted his version of the events], I'd rather have friendship than the cash."[111] And he settled on good terms with the publisher of the *Examiner*, telling Dent Robert in 1910, "I see clearly that the major responsibility lies with the N. Y. people. But please remember that I haven't any feelings against anybody. . . . Don't I know the chaos and anarchy of newspaperdom enough to understand how such things will happen!"[112] Here is yet another example of London's bohemian, authorial economics. Personal relationships were more important than money. And, no, he never got his two hundred dollars. But he gave the Chicago *Sunday Socialist* his text to show his support for socialist candidates for local offices in Illinois.[113]

When London was in Hawaii in 1907 on the *Snark*, Haywood's trial began. In a decision that surprised both the prosecution and the defense he was found not guilty. Pettibone was acquitted in January 1908, and charges against Moyer were dropped in the same month. So they were found innocent in the end, but, in a final irony, it is more likely than not that, according to the latest exhaustive research, they were in fact guilty.[114]

8 EARTHQUAKE APOCALYPSE AND BUILDING THE CITY, BOAT, AND HOUSE BEAUTIFUL

BOHEMIA DESTROYED

n the afternoon of 18 April 1906, George Sterling wrote to his friend, "Dearest Wolf: We had a hell of an earthquake in Carmel (and assumably everywhere else in America) this morning. You should have seen Carrie [his spouse] getting from her bed to the front veranda in 1½ seconds! . . . The dog was so scared that her heart hasn't stopped thumping yet, and all the hens yelled 'bloody murder.'"[1] George can't be faulted for treating the infamous event so cavalierly; he had no idea that his friends were in danger, that fires raged in San Francisco, that cities north of the bay were in ruins. According to initial reports, over two hundred people died, thousands were injured and three hundred thousand left homeless, and property loss was estimated at one hundred million dollars.[2]

In San Francisco, a principal locus of American bohemia, the Montgomery Block, survived; it housed Coppa's Restaurant as well as the apartments and studios of bohemians like Xavier Martinez, who hosted London when Jack needed to recover from a night out and where London and Sterling probably first met.[3] The restaurant was left vacant, except for one night devoted to a final meal for Bohemia: "They brought their own food, vino and coffee from their places of refuge in the east Bay and consumed it cold from paper plates and cups, held on their laps. Permission was obtained from a Colonel Clem of the State Militia for candlelight. So, with a sentry posted outside, the Coppans lit their candles as the night came on and recited their odes and made their toasts. Then the crowd dispersed to the East Bay ferry. From there, some went on to New York, some to Carmel and a few, such as Maynard Dixon, to a temporary shelter until Papa [Coppa] should open a new restaurant" (*Coppa Murals*, 55). London was a frequenter at Coppa's. On the second night of the Londons' return from the lecture tour in 1906, they, with Sterling, Martinez, Laffler, Garnett, Austin

Lewis, and "fool women" (!) had dinner at Coppa's and a "general racket."[4] Coppa's even threw the Londons a farewell dinner on 14 March 1907 before the *Snark* sailed, entitled "Just Meat for White Fangs," featuring spaghetti with "Children of the Abyss Dressing," and "The Call of the Wild Salad."[5]

But those happy times were over. The Bohemian Club, with its new exhibition of Old Masters—including a Rembrandt—burned completely.[6] Arnold Genthe lost his studio, his negatives, and his equipment. Maynard Dixon and William Keith lost nearly all their paintings. Ina Coolbrith (first Poet Laureate of California and an early mentor to young readers such as London during her employment at the Oakland city library) lost her manuscripts, three thousand books, and years of correspondence; especially noteworthy were her letters to all those in the first *Overland Monthly* crowd. Jerome Hart and his *Argonaut* had to move to San Jose. The manuscript of *The Sea-Wolf*, locked in a safe, nonetheless burned beyond use for future scholars. Daniel Burnham's plan to turn San Francisco into a City Beautiful had been deposited the day before and burned with city hall. Sterling lost nearly all printed copies of his books, and Charles Warren Stoddard lost all copies of two of his, as well as his publisher's entire operation. Henry Laffler lost his house, Xavier Martinez his studio. The Mark Hopkins Institute of Art and its thirty-five-year-old collection of paintings, books, and sculptures were gone. The Arts and Crafts furniture maker Frederick H. Meyer (who had worked with the architect Bernard Maybeck) lost his shop. The buildings of the three major newspapers and the offices and printer for *Sunset Magazine* were destroyed or severely damaged, as were all the theaters, libraries, and the Grand Opera House. Cultural San Francisco had been devastated.

Porter Garnet, Martinez, Maynard and Lillian Dixon, Allan Dunn, and Mary Edith Griswold—all writers and artists who formed a sizable portion of the bohemian core of the city—sought each other out on the eighteenth to help and console. Isabel Fraser, anointed the Queen of Bohemia by the bohemian cultural workers in 1902, told London three years after the quake that her identity as queen "was killed in the quake, burned in the fire, and from her ashes has risen one, Cholly Francisco [her nom de plume as a feature writer for the *San Francisco Examiner*]," signaling the death of an era, but not of the eternal bohemian spirit.[7] Many artists and writers were among the thousands displaced, and they gravitated toward bohemian oases like Monterey and the Sterlings' own encampment there.

But what the earthquake and fire took away with one hand, it gave with the other. As Fraser said, bohemia never dies. The event generated an immediate flowering of writing and photography, like blooms in cooled volcanic lava, the beginnings of a cultural renaissance. It began with the multiple stories of the earthquake and fire and thousands of photographs, among which we find London's contribution "The Story of an Eye-Witness" and his own photographs of ruins taken in May. (He did not take any photos on the eighteenth and nineteenth.)[8] His friend and editor Bailey Millard, in his 1924 three-volume *History of the San Francisco Bay Region*, noted that after several disastrous fires in the city's early days, the city council created a seal with the image of a phoenix rising from the ashes.[9] Once again, the phoenix rose. Maynard Dixon imagined the spirit of the city, not as a mythological bird but as a mythological spirit. For both the cover of the "New San Francisco Emergency Edition" and the June–July edition of *Sunset*, he painted a nude woman looking skyward in hope with the city's ruins strewn about at her waist. For the latter, he added a rebuilt white city cradled in her arms, the first vision of what the future city would look like. The city was resurrected, Millard made clear, because all through the April days of devastation "never was the community spirit in stronger evidence anywhere. A dozen eggs would be divided among three or four families. A loaf of bread would be cut in two. Nobody was permitted to go hungry" (499). In one of his few emotional outbursts, Millard, wrote, "It is doubtful if there was in all history a better spirit of cooperation during a great calamity" (507). He meant that this "true communistic way" was expressed nationally, for he noted how many other cities helped immediately in relief work. Much of the rest of his historical essay then reprints his immediate impressions published in *Cosmopolitan* as "When Altruria Awoke."[10] He clearly suffered from a nostalgia for catastrophe, a kind of posttraumatic syndrome. As early as July 1906, when he had lived in New York City for a month or so, working at *Cosmopolitan*, he told London that he was "simply vegetating and degenerating here. Should like to have an earthquake or something to wake me up. Never feel '*alerted*' as Whitman says."[11] As awful as the event was, the earthquake, like a combat situation, made him feel alive and awake in a way he not only never had felt before but also would never feel again. It was, as the quotation from Whitman indicates, a peak bohemian experience, never to be repeated.

"When Altruria Awoke": The telling title speaks to the communal spirit of the region, of which bohemia was a significant part. Altruria was a utopian community near Santa Rosa that supplied food to cooperative grocery stores run by socialists in Oakland and San Francisco. Millard highlights the bohemian economics of Altruria—of both the commune founded by Edward Payne and others as well as the ideal construct—as he recounts individual instances of selfless behavior: "I saw intrepid men and women rush into tottering houses to grasp their own or their neighbors' kin out of the stiff grip of Death. I saw fire-fighters do deeds that made one feel they were eager to give their lives to save the city. . . . What an amazing picture was there—the picture of *self-effacement*." This was the lesson of the calamity: "Here was a luminous lesson in Utopian economics—a lesson for the whole doubting, artificial, selfish world—a dropping off of all mean play at precedence and all the cunning trickery of gain." Not a particularly religious man, Millard nonetheless saw all this lack of egoism as a sign that "the dream of Christ [had] come true."[12] To a skeptic like Mother Jones, who was not there, the whole event would be converted by "the sky pilots" into something quite opposite: "the wickedness of the people of the City."[13]

Millard was not a socialist, but his words could easily become the rhetoric of anticapitalism. Herman Whitaker, London's friend and fellow author, appealed to the rest of the nation in *Harper's Weekly* that if it would help San Francisco then it would furnish "the world with proof that, in our time, 'brotherhood of man' was not an empty phrase."[14] Whitaker, we remember, ran a socialist grocery store in Oakland where London first encountered serious political debate. On the second day of the earthquake and fire, he toured the grocery stores in the East Bay to see if they were charging inflated prices; only one was—another instance of what Millard called "Utopian economics."

For Whitaker and Millard, as for London in "What Communities Lose by the Competitive System," it was a contest between competition and altruism and the latter won—"to compete with one another only in heroism, were the unfailing acts of those altruists by the Golden Gate," effused Millard.[15] Carl Sandburg, writing from Chicago, gloried in the reports that "the San Francisco horror has shown that underlying all their hot rivalries and fierce contentions the human race is at the last a brotherhood, a solidarity."[16] In the same issue of *To-Morrow Magazine*, Parker Sercombe, the editor, ran a one-page statement from Maxim Gorky. He seized the moment to, on the one hand, sympathize with San Francisco and its people, and, on the other hand, to call for help from America to relieve the suffering of Russia. "Misfortunes must teach us brotherhood," he wrote. "Not for power over each other must we think, not for wealth, but how to be masters of the whole power of the earth."[17] In a short story published in *Sunset* two months after the event, Charles Gilman Norris (Kathleen Norris's husband and Frank Norris's brother) portrayed the clichéd but dramatic turn in his main character's life as a turn from selfishness to altruism; spurned by the woman he loved, he tries to commit suicide only to be frustrated by the earthquake. When he realizes that thousands of people need medical attention, Claxton, a doctor, decides to live: "In the face of such far greater sorrow, his own selfish desires seemed puny and contemptible." He decides to help save "the heart of Bohemia," the city of San Francisco.[18]

Altruism was not dead, though perhaps it was activated only by severe crisis, as a mode only of survival. In fact, Gaylord Wilshire predicted to London that the earthquake and fire would instigate "the greatest boon in real estate that ever happened in the city, and I am sure that labor is never going to be as well paid in San Francisco for the next six months as it will be again in the next century."[19] I don't mean to portray Wilshire as heartless. His letter begins, "It must have been something terrific, the scene, yesterday when the thing was going on and I suppose even today it is something very terrible." But from the East Coast one could take a more objective point of view, and Wilshire predicted that those with money to invest would make a killing. Some saw a phoenix rise from the ashes, others smelled the sweet smell of money. Once again bohemia would be co-opted by capitalism.

James Hopper created a first-person, hour-by-hour narrative of what he experienced. He was London's friend, a bohemian, a reporter for the *San Francisco Call*, and a short-story writer, who would in a year supply the crew of the *Snark* with his Cal football jersey as a kind of banner. Like Millard, he lived in the city and was lying in bed. The quake struck and he flipped about like "a fish in a frying-pan." His essay in *Everybody's*, which London and Sterling thought the best of all the bunch, is poignant and strong because he captured the psychological impact of the disaster, both on himself and others.[20] An old man, obviously traumatized, tried to read with broken glasses the inscription on the Dewey monument in Union Square hours after the quake struck, as if he had never seen the statue before. A man in "pink pajamas, a pink-bathrobe, carrying a pink comforter," walked barefoot across the gravelly square. Hopper saw people sit in the street, exhausted, resigned to burn to death. He saw groups of people in empty lots, sitting on their trunks and suitcases, waiting to die. Hopper himself pulled bodies from under stone and brick, both alive and dead. Disbelief and denial—"the twisted vision of us all"—characterized the general human reaction to the devastation.[21] Mentally as well as physically people had lost their grounding.

Mary Edith Griswold—a writer and editor for *Sunset* and, before she married the former Rough Rider Edwin Emerson, the roommate of Isabel the "Queen of Bohemia" Fraser—wrote what I feel is the best account of the three days of the fire, though it ends somewhat abruptly.[22] She leaves the reader with the anxiety and fear that everyone in the city must have felt with the resolution of the fire still unknown. Written in the form of a diary and seemingly during the events she describes, her account has a powerful immediacy because of her command of the telling detail, both within and without herself, and because of her use of the present tense: "The fire is within two blocks of my house. . . . The firemen are frantic. If they don't stop the fire now the whole Western Addition will go—a policeman with a red face is running up and down in front of the house. A dead Italian lies in the middle of the street opposite my house. Members of his family sit around his body in a circle. I got so scared I couldn't swallow a glass of water. The heat on the balcony was intense—too hot to stay out there. The paint on the woodwork was blistering. Everyone was fire mad. My home will surely go." That's the ending, written at Fort Mason while waiting for a boat to take her to the Oakland ferry. She writes without a message, without the need to reassure, to partake in boosterism. She captures both the need to save oneself and help others but also the desire to see the fire at work, to confront the monster. Her friends Maynard and Lillian Dixon were insistent on taking her to their home in Sausalito, but she wanted to stay: "I know now why the people who live at the foot of Vesuvius all stay till it is too late to escape the lava." She had checked on the writers, editors, and artists of bohemia, but she managed to talk with and observe the ordinary people of the city: the Chinese employee at the Palace Hotel who was dusting; the African American street preacher who regretted prophesying the fire and brimstone to be visited upon a sinful city; the white upper-class woman "of stunning style who walked between two men, her hands in her muff." Others, like London, observed the refugees pulling their trunks along as they escaped the fire. Only Griswold noted the sound: "The screeching sound of the trunks dragging on the cable slots went to my marrow."[23]

One would think London would follow in Millard's and Whitaker's shoes and write the story of the event from a socialist perspective. Alternatively, he might have followed Hopper and Griswold and written it as a straight realist, first-person narrative with a strong psychological undertone. No, he aimed differently. He does mention that "never, in all San Francisco's history, were her people so kind and courteous as on this night of terror," but he doesn't detail any instances of kindness, and he certainly doesn't equate it with altruism. It's as if he had read Millard and Whitaker and Hopper and drawn this conclusion from them, not from his own experience.

The greatest surprise in reading London's "The Story of an Eye-Witness," and especially in viewing his photographs, is the absence of individuals. In his written text, London, having cemented his reputation as a national figure, now began envisioning the effect of national events upon the global scene. He could easily have contributed to *Sunset* or *Pacific Monthly* or *Overland Monthly* and emphasized his natal geography. Reading Hopper and others, London could see how references to actual people and places cut two ways: they make the report as close to photographic realism as possible—a positive quality because it conveys immediacy and authority—but it also makes the report parochial. He imagined instead a national audience's take on the event. His article is the story of the fall of "the imperial city." You may think that San Francisco was only an adult version of a gold rush town, the sophisticated habitat of those who had profited from mining in the fifties, he says to his audience. Or you might think of it as a gateway to the Pacific world. It's both of those, of course, but it is also the capital of, at least, the vast western American empire, and maybe of the empire as a whole, making Washington DC merely the capitol of the nation. This is how London generalized the event. *Imperial* can connote cosmopolitan to be sure, a tamer persona for a global city. But it mostly connotes Rome and its world domination. Either way, the earthquake and fire had far-reaching effects: on world trade, on world migration. Instead of fire and brimstone being visited on a sinful city, London imagines San Francisco paying for its capitalism.

He is the eyewitness; oddly, he erases Charmian from the narrative, probably thinking that the singular first-person pronoun was more effective than the plural. He witnessed the destruction, and though Jimmy Hopper gave a better account of it, he witnessed how "the heated air rising made an enormous suck. Thus did the fire of itself build its own colossal chimney through the atmosphere. Day and night this dead calm continued, and yet, near to the flames, the wind was often half a gale, so mighty was the suck." But instances of reporting a single person's fate, a single fire chimney, are few. London is dealing in generalities: streets, not a street; refugees, not a refugee. He creates, not a typology like that of pseudo-anthropological clans like the Sons of the Wolf, the Daughters of the Snow, but rather categories of destruction and suffering. We don't feel the need to look at a map of the city as we do to trace Griswold's and Hopper's and Whitaker's movements during those days; we don't need to know where Market Street is, only that south of it is where "the working-class ghetto was." This report is for the eyes of the world, not an account to let the people who lived through it know what exactly had happened beyond their immediate sphere of observation. "The hills of San Francisco are steep," he says, describing the refugees carrying their personal effects away from the fire; no kidding! says the native San Franciscan, but for the reader outside the United States this would be an important detail.

London positions himself not as a native of the city but as disinterested observer; there is no hint of emotion as he views scenes of his life destroyed by the fire. London wants to stand apart in order to write for the world, but by portraying himself as a witness, and by writing in generalities, he creates the impression of being a disaster tourist. Millard praised his essay but reminded him that he had actually lived through the quake and the entirety of the fire; London had spent at most sixteen hours in it. Millard had participated; London had traveled to see it. He left the city on the morning of the second day, though he does not tell his reader that, and in the final paragraphs of his report he tells us of events on Thursday and Friday that he himself did not witness. And he closes with an understatement that reveals why he did not follow Griswold and Hopper and Whitaker: "The government has the situation in hand, and, thanks to the immediate relief given by the whole United States, there is not the slightest possibility of a famine. The bankers and business men have already set about making preparations to rebuild San Francisco."

London makes no attempt at promoting the civic pride in the residents' resilience, in their selflessness, in their humanity. Instead, as if taking a cue from Mother Jones and Gaylord Wilshire, he sees a simple and dispassionate economic cycle of bust and boom. Those who were rich—and his only two interviews are with rich men—are no longer, but will undoubtedly be soon. As he wrote to his friend Ida Winship, the "earthquake and fire, by destroying so much wealth (surplus product), set back the coming of socialism in U.S. fully six months."[24] As long as everyone is poor together, he seems to be saying, though with a certain amount of tongue in his cheek, there is no need for a political system built on economic equality, but the rich won't stay poor long. London passed on a chance to convey what it was like for the working class to live through a monumental disaster in favor of conveying to the world the essence of the apocalypse. It was part and parcel of his new authorial role, to make the transition from a national to a global author.

His report is, after all, entitled "A *Story* of an Eye-Witness," and we can remember his very first published work, in the fall of 1893, "Story of a Typhoon off the Coast of Japan." The latter was very much a nonfiction work, yet, at the same time, its emotional charge comes from the adept way London selected, ordered, and framed the events to such an extent that we felt we were looking at a Turner painting that conveyed the emotional, but not factual, import of the events he participated in. In 1906, London says he was an eyewitness to events he was far away from, he generalizes when he could write with detailed accuracy, and he thus creates a very different kind of emotional or human document than one conveying the truth of the quake, principally, the terror of being at the mercy of unseen and overwhelming natural forces.

One gets the same impression from his photographs, which seem more like postcards of a disaster than a recording of damage done. On 29 May, Charmian wrote in her diary, "Went [to] city taking Manyoungi. Spent over 3 hours in auto, seeing city and taking pictures."[25] Hopper, on the eighteenth, also rode in a car, commandeered so that he could speed from place to place and report on as many scenes as possible. But with the Londons and their servant, one senses their distance from the wreckage. In the photographs in which one can discern people, they either have their backs to the camera, or have their faces obscured in shadow, or are in such small scale in relation to the ruins that they appear only as filler. It comes as a surprise and disappointment that in neither written nor visual text did he render the catastrophe's effects on the individual Californian.[26]

So the earthquake was a lesson to the imperialists about the fragility of their creation, but it was also a challenge to those who embraced the age's benefits. The quake had lasting effects on London's ideas about the future of man, especially the future of the cooperative commonwealth. There is a hint or two of the earthquake in *Before Adam*. Perhaps when the Fire People smoke the Folk out of their caves, he couldn't help but recall the masses of flames and the never-ending smoke of the fire he and Charmian had walked around on Earthquake Day. When Lop-Ear, Swift One, Big-Tooth, and Hair-Face escape the fire and smoke, and wander in the swamp, he imagines them as "a handful of survivors after the day of the end of the world," a line he had used in "Story of an Eye-Witness."[27] This was not exaggeration, though it would quickly become a cliché. As Millard noted in his history, many people believed that the end of the world had occurred. Hundreds went to church to pray. Hopper thought it was "the end" as he was shaken out of bed.[28] Charmian felt "very lonely in the conviction that my end was approaching in leaps and bounds."[29] Of course if the world had actually ended, there would not be a day after nor an author to write about it. Of course he means that the world as they knew it had ended, and like the Queen of Bohemia, resurrection from the ashes was possible. The empire had fallen, but in all likelihood it would return in a different shape. After all, a new and different economic order wouldn't come about from physical devastation.

RED ESSAYS

Charmian London captured the physical apocalypse in her diary in two short words: she saw the "burning streets" of the city. (London's repeated "wall of flames" seems trite in comparison.) It wasn't a metaphor. Their friend Jim Whitaker reported in his story "Human Drama at San Francisco" that the bricks and cobblestones of the streets "actually burned like coal."[30] We can see the red flames in her word-picture, and certainly when London interrupted the writing of *Before Adam* again to write a 136-word introduction to his choice of his best short story for *Grand Magazine*, redness and destruction were foremost in his mind. His British agent, James Pinker, wrote London in mid-April that the editor of *Grand Magazine* would pay ten and a half pounds for "two or three lines" and the right to reprint the story as part of a long continuing series that had already included Joseph Conrad and Arthur Conan Doyle.[31] His choice was "The League of the Old Men," and he sent the typescript and introduction off at once. In its published form the introduction is only 116 words; the editors cut the first sentence ("I incline to the opinion that 'The League of the Old Men' is the best short story I have written.") and rewrote a few others. Though brief, it is one of London's few public statements about his own work and why he finds merit in it: "It has no love-motif, but that is not my reason for thinking it my best story." To begin with, that is an odd formulation. Why would a story that is not a love story necessarily be a great story? Especially to the audience of a pulp magazine like *Grand*?

Unless he meant that to be a great story one would have to frustrate popular expectations and write something against the grain of the public's desire, which is what he wrote in a 1907 piece for the *Editor*. "I should advise the young story-writer to study the stories in the current magazines. . . . But I must append this warning: HE WILL SUCCEED WITH THE EDITORS OF TO-DAY; BUT IN THE CENTURIES TO COME HE WILL NOT HIMSELF BE ACCREDITED A MASTER OF LITERATURE."[32] London is repeating Brett's injunction to write material worthy of a "real place in the permanent world of literature," and a conventional love story simply provides entertainment in the present, not repeated readings in the future. Thus, we remember that he felt compelled to include a love story in *The Sea-Wolf*, but only an entirely unconventional one. The terrible and tragic may not sell, but it will lead to canonization.

The second criterion points more explicitly to a timelessness of theme: "The voices of millions are in the voice of old Imber, and the tears and sorrows of millions are in his throat as he tells his story; and his story epitomizes the whole vast tragedy of the contact of the Indian with the white man."[33] When Imber is caught and put on trial, he confesses to his crimes, and as he does so, the judge is made to see the Anglo-Saxon race as "a mighty phantasmagoria" that had bloodied the very landscape of the entire world: "He saw it dawn red-flickering across the dark forests and sullen seas; he saw it blaze, bloody and red, to full and triumphant noon; and down the shaded slope he saw the blood-red sands dropping into night."[34] We might recall that London pronounced, in his defense of Rudyard Kipling's treatment of the Anglo-Saxon, that "the color of tragedy is red."[35] London emblematized the Anglo-Saxon with the violent Red-Eye. But the principal tool of the Anglo-Saxon in the Machine Age wasn't the sword but rather "trade! trade! all the time was it trade!" (818). The white capitalists had conquered the Whitefish and other First Peoples by introducing capitalism into their socialistic world. And though the old men "called ourselves brothers" and fought back, it was no use. Read as a parable for the politics of 1906 America, "The League of the Old Men" tells us that murdering the ex-governor of Idaho or Andrew Carnegie or performing any act of red anarchistic terror is anger misdirected and political action rendered ineffectual. In 1904 he told Brett that *Children of the Frost* was "by far my best collection of short stories" and in it "'League of Old Men' is one of my best two short stories."[36] We remember William Dall's judgment of London's characterizations of First Peoples—"they are unlike any Indians whatsoever"—and certainly London borrows from the myth of the Noble Savage. But what redeems his portrait of Imber is the political allegory of the tale. Yes, he stands for the "millions" slaughtered by whites; but he also stands as martyr to the socialist cause, a reminder, even to the judge, that blood-red economic competition leads to murder, which can only be fought by instituting a new economic order, not murder in kind.

Not surprisingly, then, redness blazes forth in his next piece of writing, the first he undertook after he completed *Before Adam*, with its red atavistic rage. He sent "The Somnambulists," completed 13 June, written unbidden, to four top magazines, all of whom rejected it. Hamilton Holt of the *Independent* took it without fanfare, paid thirty dollars and published it during Christmas time. London saw how it could fit into a projected volume led off by "Revolution," a book of essays that needed three more before completion and publication in 1910.

"The Somnambulists" is a direct outgrowth of his work on *Before Adam*. It is a vessel containing the overflow of ideas that could not be directly expressed in the novel, thus exposing the underlying biopolitics of that novel. It is an essayistic rant against humankind, or at least those who deny their savage, cave-dwelling origins and their apelike character still in residence under the veneer of civilization. London's argument is that the vast majority of society are sleepwalkers, like Frank Zappa's pajama people. They sleepwalk because they are in denial, and the denial allows them to "dream drunken dreams of self-exaltation."[37] All humans are "red" animals. In a master stroke that combines this essay with both *Before Adam* and "Story of an Eye-Witness," he writes, "The raw animal crouching within him is like the earthquake monster pent in the crust of the earth. As he persuades himself against the latter till it arouses and shakes down a city, so does he persuade himself against the former until it shakes him out of his dreaming and he stands undisguised, a brute like any other brute" (42).

Here is a further development of the effects of the quake: not only does it expose the thin veil of civilization that can be destroyed in a moment by natural forces, but now he's linking the veneer of civilization to a psychological state of denial. The fear of natural destruction—if it happened once, it can happen again—and the fear of one's worst instincts, those embodied by Red-Eye, are the same, and, if London were a psychologist, he would want us to work through that fear and wither the denial. But he's a social activist, so he exploits the bourgeois fears, taking the fear of earthquakes and tying it to the fear of the primitive, hoping that in this conjunction the bourgeois will be made to see how asleep they really are, so they can awake to socialism. Socialists are "clean, noble, and alive."

But only the right-thinking red animals feel this fear. The prize fighter, the reddest of animals (we remember that Red-Eye is linked to a pugilist), is the figure for those who are at least partially awake. He becomes the central figure for the relationship between the primitive instincts inside the body and the somatic veil that covers those red instincts. A prize fighter accepts the body; he accepts the somatic foundation of human being. Those who are completely asleep—the capitalists, the professors, the college students, the independently wealthy, the sky pilots, the politicians—deny the body and glory the spirit. So they are the most dangerous because they are the ones living most fully their lives of illusion and have created the most fully developed rhetoric of the spirit, sacrificing the real glory of the body. Bohemian authors who celebrate and practice boxing, on the other hand, are a blend of soma and machine. This is the political message of *Before Adam*, the material he could not make room for in a fictional, absorptive narrative. In all of the published letters by Eugene Debs, only one mentions Jack London, and it concerns "The Somnambulists": "It is Jack London at his best," he told his brother Theodore, and he suggested that Theodore pass the essay to their friend Stephen Reynolds so that it might be read by the Terre Haute Club. "How it would make the dry bones rattle!"[38] And so the targets of *Before Adam* and "The Somnambulists" become the targets of his futuristic novel, *The Iron Heel*.

CREATED HE THEM

As a prelude to *The Iron Heel*, he wrote several short stories after "The Somnambulists": "Created He Them," "A Wicked Woman" (both the story and the one-act play), "The Wit of Porportuk," "Finis," and "Just Meat."

In between the third and the fourth, he wrote two essays: "The House Beautiful" and the foreword to *The Cruise of the* Snark. One might think he was writing stories merely to earn the money that he needed to build the *Snark*, and yet in September 1906 he had $8,882.67 in his bank account, or approximately $240,000 in 2016 dollars. So he didn't hesitate when he wrote to two comrades in Oakland, telling them that he would lend them one hundred dollars, a fifth of what they needed to purchase a printing press for socialist publications, including the *Socialist Voice*. Whenever he lent socialists money, he never expected to get paid back.[39]

The first story shows how much continuity there is in London's writings from, at least, *White Fang* through the lecture tour to "The Apostate" to *Before Adam* and all the essays he wrote during the writing of the latter. In fact, "Created He Them" might be called "Just after *Before Adam*"—"Male and female created he them, and called their name Adam, in the day they were created" (Gen. 5:2)—as London again expands upon his interest in past time to include the mythical moment of creation, a competing origin narrative to evolutionary theory.

"Created He Them" is a significant story because its title was also the title of a serial—a series of short stories—London contemplated, perhaps in reaction to McClure's almost monthly insistence in 1905 that he write such a work for the magazine. "A Wicked Woman" would also be a part of the series. He completed only those two stories and then included them with ten other non-Klondike stories to comprise *When God Laughs, and Other Stories*.

But he left behind notes for twenty-five stories and a one-act play. Four clues indicate he wrote most of the notes in 1905: first, he told George Brett in July 1905 that he had "mapped out for myself to write a series of brief, nervous, strong, dramatic sketches." He often declared that his planned work would be radically different from anything he had written previously, and this is how he characterized these stories.[40] Yet in December 1905 he confessed that, while on the road for his lecture tour, he was unable to work on "that set of 'Created He Them' sketches."[41] Second, he clipped a newspaper article from June 1905 about a Vermont woman who had murdered her husband and attached it to a typewritten sheet with "Created He Them" written at the top. Third, a number of stories involve plot lines from the life of Charmian's Aunt Netta Wiley Eames, and since she appears in "Planchette," written in the summer of 1905, a narrative based on Charmian's idea, one can easily imagine the four of them—Jack, Charmian, Netta, and Roscoe—sitting 'round the fire in Glen Ellen swapping plot ideas. (In their idyllic surroundings, they hatched Hitchcockian stories of murder, disappointment, and tragedy.) Fourth, he planned for one of the *Created He Them* story ideas to also be a curtain raiser that London intended for Blanche Bates, the actress he hoped would star in *Scorn of Women*, the play he worked on from late 1904 through June 1906. "A Wicked Woman," the one-act play found in these notes—based on the story by the same name—is on a continuum with *Scorn of Women* and his general interest in 1904 through 1906 to write a successful theatrical production. One can see London developing these story ideas as he is writing "Planchette" and *White Fang*.

The lecture tour interrupted all his writing plans. As the afterglow of the tour and his national prominence as a socialist spokesperson wore off, he settled into writing pure absorptive short stories again, and now he consulted his batch of notes for *Created He Them*. We remember that "When God Laughs," the second story he completed after his return, is a disquisition upon relationships between men and women. It is a story that could have fit well with the projected theme of *Created He Them*, and, not surprisingly, he grouped it, "Created He Them," and "A Wicked Woman" into *When God Laughs, and Other Stories*, after he realized he could never finish *Created He Them*. Given that the stories for this series were first dreamt of in 1905, that is, before his electrified interest in the primitive and the elasticity and infiniteness of time produced *White Fang*, *Before Adam*, and *The Iron Heel*, it is not surprising that the plots he had on hand in that summer of 1906 did not result in finished products beyond "Created He Them" and "A Wicked Woman." He was too preoccupied with creating his pair of time-traveling novels.

There may have been another reason why he didn't complete the serial. He could not decide on the general tenor of the series. In 1905 Charmian helped him type up some general observations about *Created He Them*.[42] He envisioned a series of "short, sharp, trenchant" stories of between two and three thousand words (though "Created He Them" turned out to be 3,800 words). "Tense and terse all the way through," they would all be tragic, but in different ways: "business tragedy; political tragedy; tramp tragedy; criminal tragedy; working-class tragedy; slum tragedy."[43] But after the double, lengthy interruptions of the lecture tour and then the *Snark* voyage, he turned away from the idea of a series of differently inflected tragic stories and wanted to "keep sexual stories together under title of 'Created He Them.'" Then, for the first time, he named a second collection growing out of the first: "Maybe collect the other stories under the title of 'The Smoke of Life.'"[44] It's not clear what those "other stories" are. But in 1905-6 and again in 1909 he was vacillating and could not come to a clear resolution for the thematic content for either title.

Created He Them is more thematically cohesive than *The Smoke of Life*. Several plots for the "sexual stories" came from Netta, who, we may remember, was a bohemian magazine and newspaper writer whose lover and future husband Edward Payne had helped found Altruria. Netta's relations with men, in particular Payne and her first husband, Roscoe Eames (who captained the *Snark* from San Francisco to Hawaii), were free and unconventional; the three formed a ménage a trois for many years, with each also taking lovers from outside their circle.[45] We remember that she and Roscoe were figures in "Planchette," and she was the source for four of the stories in *Created He Them*, one of which would become both a short story and play entitled "A Wicked Woman," which I will discuss a little later.

Three have to do with her "innocence," her life before she became a free-love practitioner. In one, she is an author figure who attracts a young man interested only in sex. He moves on to another, and the story ends with tears. London considered writing a novel with this story as a chapter. Based on the "development of Aunt Netta from girlhood," the story ends with "Netta's" marriage to a Roscoe figure.[46]

Netta also told London a story that he entitled "Mormon Harry and the Woman Professor." The story involves a professor, a painter, and a photographer; the painter is Mormon Harry. The professor is unhappily married, she kisses the painter, and then falls into violent self-recrimination, comforted only by the photographer. There is no resolution, only tears, again. We never find out why it is important that the painter is a Mormon.[47]

Anna Strunsky and her refusal to marry London was also on his mind. In a page-long note on another *Created He Them* story, Anna is named and characterized as an admirable martyr to her attraction to "the man [to be drawn "dimly and colossally"] Anna really loved all the time." This man is unavailable, not because he is married and has a daughter, but because he is dead. She marries one of two suitors, but both are aware of her true love, and presumably the story ends with Anna (an author figure) haunted by the ghost of the man who died.

There is a sex story that, again, may have been inspired by the broken love affair between Jack and Anna. This time the man is unavailable because of a wife and child. Because she is so damned ethical, and strong, and self-sacrificing, they separate forever, but not before, at the moment of final departure, she takes him into her bedroom, "makes him lie down with head on her pillow," and while he "lies there for a moment in torture," she "looks at him with infinite yearning, imprinting on her mind the picture of him lying there." It is enough. She leads him back to the door, they say good-bye, and she returns to the bed "to kiss passionately the pillow, and in the morning to kiss it again."[48] It's this kind of unfulfilled desire, this sexual frustration that marks these stories as not quite Victorian, not quite modern. London's characters exist in a sexual gray area where convention wars with desire, and lack of resolution in these stories mirrors the constant and unresolved sexual tensions between men and women.

Another plot was perhaps inspired by Netta, but no personal names appear in the notes. It's another ménage a trois: "Wife,—say a happy wife—blunders into her husband and her best woman-friend in the act. Showdown for all three." They are "intellectual" and possess "super-fineness and nobility," so they discuss the event. The story is about their "psychologies," and there is no resolution, merely a devising of "some sort of satisfaction with the various standpoints of the actors." Although London didn't write any of these ménage a trois stories, they are forerunners for his big novel of infidelity, *The Little Lady of the Big House.*

Mothers are creators, not so different from author figures, and, apart from the treatment of sexuality and sexual relations, this series is focused on women as either authors or author figures. Given the title of the collection, we should not be surprised at this focus: God as author who names His, or Her, first characters Adam and Eve. Sex and authorship come together in a story note concerning the lie a woman tells her new husband: she tells him she is a virgin. He believes her, although he says, "This is the one thing she has the right to lie about." Then "some man" tells the husband with "excellent and convincing evidence" that she did in fact lie. The husband lies in his turn, telling him that he knew this already because his wife had been truthful about her sexual experiences in the past. "Make very dramatic," writes London, "after man goes, husband sits a few minutes; then sighs with resignation." He feels "a hurt in his palm" and looks down at his hands. "He has driven his nails into the flesh." The story is about the sexual relations between a man and a woman, about conventionality and unconventionality and the prices one pays, but most importantly the psychological damage occasioned by telling fictions.

Some of his story notes are mere fragments. In one we have a Mrs. Burton who is forced to choose between her two children, to be separated by divorce, one to her and one to her ex—"an Eastern divorce proceeding."[49] This is Machine Age domestic living. This story seems connected to a different, somewhat anomalous story note of two lines: "The old maid who holds baby to her breast to suckle, when no one is around. Make splendid development of character, situation, history, before this culminating act." We usually think of London as one of America's preeminent defenders of children, especially of children exploited by capitalism, but these notes show how focused London was on the possible tragedies of motherhood, though its manifestations are only barely hinted at.

Infidelity and suicide are recurrent plot devices in *Created He Them*. One of the stories involves a "consumptive, an artist or poet"—foreshadowing Brissenden in *Martin Eden*—who is about to shoot himself when his wife finds him. Giving into his determination, "she goes out [of the room] and lets him do it."[50] This may be a variation on an idea based on his friend Frank Strawn-Hamilton's life: "Sketch Hamilton's nature. His oft-repeated threats of suicide." A friend hands him a gun and tells him, forcefully, go ahead, but do it outside so you "don't make a mess on the carpet." The story ends with Hamilton writhing "on the floor in agony of cowardice," trapped in the aporia of too sick to live, too afraid to die. Then there's the three-line story idea involving a married woman who brings a young girl into her house (a domestic situation similar to Netta's before she married Roscoe) only to see her hook up with the husband. The woman "compels" the girl to commit suicide and then, as a final touch, says only "nice things about the dead girl" to her mother at the funeral.

The only story that doesn't involve infidelity and/or suicide is a kind of jokey tale of "a typical criminal" who kills a shopkeeper in his store and then hangs a sign on the door, saying, "Closed on Account of Death of the Proprietor." Is it revenge? Randomness? The red rage? We'll never know. The story ends anticlimactically: "His footfalls on quiet street." This murderer gets away.

He drew on the lives of three historical figures outside of his circle of family, friends, and acquaintances for two other stories that make *Created He*

Them truly a reflection of this in-between age. In one, he takes Edward Aveling and Eleanor Marx—the daughter and son-in-law of Karl Marx—"a pair of free-lovers" and destroys them. Aveling has fallen for another woman, tells Eleanor, and then leaves the house so that she can commit suicide. "Have reader accompany him on walk, and return with him to find her dead."[51] Eleanor Marx did discover her husband in love with another woman, and she did commit suicide.

Another tragic historical figure that London used was the California poet and editor Madge Morris, a mother–author figure. He may have heard about her life from Joaquin Miller, who was a mentor and promoted her work. Not much is known of her life before she married Harr Wagner, the editor of the *Golden Era* and biographer of Joaquin Miller.[52] These life details, London told himself, should be told in "condensed realism," a fascinating variation on his better-known expression "impassioned realism." The terms overlap. Writerly realism, as opposed to photographic realism, cannot represent every object with exact fidelity in a frame created by the author, nor should it. Much has to be left out; the entire picture has to be condensed, and the selection process has to be motivated by the best way to convey intense emotion to the reader.

London selected details from the life of Madge Morris that showed the difficulties of a mother trying to become a successful cultural worker. She was born "in the mountains"; her family was traveling to California in a covered wagon. A "wandering taxidermist" taught her how to read and write. Still living in those mountains—most likely the goldfields of the Sierra— she walked seven miles to school and read only newspaper poetry. Her mother was illiterate and smoked a pipe, "a sheer animal of a woman." When Madge was fourteen, her mother arranged a marriage between her and Jem, a less than ambitious "crevice (one who crevices like a pig for gold)." By the time she was twenty-two, she had given birth to seven children, five of whom died. She left Jem and took the two children to San Jose, where she decided to write and submit poetry. The editor of the *San Jose Mercury* liked them, interviewed her ("outrageously clad in a faded calico") for a job as a reporter, and helped her divorce Jem. This was sometime in the late 1870s, early 1880s. Her Fourth of July poem for 1882 "rings all over U.S.," and with the help of Wagner, she eventually becomes a regular contributor to the *Golden Era* (sometimes publishing in the same issues as Brett Harte, Ambrose Bierce, and Mark Twain) and publishes several volumes of poetry and a novel. But London's story (which says she marries the editor of the *Mercury*) ends before her success. The "final scene" is the funeral for one of her remaining two children. Jem and her mother arrive from the mountains: "They sat one at head and one at foot of dead child, smoking pipes." Her sexual subjugation by her husband is the principal barrier to her authorial drive, but London's emphasis is on the combination of authorship and death, the tragedies of the writing life.

A particular tragedy of his own writer's life appears in a two-paragraph note: "a young fellow of twenty, [gone] wild at college." He comes home to meet his uncle, "incensed at being uncle's bastard." But his uncle tells him that he is a bastard, but "not HIS bastard, as doubtless he had often heard whispered."[53] It sounds, sadly, like a confrontation between Jack and his stepfather, John London.

Another story of betrayal features a man and a woman who first argue whether "any woman in the world will go in under another woman's guns to cut out the man she loves." She denies it and then does exactly that to get him to love her. "Then a tragic awakening for the woman" as she realizes what she has done. The self-realization is the tragedy, for the story ends with her "putting her arms around him, 'Yes, dear; you're right.'" "Instinct compels." Fighting biology is futile.[54]

Biology, race, and insanity are central themes of a story that resonates with *Before Adam*. We remember that Red-Eye in that novel was portrayed as partially insane. Here, the story note begins, "Insane asylum sketch. Napa," where his friend Bamford had stayed. The story concerns three characters: a Jew, a professional gambler, and "a man of violence," obviously a modern-day Red-Eye who is "the biggest toad in the puddle" and, like the others, insane. The Jew loans money to the gambler, who wins big only to lose his money, as does the Jew, to the insane toad who robs them both. The asylum is a kind of Southland Devil's Dice Box, the pit where London's imagination resides—death, chance, gold. There's an added twist, though, an explicit political charge to the story: the Jew and gambler "are both capitalists, the only two in asylum." The rest, we presume, are apolitical or unaligned individualists, like the toad who is out to enrich only himself by thievery. London originally designated this idea for *Created He Them*, but at some point he crossed out the series title and wrote, simply, "Short Story." On the typescript he added "(Humorous)."[55] Again, we wish for more development of this fascinating sketch, for it would be interesting to know if London was warming up for a story to be called "Told in the Drooling Ward" or if he was imagining that the whole nation had gone psycho and the Napa Sanitarium was a microcosm, a forerunner to Ken Kesey's unnamed hospital in *One Flew over the Cuckoo's Nest*. The title *Created He Them* certainly has cosmic potential.

After 1909 London still thought he would do a series entitled *Created He Them*, and he jotted down four ideas. First, there is a one-line note about a robbery: "A thief-cashier caught, and scene with Directors." A second, also brief note concerns "a leader of the people, sincere, honest, altruistic, etc.," in short, a respectable socialist, who is then "turned upon by the very people he wished to save, and reviled, and even physically abused." A third, somewhat longer note treats a scene in "the Home for Feeble-Minded children." First he wanted to "work up the five or six girls individually. The stigmata, the vacuousness of each, the peculiarities of each." The focus would be on the irony of the girls' lack of self-knowledge, each one asserting, as they waitress for the entire home, that "Thank God I am not feeble-minded." It's a joke on the surface of things, a tragedy below. London will use the word *stigmata* in another story note, this time about a criminal, betraying his belief that merely by looking at someone he could tell that he or she were criminal or insane. The final idea comes from a newspaper article entitled "The Case of Mrs. Rogers and the Death Penalty." Rogers and her lover kill her husband. He called it, simply, *Man*, or *The Brute*: "for the brute that is in man, quote verbatim from confession of murderers, Mrs. Rogers, filed away in 'Created He Them' material." This book idea centered on the conceptual integrity of combining insanity, rage, murder, and the primitive: "Show how close to the brute—insane—feeble-minded." But then there is "Temporary insanity—common to all in bursts, when suddenly all things are muddled, the mind is obfuscated, there is a flutter, it is seen in the change of the eyes, etc., and the harsh or silly word is spoken—everybody this way."

A fifth story idea that can be traced reliably to the post-1909 period is the only note that is headlined "Smoke of Life or Created He Them," thus providing hard evidence that the two serials were linked in his mind. It features a Dr. Burton, close to death from consumption, who travels to Arizona, presumably to get well. But he's so close to dying that "death took shape before him in a half-breed Indian. Spitting blood in the face of death." Nonetheless, he is "a fighter" and determined to see another sunrise, does so, and lives.[56]

The Smoke of Life seems conceived as merely a kind of catch basin for stories related to but not to be included in *Created He Them*. Seven of *The Smoke of Life* stories are clearly labeled as first conceived for the earlier collection, and they were filed with a newspaper article entitled "Feigned Insanity to Get into the Madhouse and Now She Can't Get Out," published in a Bay Area newspaper around the first of June 1905; here is another indication that London was concerned about the borders between sanity and insanity that got expressed in *Before Adam*. One story narrates a rape of an "old maid, not pretty, middle-class, never had known satisfaction of passion." After she sinks back "with a satisfied sigh," the rapist robs her, and the final line of the notes reads, "Must make her disappointment dramatic."[57] She thought love, not theft, followed from rape.

A similar story comes from an incident in Upton Sinclair's 1907 *The Industrial Republic*. A poor, orphaned young woman is refused entry to the House of the Good Shepherd because they take only "fallen women" who want to redeem themselves. So that night she sleeps with a man for money and then comes back. In another story idea, a man and a woman agree to commit suicide together, only the man chickens out and the woman "stares at him reproachfully" as she dies. A brief sketch based on Robert Browning's *The Ring and the Book* is a *Rashomon*-like story, with the same plot told by two different people with two different "psychologies." Another story is simply "Sterling's father's conversion to Catholicism." Then there is a Kananka's schooner's captain who loses his feet to sharks, is saved, and then begs to be "thrown back in," which he is; this idea is congruent with a series called "Sharks" that he was putting together during the *Snark* voyage. And finally there is a man named O'Brien (an idea unrelated to the 1907 short story "The Passing of Marcus O'Brien") killed for some reason by unnamed men on an island, who do not notice "the vessel" coming toward them that will expose their deed. Most likely, in the completed telling of these ideas we would be able to see what differentiates them from the stories in *Created He Them*. But the significant fact we glean from this set of notes is that London was contemplating a series related to *Created He Them* and that he still considered the latter to be a viable project four or more years after its inception.

Finally, we have come to the short story whose title would also name the proposed collection: "Created He Them." It may seem like a decade of London's life has passed since he wrote his last short story—"The Apostate"— because we have discussed a major novel and four complicated, age-defining essays, but it has only been two and a half months. The notes for the story have a number of elements in common with the notes we have been discussing. Insanity is replaced by alcoholism (considered a subset of insanity in most medical literature at the time), and we have suicide as well, a suicide scene that London had tested in the two short notes about a man—one based on Frank Strawn-Hamilton and one unnamed—who are all but encouraged to shoot themselves. In one set of notes for the story, George arrives at his brother's house to take him, Wick, to the Livermore Sanitorium. Wick doesn't want to go. They take a streetcar to a train station, and there, across the street, George gets a bottle of whiskey and almost misses the train. At Livermore, they walk the grounds until it's time for George to go. Wick announces he won't leave. George takes out a gun, gives it to Wick, and tells him to go off to a thicket and shoot himself. Wick goes off but can't do it and says he'll stay. George leaves and the story ends. In the second set of notes, written at a different time on a different sort of note paper, the story begins the same way with George arriving at his brother's house, who, this time, is named Al.

London used both sets to write the story, for phrases from both appear in the story; both story ideas, though each is incomplete, together form nearly the whole of the finished manuscript. From the first set, George, at the moment he hands Wick the gun, says, "'Then there is only one thing for you to do.' Points to thicket. 'If you don't I'll have to do it for you.'" When Wick decides not to kill himself, George hears "Wick's voice—at sound, George starts as though it had been revolver." In the second set, he sees George meeting Al's wife at the beginning, a refinement of the first set and retained in the story. "Describe her and children, her haunted eyes, the lines on her young face that were not the handiwork of mere worry." Small wonder that she is haunted by an alcoholic, a significant detail indicating her status as an authorial figure, though her work is never mentioned. George tells Al that if he doesn't go he'll lose his job, his marriage, and his children. Al agrees to go, leaves the room, George follows him, and finds him drinking whiskey. Al "smashes glass and bottle to the floor. A look like a wild beast in eyes of Al." They hear Al's wife "sob as they go out the front door." As in the first set and the finished story, George almost misses the train when he buys Al a new bottle. The final pages for these notes are missing, but presumably they treat the scenes at the sanitarium: walking the beautiful grounds, Al deciding to leave, George giving him the gun, and Al unable to shoot himself. It's a domestic tragedy and shows London's preoccupation with alcohol, suicide, and the tribulations of a wife-mother. It retains the irony of the series' title: What sort of God would do this to humans?

Understandably, none of the mainstream magazines wanted such a challenging story. Even the magazine that eventually published it, the *Pacific Monthly*, at first rejected it. His first four choices passed, and, because he had promised a story to Hayden Carruth at *Woman's Home Companion*, he sent it to him even though he knew it was "too harsh" for him.[58] Indeed. So, next he sent it to John Fleming Wilson of *Pacific Monthly*, who had just written to him, proud of his magazine's newly accomplished success and desire to be "literary" as well as "picturesque." Now he could afford a London story, but he returned both "When God Laughs" and "Created He Them" with the injunction to send him a "story of the West . . . something in your own distinctive field of the big Northwest," meaning a Klondike story. He would even pay five hundred dollars for a three- to five-thousand-word story . . . or, oddly, he offered to take back "Created He Them," even though he liked "When God Laughs" better, but for two hundred fifty dollars for a 3,800-word story.[59] The choice was fortunate because Paul Reynolds had just sold "When God Laughs" to the *Smart Set*, though for only two hundred dollars.[60] London took it immediately, even though it was far below what he now expected to be paid. The transaction turned out to be important for future work. The *Pacific Monthly* would publish the final six essays in *The Cruise of the* Snark, essays no one else would touch.

The final story of this complicated and deep set of notes is called "A Wicked Woman." He finished it a week after "Created He Them," and its plot came from Netta. The notes outline the bare bones of the story: Netta and Roscoe live in Los Angeles where they have a romantic interlude during which she allows him to kiss her. This moment convinces her she is a "wicked woman" because "she thought a woman ought to marry a man if she allowed him to kiss her." She didn't love him, he "cried all night" when she told him so, and her family sends her off to Santa Barbara. Her family—Captain Kitt and two sisters—write her letters, telling her not to marry Roscoe. In Santa Barbara, after receiving the letters, she tells her friend Ned that "she has sinned," and Ned storms about, insisting Roscoe ("the scoundrel! . . . . the villain!") marry her. But then he realizes she and Roscoe didn't have sex, and he calms down, having "realize[d] that she is a perfectly innocent woman of twenty." The story ends with "his shaken faith restored . . .

speaking soothing, cheering words." Virginity once more decides the fate of a relationship between a man and a woman.

The story itself adheres to this rough outline but is more complicated if only because there are so many more characters. Netta becomes Loretta; Roscoe is Billy; a sister, Daisy, has a small role; and Captain Kitt becomes Daisy's husband. Loretta has broken up with Billy and, after being consoled by Kitt and Daisy, they all decide Loretta should go to Santa Clara and visit Mrs. Hemingway and her husband, Jack. We are told that "Loretta was so innocent a young thing that were it not for her sweet guilelessness she would be positively stupid."[61] Daisy and Kitt, then, decide to set her up with someone who could appreciate her innocence: Ned Bashford. Ned, instead of being based on Edward Payne, is now based on George Sterling, of all people, and we learn why he was nicknamed the Greek, if only indirectly and circumstantially. In direct contrast with Loretta, he was a jaded, cynical young man who, not surprisingly, lived, not at the Bohemian Club (as George did), but at the Athenian Club. He was "artistically and temperamentally . . . a Greek." That is, following the Nietzsche of *The Gay Science*, he "had passed through the long sickness that follows upon the ardent search for truth" and found there was none. He quoted Nietzsche: "To worship appearance, to believe in forms, in tones, in words, in the whole Olympus of appearance! . . . Those Greeks were superficial—*out of profundity!*" (73-74). To give up on a unifying source of all truth, like God, or even biology, or any other science, is to be "brave," and shows one knows "how to *live.*" Only one kind of person can achieve this: "worshippers of shapes, tones, words." In other words, "artists."[62] This is the redemption that London felt after completing his own search for truth—his own "long sickness"—and obviously it was something Sterling went through as well, cementing the bond between the Greek and the Wolf.

When London sent the manuscript to George for commentary, George wrote, "'A Wicked Woman' is daring, and decidedly amusing, but so much out of your vein that coming from *you* it seems trivial," but Sterling misses London's philosophical point.[63] True, it seems a conventional story. Loretta and Ned eventually fall for each other and seem destined to marry until Loretta receives a letter from Billy (Roscoe) that tells her she ought to be ashamed for not marrying him since she had kissed him. Loretta is thrown into great confusion, being such an innocent, and believes Billy when he says, "Our kisses were terrible if we didn't get married. . . . When a woman

allowed a man to kiss her, she always married him. . . . It was the custom."
(1147). Ned, relieved that they didn't have intercourse, consoles her and then
quickly proposes. In what is meant to be a perfectly innocent and charming ending, they end up in each other's arms, kissing, defying convention
and planning their marriage.

If that was all there was to the story, then, yes, Sterling would be right.
The plot *is* trivial. But the psychology is not. London wants to create a set
of Machine Age lovers; in the theatrical version of this plot, Ned even says
about Loretta that "it is remarkable to find such a woman in this age."[64]
The last sentence is crossed out only because London then decided to put
those words in Mrs. Hemingway's mouth so that Ned can agree with her.
Ned, before he meets Loretta, believed "women were faithless and unvera-
cious," but, "faithful to his German master, he did not strip from them the
airy gauzes that veiled their untruth" (74). Thus he can play with Loretta,
relishing the appearances and unafraid not to look underneath the illusion. George Bernard Shaw even makes an appearance as another of Ned's
authorities on women and sexual relations, and another tie-in to *Scorn of
Women*. But then he truly, madly falls in love: "He confused superficiality
with profundity, and entangled appearance with reality until he accounted
them one" (77). To see how a single woman is different from all other "faithless" women means one has fallen in love. When he tells Mrs. Hemingway
that Loretta "was different from other women. There was no masquerade
about her. She was real," she agrees and then winks knowingly at her husband (77). Ned's philosophy has fallen apart—until the letter arrives and for
a moment he is right back where he started: disillusioned by the nefarious
duplicity of Woman. So this seemingly conventional courtship, trivial in
nature, is itself a mask over the very real philosophical questions about the
relations between men and women. What is attraction? What is trust? What
is the role of sex? What is the social determination of such a relationship?

London sent the story first to *Collier's*, then to *Life*, and finally to *Smart
Set*, knowing full well that a top-notch fiction magazine like *McClure's* or
Harper's or *Atlantic Monthly* would reject it outright. *Smart Set*, though
they seemingly missed the philosophical thread that London had woven
into the trivial plot, accepted it somewhat reluctantly, saying, "Frankly,
we should have preferred to receive the type of story that has come to be
particularly identified with your name," that is, a rugged, manly Klondike
story. They offered a mere sixty dollars, which London took.[65] There was a

slight misunderstanding between author and magazine, though. London had instructed his English agent, James Pinker, to sell the story in England per their usual arrangement; Pinker, however, alerted London that *Smart Set* may have retained world rights, and, in fact, they had. Without realizing it, London had not only received a mere five cents per word—he was asking fifteen cents a word now—but also cheated himself out of the extra income that came from UK sales. It is possible that no other magazine would have bought this story, but in the future he and Pinker would terminate their relationship because of a mix-up involving another short-story sale to *Smart Set*, as if they hadn't learned their lesson from the sale of "A Wicked Woman."

Out of this story came a one-act play by the same title, as London brought his purely theatrical mode to the front burner. The notes for the play show he wanted to deviate in a number of ways from the short story, but the finished manuscript shows he decided not to. He played with the title: "Innocence"; "Miss Innocence"; "A Young Thing"; "Little Miss Innocence," until he decided on "A Wicked Woman."[66] At first he thought it should be set in a "Country House in Santa Barbara," and then decided on Santa Clara, as in the short story. In his notes for the play, Ned, "a young and jaded man of the world who has lost hope and faith in woman, and who is in love with Netta," and Netta (he uses only one word to describe her: "innocence"), who may or may not be in love with him, meet in the living room with the Lady of the House (in the published version Mrs. Alice Hemingway, as in the story, a reprise of the Mrs. Effingham character from *Scorn of Women*, which, again, he was polishing up for publication). We witness Netta come in, open mail, and relapse into a troubled state of mind. "Roscoe arrives," and Netta, "fortified by letters" (apparently borrowing from the notes for the story that he didn't use, London is using the letters from Kitt and her sisters urging her not to marry Roscoe), refuses Roscoe. "Why did you kiss me?" he asks, and they argue until Ned enters and she sends Roscoe away. Ned, discovering "her virtue," proposes marriage and she accepts. Curtain. It's a romantic comedy, pure and simple now.

In the published version of the play, the references to Nietzsche are gone, and the absorptive qualities of the short story are washed away in the floodlights of theater. If women didn't like *Before Adam*, presumably they would love *A Wicked Woman*, with its Huck Finn–like self-condemnation for trying to overturn convention; Netta hates herself for thinking she should not marry Billy. They would love how Loretta, in her innocent way (maybe she isn't as innocent as Ned thinks she is), tries to get Ned to say that he thought she and Billy had had intercourse and that's why he had thought originally that they had to marry. But she relents without him saying it, and they kiss and, with Jack and Alice Hemingway looking on, expecting her to be embarrassed, she utters the final line of the play: "I don't care." She doesn't care if they know, she doesn't care about convention, she doesn't care what her family thinks. Loretta is the original Nasty Woman.

We have, in the end, two complicated sets of notes that yield very little in the way of published material. Like the novel about Jesus and other nearly fully formulated novels, here is yet another significant work of art—two if you count *The Smoke of Life*—left on the cutting-room floor. Yet all these works are interconnected, some serving as rough drafts for others. Having returned from Korea in 1904 and anxious to write a play, London converts "The Scorn of Women" into his first three-act theatrical production, from which he turns to write a fully absorptive novel, *White Fang*, which is thematically connected to "Planchette." This story, told to him by Charmian and featuring characters loosely modeled on her aunt and uncle, is then connected to the short story series *Created He Them* through a common source of plot, namely, Netta Eames, who provides the plot for "A Wicked Woman," which London converts into a one-act curtain raiser by the same title. It is completed four days after he mails Brett the finished manuscript of *The Scorn of Women*. That is, in June 1906, in between the writing of *Before Adam* and *The Iron Heel* (two novels intimately linked and together forming a thematic and linguistic triangle with "Revolution" in their concerns with the failure of capitalism to elevate humans' conditions above that of the Bone Age), he had been deeply engrossed in writing and rewriting and publishing plays. This period of switching between modes and genres of writing, of testing the limits of traditional authorial practice, is, as we have seen, not new in his career. His juggling of forms of writing defines his career.

ABSORPTION IN 1906

The pendulum of London's compositional practice swung back to the absorptive, and in July he wrote a Klondike tale, "The Wit of Porportuk." This would be the second of only four short stories he wrote in 1906 that took place in the North. The main character, El-Soo, is "a full-blooded Indian," and, in an odd moment of hyperbole, London describes her as "fire, the living flame of life." Picked out of her village after her mother died—and, though her father, a chief, still lived—she was taken by a nun to the mission at Holy Cross, to which Sitka Charley had given money in the 1905 story "The Sun-Dog Trail." She learned to read and write and "excelled in mathematics." She also was an artist and in a different place and time "she would have made literature or music."[67] Out of the mess of stories in *Created He Them*, an assortment London could not unify, he brought the idea—now almost an obsession—of the woman author figure.

But this author figure had had her creativity, her fire, cauterized by religion, by the nuns of the mission. Instead of learning to create, she learned "cleanliness and righteousness" and Catholicism, and we will see what London thought of "cleanliness" when we next turn to the essay "The House Beautiful." She carried her education and her fire back home to tend her sick father in his bohemian enclave, a "large log house," "a bacchanalian ruin" (194, 198) which "shook with the roar of wassail and of song," "a cosmopolitan atmosphere" where men and women of all nationalities met and drank and carried on (196). The house, though barely described, sounds very much like the house London himself wanted to build; he must have been thinking about it because within a week he would write "The House Beautiful." "The latchstring to the large house was always out," says the narrator of "The Wit of Porportuk," repeating a phrase London often used in his letters to potential visitors to his ranch (196).

Porportuk is the richest Native American in Alaska, "bourgeois," "a money-lender and a usurer" (195). He lent money, Klakee-Nah spent it, and El-Soo was "as disdainful of money as he" (199). The two good bohemians—Klakee-Nah and El-Soo—slowly come into debt to Porportuk, and that is their doom. To repay the debts her father owed Porportuk after Klakee-Nah dies, El-Soo sells herself to the highest bidder, who happens to be the moneylender. Having promised him that she would never marry him—only her beloved Akoon—she runs away on the principle that Porportuk bought her as if she were a dog, and, now, being his dog, she runs away with Akoon. But eventually she is caught, and though Porportuk gives up and hands her to Akoon, he shoots El-Soo through the ankles so that she may never run away again. It is a premeditated act of cruelty, and the story ends with Porportuk grinning, thinking he has found the wit to match that of his foe. He has only demonstrated that capitalists win against bohemians every time and that the winners use an awful kind of violence for their ends. What we as readers had hoped would be the success of an accomplished and powerful young woman author figure turns out to be only a setup to make El-Soo's fall all the more tragic. Yet the capitalists win only in the economic arena. The poor and oppressed still win in the realm of love, as the story ends with El-Soo and Akoon staring into each other's eyes and he promising never to leave her. These are the hints of the forthcoming *The Iron Heel*.

The publication of "The Wit of Porportuk" is the story of the dark side of the boom in American magazine publishing at the turn of the century, its so-called golden age. "The Wit of Porportuk" is a long short story, 9,728 words, a "Planchette"-sized effort. At first rejected by *McClure's*, the story was asked for and accepted by, of all people, James Randolph Walker, the son of *Cosmopolitan* editor John Brisben Walker, who had famously granted London's essay "What Communities Lose under the Competitive System" first prize in his 1899 essay contest and subsequently offered London a job back East at the magazine. James Walker, when he had worked for his father in the *Cosmopolitan* office in 1905, had implored London for short fiction, and when London informed him that all he had available was "Revolution," the Walkers accepted it, yet never published it.

So it may have been with some glee mixed with trepidation that London received James Walker's plea to have a story from him a year later. This time Walker *fils* was editor of a new magazine, the *Times Magazine*, and he was decidedly a fan of London's work; in a December 1904 profile in the *Editor* he boasted (somewhat untruthfully) that "Jack London . . . was a contributor to *The Cosmopolitan* before he was recognized elsewhere."[68] He needed a story from London quickly and so sent a telegram: "Getting out New Magazine Must have short story from you Initial number."[69] London sent him the violent and uncompromising "The Wit of Porportuk," as almost a dare, and he insisted on fifteen cents a word, nearly fifteen hundred dollars.[70] Walker offered eight hundred and asked that London cut the story down.[71] When London balked at the low price, Walker raised it to a cool one thousand dollars.[72] And then never paid. London wrote over four times to recover his money, but, after the story appeared in December, James Walker explained that he himself was owed money from the owner of the *Times Magazine*, had left the magazine, and gave London the name and address of his lawyer.[73] London even asked Upton Sinclair for advice, who told London that he had been promised five hundred dollars for an essay for the *Times Magazine* and was paid only about half. Sinclair managed to squeeze his money out of Frederick A. Richardson, who owned the magazine. Sinclair told London to assign him power of attorney, and he would get London's money for him.[74] London never did. The supremely busy London felt there was only so much he was willing to do to earn his money. Shades of Klakee-Nah.[75]

To make the matter worse, James Walker, on the same day he offered a bargain rate of eight hundred dollars for "The Wit of Porportuk," asked London about the availability of "Revolution."[76] London must have been floored by the man's audacity, for the Walkers had refused to publish the essay because of its politics. James Walker knew that *Collier's* had taken the essay but had also decided against publication. London told Walker to ask *Collier's* whether they would release it, and then, disregarding any sour taste he may have had left over from dealing with the Walkers in the past, he told Walker, "If you get around to using it, you have my full consent to disavow all responsibility for it, and belief in the content of it, just as long as you publish it."[77] He didn't. *Collier's* neither released the manuscript nor published the essay.

When London returned from the South Seas in 1908 and sorted through his outstanding business deals, he decided he would never get satisfaction from the *Times Magazine*. So he enacted a kind of revenge and sold the story again to *Sunset* for three hundred dollars' worth of railroad tickets, which he gave part of to his friend Elwyn Hoffman.[78] The *Times Magazine* lasted about a year, probably because Richardson was too stingy to attract authors of London's pay grade, and he had hurt his own reputation by never paying Walker the money he was owed. On this anticlimactic and dark note, the Walkers' participation in London's authorial career ended.

Perhaps it is a sign of London's faith in the quality of "The Wit of Porportuk" that he wrote a rough draft of a letter to "managers" who might be interested in dramatizing the story. "It is absolutely fresh, new, and different," he expostulated to himself, in redundant terms. "To tackle it, you require nerve. . . . Got to have good actors. Got to get audience off its feet[.] If it goes, it'll go clean to hell and back again and keep on hitting the high places to kingdom come." If that wasn't enough, he imagined that "managers" would be taken by "the gorgeous and bizarre and primitive and modern coloring in costume and type."[79] Both modern and primitive, beautiful and terrifying, "The Wit of Porportuk" on stage would have transcended its locale to present the evils of capitalism, the strength of love's resistance, and the glories of bohemia.

It may still be hard to imagine London as a bohemian, so consider the continuity in his choice of housing from 1902 to the end of his life. One of the qualities of bohemianism is a respect for land and a desire to inhabit it with as little human interference as possible. This is not to disregard urban bohemian enclaves, which could (as much as it was possible) demonstrate a respect and bond with the landscape. Consider various San Francisco enclaves of late nineteenth-century shacklike houses on Telegraph and Russian Hills, especially a cluster of houses built by Edmund Vischer on Pine Street (all of which burned in 1906). The *San Francisco Chronicle* called it a "most romantic retreat," and it housed "a small colony of writers, painters, and diplomats. Beyond the street lay interior courts with lush, unkempt gardens reached by narrow, stepped passages—it was 'a veritable wilderness' now tenuously perched at the edge of the expanding commercial center." Here and Russian Hill were considered "Bohemian enclave[s]."[80]

Joseph Worcester and Willis Polk had built homes across the street from each other on Russian Hill. Worcester, a Swedenborgian minister, was an amateur architect, heavily influenced by the Arts and Crafts movement. In fact, the mission style originated with a chair designed by A. Page Brown for Worcester's San Francisco Swedenborgian Church in 1894; seven years later *House Beautiful* praised the church's chairs.[81] Worcester was a major influence on Polk (who designed during his long career the shield for the Sierra Club) as was another important San Francisco architect, Ernest Coxhead. Worcester, who had moved to the Bay Area from Massachusetts in 1868, was in turn heavily influenced by Emerson's and Thoreau's concepts of economy and simplicity. He was a strong advocate for "a simple, harmonious relationship between nature and design" and "became a spiritual leader to many of the young artists and intellectuals working in the region."[82] In 1876 he designed and built a cottage "that was perhaps the first dwelling in California to cultivate rustic qualities."[83] Marked by a hip roof above a long porch, the absence of any decoration, and especially its exterior shingles, the house afforded a physically and spiritually expansive view; he could sit on his porch and contemplate nature above the cities of San Francisco and Oakland. More than merely "rustic," this house was probably the first shingle-style domicile in the West, a design that was an expression of American rural simplicity and that had strong ties to the Shakers, Gustav Stickley, and mission design. Twenty-six years later, Jack London and his family rented the house and moved in.

London wrote to Cloudesley Johns: "We have a big living room, every inch of it, floor & ceiling, finished in redwood. . . . The rest of the house is finished in redwood, too, & is very, very comfortable. . . . A most famous porch, broad & long & cool, a big clump of magnificent pines, flowers & flowers & flowers galore."[84] If a photograph of the enormous fireplace in Worcester's San Francisco home is any evidence, London's hearth dominated the living room. One visitor noted the "fireplaces for damp weather, a piano, and great crystal-clear windows, framed in swaying trumpet vines" and "big, cheerful rooms [that] have the sweet, fresh smell of the woodland. The entire interior finish is of redwood, the floors covered with rugs deep and soft as velvet." Typical of an Arts and Crafts interior, "comfortable lounging places and nooks beguile one to the luxurious and continued idleness which is the peculiar seduction of the dreamy Pacific." The visitor called it "the ideal abode of a poet."[85] One could not wish for a better description of the combination of the Arts and Crafts movement and bohemianism. This is the property with fields of California poppies that the Oakland masses devastated and that London sought to preserve and wrote about in his essay "The Golden Poppy." Despite the conflict with flower pickers, London embraced the natural setting that enabled a bohemian lifestyle equal to that lived in an artist's studio and Coppa's in the Montgomery Block. London could have learned all about Worcester and Polk and Coxhead and the influence of the Arts and Crafts movement from their friend Ernest Peixotto's wife, Jessica, who was a regular member of the Ruskin Club and a friend of Austin Lewis. A photograph from 1912 shows Ernest Peixotto sitting on a bench with Polk at the Bohemian Grove for the annual High Jinx, which London attended.[86]

"The House Beautiful," composed immediately after "The Wit of Porportuk," is a clear statement of London's bohemian life aesthetics and exhibits the love he had for his shingle-style cottage; "I never loved a habitation so greatly in my life," he wrote.[87] And we can see Worcester's values embodied in the cottage re-created in this new essay, in the building of the *Snark*, and in the Wolf House, completed and then burned in 1913. A celebration of the Arts and Crafts movement, the essay promotes the kind of back-to-the-land movement we recognize as characteristic of 1960s bohemia, which had its roots (at least in California) in utopian colonies like Altruria as well as in more bourgeois but still bohemian aesthetic manifestations like the bungalows of Greene and Greene in Pasadena.

London was attracted to the Arts and Crafts movement not simply because it accorded with his notions of beauty but also because it was politically simpatico. Supported by the politics of John Ruskin and William Morris, the Arts and Crafts movement united art and socialism. As Oscar Lovell Triggs wrote (in a book published by Chicago's Bohemia Guild of the Industrial Art League), "The primary motive of the arts and crafts movement is, as the name implies, the association of art and labor."[88] More explicitly, he said the movement was "an industrial tendency springing from the economical teachings of Carlyle, Ruskin, and William Morris. . . . Carlyle announced the doctrine, Ruskin elaborated the system, and Morris gave the first practical example."[89] Julia Bracken, an artist in the Bohemia Guild, designed and executed three large wall plaques featuring the profiles of Carlyle, Ruskin, and Morris and trenchant quotations: "On the whole we do entirely agree with those old monks. Laborare est orare. Work is worship"; "Life without labor is guilt. Labor without art is brutality"; "One day we shall win back art again to our daily labor. Win back art, that is to say, the pleasure of life to the people."[90] The images were Arts and Crafts, the words, socialist. We see the same blending of word and image, art and politics on the May 1902 cover of the *Comrade*, the monthly socialist magazine.[91] It was not only London who believed that revolutionary socialism could be blended with the Arts and Crafts movement's aesthetics of architecture and design, even if tamer, Fabian-like politics were present at the birth of the movement. Many socialists thought that the houses of cooperative commonwealths should be indebted to the Arts and Crafts movement.

There are a number of clues in London's work that anticipate the ideas in "The House Beautiful." As I said, El-Soo and her father live in a house that London was imagining for himself. Second, he and Charmian were building the *Snark*, their new home for what they hoped would be seven or more years. So London had interior design and architecture on his mind when, out of the blue sky that fame sometimes created, he received a letter of solicitation from Herbert Stone, the publisher of *House Beautiful*: "I am anxious to run in The House Beautiful magazine four or five articles entitled 'My Castle in Spain.'" He planned to ask Richard Le Gallienne, Edith Wharton, and others. "What I want is a description of your ideal home and its contents and surroundings. Every man plans to have a home of his own at one time or another and every man has ideas as to what that home shall be and mean."[92] As Frank Luther Mott wrote, Stone "had an almost religious devotion to simple beauty, an abhorrence of display and blatancy in modern life, and a special interest in the development of new art forms and the revival of old ones as he found them within the framework of beauty and suitability."[93] *House Beautiful*'s slogan was Thoreauvian: "Simplicity, Economy and Appropriateness in the Home."[94] On the cover of the January 1908 issue of *House Beautiful*, we see a close up of a typical Arts and Crafts hearth, flanked by simple Stickley chairs, Arts and Crafts pottery on the mantel, and the Scottish injunction "East, West, Hame's the Best" carved into the lintel above the mantel.[95] El-Soo and London would have felt at home here.

On the first page of the March 1902 issue of *House Beautiful*, Stone published a stanza from James Thomson's "The Castle of Indolence" and titled it "A Castle in Spain." Here we find another link between bohemia and the castle-home. At first, in the 1300s, the phrase "castle in Spain" simply meant "improbable dreams," or dreams one has about things too impossible to come true. Over the centuries the dream's realization became less and less remote; Henry David Thoreau probably wasn't the first to instruct dreamers to get practical, but his instruction to build foundations under airy castles is indicative of the phrase's shift in meaning.[96] We do not know if London read *Walden*, but London's cover letter to Stone accompanying the manuscript sounds very Thoreauvian: "I have boiled down into it all my thoughts of what a livable house in general should be. In fact, ... I think I've given the ethics of my house beautiful. There are lots of people, I'll wager, who do not imagine that ethics and architecture are at all related."[97] Thoreau was not one of those people. When he placed a foundation under his castle in the air, like London, he first "considered what a house is." He inveighed against "empty guest chambers for empty guests," against the "morning work" of dusting ("I would rather sit in the open air, for no dust gathers on the grass"), against thoughtless ornamentation ("not that all architectural ornament is to be neglected").[98] Simplicity does not demand that we live in caves, but modern architecture and interior design as conceived by Thoreau's antagonists do nothing to elevate us from our primitive beginnings: "The effect of our art is merely to make this low state comfortable and that higher state to be forgotten." I do not mean to turn Thoreau into a modernist, like London. One can sense the abyss between the two authors when one considers what sort of imaginary beings Thoreau sees in the humanly uninhabited woods: "Such was Caucasus and the rock where Prometheus was bound. Aeschylus had no doubt visited such scenery as this" (64). One senses how close to the classical age Thoreau was. It's a difference that shows how far removed London was from Thoreau's major intellectual and cultural influences. Further, their attitudes toward Native Americans could not have been more different. London portrayed First Peoples in conflict with others, while Thoreau, in general, saw Native Americans as part of the natural world.

Still, it's as if Thoreau had written *Before Adam* before composing "Shelter": "the civilized man is a more experienced and wiser savage," but, nonetheless, a savage with a tendency to regress, atavistically (40). The trick is to build a house that advances one's spiritual state. Before we analyze London's essay, consider the future imagined by London through his mouthpiece Anthony Meredith in *The Iron Heel*. Simplicity will rule. In the past, he says, "it was still the custom to fill the living rooms with bric-a-brac. They had not discovered simplicity of living. Such rooms were museums, entailing endless labor to keep clean. The dust-demon was the lord of the household. There were a myriad devices for catching dust, and only a few devices for getting rid of it" (72). Dust is eternal, it seems, and the problem of ridding our homes of it requires both an aesthetic-design solution as well as a political solution. Socialism, not capitalism, advocates simplicity.

Thoreau had solved that problem (he tells us in *Walden* how he built his house, precisely, with lists), and, in the next couple of generations, it was solved by Oscar Lovell Triggs, Elbert Hubbard, and others who combined simplicity, design, beauty, and—unlike Thoreau—community. These were the Machine Age community members of Brook Farmists who combined colony building—even socialist cooperative communities—with a consciousness of art and design. Hubbard, the founder of the Roycrofters community and later, in 1910, a critic of London's revolutionary socialism, would not have been able to see how London's politics allowed for the simple beauty of design that he advocated.

But Triggs, Sercombe, Sandburg, and other denizens of "To-Morrowland" (as Charmian called their bohemian enclave in Chicago, riffing on the title of their magazine) were perfectly attuned to the combination of Arts and Crafts aesthetics and American socialist ideology.[99] By the time the Londons arrived in Chicago in 1906 at the end of their tour, Triggs had disappeared from the scene and Sandburg was out of town, but Sercombe drove them around the city and fed them at his "'To-Morrow' house." The continuity of art and politics is reflected in their itinerary, for on the next day London gave "Revolution" at the University of Chicago, and A. M. Simons gave them a tour of the stockyards on the day after that.[100] Upton Sinclair was present in spirit, as *The Jungle* was being talked about everywhere.

So, too, was Walt Whitman, one of the principal guiding lights of To-Morrowland. Within the Arts and Crafts movement, Thoreau represented the desirable simple, minimalist aesthetic, and Whitman represented the expansive spiritual inner being and a new kind of poetry. According to Amy Lowell, in an essay published in Gustave Stickley's the *Craftsman*, Whitman and Poe were the only "truly American" poets, and she praised Whitman for being "a pagan moralist."[101] When the movement was beginning in England, Charles Robert Ashbee, "the most successful and the most enigmatic exponent of the ideology of the Arts and Crafts Movement," reprinted Whitman for his Essex House Press. Whitman's "words might almost be said to be the inspirational expression of the ideas which led Ashbee to found the Guild and School of Handicrafts."[102] In Chicago, Triggs, in his history of the movement, quoted Ashbee's *Chapters in Workshop Reconstruction and Citizenship* at length, including this crucial passage: "The Whitmanic love of comrades is [the new citizenship's] modern expression, democracy—as socially, not politically, conceived—its basis."[103] Ashbee, Morris, Triggs, and the rest were not political democrats; they were socialists, and the new citizen would be too. Thus Whitman's conception of brotherly love was to form the basis for both the new political and the new aesthetic realm; a cooperative commonwealth and the Brotherhood of Man could not exist without a little "Whitmanic love." Ashbee, still quoted by Triggs, concludes, "The thought as to how much of the solidarity of labor and the modern trade-union movement may be due to an unconscious faith in this principle of comradeship is no idle one" (146). And, Triggs concludes, "Hence the Arts and Crafts movement, with its principle of co-operative individualism, is brought into harmony with some of the deepest thought tendencies of the times," and he includes *Leaves of Grass* with work by Kropotkin, Tolstoy, Henry George, and others. Capitalism frustrates the creation of art, but the new individual will bond with others in "Whitmanic love," forming guilds and workshops to take the place of the factory, which "is organized to the end of making profits for some owner and director. . . .

The wage slavery of the factory forbids art; the machine forbids it; competition forbids it" (158). In a denouement that makes perfect sense, Triggs, after being caught making love with a woman not his wife in a room in the Spencer-Whitman Institute on Calumet Avenue in Chicago, was divorced and moved with his new wife—a former student from the University of Chicago—to Saugatuck, Michigan, where he formed the People's Industrial College, a Morris-inspired community of craftsmen. From there, the couple moved to California, where they farmed and won a prize at the Sonoma-Marin County Fair, in 1914, for their Shetland pony. At some point they moved to the utopian community in Point Loma, Tingley Colony, a move entirely consistent with his politics and aesthetics. Amazingly, it seems he never ran into the Londons.[104]

As advertised in Triggs's and Sercombe's *To-Morrow*, the Spencer-Whitman Institute was "a club house and inn where free souls and advanced thinkers may lodge, dine and commune with their kind."[105] But besides making love to women at the institute, Triggs promoted Whitman in other ways. In the *Conservator*, Horace Traubel's newsletter of all things Whitman and of his legacy, Triggs's endorsement leads the table of contents of the June 1906 issue: "The Conservator is the organ of the most liberal and advanced opinion in America. It is almost the only advocate of freedom and justice as determined by right reason and unaffected by money or position."[106] Eugene Debs was a great admirer of Traubel, and Debs in turn published "Whitman's Optimism and Love" in the July 1908 *Conservator*.[107] Each issue began with a long quotation and the May 1906 issue begins with a paragraph from Joaquin Miller's *Building the City Beautiful*, a book that illustrated what sort of city Miller hoped post-earthquake San Francisco would become. It would be a bohemian city: "When all men toil, no man need work hard or beyond his strength. Work, in fact, has become a recreation, a necessity of perfect enjoyment." Here is a foundation stone of London's own bohemian economics.[108] Miller, who cultivated a persona and look akin to Whitman, was as much a father figure to Bay Area bohemians as Whitman was to, first, New York City bohemians and then others, like Triggs and Sercombe, nationally.[109] He lived within easy reach of London in Piedmont.

Miller did not compose poetry similar to Whitman's verse, but Charles Warren Stoddard did. He was a staunch admirer of the *Conservator* and peer and friend of Miller, London, and the rest of Bay Area bohemia. He wrote free verse in the manner of Whitman for the *Golden Era* in the late nineteenth century, heavily influenced by *Leaves of Grass* and especially "Cala-mus." London called him Dad, and in 1906 Stoddard sent him a copy of the *Conservator*. "Traubel is one of the finest—I wish he knew *you!*" Stoddard told his favorite son. London in turn wrote, "Sure, I know Traubel. I had a copy of 'Conservator,' but was glad to get an extra one."[110] From June 1905 till at least February 1907, Traubel published this blurb from London on the back page of his magazine: "I want to thank you at this late day for the reviews you have given me in The Conservator. Leaving out everything else, you have done what not one in a hundred reviewers has done—grasped the innermost meaning of my work." Traubel had reviewed *War of the Classes* favorably without qualification, and London returned the favor by writing a paragraph for the *Conservator* praising Traubel's *Chants Communal*: "It supplies a crying need of the socialist movement," he wrote, concluding, "It is twentieth century thought and it is alive. And for me that is the best I can say of anything, that it is alive."[111] As for Sercombe, London wrote to him in 1906, "Say, old man, here's what we've got to do:—We've got to swap autographed copies of our Cave Dwellers stories. If 'Chicago Cave Dwell-ers' is out, shove your fist into it and send it along, and I'll do the same to you with 'Before Adam' as soon as it comes out in book form, which will be in February." Exchanging art objects—crafted by bohemian hands—was entirely natural to these socialist men and women.[112]

And then there was the third prominent member of the Chicago bohe-mian world, Carl Sandburg. Sandburg missed London in Chicago in Feb-ruary, but his profile of the famous author appeared in the April 1906 issue of *To-Morrow*. His essay, like Traubel's review of *War of the Classes*, takes off from *The People of the Abyss* and applauds London's politics. He calls *The Call of the Wild* and *The Sea-Wolf* masterpieces, and then exposes the politics inherent in those two works: "Wolf Larsen is The System incar-nate."[113] Decades later and now billed as "the elder statesman of American letters," Sandburg was once asked what he thought of the "beatnik move-ment." Carl said in his creaky voice, "I think there should be a beatnik move-ment in every generation. I was a part of a beatnik movement from 1915 to 1925. Some of my work is a challenge to the beatniks."[114] He has his dates wrong—1905, not 1915, is more like it—but his point is clear. He—and Triggs and Sercombe and Moore and others in Chicago, as well as London and his cohort—were the precursors to the Beats and formed the third gener-ation of American bohemians.

The links among socialist thought, Whitman's ideas of poetry and citizenship, and the Arts and Crafts movement were manifold, three-dimensional. This was the intellectual and cultural cathexis out of which London's "House Beautiful" grew. We remember that Robert Collier, in making his pitch to London to tour and write about the nation, likened him to Whitman. London acknowledged the inheritors of Whitman as living according to right principles. That is, London's socialism was larger than just a set of economic paradigms. He meant it as a new, better way of living. It led him to think about the Arts and Crafts movement, or at least ideas that were embraced by that movement and, independently, by socialists. As his friend A. M. Simons wrote, "The chief aim of social workers should be to make society artistic." Art and labor must be united, and labor must be governed by socialist principles because "Capitalism presents a hostile attitude toward all efforts to restore the conditions of healthful, pleasurable, beautiful workmanship." In fact, "under these conditions any movement toward the revival of the beautiful, the pleasant, and the good,—in short of the artistic,—which does not connect itself with the great revolutionary movement of the proletariat, has cut itself off from the only hope of realizing its own ideal." [115] This is why London was so attractive and important to socialists like Simons. He was building an artful life as a proletariat. They all agreed: Art is life.

When Sercombe showed London around Chicago in early 1906, they must have talked about such foundational concepts and specifically the links between the Arts and Crafts movement and socialism. London may have first come across the phrase "my castle in Spain" and its link to the Arts and Crafts movement in Nixon Waterman's *A Book of Verses*; Waterman was a friend of London's aunt and one of the first editors London ever met. The book is beautifully designed with an Arts and Crafts flower-and-thistle cover. His poem "My Castle in Spain," with its "delicious nests" and places "forgetful of care and pain," is evident in the stage directions for "A Wicked Woman."[116] The description of the set reads: "The room is remarkable for magnificent stone fireplace at rear center. On either side of fireplace are generous diamond-paned windows. Wide, curtained doorways to right and left. To left, front, table with vase of flowers and chairs. To right, front, grand piano." One of the chairs is a Morris chair. The fireplace is central because it is the material manifestation of the ideals of domesticity, whether masculine or feminine.

Given London's aesthetic, the reader of his "The House Beautiful" essay is initially puzzled after London announces in his first sentence, "Speaking of homes, I am building one now." The "home" seems unnecessarily constrained, unwelcoming in fact. There will be no "fences, lawns, nor flowers," nor a veranda. If the reader doesn't pause at London's clue that he is not describing a house but a "home," then he or she won't realize until the fourth paragraph that London has deployed one of his favorite rhetorical devices, one that he used to begin *The Call of the Wild*. He withholds the most crucial fact about what he is describing. "Oh, I forgot to tell you," he says in his most theatrical fashion, "that this home I am describing is to be a floating home."[117]

His "land house," however, will not be that much different. Like the boat, it will be built according to three principles: it will be lived in, it will combine utility and beauty, and it will combine "construction and decoration." This latter "idea is more important than the building of the house, for without the idea the house so built is certain to be an insult to intelligence and beauty-love" (164). These are Arts and Crafts principles, especially the second one, which echoes Morris: "Have nothing in your houses that you do not know to be useful, or believe to be beautiful."[118] No columns that don't support weight.

London's conception of the house beautiful includes a direct link between fireplaces and, not just domesticity, but clean, fresh air. "The fireplaces of my house will be many and large. . . . With large fireplaces and generous heat, some windows may be open all the time, and without hardship all the windows can be opened every little while and the rooms flushed with clean pure air." The house will be like a cave, in a way, because (with *Before Adam* still on his mind) "for countless thousands of years my ancestors have lived and died and drawn all their breaths in the open air." There will be "large verandas" and even they will have fireplaces for comfort in the frosty evenings. "I've got only one pair of lungs," he writes playfully, "and I haven't the address of any repair shop" (175). One might almost forget that he was a chain smoker.

The materials of the house have to be selected according to similar principles, one of which is Keatsian in its formulation: "A thing must be true, or it is not beautiful" (166). Partly London is thinking of the banality of not using shoddy material, like that which was used for the barn on his property that fell in the earthquake. The earthquake makes a reappearance in this essay. He notes, as many did, that the new city hall in San Francisco fell because "the mortar was not honest" (168). It's significant that he doesn't stay on the material plane but rather ascribes an ethics to rotten materials. The ethical consideration lies in the choices builders make, and if they choose cheap material they are dishonest. But there's more. The materials have to fit the idea of the building. A skyscraper "should not bulk on the cityscape like Leviathan; it should rise and soar, light and airy and fairy-like." Thus the earthquake was "a punishment for sin; but it was not for sin against God. The people of San Francisco sinned against themselves" (168). London convicts his city for being capitalistic. Architecture, like all art forms, should be based on socialism: "clean, noble, alive."

As he deals with the past, so too he addresses the future, as he warms up for *The Iron Heel*. "I often regret that I was born in this particular period of the world. In the matter of servants, how I wish I were living in the golden future of the world, where there will be no servants—naught but service of love," an echo of Miller's *Building the City Beautiful*. London expounds on a larger point, one that incorporates a Whitmanesque brotherly love. Just because servants are required by "the rationality and the necessity of the division of labor" doesn't "justify me in lack of consideration for them." Given that "one of the great and selfish objections to chattel slavery was the effect on the masters themselves," it is unethical to demean servants by refusing them decent habitation. "Heaven in the drawing-room and hell in the kitchen" is an antithetical principle to the house beautiful in the time of the Brotherhood of Man. Furthermore, servants' work will not include cleaning. "It will be no spick and span and polished house." The "philosophy of spick and span" is built on a hierarchy not just of labor but of being. Minorities of both class and race suffer because of this. "The Korean drone flaunts his clean white clothes, for the same reason that the Chinese flaunts his monstrous finger-nails, and the white man and woman flaunt the spick-and-spanness of their spotless houses" (171–74). We can fault London for not taking a more active role in the early civil rights movement, as did his friend William English Walling, who helped found the NAACP. But we can applaud his anticlassism in "The House Beautiful."

Comfort, beauty, and leisure are all qualities he required for his house, especially the laughter and good times that come when guests and hosts are comfortable in an aesthetically pleasing environment. "It will be a house of air and sunshine and laughter" (176); as Simons had pointed out in his essay for the *Craftsman*, play was a crucial component of the artistic life, endorsed by both the Arts and Crafts movement and by revolutionary socialism. London foresaw an eternity of pleasured progeny living in his house, as great a lasting gift as he hoped his writings would be. The essay concludes, "I have a thousand generations in my loins. Laughter that is decadent is not good for these thousand generations."[119]

Except those aren't the words that got published in either "The House Beautiful" or in *Revolution, and Other Essays*. Stone revised the penultimate sentence to read, "I have in me a thousand generations." "Loins" was too suggestive a word for the magazine, and we may assume that it catered to people like Corra Harris, a novelist and book reviewer for the *Independent*. London may have sent her a copy of the manuscript because she had recently published an appraisal of his work thus far. Entitled "The Walking Delegate Novelist," she wrote in her southern way, "Properly speaking, Jack London is a 'hobo' novelist. This is not so bad as it sounds, nor nearly so bad as it used to be." She goes even further and agrees that he is a "genius," but a genius with an "elk-nature" and "mental obstreperousness" that makes him and others of his elk ilk "not novelists at all, but unscrupulous speculators in law and life. They are not simply the sons of their own fathers, but they are often the ramping intellectual posterity of Walt Whitman and of half a dozen other erratic geniuses."[120] Perhaps now that we have tracked how the aesthetics of Whitman and London overlapped, we are not surprised that a contemporary reviewer thought to lump the two together.

She was appalled by his new essay. She was so offended by that word *loins* that she sent him a "written-out apology form" for him to fill out. He attempted in his reply to remain on light and friendly terms, but she was too offended to be pen pals. In 1914, on his way to New York City, where she was living at the time, he wrote her to set up an appointment, "to arrange a truce or loose the dogs of war according to your heart's desire."[121] They met at an Author's Guild dinner. "I was astonished," she said. "He was pale, dressed like a mechanic in his Saturday-afternoon clothes." In her view, though, he had stepped up, but barely, from being a hobo-author to being a mechanic author.[122]

They of course disagreed about politics. Her friend and editor Hamilton Holt wrote to London a number of times to persuade him to let him publish the correspondence between the southerner and the westerner, most of which appears to be lost. In 1907 he wrote to London, saying, "I have seldom come across such an electric controversy in my life, and it is too good to remain unpublished."[123] But London said no. So Holt tried again two years later: "By the way, I wonder if the last two or three years have not cooled you and Mrs. Harris off enough so that you will both re-edit the correspondence on Socialism. It was the best bit of controversy I have ever happened to know on which both sides came out victorious. Why won't you change your mind and let it be printed?"[124] And, again, London said no. Though London was "universal" enough to make up with her, she was not.[125] In her memoir, she again likened him to a primitive beast, recalling the time when "Jack London charged, pawing and bellowing, into the arena of American fiction." She did not separate manners and the quality of one's fiction. Harris was one righteous church lady from the South, the wife of a Methodist preacher, and momma don't allow no "loins" in her house.

London had intimated in his essay that in seven years or so he would build his house beautiful, and he did just that. It was designed by Albert Farr, whose work drew "directly from recent English arts-and-crafts examples."[126] Wolf House was comprised of five local materials: "redwood trees, a deep chocolate-maroon volcanic rock, blue slate, boulders and concrete," as George Wharton James described it. The boulders were dynamited out of the ground and then hauled into place, not chiseled or otherwise worked upon. The redwood logs kept their bark. Thoreau would have been proud. "We certainly leave the handsomest paint and clapboards behind in the woods, when we strip off the bark and poison ourselves with white-lead in the towns," he wrote in *Maine Woods*. London himself could have written the next words: "For beauty, give me trees with the fur on."[127]

In keeping with the ideals of the Arts and Crafts movement, James noted that the centerpiece, an immense living room with a large fireplace, "will give [the house] a cheerful, homelike, though vast and medieval appearance."[128] London could well have remembered the medieval Arts and Crafts designs in glass and stone that he saw in Mandel Hall at the University of Chicago, among other places. As Stickley once wrote, "The Middle Ages [were the] golden period of the arts and crafts." With all the workmen on site at London's Beauty Ranch—the carpenters, the stone masons, the carters, and so on—it's as if he had re-created, on a small scale and solely for the purpose of building his house, several of the craft guilds from the Middle Ages and duplicated in America in the twentieth century at places like Rose Valley, Pennsylvania, and Roycroft, New York.

If the *Snark* was a house, then his house was a ship. Some think of the Wolf House as a rich man's house, perched on a domineering position on a hillside, commanding a wide view. That must be the conclusion you come to if you take Wolf House as the exhibition of an outsized ego, a selfish undertaking compensating for all his perceived sacrifices on behalf of the cause. Yet James wrote that the house was actually nearly invisible to the public. He overheard a visitor exclaim, "What fools they are! building such a glorious house where none can see it!"[129] If we follow this rhetorical exchange between ship and house, and if we keep in mind how the house's natural and local building materials made it seem as if it grew organically from the hillside, and that it was backed by a large redwood grove as if it were masts, then the Wolf House becomes the equivalent of the highest point on a ship, a sailing ship, and the highest point is the topmost sail called the skysail. Jack's writing desk would be at the equivalent height to the eagle's nest. Skysail Jack was the name London gave to a companion of 'Frisco Kid in "And 'Frisco Kid Came Back." London sometimes went by Sailor Jack on the road, and the two names—Skysail Jack and Sailor Jack— seem interchangeable nomenclature for an author. Skysail Jack does the cooking in the 'Frisco Kid story at the hobo camp, the epitome of male domesticity. Skysail Jack was the name of the hobo he chased across Canada in 1894—the ghost that is his imagination. Author under sail, indeed.

The interchange between house and boat continues with the very next piece of writing, the foreword to *The Cruise of the* Snark. Given that the boat's completion was still in doubt, it may seem a gratuitous choice of essay topic. Yet the house and boat essays are really cut from the same cloth, metaphorically designed by William Morris. For London sailed an Arts and Crafts boat to the South Seas. When he described the *Snark* in "The House Beautiful," he made it clear that his house would follow from the principles he adhered to in building the boat. London strove for Thoreauvian simplicity, but not Thoreauvian economy in his designs for both, and in his written style as well. The *Snark* would be simple, but expensive. He had many needs—a large engine and two smaller ones, a bathroom, a large cockpit, a "dynamo," "a storage battery," even an ice machine, and, especially, a crew. In the span of six sentences London goes from writing "There will be no crew" to "Of course there will be a cook and a cabinboy."[130] This is not Thoreauvian economy. Thoreau would have tried to manage to do it all himself. But servants enable a division of labor in London's mind—after all, if a servant leaves out his clothes and cleans up after him, then he has more time to write and for bohemian comfort. "Why should we stew over a stove, wash dishes, and set the table?" London asks. Jack and Charmian's work—writing—was their pleasure. The others would get their chance at comfort, as soon as they finished putting the dishes away. Still, as with Triggs and others, London sincerely wanted his crew bonded in Whitmanesque comradeship, not, say, in Melvillian democratic citizenship. Whitman was the founder of the spirituality that sustained the Arts and Crafts movement. That influence, Jack and Charmian hoped, would continue with their voyage. They wanted to be "alerted," as Millard had said about his earthquake experience.

To write a foreword to a book that doesn't yet exist is not such a fanciful undertaking. But to write a foreword for a book to be based on an expedition that may or may not happen, now that's a risky and impatient project. In July 1906 London had no guarantee that the boat would actually be completed. His editor at *Cosmopolitan*, Bailey Millard, now back in New York, who was apprised with everyone else in the country about the progress of the boat's construction, was surprised to receive the essay.[131] But the foreword is all about London's impetuous nature. How wonderful would it be to sail around the world: that is how the essay begins, as Charmian, Jack, and Roscoe swim in the ranch's lake. London's notes for the essay begin with a single word: "World."[132] "Let us do it," they say. But domestic affairs come first, he says, at least initially. He has a house to build, even though he had just told his national audience that he was building a boat first, then a house. He wrote an essay about a house that is actually a boat. And then he writes an essay about a boat trip that can't be taken because he needs to build a house. It's as if he can't decide which to do first, so he combines the two so that he can do both simultaneously. Their interchangeability also signals their indebtedness to the same aesthetic principles.

The first paragraph contains at least two falsehoods, though London's audience would not have been aware of them. First, the idea of the trip came to Jack and Charmian before they ever discussed it with Roscoe; Charmian wrote in her diary for 9 August 1905, "Starting Capt. Slocum's book. Planning our trip around the world."[133] We know for certain that London was thinking of a long South Pacific sea voyage in February 1903 when he told Brett that he would take the money from *The Saturday Evening Post*'s serialization of *The Call of the Wild* and write *The Sea-Wolf* aboard ship;

he repeated his intention to go around the world in seven years to Anna Strunsky in September 1903.[134] Interestingly, Slocum's book cover features an anchor on which two sea horses are intertwined; a sea horse might be envisioned as the peaceable side of a coin on which the other side is a sea wolf. The cover, then, may have been a source for the title of Jack's sea story. In any case, Jack's plan outlined to Brett in 1903 does not follow Slocum's book, though it dovetails with it. In fact, a month later he bought a boat and named it after Slocum's: the *Spray*.

Second, London says they came up with the name *Snark* "because we could not think of any other name" (2). Actually, their first choice was *Gull*, which was then abandoned despite George Sterling's plea that they do not choose such an ill-fated name as *Snark*.[135] London says in his foreword there was nothing "occult in the name," disavowing a spiritualist or ghostly aura surrounding the boat. Despite his protestations, the name *is* weird.[136] Lewis Carroll's poem is about a ship and its crew that hunts something that turns out to be terrible and tragic. The Snark turns out to be a Boojum, and if you meet the Boojum, as one crew member does, you will disappear—"softly and suddenly vanish away"—like a ghost. Boo!—jum. In their Arts and Crafts boat, named after an imaginary entity that Carroll consulted Ruskin about, the *Snark* crew enact a Victorian ghost story. The ship is named after the object of a hunt, but the ship is doing the hunting. London might as well have been sailing a ship called the *Ghost*.

London feels compelled to say why they are undertaking the trip. For him, this question demands an exactitude that no other legitimate question— Where are they going? When will they be back? How on earth will they survive?—demands. And yet he dismisses the question outright as a matter of egotism. Not his, but that of the questioners. Egotism is a failure of imagination, according to London. It is an inability to imagine others' "desires, likes, and dislikes," and so one uses one's own thoughts as the measure of what is normal, sane, productive (2). In any case, egotism is different from London's famous statement of why he did go: "I Like." *Like* explains ambition, addiction, and religious extremes. It is "the line of least resistance" to fulfill one's deepest needs. It is desire, motivation, and the object of philosophy. It is a "set of values." It is, finally, who we are, which requires no explanation after all. Like Lewis Carroll's Bellman—who said, "They think I am crazy," though the "utter inanity" of his "words . . . proved his insanity"— London's words fail to prove his sanity. As with *Before Adam, Created He*

Them, and even the effects of the earthquake, soundness of mind is a principal concern in the foreword. We are not insane, asserts London, before he headed off into the ocean without a navigator or working engine or a watertight ship.

He once told the managing editor of *Success Magazine*, when the latter had counseled taking a clipper ship instead of a small boat, "But gee—think of it—achievement! Think of going around the world yourself, *taking* yourself around the world,—doing it with your own hands and head. I think that's the biggest thing of all that can be said in favor of the small boat."[137] Anybody can sail on a clipper ship. Anybody can be the tourist. Tourism is not an accomplishment, it's imperialistic dilettantism. "The thing I like most of all," he writes in the foreword, "is personal achievement." What he achieves "must be concrete." Writing books is concrete but writing "the great American novel" is not (3). Who is to say, after all, whether *The Sea-Wolf* placed London in the pantheon of America's greatest writers, that he had lived up to the expectations of his publisher George Brett? He isn't denigrating the act of writing. He is denigrating the act of criticism, which is egotism. He writes because it represents his "set of values." He has a "water-fight" because that is a bohemian act as well. And he would rather be a water-fighting, kite-flying author than write something that all critics would herald as the Great American Novel. He will write what he wants, when he wants, and not be held to conventional or critical examination, especially by people like Corra Harris.

In a touching moment of self-examination and self-revelation, London admits "that I do like a small audience." It must be composed of those he loves and in turn who love him. In an absolutely honest and startling pronouncement, he says, "When I then accomplish personal achievement, I have a feeling that I am justifying their love for me" (5). His greatest fear is not being unloved but in failing and disappointing those who love him. If he fails, he would end up outside his family, community, his brotherhood. It is an immature conception of love, though its confession is mature. More than anything else it articulates his famous boyishness.

At the same time, he is perfectly happy accomplishing something that only he is aware of. "The delight of the achievement itself . . . does not depend upon witnesses" (5). It is the ultimate satisfaction to know that he has adjusted "to environment." This is the very definition of "success." Success is not a matter of material gain or public recognition. To write is to live. To write is to succeed. Not to write is to fail. To fail is to die, and, again, writing is a life-or-death matter. "Life that lives is life successful, and success is the breath of its nostrils" (5). Success, in fact, is the breath or spirit emanating from the living being. To write is to live is to have the spirit.

He could have stayed home, but "he was not made that way." He needed the ultimate challenge. He needed to be "alerted." He says, humbly, "I am so made." He has no choice, just as others have no choice in staying home and not sailing around the world. It is enough for them to adjust to their immediate circumstances again and again, day after day. But London needs the novel environment, the "big moments of living." "Being alive, I want to see," he says (7). Vision, writing, success, and community are all bound up together in this voyage. One cannot happen without the other.

So far the foreword is surprisingly similar to confessional literature like *John Barleycorn*. It is in this sense a warmup for the book he would write after *The Iron Heel—The Road*. He is not exposing his fears and psychological structure because he thinks there is an audience for it. He expects the same from any adventurer. If you don't know why you are putting yourself in danger, if you don't know why you are leaving your home and loved ones and community, then you are truly insane. He is telling his audience through the mode of confession that he is worthy of the trip, and if he convinces them of this basic truth, then they will follow his every step. For the trip is no less an engagement by a mere mortal—"fallible and frail, a bit of pulsating, jelly-like life"—with death. Jack London may seem like a great man, one of the most famous authors of all time, but in reality he is just "a little animal called a man—a bit of vitalized matter, one hundred and sixty-five pounds of meat and blood, nerve, sinew, bones, and brain." And the trip will take this bit of organic flotsam into the giant maw of "great natural forces—colossal menaces, Titans of destruction, unsentimental, unethical, mathematical monsters that have less concern for me than I have for the grain of sand I crush under my foot." Death can take many forms: "cyclones and tornadoes, lightning flashes and cloud bursts, tide rips and tidal waves, undertows and waterspouts, great whirls and sucks and eddies, earthquakes and volcanoes, surfs that thunder on rock-ribbed coasts and seas that leap aboard the largest crafts that float, crushing humans to pulp or licking them off into the sea to death" (6). In his notes for the foreword he wanted, first of all, to explain this psychology: "psychology of the trip. The smallness of man—his monkey origin, etc. the earthquakes and shooting stars striking earth." He then refers himself to Meyer's *The End of the World* and its discussion of comets hitting earth. "What I have seen of the sea and the elements—pictures of colossal sea disturbances caused by earthquake, etc. Work in unbelief in immortality. And then the challenge of my soul to the wild forces—we'll do it. What if we die? etc. Also with my own hands I did it!" . . . "Work in my worship of personal achievement. Rather be champion prize fighter of world, than president of the U.S. . . . Two of the proudest achievements of my life—not 'Call of the Wild' etc., but the stone water-trough on ranch and the time I steered the Sophie Sutherland in typhoon."[138] To flaunt death seems insane, but he has now examined his soul and his mind and found himself intact and stable. It is egotism on the part of others if they judge otherwise.

The foreword closes with a litany of mechanical problems that frustrate an easy construction of the *Snark*. There's the engine, the rigging, the lighting, and so on. All these demand complicated answers. But none rivals the matter of navigating, and his audience must be appalled that the ship is sailing off into the Pacific without either the captain or the owner knowing how to navigate. In his notes, London imagined a bit of dialogue to accompany the disquisition of this problem: "Neither knows navigation. 'I'm rushed to death [!], Roscoe.' You learn this summer and teach me after we start." In the published version, London solves the problem by saying they'll learn on the way, but "there's one unfortunate and perplexing phase of the voyage" that apparently London cannot solve. That is, he and Roscoe disagree about "cosmology" (15). Roscoe believes the earth is concave, like a bowl, and the sky and universe are in the middle. He learned this from the writings of Cyrus Teed, who founded a system of beliefs called Koreshanity and established utopian colonies first in New York, then in Chicago and San Francisco, and finally in Florida. Perhaps Roscoe had been a member of the San Francisco colony. In any case, it is a mildly amusing belief system, and London uses it to end the essay on a light and humorous note, so necessary for rhetorical balance after the confessional mode and the litany of death-dealing natural forces. Unbeknownst to his readership, however, he had written to his good friend the librarian, Fred Bamford, to find out if there was scientific evidence to dispute Teed's hollow sphere theory.[139] Bamford apparently supplied the necessary counterarguments. London did not actually believe Roscoe could be right, but he needed to convince him that he, London, was right. As it turned out, it was he, not

Roscoe, who learned how to navigate, in a way proving that his "cosmology" was correct. It turns out that Captain Roscoe was crazy, and London was crazy enough to hire him.

PRELUDE TO *THE IRON HEEL*

As he wrote the foreword to *The Cruise of the* Snark, "House Beautiful," "The Wit of Porportuk," "A Wicked Woman," "Created He Them," "The Somnambulists," his reports on the earthquake and on the Haywood-Moyer-Pettibone kidnapping, "My Best Story and Why I Wrote It," and *Before Adam*, the composition of *The Iron Heel* composted in his mind. Before he began it, though, he needed to return to the short story. Thus, he wrote "Finis" and "Just Meat."

"Finis" was published under the title "Morganson's Finish" in *Success Magazine*. The story begins with an end, the end of a Klondiker's food as he sits in his camp, but also a beginning. He has made a decision. "It was the last of Morganson's bacon. He had begun with sopping his biscuit in the grease on the bottom of the frying-pan, and he had finished with polishing the pan with the biscuit."[140] It's a clever rhetorical trick to show him nearly out of food, without dogs, and ill with scurvy. We don't learn the exact nature of his decision until much later in the story, so, at the beginning, because of his condition, we sympathize. And then when we learn the nature of his decision, we learn that we are sympathizing with a murderer.

He is also haunted. We learn that "his pale blue eyes were troubled. There was that in them that showed the haunting imminence of something terrible."[141] And tragic. It is the dawning of his knowledge of his impending death. Alive, he is haunted by the ghosts in the white silence. Yes, we are indeed in the heart of ghostland. Later, when the scurvy had progressed horribly, he looked in a pocket mirror and scared himself. "That vision of himself haunted him day and night."[142] Not only is he now a ghost of himself, but the ghost that haunts the land is in turn haunted by itself. Still later, when he returns to the town of Minto, the bartender says he thought he was dead. "You've been dead for more 'n two months, now," as if Morganson is there, but not there (206). This is the awful fate of the dying in ghostland. Not only that, but the main action takes place on that day so fraught with terrible meaning for London, Christmas.

Dead as a ghost, Morganson lies to the bartender, fabricating an entire story of his life for the last two months, thus exposing himself as a false author figure, a kind of a ghost of a real author. By now we strongly suspect he wants to kill someone on the trail; life has been unfair to him, we have learned. He wants revenge against Chance, against Life. As London wrote in his notes to the story, "Beginning of second movement Morganson has his mind made up. Fixed resolve, though show not its nature."[143] London hides Morganson's motivation because it's imperative that we initially identify with and sympathize with this ghost–false author–murderer. Part of the message of the story is that an individual such as Morganson must learn to adjust to the environment or else die. It could be us. We all need to learn this lesson. Or, in political terms, if we are as frustrated and angry with the capitalist system as London was, we still need to be reminded that a single assassin cannot accomplish the downfall of wealthy capitalists like the Swede and John Thompson; anarchism is not the answer. We recall the money these two successful miners have and how it becomes a horrible fixation for Morganson: "A vision of life before him . . . took the form of a roll of hundred-dollar bills" (210). Adjustment in socialist terms means uniting with others in order to effect the equal distribution of wealth. At the end, in a passage that echoes the earlier story "When God Laughs," he discovers "the lies and frauds of life." As he dies he finds relief; death is a "sweet sleep." Life had told him before that death was something to fear, but "death did not hurt" (219). And this is the final indictment of the ghost–false author. Life lies, yes, but only to perpetuate itself. The lies are necessary for those who want to live. Only the morally corrupt wish to die and accept death's realism for the final truth.

London had as much trouble placing this story with a magazine as he did in one of his own story collections; not thematically suitable for *When God Laughs, and Other Stories*, it sat idle until the teens when he first thought of collecting it with "The Tar Pot" in a volume by that name. Then he stitched together a table of contents for a volume to be called either *The Hobo and the Fairy* or *Told in the Drooling Ward*. The contents for the volume changed over time, and its title became *The Turtles of Tasman*, but it finally included "Finis," placed between "The First Poet" and "The End of the Story," all titles marking time.

His travails with magazines began with Caspar Whitney of *Outing* and Perriton Maxwell of *Cosmopolitan*, both of whom rejected it because it was too long; as Maxwell wrote, "I am forced to return your splendid story 'Finis' for the reason that it cannot be divided into a two-part story with sustained interest and it is much too long to go in a single number of the magazine."[144] Finally, after four more rejections, he turned to an outlet with which he already had a contract. Robert MacKay had just become managing editor of *Success Magazine* at time when the magazine had risen to the top ranks in circulation and advertising income. It had shifted its main focus from the lives of famous and powerful men and how they attained "success" to fiction and muckraking. The magazine had been founded by Orison Swett Marden, one of the most prominent New Thought advocates in the U.S. and author of *Pushing to the Front*. He also wrote books entitled *Kill Worry and Live Longer, He Can Who Thinks He Can,* and *Be Good to Yourself.* It's hard to imagine that such a man would have accepted a story of a Klondiker who succeeds in murdering two men because he is so single-mindedly good to himself, but choices in the world of fiction manuscripts fell to his new editor, a task Marden must have felt himself unsuited for. MacKay was obviously intent on competing with first-rank fiction magazines, so he sought out and signed London, in November 1906, to a contract to publish two five-thousand-word stories at fifteen cents a word or $750 each.[145] The contract emphasized two conditions: first, that the length be five thousand words, more or less, and, second, that "I hope you will give us some good, strong stories, something like 'The Love of Life.' . . . Do not think that our magazine is not capable of being sufficiently broad in its policy to present such a story."[146] No fear about that second condition. London of course would send what he wanted.

Imagine MacKay's surprise and/or consternation in February 1907 when London sent him the 9,465-word "Finis." London's cover letter expresses worry—but not much worry—about two matters. First, he confessed that "'Finis' is not a story of success." Nonetheless, he considered it one of his "very best." Following MacKay's lead, he compared it to "Love of Life" with one significant difference: "'Love of Life' was the song of success, while this is a song of failure." No kidding. But he also told MacKay that other magazines did not take it because it *was* about failure, implying that MacKay had a chance to publish one of Jack London's finest stories because other magazines were too hesitant and pusillanimous. Clearly, he was testing MacKay's assertion that their editorial policy was broad enough to accept a story about willful murder and bloody death in the snow. To MacKay's credit, he lived up to his promise in that regard. In fact, when he received the story and cover letter, he told London, "I am not opposed to a story of failure, for in failure we often find the best elements of success. . . . We are publishing a big, strong fighting machine, broadminded and purposeful. Ours in not modeled for the Sunday school, but for the active men and women of the moment."[147] When he advertised the story, he used the connection to "Love of Life" to sell it but argued in the copy that their story was "more powerful, more vivid, more realistic."[148] Still, no one missed the irony that a story about death appeared in a magazine about success.

Second, because the story was double the length of what they had discussed, London offered it for $750, "a straight cut of 50% in the price." He knew that money was not so much the issue; MacKay earlier had exclaimed that fifteen cents was higher than he had expected but that he was "game."[149] But the story's length could be a problem, so he was willing to accept approximately eight cents a word even though he had just bragged to *Cosmopolitan* that he was getting fifteen cents a word from *Success Magazine*.[150] He did not offer MacKay the opportunity to cut the story down to five thousand words, but MacKay had to fit the story to his space, which he did after he accepted the story, though telling London only that he wanted to change the title to "Morganson's Finish."[151] The pattern of excision indicates a cutting in order to keep down the word count for a better fit for the magazine trade and not an artistic imperative to make the story better.

MacKay, it turns out, was much too sanguine about his readers' tastes and the compatibility of his own editorial policy with that of his boss, Orison Marden. When London sent him a brand-new story from Hawaii, MacKay turned it down. "Forgive me for sending back this excellent story," he wrote. "But it is, we fear, altogether too grewsome. The fact of the matter is, 'Morganson's Finish' gave our readers a shock from which they do not seem to recover as readily as I had anticipated, judging from the letters that are swarming to the office. Haven't you something else less grewsome,—something in which death does not play a part?"[152] He even offered to market the story for London, but London, always reasonable, sent him a tamer story—"That Spot"—and asked his agent, Paul Reynolds, to find a home for the story MacKay and his boss so feared, "To Build a Fire." Cowardly and conventional, they missed out on the opportunity to publish one of the quintessential short stories of twentieth-century America. Success, indeed.

In what may have been his final act at *Cosmopolitan*, Bailey Millard accepted "Just Meat," London's final story before he composed *The Iron Heel*. London completed "Just Meat" on 18 August, and nine days later London received the acceptance.[153] And then Perriton Maxwell took over as editor. No one told London about the change in editors, a lack of communication that carried into November when the exasperated author—pissed off over several related issues, including the exclusivity of his work about the *Snark*; payment for photographs taken during the voyage; and the calculation of word count and payment for "Just Meat"—asked, "First of all, I want to know who *is* the editor of *Cosmopolitan*." Maxwell, diplomatically, cleared up all the matters for him, only to be stymied a week later when an angry London complained about the intrusive copyediting performed on "Just Meat." "I don't like the way you have taken liberties with my copy." Without foreknowledge of what would happen to "Finis," he continued, "No one man in a million, including office-boys, is to be found in the magazine offices, who is able properly to revise by elimination the work of a professional author." The letter is London at his angriest: "Just think of it. Wading into my exposition and cutting out the premises or proofs or anything else just to suit your length of an article, or the space, rather, that you see fit to give such article. Who in the dickens are you, any of you, to think that you can better my work!" He concluded with the warning that he would cease sending them material if they did not agree to leave his manuscripts alone.[154]

Three months later, he wrote to MacKay: if they published *The Iron Heel* he gave his "full permission,—a free fist—in which case, if 'Success' does run THE IRON HEEL, I'll leave the blue-penciling to you, with an earnest plea not to ruin me entirely." The immediate concern was how to deal with the novel's footnotes, which MacKay hoped he could run in the text proper somehow. London agreed to that plan, recognizing that "they would certainly be awkward in the large pages of a magazine." They could be placed in parentheses or in italics, he says, and then leaves it up to MacKay—if he decided to accepted it for serialization (he didn't).[155]

But the real issue is how London viewed editorial interference. On the one hand, he objected to "blue-penciling" when it entailed the willy-nilly excision of text or the nonsensical substitution of one word for another; in the case of "Just Meat," he objected to the copy editor's substitution of "crimp" for "kibosh" in the sentence, "I put the kibosh on his time." A copy editor had also cut portions of the foreword to *The Cruise of the* Snark.[156] But those changes were different from the kind he felt he was allowing in the case of *The Iron Heel*. Further, by March 1907 London instinctively felt no one would serialize *The Iron Heel* and so tried to make it as easy as possible for MacKay to publish it. He understood the needs of magazines, but he could not stomach what seemed to him irrational changes or changes made simply to fit material into limited space.

London wrote "Just Meat" to add another story to the collection *When God Laughs, and Other Stories*, stories of chance and impersonal forces that make a mockery of human action in the Southland. The situation may seem a radical departure from all that London had written so far: two professional burglars rob a private residence of diamonds, and then suspecting each other of duplicity, poison each other and watch the other as both die, "grewsomely," as MacKay might have said. Yet in his notes for the story, London connects it to "The Story of Jees Uck" and uses the description in that story for his description of death by strychnine in this one, blurring, like the story "When God Laughs," the line between Northland and Southland and thus making it in yet another way a suitable piece for *When God Laughs*.[157] It's a theatrical piece, preoccupied with the moment, a dive into present conditions, a break with his concerns for the eternity of the past and of the future. As with nearly all of his theatrical short stories, it provided a relief from the intensity of an absorptive tale like "Finis."

So readily snapped up by *Cosmopolitan* because it was perfectly hewn for a magazine, it carries an important political message: the denizens south of the slot who think they can create economic equality through crime simply mimic the more powerful, more successful white-collar criminals who hide behind trusts and other manifestations of the competitive system. There's a hint of the political when Jim realizes he has been poisoned and he rebels against it: "This was revolution within himself, this was anarchy" (1198). The body politic, says London, is diseased and only its death can bring rebirth. But the hint is clearer when Matt explains capitalism to Jim, "I guess there's just as many thieves among honest men as there is among thieves," without realizing the contradiction he employs nor the fact that the man he had killed to get the jewels had just robbed his own partner. "You read about such things in the papers, Jim. Pardners is always knifin' each other."[158] Unlike the sane London who used his riches to build a morally upstanding, honest house and boat, these two criminals are brought to the edge of insanity by their wealth. "But in [the diamonds, Jim's] swift imagination visioned the joys of life they would buy, and all the desires and appetites of his diseased mind and sickly flesh were tickled by the promise they extended. He built wondrous, orgy-haunted castles out of their brilliant fires, and was appalled at what he builded. Then it was that he giggled. It was all too impossible to be real" (106). In his sly way, London secretly connects this story to his recently completed essay "The House Beautiful" and the foreword to the *Snark*. The diamonds are real, but these two possess a fevered, impoverished imagination, not the imagination of an author. The burglars' illusions are heartbreaking, so London's story tells us. Upon examining the diamonds for the first time, Jim exclaims, "Wake me up! I'm dreamin'! . . . We're rich men Matt—we'll be regular swells" (102). Just as they stole as capitalists steal, they realize that they will kill just as plutocrats "is always knifin' each other." They are wolves, intellectually inferior to Wolf Larsen but equal to his rapaciousness. But they are, as they realize at the end, "just meat" in their own eyes and in the eyes of society. Only a complete reformation of American economics will truly help the poor.

From John Brisben Walker's acceptance of "What Communities Lose by the Competitive System" to Millard and Maxwell's acceptance of "Just Meat," *Cosmopolitan* had been instrumental in providing London with a national platform for his socialism. They would do more. They had already accepted London's offer to publish material from his *Snark* trip, and the acceptance of this story was part of a larger strategy. With the magazine on the (meat) hook for *Snark* articles and then, as a replacement, for the serialization of *The Road*—arrangements that we will get to in the next chapter—Maxwell, Millard, and the other editorial workers at the magazine were laying the groundwork for a relationship with London that would become steadier and steadier until it became exclusive in the final years of London's career. It would be rocky at the beginning, but they were building a trust between author and publisher that would rival that between London and George Brett.

THE FUTURE OF SOCIALISM AND
THE DEATH OF THE INDIVIDUAL

FUTURE STUNTS

The Iron Heel is Jack London's only explicitly socialist novel—if you can call it a novel, a question of genre that we will return to. Unlike any other of his novels before and after, its main characters fight for the socialist cause, and the plot deals with socioeconomic problems that, in the mind of the author, can be resolved only by the Socialist Party. It is surprising that an author—so committed to his political ideals—who professed that socialism was the ground for all good art should write only one such work. As long as he was able to incorporate socialist themes in his fiction, as he did with "Just Meat," he was content not to write more novels that explicitly advocated his political views.

The timing of The Iron Heel's composition is important. In 1899 he first articulated a plan to write a novel based entirely on class warfare; but because he had just returned from the Klondike with a veritable suitcase of story ideas, he wanted to establish himself as a fiction writer before he became known as a socialist fiction writer. Absorption, not theatricality, was his first priority.

One might think that, given the success of the 1904 election and the enthusiasm for the cause that it generated, he would have written a socialist novel in 1904 or 1905. When Joan London was writing her biography of her father, she asked Ernest Untermann, London's friend and fellow socialist, what the impact of the 1905 Russian Revolution was on Jack. He told her that "most of us did not expect much from it. . . . Our sympathies of course were with the Russian masses in 1905, but some of us had little confidence in the Russian revolutionists, because we knew they did not stick together, and that their conspiratory psychology made them suspicious of each other as much as of the czarist agents."[1] Newspaper headlines told American readers the superficial facts of the matter, but for a number of years Americans would be ignorant of the motivations of the revolutionaries and their opposition. Thus, we find just a few clippings on the event in London's files. He contemplated a "Russian Revolution Short Story," but the notes are accompanied by a smattering of unrelated clippings, and he never got beyond a sketchy outline.[2] There is no hint of a tie-in to *The Iron Heel*.

London, of course, was perhaps more familiar than most with events in Russia because Anna Strunsky Walling and William English Walling were there, and Austin Lewis had critiqued her article on the revolution. In line with Untermann's latter-day analysis, London wrote to Anna, "Austin Lewis quarreled with you over your revolutionary article because he doesn't believe much in the immediate success of the Russian Revolution."[3] London doesn't tip his hand here (but I think you can hear his agreement with Lewis) or anywhere else, for that matter. If 1905 did influence London in the writing of *The Iron Heel*, then it was in the way that Philip Foner has surmised: "The brutal suppression of the Russian Revolution of 1905 convinced him that the socialists had to face a fierce and violent struggle by the capitalists to maintain their power."[4] Yet when the historian in *The Iron Heel*, Anthony Meredith, explains what the Black Hundreds were—a group of Russian antisemitic and antirevolutionary ultranationalists—he says "the name [Black Hundreds] only, and not the idea, was imported from Russia."[5] London was not interested in Russian nationalism and identity. He was interested in the specific American conditions of class warfare. Besides, London did not need to read about the failure of 1905 to know that socialists faced the likelihood of violent oppression. "Revolution" speaks to this issue.

One more point: the *Socialist*, a national newspaper, solicited commentary from a wide spectrum of writers, including London, to commemorate the thirty-fifth anniversary of the Paris Commune. Eugene Debs, George Herron, John Spargo, and others contributed, but London declined, pleading overwork.[6] It seems he was just not that committed to the Russian Revolution.

He had something besides a celebratory theme in mind for his one and only socialist novel, something that would have more meaning than a simple shout of praise and support for the Russian revolutionary movement. His socialist novel would even be about more than the cause as it existed in the United States at the time. His socialist essays and book reviews fulfilled that function. His novel would do something different. It is that difference that we have to examine to understand *The Iron Heel*'s unique place in London's long fiction.

London, his sense of time exploded by the meaning and ramifications of evolution, was ready in 1906 to write about the infinite future, now that he had dealt with the infinite past in *Before Adam*. *The Iron Heel* was the first in a series of stories that take place in the future, a series that includes the projected novel "A Farthest Distant" as well as the futuristic short stories written after *The Iron Heel*, in early 1907: "Goliah," "The Dream of Debs," "The Enemy of All the World," "The Unparalleled Invasion," and "A Curious Fragment." Three months after Jack London had completed *The Iron Heel*, he wrote to Robert MacKay: "I am sending you this mail the manuscript of a freak short story of mine entitled 'The Unparalleled Invasion.' Just now I've got the future stunts on the brain."[7] It's an odd turn of phrase, "future stunts," but it indicates how invested he was in projecting his imagination into the future and creating worlds that may or may not be logical outgrowths of the present. This impetus is not wish fulfillment. It is a form of social engineering accomplished through fiction writing. Better, it indicates a new authorial model that London took upon himself that could work in conjunction with the model that replaced the hobo-author: the sailor-author. Now recognized as a preeminent national author, buoyed by the reception he had received on tour, he was encouraged to think of his stature in world literature. As Anthony Meredith writes in his introduction, "We enter into the minds of the actors in that long-ago world-drama" (6). We note the theatrical terms—"actors," "drama"—which will be taken up again later, but the emphasis here falls on "world."

I want to stress how London was reimagining himself as an international author on the eve of his worldwide trip. One of the very first footnotes in the novel attests to his concern to address not just his nation but the world. When Anthony Meredith speaks of the Second Revolt, which Ernest Everhard helped to plan and during which Avis Everhard is executed, he speaks of its "truly international" nature. "It was a colossal plan. . . . Labor, in all the oligarchies of the world, was prepared to rise at the signal." He lists the "socialist states" that helped the revolutionaries. "It was for this reason, when the Second Revolt was crushed, that they, too, were crushed by the united oligarchies of the world" (10). Later in the book, in the chapters "The General Strike" and "The Beginning of the End," London uses the international situation to show how a worldwide united labor force can prevent a war and a fragmented worldwide labor force can allow the oligarchies to succeed. To fulfill his goal of speaking to the world, he chose the role of prophet. But he would write, not prophecy, but a jeremiad. Like W. J. Ghent's *Our Benevolent Feudalism, The Iron Heel* is an economic jeremiad, a warning to capitalists that their control will end and to socialists that an easy victory is not possible. Leon Trotsky called the novel prophecy, but he sensed how it really worked as a jeremiad when he wrote, "London is an optimist, only a penetrating and farsighted one. 'Look at what kind of abyss the bourgeoisie will hurl you down, if you don't finish with them.' This is his thought."[8] Two years after the 1904 election, he was more conscious than ever of the immensity of the future and of the power of those in control. London saw the inevitability of multiple bloody revolts that would ultimately result in the success of the Brotherhood of Man.

In one of those odd moments generated by his fame, London received a letter from a woman unknown to him in the summer of 1906 that struck a note of patience, of waiting for the ideal state to form itself; revolution would only generate bloodshed and more severe oppression. Clara F. McIntyre wrote, "I think that the socialistic ideal of a state where each man has enough for his wants and comforts . . . is very beautiful, but it is the practical side which troubles me. Would this not require ideal men to do their part? Is it not, after all, an ideal, toward which we must work, for centuries perhaps, pulling up a little here, and a little there, all along the line, till we begin to approach it?"[9] Her view of the future is his view, her sense of futurity is his, and London's viewpoint was always practical, but his practicality entailed gunpowder: "Please reread my *Iron Heel*," he told the critic Philo Buck in 1913, "and among many other things note how my hero, in reply to announcements of all socialist political successes, invariably inquired the price of gunpowder."[10] Two months earlier, in an interview with Emanuel Julius (later Emanuel Haldeman-Julius), he advocated for both political and for direct action. "I believe there is much to be gained by entering political campaigns" because the working class can then be educated through defeat and come to understand "the wrongs of the present system and the meaning of class consciousness." Given that view, Julius asked him if he supported syndicalists and sabotage. "Hopelessly so. I have believed in them for twenty years," and that mention of a long time span coupled with the adverb "hopelessly" shows he was not sure how violence could achieve its end but that he was still committed to it. The capitalists would never be simply voted out of office. "The capitalists own the governments, the armies and the militia." Education and violence were the twin tactics he favored. "There is a mighty ruling class that intends to hold fast to its possessions. I see years and years of bloodshed. I see the master class hiring armies of murderers to keep the workers in subjection, to beat them back should they attempt to dispossess the capitalists."[11] One year after the date he had set in *The Iron Heel* for the Peasant Revolt and Chicago Commune, he must have felt vindicated, though unhappy with the silence or resignation that had apparently greeted his jeremiad.

THE SOCIALIST JEREMIAD

The form of the novel is one of its most interesting features. It is the perfect vehicle to help express London's sense of futurity. It is, in and of itself, a futuristic construction. We know that *The Iron Heel* is London's clearest statement of the Shavian aesthetic principal that all art comes from socialism, even if it is so deeply personal that it is also a self-reflective narrative about author figures creating stories. But its form is nearly impossible to classify, and, throwing our hands in the air, we classify it as a novel only because that form is so capacious.

To construe this mystery in a positive light, however, is not so difficult. London's sense of his form's indeterminacy is a reflection of his own inability to answer the central question of his authorial identity: Why do I write? When he was in need of a shorthand answer, he said he did it for the money. Obviously, one does not write a socialist novel for money, especially after years of explaining to fellow socialists that writing was a form of donation, of self-denial, for the cause. Haunted by forces he could not understand, he felt freed from conventions of genre and even the concept itself. There is no such thing as a genre or, rather, like a ghost, it exists and yet doesn't exist. London could make up his own genre, creating a hybrid from the parts of narrative form that appealed to him. Like Jeff Wall and his hybridization of photography, history, and painting, he was dissolving the concept of genre. A novel could be a play could be a history could be a jeremiad.

One would be excused for thinking that it is of the prophetic mode, but London himself denied it. "I *didn't* write the thing as a prophecy at all. I really don't think these things are going to happen in the United States. I believe the increasing socialist vote will prevent—hope for it anyway."[12] He took this stance for two reasons. One, it was a way to counter expected criticism from more conservative socialists like John Spargo and others who read *The Iron Heel* "as a lapse into the scientifically outmoded theory of 'cataclysmic' social transformation."[13] Two, he didn't want to fall into the category of those who, like Ghent, had prophesized the triumph of the oligarchies and ways that they would always defeat the socialists. We will return to Spargo's and Ghent's influence on the writing of *The Iron Heel*, but here we need only cite the one time Ghent is mentioned in the book: "It has always been insisted that Ghent put the idea of the Oligarchy into the minds of the great capitalists. . . . To-day we know better, but our knowledge does not overcome the fact that Ghent remains the most abused innocent man in all history" (219). It is a startling but obviously exaggerated characterization, most likely constructed out of fear of becoming the second "most abused innocent man in all history."

Instead of prophecy, he deployed the jeremiad. In the same conversation reported by Charmian, he told her, "But I will say that I sent out, in 'The Iron Heel,' a warning of what I think *might* happen if they don't look to their votes."[14] I use the term *jeremiad* in the classic literary sense. Like the election-day sermons of the Puritan clergy in New England, *The Iron Heel* combines a secular and religious history both to warn London's contemporaries of the consequences of allowing capitalism its ascendency and to confirm the socialists' belief in the righteousness and inevitable victory of the cause. It fits in Sacvan Bercovitch's genealogy of the American jeremiad as a "latter-day jeremiad." As one of the "left-wing polemics proving that capitalism was a betrayal of the country's sacred origins," *The Iron Heel* takes its place in a line of texts from John Winthrop's *A Model of Christian Charity* to Thoreau, Whitman, and Martin Luther King's works.[15] The American jeremiad asked, When will our utopia be realized? London, in his attempt to provide hope to his fellow revolutionists, gives them an answer they do not want to hear: The Brotherhood of Man will come, but not for another seven hundred years.

The form of the novel is interesting in two other ways. First, it allows him to place his interest in the future at the forefront; this is the function of the introduction, which sets the tone for the entire novel and of the footnotes. Second, it allows him to create what people were calling a human document. That is, he wanted to come as close as possible to writing a documentary of his time, a documentary that someone—a twenty-first-century biographer, perhaps—would discover in the same fashion that someone had discovered Avis's document. Of course, they are one and the same, but this conflation of authorship, manuscript, and time is nothing new to

London. He had simply found the best possible form to express that conflation. He would retreat from this experiment in form in his next works, returning to more traditional nineteenth-century novelistic form until 1913. With *The Star Rover*, he again tried an experiment.

Futurity did not equal jeremiad alone. It did not simply represent a time zone in which to displace one's political ambitions for the day. It also represented a time of inevitability. London used the future as a teleological construct. True, in "What Life Means to Me" he wrote, "My faith is in the working class. As some Frenchman has said, 'The stairway of time is ever echoing with the wooden shoe going up, the polished boot descending.'" But I think it would be a mistake to take this as a statement of endless repetition. If it were, he would never have prefaced that remark about "the stairway of time" with a faith in the proletariat. In the future, the boot would no longer crush the shoe.

The form may be experimental, but the content of the novel is nothing new. It is simply an exposition and sometimes a re-presentation of previously written essays. This is not meant to be a criticism of the novel. Rather, the incorporation of "The Question of the Maximum" and "Revolution"—two essays he explicitly reminded himself about in his notes for *The Iron Heel*—shows how he conceived of the novel as a kind of scrapbook to illustrate all his previous theoretical writings in sociology. At one point he thought it best to create not an experimental novel but a conventional "series of half-dozen short articles, not strongly socialistic at all, but condemnatory of present industrial society." The topics make this note sound like an outline for *The Iron Heel*: "The Twentieth Century machine-breakers—the men who oppose the trust in all its forms. CHILD LABOR. WOMAN LABOR. The Morality of Capitalism. The dear little moralities. The Persistence of the Established. Rapid resume of surplus value (QUESTION OF THE MAXIMUM). Why the struggle between labor and capital is irreconcilable. If labor be given higher standard of living, the only result will be that labor will want a still higher standard of living."[16] Each of these topic headings could be considered chapter titles, as the very first one is. I have discussed "Persistence of the Established," but we will see how London borrowed from its documentary background to write *The Iron Heel*.

An undated note to himself that pertains directly to *The Iron Heel* is a reminder both to stick to his experimentalist guns and to create enough of a recognizable novelistic form to keep his audience enthralled: "What scenes are *given*, let them be striking, to make up for absence of regular novel features—

> make striking:
> The Bishop's break
> Congress
> Chicago Commune
> etc. etc."

These traditional novelistic scenes would be interwoven with theatrical scenes—scenes that emphasize dialogue, disputation, and monologue. As London wrote *The Iron Heel*, he was also correcting page proof for the book publication of his play *The Scorn of Women*. Two months previous to the beginning date of *The Iron Heel*—19 August 1906—he had completed his second play, *A Wicked Woman*. Scene, dialogue, and character were not only very much on his mind, but so were ways to improve his theatrical skills and to experiment with them.[17] Thus, in *The Iron Heel* London uses theater to convey a jeremiad. The theatrical mode is more effective than the absorptive to articulate a message to an audience, of course, but it is also the most direct and efficient way to create emotion in an audience. It courts melodrama, the genre he praised in calling *The Jungle* an equivalent to *Uncle Tom's Cabin*. At the same time it can employ the facticity of realism. We might call this combination of emotionalism and realism *autodrama*, an appellation I will explore later once we add in London's Nietzschean impulse for autobiography.

To return to the theatrical mode: This is theater in the round with a split stage. On one half of the stage, actors play the heroic socialist leader, his lover, her father, a bishop, laborers, oligarchs, and others. Half of the audience sees this drama of the present day. The other half of the audience is addressed by a single actor, who plays a historian from the future. The action in the first half is broken from time to time by pauses, which are then filled by the commentary, in the form of textual footnotes, by the historian Anthony Meredith. As Leon Trotsky pointed out, "The form of the novel here represents only an armor for social analysis and prognosis."[18] Although Trotsky doesn't call it theater, he is recognizing its theatrical form. He understood how, like all of London's theatrical writings, it appeals directly to the audience.

As with another theatrical production, *The People of the Abyss*, the Fireside Poets provide a kind of spiritual foundation for *The Iron Heel*. One Fireside Poet is mentioned in London's notes: James Russell Lowell and his poem "A Glance behind the Curtain." Actually, he quotes the poem from memory and then charges himself to verify the quotation. "The times are rotten ripe for change. Then let it come." Close enough. He must also have been thinking of the lines that follow:

> He who would win the name of truly great
> Must understand his own age and the next,
> And make the present ready to fulfil
> Its prophecy, and with the future merge
> Gently and peacefully, as wave with wave. . . .
> Let us speak plain: . . .
> Let us call tyrants "tyrants," and maintain
> That only freedom comes by grace of God,

London, of course, is no Christian Socialist, but he is unafraid to find his truths in the works of disparate thinkers. Thus, Meredith speaks of capitalism as "the ripened fruit of the bourgeois revolution" that all expected to "decay" and bring forth socialism. Instead, "capitalism, rotten-ripe, sent forth that monstrous offshoot, the Oligarchy." God may not have instructed London to call a tyrant a tyrant, but historical materialism does.

A different poet, Tennyson, provides the novel's epigraph. This one is not about truth telling, but it is very much about futurity and theater, and the poetic expression of that combination encapsulates the novel as a whole:

> At first, this Earth, a stage so gloomed with woe
> You almost sicken at the shifting of the scenes.
> And yet be patient. Our Playwright may show
> In some fifth act what this Wild Drama means.

The epigraph speaks to futurity. It speaks to stagecraft. Typically, it is read in terms of the former, but London gives the latter equal emphasis. The events of 1912 to 1932 are the "shifting scenes" of "woe." The time of Anthony Meredith is the "fifth Act." The final result of the play will be revealed by God, the playwright. But if London is the playwright, the "shifting scenes" are the present and the "fifth Act" is the destruction of capitalism. The novel is a jeremiad is a play. *The Iron Heel* is consciously theatrical, a historical word-painting. The very first line of the introduction makes this clear as Meredith passes critical judgment upon the worth of Avis Everhard's manuscript: "It cannot be said that the Everhard Manuscript is an important historical document." But his judgment takes nothing away from the fact that this is a historical document and that its proper mode of writing is theatrical.

THE COLERIDGEAN WELL

Avis Everhard has written a kind of play based on fact. She has dramatized fact. Anthony Meredith has written a partial history based on a play based on fact. In London's notes for the novel, Meredith is always referred to as "the historian." In writing that history, he has "factualized" drama. He has the hindsight that provides truthful corrective when Avis has over-dramatized. At the same time, his footnotes lend credence and thus authority to Avis's record. London conveys that truth through the footnotes, and they have absorbed much of the attention of readers and scholars. It is traditional in the critical reception of this history/play to identify and elaborate upon the facts, the sources. Following John Livingston Lowes's identification and elaboration of Samuel Taylor Coleridge's sources for "Kubla Khan" and "The Rime of the Ancient Mariner," we might call this intellectual pursuit the road to Ardis.[19] In London's voracious reading, like Coleridge's, we find the first visible traces of the workings of his imagination for *The Iron Heel*. Most of the sources will be familiar, for the vast majority of them have already been identified by scholars. Often, he mentions his sources in either his notes for the novel or in the novel itself.

There are two general categories of sources, though they sometimes overlap: those that he used for particulars, and those that provided either reinforcement for, or a reminder of, ideas and concepts that would appear in the novel, sometimes under contestation. We'll deal with the latter category first. These are, more often than not, books and articles that had deeply influenced him from an earlier time or that he had reread or read for the first time immediately before and during the composition of the novel, books that confirmed that he was on the right intellectual path, whether he followed a particular author's path or not.

But first we should remind ourselves that a foundational text for *The Iron Heel*, as well as for all his socialist writings, was Laurence Gronlund's *The Co-operative Commonwealth*. By foundational I mean that Gronlund's work, the *Communist Manifesto*, and an 1897 ten-page booklet featuring a translation of a part of *Capital* were three of the very first texts that London read on socialism.[20] They informed, silently and reflexively, all his political writings. Gronlund seeks to differentiate socialism from communism, an important distinction for someone like London who was new to political philosophy and had just read Marx and Engels for the first time. Gronlund's definition of socialism as an antagonist of sorts to communism appears in London's 1895 essay "What Socialism Is," and I have italicized the words that London himself underlined:

> It is evident that this New Order—where every worker will be remu-nerated according to *results*—is in no sense *communistic*. Socialism and Communism are, in fact, two radically different systems, and yet they are confounded, even by well-informed people. . . . A form of Communism is practiced by the Shakers and similar religious bodies. We believe that to retire from the world, as they do, is a poor way of reforming the world. We believe that reformers are like yeast, which must be mixed with the dough to act upon it: if kept to itself, it spoils. Their principles:—in which they agree with political communists— are diametrically opposed to ours. Communists make all property common, while our Commonwealth will *place only* the *instruments of production*—land, machinery, raw materials, etc.—under col-lective control. They require every one to do his share of labour, and allow him to consume as he needs. Our Commonwealth leaves everybody at perfect liberty *to work as much or as little as he please*, or not at all, but makes his consumption exactly commensurate with his performances. Adam Smith observed that "the produce of labour is the natural recompense of Labour"; and St. Paul declared that "if a man will not work, neither shall he eat." The New System—as our definition points out—will put these doctrines into practice.
>
> In short, the motto of Socialism is "To everybody according to his *deeds*": that of Communism, "To everybody according *to his needs*." The communist motto is undoubtedly more generous than ours, but

our motto is more just, taking human nature as it is—and the fact that Socialists take human nature as it is, is just their merit.[21]

Here we find some of London's fundamental commitments in the realm of political philosophy. In "What Socialism Is," he quotes Gronlund's "motto" for socialism, he follows Gronlund's disparagement of reform and reformers, he concurs with Gronlund's practicality, and he shares Gronlund's distaste for utopias and utopians. Gronlund was one of the first to expose to London Marx's four historical stages of human society: slavery, feudalism, capitalism, and socialism.[22] It's possible that Ernest Everhard's speech on surplus value and foreign markets owes quite a bit to Gronlund's first chapter on value or, rather, that London is drawing on "The Question of the Maximum" from 1899, which in turn relies on Gronlund.[23] What London is calling surplus value Gronlund calls overproduction.

London also read in Gronlund, probably for the first time, the idea that socialism was social evolution. A passage from "What Socialism Is" underlies the thinking behind *The Iron Heel*: "Socialism . . . is a vision of the future, while its agents are actively working in the present. It is a product of social evolution. . . . Whether this generation will see it is uncertain."[24] Gronlund's work may have in fact prompted London to write his novel of multiple revolts, repressions, and the ultimate triumph of the proletariat. In the final chapter of *The Co-operative Commonwealth*, Gronlund wrote, "Most Americans remember the rising of the workingmen in July 1877. That rising was to all Socialists a most promising sign. It was the first revolt of American white slaves against their task-masters. . . . Before long we shall have another series of years of hard time. . . . We may expect another revolt then, more serious than the first. It most likely will also be suppressed with comparative ease. A few years will elapse; the inevitable crisis will recur; and another most serious revolt will follow. Possibly powder and shot will suppress that too. But in the fullness of time we shall have a labour revolt that will not be put down."[25] Gronlund owed his largest intellectual debt to Marx, though Marx's name does not appear in *The Co-operative Commonwealth*. Because of the paucity in nineteenth-century America of published works on socialism, and especially ones that addressed American conditions, Gronlund's book and Bellamy's *Looking Backward* "were the most significant American socialist treatises of the late nineteenth century," though we have to add that booklet containing pages of *Capital*.[26] Hence the success of Charles Kerr and his publishing house.

London's work walks a fine line between socialism as revolution and socialism as evolution. He wanted it to be both: revolutionary action was evolutionarily necessary. But like many of those he read in preparation for writing *The Iron Heel*, he was not a social architect. London was not interested in outlining the specifics of a socialist society. That was not his job. It was enough to advocate for radical change. Evolutionary socialism requires social architects. But social architects such as St. Simon and Fourier—the French school of socialism as opposed to the German school—are utopians. Besides, social evolution was too passive and seemed to contradict the value Gronlund placed on deeds. Furthermore, London and Gronlund differed on one essential point; the latter rejected the idea that socialism was a class-based movement; the proletariat should not be given a privileged status. No wonder, then, that Gronlund eventually turned to Christian Socialism. Although his book was influential, it appears neither in *The Iron Heel* nor in the notes for the novel.

Most likely, the first book that London read as direct preparation for writing *The Iron Heel* was H. G. Wells's *Mankind in the Making*. Charmian kept track of their reading in her diary, and on 19 July, a full month ahead of the day he began to write notes for the novel, she mentions Wells's book.[27] From it, London drew at least the confidence that he was not alone in predicting the inevitable change from capitalism to socialism; Wells wrote, "The general aspect of all our social and co-operative undertakings, is to prepare as well as we possibly can a succeeding generation, which shall prepare still more capably for still better generations to follow. We are passing as a race out of a state of affairs when the unconscious building of the future was attained by individualistic self-seeking . . . into a clear consciousness of our co-operative share in that process."[28] Both Wells and London did not share in the Victorian belief in organic inevitable political change, as did, say, Charles Dickens. They believed that the lower classes had to fight for the dissolution of the monarchy, for economic equality. And Wells writes that if the electoral process in both England and America is not changed, those countries will "see a government *de facto* of rich business organizers override the government *de jure*, or to relapse upon a practical oligarchy of officials" (257–58). Wells imagined this oligarchy becoming inefficient in a number of years, but London, who had first used the term *oligarchy* in 1899 in "The Question of the Maximum," imagined the oligarchy as ruthlessly efficient. However, they both believed the fight against the oligarchy would yield a future of inevitable political and scientific progress. Socialism could not lose.

Mankind in the Making and Wells's earlier work *Anticipations* make their appearance in chapter 17 of *The Iron Heel*. When Ernest, now a congressman, debates a socialist-sponsored bill for the unemployed and the starving masses, Avis writes that "we called these wretched people the people of the abyss" (180). It is a clear-enough statement, a picture-perfect phrase. But there's a footnote, seemingly gratuitous, that simply touts Wells's "genius." He "was a sociological seer, sane and normal as well as warm human." Earlier in the year, London had used the phrase "warm human" in "When God Laughs" to describe Ethel Baird and Marvin Fiske, the lovers whose "blood" "glowed" "sunset red." He also described Ernest Everhard, the waver of the red flag of revolution and just as mad with love, as "warm and human" in his notes. In the novel, not Ernest, but the people of the abyss are "the Holy Grail, Christ's own Grail, the warm human, long-suffering and maltreated but to be rescued and saved at the last" (61). When Wells uses "people of the Abyss" in *Mankind in the Making*, Charmian marked it in the margins (103). All this notation is partly meant to cement the connections between London's own *The People of the Abyss* and *The Iron Heel*. Wells would have been entirely sympathetic to London's treatment of the monarchy and the coronation in *The People of the Abyss* because his new republicanism, a sort of liberal socialism, was vehemently antimonarchy. That is, Wells and London agreed on the foundational aspect of class difference and the need for its abolition; whether Wells agreed with London's notions of class warfare is another matter. London's solution to the seeming endlessness of dire poverty in urban centers was to bulldoze the cities and replace them, perhaps with Wells's "pleasure-cities," which Meredith brings up in his footnote. It's as if London intended *The Iron Heel* to be a projection of what would happen if a socialist society had decided to fulfill his plan for an entire societal makeover. Wells and London may not have agreed on this plan and on the long evolution of its accomplishment, but they did agree on a different foundational principal enunciated by Wells: "The United States theory of the essential equality of all men is equally not in accordance with the reality of life," as is the British system of class distinction (240–41).

After Wells's *Mankind in the Making*, the next sociopolitical book Charmian cites in her diary is Ernest Untermann's *Science and Evolution*. It is a brief history of philosophy constructed to show the superiority—that is, the pure antimetaphysical nature—of Marxist materialism. Untermann's starting point is "proletarian science," a concept, I believe, that he originated and that became something quite different when the Soviet agronomist and biologist Trofim Denisovich Lysenko and his proponents in the cold-war battle against "classical" genetics usurped it. For Untermann, the concept meant "historical materialism," a materialistic conception of both science and history that began with two premises: that the human must be conceived as a bodily entity and that any discussion of soul or mind must begin with the brain. "And if I use the terms mind and soul occasionally I refer to them simply as brain activities, identical so far as our discussion is concerned with any other brain activity connected with thought."[29] In a passage marked by London, Untermann writes that they are like unknown quantities in an algebraic formula and that sometimes x and y equal zero (14). But the key to Untermann's analysis is the presumption that a member of the proletariat who is interested in science will take concepts like the unknown, the mind, and the soul as ideological constructs. "Materialism is the handmaid of revolution, and without it no proletarian movement complies with the historical requirements of its evolution" (26). Mysticism is the enemy of the revolution. Further, when London writes Fannie Hamilton just before starting the novel that he is "a materialistic monist," he is following or paralleling Untermann.[30] For that matter, he echoes Marx: "It is a fact, which explains itself out of the historical conditions of proletarian evolution, that the scientific socialists are the only consistent monist materialists of the present day" (55). In two more passages that London marked, Untermann derived from one of his heroes, Francis Bacon, that "all human understanding arises from the world of sensations" and placed John Locke as Bacon's successor. In W. J. Ghent's *Mass and Class*, which we will turn to in full later, London read that "historic materialism is concerned with the play of causes and effects among social phenomena, but it does not touch the question of the primary cause of the cosmic process."[31] Nothing comes from the realm of the Unknown. Meredith, whose first task is to place Avis's portrayal of her husband in the correct historical perspective, notes that perhaps Everhard's longest-lasting contribution was "his elaboration and interpretation of working-class philosophy. 'Proletarian science' and 'proletarian philosophy' were his phrases for it" (5). These labels point to what historians of science now regard as the ideological construction of scientific paradigms. Untermann's definition of the terms is not only very modern but transparent about his own ideology: "Proletarian science is the Declaration of Independence of the proletarian mind from the control of the capitalist mind. And since the proletariat is historically the most revolutionary class in society, and the future man in embryo, proletarian science is the most revolutionary science and the embryo of the future world philosophy" (8).

We have been tracking a significant change in London's thinking about the relation between biology and class. That is, he was incorporating more and more the importance of environment on class formation. In reading Untermann, he furthered his education in this direction, and if *The Iron Heel* stands as a kind of reformation of his thinking on this relation, then we see another reason why he wrote this book at this particular time. In part, the book signals his goodbyes to the Socialist Party as he gets ready to voyage around the world; partly he is indicating the length of time it would take for the proletariat revolution to succeed; but partly he is working out this new development in his thought. He needed to write *The Iron Heel* to update his own socialist work, and Untermann was a principal influence. London's readers would immediately have linked Ernest Everhard with Ernest Untermann. London himself once asserted that Everhard was loosely modeled on himself, Untermann, and Eugene Debs.[32] In London's notes, as he developed Everhard's character, he wrote, "Had educated himself in German and French—at that time was making a meager living by translating for struggling socialist pub house in Chicago, and from small sales of his own works—philosophical works from standpoint of working class a la Untermann."[33] Untermann was a native German speaker and published with Charles H. Kerr in Chicago. This is the extent of Untermann's life history infusing Everhard's character.

Untermann wasn't quite the Noam Chomsky of his age, but he might be considered a prototype. He was more original than other socialist thinkers like John Spargo.[34] He "was the most ambitious American theorist yet to address the question of evolution, and his writings reflected both his scholarly ability and his political centrism."[35] Born and raised in Germany, he was a Socialist Party centrist. Like A. M. Simons's work, for whose *International Socialist Review* he wrote numerous book reviews and serialized his influential *Science and Revolution*, Untermann's work was rejected by the next generation of socialists. Simons had turned against the cause, but Untermann's work was considered reductive because it subsumed all intellectual endeavor under economic (and behind that natural historical) considerations. Thus he dismissed Aristotle, Socrates, and Plato for being in the service of the Greek master class who kept slaves. According to Untermann, the first proletarian revolution was led by Jesus and supported by working-class Jews. The later theorists who dismissed Untermann and Simons instead worked in more discipline specific ways and "studied social science and philosophy on those disciplines' own terms."[36] A grand unifier of knowledge like Herbert Spencer, a major influence on Untermann, had become suspect.

London missed meeting Untermann in Chicago in February 1906, either at a dinner at Hull House or when the Londons visited the office of the *International Socialist Review* with Simons, though those were likely hangouts for Untermann a little later in life.[37] In 1906, though, he was most likely on his chicken farm in Orlando, Florida, scratching out a living as a translator of Marx's *Capital*. But eventually they did meet, and, beginning in 1910, Untermann lived for several years on the Londons' ranch while he translated *Before Adam* and "An Odyssey of the North" into German; at the same time they "straighten[ed] out their mutual ideas on Socialist theory and practice."[38] In 1906, when London finished reading *Science and Evolution*, London wrote to him to praise the book, and thus their friendship, which ended only with Jack's death, began.[39] Untermann could be difficult and got into spats not only with London (over an essay contest) but also with Eugene Debs and others. However, he was incredibly productive in writings and translations. Untermann had even spent a considerable amount of time as a deep-water sailor, being shipwrecked thrice in the Pacific and the North Sea.[40] But London and Untermann had their differences in degree, and London, unlike Untermann, was more tolerant of a field like psychology; Untermann believed in "the difference between conscious and unconscious, or subconscious, though it is purely one of the intensity of stimuli and reaction" (152). That was the close of the matter for Untermann, but London found the unconscious to be both material and mysterious and explored it enthusiastically. He was unwilling to assign it to a material condition and leave it at that.

Spencer was a heavy influence on both London and Untermann, but in different ways. Both embraced Spencer's evolutionary science and his materialism—centered on concepts of persistence, force, and matter. (Spencer, pigheadedly, never would exchange his term *persistence* for the standard scientific term, even in his own day, of *conservation*.) But London struggled with Spencer's metaphysics, despite his disavowal of that philosophical path; Untermann simply ignored it. London reread parts of *First Principles* on and off in the summer and fall of 1906, picking it up next after he had finished with *Science and Evolution*. He read aloud to Charmian for several days straight while making notes for *The Iron Heel*; she listened one day while "sewing on underclothes," happy after morning sex.[41] The previous month Fannie K. Hamilton, who had interviewed him three years earlier and had become friendly with the Londons, had informed him that she had been rereading Spencer. "Though I am not classed as a follower of his," he instructed her, "his thinking has profoundly affected my life." He then labels himself, with an appellation we have already heard: "Technically, I am a materialistic monist," a follower of sorts of Ernest Untermann. "The idealists and all the rest of the metaphysicians have vainly struggled to win me," a battle that finds expression in the first chapter of *The Iron Heel*. They failed with London (and with Everhard) in part because of his politics; Spencer was adamantly opposed to socialism, an antagonism that Meredith notes in his introduction; London certainly read—though it is impossible to say when—a five-page prospectus for the *International Socialist Review* published in the back of Untermann's translation of Wilhelm Liebknecht's *Karl Marx: Biographical Memoirs*, which begins, "Even Herbert Spencer, its greatest opponent, was forced to admit in his last volume that 'Socialism is inevitable.'"[42] John Spargo, in *Socialism*, which London read in 1906, also made great use of Spencer's confession.[43] Interestingly, Fannie Hamilton had also questioned London's political commitments, as if his general approbation of Spencer had compromised his politics. London emphasized that he "was the same revolutionary socialist. I have not clipped nor moderated my utterance. And I am more irritated than ever by the smug and brutal bourgeoisie," an irritation that accounts for the vehement declarations made by Everhard. But Everhard, like London, picked and chose from *First Principles*. To be "profoundly affected" meant London used Spencer's worldview as a starting point for the development of his own thoughts on biology, politics, and other fields of inquiry.

Back in 1899, London had chastised Cloudesley Johns for being "rabid" and "narrow," for failing to recognize that "the infidel that positively asserts that there is no God, no first cause, is just as imbecile a creature as the deist that asserts positively that there is a God, a first cause."[44] This is the common-sense philosophy of Herbert Spencer straight from *First Principles*.[45] The first step in his "general Theory of Things" was to assert "that in opinions seeming to be absolutely and supremely wrong something right is yet to be found." Following this, we have the method to reconcile religion and science: "Compare all opinions of the same genus; to set aside as more or less discrediting one another those various special and concrete elements in which such opinions disagree; to observe what remains after the discordant constituents have been eliminated; and to find for this remaining constituent that abstract expression which holds true throughout its divergent modifications."[46] That is, a philosopher should disregard all the particular manifestations of each religion and disregard all the various ways scientists have come to understand the physical universe in order to see what abstract notion lies at the very foundation of each discipline. That notion is mystery or force. Both religion and science start from exactly the same point: that which cannot be known. By ignoring the scientific method (at least initially) and by ignoring a belief in the revealed word of God and the literal nature of the Bible, Spencer can call that which religionists and scientists both acknowledged as unknown as the Unknowable. If so many people throughout history have faith in something unseen, then what is important is not the faith and its expression but the very fact that there is faith and that it had been maintained by diverse peoples throughout the ages. This common-sense viewpoint proves the equality of religion with science. "Religion, every where present as a weft running through the warp of human history, expresses some eternal fact; while it is almost a truism to say of Science that it is an organized mass of facts, ever growing, and ever being more completely purified from errors. And if both have bases in the reality of things, then between them there must be fundamental harmony." There cannot be, according to this common-sense view, "two orders of truth, in absolute and everlasting opposition." This would be Manicheanism, which, on the mere face of it, must be rejected. No, there is a whole that is truth, a perfect sphere one might say, and "Science and Religion express opposite sides of the same fact—the one its near or visible side, and the other its remote or invisible side."[47] Thus they are not "symbiotic," but rather familial.[48]

Having thus proved Johns's blindness to the holistic conception of truth, London then affirmed the apparently unconscious duality of Spencer's *First Principles*. "Have you ever read Herbert Spencer's *First Principles* of synthetic philosophy," he asked in the next sentence, "and noted the line, the adamantine line of demarcation he draws between the knowable and the unknowable." Spencer himself did not draw such a line at the most abstract level of philosophical thought. When he considers "what is it that we know"—when we get into the particulars of what science can teach us—then we see how religion and science are irreconcilable. But Spencer does not admit to this. He begins the second section of *First Principles* by talking about, not the Knowable but rather "the manifestations of the Unknowable." He naturally has to state the near tautology that "we have abandoned as futile the attempt to learn anything respecting the nature of that Power," that is, the Unknowable.[49] Philosophy—a key word in Everhard's first debate—concerns itself with the relationships among the various sciences, not with metaphysics. At the same time, defining and employing philosophy means effectively turning one's back on the Unknowable. Yes, all the data of science come from an ultimate power. But in ignoring any attempt to define that power means there is a sharp division between the work of religion and the work of philosophy and science. Though Spencer does not make this point, London makes it for him. Reconciliation is temporary, and when Spencer brackets the Unknowable, London seizes on that intellectual move and then asserts the primacy of the Knowable.

Everyone had read Spencer, and many found him to be more of a metaphysician than a materialist. As his newest biographer puts it, "To most of his readers, and to himself, his endeavours were always pregnant with spiritual vitality. Spencer's worship of the 'Unknown' provided solace to those who feared that the universe was only a collection of lifeless material objects and physical laws."[50] One of the most common attacks on him and his metaphysics was the statement, "There is no god but the Unknowable, and Herbert Spencer is his prophet." It is quoted in *Martin Eden* by "a sneering socialist" and paraphrased in *The Iron Heel* by one of Avis Everhard's father's friends in the first chapter. Dr. Ballingford, probably sneeringly as well, says about Ernest, "There is no God but Fact, and Mr. Everhard is its prophet" (18). Spencer was an intuitionist, not a British empiricist. An adherent of the philosophy of William Hamilton—whose law of parsimony is cited by Darrell Standing in *The Star Rover*—Spencer attributed his reconciliation of religion and science to the previous work of Hamilton. The intuitionists and those who followed them applauded the metaphysical nature of *First Principles*, but London and other empiricists—like Ernest

Everhard—focused instead on what was a philosophical difficulty for Spencer: "He wished his metaphysics to remain unchanged while he gained support for his data-laden views on science."[51] Even if there were a holistic notion of truth, London realized that Spencer had drawn an "adamantine line" between the two halves. If Everhard is a Spencerian—like Martin Eden—he is one because he uses one half of Spencer to attack the other.

In the next decade, London would discover William James and *The Varieties of Religious Experience*, which would ground his metaphysical tendencies in the personal experience of those who substantiated James's claim that "although all the special manifestations of religion may have been absurd (I mean its creeds and theories), yet the life of it as a whole is mankind's most important function." Though the first clause is very Spencerian, the second clause is a refutation of Spencer's intuitionism in favor of James's pragmatism; his task was "to defend 'experience' against 'philosophy' as being the real backbone of the world's religious life."[52] Science takes a back seat when religious experience is favored. "In my belief," asserts James, "that a large acquaintance with particulars often makes us wiser than the possession of abstract formulas, however deep, I have loaded the lectures with concrete examples."[53] This is what the "prophet" Everhard and his creator stood for when discussing the Unknowable. One cannot let it stand on its own. The interior life of the spiritualist must be examined, and London would find that dynamic psychology in conjunction with art—fiction writing and cinema—was the best method for that examination. For London, but not for London's understanding of Spencer (if not for Spencer himself), the Knowable and the Unknowable were indeed symbiotic.

But we are getting ahead of ourselves. Everhard cites Spencer in the first chapter as the authority for inductive philosophy: "As Spencer says, the data of any particular science are partially unified knowledge. Philosophy unifies the knowledge that is contributed by all the sciences," though Spencer would have included religion, not just the sciences, in that statement (16). When London read Spencer he focused on his materialism, though he quickly grasped the significance of August Weismann's work in undermining Spencer's neo-Lamarckian biology. London once told Johns, in one of his rare, beautifully written epistolary lines—he was usually too rushed to write well in his letters—"To be well fitted for the tragedy of existence (intellectual existence), one must have a working philosophy, a synthesis of things." When London told beginning writers that they must have a philosophy of life, he was offering advice that he himself adhered to. Here London is blending two phrases from Spencer, *a system of synthetic philosophy*, which was his meta-title for all his volumes on first principles, biology, psychology, sociology, and morality, and a "general Theory of Things," his name for his unified theory. In his letter to Johns he paraphrases the table of contents of *First Principles*: "Do you write, and talk, and build upon a foundation which you know is securely laid? . . . In token of this: What significance do the following generalities have for you:—Matter is indestructible; motion is continuous; Force is persistent; the relations among forces are persistent; the transformation of forces is the equivalence of forces; etc. etc.?"[54] But these are some of the chapter headings for only the second half of *First Principles*. Like Everhard, London ignored the smaller first section called "The Unknowable." Even though the general reader of Spencer found his metaphysics reassuring, London read against the grain, and in perfect sympathy with Spencer as scientist, and ignored the Unknowable in favor of the Knowable.

It is difficult to tell if London is still referring to Spencer when he tells Fannie Hamilton that the "idealists" and "metaphysicians" were his opponents. Even though in 1899 and 1900 he thought of Spencer as an evolutionist and explicator of natural forces, at the same time, he wrote futuristic, dreamworld, metaphysically inclined short stories that seemed to be instigated by Spencer; he seems to have been engaged in a kind of antagonistic reading, using the friction between Spencer's ideas and his own to create fiction that ran counter to Spencerian philosophy. The author-protagonist of "The Strange Experiences of a Misogynist" dreams of the disappearance of all women, an event that erases "the adamantine division between the knowable and the unknowable." The story suggests that London saw Spencer's metaphysics as refutable, an attitude that I believe accounts for his dismissive attitude toward the first section of *First Principles*. If one could conduct the thought experiment of this short story, then one could imagine how Spencer's "adamantine line" was in reality permeable. Or, to put it in Spencerian language, mystery was the great unifier of religion and science and thus there was no line. London worked on his own conception of the mystery of all things, for it had to account for the ghost within, that ultimate personally challenging mystery, the nature of the imagination.

At the same time, sociologically—that is, theatrically—that line had to remain in place. To write *The Iron Heel* he wanted to remind himself how he could not be a prophet of the Unknowable. The socialist must attack religion and all ideas whose results cannot be placed in the palm of the Texan's hand, and Ernest could be called another Cloudesley Johns, or, rather, London always had seen part of himself in Johns even as he sought to refute Johns's atheism. When Anthony Meredith, in his introduction, explains who Herbert Spencer was, he calls him one of the "intellectual and antagonistic giants" to socialism who nonetheless accepted that socialism was a natural outgrowth of capitalism, not foreseeing the rise of the Iron Heel (7). Thus, even when London "applauds" Spencer he resists him. In the same way that London allowed his public to think he was a devotee of Spencer's philosophy of composition, so too did he allow it to see him intellectually indebted to Spencer. This sleight of hand was dangerous, for it encouraged people to read *The Sea-Wolf* and *Martin Eden* (as well as other works) as supportive, not antagonistic to Spencer.

The emphasis on religion and its proponents, like Bishop Morehouse, is present in *The Iron Heel* because of its centrality in Nietzsche, Marx, and the philosophers like Kant and Hegel with whom Marx debated. As Untermann had noted, Marx wrote, "Religion 'is the self-consciousness of a human being that has either not yet found itself or again lost itself. . . . Religion is the sigh of the oppressed creatures, the mind of a heartless world, the spirit of spiritless conditions. It is the opium of the people. . . . The abolition of religion as the illusory happiness of the people signifies their demand for real happiness'" (111). London agreed, but we have to remember that *The Iron Heel*, despite the infusion of philosophy and theoretical sociology, is not a treatise but a work of art. London, unlike Marx and Untermann, treats the relation between religion and politics simplistically. Within his given genre religion becomes simply a tool of the oppressors, and we should expect nothing more—or less.

For it is a powerful critique, not just of established religion as a mouthpiece for the Oligarchy but as a critique of any socialism—especially the Christian Socialist movement—that advocates social change that retains the Christian message. London wrote humorously about the Holy Jumpers because he found them tame, harmless. But he had lost patience with the Christian Socialism movement—as had Untermann—and with reformists of all kinds. This is a proclamation of war. Nonviolent means to social justice will fail in the face of the capitalists' unwillingness to negotiate power. Turning the other cheek invites death.

Perhaps the most important book that London cited in either his notes or in the novel is W. J. Ghent's *Our Benevolent Feudalism*; in fact, London's response to Ghent provides a clue to why London chose 1906 as the correct time to write his novel. In his notes to *The Iron Heel*, London tells himself, "Give the rise of socialism, and the struggle of the two sides for the U.S. and for the world. And how socialism is knocked, by formation of the Oligarchy. This idea was evolutionary, yet had been crystalized stamped in book, by Ghent,—and made clear to the capitalist minds. The paradox of Ghent, a socialist, by this book, defeating the Cause."[55] Before this, London had thought Ghent's cynicism was defeatist and, even worse, perhaps collaborationist. Now, in 1906, was the time to offer a corrective. If the capitalists thought they could find a justification for their actions in Ghent, they would find a countervailing thesis in *The Iron Heel*. Ghent did not forecast the defeat of the new feudalism, only its ascendency and defeat of socialism. Ghent once wrote to Joan London, "As to *Our Benevolent Feudalism*, I have always understood that it furnished the inspiration for *The Iron Heel*, though I do not recall any specific conversation on the subject with your father. Still, we talked about many, many things."[56] London wrote *The Iron Heel* partly to reverse his estimation of Ghent. In this way, Ghent was correct to say that *Our Benevolent Feudalism* was the inspiration for *The Iron Heel*.

In order to restore Ghent's reputation as a qualified socialist writer, London drew on Ghent's *Mass and Class* repeatedly in his notes and in the novel. He found this book more in tune with his own optimism and with Untermann's work, who is cited almost immediately by Ghent. Ghent himself, in the third edition of *Our Benevolent Feudalism*, had already acknowledged the unintentional consequences of his "satirical interpretation of the facts and tendencies of the time." *Mass and Class* was meant to correct those who, like London, had misunderstood the full import of his work and his dedication to the cause. "I have no excuses or apologies to offer for that work," he wrote in his preface to his new book. "As a warning alike to the apathetic and to the oversanguine, it served, I hope, a useful purpose," much like *The Iron Heel* was to effect. London, the more accomplished writer, chose romance rather than satire to leaven his sociological analyses and forecasts, and thus did not court misunderstanding. Everhard is harsh with Ghent, saying, "Ghent has taught the oligarchs" how to combine with labor unions. "I'll wager they've made a text-book out of his 'Benevolent Feudalism'" (157). This was Jack's position in 1903. But, after reading

Mass and Class in October 1904, he modified his tune.[57] As played now by Anthony Meredith: "It has always been insisted that Ghent put the idea of the Oligarchy into the minds of the great capitalists. . . . To-day we know better, but our knowledge does not over come the fact that Ghent remains the most abused innocent man in all history" (219). Ghent must have been relieved to hear that his guilty plea had been overturned in the socialist writers' court, for he concluded his preface of *Mass and Class* with these words: "In my present work I have sought . . . to indicate the current of social progress which, in spite of the blindness of the workers, the rapacity of the masters, and the subservience of the retainers, makes ever for an ultimate of social justice."[58] Ghent's cynicism toward all classes dissipates in a straightforward affirmation of the optimistic strain in—that is, a belief in the inevitability of—American socialism.

In the final text of *The Iron Heel*, London not only absolves Ghent but shows how an accurate prediction of the Oligarchy is impossible; no longer evolutionary, the rise and sustained violence of the Oligarchy was, in Meredith's words, "not inevitable." Not even Ghent could have foreseen it: "In the orderly procedure of social evolution there was no place for it" (7) as there was for the dissolution of capitalism. Before he had named his male central character, London wrote his core beliefs: "The hero bases his faith, on the generalization that every system contains within itself the germs of its own decay."[59] The Oligarchy and capitalism would ultimately destroy themselves, but this was not a fast-acting cancer.

Another note reminds himself to pull *Our Benevolent Feudalism* and *Mass and Class* off his bookshelf. And then he gets more specific: "See Mass and Class, Index, for ethics of business men, private property, etc. For the retainers (divisions of the castes) see Mass and Class p. 85."[60] Indeed, the index and page 85 are marked, though not annotated; the only annotation is at the back: "234—more yearly railroad deaths than Gettysburg—precariousness of life," a remark perhaps intended for some other work. But in *Mass and Class* we find, among other things, a reference to E. R. A. Seligman's 1902 *The Economic Interpretation of History*, a book London read and annotated and that coincided with Untermann's and Ghent's undertaking; that is, history should be about social relationships expressed through economics. This is a historiography for which London could advocate. "History, which once was the record of little more than the doings and sayings of warriors and kings, comes now to be the record of human society. . . . From the emphasis of the individual it passed to emphasis of the state, which now it tends to lay the greater stress upon the social body," reads Ghent's first sentences.[61] We see in part why Meredith downplays Everhard's role in the Second Revolt. Especially in the history of socialism, we should emphasize the role of the many, and not the performances of the few.

When Meredith footnotes Avis's statement that "the strength of the Oligarchy lies in its satisfied conception of its own righteousness" (216), he relies on *Mass and Class* and the pages on ethics that London marked. When Meredith quotes from John Stuart Mill's *On Liberty* to support Avis's explication of "the aristocratic ethic or the master ethic," London had pulled this quotation—"whenever there is an ascendant class, a large portion of the morality emanates from its class interests and its class feelings of superiority" (53)—from *Mass and Class*.[62] Ghent carefully analyzes the constitution and mindset—the instinct and consciousness—of each of six classes. From him we learn that a handicraftsman like Ernest Everhard—an unemployed horseshoer—is the victim of modernization and "the full development of the system of capitalist production."[63] Avis calls him "working-class," which is generally true, but, as Ghent would have it, "in him [the handicraftsman] the interest and function of the producer is qualified by the interest and function of the trader." These interests and functions are different from the proletariat. Avis gives his occupation as "social philosopher," making him a displaced person from the capitalist system of production and distribution. As such, and despite Avis's initial recoil from his breaching of class lines to shake her hand when they first meet, he is able to romance someone outside his class, and she, in turn, is able to accept that romantic "presumption." "You see," she says, somewhat shamefacedly but cognizant of how her class consciousness had been formed by the system, "I was a creature of environment, and at that time had strong class instincts. Such boldness on the part of a man of my own class would have been almost unforgiveable" (12). Ghent calls philosophers, artists, educators, and clergy members of "the Social Servants." They can be divided into two subclasses: the "normal" and the "perverted." How a member of this class conducts himself or herself in relation to the trading class defines one's subgroup. Because Everhard is a socialist and advocates for the nonwage earners (tramps, criminals, stay-at-home women, and children) and the self-employing producers (or handicraftsmen) he is thus a normal member of his class. *The Iron Heel*'s first chapters are about the intellectual warfare between the normal and the perverted.

Everhard simplifies Ghent's class structure, limiting the number of classes to the traditional three: the proletariat (of which he classes himself), the middle class, and the oligarchy or plutocracy. Simplification allows for direct action, for a clearer statement of the us-versus-them rhetoric for the revolutionary overthrow of the ruling class. Besides, *The Iron Heel* is indebted to, but not of the same genre of, a sociological monograph like *Mass and Class*. We should be aware that London's indebtedness to Ghent (and others) was limited by his own artistic, theatrical demands. To convince his readership that the proletariat had a chance to win the economic fight, he had to make the enemy one-dimensional. So all members of the social-service class are perverted. And, despite Ghent's accurate assessment of past writers' vagaries about what actually defines the middle class, London nonetheless allowed that common, easily graspable term to stand. If you weren't an owner of the means of production, asks London, then why aren't you fighting against the capitalists? In the end, as powerful as Ghent's analysis may have been to London, and as powerful as Ghent's switch from irony to literalness was, *Mass and Class* was all too vague about the nature of the revolution necessary to overthrow the dominant class. Ghent foresaw the necessity of the cooperative commonwealth because people in general cannot stand graft, corruption, and greed for long—his final four chapters are a Homeric catalogue of such—but he does not take into account the factor that Everhard preaches the most: the violence to which capitalists will stoop to protect their profits and status.

Friedrich Nietzsche's work influenced *The People of the Abyss* and *The Sea-Wolf*, but his influence seems more pronounced, if only because more explicit, in 1906. Before we turn to a full analysis of Friedrich Nietzsche's presence in *The Iron Heel*, which will lead us in turn to George Bernard Shaw's *Man and Superman*, we need to look closely at the beginning of the novel.

The Iron Heel, like *The Call of the Wild*, begins in an idyllic northern California setting. If we have read "Planchette," *White Fang*, and "All Gold Canyon," we will recognize the dreaminess of the locale and dread what will be revealed. Instead of possessed horses, escaped convicts, and murderous miners we have imminent worldwide revolution, "that mad maelstrom of death and destruction so soon to burst forth," "the marring and mangling of the sweet, beautiful flesh, and the souls torn with violence from proud bodies and hurled to God" (9). Both materially and spiritually, humans will be destroyed, says Avis, as "the soft summer wind stirs the redwoods, and Wild-Water ripples sweet cadences over its mossy stones. There are butterflies in the sunshine, and from everywhere arises the drowsy hum of bees." Ernest Everhard is dead, and, along with the b(r)eezy buzz, other sounds compete for Avis's attention. In her bower she can hear "the cries of the stricken," and she can see the killing (9). Presumably she is thinking of the "secret execution" of her husband (9), and then, because she cannot separate the idea of the Second Revolt from thoughts of her husband, she thinks of his life as she knew it. In other words, the "Sonoma Hills" harbor the ghost not just of Everhard but of all those who have died so far in the name of the cause, a roll call that will soon include her own name (9). Because she hides her manuscript in "the ancient oak at Wake Robin Lodge" (8), this terrifying, idyllic place is the residence of London's imagination. As forecast by *White Fang* and other stories, London has turned away from the Klondike abyss where chance, death, gold, and writing combine to make an artist write. Instead of a cabin in an abyss surrounded by the deathly white silence, it is a hole in a tree surrounded by ghosts warmed by the California sunshine.

Everhard, as the eighth footnote tells us indirectly, is a ghost in a different, Nietzschean sense. "The modern Zarathustra . . . is neither an historical nor a mythical person," says Alexander Tille in his introduction to the text of *Thus Spake Zarathustra* that London read, "but a 'ghost,' as Nietzsche would have called him, a type existing nowhere, and yet the incorporation of wishes and aspirations; an ideal reflected in a human image; a man as man should be in Nietzsche's opinion, and as he would have liked to be himself."[64] There is more to say about the ghostliness of the superman, but first consider how the autobiographical element in *Thus Spake Zarathustra* might have legitimated London's deployment of it. If Nietzsche could imagine his own ideal self as an Übermensch, then certainly London would have felt empowered to do the same, albeit with his own creative re-creation of the genre at work. It is no mere ego trip for London to imagine himself as Ernest Everhard, so-called hero of the Second Revolt, especially given Meredith's reassessment of his historical importance.

London had discovered a new genre for himself, one that is suited to a third sense in which Everhard can be figured as a ghost. Having died before the time in which Avis writes her book, Ernest thus returns from the dead to be the main character in her memoir. She brings him back to life, hovering about her as a disembodied presence. Ernest, says Avis—and we remember that the Übermensch has two companions, the eagle (Avis) and the serpent (the masses or proletariat)—is an aristocrat, not of that class, but of temperament, of soul. This is exactly how Nietzsche conceived it. And his blondness is a kind of whiteness like a ghost. *Super* as a prefix then means a "beyondness" that exists apart from bodily presence.

Finally, there is a fourth way that Ernest—and Avis—are figured as ghosts. In order to effect the First Revolt, they must undergo disguise and sometimes physical alteration. They then can assume new identities as members of the Oligarchy. As Meredith tells us, "disguise did become a veritable art during that period. The revolutionists maintained schools of acting in all their refuge" (198), and here we have the conjunction of drama and ghostliness. For not only do Avis, Ernest, and all the socialists who infiltrate the Oligarchy become actors, but they also become ghosts. One kills one's old self in order to become a new self. "You must make yourself over again," Ernest tells Avis, "You must cease to be" (197). Avis is so accomplished at the makeover that she thinks of her old self as a dream: "One must become so adept as to deceive oneself," she writes.[65] The acting self displaces the biological self. The biological self, by definition, dies, but the acting self lives on as a ghost. Avis, Ernest, and their comrades became "agents-provocateurs": "like ghosts the agents came and went" (218). The story of the resistance to the Iron Heel is a ghost story, and that makes it a story about writing and the imagination.

Ghostliness or imagination—Ernest the ghost inspires Avis's work—and the ghost that is the imagination is necessary because it serves a critical function in addition to inspiration. Having the ghost present, paradoxically, gives life or the feel of life to the work itself. Another way to put this is to say that there is a congruence between autobiography and emotion. Earlier, I suggested we might call it *autodrama*. As Meredith says of Avis's manuscript,

Especially valuable is it in communicating to us the *feel* of those terrible times. Nowhere do we find more vividly portrayed the psychology of the persons that lived in that turbulent period embraced between the years 1912 and 1932—their mistakes and ignorance, their doubts and fears and misapprehensions, their ethical delusions, their inconceivable sordidness and selfishness. . . . History tells us that these things were, and biology and psychology tells us why they were; but history and biology and psychology do not make these things alive. We accept them as facts, but we are left without sympathetic comprehension of them.[66]

In other words, Avis's biography—which is, after all, London's autodrama—is one half of a human document. Meredith's introduction and footnotes provide the other half: the history, the biology, and the psychology. Now we see London further refining his concept of the human document. A human document is a fiction used to answer the what and why of human history. We realize that this autobiographical impulse—given a literary form inspired and legitimated by Nietzsche—provides the bridge between *The Iron Heel* and London's two subsequent novels, *The Road* and *Martin Eden*. We have to remember, however, that none of the three novels is the autobiography of the Übermensch or the blond beast. London's "autobiographies" are very much a critique of those concepts.

There is also the matter of when London actually read Nietzsche. In 1915, with characteristic hyperbole, he told a fan, "I have been more stimulated by Nietzsche than by any other writer in the world." The hyperbole is meant to set up the next sentence: "At the same time I have been an intellectual enemy to Nietzsche," and he cites *The Sea-Wolf* and *Martin Eden* (but not *The Iron* Heel) as proof.[67] Still, we have to take his hyperbole seriously. When London read Nietzsche is a question of some controversy. There is, first, the conservative approach, defined as a reliance on documents (not London's published works) that explicitly mention his reading Nietzsche. The earliest such document is a September 1904 letter to Charmian: "Have been getting hold of some of Nietzsche. I'll turn you loose first on his *Genealogy of Morals*—after that, something you'll like—*Thus Spake Zarathustra*."[68] I take a more liberal approach and use London's writings as well as the documents. In all of his published works, the word *superman* appears once: in *The Iron Heel*. But the words *blond beast* appear a number of times before *The Iron Heel*: in *The People of the Abyss*, *The Sea-Wolf*, and "How I Became a Socialist." The first was written in the fall of 1902, the latter two in early 1903 (February and April through January 1904). I believe that London first read *A Genealogy of Morals* in the spring or summer of 1902, and then he either read or reread the other works beginning in 1904 and continuing through 1906. In his copy of *A Genealogy of Morals*, he placed a 1906 article by Vernon Lee from the *North American Review*. The fact that he read it and clipped it indicates his direct involvement—whether it was a rereading or a skimming—with the book.

It's not just that the phrase appears in his texts; in using it, he exhibits a clear understanding of the term. At the same time, however, as we briefly go through the texts in which he does use *blond beast*, we see how London changed the concept. First, in *The People of the Abyss*, having described the poor people of Kent, he writes,

> Such hordes of beastly wretchedness and inarticulate misery are no compensation for a millionaire brewer who lives in a West End palace, sates himself with the sensuous delights of London's golden theatres, hobnobs with lordlings and princelings, and is knighted by the king. Wins his spurs—God forbid! In old time the great blonde beasts rode in the battle's van and won their spurs by cleaving men from pate to chine. And, after all, it is far finer to kill a strong man with a clean-slicing blow of singing steel than to make a beast of him, and of his seed through the generations, by the artful and spidery manipulation of industry and politics.[69]

This is a straightforward borrowing from Nietzsche and is, I believe, strong enough evidence to show that he read *Genealogy* in 1902, or perhaps before. (He had met Frank Strawn-Hamilton in the late nineties, someone who was conversant with Nietzsche, as others like Austin Lewis or anyone familiar with critics of socialism might be.) I quote the passage in full because it conveys not just the admiration both Nietzsche and London felt toward "great blond beasts" but the conviction that the veneer of civilization was corrupted and had wrongly succeeded the bloodthirsty Vikings or Germanics or whatever race happens to embody the blond beast. London must have been nodding his head (besides marking a bar in the margin) when he read in *Genealogy*, "This is the very *sense of all civilization*: to change and rear the beast of prey of 'man' into a tame and civilized animal, a *domestic animal*."[70] London had arrived at his own conception of the antagonistic pairing of savagery and civilization, but he could imagine it as coincident with Nietzsche's.

The next appearance of *blond beast* occurs in February 1903 in the third paragraph of "How I Became a Socialist." He explains his state of mind and body before he became a socialist: "I was a rampant individualist. . . . I could see myself only raging through life without end like one of Nietzsche's *blond beasts*, lustfully roving and conquering by sheer superiority and strength."[71] Further along in the essay, he repeats the phrase twice. When he says he went hoboing, he calls it "a new *blond-beast* adventure" (273). And on the road, who should he meet but "all sorts of men, many of whom had once been as good as myself and just as *blond-beastly*" (273). This is a reinvention of the term (though we do have to admire his conversion of the nominative into an adverb). Nietzsche would never use his term to define hoboing or any like "adventure" as something a blond beast would undertake. And Nietzsche's blond beasts were not tamed and then crippled by the Industrial Revolution. Whatever civilization existed was enough. Napoleon—whose appearance in London's essay can only be explained by his appearance in Nietzsche's book (see 58; marked by London)—though he was a problematic character was nonetheless a blond beast gone bad, though more from being a "synthesis of monster and *beyondman*," which, incidentally, is the only appearance of Übermensch in *A Genealogy of Morals*. Not only does Nietzsche not explain this "synthesis" but he also does not explain the apparent conflation of blond beast and Übermensch, a conflation decidedly not intended by all other discussions of both concepts, a matter we will return to shortly.

Further textual proof that London was relying heavily on Nietzsche is this subsequent sentence in "How I Became a Socialist": "I hope I have made it clear that I was proud to be one of Nature's strong-armed noblemen." "Strong-armed noblemen" is Nietzsche's synonym for blond beast. And then there is a final, misappropriation: "In short, my joyous individualism was dominated by the orthodox bourgeois ethics. I read the bourgeois papers, listened to the bourgeois preachers, and shouted at the sonorous platitudes of the bourgeois politicians" (271). This is not Nietzschean individualism. A blond beast exists under, that is, apart, from bourgeois ethics. He is opposed to them. But London mistakes nobility for bourgeois. And here his notion of the beastliness of man departs as well from Nietzsche. For Nietzsche, the noble man is a beast because he has been categorized and thus demeaned by the civilized man. It is ironic in this way, because although he is a fierce warrior shedding blood with sword and army, he is also a beast because he is a force to be reckoned with. For London, however, the beastliness of the blond beast is synonymous with primitive man, with the cave dweller, the man just risen from the other primates. *Beast* is a term from Darwin, a thinker Nietzsche derided.

The Sea-Wolf, as London famously has said, was meant as a critique of Nietzschean individualism, and what better way to critique an author both admired and rejected than to re-create him as one of the central figures of a novel. When London wrote of the death of Wolf Larsen, Charles Watson argues that "there is good reason to believe that London had in mind the symptoms of advanced syphilis of which Nietzsche had died in 1900."[72] If so, the ideal that is Larsen is coincident with the ideal that is Nietzsche; that is, the superman is both how Nietzsche imagined his best self and how London imagined Wolf Larsen. Whereas Humphrey Van Weyden's friend Charley Furuseth reads Nietzsche (as we learn in the first paragraph), Hump encounters the man himself. Wolf Larsen is, as one contemporary reviewer noted, "a very startling embodiment of Nietzsche's ideal of the Uebermensch."[73] Another reviewer called him "no mere symbol" but "very much alive," "a typical Superman, the great blond beast of Nietzsche."[74] We can ignore that reviewer's mistaken conflation of two concepts, the Übermensch and the blond beast, and still agree that he is a "superman" character. After using the term *blond beast* in *The People of the Abyss*, London chose the next significant term he was interested in, the Übermensch. He didn't need to say it out loud. It was obvious enough to be left unstated.

What isn't obvious and requires a careful reading of *A Genealogy of Morals* is how London patterned Larsen off of Nietzsche's characterization of Napoleon: "Napoleon, that most isolated and latest-born of men that ever was; and in him appeared the incarnate problem of the *noble ideal as such.* Let it be well considered *what* kind of problem this is: Napoleon, this synthesis of monster and *beyondman*" (58). We saw how London pictured Larsen as a monster, half man, half leopard (or some such killing animal). Now we see the philosophical underpinning for this characterization. Napoleon is not a "beyondman" because he is a monster. He is a monster as well as a beyondman. The problem does not reside with London's elaboration of this conception. It lies in Nietzsche's formulation, a problem London ignored, probably because he read *Thus Spake Zarathustra* after he read *Genealogy*. In the former, the Übermensch is supposed to be a figure of the future, someone who will arrive. Nietzsche does not elaborate on the idea that Napoleon, even if he is the "latest-born of men," is actually an Übermensch. But it does seem he has modified the idea, perhaps in response to judgments that would later be articulated by readers such as Erich Heller who saw a fatal contradiction between the concept of the Übermensch and the concept of the eternal recurrence of events. If indeed Napoleon is an Übermensch, he could then recur.

But Ernest is not, in the strict Nietzschean sense, an Übermensch. Avis says that "he was a natural aristocrat—and this in spite of the fact that he was in the camp of the non-aristocrats." This much synchs with Nietzsche; he uses the words *noble* and *gentleman* in *A Genealogy of Morals*; a sample phrase might be "the conquering and *gentleman race*, the race of the Aryans" (26). But then Avis goes off the Nietzschean track in *The Iron Heel* and writes, "He was a super-man, a blond beast such as Nietzsche has described, and in addition he was aflame with democracy" (12). Nietzsche of course dismissed democracy as a mob-ruled system, a mob defined by resentment and the opposite of the interiority of the Übermensch. For all of Napoleon's problematic combination of "monster and *beyondman*," he was, for Nietzsche, the ideal that opposed "the old, false battle-cry of resentment about the *right of the most*, [he was] against the will to the grading, degradation, and leveling, to the downward and dusk-ward of man." Democracy entailed the "leveling" of all men. The "*beyondman*" issued "the terrible and rapturous counter-cry of the *privilege of the fewest!*" (58). In *A Genealogy of Morals*, Nietzsche explicitly enunciated his distaste for socialism and the cooperative commonwealth, a distaste that cared little for distinctions not only between democracy and socialism but also among those twin political concepts: "Who will guarantee that modern democracy, anarchy, which is still more modern, and especially the hankering for *la commune*, the most primitive form of society—which is held in common by all our European socialists[—]do not represent in the main an immense *afterclap*, and that the conquering and *gentleman race*, the race of the Aryans, is not among other things physiologically succumbing?" (26). The noble, Aryan race is being supplanted by the "pre-Aryan," "an essentially dark-haired population" (25, 26). In the attempt to rectify the wrongs of political oppression, socialists have lost the true meaning of morals and ignore the need for "the blond beast."

Yet London must have felt that there was nothing that prevented blond beasts from forming a social organization that might approximate or even realize socialism's goals. London agreed with Nietzsche that the majority of people were of the "slave mentality." Such people are passive and prudent or act only out of resentment; they are the herd and are conventional. "Noble men," declares Nietzsche in *Genealogy*, believe in "the perfect reliableness

of function of the regulating, *unconscious* instincts or even a certain impru-
dence, such as readiness to encounter things—whether danger or an enemy—or that eccentric suddenness of anger, love, reverence, gratitude and
revenge by which noble souls at all times have recognized themselves as
such" (38). They do away with the morbidity of Schopenhauer. "The positive fundamental concept of the noble valuation . . . is thoroughly saturated
with life and passion and says: 'We, the noble, we, the good, we, the fair,
we, the happy'" (35-36). "They could never sever happiness from action"
(37). In quite the opposite manner, the "common man" (36) feels happiness
only as "narcosis, numbness, rest, peace, 'Sabbath,' unharnessing of mind,
and stretching of limbs" (37). Even if London, in a later work like *The Valley of the Moon*, draws with great sympathy the recreational habits of the
working class, he nonetheless knew his former class was fundamentally
unhappy. The "noble man is self-confident and self-sincere" (37), according to Nietzsche. The common man, "the man of resentment," "is neither
sincere, nor naïve, neither honest nor straightforward against himself. . . .
He is the mast in the art of keeping silence, of forgetting nothing, of waiting, of provisional diminution, of self-humiliation" (38). London marked
that passage in the margin as if in anticipation of creating a character like
Ernest Everhard, who is a dedicated man of action, who courts danger and
his enemies, who is sincere and honest, joyful, capable of sudden love. He
is alive, as well as clean and noble.

At the same time, "in the first decades of the century, many of the Übermensch's most vocal enthusiasts were socialists."[75] They seemed not to find
a contradiction between their avowal of reform and/or revolutionary politics and a figure who was opposed to the rights of the majority. London,
however, transformed his initial appropriation of the Übermensch for *The
Sea-Wolf* and emphasized not the individualistic Übermensch but the warrior Übermensch who fights against convention, against bourgeois ethics,
against the oligarchy.

Nietzsche's influence on London developed along a curious line: from
the blond beasts of *The People of the Abyss* to Martin Eden as a proud blond
beast. The great irony of Nietzsche's influence is that two of London's fullest and thus greatest characters are modeled after the same philosophic
principle—the blond beast—and yet could not be more different in elicit-
ing our own reactions. Having read Nietzsche, he converted that concept

into something serving not just his own personal conception of himself but of that ideal which would bring revolutionary socialism to its fruition.

Wolf Larsen and Ernest Everhard do share an attribute of the blond beast. To bourgeois society, they are, as Nietzsche describes them in *Genealogy*, "not much better than so many disengaged beasts of prey. Here they enjoy liberty from all social restraint; the wilderness must compensate them for the tension produced by a long incarceration and impalement in the 'peace' of society." Having escaped that false "peace," the blond beasts—who seem like "beasts of prey" but "among one another prove themselves so inventive in regardfulness, self-restraint, delicacy, faith, pride and friendship" (40)— "step *back* into the innocence of the conscience of the beast of prey, as exultant monsters, which, perhaps, walk away from an abominable sequence of murder, burning down, violation, torture, with such wantonness and equanimity, . . . with the conviction that now for a long time again the poets will have something to celebrate and sing of. At the ground of all these noble races, the beast of prey, the splendid, *blond beast*, lustfully roving in search of spoils and victory cannot be mistaken" (41). Here is Nietzsche's very first use of the phrase *blond beast*. The "noble race" might be "Roman, Arabian, Germanic, Japanese nobility, Homeric heroes, Scandinavian Vikings," but they all have a "boldness." They are "foolhardy, absurd, sudden." They are thought of by the ignoble, by their opposites—those who established right and wrong, good and evil as social goods—as being characterized by "their indifference and contempt for safety, life, body, comfort; their terrible gaiety and profundity of delight in all destruction, in all blisses of victory and cruelty."[76] To create Ernest, London took Wolf Larsen and subtracted out the "contempt for . . . life," the "delight in *all* destruction" (Ernest certainly delights in the destruction of the oligarchy), "in *all* . . . cruelty." Wolf is cruel toward all; Ernest is cruel to those who oppose him.

Like many Americans at the time, London may have used the word *superman*—not *Übermensch* or, as it is translated in the text he read, *beyondman*—because of George Bernard Shaw's *Man and Superman*. As one historian puts it, "Shaw's protagonist helped popularize the image of the Übermensch as a vitalist hero flouting Victorian morality."[77] We remember that in the fall of 1904, while London was writing his first play, *The Scorn of Women*, he had read *Man and Superman* with Charmian and sent a copy to Blanche Partington. The superman is Shaw's touchstone for advocating a personal philosophy, just as it was for London, and for both authors having a central figure with whom one must argue is fundamental for the production of art. We recall that in 1905 London told a reporter, while discussing Shaw, that "you have got to get right down to the root of a subject and you will find socialism the basis of art." This principle thus seems to owe its generation from Shaw's introduction to *Man and Superman*.

It's not that Shaw placed socialism as the foundation stone for all art, though he was indeed a socialist, albeit of a different kind from London. It's that he placed a philosophy, any philosophy, in that place of beginnings. "This is the true joy in life," he wrote, "the being used for a purpose recognized by yourself as a mighty one." In a sentence that sounds exactly like London's famous credo—"I would rather be ashes than dust"—Shaw elaborates on that purpose: "the being thoroughly worn out before you are thrown on the scrap heap; the being of a force of Nature instead of a feverish selfish little clod of ailments and grievances." "The only real tragedy in life," says Shaw, "is the being used by personally minded men for purposes which you recognize as base." To revolt against that which is equivalent to slavery, Shaw argues in *Man and Superman*, "is the only force that offers a man's work to the poor artist" (xxxii). Need I mention that this passage was the only one in Shaw's introduction that London marked?

Shaw thought it was a short distance between John Bunyan and Friedrich Nietzsche, even given "the difference between their conclusions," as he says in his introduction to the play, and London agreed (xxxii). "The artist-philosophers," a group in which Shaw included himself, coordinate their "demonstrations of life" with a "philosophy or religion" (xxviii–xxix). Against Dickens and Shakespeare and other "romantic playwrights," Shaw opposes his top four—"Bunyan, Blake, Hogarth, and Turner"—as well as "Goethe, Shelley, Schopenhauer, Wagner, Ibsen, Morris, Tolstoy, and Nietzsche" (xxviii). We note how the last five were also major influences for London. The point is that for both Shaw and London, "the main thing in determining the artistic quality of a book is not the opinions it propagates, but the fact that the writer has opinions." This is the same conclusion London reached in his very first essay on the office of the author, "On the Writer's Philosophy of Life." Art is formed out of the "ordinary working philosophy of life," and that philosophy should be socialistic in content. In that essay he said that "a philosophy does not imply yielding to the didactic impulse," but in London's work it often does. Certainly in *The Iron Heel* it does, and upon reading Shaw, London would have found affirmation for the theatrical, "didactic impulse"; in one footnote, Anthony Meredith proclaims that "the flower of the artistic and intellectual world were revolutionists" (208). In an acerbic comment on present-day artists, Shaw writes, "And when [the artist] declares that art should not be didactic, all the people who have nothing to teach and all the people who don't want to learn agree with him emphatically" (xxxvi). Reading Nietzsche, London needed to instruct the world about the dangers of Nietzschean individualism if there was any hope of establishing the cooperative commonwealth.

There is a world of difference between Shaw's understanding of the superman and London's. For Shaw, the superman turns his back on the devil, hell, and all activities that merely add pleasure and ease to life. In *Man and Superman*, Jack Tanner believes instead in following "the Life Force" that leads him toward self-knowledge and the self's "destination" (134). In act 3, Tanner is asked by the devil, "What is the use of knowing?" and Tanner answers, "to be able to choose the line of greatest advantage instead of yielding in the direction of the least resistance." So far, London would agree. In the next decade, London, like Shaw, would embrace Henri Bergson's concept of the élan vital. And then, in words that must have rung especially pertinent to a sailor-author ready to embark on a voyage around the world by boat, Tanner says, "Does a ship sail to its destination no better than a log drifts nowhither? The philosopher is Nature's pilot. And there you have our difference: to be in hell is to drift: to be in heaven is to steer" (134). The Nietzschean superman is a man of action, not a passive receptacle of society's directives. And yet London was convinced that the superman is inimical to the proper construction of society. Shaw parodies the Left by staging arguments among his caricatures of an anarchist, social democrats, and the like; we remember a similar scene in London's story "Two Children of Abraham" where London lovingly pits one Left faction against another. But London thought there was hope that all factions, except, perhaps, Christian Socialists and other unthinking reformists, could eventually be united in the service of revolutionary socialism. The superman, someone like Ernest Everhard, cannot do this. He is too much of an individualist to steer the new ship of state.

Man and Superman's philosophical debate is between the devil and Don Juan, a debate that the superman wins. It takes place, however, while a third, significant party sleeps. Henry Straker is, according to Shaw, the rarest of theatrical creations. In his introduction to the play, Shaw observes that "on the stage" "the workers are all footmen, parlourmaids, comic lodging-letters and fashionable professional men" (xxv). Thus Henry Straker is regarded as an equal by the hero, Jack Tanner. *The Iron Heel* owes a debt to Shaw's insistence that modern drama must stage real-life workingmen. But there is a frustrating contradiction in the play, a contradiction that London sought to resolve. Straker is not simply a new creation, the real-life worker. He is, as Tanner calls him, the New Man. He is engrossed by the automobile and by speed, twin attributes of the new century. But that is all he is about. When it comes time for a choice between pleasure and philosophical monasticism (a subjectivity that Tanner himself cannot live up to) the New Man chooses pleasure. But what makes the New Man a special theatrical creation is his position vis-à-vis Tanner. The latter treats his chauffeur as an equal. Yet Tanner is the superman, and they should be in opposition. In *The Revolutionist's Handbook*, Tanner (that is, Shaw) writes, "Does any man seriously believe that the *chauffeur* who drives a motor car from Paris to Berlin is a more highly evolved man than the charioteer of Achilles? . . . We must replace the Man by the Superman. . . . Poets who plan Utopias and prove that nothing is necessary for their realization but that Man should will them, perceive at last, like Richard Wagner, that the fact to be faced is that Man does not effectively will them. And he never will until he becomes Superman. And so we arrive at the end of the Socialist's dream of 'the socialization of the means of production and exchange'" and, in a clause that seems directly pointed at London and Everhard, "of the Positivist's dream of moralizing the capitalist."[78] This contradiction becomes in *The Iron Heel* a dialectic resolved by the creation of the working-class superman, even if he is ineffectual.

Shaw would later write that he had produced, in some unnamed way, a "careful demonstration of the folly of . . . [looking for] the salvation of society to the despotism of a single Napoleonic Superman."[79] And although the Devil, seemingly with Shaw's blessing, warns Don Juan, "Beware of the pursuit of the Superhuman: it leads to an indiscriminate contempt for the Human," and although Tanner chooses marriage not through the exercise of his independent will—his will is to run like a madman from Ann—but because he is to some extent shamed into it, *Man and Superman* does create the contradiction between the glorification of the working class and proselytizing for the superman.[80] London avoids this contradiction by making the New Man—Ernest Everhard—the superman himself. By borrowing the word *superman* from Shaw, then, and expanding upon that borrowing to enter into the world of aesthetics, we see how *The Iron Heel* is theatrical in content as well as structure.

Both works, too, are experimental theatrical productions. A novel with footnotes found part of its inspiration in an unusually long "romantic comedy" centered with "a philosophic interlude of dramatic interest."[81] Further, Shaw makes a point of answering a critique about "romancers," meaning writers such as himself: they "announce their hero as a man of extraordinary genius, and to leave his works entirely to the reader's imagination" (xxv–xxvi). How true. So he makes Tanner the author of a book entitled *A Revolutionist's Handbook* and then wrote the book and included it as an appendix to *Man and Superman*. London did not exactly follow this path, but he did give Everhard his own analysis of surplus value and then hoped the reader would find those thoughts in "The Question of the Maximum."[82] And he gives Everhard lines from "Revolution" and considered, but resisted, publishing the essay as an appendix to the novel. As he said in his notes for *The Iron Heel*, "In course of story, have a revolutionary speech made (my Revolution)—give brief excerpts and much description. Then—in appendix, give complete speech, a la Shaw's Revolutionist's Handbook and give him credit for the idea."[83] This is the mark of what Shaw calls his "drama of ideas."[84]

The subtitle of Shaw's drama is *A Comedy and a Philosophy*. We have dealt with the philosophy. The play is a comedy in the classical sense: it requires a marriage for its ending. This kind of play, however, needs a special kind of marriage. It must acknowledge the Life Force, the sexual instinct, the natural necessity of the reproduction of the species. Ann Whitefield protests, but as Tanner (now speaking as Don Juan) explains, "The plain-spoken marriage services of the vernacular Churches will no longer be abbreviated and half suppressed as indelicate. The sober decency, earnestness and authority of their declaration of the real purpose of marriage will be honored and accepted, whilst their romantic vowings and pledgings and until-death-do-us partings and the like will be expunged as unbearable frivolities."[85] Ann dismisses Octavius because he vows and pledges romantically. And when Tanner and Ann agree to marry, he announces that they have sacrificed everything but "the cares of a household and a family" (175). This is domestic supermanishness, and it is not Nietzschean. It is more in line with a new masculine domesticity. Known as a superman for following the Life Force, Tanner becomes instead its "victim" when it is embodied in a woman. Tanner has apparently given up on resisting the castrating effects of a woman upon the creative artist. He cedes the creative impulse to the woman, who produces children. This is neither consistent with his ideas nor is it Nietzschean; in "The Revolutionist's Handbook," he says, "Marriage, whilst it is made an indispensable condition of mating, will delay the advent of the Superman." But it is consistent with an inchoate advocacy of eugenics. For, like Herbert Wace in London's *The Kempton-Wace Letters*, Tanner "advocates careful 'breeding [of] the race, ay, breeding it to heights now deemed superhuman.'"[86]

The play, in its final move, is as much anti-Nietzschean as *The Iron Heel*, and a strong, creative woman is the cause. Either we take Shaw's identification with Tanner as complete (and regard "The Revolutionist's Handbook" as his own), or we take Shaw at his word later in life as an antagonist to the Nietzschean superman. It wasn't incumbent upon London to make either choice. It is enough for him to reject both the way the superman concept is upheld in the play and the way that love and marriage are disparaged; as Silver notes in his study of Shaw's plays, in *Man and Superman* "love is merely vestigial, and in the Superman it will be totally absent." By marrying Charmian Kittredge, London emphatically rejected his previous arguments as Wace. But, more important, he creates a space for a woman in the world of authorship. This is not simply an act of early twentieth-century feminism. It is a statement against the Nietzschean superman.

Two other works of fiction are usually cited as influences when discussing *The Iron Heel*: H. G. Wells's *When the Sleeper Wakes* and Ignatius Donnelly's *Caesar's Column*. Apart from some minor congruences, these works bear little resemblance to London's work. In fact, their major conceptual designs are as different as can be from London's. Wells and Donnelly imagine the future in terms of the advancement of technology. One interesting overlap between the two is the imagining of a worldwide news and movie service accessed through iPad-like devices and that will displace the novel as a favored form of entertainment. For Donnelly, who doesn't consider one medium's replacement of another, the prototype for the internet and iPad is a series of "telephone tubes" into which one speaks and then receives an answer in what the main character "had supposed to be a mirror" where a requested news item appears (33). In both novels transportation is always elevated: airships and rails cruise through the sky, and skyscrapers are prodigiously high. Futurity, in other words, is defined as airborne technology.

For London, futurity is a matter of ideas, not technology. Those ideas are always about the betterment of mankind through revised economic relationships. In Donnelly's novel, the Brotherhood is not the Brotherhood of Man; it is the Brotherhood of Destruction, the violent proletariat who eventually rebel in ferocious combat against what he calls the Oligarchy. The Oligarchy, however, is simply a dozen or so men who run everything, a creation from the perspective of a deeply frustrated Christian reformist, not from the socioeconomic principles of a revolutionary socialist. True, Donnelly (sparingly) uses footnotes to document certain sections, as when Maximillian, a leader of the Brotherhood, cites magazine articles from 1889 about the disastrous effects of the concentration of wealth and the predictions of violence made by right-thinking bishops. And, true, he imagines rebels throwing grenades from airships and a bloody fight between a crazed proletariat and everyone else. But beyond these insignificant details, Donnelly, a reform-minded populist from Minnesota, shared no ideas in common with London. The novel is heavily influenced by the Civil War and the assassination of Lincoln, events that held much less meaning for London's generation. Donnelly's novel is in fact a lesson, not in the awful power of the Oligarchy, but the murderous anarchy of the proletariat if they were ever allowed to take control. The warfare they wage is more like civil war than class struggle.

Wells's politics are closer to London's, but different in significant ways. In *When the Sleeper Wakes* the brotherhood is more like the Brotherhood of Man than the Brotherhood of Destruction, but it is as corrupted and just as autocratic as the oligarchy it replaces. Again, the lesson is that reform is preferred to cataclysmic change. One might think that Donnelly's and Wells's novels are more entertaining, but they are in fact duller. Donnelly's novel is more a melodrama about the necessary protection of virginity than a political statement; for someone like London who witnessed young girls in cages hung up for display and purchase in San Francisco, Donnelly's conventional sex morals must have struck him as quaint and his reformist, anticataclysmic politics naïve. Wells's morality, given his reading in Nietzsche and his reaction against how he (mis)understood the philosopher, is more in tune with London's. Both of them rejected the idea that the "common man" was merely "weak and bestial" and needed the aristocratic *beyondman* to take charge of society. Both thus favored a political system that Nietzsche detested. In sum, though London's work seems more abstract in conception than either Wells's or Donnelly's, it is highly dramatic. In it, one can sense the influence of the several years of thinking about and writing plays. All three works are theatrical, but only London's creates drama through dialogue.

No, the fiction and essays that most influenced the writing of *The Iron Heel* were all written by Jack London, except George Bernard Shaw's *Man and Superman*, which one may classify as either a play or a pamphlet or some odd combination of the two, like *The Iron Heel*.[87]

John Spargo provided London with similar kinds of information for the novel. By including Spargo, and his fellow centrist Robert Hunter (who is briefly cited in a footnote) side by side with more radical socialists like Ernest Untermann, by sounding (and critiquing) themes that were advanced by revolutionaries and Christian Socialists, conservatives as well as progressives, London tried to unite, rhetorically, all the diverse factions of the Left. It's as if the ISS had commissioned the book. The novel then is a kind of rhetorical illustration of the similarities among them all. It was an important facet of his temporary farewell message to the American socialists. To defeat capitalism we must be united, London subtly proclaimed. Echoing one of his heroes and "the great humanist" Abraham Lincoln, who is cited as such in one of Meredith's footnotes, London is calling for the leftist house divided against itself to find common ground.[88] Only in that way will the Oligarchy be defeated. In fact, in the mid-aughts, the socialist program began to overlap with the reformist parties, including mainstream Democrats. "Municipal ownership of public utilities, the ending of graft, the initiative and referendum, and municipal home rule" had entered mainstream politics.[89] What London had not foreseen was that mainstream progressive politics would rob revolutionary socialism of its will to continue. But that realization would not become painful and his involvement in the world of leftist politics unsustainable until 1916.

Spargo's influence came from his two 1906 books: *Socialism* and *The Bitter Cry of the Children*. The former appears twice in London's notes. From *Socialism*, London learned, if he hadn't already from some other unknown source, that Columbus discovered America because the eastern trade routes had been blocked by the Turks, an example of the materialist conception of history.[90] The latter, introduced by Hunter, appears once, in London's notes, in conjunction with a reference to Hunter: "Footnotes Historian gives summaries figures from books like 'Poverty' 'Bitter Cry of Children' etc. A book written at the beginning of this era by John Spargo, etc."[91] London marked passages that documented the capitalist exploitation of child labor and its deleterious effects on health. He would have found the 1900 census figure for the number of child laborers that Everhard cites in his speech to the Philomath Club.[92] Although Spargo's name does not appear in *The Iron Heel*, Spargo's book reinforced London's newfound conviction that environment was as important as heredity to human development; the first passage he marked reads, "The number of children born healthy and strong is not greater among the well-to-do classes than among the very poorest," and then he marked a passage in appendix c (the recorded testimony of one of England's school inspectors, devoted to the question of heredity versus environment) concluding that class did not determine the health of a baby at birth, only after it was born.[93]

In a 1921 letter to Charmian, Spargo praises her biography and then says, "It made me proud to come across the inclusion of my name in the list of his 'intellectual friends'"; he is referring to Charmian's list in her biography: "Walling, Spargo, Hunter, Stokes, Heron."[94] Spargo goes on: "Just as it made me proud to find, when I first read 'The Iron Heel,' that the definition of Socialism he gave had been taken from my 'Socialism,' and I have proudly remembered the kind words he wrote me."[95] The definition he is referring to seems to be socialism as "social evolution," a phrase that appears repeatedly in Meredith's foreword, though it is a phrase London could have picked up from any number of sources. Spargo, however, had forgotten that when he had written his lukewarm review of the novel in the *International Socialist Review*, he had found that the passages from Everhard's book *Working-class Philosophy* that Ernest reads aloud in the second chapter are in fact quotations from *Socialism*; Ernest even gives the correct page numbers.[96] Still, it is a testament to Spargo's magnanimity (and perhaps egotism) or desire to unite all factions of socialists that he wrote such an unequivocally positive letter to Charmian. It was a different time, post–World War I, and he no longer had a need to separate himself from revolutionaries like London. That factional strife was all in the distant past.

We can now turn to those explicit references to source material that appear either in London's notes or in the novel itself or both. The number of sources cited in Meredith's footnotes is not quite as large as one might expect, and it is interesting to note what names and events in Avis's manuscript are not opened out for explanation or, in the case of the phrase *Iron*

Heel, obscured. Although Meredith says that the title of the manuscript "originated in Ernest Everhard's mind," it in fact appeared as early as *Huckleberry Finn*; the duke complains that "'Tis my fate to be always ground into the mire under the iron heel of oppression."[97] We should also remember that London used the phrase in his 1900 notes for his Christ novel, as in "the iron heel of Rome."[98] Place names such as Berkeley, Missouri, Texas, and Constantinople; historical periods such as the Middle Ages; figures of the past such as Herbert Spencer and an "Indian medicine-man" (14); adjectives like "Mephistophelian," "lick-spittlers," and "panderers," and nouns like "scab" and "labor-ghettos" (36, 181, 42, 217) all could have been footnoted in the way that "peddler," "people of the abyss," "fake," and "grub" are. We know that London as author makes a telling political or linguistic point (London is forever committed to the beauty and functionality of language) with each footnote, but Meredith's choices sometimes seem random and certainly not as thorough as we might expect. Berkeley will exist in 2638? We will know what a lick-spittler is but not a peddler? Those words and phrases that are footnoted may be as obscure to us (and to past and future readers) as Meredith imagined they would be, and so we have to accept on faith that Meredith knows his present readers well. We may then assume that every word and phrase that seems to call for a footnote, whether one is provided or not, indicates exactly what the future will look like. What Meredith doesn't tell us are things he knows his readers already know. On the other hand, there seems to be a principal of economy at work in Meredith's research, but it is unclear and speaks to London's neglect to fully characterize one of his two narrators.

A little over two months into the writing of the novel, London received a copy of Ambrose Bierce's first volume of *The Cynic's Word Book* from George Sterling, with the inscription, "I believe you can stand for even the definition of 'Grapeshot'!"[99] London went back to chapter 5 and plugged in the footnote for Wickson's prediction that socialists will be beaten with military force. Bierce, as Meredith (and London) called him, may have been a "misanthrope" (and London intends by that word to indicate Bierce as an antisocialist—he thought all socialists to be utopian dreamers), but he accurately predicted capitalism's answer to political dissent.

Henry Van Dyke's *Essays in Application* provided Meredith with a perfect example of "bourgeois thinking." Van Dyke was the belletristic Presbyterian minister at Princeton University for over twenty years, someone who sermonized against "the vulgarity of organized business" but found biblical justification for private property and capitalism.[100] Van Dyke argued against the notion that Jesus was a socialist or communist (terms Van Dyke uses interchangeably) by saying that (a) Jesus said the poor shall always be with us and (b) the source of poverty is "the selfish and willful evil that dwells in the heart of man" that requires "the use and control of [private property] by the spirit of fair play and wise love." He may well have been a model for Bishop Morehouse before his conversion. They both certainly believed in the possibility of "fair play" under capitalism.[101] Unlike Van Dyke, Morehouse saw the light.

London read Joseph R. Buchanan's *The Story of a Labor Agitator* in 1905. London marked Buchanan's account of hearing the live reports via phone of the hanging of the Haymarket Square anarchists as well as copies of the letters that four of the imprisoned men sent to Governor Altgeld protesting their innocence and the justice of their cause (see pages 382–87, 412–15). In his notes for *The Iron Heel*, London wrote, "Thousands were killed Many were executed—a la Chicago Anarchists (draw material from speeches)," and he may have been referencing these letters; but he decided against using them, limiting himself to a brief mention in the novel of the Haymarket Square anarchists' executions as an example of the power of the Iron Heel. Given that either he or Charmian typed out several paragraphs from the book and then placed the typed sheet in his "Persistence of the Established" file, Buchanan's book seems most likely a source for that uncompleted project, not *The Iron Heel* (see p. 186 of *Story of a Labor Agitator*).

Charles Watson has pointed out a number of sources for *The Iron Heel's* minor characters. There is Anna Roylston, called the Red Virgin, a sobriquet first used for Louise Michel, the famous anarchist of the Paris Commune of 1871. As Watson notes, London had clipped a profile of her occasioned by her death in January 1905, planning to use it for a lecture that would reverse the meaning of *anarchy* and "hold Louise Michel up as a better type of human than a woman of the bourgeoisie, fat and selfish and dead."[102] London's lecture on anarchy was to argue that true anarchy was practiced by competitive capitalists and that "socialists who go the trusts one better in law and order, are assailed bitterly, and even called anarchists by these misguided anarchists." The first line of his notes is "See 'Diseases of Society,'" G. Frank Lydston's 1904 work on criminal anthropology. In his chapter "Anarchy and Its Relations to Crime," Lydston provides London with the intellectual underpinning necessary to rework the popular idea of anarchy. As Lydston writes, "Every criminal may be justly termed an anarchist in action, whatever his theories of social conditions may be," for the criminal and the anarchist think only of self-preservation and egotism, not "the social instinct," "the highest, most altruistic phase of the instinct of self-preservation." In fact, "the true anarchist is not a firebrand, but a mistaken, misguided philosopher, an idealist whose conceptions of what ought to be are not in harmony with what is." Thus London could imagine the capitalist as an anarchist, someone willing to sacrifice the good of the people for the sake of personal profit.[103]

The speech was to conclude with the portrait of Louise Michel, taken to be an exemplar of the altruistic person, the antithesis to the anarchist. But it is likely that in *The Iron Heel* he used and modified (or simply could not spell) Jane Roulston's last name and then used Sterling Heilig's characterization of Michel for the character of his own Red Virgin.[104] After all, Joan London (who is following her source, Austin Lewis's memoir, very closely) describes Roulston as "retiring, almost old maidish in her ultra-respectable, typically Eastern bearing," a description that does not match Anna Roylston, whose first name is most assuredly taken from Jane Roulston's and Jack's good friend Anna Strunsky Walling.[105] Like Michel, Roylston was an assassin; Michel had tried and failed to murder both Thiers and Napoleon III, whereas Roylston successfully murders the oligarch Timothy Donnelly. One sentence in Heilig's piece must have appeared to London as if in bold and forty-eight-point type: Michel "had revolted against society because it leaves wizened children to wear their lives out in factories or starve in the street."[106] The American anarchist Emma Goldman, who had so fervently spoken on behalf of child laborers in front of London earlier in 1906, may have been a kind of silent, perhaps unconscious source for Anna Roylston as well.

I mentioned in chapter 5 that one of London's notes in the back of Henry George's *The Menace of Privilege* was intended for *The Iron Heel*; the rest were for his never-completed essay "The Persistence of the Established," meaning that he had not abandoned the latter for the former. On the back cover of *The Menace of Privilege*, he wrote "165–6 Quote for Future Novel." These pages find their rearticulation in Meredith's footnote in chapter 15 of *The Iron Heel* on P. M. Arthur, the head of the union of locomotive engineers. In his chapter called "The Dangers of Unionism," George writes that Arthur, after "the Pittsburg strike and riot of 1877," had devised "a scheme to have the engineers, as a union, make the best terms possible with the railroad companies and 'go it alone,' regardless of public rights the railroads were overriding." London reworked this as "he broached a scheme to have the Locomotive Engineers make terms with the railroads and to 'go it alone' so far as the rest of the labor unions were concerned" (165). But then London adds a typical rhetorical flourish and invents the term "arthurization" to further demonize the union traitor.

One source earned London unwanted publicity and another charge of plagiarism. London used a report from the Chicago-based *Socialist Spirit* for Bishop Morehouse's speech in chapter 7. As had been retold many times, the British novelist and editor Frank Harris imagined the Bishop of London giving a speech, not placating the materialism and complacency of his congregation, but rather as if he "had suddenly become a Christian." He published it in his magazine the *Candid Friend* in 1901. The *Socialist Spirit*, based in Chicago, reprinted the speech as a straight news item later the same year. London clipped the article, filed it, and then six years later pulled it out for his new novel.[107] He then drafted a few lines in the margin to rewrite a passage in which Harris mentions a London locale, changing it to a generic allusion: "I live in such locality It is a mansion. It is a palace. I never knew what palaces were good for—."[108] He incorporated six paragraphs nearly word for word but added three paragraphs and a sonnet by Oscar Wilde to complete the bishop's speech. When the novel was published and Harris had read it, he published "How Mr. Jack London Writes a Novel," in which he showed, by printing the pertinent passages side by side, how London had used his bishop's speech. The American newspapers then turned the event into a scandal about plagiarism, sometimes highlighting previous charges against London. In his defense, London explained he had believed the item in the *Socialist Spirit* to have been a straight news story. Who could blame him, given the introduction written by an editor of the *Socialist Spirit*: "At a meeting in London the other evening, called to consider public immorality and the remedy for it, the new bishop of London, Dr. Winnington Ingram, presided. By his side were the bishop of Southwark, Sir Edward Clarke, and H. H. Asquith, the liberal leader. All was perfectly convention until Bishop Ingram arose, evidently in a condition of high nervous tension, and, without any introduction, abruptly started off."[109] London told his public, "I thought I had a human document."[110] Even in 1901 he was tired of being accused by editors and readers of falsifying events upon which he based his fiction, so "with much glee I used it word for word, and again filed the clipping against the possibility of being charged in the future with having stretched realism and human probability."[111] Both London and Harris refused to budge from their respective positions.

The event is less important, however, for understanding London's compositional techniques—we have already seen how he borrows and rewrites from various sources—than it is for the magic phrase he uses to describe his source. "I thought I had a human document." Magazines, especially *McClure's*, sought out human documents, texts that spoke from fact to our emotions, and London used the phrase to characterize his own texts of impassioned realism as well as his sources for those texts. We see it again in connection with *The Iron Heel*. When it was published, he sent a copy to a friend of his and Charmian, Elizabeth Bull, a bourgeois woman from the Bay Area who was interested in learning about socialism. "Walk with me here a bit," London wrote her on the flyleaf, "a[nd] learn a few things on the other side. Remember, however, that this is not my prophecy. It is my fiction. The things that happen are my story. But remember, too, that the story is based upon facts. These facts I vouch for." Interestingly, his facts about the bishop's speech—the source he thought was a human document—turned out to be fiction and yet changed not a whit the force of what he wrote. Harris had complained that London had stolen not only his words but also his "idea," but clearly London's source only buttressed the theoretical points he had gleaned from his socialist reading about the corruption of organized religion and its collusion with capitalism.[112]

In a minor key, London borrowed words and phrases from an essay by Austin Lewis; in this case, however, London actually cites Lewis by name in the novel and in his notes.[113] London drew on a number of articles he had originally set aside for "The Persistence of the Established" and "The Disappearing Class." For London's footnote on patent medicines, he relied on an article entitled "The Great American Fraud" in the *Pandex*.[114] For his long footnote quoting David Graham Phillips in chapter 19, he pulled an article from *Wayland's Monthly* out of his "The Disappearing Class" file that provided him with the quotation from Phillips and the *Saturday Evening Post*. And for the footnote on "the eleven groups [that] dominated the country" he drew on an article in *Twentieth Century*, using it word for word at one point.[115] Apart from articles he cites in the footnotes from *Out-*

look and the *Saturday Evening Post*, other information Meredith provides most likely came from similar clippings from newspapers and magazines that have yet to be located.

As I have noted, Meredith's footnotes provide a factual basis for Avis's emotional appeals to her audience; fact plus story equals human document. But they also play with our sense of time. As much as this novel is about the present as past, it is also about the future. True to London's revolutionary socialist mindset, he will not tell us specifics of Meredith's life. We learn through indirection. There are "pleasure-cities," and Meredith likens them to Wells's "wonder-cities." The city of Ardis has a "National Library," so there is still the concept of nation and its need for an archive and print still is in use (thank God!), not replaced by Wells's new information technology. Food is prepared in laboratories, we learn, as Meredith explains, that in the past "cream and butter were still crudely extracted from cow's milk," another indication of the crucial imbrication of food and politics for socialists (208).[116] There is no more economic slavery, though Meredith warns current "political theorists" that the case of the Iron Heel— unpredicted, unnecessary, and an aberration in social evolution—proves society could always regress; this is of course part of the strategy of jeremiad that London employs. There is no such thing as insurance. In a sly reference to his recent essay "The House Beautiful," London as Meredith says that homeowners in the twentieth century collected bric-a-brac that in turn collected dust: "They had not discovered simplicity of living" (57).

Some of these changes over time are trivial, but some, like the last, indicate a change in human behavior. In the foreword, Meredith writes that by reading Avis's manuscript we learn about "the psychology of the persons that lived in that turbulent period" (6), characteristics "that are so hard for us of this enlightened age to understand" (6). They are presented as things of the past, and only by reading Avis's book can the people understand the past's "mistakes and ignorance, their doubts and fears and misapprehensions, their ethical delusions, their violent passions, their inconceivable sordidness and selfishness" (6). That is, the people of the future apparently are not ignorant, don't have doubt and fears, are not ethically deluded, are not violent, sordid, or selfish; Meredith even has to explain not only the violence between labor and capitalists but also the violence between married folk (see 29). "We," says Meredith to his audience, "who by personal experience know nothing of bloodshed," are handicapped in trying to come to terms with our ancestors (178). Human traits are "facts" about the past, but in the future the factual nature of humankind has changed so momentously that human psychology apparently has been perfected. All are self-actualized, all are compassionate, peaceful, delightful, and delighted in life. London imagines that economic equality is a worthy goal, but it is actually the means to a higher goal, that of the perfection of human nature. No wonder he gives his species seven hundred years to attain that goal.

COMPOSITION AND STRUCTURE

London began to gather and make notes for *The Iron Heel* in August 1906, but the idea for the novel had been long in the making, cooking in the imagination for years, as we have seen by the dates of his sources. Sometime in 1899, he wrote two entries in his idea notebook for a socialist novel or two. The first reads, "Perhaps write a novel, a la Wells, out of idea of wage-slaves, ruled by industrial oligarchs, finally ceasing to reproduce. And either figure out new way of penetrating the future, or begin far ahead of the actual time of the story, by having the writing dug up by the people of a new and very immature civilization. Begin: I without place in the present, write this for the future, if future there be." The second entry reads, "Novel—CAPTAINS OF INDUSTRY. Industrial oligarchs controlling the world, terrible struggles of workmen; some big city center of some scene like the Paris Commune. Read up." There are several important points here. We see London had a generally expansive sense of time as well as the impulse to fictively represent that sense of time even before he had begun *Before Adam*. Second, Wells's work stands for, not so much a model to follow but as a trail blazer. For a long time, then, London was preparing to write *The Iron Heel*. What is missing from his sources and from his 1899 notes is the conception for his main characters: Meredith and the Everhards. That is what he seemed most focused on in 1906—the development through fictional characters of a history play of American socialism.

London's notes apart from those he took on potential sources can be roughly divided into two piles: the very early 1906 notes, in which he is feeling his way toward a beginning, toward the proper role for Avis, and for the plot line; and the later, more confident notes that match sometimes word for word what he ended up writing. The latter come after he has his character names more or less firmly in mind, and he notes down material for the foreword, the episode of Jackson's arm (first called Thompson), the significance of the Moyer-Haywood-Pettibone case (another link to what he had been writing in 1906), Ernest's election to Congress, the Chicago Commune and premature revolt (for which he used the subhead "Chicago: City of Blood"), and a few of Ernest's rhetorical battles.

For the creation of Meredith, he merely needed a two-dimensional character, a disembodied voice, a kind of voiceover for the docudrama of the Everhards' lives. He is an intellectual, a kind of conglomeration of all of London's sources. There is no indication that London put much thought into Meredith's creation. His name does not even appear in the notes. At some point London did write notes for a foreword, but they describe a different sort of beginning: "Foreword The finding of the manuscript in the heart of an oak, blown down by the wind—hidden, undoubtedly in year so-and-so, at the terrible break-down of what the historians call the Second Revolt—when the United Oligarchies of the world drown in seas of blood the movement toward liberty (better) Little did Avis Everhard realize that the slow and torturous evolution of the ages that there was to be a Second Revolt, a Third Revolt, etc.—before the change."[117] We can hear how London was creating Meredith's voice, a kind of third-person narrator become first-person commentator. But we cannot lose sight of one of London's central conceits. That is, while Avis wrote the manuscript that is found in a tree—interestingly foreshadowed by the tree that elevates and helps transform Johnny in "The Apostate"—Anthony Meredith is the author (or author-editor) of the book that we read: *The Iron Heel*. By adding all of his paratextual material to Avis's manuscript, Meredith creates this hybrid of novel, memoir, autobiography, history, jeremiad, and play.

Ernest Everhard is Johnny from "The Apostate" all grown up. We left Johnny, just a few months previously, no longer bitter about the death of God or capitalism, which amounted to the same thing. He had found peace in the country, waiting for a train; he was "becoming a tramp," as London says in his notes.[118] He is recovering from, among other things, the sound of the daily factory steam whistle, which is footnoted in *The Iron Heel* ("the laborers were called to work and dismissed by savage, screaming, nerve-racking steam-whistles," which helped dehumanize the workers [38]). His revolt against God is made theoretical in a number of footnotes in *The Iron Heel*, particularly on pages 32–33, concerning the partnership between Christianity and capitalism, as well as the storyline for Bishop Morehouse. Note, too, how Meredith dates the election of 1906 as a year in "the Christian era," as opposed to the current era of the Brotherhood of Man. Even a seemingly innocuous sentence in *The Iron Heel* shows the rhetorical continuity between the two works. When Avis is describing her meeting with Jackson, she says, "He ripped out a savage oath." This sentence earns a footnote from Meredith: "It is interesting to note the virilities of language that were common speech in that day, as indicative of the life, 'red of claw and fang,' that was then lived. Reference is here made, of course, not to the oath of Smith, but to the verb ripped used by Avis Everhard" (44). Though *ripped* doesn't appear in "The Apostate," it does in London's notes for the story and in the same context: describing Johnny as he watched his younger brother play out front, London writes, "He was peevish and irritable—rips out a snarling curse when younger brother teases him."[119] Both Johnny and Ernest worked in the same kind of factory at approximately the same age; Johnny was born in the mill, and Ernest started there at age ten. With London's own life experiences providing some of the characterization of Everhard, we shouldn't be surprised that Johnny would undergo a conversion to socialism while on the road and, reborn with the new name Ernest, become a socialist leader and author.

Not only do London's experiences provide this continuity between the two stories. Consider the sunny, life-affirming setting at the end of "The Apostate" and note its continuation into the beginning of *The Iron Heel*. Bohemianism and tramping are enough to save the soul of one child-man; we remember how the imagination, figured by Johnny's vision of the tree (whose "brother" then holds the manuscript of *The Iron Heel*), saves his life, making him into a creative entity. Once again, writing is a life-and-death matter for the individual. But when London wants to promulgate a systemic solution to capitalism's tyranny, then the bohemian, radicalized, must leave the sunlight and reenter the war of the classes in the cities, just as Everhard does.

I have talked about Ernest as a ghost, as a Nietzschean blond beast, and as a superman, but his primary identity—as we see in the continuity with "The Apostate"—is as a proletariat. We might be surprised that London thought of Lincoln as a model for Ernest, but because Lincoln's role as the Great Emancipator lost potency for London's generation, he became something else. London and other socialists could see Lincoln, like Jesus, as a working-class figure, a proletariat. Thus we get a long quotation in chapter 6 from one of Everhard's letters, warning of the threat to the United States created by corporations, the aggregation of wealth, and "the money-power of the country" (78). In one of London's early notes, he describes Ernest as "a horseshoer originally, a Lincoln type of man, warm and human, and great," self-educated, his speech marked by "homely use of figures, a la Lincoln." Typical of London, he creates a character through his speech patterns, and language is central to Ernest's nature. "He was a poet," says Avis, "a singer in deeds." In this way he is like Buck, and Avis uses a verbal construction very much like London's description of Buck: "And all his life he sang the song of man. And he did it out of sheer love of man" (182). This is not to say that Ernest howled like a dog, but rather the dog sang like a socialist leader of the pack. Note how many times Meredith alludes to wolves in his footnotes to characterize economic man. Ernest's song implores men to turn away from their wolfish nature and become truly human. But like Lincoln and Jesus, "for man," says Avis in language straight from the King James version of the Bible, "he gave his life and was crucified."

Avis is the central figure because she is the primary author figure in a work filled with them. After all, she writes the book that London writes, making her at least as much a part of London's psyche as Ernest is. To that point, initially, she was to be a proletariat author. The story of Avis's father was to be the starting point of the novel before London decided to relegate him to a footnote and to the role of facilitator and observer—quite like a stage manager. In a note labeled "Beginning" (which he then crossed out when he realized he had a better idea), he imagined his novel would start with Cunningham's demise as "a broken professor—develop why he was broken. He was of independent income as well. Straight old Mayflower stock. He was broken at the beginning of the combination of large capitalists with the labor unions. The story begins right here—giving causes for breaking him, current events, etc." The result would entail Avis going to work in a "sweatshop."[120] London abandoned that plot line before he envisioned its end, but he never let go of his conception of Avis as an authorial figure. Cunningham, interestingly, retains his "stout old *Mayflower* stock," but Meredith not only denigrates how Americans in the twentieth century were "inordinately proud of their genealogy" but also points out how "the blood [of the original colonists] became so widely diffused that it ran in the veins practically of all Americans" (129). This footnote is similar to an earlier one in which Meredith writes that "the distinction between being native-born and foreign-born was sharp and invidious in those days," a sharp commentary on twenty-first-century immigration debates in the United States. I have mentioned how London, by using a woman narrator, rejected his views in *Kempton-Wace Letters* as well as the Nietzschean views of marriage. Now, in an oblique way, we see the maturation of London's views on the importance of blood and race. In fact, *The Iron Heel* contains some of London's strongest antiracist rhetoric. Note in particular Meredith's footnote on the word *leg-bar*. In the future, London imagines, distinction by race will not matter to the perfected human species. We will be all one.

As he considered the beginning to be an exposition of how labor and capitalists united, he made notes with the subhead "Love." This would be the story of Avis and Ernest, though at first she would be Avis Selfridge or maybe Elsa or Herda, and Ernest would be Ernest Blenheim or maybe Bartholomew; he would be twenty-eight, she twenty-four. She would write a foreword much like Meredith's but explaining why she needed to write a history of the time. The time period would be different—1914–75, not 1912–32—and Avis's account would show how what "was mysterious at time of occurrence afterward cleared up." Very early on, when he first had the title in mind but not any names, he tried out an entirely different beginning: "Iron Heel Very concrete, begin most likely with him—the leader of the people—his surroundings, his home, etc. etc. At the end, dying, the word is brought him that the world war is afoot. The Germans, the French, English, Italians, Russians, etc., and the final liberation comes."[121] Avis seems very much a background character, the narrative a straightforward account of the successful worldwide socialist revolution for which Ernest would be martyred. Avis evolved, then, in London's notes, becoming more and more prominent, and then less and less an authoritative historical voice and more of an impassioned memoirist. As London was able to weave the love story into the dramatic dialogues that constitute the first several chapters, Avis gave birth to Meredith, and Ernest ended up in her shadow.

Avis is the hero of Anthony Meredith's novel *The Iron Heel*, and Ernest is the hero of Avis's untitled memoir. By denigrating Ernest's role in the revolution, Meredith elevates Avis's stature. London's source material for *The Iron Heel* reiterated time and again the necessity of treating men and women equally in all realms of life, especially the economic one. The official platform for the Socialist Party, in its list of "Immediate Demands," called for "equal civil and political rights for men and women."[122] London, Gronlund, Spargo, and others all agreed on the importance of the role of women in the movement, something that American socialists did not in large numbers favor.[123] That two major figures in the novel are women should be very striking to us and would have been to London's readers. Remember that Gronlund's *Co-Operative Commonwealth* argued for the equal status of women—not universal suffrage, but equal pay for equal work. Voting was "bourgeois reform" and would matter little in the long (really long) run.

Political principle is coupled with a private willingness to admit Charmian into his authorial practice—if only in a limited and intermittent way. It is not surprising to see London return to the creation of a strong, independent, female, central character. Unlike Frona Welse, though, Avis is explicitly an author figure. London's choice of reflector is thus politically motivated.

She is very much modeled on the one woman he had closest at hand, the only one whom he could imagine paired with Ernest: Charmian Kittredge London. In *The Iron Heel*, Avis even had "a writer friend" who had owned the property where she hid out in Sonoma County; "he, too, had become a revolutionist," but he died, most likely killed by the Oligarchy (chapter 18). Avis and Ernest's love story is somewhat problematic from a twenty-first-century point of view. Despite Ernest being "overworked," says Avis, "he found time in which to love me and make me happy. But this was accomplished only through my merging my life completely into his." Like Charmian, Avis used shorthand and typing to stay close to her man or, as she says, "Our interests became mutual, and we worked together and played together" (136). At first sight, the relationship seems only to benefit him, and yet in the next paragraph it sounds as if they lived the perfect couple's life that would be realized for all in Meredith's time: "We lived on the heights, where the air was keen and sparkling, where the toil was for humanity, and where sordidness and selfishness never entered. We loved love" (136). When we realize that Charmian was more than a typist and actively collaborated on his work, including changing words in the manuscript of *The Iron Heel*, we see what London meant by Avis and Ernest working together. It isn't quite the same degree of collaboration that Anna Strunsky and Jack effected with *The Kempton-Wace Letters*, but it is the same kind.

In an interesting manipulation of time, London creates the illusion that we get the full account of Ernest and Avis's conjoined lives. Yet because the manuscript begins with their meeting in February 1912 and ends with the failure of the First Revolt in 1917, and because Avis composes the manuscript in 1932, we realize we have a record of only a fifth of their time together.

The Iron Heel, thus, is not so much a love story as it is a first-love story. It's as if Maude Brewster and Humphrey Van Weyden had to live their love life hidden from the sight of Wolf Larsen, who only grows stronger, not weaker; the link between Larsen and the Oligarchy is not so far-fetched given the constant allusion to the wolfish nature of capitalism in *The Iron Heel*.

By changing the starting point of his novel, London was able to allow the drama of the ascendency of the Iron Heel as well as that of the lovers to slowly increase. Mr. Wickson does not warn Cunningham of his eventual social and financial destruction until the eleventh chapter. This allows London to convey both the strength of the socialists and of the oligarchs through staged conversations and to build drama through dialogue. The structure of the first part of the novel, like a play, is built around monologues and arguments among antagonists about economics and politics. It moves from Everhard's debate with Dr. Hammerfield about scientific and philosophic truth; to his debate with Bishop Morehouse about Christianity and socialism; to the dialogue between Everhard and Avis about Jackson's injury and profit; to Everhard's speech to the Philomath Club and the subsequent debate; to Morehouse's speech; to Everhard's speech at Avis's father's "Profit and Loss" dinner and the debate about surplus value. Chapter 10, "The Vortex," begins what might be called act 2. In this section, static speechifying and debate give way to action (as implied by the title of the chapter) and a more conventional novelistic narrative. Avis sums up her father's dismissal from the university and the suppression of his book, the defeat of labor's strikes, the crushing of the middle class, and the hope and defeat of political action—all the stages of socioeconomic and political resistance that London himself had tried out in theory and practice and decided would be ineffectual compared to outright revolution. Act 3 begins with chapter 15, "Last Days," and the tempo of the dramatic action begins to accelerate. The final act is a mix of the theatrical and the absorptive. Everhard debates with O'Connor the labor leader about the value of socialists and unions standing together, which results in Everhard's vision of the future battle between the labor castes and the Oligarchy and its relation to surplus value. These are the days of the international rise of the Iron Heel, the destruction of the Grangers and the coal miners' union in the U.S., and the underground warfare between socialist secret agents and the agents of the Iron Heel. All this is told by Avis in broad strokes until she alights on the bombing of Congress, the arrest and conviction of Everhard (and its comparison to the Haywood-Moyer-Pettibone case), Avis's residence in the socialist hideout in Glen Ellen, the grand jailbreak and reunification of the two lovers, the preparations for the First Revolt, and its failure. The chapters seem to grow shorter and shorter until, like the vortex forecasted in chapter 10, we get to the bottom tip of the funnel and the end of the manuscript. As the dystopic elements of American sociopolitical life increase, so, too, does the romance between the two protagonists. Love does not triumph so much as hold in abeyance the despair wrought by capitalism.

THE PRODUCTION OF THE JEREMIAD

Charmian worked hard typing the novel throughout the fall, but rarely noted her exact progress. On the other hand, each day between the nineteenth—the day after he had completed his final short story of the year, "Just Meat"—and the twenty-fifth of August she wrote that London was "working up" his notes and gathering his research materials for *The Iron Heel*, a rather long period for preparation. On the twenty-fifth, he began the introduction, finished it the next day, and she typed it on the twenty-seventh as "Mate began novel proper."[124] A month later she completed chapter 7, "The Bishop's Vision," a little less than a third of the way through. She contributed only a few revisions in the manuscript, fewer than in *Before Adam*. In the first chapter she changed "demanded testily" to "repeated impatiently" to avoid a repetition of "demanded." In chapter 2 she helped him place the long footnote on Christian support for slavery. And in chapter 21 she added a few clarifying words in its first chapter.[125] She was not as emotionally moved by this work as she was by, say, later novels such as *The Valley of the Moon* and *The Little Lady of the Big House*.

But she was sharing in his good mood. They were having sex on a regular basis, and London wrote to a friend (Zoe Greene Radcliffe) that "you hear aright. I am very happy these days. Everybody mistakes the radiance of happiness in my face, for avoirdupois, and tells me I am getting fat."[126] When, as he was writing, he reached a point that needed a footnote, he would draw a line across the page at some point below, estimating the length of the footnote. If he misjudged, he would simply write out the rest of the footnote text, cut it from that new sheet, and pin it to the bottom. Sometimes he constructed the footnotes on the same day as he wrote the text that called for the footnote; sometimes, when he revisited the text, usually on the following day of writing, he added the note by writing it on a separate piece of paper and then attaching it to the bottom of the correct sheet of manuscript with pins.

By mid-September, he told Cloudesley Johns that he was an eighth of the way done, though he was further along than he thought; he originally projected the length to be over one hundred thousand words, but he finished it under that count.[127] To Johns, he enthusiastically made his first description of his new work: "It is a socialistic-capitalistic novel. The Iron Heel is the oligarchy of the master capitalists. The period covered is between 1912 and 1932—the twenty years that begin with the Peasant Revolt & Chicago Commune, and that culminated in the Second Revolt in 1932. But know that this Second Revolt was a failure, and that the Iron Heel ruled three centuries longer. Then came the new era of the Brotherhood of Man, and it was in the fourth century B.O.M. that the manuscript was discovered & published—seven centuries after it was written." He was excited simply about the plot line, happy to have finally worked out his complicated time sequence. He also talked as if the novel's events were actual historical occurrences: the Peasant Revolt, the Chicago Commune, the Second Revolt. He is very much into the role of Anthony Meredith.

"Of course, there is a foreword written by a historian," he next tells Johns, as if Johns had earlier insisted that a novel like this—a novel that has no precedent—would require a historian's point of view. "The book is copiously annotated by said historian, & you can imagine, with his seven centuries of perspective, the delicious slings he takes at the irrational and anarchic organization & management of society to-day."[128] Here is his principal delight, critiquing the present from an unassailable point of view, though as he continued working through the relationship between Meredith and the manuscript he found he could use the manuscript to critique the humorless, hyperrational Meredith and so create a character whose life may be in perfect balance and in harmony with all others—as they are with him—but who seems soulless. Meredith is supposed to be flat, a two-dimensional creation whose accurate pronouncements do not mask the gaps in his knowledge or his inability to grasp some of the subtleties of Avis's rhetoric. London didn't want to make the future seem too perfect and thus had found a fictional form that truly delighted him. "I'm having the time of my life writing the story," he tells Johns at the end of his letter to him. Living with the daily stress of building the *Snark* under demanding circumstances—the scarcity of materials, the rising costs of everything, the prospect of sailing across the Pacific without knowing how to navigate—he found solace in his authorial practice. It was never about the money.

He also emphasized Meredith's role and his "foreword and copious footnotes" to George Brett in September. At the same time that he told his agent, Paul Reynolds, that he was ready to market the story serially and would send him the first twenty-five thousand words soon, he told Brett about the new project and his progress—now up to twenty-two thousand words, having written two thousand in the day after writing Reynolds.[129] Because he thought Reynolds would never be able to sell it to a magazine, he told Brett they might try Brett's experiment of bringing a book out without serialization to see if his book sales were hurt by previous publication. It did not occur to him, apparently, that the reason the book could not be serialized may be a principal reason for the book doing poorly. It was after all "something entirely different from anything I have done!" and though he admitted he often said this, *The Iron Heel* was indeed something completely different.[130]

Eleven days later he had written ten thousand more words. "If it hits the American public at the psychological moment, it will make a ten-strike," said London the marketing exec. "In many ways, it is the most daring book I have ever attempted."[131] Then he stopped his puffery and limited himself to reporting to Brett and Reynolds how far along he was: by 16 October he had done fifty thousand words, by 31 October he had completed sixty thousand, and by 16 November he had written seventy thousand.[132] In October, though, he pitched his novel to Frederick Bamford as more of an essay on the "the perishing middle class," "surplus value," and "the inevitable breakdown of capitalism under the structure of profits it has reared," something suitable to be read to the Ruskin Club.[133]

As London kept Brett abreast of his progress, they were negotiating, among other matters, advances and a new contract. Both parties wanted to continue the contractual arrangement as it had stood for the last several years, so that wasn't creating any tension. And the question of advances was easily resolved in London's favor; even though Brett asked him to "go easy" and reminded him that he was around twenty-two hundred dollars overdrawn since July 1905, he told London the sales of both *White Fang* and *Before Adam* would cover the past deficit and create a solid cushion for the future. So London hit him up for five thousand dollars at the same time that he unintentionally deflated Brett's expectations for *The Iron Heel*. Brett had written that if the new book was a novel about a utopia—an update of, say,

Looking Backward—then, as a "very clever fellow" had told him recently, "the public would give more for a story of a Utopia than for anything else."[134] London signed, sealed, and delivered the new contract, asked for the five grand, and told him "*The Iron Heel*, by the way, deals, not with a Utopia, but with an Oligarchy."[135] Rats, thought Brett; I thought I might have another best seller. Nonetheless, he told London that if *The Iron Heel* was as artfully accomplished as *White Fang*, "there should then be no limit to what you will be able to do and the public that you will be able to command."[136] Brett had no idea of the extent to which London had not only promoted radical socialist ideals but also experimented with the novelistic form. If he had known, in the interest of maintaining a nurturing and permanent relationship with London, he still would have supported his author.

He even backed away from the idea of publishing a novel without serialization. He pointed out that if he received the manuscript in December, there would be nearly a year before its book publication, providing plenty of time for its magazine appearance. Sensing that the book might be something entirely new, he reminded London of the "multiplicity of magazines" that allowed not only for expanded opportunity but for getting "a very good price for it indeed," and he offered to handle the negotiations himself; he once told London that he thought agents were parasites, but useful when there were so many magazines to deal with.[137] Reynolds, though, had made the same offer, and London let him do it, thinking he might get $10,000 for it; later, after Reynolds asked if he would be willing to cut material like the characterization of William Randolph Hearst, he thought he might get $5,000. In the meantime, A. M. Simons at the *Appeal to Reason* asked for the privilege of publishing it, but London begged off, hoping to not have to donate it to the cause. "On the other hand," he wrote, "there is a large likelihood that the stuff will be too strong for any of the conventional magazines."[138] It would all be resolved shortly because he predicted that he would complete the manuscript on 15 December.[139] He finished it two days ahead of schedule; "It is only 90,000 words long," he told Brett. "I didn't dare an anti-climax after The Chicago Commune. So I cut it short right there."[140]

It may have been the best aesthetic choice, but he wondered if the book had turned out to be a generally unappealing artwork. He sent it first to Reynolds with hesitant promotion: "It will puzzle you and the editors, I am sure. Nevertheless, if the editors will only realize how live a question socialism is right now, they won't be so backward in accepting it. But how the dickens are you going to make them realize it?"[141] As we've seen, Reynolds's strategy was to cut all the offensive material out. London repeated his doubts when he sent it to Simons for feedback. He was not hopeful about its chances in the magazine market, even those publications like *Appeal to Reason* that were politically sympathetic. As he told Simons, "The more I think about it, the more impossible it seems to me that the story is even for a socialist publication like THE APPEAL TO REASON. It runs such a strong liability of being misunderstood, and hence, instead of being a help, it would turn out a hurt, to the propaganda."[142] When he sent it to Brett, he was only slightly more upbeat, wanting Brett to be critical if need be but hoping that he would see how "the widespread interest in socialism" would make it "a hit."[143] It wasn't so much, then, about getting paid. London now realized that he had written a book that may have appealed only to him. He had unintentionally undermined his mission to help unite the American Left.

Brett had other concerns. Initially, he told London he would read it when it appeared in print.[144] Then, in January, he sent London one of his longest personal reports on a manuscript and asked London to address three issues. First, he thought the novel would succeed or fail based on the reader's ability to imagine himself as a reader in the time of Anthony Meredith. To do that, he asked London to beef up the characterization of that future time. Add more detail, make the reader feel as if he or she belongs. "Without such a knowledge of the times," Brett insisted, "however vague, it is difficult for them to approach the story in the right attitude, and they must approach it in the right attitude or the whole fact of the invention or discovery is lost." London, in response, fell back on the artist's right to describe by indirection, in an "austere way," with "many hints and suggestions of that far future time." His choices were dictated "by the form of the narrative," which did not necessarily take into account the construction of a person of a future reader. In fact, it is quite apparent that London wanted his readers to be aware of current critiques of capitalism more than to be knowledgeable about the future. He had written this book for the present; no knowledge of the future was necessary to understand how capitalism had failed and would continue to fail. As Meredith wrote, "Avis Everhard took for granted that her narrative would be read in her own day" (182). Brett simply missed the implications of that footnote.

His second challenge to the manuscript caused London to delete a particularly acerbic sentence. In chapter 14, Meredith gives three examples of "decisions of the courts adverse to labor": one concerning a child labor law in Pennsylvania, one concerning the hours that women and children could be forced to work, and one concerning the number of hours bakers could be required to work. After quoting the Supreme Court's decision upholding employers in all three cases, London wrote, "Such inane verbiage well illustrates the absurdities the Bench perpetrated in its efforts to mask its venality by legal show."[145] Brett was worried that such a statement could be construed as "contempt of court" and asked London to modify it. London refused, but when Brett pointed out that the courts could block publication, he agreed to "change the foot-note in the proofs."[146]

The third issue was a minor one. Brett asked London to revise the way "the Doctor"—meaning Avis's father—loses his house and stock: "There are lots of ways in these times by which a man can be deprived of his property without any necessity for leaving the matter as uncertain as it is here; and anything that is uncertain in a story of this kind and which makes it possible for anyone inclined to criticize it to be able to do so is a decided disadvantage."[147] In all three requests, and especially in the last one, Brett shows his sympathy for London's politics; he was looking for ways to make London's socioeconomic jeremiad beyond reproach, even to the uninitiated. London said he would "try to figure out a more ingenious way of ridding the Doctor of his home and stock," but gave up the attempt and made no change in the subplot.[148] In any case, after Brett knew London would make only minimal changes—he knew this would happen, having prefaced his suggestions with a reluctance to make them—he told London that it was "a really great piece of work." In his opinion, it outlined "better and more fully than anyone else has ever thought of doing the future of development in America. For however wrong in some detail such a book must be, there is no doubt that such a wonderful a picture has never been projected or even thought of." How strange and prescient Brett is to use a cinematic analogy to describe the novel. Here is the voice of the man who without hesitation published *War of the Classes* and *Revolution*.

Nonetheless, he was quite aware of the novel's lack of appeal to a general public. After speaking with Reynolds, who told him he had tried to place it with Lorimer at *Saturday Evening Post*, Brett suggested *Collier's* or *Everybody's*. He was now coming around to London's pessimistic assessment of its marketability. "With you," he said, " I have not very much hope that the story can be sold serially to the regular magazines. These are too much like the daily newspapers to warrant the belief that they would dare to print a story that contained so much truth about conditions of the time and containing so many facts damaging or unfavorable to their regular readers."[149] Not only that, but he feared that the newspapers and magazines would not even review the book, let alone look upon it positively. "You, as well as Ghent and other writers, find in the press today an indisposition to be fair to Socialism and Socialistic writers and I am inclined to agree with you that this is really the case." He asked London if he would consent to issuing the book, not in the usual hard cover, $1.50 edition, but rather as a cheap edition costing fifty cents in paper, seventy-five cents in hardcover. London said no, thinking he had a substantial enough readership of "several thousand strong."[150] Brett backed down, saying he admired his courage in appealing without compromise to the general public. London had compared *The Iron Heel* to *The Jungle*, perhaps forgetting Upton Sinclair's losing fight with Brett to publish it. Brett hadn't forgotten: "I think you are willfully belittling your book when you compare it with such a sordid piece of realism as 'The Jungle,' a book which owed its success wholly, in my opinion, to the facts on which it was founded and which might have been better handled, it seems to me, in almost every way than they were in this particular book." Brett still couldn't believe Sinclair had succeeded. "To compare your book to this one is like, I think, comparing a piece of creative imagination with the reporter's story of what he saw in the case of any incident or accident." Sinclair was no novelist, at least at this stage in his career, and Brett found the merely factual to be inferior to the emotion-laden, factually secure sociological analyses by London, Ghent, and others.[151]

After Lorimer turned it down, Reynolds sent it to Robert MacKay of *Success*, who had just published the long short story "Finis."[152] MacKay had reservations about how to publish a manuscript with footnotes, and, though he liked the work well enough to recommend "it highly for publication," his boss, Orison Marden, rejected it.[153] Reynolds finally gave up trying to place the manuscript with a magazine in November.[154] And though London thought of *Appeal to Reason* as his safety net, Simons never did publish it, simply because the book came out before had a chance to.

It appeared in February 1908, Brett having given Reynolds plenty of time to sell it. The cover of *The Iron Heel*, minimalist in conception, is quite powerful. Within a T-shaped frame, three pairs of hands and forearms—colored dark blue—extend upward between two parallel slopes of an abyss or pit.

They are reaching toward the sun, centered above the pit, with its golden rays extending from the middle in all directions. The picture aptly and simply captures the present/future dynamic of the narrative: the strong hands of socialism that London always cites in his revolutionary writings yearning for the sun, the power that will lift the proletariat out of darkness.

Despite the cover's aspirational quality and the book's ultimate message of triumph for the people, *The Iron Heel* did not sell well or receive consistently good press.[155] When Joan London was researching her biography and asked Untermann about its lukewarm reception among socialist leaders, Untermann told her, "You are right in assuming that Jack's 'Iron Heel' did not please many leaders of the American Socialist Party. It outlined a future development of the party which held out no hope whatever for the rise of this party to permanent power and victory." In a bit of resentful egoism, he also claimed that Hillquit, Berger, Meyer London, and others faulted London for creating a hero—that is, Ernest Everhard, not Avis—modeled, not on them, but on himself, London, and Debs.[156] It is interesting that he did not include Spargo in that list, thus indirectly confirming Spargo's 1920s support for London and the novel.

In a 1914 letter London pasted into his copy of the novel, he told a comrade who had written a letter praising the book that not only did the book not sell but that socialists had found serious fault with it: "The book-buying public would have nothing to do with it, and I got nothing but knocks from the socialists."[157] It was "a dead failure," said the gloomy author, but the rank and file had heeded his jeremiad. In another letter also pasted into his *The Iron Heel*, W. G. Henry told London, in 1911, that he had staged a three-act play based on the book and hoped London could attend a performance at the Dietz Opera House in Oakland. "About a month ago we put on one act (The first) to see how it would go and they simply ate it up and kicked for more. . . . I think that you would be pleased by the manner in which even a company of rough-necks will handle your splendid book."[158] The three acts are each centered on the early debates between Everhard and those at Avis's father's dinner, between Everhard and the "machine breakers," and Everhard and the Philomath Club, the moments of pure theatrical content. One hundred and five years later, one of London's descendants, Tarnel Abbott, also staged a dramatization of the book. She successfully captured London's intent to dramatize the scary future for America if it did not act to forestall the rise of homegrown fascism.

10   THE ROAD NEVER ENDS

FUTURE TIME, FUTURE SPACE

t is not typical to class *The Iron Heel* as science fiction, but the novel fits, if somewhat incompletely, in that genre.[1] Not only was the future the time of both the seeming endless rule of the Oligarchy and then the inevitability of socialism's victory over capitalism, it was also the moment when London and a number of his contemporaries foresaw man's exploration of space and, especially, of Mars; one can imagine Anthony Meredith as someone who had served time in a colony on Mars and returned to earth in his new position as historian. Given what he thought was the inevitability of man's successful exploration of outer space and planetary travel, London meant to accomplish two things: highlight the important scientific achievements of his day and to inspire the people of his day to work harder toward a goal humanity was fated to achieve. Man was meant to walk on Mars because adventure was simply a part of human nature. Traveling to Mars was an extension of sailing across oceans. To promote mankind's destiny, he wrote notes for a novel of the future called "A Farthest Distant," a work that shares a familial resemblance to *The Iron Heel*.

We get a hint of London's interest in the future in *White Fang*, and perhaps even the first trace of his reading of the material that he thought would make up "A Farthest Distant." When, at the beginning of his story, White Fang falls out of his cave and gets up and looks around, London makes a telling comparison: "He sat up and gazed about him, as might the first man of the earth who landed upon Mars. The cub had broken through the wall of the world, the unknown had let go its hold of him, and here he was without hurt. But the first man on Mars would have experienced less unfamiliarity than did he" (89). The connection between Mars and the Klondike is not so fanciful. As John Hay has pointed out, the "wastes of the Arctic" are similar to outer space, and we can point to the similarities of temperature and silence and the psychological effects of both.[2] We should also remember that Brown Wolf is likened to "a traveller from another planet."

[539

There are moments where London's parallel project, "A Farthest Distant," bleeds into *The Iron Heel*. In two notes probably composed in 1910 or 1911, London imagined a series of novels that would tell the history of man as a history of class struggle; *The Iron Heel* would be the penultimate novel and "A Farthest Distant" would be the ultimate in the series. More specifically, these two projects are united by their concerns with space exploration and physics. Meredith tells us that certain "historical events" (6) were as easy to predict as "the outcome of the movement of stars" by "astronomers to-day" (7). He also tells us that Avis's father was a physicist who "established, beyond cavil and for all time, that the ultimate unit of matter and the ultimate unit of force were identical," something that "Sir Oliver Lodge and other students in the new field of radio-activity" had "earlier advanced" (11). If we substitute *energy* for *force*, we get the timelessness of Albert Einstein's theories.

Jumping ahead a bit, we see London marking passages related to Einstein's theories in C. W. Saleeby's 1904 collection of essays entitled *The Cycle of Life*; he may have read this work before he left for Hawaii, but Charmian notes he was reading it aloud on the *Snark* in 1907. There are many marginal notations to "Farthest Distant." In Saleeby's essay "The World Is Young," he marked passages about a possible correlation between the growth of a child and the growth of the human race, showing that, given the projected age of the race as three million years, the race is indeed but a child. Related to this, Saleeby discussed the future of population growth and reproduction and its connection to altruism. In the margins of "Science and Sin," London wrote, "the idea of the ancients that we were a fallen race—the conception of original sin," apparently imagining this as a relic of immature human morality. But the passages on the new physics are the most pertinent here. Paraphrasing an essay by Maeterlinck, Saleeby imagines the secret of gravity solved, enabling humans to navigate planets through space. Second, London marked Saleeby's incredible forecast that new discoveries about the nature of the atom show "that the most abundant source of energy in the universe—a source all but inexhaustible—is to be found *within* the atom, where until recently no energy was suspected. Some day we may expect to tap it, and then we need not deplore our exhausted coal-mines or nitrate-fields."[3]

London initially wanted to incorporate these new ideas about matter, space, and time to explicitly motivate the love story in *The Iron Heel*; his early notes spell out the argument between Ernest and Dr. Ballingford about Aristotle and the Dark Ages—"a period wherein science was raped by the metaphysicians, wherein physics became a search for the Philosopher's Stone," says Ernest, winning the argument (17)—and conclude, "and she falls in love with him," a kind of father figure now. But London finally let the ideas and the father-lover dynamic work implicitly. To some extent these ideas were transferred to "Farthest Distant." He thus locked together his published novel about future time with a projected novel about future space.

On 21 January 1907, London—probably in the company of Charmian—attended a song recital by Mme. Schumann-Heink accompanied by the University (of California) Orchestra at the Greek Theatre. He may have been paying attention to the music, but his program shows he was occupied with thoughts of "Farthest Distant." He had been clipping articles for it as early as September 1906 while writing *The Iron Heel*. The notes on the program concern one of his major preoccupations in just about any work he wrote: how people in his stories communicate. "Farthest Distant | Speech, these men—like a flower's petal falling upon the wind—etc. Enlarge the telepathy. etc. But, for record, written language was employed—& for telepathy a language with vocabulary was essential. These men spake in a strange tongue—-such as was never dreamed of in the younger world." We are clearly in a time even further removed from our own than that of Anthony Meredith and his civilization. London's final words written on the program say, "Begin, very beginning, of book—of these three men speaking by telepathy, as they prepared to start the record of the past through the machine. Get splendid touch on telepathy at the very very first." If we thought he had traveled into the future in *The Iron Heel*, he in fact was now further out in the space-time continuum than ever before. One note read, "I must increase the lapse of time of the cooling of the earth after 8000 centuries of brotherhood of man, must get a new and tremendous era with new name. Include the era of the Iron Heel, between A.D. & Brotherhood of Man." Still thinking like Meredith, he imagined himself a historian not simply of our time but of all time, if that indeed were possible.

Unlike *The Iron Heel*, "Farthest Distant" primarily concerns advances in technology, though one magazine article that discussed future food production—specifically how "our milk, eggs and flour will eventually be made in factories"—found its way into one of Anthony Meredith's footnotes.[4] From the same issue of the *Arena* he found an article on the coming of the next ice age and the concomitant migration of people from North America to South America. He clipped an article in 1906 on new ways of generating light without heat. A week after the performance at the Greek Theatre he clipped an article from *Literary Digest* called "Growth without Life," showcasing work done in France with sugar solutions that seemed to mimic plant germination. In the next month he found a letter to the editor of *Scientific American* about the orbit of the solar system. He clipped an article about the electromagnetic, not mechanical, reproduction of speech, about storing water in glaciers, about the rigidity of the earth's crust, about the characteristics of the new element radium, about channeling heat from the earth's core, about an all-electric house (which included an electric camera obscura that allowed the house occupants to view a visitor knocking at the door!).[5] There are also three short articles about producing artificial nitrates from air and how this would help alleviate world hunger. One double-page insert into a 1907 Sunday *San Francisco Examiner* touted "Six Startling Problems Scientists Are Now Solving": the conversion of sewage into drinkable water; the vacuuming of the air to make it cleaner; the manipulation of the weather to make it temperate across the nation; the chemical manufacture of food; the elimination of our need for sleep; and the telegraphic transmission of mail. Only one article was generally about the future, and it seemed to have made an impact on London. Written by Hudson Maxim, author of *The Science of Poetry and the Philosophy of Language*, he uses John Milton, Herbert Spencer, and others to meditate on infinite time and space and cycles of human life and the time spans of celestial bodies. Clipped in February 1907, it served to validate his own ruminations about infinity and authorized his continued interest in the future.

To save himself from getting lost in metaphysical speculations or in the plethora of scientific advancements of his age and what they portended, he focused on Mars. He clipped "Is Mars Inhabited?" by Percival Lowell, whose *Mars and Its Canals* he also owned.[6] Lowell's work popularized the existence of the network of nonnatural canals on the planet and thus life. Lowell was brother to Amy Lowell, the poet, and graduated from Harvard University with a degree in mathematics. Coming from a wealthy family, Lowell founded Lowell Observatory in Flagstaff, Arizona, where modern-day astronomers first detected evidence of the expanding universe and discovered Pluto.[7] He was a careful researcher and dedicated student of Mars. Still, even though he carefully took into account Earth's atmosphere, the limitations of telescopes, and even an individual's eyesight and physicality of his or her eyes, he nonetheless mapped out the canal system on Mars that later astronomers with better technology showed was actually a reproduction of Lowell's own eyes' vein structure, which he was seeing superimposed on Mars.[8] His work and photograph were featured in the second article London collected: Waldemar Kaempffert's "What We Know about Mars," published in *McClure's* in March 1907. Kaempffert promoted Lowell's theories and then took them a step further: What would living Martians look like?

"A Farthest Distant," in one iteration, would answer that question.[9] On the last page of Kaempffert's article, London wrote notes addressing two elements of the story in the works—the physical attributes of his characters and the method by which a form of space travel was effected: "For long the problem—how to transfer inhabitants from one world to another. The fictional methods of Verne, etc. The way it was done: Come alongside after signaling, bringing ends of axes together. First time, quite a smash. Later learned to control perfectly. (The two boys are both visitors from other planets—one planet which had disappeared totally off on long journey. Describe radical physical difference between two boys. One with attenae very long and sensitive.)"[10] Despite the mention of Jules Verne, it seems London was not attuned to literary representations of Martian life or alien beings, though nine years later he would lament to an aspiring writer of socialist science fiction that he had "failed, and have failed utterly, in every attempt I made at the pseudo-scientific, and the sociological, when embodied in fiction form." And now, he tells his fan, "The public seems to be no longer interested in stories of the Jules Verne variety."[11] Here, the name Jules Verne appears as a generic category and not a specific influence. Surprisingly, H. G. Wells's "Intelligence on Mars" and *War of the Worlds* appear nowhere in London's notes.

This first set of notes shows London holding several titles and several ideas about narration and plot in mind at the same time. His first choice, used as the title for the three sheets he numbered consecutively, was "Farthest Distant: The Last Novel of All"; he may have been thinking that either no other novels would be written after the time period in which this story would take place, or he may have thought it would be his own final novel. It seems the former is more logical, for going to sea was synonymous with writing novels in his mind and within a year he began *Martin Eden*.

These notes begin with confidence and a clear-eyed view of the plot. He uses a similar time sequence as that in *The Iron Heel*: "Dealing with a vastly distant time; yet written at a far more vastly distant time." So, again, we are dealing with three different time periods—our present (of which *The Iron Heel* and "Farthest Distant" are critiques), a future, and that future's future. Rather than advocating for a time in which the human race would have reached a sociopolitical perfection, this novel would picture a time of evolutionary perfection: "Physical evolution had ceased. The change was in the direction of mental evolution—evolution not in the physical structure of the brain, but in the mental and moral concepts gained by humans after they were born, from the accumulated wisdom of the race, through education. . . . The children were all educated scientifically; it was quite natural for them to be all scientists. They had to be scientists in order to manage all the marvelous forces that did the labor for them at that time." There is a narrator who, like Meredith, "looks back with amusement on the men of the 8th thousandth century after The Brotherhood of Man, which era began at the end of the twentieth century after Christ. During the 20th Century A.D., or rather, the men of that period are referred to as unthinkable savages (dandy chance for satire upon existing weaknesses); and before that time are referred to almost as slime." The people now live from 300 years to 1,684 (the oldest living being); "in a foot-note, . . . have narrator look back pityingly upon the 150-year generation at the end of the era of the Brotherhood of Man." A later, handwritten note on the third page adds to this chronology: "Include the era of the Iron Heel, between A.D. & Brotherhood of Man." This note not only helps date these notes as sometime in 1906 when he was writing *The Iron Heel*, or shortly after finishing, but also shows how the two novels work hand in glove in genre, structure, and content. Thinking of this timeline, London considered a different title: "A Child's History of the Planet—a sort of text-book popularized for very young children," which they read as they become educated as scientists. Physical evolution is a dead issue, and we can see how London, as he was in *Before Adam*, was becoming more and more interested in the mysteries of human psychology than anything else. Just as he was abandoning evolutionary science in favor of depth psychology, so too was he becoming less interested in picturing a perfect political world and more concerned with a postpolitical future world, a time beyond the Brotherhood of Man. Unlimited time in an unlimited space.

It's unclear if London thought the satiric narrator would be the author of this history of the planet or if London was actually working on two possibilities at the same time; I believe it is the latter. In any case, a history of the planet is necessary for these children—and the grossly expanded timeline of eight hundred thousand years—because the narrator is "looking back upon a time when the world was growing colder and colder. And the people were being driven to the equator to shiver for warmth." The sun was losing power. "A daring theorist" devised a way to move the Earth closer, and London imagined collisions with other planets. However, after several thousand years, the Earth again was getting too cold for habitation, and then we come to the central conceit that drives both versions of the novel: after arguments among "politicians," those who sided with a group of "young adventurers—a group of daring young scientists"—convinced the rest to "abandon the perishing sun, and go voyaging through space from sun to sun until they found one to their liking." The history would then become a narrative of "the thousands of years journeying through space, the milky way, the various constellations." They encounter another planet traveling through space. They meet "other populated worlds, populated with low orders of life and high orders of life." Footnotes, addressed to the children—in the same manner that Meredith addresses his contemporaneous readers—would explain much of the factual material, at the same time "giving verisimilitude and conviction to the reader of to-day." When he wrote that line, he thought of changing the title to "Farthest Distant."

In a second iteration of the novel, of which his notes on the Greek Theatre program are a part, he kept the idea of a traveling Earth through space seeking new forms of energy. Earth travels among "thousands of navigated worlds," which have formed a "concourse of ultra-civilized worlds." Earth, a newcomer to this planetary consortium, is "a little hayseed, a mere provincial" because it came from "far off on the fringe of the inhabited universe." It's all a "tremendous social mass" of traveling planets, and Earth is like a "yacht" among "crowded moorings." To avoid collisions, the planets communicated with "wireless messages." Or "perhaps they had what resembles a Harbor Master; and permission had to be received to move." And here we might have a clue to what instigated this rather bizarre future tale. London, imagining himself on the *Snark*, sailing from the edge—the West Coast—of the world, finds himself among other travelers and other (strange) worlds. Space, then, is a metaphor for the ocean, for both vertically—sky and the depths of the ocean—and horizontally—the ocean's seeming unlimited expanse—the ocean resembles the infinity of space and time.

"Finding beneficent suns emanating tremendous quantities of radium, or of something vastly better than radium." He names two scientists—Henry Mersfeldter and Katherine Ingleby—who figure out the nature of the new energy and how to capture and store it. The Earth would suffer during "the first centuries of wandering" from earthquakes and other changes in its geology. Apparently, these problems would be solved because of "their astounding mastery of matter," which, paradoxically, yields even greater mysteries. Typical of London, as much as he was enamored of technological advancements, he was more interested in epistemology. Thinking more about communication, he had the three men communicating via telepathy "prepare to start the record of the past through the machine." London does not tell us what the "machine" is, but the three men now appear as historians, telling their fellow Earthlings about their past. Whether narrated by one or by three historians, London wanted to retain that structure.

In fact, in the first iteration, he thought of having the book—including the footnotes by the historian(s)—framed by yet a different device: "Maybe a brief description, describing the two boys who are studying the ancient and obsolete art of reading (just as to-day men study Sanskrit and Egyptian Hieroglyphics)." Again, London seems most interested in knowledge and its transmission. At the same time, it provided an opportunity for both "a still further expansion of time"—because the boys would be reading the text in an era beyond that of the historian(s)—and for humor: the boys would "think the writer of the text-book an old fogy, and rather ignorant of a lot of things." This last idea triggered an all-caps reminder to himself: "THINK WELL OVER ADOPTING THE FOREGOING AS THE MEDIUM OF NARRATION." The transmission of knowledge is of course a matter of rhetoric, and "Farthest Distant" would be about storytellers and storytelling in typical Londonian fashion.

In the second iteration he vacillated between having the three historians speaking by telepathy as they prepare their book and having a single narrator who would be "maybe, a scholar, [who] sits and listens to a long, fine wire, running by radium, that tells the whole history of the Earth's travels." Again he instructed himself, "Must work hard for right medium for telling story." Or maybe the boys would still be reading the book, and "at the beginning of the story the boys read: 'Far beyond the farthest star, once revolved the earth.[']" He elaborated more adventures of the space yacht Earth. Besides ending up among other spaceship planets jockeying for position like so many yachts, the Earth had troubles initially with encountering a desired new sun. "Great floods, etc. when they arrive at some new sun. they learn to do it gradually, after one terrible and too-sudden thaw that destroyed many vast glass cities. They learn to stop far away, and to thaw out gradually." The cities were made of glass to help retain heat; "the earth outside [was] a frozen desert." Once, Earth stopped next to a satisfactory sun, but the adventurers wanted to continue for the sake of traveling through the universe, so they did, much like the *Snark* sailing from port to port for the experience of seeing the world. This desire to simply see became something of even greater import. "The great universe-journey," writes London, "took on a sort of sacred significance. It was something that must be carried out. The carrying out being the highest patriotic, ethical, and religious form of conduct—all for science and knowledge."

Paradoxically, "that with their astounding mastery of matter, the mysteries of living matter, life, and the universe, are more profound than ever. The more they knew, the more colossal the mystery." This paradox of knowledge-acquisition is similar "to that adventure of the Slime, in the early World, when the vitalized Slime reared Heaven, and made God." Then, discovering the fictitious nature of God, "recoiling upon itself, all its proud self-projections crushed, itself crushed by the immensity of the Unknown," yields to depression and pessimism. The "Pessimists" all then commit suicide and the "Optimists" take over. These are "the lovers of life that kept the face of truth veiled, a la Nietzsche. But they, in turn, in that Far Distant time, know naught but that all is mystery and apparently eternally non-understandable." In this narrative of space travel, we end up as London did, embracing the lies we tell ourselves to keep from committing suicide, aware that intellectual development—even eight hundred thousand years of mental evolution—will not be enough to reveal life's secrets.

By writing of the future, not only was London returning to a critique of its past—his present—but he was brought face-to-face with his own intellectual debates, conflicts, and impartial and unsatisfactory resolutions. This may be part of the reason he abandoned the project. He did try to mitigate the emotional effect of the frustrating search for truth by incorporating humanizing and entertaining elements into the story. In the second iteration, the boys who were reading the book get fleshed out a bit more. One is from Mars. He is "the Mars boy" who was among the Martians who met the first Earthlings to visit their planet. He might need "a portable apparatus for thinning air when he went out." He feels "sluggish on earth; tells what he could toss on a shovel on Mars." This allusion to physical labor is taken from Kaempffert's article on Mars; he writes that the Martian atmosphere would make Martians seem superhuman. After enumerating several amazing athletic feats that would be ordinary for a Martian—all of which London ignored—he chooses one he could readily identify with: "A Martian laborer could perform as much work in a given time as fifty or sixty terrestrial ditch diggers, and keep pace with a powerful Panama dredger. Two and one-half tons would be the average load that he could toss over his shoulder." Here is one of the reasons London is such an attractive thinker and writer. He always wants to represent the proletariat—Earthling, Martian, whatever.

Or maybe the Mars boy would actually be "earthborn, his father from Mars, his mother from Earth, and he inherited from father antennae and other things." His father had come to Earth because "maybe lost Mars had had some accident, and was destroyed, or was chained a prisoner by some stellar monster." Maybe some unknown cause destroyed Mars' people, a cause that "Earth's inhabitants would avoid . . . by getting out." And then, in an epistemological shift, London identified the referent of "farthest distant"—not the time in which the historian(s) write or the boys read, but rather it is our time. "Farthest distant" is how people eight hundred thousand years from now will refer to us. With this shift of perspective, London would make his readers feel the full effect of being just a speck in the universe, our lifetimes a mere second of life in the infinity of time.[12]

There may be another reason why he did not complete this tale of interplanetary travel, which may have actually supplied him with the general idea of time and space travel that finds expression in *The Star Rover*. In his second iteration of notes, he becomes sidetracked for a moment while he contemplates how the human race achieved such lengthy lifespans. It was simple: "The length of life had increased because disease had been conquered; germs destroyed by other germs—the battle of the bacilli, of the microbes." But he wasn't interested in medical science. He began thinking seriously about unlimited space in the microscopic world. "The battle of the unseen world of microscopic things. And in this unseen world, controlled and directed by man, took place the bloodiest wars." Why London thought these wars would be bloodier than, say, the Chicago Commune, is unknown, but he wanted to meditate on it: "Man, who did not by his ordinary senses, know this unseen world, nevertheless planned and carried out vast campaigns in it, aided by minute and microscopic auxiliaries." London miniaturized warfare in this imagined intercellular space, and then, in *The Scarlet Plague* (1912), considered other possible effects of germ warfare and the spread of a worldwide disease. As John Hay writes, works like *The Scarlet Plague* and *The Star Rover* not only connect to his Klondike stories because of the likeness of Arctic wastelands to deep space but express "a coherent position regarding the relationship between individuality and nationalism," a major theme, of course, of *The Iron Heel*. In his notes for "A Farthest Distant," he had not yet figured how to incorporate that theme.

There was another avenue open to him that he could not bring himself to follow. Having just completed a novel of conditional hope, he also seemed unable to contradict or supplement that hope with a postpolitical narrative. And then there was a matter of aesthetics and the construction of this novel. For all his enthusiasm about future technology, he could not seem to construct a coherent narrative from the facts he was garnering from the papers and magazines. He played with the number and characterization of narrators without reaching a complete picture of any of them. He couldn't settle upon the best way to characterize the boys or how to place them in the narrative. Should they be narrators? Where should they come from? He doesn't even get to the character of the second boy. He played with the plot, but it never reached a conclusion. Untethered from politics, the narrative devolved into a Nietzschean imperative to dance in the face of existential terror. Fascinated with scientific innovation and the advancements of his age, London nonetheless could not commit to a narrative that would merely celebrate those achievements. His stories had to mean more, and we should note that the weird interstellar space/time travel in *The Star Rover* only happens because the whole of the novel's narrative is centered on America's corrupt treatment of its prisoners and the inhumanity of capital punishment.

So he postponed the writing of "A Farthest Distant," taking his notes with him on the *Snark* but even then turning away from the future to write about his past: *Martin Eden*. But first he would complete his last long work before he left on his yacht: *The Road*. Beyond its literal meaning—railroad or highway—its metaphorical meaning applies equally well to both ocean and space travel.

As in *White Fang*, London's future stunts bubble to the surface of *The Road*. Just as White Fang is like a Martian, so too is the narrator of London's "tramp reminiscences." The final chapter begins with an imagined future: what if all the hobos disappeared? It would only happen, as he said in his essay "The Tramp," with the end of capitalism, for capitalism needs surplus labor. But the sense of futurity governs the end of the book. London imagines that he is like "the man from Mars" in two of the episodes that make up "Bulls." It is another mark of his modernity. American literature of his recent past would imagine visitors from another time and place to be classical-era demigods. As Henry David Thoreau imagined in *The Main Woods*, "The summit of [Ktaadn] had a singularly flat, table-land appearance, like a short highway, where a demigod might be let down to take a turn or two in an afternoon, to settle his dinner."[13] Mars, to Thoreau and others, was simply a brighter speck of light in the heavens populated by images of mythological beings.

Ostensibly, London's final chapter in *The Road* is about his encounters with railroad police and the symbiotic relationship between the hobo and "society's watch-dogs" (197). It's almost a description of the relationship between author and editor; we can easily describe London's early essays on the writing game—essays like "Getting into Print" and "Editorial Crimes"— with their first-person narration and dramatic flourishes, as prototypes for sections of *The Road*. First, like the writing game, the pursuit and the escape from capture are "all in the game" (197). "The hobo," like the artist, "defies society," and "society's watch-dogs," like editors, "make a living out of" the hobo. And sometimes when the police catch a hobo, the "constables" sometimes "split their fees with the hoboes they arrest" or publish. This happens rarely, though, and being arrested is more like having a manuscript rejected. London notes a number of times he tells a "story" (a beautiful, untrue thing, as Oscar Wilde has it) only to have the cop disbelieve it and reject it.

In the two man-from-Mars episodes, one lie is believed and one cannot even be told because of the urgency for escape. In the first, London pictures himself riding between two boxcars traveling at full speed, at night. Standing straight up and facing neither front nor back but to the side, his feet resting on narrow pieces of metal on either side of the coupling, his hands outstretched and pressed against the sides of each car, his body was jerked constantly by the cars up-and-down and side-to-side motions. He is in an impossible, thrill-seeking, death-defying position, much like a sailor on a storm-tossed sea or an author embarked on a crazy adventure-writing spree. No longer able to maintain his balance, London swung around a corner of a car and held on to an iron ladder. At the right moment, he lets go and, his momentum carrying him uncontrollably forward, runs right into a cop. "If that bull had any imagination, he must have thought me a traveller from other worlds, the man from Mars just arriving" (217). Futurity and the imagination go hand in hand, and the author, of course, knows both and then combines them. The author is from Mars (or some other distant world) because he possesses knowledge in the form of a narrative that is not only unknown to the cop but also at risk of being disbelieved. Even though the cop is knocked down and wants to arrest him, London tells him a "story," and because "he was a really good bull at heart," he lets London go. The boy from Mars brings news from his planet that soothes the savage cop soul.

The second episode involves a wild chase from a train to an empty lot and over a wall that hid a drop of nine or ten feet on the other side. London jumps the wall and almost lands on a policeman. "It was the man-from-Mars stunt over again." No words are exchanged—though we are now prepared to imagine what they would have been—and London escapes. He boards a new train and ends up, by mistake, back where he had started. *The Road* then concludes with our storyteller from Mars catching a train going in the right direction. London the space hobo-sailor-author has infinite time and space to travel in. Neither the road nor the stories ever end.

This isn't the only connection between *The Road* and his immediate past work. In a rather obscure footnote in *The Iron Heel*, London, as the historian Anthony Meredith, pays homage to Oscar Wilde: "Oscar Wilde, one of the lords of language of the nineteenth century of the Christian Era." To Bishop Morehouse, Wilde is "an erring soul," and then he quotes from Wilde's sonnet "Easter Day" and uses the poem as a springboard to continue his excoriation of religious hypocrisy (84–85). If Wilde's presence in the novel is noticed at all, he appears as one more critic of organized religion, a socialist's take on how capitalism has corrupted true Christianity. But Wilde serves a dual purpose; he is remembered by the people of the Brotherhood of Man as a "lord of language," not a social commentator. We should not be surprised. Of the 123 footnotes, 23 are concerned with either literature or vocabulary; sometimes one feels Meredith is providing a glossary for the archaic language of the twentieth century. Citations to Wilde and Ambrose Bierce are fundamental to this aspect of the novel, an aspect that works in tandem with its socialist critique. As in "A Farthest Distant," London is principally concerned with communication and epistemology.

It is in this second role as master of language that Wilde forms a link between *The Iron Heel* and *The Road*. Fresh from his appearance in *The Iron Heel*, Wilde stars in the first chapter of London's "autobiography" of his hobo life. In fact, London began the latter one or two days after completing *The Iron Heel*, suggesting that Wilde was uppermost in his mind. Wilde's theorizing of the difference between truth and lie governs not only the construction but the aesthetics of *The Road*. After being so concerned with the difference between fact and fiction in *The Iron Heel*, London now turns upon himself and, using Wilde, ruminates on the gray areas between the two, hoping that his concept of sincerity would help him negotiate this principal tension in his authorial life. The historian-author cannot concern himself with such a literary matter, and so none of the doubts and uneasiness about a lie-telling author come up in *The Iron Heel*. Only the hobo-author (who is in the process of becoming the sailor-author) is capable of exploring the boundaries and limitations of fact. *The Road* is a philosophical assessment of *The Iron Heel*.

The importance of Wilde and his essay is underlined by the fact that in London's final month of life he clipped an essay from *Vanity Fair* by Arthur Symons called "On the Value of a Lie: The Intellectual Somersaults of Oscar Wilde." He thought it might work as background philosophical material for a story to be entitled "The Eternal Enemy," which he began clipping articles for in 1913, two months after composing *John Barleycorn*; in fact, this story could be considered a continuation of his "alcoholic memoirs." It features a "a writer of successful love stories." He was popular because he created illusions for women that they were better people than they really were. He "helps them to the illusion that will hide the cruel, unmoral reality of themselves from themselves," an illusion that London likens to Fourth of July "spread eagle oratory." We also are reminded of the Seaside Library that he excoriates in *The Iron Heel*. But romance novels aren't the only way people avoid their true nature: "Others drink for the same purpose, take drugs, lose themselves in music and the arts, construct metaphysical philosophies, etc. All engaged in fleeing from their not-likeable and ugly real selves."[14]

London reminds himself to read Edgar Saltus's *The Philosophy of Disenchantment.* He might have also referred himself to Vernon Lee's *Vital Lies*, which would play a crucial role in writing *John Barleycorn.* The point is that he would eventually displace this 1907 interest in outer space and infinite time to a study of the endless depths of the psyche or, as he was calling it in the notes for this story, the eternal enemy. Besides Saltus, he wanted to incorporate Carl Jung's *The Psychology of the Unconscious* (1916). He wasn't interested in Jung's mythopoeticism but rather his definition of the underlying cause of neuroses: "a refusal or failure to meet the difficulties and dangers of life in the actual world," a quotation London underlined in an undated, unsigned review that he put in the same file as his outline for the story. In Symons's appreciation of Wilde, he makes much of Wilde's "The Decay of Lying" as artistic statement, but he concludes with a statement that paralleled London's expanded sense of the function of lying: "Wilde was . . . alike in the art of life and the art of literature," saying untrue things to combine wit and truth.[15] Wilde would always have this fascination for London as long as he explored the distinctions and similarities between fact and fiction, the beautiful untrue things. Then lying became something more than an aesthetic principal for London in the second decade of the twentieth century. It was a philosophical choice for living in a particular way, a way that allowed for the creation of art that nonetheless recognized the bitter realities of life.

Wilde, and the general model of the Byronic romantic artistic genius, validated London's conception of art as transgressive. If, as he had told beginning writers, you want to succeed in the market, simply adhere to the conventions of storytelling that can be found in any mass-market magazine. But if you want to write true art, then one must break those conventions, as he had done with his experimentation with form in *The Iron Heel.* This experimentation continued with *The Road.* As he radically blended fact with fiction to the extent that you could no longer tell which was which, he sought for the appropriate narrative form. This new form could very well become the conventional form of the future, the way that all successful novelists would then follow as the capitalist market for fiction adapted to the production of solitary romantic geniuses.

"Pictures" is the title of the third chapter of *The Road.* "Pictures! Pictures! Pictures!" begins *Before Adam*, a word indicating the form that dreams take in the mind of the protagonist. In two undated though related set of notes, he imagined how to write a series of "pictures" both from his own life and for a short story he conceived post-1910. In the first, he wrote, "Some time write a volume of pictures—from my own life—visions I recall snatches from the past"; this would be a volume that would include "tramp visions." None of these sketched-out "visions" were included in *The Road*, but they are similar. One "vision" would center on "when I came on the Umatilla that dark night at Vancouver—how we work—First officer overboard." And he remembered "a lodging house in Chicago underground" as well as "a vision at the table at Mercersburg Pa—the schoolmaster and his beautiful aristocratic wife." Finally, in a note that is bafflingly incomplete he would portray "Kelly's army—the time we cooked grub on the slide and everything slid." In the second set, basing the story on pages from the Prison Reform League's 1910 *Crime and Criminals*, he began, "develop boyhood of this boy in quick sharp sketches—each, a detail-picture, vivid, nervous, (my very best), a la French short story."[16] And then he listed five pictures illustrating the boy's life as he progresses from innocent to soon-to-be-executed convict in San Quentin. We immediately see the link between this new way of constructing a book and its fruition in *The Star Rover*.

When he uses the word *pictures* he means photographs, as in the phrase "moving pictures," just as he had done in the first sentence to *Before Adam*. *The Road*'s narrator in the third chapter describes life in Hobo Land as "an ever changing phantasmagoria, where the impossible happens and the unexpected jumps out of the bushes at every turn of the road." He "lives only in the present moment," and his book is "a record of swift-moving pictures." A photograph (or, since London seems to be employing the new vocabulary of the cinema, a moving-picture show) as a model grants the viewer instantaneous knowledge of a moment. This surprising and abrupt moment is akin to the cinema of attraction, the highly theatrical nature of the earliest movies.

For a story to be like a photograph, one might assume that it must be short, something like a Donald Barthelme short story or some other postmodern construction. Barthelme conceived of the minimalist conception of a short story. Length and syntax, metaphor and structure all are to be subverted. London, not a postmodernist but instead a modernist, asked, How can a piece of fiction writing be like a photograph? He wants to capture a moment and present it so that it strikes the reader instantaneously. Yet he is relying on words, not images, so by necessity the description of word-pictures will be drawn out. But the pictures will be juxtaposed, not joined by a running narrative.

Here is where London and Barthelme actually come into contact. Both believed in the value of the collage. Though they had different ideas of what constituted collage—London never uses the word and was working at a time when the idea of collage as an aesthetic choice was still developing and found only in painting—nonetheless *The Iron Heel* and *The Road* partake of the seemingly disjointed organization of the collage. The difference between these two works, in terms of their experimentation with form, is that the former is a frame story. *The Road* portrays action as a series of pictures just as *The Iron Heel* does, but it dispenses with the frame all together. There is no hobo finding a lost manuscript. The manuscript simply is. It is "a swift succession of pictures" unified only by the point of view of one who lived inside those pictures. The frame, if you can call it that, is the psyche of the author.

The conventional form that most closely matches the innovation of *The Road* is the collection of related short stories, something like *A Son of the Wolf*. But we wouldn't call each of those stories elements in a collage; for one thing, many of them are frame stories, meaning that they are able to stand on their own. In *The Road*, London wanted to create a series of stories, unified by the narrator's voice and experience, but by nothing else. On the road, life is lived as a series of present moments that take place by chance. To impose more of an order than a collage imposes would be unfaithful to the nature of chance. This is a radical choice. He advocates for a new way to order stories, dispensing with traditional modes of connective narrative events. For a book on life on the road, this is entirely apt. For the road never ends, there will always be another present moment. If we consider how much *The Road* tells the story of London's 1894 hobo trip, then the book ends in medias res. "So I caught the next train out, and ate my breakfast in Baltimore" is the final sentence. There is no resolution, no loose ends tied. There is no grand conclusion about what life on the road means. There is no Spencerian grand unified theory of hoboing. But there will always be a next train.

One way to create instantaneous images in words is to write of violent human interactions. One of the most uncomfortable moments in *The Road* takes place in the chapter called "Pictures," though violence is the hallmark of "Pinched" and especially "The Pen." Before we get to the moment itself, consider that one of the governing metaphors is that a moment like this is like a page in a book. Here we see the beginnings of London's conflation of word and photographic image, so crucial to his developing definition of what a human document is. So when the moment is over, London the narrator says, "It was a page out of life, that's all; and there are many pages worse, far worse, that I have seen." That last word—shouldn't it be "read," not "seen"? No, not if the author is melding two mediums. And when the chapter ends, he writes, "The whistle sounded. The page was done." The reader/viewer turns the page/photograph over to reveal the next moment, the next page, the next photograph. As London says later in the chapter, "and so the book of life goes on, page after page and pages without end— when one is young" (71).

The cliché gains force of expression when one considers how London described the Klondike trail as if it were a black pen writing on a white sheet of paper, of how nearly every work is about authorship, and of how writing and death and ghosts seem inextricably tied, even here in such a light-hearted humorous autodrama like *The Road*. For when London expounds on the relation between hoboing and authorship and pictures himself telling stories to the lady in Reno, he incorporates a third figure, almost unnoticed, at the table. He isn't the audience for London's stories, for London is talking to the lady. He is the lady's son who has suffered an injury to his head, which is wrapped in white, ghostly bandages: "And all the while, like a death's-head at the feast, silent and motionless. . . . I could not forebear, once or twice, from wondering if he saw through me down to the bottom of my mendacious heart" (19-20). Guilty of writing fiction, London is accompanied by death.

The deathly violent moment that forms the principal subject matter of "Pictures" occurs outside Harrisburg, Pennsylvania, when London witnesses a man whip two boys and a woman. Violence is a way to fix our attention on what happens in a London story. It's a way to focus when our eyes wander between fact and fiction. When we are confused by the blurring of that boundary, violence strikes us in the face. It is the epitome of theatricality, which we need to anchor us when we might become too absorbed, too deep inside the thoughts and feelings of the narrative. Violent narrative moments keep us aware of our surroundings, and in this heightened frame of mind we become aware of the necessity of socialism as the solution to violence. Again, we see how socialism is the basis of all art for London.

The hobo is not a political being, let alone a socialist. He is a bohemian. London may have been radicalized on the road, but he didn't become a socialist until he arrived home, read Gronlund, Marx, Lewis, and others and then joined the party. So his hobo refrains from interfering in the beating of children and of a woman. When the narrator says that he has seen worse "pages," he then references "child labor in the United States." The conclusion is not an advocacy for revolution or even for membership in the Socialist Party. It is rather an admission that "all of us, profit-mongers that we are, are typesetters and printers of worse pages of life than that mere page of wife-beating on the Susquehanna" (68–69). This assertion that London, one of the most prominent socialists in America and one of America's representative socialists to the world at large, would admit to being a "profit-monger" should come as a violent shock in its own right. Still, we readily see the strategy. Just as London the hobo first seeks out the character of his audience before he tells his story, so he admits to his capitalist nature in order to bind himself to his audience so that they can more easily believe him. He isn't disowning what he had just written in *The Iron Heel.* He is trying to make it more palatable to those who have yet to be enlightened. More importantly, he continues the religious metaphor of his political conversion by emphasizing his numerous confessions.

London reworks scenes from his life that he had previously used to write both the 'Frisco Kid stories and his previous hobo stories and essays. The first chapter of *The Road* is about how London writes fiction and what sort of authorial model he follows. For the remainder of the book, we the audience are both in the know—we know that London exaggerates the truth in order to get at the Truth of a matter—and out of it. That is, we become hypnotized—or deeply absorbed—by the rest of the pictures. This is why the first chapter is called "Confession"; he is confessing to the secular sin of lying to earn food, clothing, and shelter—that is, lying to earn a living as an author—and, as we will see, he has other sins to confess. Once inside the telling of a picture, we can no more recognize the art of its construction than can those he is describing as listening to his hobo-author tales. We may not even notice that the first chapter takes place in 1892 when London is sixteen and will write about that initial time of hoboing in "'Frisco Kid" and "The 'Frisco Kid Comes Back." In chapter 2, which takes place in 1894, we learn how to ride the rails and the ways the police would try to thwart us. We're still in 1894 in "Pictures," and here we get the violent whipping scene and the reunion of Jack and a fellow jailbird from Buffalo over a game of cards. We don't know it yet, though we may have had an inkling, but the narrative does not follow a chronological path. It's in the next chapter, "Pinched," that we get the story of how he knows his fellow cardplayer and ex-con.

In "Pen," chapter 5, London continues his narrative begun in chapter 4 of being arrested for vagrancy and locked up for thirty days in the Erie County Penitentiary. If the structure of the book has a fault, it is here, for London temporarily abandons the quick, instantaneous communication of a scene for a classically styled narrative of his humbled accommodation to the life of a prisoner and, again, his assumption of the role of a wolfish capitalist; for the prisoners trade and barter with London and the other hallmen who take advantage for their own profit. "We were wolves, believe me—just like the fellows who do business in Wall Street" (104). He turns to his readers for a moment, and in a theatrical gesture, states, "It was like taking candy from a baby, but would you?" No amount of sarcasm or irony—"besides, we but patterned ourselves after our betters outside the walls, who, on a larger scale, and under the respectable disguise of merchants, bankers, and captains of industry, did precisely what we were doing" (101). London is able to work in the message of *The Iron Heel* (which, of course, has a footnote explaining what Wall Street was) by making his readers sick to their stomachs with the sight of economic exploitation, even if it means he, too, participated. This is another of his confessions. We recall from "How I Became a Socialist" that he converted to the politics of socialism as if it were a religious conversion. Confession is the necessary first step: We admit that we were powerless over profit, that our lives had become obscenely selfish.

Chapter 6 continues the linguistic theme and informs us of the noms-de-rail of many a hobo, neatly categorized and filed away by this collector of nouns, verbs, and modifiers, this "master of language." But in chapter 6 we also get an idea of the loose structure of the visions and how they are tied together. He tells us that he was following a "ghost" hobo across Canada and ended up west of Ottawa. We easily remember that he has already told us a story about Ottawa and his initial note to write up this ride from the capitol. It is a fine physical feat, but not more noteworthy than some of his others. What, then, makes this particular adventure so important that it was one of the first structuring devices he thought of? That phrase "ghost hobo" is a clue. London finds himself chasing a signature, that of Skysail

Jack, that he first encounters inscribed on a water tank in Montreal. His own signature was Sailor Jack. Now, it is true that, because of this system of writing one's name on water tanks and other surfaces that all hoboes, at one time or another, found themselves trailing other hobos they never see; London tells us, "I have met hoboes who, in trying to catch a pal, had pursued clear across the continent and back again, and were still going" (26). But here London turns his entire journey back home into a tale of chasing himself or someone just like himself. He even tells us that he met a road kid from Oakland who had been part of the same gang as he that tells him about Skysail Jack. Skysail ends up on a ship out of Vancouver "flying west on his world-adventure," a trip his alter ego, Sailor Jack, would soon be taking on the *Snark*. Skysail Jack is the ghost of his imagination.

It's not until chapter 7 that London tries to explain why he went on the road to his readers who know that he is a prominent author and socialist. "Every once in a while," he writes, "in newspapers, magazines, and biographical dictionaries"—he is indeed very famous—"I run upon sketches of my life, wherein, delicately phrased, I learn that it was in order to study sociology that I became a tramp" (152). We might forget how controversial it was for someone famous to confess—his third confession—that he had lived hand-to-mouth, begging on the streets, traveling illegally on trains, guiltlessly stealing firemen's gloves, and spending thirty days in a penitentiary for vagrancy. So here at the beginning of the third-to-last chapter, he comes clean because the audience by now is in his corner. They have identified with him as he has identified with them. He may be a radical political activist, but, then, "sociology was merely incidental." He is in fact undermining his own publishers' marketing program, which tried to turn this former tramp and convict into a sociological experimenter and researcher. No, says London. He went on the road "because it was easier to than not to." We hear the echo of his essay from the previous summer, his foreword to *The Cruise of the* Snark. "I like," the statement of traveling the line of least resistance, is not egotism; egotism is the failure of imagination, the failure of others to understand why someone might adventure. "I went on 'The Road' because I couldn't keep away from it" (152). It is the following of one's ghost, of one's imagination. He is incapable of holding a "real" job. He is, by constitution, bohemian.

Chapter 7 tells the story of the first time he went on the road, the trip that laid the foundation for his earliest stories in the *Aegis*. It is tied up in criminality, learning the new language of the road, and the metaphor of the wolf to describe the road kids who prey on the weak and vulnerable. Kids are wolves because they are baby capitalists, or, rather, they are imitating their adult role models. They go where they want, they rob who they want, they loaf when they want. This is why London calls the professional hobo "the blond beasts so beloved of Nietzsche." The profesh "are the lords and masters, the aggressive men, the primordial noblemen" (173). Note that he does not label them supermen, as he did with Ernest Everhard. Road kids are like the Vikings that Nietzsche described, murderous adventurers. London links the blond beast with John Milton's Satan—"better to reign in hell than serve in heaven" (153)—and though we hear a note of admiration in London's description and also sense nostalgia in his account, London clearly uses the violence of these kids to distance himself from them. A violent life leads to death or jail or both, and London left the road for brain work that would put the road life securely in the past. Writing *The Road* was part of his project of sealing off that past from his present.

When, in chapter 8, he quotes from his tramp diary of 1894, turning it into a human document that underlies *The Road*, he is honest about his "desertion" from Kelly's Army, his own beastliness, his "cussedness" (192). His diary becomes evidence of his sincerity. He confesses to his criminality and honors Kelly and George Speed for being "heroes" (192). London apologizes to them. That's one of the unstated reasons he wrote this book. His guilt finally caught up with him, and before he left the United States he needed to unburden himself. Apart from the aesthetic and biographical reasons for writing this book at this particular moment, he was also anticipating his future ocean voyage. The future was to the west, the past to the east. He faces east only then to be able to turn his back on it.

The structure of *The Road* is subtle, a matter of first telling his readers what it means to be an author, then posting signs of stories to come—the time in jail, the Canada crossing with a focus on Ottawa, the time with Kelly's Army, his aim to go to Baltimore—and then relating those stories. The structure intentionally appears haphazard, each anecdote or vision coming as if in a dream, but in reality the structure intentionally mirrors life on the road, a succession of events determined mostly by chance but always driven by a larger purpose, which is simply to get to one end of the country and then back. He is replaying his socialist lecture tour—on which he sometimes talked about his tramping experiences—but this time as simply another naïve American capitalist before his conversion to socialism. Being boyishly naïve, he can be humorous. I didn't know any better, he is telling us, as he describes adventure after adventure.

The book's ostensible message comes at the end: "Oh, no, life on The Road is not all beer and skittles," a classic statement of the arduousness of the bohemian life (223). *The Road* is that, and it has inspired a hundred years' worth of young people to live a life unconnected to work, taking an opportunity to discover oneself and develop other romantic notions. But London is ultimately a deadly serious, political writer. *The Road* relates a tale of self-realization, the awakening, conversion, and confessions of a political being. He now sees why Kelly and Speed, friends of the unemployed worker, were heroes. He wasn't radicalized simply by being denied his rights when he was arrested for vagrancy. It was his Althusserian moment of interpellation. He thought he was simply walking down an American street, harmlessly desiring to see again Niagara Falls. Then he is hailed by the state, as Louis Althusser would say, forever changing his relationship to state power. He was happy to escape and to continue to ride the rails home. But he could not ignore the heavy hand on his shoulder. Its grip festered. That is why the final chapter is called "Bulls." It might as well be called "The Police State." You, too, he is saying, now that he had placed himself firmly among his readers in terms of political awareness, could be persecuted in the way that I was. Only when the larger adventure was over did he realize that he no longer wanted to help typeset the pages of capitalism's tyranny. He hoped his readership would strike with him.

IN DEFENSE OF HIS PAST

"Did you ever write up your road experience?" asked George Smith in 1905, London's traveling partner on the road in 1894.[17] London must have opened this letter when he returned from his tour in February 1906, and it may have prompted his "reminiscences." That, and his return to Oakland in preparation for his *Snark* journey brought back his boyhood. He didn't really need much of a prompt, given that his life on the road was nearly always in the forefront of his mind, just waiting to be written. Consider first that *The Iron Heel* took eight days to prepare. *The Road* took a day or so. He had already written a tramp reminiscence called "Jack London in Boston." When he wrote his handbook on tramping called "Rods and Gunnels," we remember that the editor of *Everybody's*, John O'Hara Cosgrave, told him to think about writing, not another essay à la Josiah Flint's *Tramping with Tramps* and the work of Walter Wyckoff, but rather an episodic treatment of one man's life on the road, a personal narrative. "Local Color" was to be the first in such a series, based on the life of Frank Strawn-Hamilton. The main character would incorporate features of one of London's earliest creations, the 'Frisco Kid. The Kid might even be hiding, one might say, in "The Apostate," ready to reappear as the first-person storytelling voice of *The Road*. As an indication of London's supreme readiness to write this book, the manuscript of *The Road*, as well as its typescript, is noteworthy because it is so clean. Few words are scratched out and replaced; once in a great while did he add more in revision. Only once did he tack on with a pin some necessary afterthought. He was ready to write this one.

Besides the amount of tramp material he had already written and his thoughts on the centrality of the hobo as a stand-in for authorship, he set down two brief sets of notes; their brevity indicates how much he already had in mind, how much he did not need to write down before composing a fifty-two-thousand-word book. One set simply reads, "Cosmopolitan | novel Adventures of a tramp on the road—see my filed notes for novels." One of those notes, which is filed with this sheet, is equally brief: "A Tramp novel Make a striking character of a tramp—glib, etc—see other notes on tramp novels."[18] Always for London, the tramp is known linguistically. Here he is "glib," someone who, on the spur of the moment and after quickly reading his audience, is able to deliver a believable false story that is nonetheless true to human experience. It is important to emphasize how crucial language is to London in the creation of his characters and of their universes. In *The Road*, pages are peppered with slang and definitions of slang, just as *The Iron Heel* is often footnoted to explain "foreign" words and phrases. In the second set, he simply wrote, "Write up Tramping experiences Jail at Buffalo Riding a blind all night, as I did out of Ottowa."[19] These are the three unifying narrative threads he first imagined would help give structure to the bohemian work.

The day after completing *The Iron Heel*, Charmian noted in her diary that "Mate started a new short story—'Confession.'"[20] Three days later, his mind made vigorous by memories, he wrote to *Cosmopolitan*, "Now, as it happens that I have just finished my novel, *The Iron Heel*, and have just begin work on the first of a series of tramp reminiscences. I have 2,000 words of the first one of this series completed, entitled 'Confession.' In this series I am giving true personal experiences of mine of the days when I was a tramp."[21] On 21 December he finished his 5,129-word "story," and then two days later he began "Holding Her Down," having taken a day off to go to the Bohemian Club's Low Jinx. He finished those 7,130 words more quickly, on the twenty-ninth, especially considering he took at least Christmas Day off. It didn't hurt his writing routine to have completed the happiest year of his life, according to Charmian in her summation of the year in her diary. "Our life is ideal, for both of us," she wrote in private. "And now we have before us the adventure of our lives . . . and it is not too much to expect, to believe that our happiness will go with us."[22] It is not much of a spoiler to reveal that it did . . . and did not. For not only did they bring back the happy memories of sailing together, but London brought back the ill effects of diseases and their treatment, treatments that helped speed his death.

The rest of the book flowed as easily as the first chapters. "Mate rose at nine," wrote Charmian on the first day of her new 1907 diary, "even with a New Year's headache."[23] Ouch! On the next day, he completed "Pictures," and on the fifth he began "Pinched." The composition continued through the weeks in this regular fashion. Charmian's diary entry for 2 February— that she had typed 2,300 words of "Bulls"—also indicated that this would be the final story, an entry that indicates London did not break it off without thinking through the whole of the book. It is worth repeating: The ending of the road is not really an ending. London would have loved Robert Earl Keen's song: The party is never over, and the road never ends.

Cosmopolitan had no qualms about serializing *The Road*, but George Brett initially had reservations. London first told Brett about the book after *Cosmopolitan* had accepted it: "I have been at work, since coming to Oakland, on a series of reminiscences of the days when I was tramping. I have already finished 30,000 words, and when I have written 20,000 more I shall have completed a volume of these recollections, which I am thinking of entitling *The Road*, with a sub-title *Tramp Reminiscences*."[24] In his letter to *Cosmopolitan*, he had stressed the personal nature of the account, but to Brett he is emphasizing his production, though he did have a revealing comment about the title: "I think the sub-title, 'Tramp Reminiscences,' should go with it, else people will think it a collection of drummers' yarns."[25] *Cosmopolitan* had called it *My Life in the Underworld*, which highlights the dual nature of the universe of the road. London suggested *Underworld Reminiscences* to link it better with the book publication, but *Cosmopolitan* thought it important to maintain their independence as a publisher. London went along, but he didn't want to create a spatial hierarchy. Hoboes and salesmen, alike in their need to sell a product whether it be brushes or stories, occupy the same space, just differently.

Brett, for his part, fixed on the subject matter: "A good deal of nonsense has been written about tramping and in discussion of tramp experiences and I should like you to publish bye and bye a small volume giving the actuality of the matter. Something of this of course you did in 'The People of the Abyss' but next time I hope it may be done from the standpoint of this country, as we need to understand better than we do this phase of modern life and this understanding can come only, I think, from the written word of one having had the experience and thoughts of his position."[26] Once London sent it to him, on 7 February, Brett sat down and read it. Perhaps he was eager, hoping that London had a field more popular than boxing or the future of economic life in America. Perhaps he mistrusted London's taste enough to tackle his new topic immediately and so quickly steer London away from a financial disaster. Just three weeks after receiving the manuscript, Brett had his opinion ready. But before he told London directly how he judged the manuscript, he thought it best to convey his thoughts indirectly: "If I could put before you evidence—good, in my opinion—that the publication of the book in book form would be likely to damage the sale of your other books, would that affect the question of your wishing to publish this?"[27] He quickly assured London that Macmillan would publish the work whatever London's answer, but he wanted London to know that he thought the confessional aspect of the book was too revealing, perhaps even sordid. The stink of the jail cell could stick to other work. Reputation and fame was a fragile thing.

London quickly and decisively responded, and we shouldn't be surprised by his ardor: "IT WAS MY REFUSAL TO TAKE CAUTIOUS ADVICE THAT MADE ME." Although he was only guessing at Brett's reasons for being hesitant, he assured Brett that he recognizes the risks of exposing himself. The greater benefit outweighed what he thought at most would be a brief downturn in his sales. He needed to be true to himself, to "the character I have built up," "the consistent and true picture of myself" that his readership has come to know and appreciate. His persona and his readers' trust in that persona is "my big asset." Clothes make the persona, and when we look back on what he wore, especially in the East End and on his socialist tour, we realize how important his appearance was.

Note that he was not saying that it was a matter of honesty. His clothes, his language, his fields of interest are all part of how he conceived of the difference between honesty and sincerity. This distinction can be found in his choice of aesthetic principles as well. It is tied to the necessity of telling stories as a hobo tells stories, of lying in order to get to the truth. How he has presented himself to his audience both physically and linguistically is to choose sincerity as a foundational commitment of his authorial self. Without it, he is not a writer. London brings the old story of his relationship with S. S. McClure and John Phillips back to life as an example of how, at the beginning of his publishing career, he had avoided becoming something he was not. So he will not listen to "cautious advice" from publishers and editors, not from McClure and Phillips, and not even from his best friend in the publishing world, George Brett. At the end of the letter, as he calmed himself, he gratefully acknowledged Brett's careful, tactful approach. He concluded by assuring Brett that he had himself taken steps to minimize damage to his sales: "It is I who have taken the liberty of forestalling the objections you did not state."[28] You should be thankful, said the letter in between the lines. I could have been honest instead of sincere. As many a biographer has wondered, what exactly did he leave out?

What he did leave out, we can be assured, would have been sensational and would have detracted from the larger purposes of the book. If it were sex scenes among convicts or hobos, they would have only duplicated the moments that Brett and other bourgeois readers found objectionable. In any case, Brett went ahead as promised and published the damn thing. It didn't affect their contractual agreement at all: when London wrote from Honolulu in May that he had more new work to tell him about but needed another five thousand dollars in advance, Brett resolutely sent the money and renewed their contract.

Brett couldn't keep quiet about the publication of *The Road*, though. In June, he assured London that the book would come out once the serialization in *Cosmopolitan* was complete. But, he wrote, "I happened however to come across in the New York Times, the other day, a letter from a person of whom I have never heard and which represents my own feeling in regard to the effect that the publication of this book may have on the sale of your other books." The letter, from E. F. Allen of Redlands, California, complains that, instead of humbly acknowledging his "rise" "from the status of a common tramp to that of a successful novelist," London has committed the sin of immodesty. "He glories in the facts that he lived by begging, stole rides on trains, and was skillful in eluding the police," all things that London openly confessed to. "These memoirs are certainly not praiseworthy, and will, I think, detract from his literary reputation. It is deplorable that he should so far debase his art." Brett assured London that he was not trying to convince him to reverse his decision; he offered the clipping "as an excuse" for his letter. And then in a concluding moment of uncharacteristic lack of confidence, he called his letter "possibly ungracious and perhaps very much uncalled for."[29] London was not an author he wanted to lose, and he would even go against his best understanding—which was considerable—of books and their markets to keep London happy. Brett was quite willing to accept London's definition of artistry, and his letter to London shows his gratitude for being associated with artistic modernity. For every mass-market romance he published, he could placate his doubts about his place in forming American culture by reminding himself that he had published *The Road*, *The Iron Heel*, and other experimental fictions.

London had no intention of breaking with Brett, at least not yet, and he suavely responded to Brett's "evidence" and concerns by providing his own evidence: "As regards the clipping you have sent me, in which some man gratuitously attempts to order my life for me, I can only say that I have received dozens of similar gratuitous letters, all of which, however, have been in praise of my series of tramp articles." Even if this were not the case, London had long ago accepted the fact that some would never meet him on his own personal terms and then take the next step to a conversion to socialism. "This many-headed public is a thing that no man can really understand or keep track of." The trick, instead of appealing to the public taste, was to keep one's authorial commitments in the forefront and never betray them. "I am still firm in my belief," he said in a restatement of his commitment to sincerity, "that my strength lies in being candid, in being true to myself as I am to-day. . . . Who am I, to be ashamed of what I have experienced?" Then, in a trenchant and poetic way, he explains who he is in social evolutionary terms: "I have become what I am because of my past; and if I am ashamed of my past, logically I must be ashamed of what that past made me become."[30] We see how his sense of the fluidity of time influenced his conception of himself. The past was alive in the present and would be in the future. His past made him an author, and that is nothing to be ashamed of. Terrified by, yes. Conflicted and haunted, yes.

But ashamed? He would feel ashamed if he measured himself by the conventional morality of E. F. Allen, and that is something he was at war with. *The Road* in its theatrical mode is about confession and political conversion, but in its absorptive mode it is all about self-discovery and affirmation of that self. Looking back he saw that the road was the path he took to become a writer.

The Nietzschean idea of autobiography influences the writing of *The Road* at this moment too. Nietzsche's work validated London's instinct to use himself as a narrator, but in the fictional mode. So all the principles involved in writing a short story or bildungsroman get applied to the writing of Avis's manuscript in *The Iron Heel* and of *The Road*. Just as Avis's story gets to the "feels" of the time period, so too was London interested in conveying the feel of the road. He isn't interested in photographic verisimilitude. He is still critical of Norris's idea of realism. He cares about facts of life on the road in the way that he cared about the facts of Avis's life. He writes a new autodrama. He realized he could fictionalize his life in order to answer the question, What does it feel like to experience life the way that I have lived it? He had tried this mode in shorter works like "What Life Means to Me" and "How I Became a Socialist." Look at the title of the first in the series: "Confession." This is the most appropriate title for an autodrama. There are photographs in both the serial and book publications of *The Road*, but they are of a fictional Jack London riding fictional trains. This kind of photography is the visual equivalent of his verbal narrative. It looks factual, but it partakes strongly of the fictional. Not surprisingly, then, London's favorite genre of photography was embodied by the work of Arnold Genthe, not Jacob Riis. Is it a coincidence that at the beginning of the composition of *The Road* that Charmian and Jack "went to Genthe and had a lot of pictures taken."[31] *The Road* is an equivalent to photographic pictorialism.[32]

Brett spared little expense to make the book attractive. Singling out the railroad as the epitome of life on the road—we should always remember that the road, not simply a moniker for a highway or for a railroad line, entails life as a hobo, which includes sleeping in parks, hanging out in hobo jungles, doing time in jail, among other activities—the cover features a boxcar heading away from the viewer. That image is bracketed by stylized railroad tracks as seen from above; if taken as vertical objects, they could be mistaken for classical columns without capitals. Like *The People of the Abyss*, it's a large-format book with copious illustrations, including the photographs from *Cosmopolitan* and five drawings.[33] "I cannot tell you how much I appreciate the splendid way in which you brought out *The Road*," enthused London. Truly, he was grateful, but he couldn't help getting in the last word about its reception. He told Brett that he had received a large number of reviews in the mail—he and Charmian and the *Snark*'s crew were in Tahiti—and "I did not notice any contemptuous or sneering notes such as you anticipated, and, to tell the truth, which I myself anticipated to a certain extent." Instead, the book seemed to have been received "most genially and goodnaturedly."[34] He did not anticipate George Sterling's reaction. From Tahiti, London wrote his friend, "I can't get a line on why you wish I hadn't written *The Road*!" London exclaimed. "It is all true. It is what I have done, and it is part of the process by which I have become," which is the same argument he had made to Brett, whose bourgeois standing made it impossible for London to make the next comment to anyone except a close, bohemian friend: "Is it a lingering taint of the bourgeois in you that makes you object?" Or is it your sense of "my shamelessness"? We do not know how Sterling replied, but it is safe to assume that he was being protective of his friend, who now had made a large section of his private life a part of his public persona.

SOCIALISM IN THE PRESENT, SHORT STORIES OF THE FUTURE

During the composition of *The Road*, London wrote two connected, short, though revealing pieces on the present deleterious effects of capitalism. The first is difficult to date but was probably written in December 1906 or early 1907. It is a blurb for Nina Wood's seventy-five-page pamphlet *Crimes of the Profit Furnace*. Wood, a medical doctor and socialist activist, described a selection of the evils of capitalism that she herself had encountered, which included infanticide in Philadelphia and other horrific crimes attributable, by her, to the profit motive. London could not wait to write her a fan letter. "I have just finished reading your book, 'Crimes of the Profit Furnace.' It can not be given too wide a circulation. It will serve to open the eyes of many to the monstrous evils that arise out of the profit system and that are protected by those two great political mainstays of the profit system—the democratic and republican parties." London was not so much against politics as he was against the two-party system that precluded any real advancement by a third, socialist party. London continued, "It would seem that money is not a medium of exchange, but that it is a disease. The ravages of the money disease are well depicted in your book. . . . Congratulating you upon your good work in the cause that will some day give us an industrial system based upon production for service rather than the damnable industrial system of production for profit which now prevails."[35] London had often quoted George Sterling's definition of socialism as a political system that was "clean, noble, and alive." If capitalism was a disease—think of how gun violence is now considered a disease—and infected people with its addictive, corruptive influence, then we see what London meant by *clean* and *unclean*. Besides offering a novel approach to propaganda against the profit motive, London's letter shows how committed he was to the cause in all its particulars, even as he prepared to leave the country.

Wood's book may have influenced his other, last nonfiction piece written before he left for the South Seas. He didn't give it a title, though Charmian wrote "Material Gain" at the top of the manuscript's first page. Composed during the writing of his final chapter for *The Road*, "Material Gain" was given as a speech to the Ruskin Club on 1 February 1907 and never published. It begins with a series of questions: Do children play for profit? Do sailors "rescue shipwrecked strangers" for profit? "Did Lincoln toil with his statecraft for material gain?" Did you attend this lecture for profit? Do professors teach for profit? ("You know their average salary is less than that of skilled laborers"—not anymore!) Do scientists perform research for profit? "Did men like Spencer, Darwin, Newton, work for material gain?" Did soldiers in the Civil War fight for profit? Some of these eclectic examples are repeated from *The Iron Heel*, and the others could have been and should be deduced from it. This was his last public pronouncement on America's socioeconomic wars before he left for the South Seas, and he had chosen his home stadium, so to speak, for his venue. The Ruskin Club members would not be generally sympathetic to the revolutionary, apocalyptic socialism of *The Iron Heel*, so London needed to show his hometown that he was still very much in tune with their core beliefs.

The lecture begins with this enumeration of how altruism is part of human nature and will not be destroyed by capitalism, for he wants to put the question of *The Iron Heel* to them in a more appealing way: "Can you not conceive that mere material gain, a once useful device for the development of the human, has now fulfilled its function and is ready to be cast aside into the scrap-heap of rudimentary organs and ideas?" Of course they could. But they—being good liberal progressives, Fabian socialists, and Christian Socialists—objected to "the economic interpretation of history" formulated by Marx and Engels. They could not see, as London was trying to make them see, that in the time of the Brotherhood of Man "spiritual gains and exaltations," "righteousness and beauty and nobility" were realizable. Marxist socialists, argued London, wanted what they wanted. The only difference was that, "paradoxically," the club members and others in the same political camp argued that man was intrinsically material. Revolutionary socialists believed in a "transitory, incidental, and extraneous materialism."[36] Economics, for these liberals, entered when we defined human nature, says London. He, on the other hand, proclaimed the overthrow of the profit motive. We don't know which texts or thinkers he was arguing against specifically, but this speech is meant to be a confrontation, a challenge, a polemic, but with a sympathetic tone. Abandon your mistaken theories, he cried, and join us. This was London's final word on socialism in America before he left, a précis of *The Iron Heel*: Factions of the Left unite!

Once London finished *The Road*, he immediately began compiling notes for his next work, a long short story entitled "Goliah." Uncharacteristically, the notes begin with the nearly exact wording of the finished story: "In 1924, the city of San Francisco awoke to read in the morning papers a letter received from some crank, by Walter Fassett—signed Goliah. Then give letter."[37] *Goliah* signifies anything extraordinary large and powerful.[38] It was the name of a monster train engine on the Central Pacific Railroad that ran through the Sierra on the route London took at least twice; this story, then, has connections to both *The Road* and *The Iron Heel*.

The letter is a kind of summation of the latter: man is "the master" of matter but "has not yet mastered society." Capitalism is unclean in part because it is irrational. Profit is the misguided end when society should be "an intelligent and efficacious divide for the pursuit and capture of happiness and laughter." Showing how anxious London was to get cracking on the *Snark* voyage, the metaphor of sailing infiltrates this story as it had when he thought in "Material Gain" about sailors rescuing the shipwrecked. According to Goliah—who lives on Palgrave Island, a fictional island next to Diana Shoal, a real geologic formation among the Bahamas, which the Londons had passed on their way to Cuba in 1906—society is a ship that needs steering by a "captain" with "the intelligence and the wide vision of the skilled expert."[39] In his notes for the story, he emphasized his "vision; even secondary to that was his discovery of Energon."[40] When we replace "wide vision" with its synonym in London's lexicon *the imagination*, we see how London is further developing the idea of the sailor-author out of the model of hobo-author.

Just as Anthony Meredith had delineated the eleven men who controlled the economy and thus society as a whole, "Goliah" posits twenty. Capitalism is "the monster" now, not the captain of the *Ghost*, though we see the danger London courts as he replaces Captain Wolf Larsen, the diseased capitalist, with Captain Goliah, the clean anarchist. He proclaims his intention to be the "strong hand" that takes over, if only temporarily until society achieves its righteous telos of happiness and leisure for all. But Goliah's plan is anarchist, not socialist; killing off the captains of industry is something Alexander Berkman advocated, not the revolutionary London.

"In the slang of the day, Goliah had delivered the goods: he had warned the nine other industrialists that they would die if they did not join him to meet Goliah, and they did."[41] What is important is that London is still writing in the mode of *The Iron Heel*; the story takes place in the near future, and the narrator is concerned with addressing the people of that future who may not understand the vocabulary of 1907. London's notes for the story even mention the possibility of drawing on the material in his "Persistence of the Established" file. In the way that Meredith told the story of Avis's manuscript and life, so the unnamed narrator of "Goliah" tells the story of the mad letter writer Goliah.

In one of those moments of writing that exposes London enjoying himself by writing for the sake of writing, at one point in the story he has Goliah play on the visual homonyms *laughter* and *slaughter*. A simple *s* separates the capitalist from the socialist. I should also point out another minor similarity between "Goliah" and *The Iron Heel* and, as well, "The House Beautiful." When Goliah's perfect society is realized, "the affairs of life, such as house-cleaning, dish and window-washing, dust-removing, and scrubbing and clothes-washing . . . were simplified by invention until they became automatic" (109). "Goliah," though a short story, fits nicely into the collection *Revolution, and Other Essays*.

In addition to *The Iron Heel*, he also borrows from "Material Gain." In Goliah's second letter, London draws on the Ruskin Club speech directly. In that speech, he said, "Can you not conceive that were material gain, a once useful device for the development of the human, has now fulfilled its function and is ready to be cast aside into the scrap-heap of rudimentary organs and ideas, such as gills in the throat and belief in the divine right of kings? Can you not conceive of food and shelter becoming automatic, as safety and order have become automatic, so that higher incentives may universally obtain, incentives such as will tend to develop and make beautiful body, mind, and spirit?" Goliah writes, "The incentive of material gain . . . had now fulfilled its function and is ready to be cast aside into the scrap-heap of rudimentary vestiges such as gills in the throat and belief in the divine right of kings. . . . The time has come when mere food and shelter and similar sordid things shall be automatic" (81).[42] London had not suddenly changed his mind about the efficacy of socialism to reinvent society. But he could imagine a powerful, independently wealthy socialist-scientist who "controls radium, or some other terrific force" that had run out of patience with both the masses and the ruling classes.[43] He was back in the genre of the jeremiad.

Goliah the anarchist exists because, as London has it in his notes, "Socialism is failing benevolent feudalism is being established right now."[44] What if, thinks London, as he again contemplates the future, there were no Ernest Everhard and his merry band of revolutionary socialists who were able to effect a succession of revolts? Instead, imagine a mad scientist who can end war. Could he force the existence of socialism as if it were a plant blooming before its time? Yes. Under Goliah's direction, first child labor is abolished and then "all women factory workers were dismissed to their homes, and all the sweatshops were closed" (97). It was that simple. All means of production were nationalized. "Wall Street was dead" (99). Technology accompanied by the single-minded will of a dictator could guide society to its best end. Radium was a destructive force, but London imagines a future "wireless telegraphy" that eventually became a pocket-sized device, something we might find familiar as we reach for our cell phones to answer another text (104). We will see the importance of telegraphy in "To Build a Fire," a story he would write soon after sailing. Science isn't to blame for society's ills or to be praised for its betterment. It's neutral until placed in the hands of those whose intentions it reflects. This is certainly one of the major themes of London's futuristic, socioscientific stories of early 1907.

Goliah, with his superior scientific achievements and his cold-blooded assessment of the value of billions of lives over the lives of a few rich and powerful men, is a Nietzschean superman. The narrator labels him as such: "While the world did not minimize his discovery of Energon, it was decided that greater than that was his wide social vision. He was a superman, a scientific superman" (112). He employs blond beasts to crew for his ship the *Energon*. He is a different sort of superman from Ernest Everhard, though. He kidnaps Africans, Chinese, and Japanese workers to build his yacht and the village on his island, enslaving them in the name of a higher good. "Where had Goliah got the sinews of war? . . . By exploiting these stolen laborers," which means he is no better with his means than your average corrupt industrialist (101). This is the charge London levied against anarchists, who used the violent means of the capitalists to achieve their own ends. Goliah, in London's notes, "orders the killing off of all idiots—of all hopelessly insane—of all criminals that were really criminals," though in the final version "the hopelessly criminal and degenerate" were merely "segregated," meaning, prevented from reproducing. Everhard would never kidnap or murder, even if it meant operating according to an imagined higher order of morals. We remember that London had told Frederick Bamford a few months previous that "personally I like Nietzsche tremendously, but I cannot go all the way with him."[45] "Goliah" represents both the boundary between London and Nietzsche and London's imagining of the dissolution of that boundary.

The final links to *The Iron Heel* come at the end. Goliah reveals himself to be sixty-five-year-old Percival Stultz. The people of the world, now that they have been conned into becoming peace-loving, happy socialists, build a monument to him in the "wonder-city" of Asgard. In *The Iron Heel*, Avis tells us that Asgard will be built soon. "The walls and towers and shafts of that fair city," says Meredith, "will arise to the sound of singing, and into its beauty and wonder will be woven, not sighs and groans, but music and laughter" (304). Note, too, that "Goliah," like *The Iron Heel*, is written for a world audience by someone who is fashioning himself as a world author who is about to adventure out into the middle of it.

London did not write "Goliah" as a sequel to *The Iron Heel* or as a viable alternative for the destruction of the Iron Heel. The connections between these two works are simply examples of London taking pleasure in the hidden similarities. Once one finds these connections, though, one realizes that London is enacting his goal for socialism and the result of bohemian economics: "As Goliah had predicted, work indeed became play" (112).

The final paragraph of the story, an "editorial note" written not by Anthony Meredith but an anonymous somebody very much like him, tells us that "Goliah" was written by a fifteen-year-old named Harry Beckwith who was able to combine the three elements that London had hoped would make *The Iron Heel* and all his future work successful: "wealth of historical detail [fact], the atmosphere of the times [the feels], and the mature style of . . . composition" (116). A graduate of Lowell High School in San Francisco, Beckwith seems to be a fictional version of Henry Ralston, the Yale undergraduate who wrote the imitation London essay "Things Alive." Even more likely, he seems to have replicated London's own first publication "Story of a Typhoon off the Coast of Japan." When that work was published in the *Examiner*, it too was accompanied by an editorial note praising the accomplishment of "one so young" (116).

This story combines the theatrical with the absorptive, though it is weighted toward the former. His next story is almost purely absorptive, a break from the intensely theatrical that had preoccupied him since the summer. After spending five days in Carmel with Charmian, Sterling, James Hopper, Mary Austin, and other bohemian refugees from San Francisco, he began "The Passing of Marcus O'Brien." It takes place in the Klondike, continuing his alternation between the Southland ("Brown Wolf," "When God Laughs," "The Apostate," "Just Meat") and the Northland ("Wit of Porportuk," "Finis"). He's back in familiar and comfortable territory after traversing, as an author, so much untried and experimental ground in *The Iron Heel*, *The Road*, and "Goliah." So he begins with a tried-and-true tactic, a dialogue among characters that takes the reader immediately and deeply into the action. Judge Marcus O'Brien passes sentence on Arizona Jack, who has murdered his cabin mate, Ferguson, for singing an irritating song in an irritating voice. Arizona Jack murdered Ferguson because Jack has "artistic sensibilities." This was a fight about what is good art.[46] And so, given the extenuating circumstances, O'Brien called it manslaughter, not murder, and spared his life.

Red Cow, their camp, is located in an undefined space (neither Canada nor America) and twenty years in the past, an unrecoverable past because all of it changed in 1897. This timeless, spaceless place has its own government and laws: "So far as the law was concerned, they were in No-Man's land"(166). It's a kind of bohemian commune, not a utopia but a place where men can live without concern for convention. They make their own conventions; and even murder, when motivated by artistic judgments, is somewhat condoned. O'Brien gives Jack a lenient sentence and Percy Leclaire makes it easier for Jack by giving him more food for his enforced banishment downriver.

But Jack was the only author figure in camp, and with his departure it all falls apart under the influence of whiskey and greed. The capitalistic worldview takes over quickly when gold—O'Brien finds a streak—and alcohol—barrels of it arrive from outside—flood the community; it's not the rising Yukon River, which seems to threaten the town at the beginning of the story, that is the real danger. Nature takes a back seat to man's wickedness. Whiskey sparks the false imagination ("The more whiskey they downed, the more fertile of imagination they became" [174]), which drives the key argument of the story: should O'Brien sell his claim to Curly Jim, who, like any good capitalist, tries to trick O'Brien? Drunk beyond measure, O'Brien is played the fool by his friends who toss him into a boat and set him adrift on the river, never to return. O'Brien wakes, can't remember the night, and believes he must have killed someone without provocation; why else would he be in a boat without food? We expect him to die; instead, he survives the two-thousand-mile journey to the Bering Sea and becomes a temperance lecturer in San Francisco. Alcohol creates a false past leading to the inartistic and conventional choice of becoming a teetotaler. It's a humorous and easy tale, expertly told, a formulaic story made unconventional by its idiosyncratic moral based soundly on the evils of capitalism: 'Tis better to kill with a sound imagination than to mistakenly believe one is a murderer because of an alcoholic black out.

After that brief respite, London returned to the experimental. "The Unparalleled Invasion" is a fictional essay. It lives in the gap between the short story and nonfiction. He made up an essay, its author, and the larger work it is supposed to be a part of: Walt Mervin's "Certain Essays in History." Uncertain that this was fiction, Robert MacKay of *Success Magazine* rejected it, saying, "If it had been fiction I would have held on to it tight, but I assure you that I read it with a great deal of interest and understanding of its value."[47] London had called it a "freak short story" when he had submitted it to MacKay, but the editor, understandably, ignored London's category. It is too much like an essay. It is written in the voice of Anthony Meredith. It would have served as one of his footnotes if China had been mentioned in the novel. It is more similar to his 1904 essay "The Yellow Peril" in content than it is to any short story. Unlike "The Passing of Marcus O'Brien," but like "Goliah," "The Unparalleled Invasion" required a dozen or so sheets of notes before composition. Again, these are nearly word-for-word try-outs for the story itself. In "Goliah" he had written of Japan's eagerness to conquer the world, and he returned to that theme in "The Unparalleled Invasion." He also returns to his experiences as a war correspondent in Korea, and thus he sets the beginning of the story's action with the Russo-Japanese War in 1904. He uses terminology from "The Yellow Peril" (that is, "race egotism") and reiterates the divide based on language ("psychological speech," "thought-processes," "intimate vocabulary"). "It was all a matter of language," a barrier that the Japanese surmounted as they moved from Korea and Manchuria into China itself.[48] They assumed command of the country, turning it into a colony, only to be expelled by the Chinese once they had become as modern as every other country.

And then the great fear of China's birthrate arose, as Chinese immigrants overwhelmed nearby countries. The world was at a loss until an obscure American professor ("get striking name," reads London's notes), Jacobus Laningdale, devised a method of germ warfare that destroyed China.[49] After the complete devastation of China's population, the rest of the world took over the land, "a vast and happy intermingling of nationalities that settled down in China in 1982 . . . a tremendous and successful experiment in cross-fertilization. We know to-day the splendid mechanical, intellectual, and art output that followed" (100). The subject of that sentence is Mervin and his readers of his history, who now knew the truth behind the destruction of China. For us, however, we can only wonder—and deplore London's anti-Chinese fictional propaganda. London's fear of the Chinese grew out of his own "race egotism," an egotism that matches what he assigns to the Chinese; as he has China's leader say, "We are the most ancient, honorable, and royal of races. We have our own destiny to accomplish. It is unpleasant that our destiny does not jibe with the destiny of the rest of the world, but would you?" (87). It was one pure race against another, and the Chinese could be accepted into London's worldview only if they were mixed with other races. Note that the utopialike state of New China is accomplished by people of mixed races. Racism guides London even as he insists on the so-called irrefutability of fact. Given the fact of China's ever-increasing population, it was, according to London, only rational for other nations to curtail Chinese sexual reproduction because they wouldn't do it themselves.

London never reached a point in his thinking where science became an ideological tool, as susceptible to indeterminacy as emotions, spirituality, and other metaphysical constructs. Facts were facts, and he could argue with science if his socialist comrades broached the topic of the Brotherhood of Man. As a world author he needed to make his pronouncement on the "threat" of the millions of Chinese.

Not every experiment in form was a success, and he suspected as much. When Roland Phillips at *Cosmopolitan* rejected "The Unparalleled Invasion" in 1909, London asked him to tell him why: "Is it a good idea poorly handled, or is it an idea that in itself is of no value to magazine publications?"[50] Phillips replied diplomatically: "Personally it struck me as an exceptionally effective story, one which you would have no difficulty in placing. It proved unavailable for us on account of the fact that we happened to have two stories in hand which while not precisely like yours were similar in theme. It was for that reason we could not use it; but stories of this pseudo-scientific kind seem to be more or less popular and as I say I don't think you will have any difficulty in securing a market."[51] London would not have agreed. Thinking its pseudo-ness outweighed its science, he next sent it to *Black Cat*, and then eight more magazines before, surprise of all surprises, his old friends at *McClure's* took it for four hundred dollars in 1910.

We might think he hadn't said enough about the Chinese if we read only the title of his next story: "The Enemy of All the World." Thankfully, however, it has nothing to do with race. In the first sentence we meet another mad scientist, "that scientific wizard and archenemy of mankind, Emil Gluck," another Percy Stultz but without a mysterious and superpowerful public identity.[52] The story takes place in the decade after the end of *The Iron Heel*. It is, in essence, a biography; we learn at the end, as we did with "The Unparalleled Invasion," that this is another fictionalized essay; an editorial footnote tells us that it was taken from A. G. Burnside's *Eccentricities of Crime*. London was having way too much fun with footnotes. The story is based on a "great mass of evidence and the documents and records of the time" (101–2). We will learn how Gluck was made into the "human monster" that he was (102); clearly, London was taking seriously the lessons about environment that he had learned the previous year. The principal factor in this malforming environment was his aunt, who was assigned to care for him after his parents died when he was six. This antimother figure nearly destroys him. A brilliant student, he becomes a professor and writes *Sex and Progress.*

The title of this book is a clue to some private moments shared by Jack and Charmian, and we should pause in the analysis of the story to consider them. Charmian London noted in her diary five days before he started the story that they were reading *Sex and Character* by Otto Weininger. Otto Weininger's book was given to Jack by Everett Lloyd, the founder and editor of the first magazine for hobos. In January 1907 London wrote him a con-gratulatory letter about *Vagabond.*[53] Lloyd seems to have endorsed much of Weininger's book, including its virulent misogyny and racism. But Jack and Charmian did not, and when Charmian says in her diary that Jack was reading the book out loud to her, they must have been laughing at it. In the chapter "Woman and Her Significance," Weininger writes, "Women [unlike men] seldom carry on an intrigue with another woman's husband, except when they wish to triumph over her by making him neglect her," to which Charmian wrote in the margin, "He must have been asleep C.K.L." And Jack had written simply, "Rats."[54] It is the only marginal comment he made. That he links his evil genius Gluck to Weininger indicates, of course, how little he thought of Weininger.

David Mike Hamilton is excellent on this point. After discussing how the book came to the Londons, he quotes Charmian's glee at receiving the book; she had quoted in her biography Weininger's definition of genius: "A genius is he who is conscious of most, and of that most acutely," though she left off his corollary, which is that genius is particular to males only. Hamilton then points us to a 1914 letter Jack wrote to a correspondent that *Sex and Character* "was all about women and was very uncomplimentary to women."[55] Weininger pitched his screed as a psychological treatise and wrote on talent, memory, and genius, as well as on the fundamental infe-riority of women. So London and Charmian sorted out the sentences they found potentially agreeable all the while laughing and wincing at Weininger's sexism and racism.

London had been mulling the story over at least since the time he had received the book.[56] Not only an author figure, but an unjustly vilified author, Gluck and his sociological writings alienate him from society, isolating him at his university. He, like London and like *The Iron Heel*'s John Cunning-ham, was called an anarchist because he advocated "social revolution." He is like Goliah in that he stands for the alternative to reasonable, socialistic change wrought by the working class instead of by one strongman. Again, London is warning the country that if it does not allow the proletariat to effect social change then one brilliant scientist will figure out how to do it, and it will be regrettable. These stories of the solitary individual are precursors to *Martin Eden*.

"The Enemy of All the World" is also a meditation on the injustice of the criminal justice system. Picking up a thread from *White Fang* and articulating his accumulating material on wrongful imprisonment, on the barbarous treatment of prisoners, and the savagery of capital punishment, the story predicts that London will write—as he did in 1913—a fuller treatment of a diatribe against prisons. If violence is a disease and a result of environmental factors—especially a society predicated on preventing social innovation—then criminals should be hospitalized, not imprisoned. It's a small point in the story, but indicative of larger concerns to be expressed in the future. And in London's imagining of the future, he has Burnside say, in the voice once again of Anthony Meredith, "It is inconceivable to us of to-day—the bungling, dilatory processes of justice a generation ago" (116).

But for all its attention to social injustice, the story moves toward the climactic moment of Silas Bannerman, whom we meet for the first time in the very first sentence, figuring out that Emil Gluck was responsible for the solution to warfare and gun violence. Bannerman was presented with two seemingly unrelated events: his first sighting of Emil Gluck and then the elimination of all weapons and constructions for warfare along the U.S. eastern seaboard. "And on the instant there flashed into his mind the connection between Gluck and the destruction." Bannerman's idea was good in and of itself; it leads to the capture of Gluck. But, as Burnside tells us, "the great thing was the conception of the hypothesis, in itself an act of unconscious cerebration—a thing as unaccountable as the flashing, for instance, into Newton's mind of the principle of gravitation" (131). The story becomes a battle between author figures or, more precisely, between the imagination of the good, law-abiding author and the misunderstood, yet evil author. Bannerman formed his "hypothesis," but, like London confronted daily by his own mysterious imaginative faculty, he was completely baffled by it. By making such a point of this moment of great insight, London reveals his own anxieties, befuddlement, and confusions about the sources and machinations of that ghostly imagination that so controlled him.

So he dives deep into the absorptive in his next story, "The Dream of Debs," even employing the first-person narrator. He decided to follow a technique that Jimmy Hopper employed, beginning the action in a room and then "a la Jimmy Hopper, spread it out—enlarge the circle." The unity of the story proceeds from the narrator, Corf, encountering the effects of a national labor strike in his neighborhood, his city, and then the nation, only to be forced back to the city at the end. "Be sure," he instructed himself, "that a number of vivid country pictures are given."[57]

"The Dream of Debs" was his final choice for a title, after considering "The Great Labor Day," "When First Shall Be Last," "The Dream of Labor," "The Chaos of Order," and "When the Dreams of Labor Come True." He wanted this tale to be timeless: "Make story without any date in it," he told himself in his notes. No footnotes, no voice of the future commenting on the follies of the past (our present). He wanted to immerse himself and his readers and keep the theatrical at bay. At the same time, we learn the narrative takes place thirty years after Debs's time, and so we are back in the near future of failed revolts (*The Iron Heel*) and the evil geniuses Goliah ("Goliah") and Gluck ("The Enemy of All the World"). His narrator begins the story with a premonition, and London can't help returning again to the earthquake, that cataclysmic event that was like the death of a loved and loving parent. "I remembered that at the time of the Great Earthquake of 1906 many claimed they awakened some moments before the first shock and that during these moments they experienced strange feelings of dread."[58] We cannot overestimate the beneficial effects of taking the *Snark* voyage as a way to put this psychologically damaging event behind him.

The narrator, "a wealthy bachelor," remembers Debs's dream of a general strike, and the narrator is against it, making sure to fire his chauffeur, a member of the Chauffers' Union who refused to scab.[59] We are back in the world of *The Iron Heel*. Chapter 13, "The General Strike," imagined that unions abandoned their strategy of winning at the polls and decided to "come over to the political field of the socialists; for the general strike was a political strike" (213). It is a success and stops the war between Germany and the United States, but in the end the Oligarchy is able to take advantage of the peace and through trade subdue Germany, increasing the Oligarchy's worldwide power.

Now we see it from the point of view of Corf, a member of Clubland and of the ruling class, and we apprehend why London has chosen the first-person point of view. We laugh at his consternation that there is no cream for his morning coffee, no olive for his martini at lunch at the club. London cleverly makes the case for the strike with his blasé, independently wealthy Bertie Messener, who tells Clubland that they deserve this reaction of labor to their oppression by the ruling class. This is the heart of the story, the objective justification of the strike. Messener sounds almost like Everhard. And when labor wins and the general strike is called off, Corf sounds like a whining child when he speaks the final sentences: "The tyranny of organized labor is getting beyond human endurance. Something must be done" (176). His story has only transferred our sympathies to the successful working class.

"The Dream of Debs" repeats a story element from "The Enemy of All the World." Gluck had figured out how to focus and direct wireless telegraphic energy at bullets and bombs to make them explode. This invisible and mysterious power may have become a weapon, but fundamentally it is the power by which information is conveyed. And it is "the chiefest hardship" experienced by Corf, "this absence of knowledge of what was going on in the world" (154, 153). When the unions announce what they will do first when they win the strike, they say, "We shall open up the telegraphs" (166). This is London's "chiefest" fear, the lack of news, of documentation to back up his stories. "The Dream of Debs," like "The Enemy of All the World," reproduces another authorial anxiety. If there are no newspapers and magazines, then there will be no creative output.

Class warfare, the future, and author figures and their manuscripts are all combined once more in London's final story—"A Curious Fragment"— written before he sailed. Just as Avis's manuscript is a fragment, so is this tale called a fragment. It begins from the platform called *The Iron Heel*. Instead of a worker named Jackson losing his arm and prompting the conversion of Avis Everhard to socialism, we have a different "tale of an arm. It was the arm of Tom Dixon, and Tom Dixon was a weaver of the first class in a factory of that hell-hound and master, Roger Vanderwater."[60] Anarchist and political activist Emma Goldman would have approved of London's choice of occupation for Vanderwater; he was "the ninth in the line of the Vanderwaters that controlled for hundreds of years the cotton factories of the South." Yes, we are back in the future, but the Oligarchy has been in charge, not for three hundred years, but eight hundred. In another twist, there are no socialist supermen. London has abandoned his desire for that kind of leader; he has made a turn away from Nietzsche. For the Oligarchy's time is also known as "the dark reign of the overman, in whose speech the great mass of the people were characterized as the 'herd animals'" (257–58). It is a clever linguistic signal of his philosophic change of heart to stop using Shaw's *superman* and use a different translation of *Übermensch*: the overman.

We are eighteen hundred years after the time of Anthony Meredith, as the nameless editor of this manuscript tells us; what's a few more centuries when we're dealing with the infinite future? The manuscript is a tale banned by the "terrible industrial oligarchy" (257). Not only were all potentially subversive tales banned, but writing them down was illegal, as was instruction in reading and writing for the working class. Again we have the transmission of knowledge placed on a pedestal only to be knocked into dust by the ruling classes. Fortunately, storytelling was kept alive, and it was the storytelling "agitators" who "preached revolt to the slave class." The storyteller lectures his audience, saying, "There are many things, my brothers, that you do not know, and it is sad. It is because you do not know that you are slaves" (259). Not only is the message of socialism carried by the written and spoken word but its very enactment is made possible by authors. We may be in the year 4627, but some things never change. However, this final story of this period of London's career, because it is called a fragment, implies that it is followed by an ellipsis. More will follow, more needs to be revealed.

EXIT FROM THE AMERICAN SCENE

Charmian was reading H. G. Wells's *Man on the Moon* while Jack was writing his "future stunts." She had also read Wilde's *De profundis* while he wrote *The Road*. You can almost see what he was thinking by looking at her reading list. They worked symbiotically, even if she wasn't making changes in the manuscript. After her minimal contributions to *Before Adam* and *The Iron Heel*, she was temporarily separated from her husband at the composition stage; he was too focused, too bent on getting these new experiments done to allow for collaboration. But she would return for the longer novels in the next decade.

If evolution had opened London's mind to the infinite past, finding that the savagery of primitive man fights eternally with his civilized nature, then socialism opened him to the future, a time of possibility and enlightenment.

He was full of both hope and foreboding as he sailed off on the *Snark*. To others, however, he seemed to have turned bitter and abandoned the cause they were staying in America to fight for. London was a most reluctant public figure. At the heights of his popularity—in 1904 and again in 1907—first as a fiction writer and then as a world author, he left the country. In the first instance he decided to assume the authorial role as war correspondent and so left for Japan and Korea. In the second instance, he chose to sail the world's oceans and visit as many countries as he could in his bid to become an international author. His fundamental commitment to travel meant he could replenish the pool of scenes and characters necessary for his continuous mode of production.

Yet, when he voyaged on the *Snark*, he missed the 1908 election. He was castigated for absenting himself from the fight against capitalism. A. M. Simon told him just before he left, "You need not try to get any sympathy from me because of overwork, or anything else connected with that boat-trip. In common with most socialists I 'have it in' for that trip. I do not know whether this feeling is partly tinctured with envy for the enjoyable time that you will have (and which I fear none of us have the courage to desire marred in the least), or whether it is what we all claim—that you are leaving when we need you and need you bad."[61] Nonetheless, he continued the socialist fight while he remained in America. When Lieutenant Colonel Petrovsky was refused entry to the United States on account of his socialism, London wrote a vicious diatribe against the immigration officials; the article was passed on to the National Immigration Committee in Washington, which, according to Joseph Noel, acted immediately to allow Petrovsky to enter.[62] Further, *The Iron Heel* and its companion stories—futuristic tales of America as a cooperative commonwealth earned through death and destruction— were written in anticipation of such charges.

In his own future, he would write a series of novels that centered on entrapment, imprisonment, and an individual's opportunities for escape. His South Seas voyage had satiated his appetite for world-changing political ideas. Back home, he resurrected the lives of individuals, not independent of socioeconomic factors, but connected in the ways that men and women create their own prisons. He never gave up proselytizing for social evolution, for political revolution. The election of 1912 was at least as encouraging as the election of 1904. But like many of his fellow socialists, he felt that the dreams of economic equality were dissipating. His jeremiads had been ignored, and he was dangerously close to becoming embittered. It's not that he became more focused on Charmian and on the ranch, but he embraced them as legitimate ways to live in the face of political disappointments and a possible nightmarish eternity of capitalism. But first he went back on the road in the *Snark*, flying a socialist pennant: a white *s* on a field of red, "carrying the message of Socialism to the people of the seven seas."[63]

NOTES

ABBREVIATIONS

HEH   Henry E. Huntington Library
JL   Jack London Papers
JLE   Jack London Ephemera
MI   Joan London Miller Papers
NYPL   New York Public Library
NYU   New York University
USU   Utah State University
WSHS   Wisconsin State Historical Society

INTRODUCTION

1. See Jack London Papers (hereafter JL) 420, no. 2, box 468, Huntington Library, San Marino CA (hereafter HEH).

2. London to Johns, 22 April 1899, *The Letters of Jack London* (hereafter *Letters*), 1:67.

3. Pacific Coast Women's Press Association, "Our Youngest Writers," *Impress*, 1893.

4. Stevenson, "A Note on Realism," 69.

5. Fried, *Courbet's Realism*, 6–7.

6. Coleridge, *Biographia Literaria*, 2:5.

7. Fried, *Courbet's Realism*, 5–6.

1. HOWL, O HEAV'NLY MUSE!

1. He confessed to adultery when she became sick. This was one of three claims made in her original suit for divorce in 1904. See Franklin Walker, notes on divorce suit, HM 45261, Franklin Walker Papers, HEH. Bess London filed an amended suit later the same year in which the claim about adultery was left out.

2. It is possible that he wrote a third work, "Telic Action and Collective Stupidity," in November or December 1902. The manuscript is undated, and he did not enter it into his sales notebook. See note 21 below. The date of his return to the U.S. is given in "Annual Ladies Evening of the Ruskin Club," *Oakland Enquirer*, 15 Nov. 1902, Jack London Scrapbooks, reel 2, vol. 2, HEH.

3. London to Brett, 27 June 1905, *Letters*, 1:494.

4. London to Miller, 11 July 1903, *Letters*, 1:374.

5. London to Brisbane, 6 Apr. 1907, *Letters*, 2:682.

6. London to Putnam, 15 Nov. 1902, *Letters*, 1:317.

7. Jack London, "Simple Impressive Rite at Corner-Stone Emplacement of Hearst Memorial Mining Building," *San Francisco Examiner*, 18 Nov. 1902, 1.

8. See Watson, *Novels of Jack London*, 34–35.

9. Consider the earnings for some of his books. After three years in the marketplace, he still owed Houghton Mifflin $78.88 for advances and other charges for *A Son of the Wolf*. His next publisher, McClure, Phillips, earned a total of $67 from two books. Brett then took over. He published 3,500 copies of *Children of the Frost*, which sold a mere 900 copies in eight months. By May 1903, London still owed $11.30. By the same date, Macmillan had sold about 900 copies of his next book, the 1902 *The Cruise of* The Dazzler. See London, "Book Sales. No. 1," JL 438, Jack London Collection, HEH, and Sisson and Martens, *Jack London First Editions*, 6.

10. See Brett to London, 30 July 1903, JL 2999, HEH: "The book [is] at the moment out of stock. This means that the first edition of about 9400 copies has been disposed of, some 8500 out of that number having been actually sold." Brett then says they had printed another 10,000 copies. See also Sisson and Martens, *Jack London First Editions*, 14; they list 71,584 copies being printed, but it is impossible to tell how many printings they are counting.

11. This paragraph is indebted to and quotes extensively from E. James, "Letters from America," 170–91. See also Morgan, *House of Macmillan*, 163–64.

12. London to Brett, 21 Nov. 1902, *Letters*, 1:318.

13. See London, "Book Sales. No. 1," JL 438, Jack London Collection, HEH, and Kingman, *Jack London*, 40.

14. London to Brett, 12 Feb. 1903, *Letters*, 1:342.

15. London to Brett, 21 Nov. 1902, *Letters*, 1:318.

16. London to Brett, 21 Nov. 1902, *Letters*, 1:320.

17. Brett to London, 3 Dec. 1903, JL 2974, HEH.

18. George Brett, "A Publisher's View," *Outlook*, 5 Dec. 1903, 780–81.

19. London to Brett, 21 Nov. 1902, *Letters*, 1:320. In August 1903, he told an interviewer the same thing: "Mr. London composes slowly, turning out about four thousand words a week" (Fannie K. Hamilton, "Jack London: An Interview," *The Reader* 2, August 1903, 282).

20. London to Robinson, 11 Dec. 1902, *Letters*, 1:328. He told Robinson the same lie he told Brett: "My [upcoming] novels . . . will not be situated in the Klondike."

21. London to Robinson, 11 Dec. 1902, *Letters*, 1:328.

22. London to Brett, 10 Mar. 1903, *Letters*, 1:351.

23. London to Strunsky, 13 Mar. 1903, *Letters*, 1:352.

24. See Frankfurt, *On Bullshit*.

25. He once said that he had two dog names in mind, Buck and Bright, and Buck was "stronger." But how he came up with either one of those names is a mystery. See London to Merle Maddern, 28 Aug. 1903, *Letters*, 1:381.

26. *The Flight of the Duchess* is a bit of a puzzle; too little material survives to tell us what exactly London had in mind, indicating that he wasn't as far along as he led Brett to believe, and, further, the material that survives is somewhat contradictory.

On the one hand, he told Brett that "it will be in the Here and Now, and though situated in California, it will not be peculiarly local but will be really a world-story which might take place anywhere in the *civilized* world. It will end happily" (318). On the other hand, the only surviving note reminds himself to "see Justin McCarthy's 'History of Our Own Times,' for political and parliamentary data," but he marked nothing in it. See Hamilton, *"The Tools of My Trade,"* 199, and Justin McCarthy, *History of Our Own Times*. He collected two one-column magazine articles about jewels, inheritances, and English royalty. It seems the story would have been influenced by his time recently spent in England. The title may have come from Robert Browning's poem by the same name. See London to Strunsky, 31 July 1900, *Letters*, 1:198, for his query to her about meeting to read the poem together.

27. London to Brett, 11 Dec. 1902, *Letters*, 1:326.

28. London to Brett, 10 Mar. 1903, *Letters*, 1:351.

29. London to Brett, 12 Feb. 1903, *Letters*, 1:342.

30. London to Brett, 12 Feb. 1903, *Letters*, 342-43.

31. London to Brett, 20 Jan. 1903, *Letters*, 1:337.

32. See Franklin Walker, *Jack London and the Klondike*, 226-27.

33. London, "Bâtard," *Complete Short Stories*, 1:730.

34. London to Charles Warren Stoddard, *Letters*, 1:195. But its perfection of form wasn't enough for him to like it best of all the stories in *The Son of the Wolf*; that honor lay with "Odyssey of the North."

35. London, letter to the editor, the *Independent*, 14 Feb. 1907, 375. See Franklin Walker, *Jack London in the Klondike*, 241-43.

36. Watson, *Novels of Jack London*, 35-36.

37. If we think of sources in a different, more general way, we might look to William Wordsworth's "Ode: Intimations of Immortality from Recollections of Early Childhood," which London quotes in *The Star Rover* (1913) and which an early reviewer used as a way to discuss the connections among the subconscious, memory, racial memory, and emotions in *The Call of the Wild*. See newspaper clipping, anon., undated, no publication indicated, Jack London Scrapbooks, vol. 4. London wrote at the bottom: "How delightfully and ponderously English this is!"

38. London to John O'Hara, 25 July 1907, *Letters*, 2:701; London to O'Hara, 13 Aug. 1909, *Chicago Evening Post*; quoted in Dyer, ed., *The Call of the Wild by Jack London* with an Illustrated Reader's Companion, 102. The *Buffalo Review*, 7 Nov. 1902, 7, reprints the first four lines of O'Hara's poem, without attribution, giving support to London's claim that he had indeed read this in a newspaper and that he did not know the rest of the poem or its author. It's unlikely that London read this particular paper, but it was a custom at the time to use poetry as filler in a newspaper.

39. Consider, in contrast, how in *The Prelude* William Wordsworth conceived of his imagination:

> that glorious faculty
> That higher minds bear with them as their own.

This is the very spirit in which they deal
With the whole compass of the universe:
They from their native selves can send abroad
Kindred mutations; for themselves create
A like existence.

London wouldn't argue about the ability of poets and novelists to create new worlds based in their own interiorities, but he had grave doubts about how "glorious" that "spirit" might be.

40. London to Strunsky, 3 Apr. 1901, *Letters*, 1:244.

41. London to Maddern, 28 Aug. 1903, *Letters*, 28 Aug. 1903, 1:381.

42. Chuck Watson kindly pointed this out to me.

43. London, Story Notebook, JL 1004, HEH.

44. London, "Husky—Wolf Dog of the North," 67.

45. London, "The Road," 315.

46. London, "The Road," 317.

47. "Jack London Interviewed," *Boston Sunday Herald*, 24 Dec. 1905.

48. London, letter to the editor of the *Stockton Evening Mail*, 21 Oct. 1903, Jack London Scrapbooks, vol. 3, HEH.

49. London, "Husky," 66.

50. London, "Husky," 64.

51. London, "A Northland Miracle," 1:543.

52. London, "Where the Trail Forks," 522.

53. Tebbel, *George Horace Lorimer*, 7.

54. Tebbel, *George Horace Lorimer*, 26.

55. Tebbel, *George Horace Lorimer*, 27.

56. In the 1910s, London had quite a bit of success. Lorimer accepted not only all the David Grief stories but also "South of the Slot" (1909), "A Piece of Steak" (1909), "The Mexican" (1911), and five others. The *Saturday Evening Post* even published "The Devil's Dice Box" in 1976. Lorimer also serialized *John Barleycorn*, though he turned down *Adventure*.

57. London to Brett, 12 Feb. 1903, *Letters*, 1:342–43.

58. Tebbel, *George Horace Lorimer*, 38.

59. Charles Watson pointed out to me that I mistakenly said in *Author Under Sail* that the *Saturday Evening Post* paid London two thousand dollars for *The Call of the Wild*, not Macmillan and Company; see Williams, *Author Under Sail*, 1:449. See Watson, *Novels of Jack London* (253n3), where he was the first to correctly attribute the two-thousand-dollar payment to Brett.

60. Brett to London, 19 Feb. 1903, JL 2981, HEH.

61. Brett to London, 9 Feb. 1903, JL 2980, HEH. It was a curious idea. Brett explained that "the series would be issued in a most attractive form from the typographical point of view and we should expect in working the books to make the series feature of it much more prominent than the individual contributors' names,

so the great reputation which your books already enjoy could not, in any event, be injured by the inclusion of this short novel in our series, and the result might be most advantageous from every point of view." That is, it was a promotional device for the company, not the author. Still, if London didn't profit directly from it, he saw that what was good for Macmillan was good for him. London argued for including "The Story of Jees Uck" by insisting on its verisimilitude: "At the time it was published serially I was gratified to receive a letter from a man who had lived a wild life, and who was so convinced by the story that I could not unconvince him that I had never lived with a native wife. For only by so living, he contended, could I have got the experience necessary to write the story" (London to Brett, 16 Feb. 1903, *Letters*, 1:343–44). Brett sent it to Carpenter, who didn't think it good enough for the series: "The story by Jack London entitled 'The Story of Jees Uck' is an interesting little sketch, but it does not seem to me that it is long enough or strong enough to stand practically by itself in your series" (Carpenter to Brett, 2 Mar. 1903, Macco Records, NYPL). Brett once more went against Carpenter's advice and told London that the story would appear in the series, but not in the summer as originally planned, given that Macmillan was now publishing not only *The Kempton-Wace Letters* and *The People of the Abyss* but also *The Call of the Wild*. See Brett to London, 27 May 1903, JL 2994, HEH. In the end, London wrote this note in his sales notebook: "Decided not to publish in little novels," though who or why decided this is not known (London, Magazine Sales, no. 2, From May 1900 to Feb. 1903, USU).

62. M. C. J., 5 Mar. 1903, Macmillan Company Records, NYPL.

63. Carpenter, "A Reader's Report for *The Call of the Wild*," 231–32.

64. Brett to London, 1 Apr. 1903, JL 2991, HEH.

65. London to Brett, 10 Apr. 1903, *Letters*, 1:360.

66. *The Call of the Wild*, 132. It's not too hard to imagine that the offensive word was *damned*.

67. Frederick Macmillan to Brett, 7 Aug. 1903, Macco records, NYPL.

68. Brett to London, 5 Mar. 1903, Macco records, NYPL.

69. London to Brett, 10 Mar. 1903, *Letters*, 1:351.

70. Brett to London, 19 Mar. 1903, JL 2986, HEH.

71. London to Brett, 25 Mar. 1903, *Letters*, 1:357.

72. Brett to London, 27 Mar. 1903, JL 2988, HEH.

73. Brett to London, 1 Apr. 1903, JL 2991, HEH.

74. London to Brett, 10 Apr. 1903, *Letters*, 1:360.

75. London to Brett, 12 Feb. 1903, *Letters*, 1:343.

76. London to Brett, 10 Mar. 1903, *Letters*, 1:351.

77. Brett to London, 5 Mar. 1903, Macco records, NYPL.

78. London to Brett, 10 Mar. 1903, *Letters*, 1:351.

79. Brett to London, 19 Mar. 1903, JL 2986, HEH.

80. London to Brett, 25 Mar. 1903, *Letters*, 1:357.

81. London to Brett, 25 Mar. 1903, *Letters*, 1:358.

82. London, "In the Days of My Youth: Chapters of Autobiography CCCLXXVI," edited by James Williams, *Jack London Journal*, no. 5 (1998): 146. Interestingly, Martin Eden gets his "true perspective" on the sea.

83. London to Brett, 2 Apr. 1903, *Letters*, 1:359.

84. At the same time, here is the man who, in his very next letter to Brett, referred to *Children of the Frost* as *The Children of the Frost*. See London to Brett, 10 Apr. 1903, *Letters*, 1: 360.

85. London to Brett, 10 Sept. 1903, *Letters*, 1:386.

86. See London to Brett, 24 July 1903, *Letters*, 1:375.

87. See London, *The Call of the Wild*, 142–43.

88. Brett to London, 30 July 1903, JL 2999, HEH.

89. Brett to London, 26 Aug. 1903, JL 3000, HEH.

90. Brett to London, 20 July 1904, JL 3010, HEH.

91. Mott, *Golden Multitudes*, 235. The actual ten top sellers for 1903 included, at number one, Mrs. Humphrey Ward's *Lady Rose's Daughter*; at number three, Frank Norris's *The Pit*; and, at number eight, George Lorimer's *Letters of a Self-Made Merchant to His Son*. Lorimer recognized *The Call of the Wild* as a success because he himself had written one. See Hackett and Burke, *Eighty Years of Best Sellers*, 67.

92. See Hackett and Burke, *Eighty Years of Best Sellers*, 24.

2. JESUS IN THE THEATER OF SOCIALISM

1. London to Johns, 10 Feb. 1899, *Letters*, 1:45.

2. London to Anna Strunsky, 13 Mar. 1903, *Letters*, 1:352. He was using "The Tramp" as a template for the successful essay. See London, "Disappearing Class: [notes for a collection of essays]," JL 602, HEH, quoted below. "The Tramp" was published in January 1902, but he was still giving it as a lecture in 1903.

3. London to Spargo, 28 July 1902, *Letters*, 1:302. See also Leonard D. Abbott to Joan London, 1 Sept. 1937, AW box 1, HEH, in which he says he first met London in the summer of 1902 "as he was passing through New York City on his way to London." London stopped by the editorial office of the *Comrade*, as any good socialist would have done.

4. London to Spargo, 20 Jan. 1903, *Letters*, 1:338.

5. London's sales notebook entry for "How I Became a Socialist" reads "Comrade (a present)" (London, Magazine Sales, no. 2, From May 1900 to Feb. 1903, USU). When Spargo had finished reading Charmian London's biography, he wrote to her, praising the book highly. And then he added: "We saw little of one another, our lives being lived far apart, but I should always want to feel that there was intellectual friendship. On my part there was always more than that, an emotional attitude toward him tender out of all proportion to our association." John Spargo to Charmian London, 8 Dec. 1921, JL 18844, HEH.

6. See J. Williams, editor's introduction to William Morris, 5.

7. Leonard Abbott, "Greeting," *Comrade* 1, no. 1 (Oct. 1901): 12. Abbott turned over the editorship to Spargo beginning with the February 1902 issue.

8. Job Harriman, "How I Became a Socialist," *Comrade* 1 (May 1902): 170.

9. Frederick O. MacCartney, "How I Became a Socialist," *Comrade* 1 (Sept. 1902): 266.

10. Trachtenberg, *Incorporation of America*, 44.

11. Abbott, "Greeting," *Comrade* 1, no. 1 (Oct. 1901): 12.

12. London, quoted in Leonard Abbott and John Spargo, editorial, *Comrade* 1, no. 3 (Nov. 1901): 32.

13. The editors of the *Comrade*, perhaps unintentionally, toned down London's bohemianism by rewriting this crucial sentence as "And I have been busy ever since running away from hard bodily labor." More likely they wanted to prevent London from alienating the working class. But London means hard work of any nature. See London, "How I Became a Socialist," *Comrade* 2 (Mar. 1903): 123.

14. London to George Brett, 30 Jan. 1903, folder 1, box 63, Macmillan Company Records, NYPL. London first met Ghent in George Brett's office in November 1902 when he returned from London; see W. J. Ghent to Joan London Miller, 11 July 1937, MI 471, HEH.

15. London, "A Review," *War of the Classes*, 207.

16. See "Jack London Spurns Union: George Ade, John Burroughs and Others Do Also," *Los Angeles Times*, 23 Sept. 1916.

17. Mabie to Brett, 29 Sept. 1903, Macmillan Company Records, NYPL.

18. Ghent to Miller, 27 Aug. 1937, MI 473, HEH.

19. For some reason, London wrote notes for "The Scab" in the margins of Henry White, "Is Industrial Peace at Hand?" *Independent*, 2 Jan. 1902, 29–30, JLE 1660, box 557, Trade Unionism, Jack London Subject File, HEH. He also used these notes for "The Class Struggle."

20. London, "The Scab," 122–23. This point is made in one of London's sources for the essay: Casson, *Organized Self-Help*.

21. Casson, *Organized Self-Help*, 13–14.

22. Casson, *Organized Self-Help*, 13.

23. Casson, *Organized Self-Help*, 13.

24. See London to Brett, 13 Mar. 1905, *Letters*, 1:472.

25. Kuehl, *Hamilton Holt*, 58.

26. Kuehl, *Hamilton Holt*, 58.

27. London to Brett, 15 Aug. 1903, *Letters*, 1:379. London is quoting a letter from Holt.

28. London to Brett, 15 Aug. 1903, *Letters*, 1:379.

29. Brett to London, 31 Aug. 1903, Macmillan Company Records, NYPL.

30. London changed the title to *War of the Classes* in December 1904 when he pulled the essay "The Salt of the Earth" from the collection. See London to Brett, 8 Dec. 1904, *Letters*, 1:455.

31. Carpenter to Brett, 19 Sept. 1903, Macmillan Company Records, NYPL.

32. Mabie to Brett, 29 Sept. 1903, Macmillan Company Records, NYPL.

33. Brett to London, 3 Oct. 1903, JL 3006, HEH.

34. London, "Class Struggle," 4, 6.

35. Edward Ross made the same argument in an article in the *Independent* that London clipped for a projected essay entitled "The Disappearing Class": "The sharpest corner American society has turned since the destruction of slavery was turned in the early nineties, when the last homestead in the rain belt was taken up," though Ross looked, not to socialism, but a new spiritual frontier in Americans who will work toward a better realization of democracy and individualism. Ross, "The New Future of American Society," *Independent*, 25 May 1905, 1155.

36. London, "Class Struggle," 18. This is in line with Gronlund's analysis in *The Co-Operative Commonwealth*, 28, 41, 46–48.

37. *Socialist Spirit* 2 (Nov. 1902): 6.

38. *Appeal to Reason*, 28 Feb. 1903.

39. *Literary Digest*, 8 Nov. 1902, 587.

40. "Labor Press on the Taff-Vale Decision," *Literary Digest*, 17 Jan. 1903.

41. "Twenty Years of Strikes," *Literary Digest*, 14 June 1902, 796.

42. "Labor Unions and the National Guard," *Outlook*, 22 Nov. 1902, 674.

43. *Wilshire's Magazine* 54 (Jan. 1903): 1.

44. Henry White, "Is Industrial Peace at Hand?" *Independent*, 2 Jan. 1902, 29–30. This is the essay on which London wrote his notes for "The Scab."

45. See London, Subject File, Trade-Unionism, box 557, JLE 1641–75, HEH.

46. London, "Class Struggles: [note for series of novels]," JL 537, HEH.

47. London to Johns, 11 Nov. 1899, *Letters*, 1:123.

48. London to Johns, 21 Nov. 1899, *Letters*, 1:129.

49. London, "Disappearing Class: [notes for a collection of essays]," JL 602, HEH. London typically collected reams of data for a single essay. On one sheet of notes he typed in all capitals: "Note: For this essay. Observe the lucidity and cumulative form as exemplified in 'The Tramp,' and rather than cover too much ground. Enlarge upon concretely. A little bit less than requisite."

50. London, "Contradictory Teachers," *International Socialist Review*, 1 May 1903.

51. London, "Class Consciousness," JL 535, HEH. The Huntington Library mistakenly gave this manuscript its title. See Williams, "Life in Jewish Oakland," for a full discussion of this story.

52. London to Johns, 5 July 1899, *Letters*, 1:92.

53. In a copy of *Revolution* inscribed by Charmian to William P. Downey in 1935, she wrote, "This, you will realize, amounted to a religion to Jack London—the principle of it all," http://carl-bell.baylor.edu/JL/letters.html.

54. See Stasz, *Jack London's Women*, 3, 5–6, 17–18.

55. London, "Christ Novel: [notes]," JL 532, HEH.

56. London, "Christ Novel: [notes]," JL 532, HEH; I date this as 1900.

57. London, "Christ Novel: [notes]," JL 532, HEH.

58. London, "Christ Novel: [notes]," JL 532, HEH.

59. These notes exist in handwritten form (JL 531) and in typewritten form (JL 532), both in the Huntington Library. Since Charmian typically typed up such notes from the kind of notepaper on which these notes are written, it is certain that these notes are from the later period of 1910–13.

60. For a detailed examination of all the sources and of London's marginalia and handwritten and typed notes, see Williams, "A Critical Edition of *The Star Rover*," 46–61.

61. London, marginalia, in Allan W. Ricker, "The Political Economy of Jesus," *Wayland's Monthly*, no. 45 (Jan. 1904): 11, 19, 21, JL 1041, HEH.

62. George Miller, "Economics of Jesus," *Arena* 36 (Sept. 1906): 237.

63. See "Jewish Innocence of the Death of Jesus," *Literary Digest*, 5 May 1906, 688–89.

64. Kipnis, *The American Socialist Movement, 1897–1912*, 267.

65. Jessie Peixotto to Irving Stone, "*Sailor on Horseback*: Research and Reference: Ruskin Club," folder 31, box 415, Irving Stone Papers, BANC 95/205 cz, Bancroft Library, University of California-Berkeley.

66. See "The Ruskin Club's Ladies Night at the Piedmont Club House," *Oakland Enquirer*, 7 Dec. 1901, Jack London Scrapbooks, vol. 2, pt. 2, reel 2, HEH.

67. Peixotto to Stone, Irving Stone Papers, Bancroft Library, University of California-Berkeley.

68. London's library contained a ten-page pamphlet entitled "Karl Marx' Analysis of Money: Abridged from Das Kapital by Edmund Saxon." It was distributed by the American Socialist Party. See Holman Collection, Jack London State Park, Sonoma CA.

69. "Dinner at the Ruskin Club," *Oakland Enquirer*, 5 Oct. 1901, Jack London Scrapbooks, vol. 2, pt. 2, reel 2, HEH.

70. Joan London, *Jack London and His Times*, 213. The label was applied by Austin Lewis.

71. London to Bamford, 21 Feb. 1905, *Letters*, 1:467.

72. David Hamilton notes that this Bible traveled on the *Snark*. See Hamilton, "*The Tools of My Trade*," 63.

73. *The New Testament of Our Lord Saviour Jesus Christ*. It seems likely that London received this gift from Bamford in January 1908, when the Londons returned home for a couple of weeks during their *Snark* voyage. This is not the first Bible that London owned, nor is it the first one in which he took notes. He read a Bible published by Oxford University Press thoroughly and marked many passages from the Old Testament. Opposite the title page, he noted two passages in particular: Numbers 31 and II Kings 17.27. See *The S. S. Teacher's Edition: The Holy Bible*, edited by Henry Frowde (New York: University of Oxford Press, 1896).

74. *The New Testament of Our Lord Saviour Jesus Christ*, xxx.

75. London, "Christ Novel," JL 532, HEH.

76. Rauschenbusch, *Christianity and the Social Crisis*, 57.

77. Rauschenbusch, *Christianity and the Social Crisis*, 58.

78. London, "Novel," JL 1093, HEH; rpt. in Charmian London, *Book of Jack London*, 2:218. Charmian dates this note.

79. Renan, *Life of Jesus*, 197.

80. Charmian London, *Book of Jack London*, 2:219.

81. London, "Christ Novel: [notes]," JL 532, HEH.

3. JACK LONDON'S PLACE IN AMERICAN LITERATURE

1. See London to Brett, 20 Jan. 1903, *Letters*, 1:337.

2. See London, sales notebook no. 3, JL 934, HEH.

3. London, "Getting into Print," JL 674, HEH.

4. London, "Getting into Print," JL 674, HEH.

5. The connection between eating well and writing was not something he took lightly. "See that your pores are open and your digestion is good," he writes. "This is, I am confident, the most important rule of all." This emphasis on the right kind of foods may seem insignificant, but progressive politics included new ways of farming, food distribution, and consumption.

6. London, "Ideas for Literary Essays, or Essays on Literature: [notes]," JL 780, HEH. On the same page of notes, he refers himself to Norris's second "Salt and Sincerity" essay in the *Critic*, May 1902; Norris's series is intimately tied to London's "Again the Literary Aspirant."

7. London, "Getting into Print," JL 674, HEH. The reprint of this essay in *No Mentor but Myself* contains a significant error. Instead of "from maggot to Godhead" it reads "from magnet to Godhead." This manuscript is mistitled in the Huntington as "First Aid to Rising Authors."

In *Author Under Sail*, 1:467, I quoted from the end of "Getting into Print" and attributed the quotation to "First Aid to Rising Authors," letting myself get confused by a catalogue mistake at the Huntington. The importance of correcting the mistake is that the concept of sincerity, instead of dating back to 1900, actually becomes central to London's conscious theorizing in February 1903, right when he has completed *The Call of the Wild* and had outlined *The Sea-Wolf*.

One further topic is raised by the manuscript of "Getting into Print." London corrected page proof for this essay and cut out all original references to the *Editor*, the publication in which it appeared. These substantive changes, as well as changes he made in page proof for "What Communities Lose by the Competitive System" and "First Aid to Rising Authors" (all three of which are at hrc.contentdm.oclc.org/cdm /landingpage/collection/p15878coll31#nav_top, the Jack London Collection, Harry Ransom Center, University of Texas–Austin), show London at work as an assiduous reviser, contrary to the myth that he never revised, a myth propagated by himself and perpetuated by many scholars since.

8. London, "Getting into Print," JL 674, HEH.

9. London, "Getting into Print," JL 674, HEH.

10. Interestingly, the only time that I have found that he was honest about which magazine accepted him first occurs in a newspaper interview in 1906 while he was touring the country. Jack London Scrapbooks, vol. 7, page 82, HEH.

11. Lowes, *The Road to Xanadu*, 432.

12. The editor in the story is Ellery Sedgwick and the "young writer in Southern California" is Cloudesley Johns. The girl from the Sierras is not known, but he used her as a model for Frona Welse in *A Daughter of the Snows*. Also, his "short adventure-stories for a famous juvenile publication" are his *Tales of the Fish Patrol*; a week before he receives a letter from *Youth's Companion* questioning the veracity of the stories, he bemoans the fact that the editor found some of them unreal. See London to corresponding editor, *Youth's Companion*, 9 Mar. 1903, *Letters*, 1:348–50. The "cliff-climbing story" is "Up the Slide."

13. London, "Stranger Than Fiction," JL 1271, HEH.

14. London to Strunsky, 20 Dec. 1902, *Letters*, 1:329. Note that he wrote this letter in the midst of writing *The Call of the Wild*, another connection between his 1903 essays on writing and *Call*. Also, part of his confidence in becoming a novelist is tied to this new self-definition of his art.

15. London, "The Terrible and Tragic," JL 1298, HEH.

16. See Edgar Allan Poe to F. W. Thomas, 25 May 1842, *Letters of Poe and His Friends*, HEH 338984. This is the edition London used.

17. London, "Again the Literary Aspirant," in *No Mentor but Myself*, 51.

18. London, "Hints to Beginners: [notes for essays]," JL 750, HEH.

19. Stevenson, "Note on Realism," 66,68.

20. Said, *Beginnings*, 5.

21. Fannie K. Hamilton, "Jack London: An Interview," *The Reader* 2 (Aug. 1903), 279. Hamilton and London maintained a correspondence at least through 1909, sharing an interest in the sea and contemporary fiction, including Conrad.

22. Lowes, *Road to Xanadu*, 432.

23. London, "The Leopard Man's Story," *Complete Short Stories*, 896.

24. London, *The Sea-Wolf*, 213.

25. London to Fannie K. Hamilton, 14 Aug. 1903, *Letters*, 1:378.

26. Johns, "Who the Hell *Is* Cloudesley Johns?," 2:50.

27. Conrad, *Youth*, 45, HEH 12066. London was reading (or had read) Conrad while writing *The Call of the Wild* as well as his socialist and writing essays. The short novel form of *Youth*, as well as its partner in the same volume, *Heart of Darkness*, may have inspired London to write a short novel, too, called *The Call of the Wild*. The number of reviews that linked *The Sea-Wolf* and *Youth* is quite startling; all were positive and used Conrad as the baseline of excellence in telling sea stories that London had more than ably met.

28. Conrad, *Youth*, 41.

29. Johns, *Who the Hell Is Cloudesley Johns?*.

30. Julian Hawthorne, "Jack London in Literature," *Los Angeles Examiner*, 16 Jan. 1905, Jack London Scrapbooks, vol. 5 reel 3, HEH.

31. London, "Amplification of Synopsis of Last Half of Sea Novel," undated, folder 9, box 24, Jack London Collection, USU.

32. T. M., "Jack London on Football," *The Occident*, Jack London Scrapbooks, vol. 3, reel 2, HEH.

33. In one of her diaries, Charmian noted that the *Sophie Sutherland* was the "model for the GHOST in The Sea Wolf" (Charmian London, Diary of *Dirigo* voyage around Cape Horn, 1912, JL 208, HEH). She repeated the claim in *Jack London and Hawaii*, 9.

34. London to Brett, 20 Jan. 1903, *Letters*, 1:337–38.

35. London, "Stranger Than Fiction," JL 1271, HEH.

36. A note in the back of London's annotated copy of Albert Sonnichsen's *Deep Sea Vagabonds* reads, "learning in the fo'k'sle, referring to Wolf Larsen," a reference to a passage about one of the shipmates reading Darwin, Huxley, Spencer, Emerson, Carlyle, and Browning. But this note feels as if it were written after London had completed a fair amount of work on the novel and had found this document of life aboard ship to confirm his characterization of Larsen. In fact, London may have been led to Sonnichsen by a review of *Deep Sea Vagabonds* that appeared in October 1903, which he pasted into his scrapbook because it reviews both that book and *The Call of the Wild*, declaring that besides London "the only other California writer of the sterner sex who has attracted much attention this summer is Albert Sonnichsen."

37. Said, *Beginnings*, 50.

38. Given London's penchant for borrowing names of real people for his fictional characters, it is entirely likely that Charley Furuseth's name is an homage to Andrew Furuseth, who is nicknamed by one biographer as the Abraham Lincoln of the sea; see Berwick, *The Abraham Lincoln of the Sea*. According to another biographer, by 1893, the time of London's first sailing job, Andrew Furuseth had "begun to establish himself as an intellectual leader in San Francisco and to make his mark in the national labor movement, where he was influential in starting a national seamen's organization and launching a legislative program for seamen." Weintraub, *Andrew Furuseth*, 27. Furuseth was instrumental in unionizing, but he was no socialist. He simply wanted to ensure the safety and rights of common sailors in a time when brutality on board was commonplace: "perhaps the most notorious of these deep-sea tyrants was Bully Waterman, whose crimes are uncountable" (78). Nicknaming a violent captain "Bully" rings harmoniously with the nicknames "Wolf" and "Death," though whether London was inspired to use these nicknames while reading Sonnichsen is unknown, though possible. The comparison between slaves and seamen was repeatedly used around the turn of the century, hence, the link between Lincoln and Furuseth. London's use of the name, therefore, is highly ironic; Charley Furuseth effectively sells Hump into slavery.

39. Said, *Beginnings*, 51,

40. See *Letters*, 1:211, 251, and Hamilton, *"The Tools of My Trade,"* 16.

41. One might also count the Bricklayers' Picnic in *Martin Eden* and the trio of bricklayers in *The Mutiny of the* Elsinore as instances of the ghostly repetition, not of the figure per se, but at least of his occupational incarnation.

42. London, "The Mercy of the Sea: [notes for novel]," JL 942, HEH.

43. London, "That Dead Men Rise Up Never," JL 1301, HEH.

44. These subject positions reverse later on when London, having seen the ghost, fears that the crew will not believe the story that he would tell of its sighting. "Stranger Than Fiction," "The Terrible and Tragic," and *The Sea-Wolf* again meld. One side note: London found the stanza from Swinburne in Caleb Saleeby's *The Cycle of Life* while sailing on the *Snark* and writing *Martin Eden*. The same verse appears in that novel as well. I'm sure he had read Swinburne before 1907, but Saleeby brought this stanza to the forefront of his mind.

45. Sausalito, which was a fishing village, was also known for its bohemian tendencies. It's where William Randolph Hearst kept his mistress, Tessie "Dirty Drawers" Powers; see Proctor, *William Randolph Hearst*, 61.

46. Ambrose Bierce to George Sterling, 18 Feb. 1905, in Bierce, *Critical Reception of Jack London*, 108.

47. In the January 1903 issue of the *Atlantic Monthly* (an issue London must have had close at hand as he began *The Sea-Wolf*) a review appeared not only of two new editions of Poe's works but of London's *Children of the Frost*. See "Books New and Old: Two Sorts of Fiction," *Atlantic Monthly* 91 (Jan. 1903), 130, 133-34. Also, Alice Meynell, to whom Maud Brewster is likened, has an essay on Dickens in the same issue; see Meynell, "Charles Dickens as a Man of Letters," *Atlantic Monthly* 91 (Jan. 1903), 52-59.

48. Hamilton Wright Mabie, "Poe's Place in American Literature," *Atlantic Monthly* 84 (Dec. 1899), 735.

49. See unsigned review, "Strenuous Life in Fiction," *Springfield Republic*, 11 Dec. 1904, Jack London Scrapbooks, vol. 5, reel 3 HEH.

50. Regardless of Brewster's reaction, London must have admired Meynell to use her name as a classificatory tool for his fictional creation. Meynell once wrote an essay called "The Spirit of Place," a phrase that comes up in London's work from time to time, especially in "All Gold Canyon." Her essay singles out Milton as the greatest of poets. See Meynell, *The Spirit of Place, and Other Essays*, 7. It is highly likely that London read this volume, as well as her poetry published before 1903.

51. Unsigned paragraphs, "Borrowed Laurels," *Town Talk*, n.d., Jack London Scrapbooks, vol. 5, HEH: "There is no *permanent place in letters* for anything except originality and a strongly marked individuality" ("Borrowed Laurels"; my emphasis).

52. Davidson, "The Horror of Monsters," in *The Boundaries of Humanity*. London expanded the meaning of *monster* in "The House Beautiful," in which he writes, "A thing that enslaves is a monster, and monsters are not beautiful" (174). He is talking about carpets, not slave masters. In *The Cruise of the* Snark, the term becomes more capacious than can be treated here. See volume of 3 of the present work.

53. London, "Classic of the Sea," 102.

54. The name of the publication is unfortunately obscured by London's handwriting. See Jack London Scrapbooks, vol. 3, reel 2, HEH.

55. London, "Experiences with Reviewers and Editors: [notes for lecture]," JL 651, HEH. These are typed notes of handwritten notes on note paper, which read slightly differently; see London, "Experience with Reviewers and Editors: [Notes for Lecture]," JL 650. On the typewritten version he has other paragraphs pertaining to other "experiences": "The Sourdoughs and the Chechaquos Explain. Also explain how men in my cabin are sour-beans and soda afterward. How I Begged My First Meal [blank] Japanese Anecdotes 'Scrap imminent.' Jap thought commercial telegram, and meant pig-iron. [rest in pencil] How I learned that city folks were not wise—Irvings Alhambra. [indecipherable word] Bluff—and how I learned to hit first." These notes get repeated in other sets of notes for the "Experience" lecture, given during his lecture trip of 1905-6.

56. London, "Little Chattering Daws of Men" [notes for article on reviews of *Sea-Wolf*], JL 895, HEH.

57. See Sutherland, explanatory notes, *The Sea-Wolf*, 348-49.

58. All quotations from Wilde's pamphlet come from London's copy: Oscar Wilde, *The Soul of Man under Socialism*.

59. There is no proof that London had read Nietzsche before writing *The Sea-Wolf*, but I assume that he did. The evidence is all circumstantial, but compelling. I believe he read *A Genealogy of Morals* in the spring or summer of 1902 and continued in the fall of 1904 and through to 1906. My supposition is based on his use of the phrase *blond beast* in *The People of the Abyss*, a use that betrays an understanding of its appearance in *A Genealogy of Morals*. See chapter 19 for a discussion of Nietzsche, Wolf Larsen, and *The Iron Heel*.

60. See London, *The Sea-Wolf*, 249.

61. Unsigned review, [name of publication illegible], Philadelphia, 17 Dec. 1904, Jack London Scrapbooks, vol. 5, reel 3, HEH.

62. Unsigned review, *International Socialist Review*, n.d., but among clippings from the Feb.–Mar. 1905 issue, 508, vol. 5, reel 3, HEH.

63. Unsigned review, "Literary Notes: Jack London's Remarkable Book," *Argonaut*, 14 Nov. 1904, Jack London Scrapbooks, vol. 5, reel 3, HEH.

64. Unsigned review, *New York Tribune*, 12 Nov. 1904, Jack London Scrapbooks, vol. 5, reel 3. Other reviews that deplored the romance but forgave the "error" include an unsigned review, *New York Post*, 19 Nov. 1904, Jack London Scrapbooks, vol. 5, reel 3; "The Woman Spoils It," *St. Louis Mirror*, 17 Nov. 1904, Jack London Scrapbooks, vol. 5, reel 3; unsigned review, *Philadelphia Press*, 20 Nov. 1904, Jack London Scrapbooks, vol. 5, reel 3; unsigned review, *Richmond (Va.) Dispatch*, 26 Nov. 1904, Jack London Scrapbooks, vol. 5, reel 3; and unsigned review, *Boston Transcript*, 30 Nov. 1904, Jack London Scrapbooks, vol. 5, reel 3. All in the HEH collection.

65. See *San Francisco Chronicle*, 13 Nov. 1904(?) Jack London Scrapbooks, vol. 5, reel 3, HEH.

66. Unsigned review, *Christian Register (Boston)*, 24 Nov. 1904, Jack London Scrapbooks, vol. 5, reel 3. See also unsigned review, *Lewiston (Maine) Journal*, 3 Dec. 1904, Jack London Scrapbooks, vol. 5, reel 3; unsigned review, *Globe* (town obscured), 3 Dec. 1904, Jack London Scrapbooks, vol. 5, reel 3; and unsigned review, *Quebec Budget*, 26 Nov. 1904, Jack London Scrapbooks, vol. 5, reel 3. All in HEH collection.

67. Sonnichsen, *Deep Sea Vagabonds*, 46-47.

68. Mary Katherine Lynn, review, *Chicago Journal*, 3 Dec. 1904, Jack London Scrapbooks, vol. 5, HEH; my emphasis.

69. Julian Hawthorne, "Jack London in Literature," *Los Angeles Examiner*, 16 Jan. 1905, Jack London Scrapbooks, vol. 5, HEH.

70. See London to Brett, 10 Mar. 1903, *Letters*, 1:351.

71. London to Brett, 20 Jan. 1903, *Letters*, 1: 338.

72. Brett to London, 27 Jan. 1903, JL 2977, HEH.

73. London to Brett, 12 Feb. 1903, *Letters*, 1:343.

74. Brett to London, 19 Feb. 1903, JL 2981, HEH.

75. Brett to London, 1 Apr. 1903, JL 2991, HEH. Three months later, he repeated the point; see Brett to London, 30 July 1903, JL 2999, HEH.

76. See London to Johns, 29 May 1903, *Letters*, 1:364.

77. London to Anna Strunsky, 29 May 1903, *Letters*, 1:364.

78. See London to Brett, 10 Aug. 1903, *Letters*, 1:377.

79. There is no historical confirmation of a utopian colony located at or near Wake Robin Lodge. Edward Biron Payne, Ninetta's husband, did form an Altrurian colony in 1894 a few miles north of Santa Rosa (Glen Ellen is south of Santa Rosa), and perhaps the reporter is simply mixed up. Or it is also possible that Payne and Eames formed a kind of informal version of their earlier experiment at communal living. The earlier community did build "at least seven cottages" and attempted to build a hotel, so there is an architectural similarity between the two. Hine, *California's Utopian Colonies*, 107.

80. Lady Algy, "The Authors' Haven," *San Francisco Newsletter*, 11 June 1904, Jack London Scrapbooks, vol. 4, reel 2, HEH.

81. Yet he couldn't resist mentioning the novel and its possible serialization to John Cosgrave, a conservative friend and editor of *Everybody's*, who apparently had heard about the sea novel and wanted it. Brett wrote to London in the middle of his negotiations with Gilder that "I met Cosgrave yesterday, the Editor of Everybody's Magazine, and he told me that you had written him to say that the thing [the sea novel] could not be serialized, and when I told him in effect what the story was he seemed to shy at it very much and doubted whether he could use it at all." (Brett to London, 27 Aug. 1903, JL 3001, HEH). London wrote back, telling him that "I thought I'd make him shy at it. Work of mine he has refused for *Everybody's* I have sold promptly, and right on top of it, to the *Atlantic*" (London to Brett, 2 Sept. 1903, *Letters*, 1:384). Cosgrave's letter apparently does not survive.

82. Brett to London, 31 Aug. 1903, JL 3002, HEH.

83. London to Brett, 10 Aug. 1903, *Letters*, 1:377.

84. See Brett to London, 5 Sept. 1903, JL 3004, HEH.

85. Jeannette Leonard Gilder to London, 9 Dec. 1902, JL 6682, HEH. In an advertisement that first appeared in the *Critic* in their December 1903 issue and was repeated at least once more in early 1904, it was announced that "Jack London, author of 'The Call of the Wild,' etc., will contribute a series of stimulating papers touching on a variety of topics in his own clever and incisive manner. This will be Mr. London's first appearance as the writer of a magazine department, and he has taken up the idea with an enthusiasm that will be shared by his readers" (advertisement, the *Critic* 43 [Dec. 1903]). Perhaps he meant to do a series like "Hints to Beginners," but no correspondence on this matter exists as far as I know, and it seems he never wrote for the *Critic* in this capacity.

86. Johnson to London, 6 Sept. 1902, JL 8494, HEH. See London, "Magazine Sales. No. 2: From May 1900 to Feb. 1903," JL 934, HEH.

87. See Fischer and Salamo, introduction to *Adventures of Huckleberry Finn*, 744–57. The editors sum up the relationship between Clemens and Gilder: "Clemens apparently did give his 'full consent' to the editing of *Huckleberry Finn* for a magazine audience. . . . The editing of the *Century* episodes of *Huckleberry Finn* in almost every instance originated with the editors and was a requirement of the magazine's format and its implicit contract with its audience" (756–57). A better description of London's relationship with Gilder and other magazine editors could not be made, except to add that London, as well as Twain, did not fear magazine editorial intervention because they considered the book text final.

88. Gilder to Brett, 26 Aug. 1903, JL 6683, HEH. Brett sent this copy of the letter to London.

89. Advertisement in *Century Magazine* 66 (Oct. 1903): 46, Jack London Scrapbooks, vol. 3, reel 2, HEH.

90. Quoted in John, *Best Years of the "Century,"* 157.

91. Fischer and Salamo, introduction to *The Adventures of Huckleberry Finn*, 748n250.

92. John, *The Best Years of the "Century,"* 153.

93. London to Johns, 21 Sept. 1903, *Letters*, 1:388.

94. London, "Amplification of Synopsis of Last Half of Sea Novel," the Clifton Waller Barrett, Library Special Collections, University of Virginia Library, Charlottesville. London sent this second synopsis as well as a copy of the first to Brett to forward to Gilder. See London to Brett, 2 Sept. 1903, *Letters*, 1:383.

95. See London to Strunsky, 27 Nov. [1900], *Letters*, 1:221. London had read *Tess* in March 1900. See London to Ninetta Eames, 26 Mar. 1900, *Letters*, 1:178. It's very possible that the former was written 27 Nov. 1899, making it the first letter London wrote to Strunsky. (Jack didn't put the date on the letter.) Charmian says in *The Book of Jack London* that when they met on 10 March 1900, he had recommended *Jude* to her, as they discussed literature and what they had been reading.

96. London to Brett, 2 Sept. 1903, *Letters*, 1:383–84.

97. The ad, quoted above, and see note 89, finished off in a fashion less agreeable to the author, to whom Brett had sent the proof of the ad (see Brett to London, 11 Sept. 1903, JL 2005, HEH): "A strong love interest develops in the latter part of the story, and the plot brings out most picturesquely the triumph of the ideal over the actual phases of force and matter. In fact, the triumph of materialism is the dominant note of the first half of the book, while that of the second half is love and the triumph of idealism." That is, *Century* wanted to market it as a novel of ideas. If the arc of the narrative goes from materialism to idealism (note, there is no mention of Hump), then readers will be anticipating a rather intellectual experience. *Century* wanted to stress this point, but against London's wishes. When Gilder wanted to entitle it *The Triumph of the Spirit*, London told Brett that he himself preferred *The Sea Wolf* (no hyphen): "I do not like Mr. Gilder's title at all. The very thing he feared about the last half of the sea novel (the making of a tract of it), I fear about his title. It seems to breathe a purpose, an advertisement of a preachment; in fact, it might do for the title of a tract. . . . *The Sea Wolf* is a strong and brief title" (London to Brett, 10 Sept. 1903, *Letters*, 1:386). He reinforced the point to Robert U. Johnson; see London to Johnson, 22 Sept. 1903, *Letters*, 1:389. Johnson, explained the reasoning to London behind choosing *The Triumph of the Spirit*: "It suggests to the reader, who may be repelled by the first half of the story, that something more ideal is coming, and thus makes him patient with the piling up of detail which you yourself would, no doubt, say is in one key. Some one has suggested 'The Taming of the Sea Wolf.' This also would meet the emergency if it were only exact, but the Sea Wolf is not to be tamed" (Johnson to London, 15 Sept. 1903, JL 8495, HEH). You can be assured that Johnson and others in the office were the ones "repelled." In the end, because Brett, Johnson, and London all agreed that the same title should be used for both serial and book publication, they would use *The Sea-Wolf*.

98. Brett to London, 27 Aug. 1903, JL 3001, HEH.

99. London to Brett, 2 Sept. 1903, *Letters*, 1:383.

100. See London to Brett, 2 Sept. and 16 Sept. 1903, *Letters*, 1:383, 387.

101. London to Brett, 16 Sept. 1903, *Letters*, 1:387.

102. London to Johns, 21 Sept. 1903, *Letters*, 1:388. Macmillan even released the information that London had revised the serial text to its marketing department, who then released it to the press. In an over-the-top review, which called the book "the novel of the year in America," "it is announced that the novel has been considerably revised and rewritten since its appearance in The Century."

103. See Johns, "Who the Hell *Is* Cloudesley Johns?" 3:172–85, for a wonderful account of these days. Johns mentions at least three times that London was writing the concluding chapters of *The Sea-Wolf*, meaning that the damned novel just would not come to a close. Johns also says that London was "turning out an average of nearly a thousand words a day," but that has to be an exaggeration or else he would have finished far sooner. Finally, Johns confirms Charmian London's observation about the relation between London's time on the *Sophie Sutherland* and the writing of *The Sea-Wolf*: London had gone "aboard the sealer *Sophie Sutherland*, obtaining

experience which now, ten years later on his own sloop and with a successful literary career assured, he was writing into 'The Sea Wolf' as we sailed the tributaries of San Francisco Bay" (176).

104. See London to Brett, 9 Nov. 1903, Macmillan Company records, NYPL.

105. He also gave the final chapters to Charmian to look over and asked her to send them to George Sterling and Johns. As Johns says in his autobiography, "I received from Charmian Kittredge a carbon copy of the last chapters of 'The Sea Wolf' for criticism, and information that Jack had directed that any changes upon which she, George Sterling and I should agree should be made before sending the manuscript on to the Century Magazine, in which serial publication already had begun. Where one or two of us suggested changes, and any one of the three disapproved, the manuscript was to be left as Jack had written it. This, of course, only for serial publication, as Jack, returning from the wars, would revise final copy for book publication." Johns found a discrepancy about the presence of a Bible on board the *Ghost*, and London was delighted with his friend's proofreading powers. See Johns, "Who the Hell *Is* Cloudesley Johns?" 5:113, 114. See also London to Johns, [March 1904?], *Letters*, 1:421: "By God! Cloudesley! I wrote it, and two others went over it; but it took you to discover the Bible contradiction. I'll fix it by having him quote from it." The editors of *Letters* have given the wrong month for this letter. London tells Charmian on 1 April "Still no mail," so no one had written to London, telling him of Johns's catch before the end of March (London to Charmian Kittredge, 1 Apr. 1904, *Letters*, 1:421). London returned from Korea on 30 June. In his autobiography, Johns says he received this letter 9 July 1904. On 11 July London tells Brett that he has sent *Century* the proofs; see London to Brett, 11 July 1904, *Letters*, 1:434. So he got home, went over the proofs, saw that Johns was right, wrote to him, and then mailed off the proofs.

106. London to Johnson, 20 Dec. 1903, *Letters*, 1:400–401.

107. Tooker, *Joys and Tribulations of an Editor*, 282.

108. Brett, when he had read the manuscript in its entirety in January 1904, objected to the description of the raising of the mast, not because he felt it was inaccurate, but because it seemed "to me to be slightly forbidding from the standpoint of most women readers. Of course, you will decide in regard to its possible curtailment when you go over it, and I am accordingly bringing the matter to your attention in the hope that you may decide possibly to cut the story a little in this particular place" (Brett to London, 23 Jan. 1904, JL 3008, HEH). London decided against cutting it.

109. Brett to London, 23 Jan. 1904, JL 3008, 281, HEH. Gilder and Johnson felt they were in a battle royal with *McClure's*, so snagging a famous author was paramount. Cutting objectionable material provided a way to keep modern and please their audience, but Gilder knew the cost. "If we, for instance, should go to boasting about the Sea Wolf—some one would say, yes but they're cutting it. We know our own principles and reasons, however" (Gilder to Johnson, 2 Aug. 1904, *Century Magazine* correspondence, CM 508, HEH). Any number of letters between Gilder and staff

members testify to the competition between the magazines; see for example Gilder to *Century Magazine*, 4 Oct. 1904, CM 544, box 6, *Century Magazine* correspondence, HEH, and Gilder to Johnson, 12 Sept. 1904, CM 553, box 6, *Century Magazine* correspondence, HEH.

110. Brett to London, 31 Aug. 1903, JL 3002, HEH.

111. Brett to London, 23 Jan. 1904, JL 3008, HEH. Brett decided on a first edition of forty thousand and hoped to sell thirty thousand before the actual date of publication. See Brett to London, 26 Oct. 1904, JL 3016, HEH. He actually presold the entire first printing and part of the second of fifteen thousand; see Brett to London, 9 Nov. 1903, JL 3018, HEH. By February 1905, it had sold around fifty-two thousand copies, a creditable amount, though below what one would expect given the buzz surrounding it, in Brett's estimation; see Brett to London, 27 Feb. 1905, JL 3029, HEH. However, the sales of *The Sea-Wolf* boosted London's income considerably, and in fiscal year 1904–5 Brett estimated his book sales totaled $17,000, or close to half a million dollars in 2014 dollars. See Brett to London, 12 June 1905, JL 3038, HEH.

4. THEATER OF WAR, THEATER AT HOME

1. See London, "No. 3. Magazine Sales. Feb. 1903 to July 1907," JL 934, HEH.

2. Procter, *William Randolph Hearst*, 48.

3. London, marginalia in Ferri, *Criminal Sociology*, flyleaf.

4. Procter, *William Randolph Hearst*, 172.

5. Jack London, "What Shall Be Done with This Boy? Jack London Replies to a Vital Question," *San Francisco Examiner*, 21 June 1903, Jack London Scrapbooks, vol. 2, HEH. He received forty-six dollars for this contribution.

6. London to McClure, 10 Apr. 1906, *Letters*, 2:569–70.

7. London to McClure [January 1906?], *Letters*, 2:545.

8. John Brisben Walker to London, 21 Oct. 1903, JL 19831, HEH.

9. McClure to London, 16 Jan. 1904, JL 14215, HEH.

10. McClure to London, 9 Feb. 1904, JL 14216, HEH.

11. McClure to London, 27 July 1904, JL 14218, HEH.

12. London, "Too Much Gold," *The Faith of Men, and Other Stories*, 101. He received one hundred dollars for this story because he owed *Ainslee's* money. He read proof sheets for the story on 28–30 September and returned them on 1 October.

13. See Ghent, *Mass and Class*, 142.

14. London, "Negore, the Coward," *Complete Short Stories*, 958.

15. London sent this story to Arthur Street (whoever that may be, perhaps an agent, perhaps an editor at the *Critic*; he had never sent a story or essay to him before) who arranged payment of $250, which London received in November 1903. There was a promise that it would be published on 6 December, but apparently it never appeared, and bibliographies list its first appearance as in *Love of Life, and Other Stories*.

16. Charmian Kittredge London to Anna Strunsky, 22 June 1912, AW box 2, Anna Strunsky Walling Collection, HEH.

17. See London, "Photograph Album Two," box 487, JLP 441, contact sheets 3-5, 3-6, HEH.

18. London, "Russians Fight Japanese on the Yalu That Main Slavic Army May be Better Prepared," *San Francisco Examiner*, 11 June 1904, 7. It is extremely important to note that Hendrick and Shepard in *Jack London Reports* mistakenly added six paragraphs to London's third report, "Advancing Russians Nearing Japan's Army"—if it is indeed London's, and because of its style I believe it is not; they actually belong to Edwin Clough's report from China that appears on the same page as London's. How ironic! Because Clough is none other than Yorick, the columnist who routinely skewered London in his column in the *Examiner*.

19. See London, "Japan Puts End to Usefulness of Correspondents," *San Francisco Examiner*, 1 July 1904, 1, 3.

20. It was published as London, "Footsore, Dazed and Frozen, the Japanese Trudge through Korea," *San Francisco Examiner*, 18 Apr. 1904, 3. See London, Jack, "Up the Peking Road," 1904, holograph MS, collection 100, box 4, UCLA.

21. See Hamilton's index (*"Tools of My Trade"*) for these books, though he doesn't include Gifford, *Every-Day Life in Korea*.

22. See, for example, London, "Expenses-Addresses-Etc.," JL 21153, HEH.

23. See "American and British Sympathy for Japan Causes Irritation in St. Petersburg," *San Francisco Call*, 30 Dec. 1903, 3.

24. Kowner, *Historical Dictionary*, 406.

25. See box 470, JLP 422, photo 85, HEH.

26. Kowner, "Becoming an Honorary Civilized Nation," 36.

27. See "Decree Excludes Hebrews," *San Francisco Call*, 27 Dec. 1903, 1, and "Will Discuss Jewish Issue with President," *San Francisco Call*, 29 Dec. 1903, 1.

28. London, "Fifteen Minutes of Socialism with Jack London," *Chicago Inter-Ocean*, 26 Nov. 1905, 29, Jack London Scrapbooks, vol. 5, HEH.

29. "Smart Set Is Improving Mind," *Oakland Tribune*, Jack London Scrapbooks, vol. 5, HEH.

30. "Far Eastern Crisis Nears Settlement: Japan and Russia on Verge of Agreement," *San Francisco Call*, 2 Dec. 1903, 1.

31. See "Russia's Reply to Japan Rejected by the Council of the Elder Statesmen," *San Francisco Call*, 18 Dec. 1903, 1.

32. See London to Johns, 7 Jan. 1904, *Letters*, 1:405n1.

33. See Collier to Roosevelt, 31 Dec. 1903, Theodore Roosevelt Papers, Library of Congress Manuscript Division. www.theodorerooseveltcenter.org/Research/Digital-Library/Record.aspx?libid=043389, Theodore Roosevelt Digital Library, Dickinson State University. How Collier eventually learned that London had chosen Hearst or what the process of negotiation was among Collier, Hearst, and London is unknown, and the same goes for the other two publications London mentions, *Harper's* and the *New York Herald*.

34. Edwin Emerson, "When West Met East," *Sunset* 15 (Oct. 1905), 518.

35. Hearst, "Seven Rules," 107.

36. London, "Expenses-Addresses-Etc." JL 21153, HEH. London could have easily stayed on for any number of months and continued to bank such easy money.

37. See The Wanderer, "'Marking Time in Tokio,'" *Town Talk*, 1904, JL Scrapbooks, vol. 4, reel 2, HEH; and Davis to Roosevelt, 14 Feb. 1904, Theodore Roosevelt Papers, Library of Congress Manuscript Division, www.theodorerooseveltcenter.org /Research/Digital-Library/Record.aspx?libID=044222, Theodore Roosevelt Digital Library, Dickinson State University. Davis tells Roosevelt that he hopes the Japanese will start taking it easy on the Russians so that the war isn't over before "I can grow rich" on his *Collier's* salary. He also tells the president that he couldn't leave New York until 20 February because he was producing a play. Obviously his commitment to reporting the war is at best half-hearted, and he stayed behind the lines with his wife, John Fox, and others.

38. London and James Tuft, "Agreement with William Randolph Hearst to Act as Correspondent," 31 Dec. 1903, JL 21110, HEH.

39. London to Brett, 21 Nov. 1902, *Letters*, 318.

40. See "No War Loan for Russia: St. Petersburg Cannot Obtain the Sinews for a Conflict," *San Francisco Call*, 20 Dec. 1903, 1.

41. London, "Japan's Army Equipment Excites Great Admiration," *San Francisco Examiner*, 3 Apr. 1904, 23.

42. London, "Dr. Moffett: [article]," 13 Mar. 1904, JL 605, HEH. This dispatch was never published.

43. London to Brett, 1 June 1904, folder 2, box 63, Macmillan Company Records, NYPL.

44. London to Brett, 4 June 1904, *Letters*, 1:430.

45. In December 1904, London chopped off the final seventeen pages of his tenth dispatch—"Travel in Korea"—called it "Korean Money," and mailed it to only two outlets before he retired it. See London, "Magazine Sales. Number 3," JL 934, HEH, and London, "On the Peking Road: [Russo-Japanese war article]," JL 1020, HEH, which is a folder containing the handwritten manuscript of "On the Peking Road" and the last half of "Travel in Korea." For the first half, see London, "Travel in Korea," JL 1325, HEH. See also London, "Travel in Korea," *Jack London Reports*, 68–73. "Korean Money" describes his attempt to understand the Korean monetary system. "Travel in Korea" also shows how London would take the serious disquisitions of Isabel Bishop and make them humorous. Contrary to Hendricks and Shepard in *Jack London Reports*, "Travel in Korea" was never published; hence, London could send half of it newly entitled to magazines.

46. See London, "How We Die," JL 775, HEH; London, "The Jap," JL 818, HEH (the main character smuggles "10,000 rifles, 50 machine guns, and 8,000,000 rounds of ammunition" somewhere on the U.S. West Coast); and London, "Japanese Names," JL 820, 978, HEH.

47. He didn't give up right away on the book, for he bought a number of firsthand accounts of the war, like "O," *The Yellow War*, HEH 336999, which alternates between stories of individual Russian and Japanese soldiers and sailors; Palmer, *With Kuroki in Manchuria*, which appeared in November with excellent photographs by James Hare; Barry, *Port Arthur*, which according to David Mike Hamilton he took with him on the *Snark* "to remember old times" (though it is clear to me that given the number of books he bought after the war he was interested in writing more about the experience); McKenzie, *From Tokyo to Tiflis*, which is inscribed "to Jack London-Greeting F. A. McKenzie London, Eng. June 2, 1905"; and Hulbert, *The Passing of Korea*. Hulbert, an expert on Asian affairs, was a resident of Korea, a reporter, and editor of *Korea Review*. See his account of London's arrival in Korea in Homer Hulbert, "News Calendar," *Korea Review* 4, no. 2 (Feb. 1904), box 569, JLE 2097, HEH. For a second account of London's travels, see R. L. Dunn, "Jack London Knows Not Fear. R. L. Dunn, Commissioner to the Japanese War for 'Collier's Weekly' Eulogizes the Daring of the Great Novelist. He Arrived in Korea with Frozen Hands, Ears and Feet, but Physical Ailments Could Not Keep Him from the Front," *San Francisco Examiner* 26 June 1904, Jack London Scrapbooks, vol. 4, HEH. A third account, which re-creates the atmosphere of daring-do and fame that newly surrounded London, was printed at the top of the front page of the *San Francisco Examiner*; Jack London Scrapbooks, vol. 4, HEH.

48. London, "How the Hermit Kingdom Behaves in Time of War," *San Francisco Examiner*, 17 Apr. 1904, 19.

49. London, "Japanese in Invisible War," *San Francisco Examiner*, 12 June 1904, 41.

50. See London, photographic album 7, JLP 445, contact sheet 8, HEH.

51. London, "How We Die: [story notes]," JL 775, HEH.

52. All these reactions were most likely created by London for rhetorical effect; no portrait that survives shows any subject showing tears or fear of the camera.

53. Palmer had a negative opinion of London, though he did lend him his code book for cabling messages back to the States; see "The Telegraphic Condenser and Universal Cipher Code [code book used in Russo-Japanese War]," JL 1297. Dunn and F. A. MacKenzie, who also traveled with him, thought well of him and valued his companionship greatly. See Palmer, *With Mine Own Eyes*; F. A. MacKenzie, "The Little Brown Man: Marching North with the Japanese Army," *London Daily Mail*, 30 May 1904, Jack London Scrapbooks, vol. 4, HEH; and R. L. Dunn, "Jack London Knows Not Fear. R. L. Dunn, Commissioner to the Japanese War for 'Collier's Weekly' Eulogizes the Daring of the Great Novelist. He Arrived in Korea with Frozen Hands, Ears and Feet, but Physical Ailments Could Not Keep Him from the Front," *San Francisco Examiner*, 26 June 1904, Jack London Scrapbooks, vol. 4, HEH.

54. London to Charmian Kittredge, 15 Jan. 1904, *Letters*, 1:406.

55. London, "Fighting at Long Range Described," *San Francisco Examiner*, 5 June 1904, 49.

56. London, "Japanese Officers Consider Everything a Military Secret," *San Francisco Examiner*, 26 June 1904, 1. Part of London's style here is to exaggerate his ex-

pectations in order to highlight how little he was able to report from the front due to Japanese army restrictions.

57. London, "How Jack London Got in and out of Jail in Japan," *Jack London Reports*, 124.

58. London, "Trip to Ping Yang," *San Francisco Examiner*, 4 Apr. 1904, 3.

59. London, "Russians Fight Japanese on the Yalu That Main Slavic army May Be better Prepared," *San Francisco Examiner*, 11 June 1904, 7.

60. "Jack London Free! He Was Not a Spy! The Novelist Had Penetrated the Forbidden Zone, Was Captured and Put into Military Prison," *New York American*, 7 Feb. 1904, Jack London Scrapbooks, vol. 4, HEH. See also Griscom, *Diplomatically Speaking*, 246, for his humorous account of the incident.

61. "Regulations for Press Correspondents," in *Jack London Reports*, 25.

62. Unsigned blurb, *The Wasp*, 19 Nov. 1904, Jack London Scrapbooks, vol. 5, HEH.

63. "Jack London, Whose Books Are Better Than His Coat—and What Befalls Him," *New York Telegraph*, 30 June 1904, Jack London Scrapbooks, vol. 5, HEH.

64. "Smart Set Is Improving Mind," *Oakland Tribune*, 17 Nov. 1904, Jack London Scrapbooks, vol. 5, HEH.

65. See Jimmy Hare, "Some of the Authors," frontispiece to Lynch and Palmer, eds., *In Many Wars*, and *Letters*, photographs between 1:378 and 1:379.

66. Palmer, *With My Own Eyes*, 242. See Davis to Roosevelt, 26 May 1904, www .theodorerooseveltcenter.org/Research/Digital-Library/Record/ImageViewer?libid =045485&imageNo=1. Davis tells Roosevelt his own false version of the event, but clearly he and Roosevelt are hearing about it for the first time, and neither have been asked to do anything about it. Thanks to Ken Brandt for pointing out this letter to me.

67. London, "Jack London's Graphic Story of the Japs Driving Russians across the Yalu River," *San Francisco Examiner*, 4 June 1904.

68. *San Francisco Examiner* editor, introduction to London, "Japan Puts End to Usefulness of Correspondents," *San Francisco Examiner*, 1 July 1904, 1.

69. In "Hermit Kingdom," London describes himself as an actor in *koo-kyung*. "I no longer live an obscure and private life. All my functions, from eating to sleeping are performed in public." He might be reflecting, not so much on his current situation, but his transformed status in the U.S.

70. See "Jack London Returns from Orient, But Says It Is Not to Fight Wife's Suit for Divorce: While He Tells How He Outwitted Japan's War Lords, Law Clerk Serves Author with Summons," *San Francisco Call*, 1 July 1904, Jack London Scrapbooks, vol. 5, HEH.

71. *The Galveston Daily News*, 7 Feb. 1904, Jack London Scrapbooks, vol. 4, reel 2, HEH. I believe the one photo I've seen of London in a Stanley hat was actually a composite of man plus hat.

72. *Boston Record*, 6 Feb. 1904, Jack London Scrapbooks, vol. 4, reel 2, HEH.

73. *San Francisco Newsletter*, 6 Feb. 1904, vol. 4, reel 2, HEH.

74. *Dawson Weekly News*, 27 Nov. 1902, Jack London Scrapbooks, vol. 4, reel 2, HEH.

75. Concert Goer, "Major and Minor," *Chicago Musical Leader*, 2 July 1904, Jack London Scrapbooks, vol. 4, reel 2, HEH.

76. See Griscom, *Diplomatically Speaking*, 246.

77. London, "Jap-Russ War Notes," USU.

78. Thorstein Veblen, *The Theory of the Leisure Class*, 1. By 1904, London was thoroughly familiar with Veblen; he and Cloudesley Johns had read it out loud together; see Johns, *Who the Hell Is Cloudesley Johns? An Autobiography*, HM 42387, 404, HEH. Veblen was William English Walling's teacher at the University of Chicago, London introduced Walling to Anna Strunsky via letter to his brother Willoughby in 1900, and it's likely that in 1903, when Walling and London met, London learned of Veblen; it's also equally likely that London found Veblen on his own or that Johns introduced him to Veblen. See Boylan, *Revolutionary Lives*, 51, and London to Willoughby Walling, 31 July 1900, AW box 3a, HEH.

79. "Jack London Back," *Nashville Tenn. News*, 6 July 1904, Jack London Scrapbooks, vol. 4, reel 2, HEH.

80. "Pressmen Sympathize with Mr. London" and "Pressmen Ask for the Selling of the Camera," *Osaka Asahi*, 3 Feb. 1904, 1; trans. Eiji Tsujii, "Jack London Items in the Japanese Press of 1904," *Jack London Newsletter* 8 (May–Aug. 1975): 56.

81. Palmer, *With Kuroki in Manchuria*, 27.

82. Palmer, *With Kuroki in Manchuria*, 15.

83. In an interview back in the States, Dunn, in response to a question about how he had been treated by the Japanese, said: "We were treated almost as badly as we could be treated. The Russians are white people, the Japs are not." Very little separates Dunn's attitudes from London's. "Little Respect for Wily Japs," *Rochester (NY) Democrat and Chronicle*, July 1904, Jack London Scrapbooks, vol. 5 reel 3, HEH.

84. "Another View of the Japanese," *Oakland Tribune*, 6 Dec. 1904, Jack London Scrapbooks, vol. 5, reel 3, HEH.

85. London, "Royal Road a Sea of Mud," *San Francisco Examiner*, 7 Apr. 1904, 3.

86. Although Asians cannot understand "white man's talk," London grants an excellence to Korean poetry: "These [poems] are sweet, are they not?" he writes to Charmian. "They are the only sweet things I have seen among the Koreans." London to Kittredge, 12 Mar. 1904, *Letters*, 1:419n2.

87. London, "The Yellow Peril," *San Francisco Examiner*, 25 Sept. 1904, 45. This passage is elided and mangled in *Jack London Reports*, 347.

88. "In another collection of my essays, *Revolution*, you would have found an article entitled 'The Yellow Peril.' I go no further than this data, which covers my entire writing experience, to show you that I have never believed that war would pass away entirely from the earth." London to Baxter, 28 Oct. 1915, *Letters*, 3:1510.

89. See Nitobe, *Bushido*.

90. Nitobe, *Bushido*, 10. This sentence comes immediately after the sentences quoted by London.

91. Joan London, *Jack London and His Times*, 284.

92. London to Bailey Millard, 18 Feb. 1906, *Letters*, 1:548.

93. London, "Great Socialist Vote Explained."

94. See Alvey A. Adee to London, 28 June 1907, and "Town Talk: Local Newspaper Men Decorated," Jack London Scrapbooks, vol. 8, HEH. Adee was acting secretary of state.

95. Brett to London, 23 Jan. 1904, JL 3008, HEH.

96. London to Brett, 4 June 1904, *Letters*, 1:431.

97. London, "Brett's Idea for a Novel: [about Indians]," JL 490, HEH.

98. London to Brett, 3 Apr. 1904, *Letters*, 1:422.

99. Brett to London, 5 May 1904, JL 3009, HEH.

100. London to Brett, 17 Nov. 1904, *Letters*, 1:452.

101. Brett to London, 3 Dec. 1904, JL 3020, HEH.

102. Brett to London, 9 Nov. 1904, JL 3018, HEH.

103. London to Brett, 17 Nov. 1904, *Letters*, 1:452.

104. London to Brett, 6 Jan. 1905, *Letters*, 1:463. Later, in June, before the British publication of the volume, London told Brett that Heinemann insisted that he make changes in the text to retain "the fair name and fame of Rockefeller or Collis P. Huntington, whose misdeeds are pretty historically correct by this time." But he was adamant about how the text should appear in America: "But I do not want to see these alterations appear in any copies of *The War of the Classes* which are to be sold in America" (London to Brett, 20 June 1905, *Letters*, 1:493).

105. See Brett to London, 8 Feb. 1905, JL 3027, HEH. Between 8 February and 3 March, someone—apparently neither Brett nor London—decided on the final title change. See Brett to London, 3 Mar. 1904, JL 3030, HEH, the first letter Brett uses the final title.

106. Upton Sinclair to London [undated fragment], Oakland Public Library. See London, "The War of the Classes: [preface and table of contents]," JL 1378, HEH. See also London's heavily revised version of "What Communities Lose by the Competitive System" at hrc.contentdm.oclc.org/cdm/landingpage/collection/p15878coll31 #nav_top, the Jack London Collection, Harry Ransom Center, University of Texas-Austin. His revisions were for book publication until he decided against including the essay in *War of the Classes*.

107. See London to Brett, 8 Dec. 1904 and 22 Dec. 1904, *Letters*, 1:455, 459.

108. London, "The War of the Classes: [preface and table of contents]," JL 1378, HEH.

109. Brett to London, 20 July 1904, JL 3011, HEH.

110. See Brett to London, 4 Oct. 1904, JL 3013, HEH.

111. London to Brett, 10 Oct. 1904, *Letters*, 1:448.

112. See London, letter to Mrs. Sydney Armor, 10 Nov. 1904, www.icollector.com /Jack-London_i11898813. Sydney Armor was a member of the Ruskin Club. See also London, "Magazine Sales No. 3: Feb. 1903 to July 1907," JL 934, HEH. He entered *The Game* in his short-story sales notebook between "Negore, the Coward" and "The Nose" ("A Nose for the King"). He received $600 (around $13,000 in today's dollars) from *Metropolitan* (after being rejected by *Century* and *McClure's*) and 21 pounds

(around $100 or $2,600 in today's dollars) from *Tattler* in England, after his agent James Pinker sold it.

113. Brett to London, 20 Oct. 1904, JL 3015, HEH.

114. London to Brett, 25 Oct. 1904, *Letters*, 1:450.

115. Brett to London, 31 Oct. 1904, JL 3017, HEH.

116. See Brett to London, 3 Dec. 1904, JL 3020, HEH.

117. London to Brett, 8 Dec. 1904, *Letters*, 1:456.

118. Brett to London, 15 Dec. 1904, JL 3021, HEH.

119. London to Brett, 6 Jan. 1905, *Letters*, 1:463.

120. London to Brett, 22 Dec. 1904, *Letters*, 1:458. He didn't immediately comply with the injunction to expand; two months later he told Brett, "I shall set about expanding 'Game' to 15000 words immediately" (London to Brett, 24 Feb. 1905, folder 3, box 63, Macmillan Company Records, NYPL).

121. On 1 March, London wrote, "Here's the 'Game.' Originally 13,600 words, I have added 1200 words, making it now 14,800 words. Pretty close to the 15,000 you wanted" (London to Brett, 1 Mar. 1905, folder 3, box 63, Macmillan Company Records, NYPL). Brett only had to express minor disappointment, when receiving the manuscript on 8 March, that it was still shorter than he had hoped—about half the length of *The Call of the Wild*—for London to quickly agree to add another 1,000 words. See Brett to London, 8 Mar. 1905, JL 3031, HEH, and London to Brett, 31 Mar. 1905, *Letters*, 1:474.

122. McClure to London, 4 Nov. 1904, JL 14220, HEH.

123. Later McClure would try a different tack. London wanted the British serial rights to "Law of Life," and McClure decided to give them to him only if London would agree to give McClure first look on story manuscripts. Then he decided to add even more pressure and said he would publish "Law of Life" only until he had another story; see McClure to London, 17 Feb. 1905, JL 14223, HEH. This is the kind of business practice that London—and Brett—detested.

124. London to Brett, 17 Dec. 1905, *Letters*, 1:457.

125. Brett to London, 22 Dec. 1904, JL 3022, HEH.

126. See Brett to London, 27 Dec. 1904, JL 3024, HEH.

127. See Brett to London, 8 Feb. 1905, JL 3027, HEH.

128. Brett to London, 8 Mar. 1905, JL 3031, HEH.

129. Brett to London, 16 Jan. 1907, JL 3087, HEH. See Brett to London, 31 Jan. 1907, JL 3091, HEH.

130. London, diary, 1904, JL 594, HEH.

131. Quoted in Jay Williams, "Corrections to *The Letters of Jack London*."

132. London to Partington, 30 Aug. 1904, *Letters*, 1:440.

133. "Fifteen Minutes of Socialism with Jack London," interview with London, *Chicago Inter-Ocean*, 26 Nov. 1905, 1, Jack London Scrapbooks, vol. 5, HEH.

134. London, from "The Pessimism of Jack London," interview by Emanuel Julius, *Western Comrade*, June 1913, 91.

135. London to Partington, 2 Dec. 1915, *Letters*, 3:1526.

136. London to Strunsky [May 1900?], *Letters*, 1:187.

137. Anna Strunsky, "Memories of Jack London," *Greenwich Village Lantern* 1 (Dec. 1960): 8.

138. London to Brett, 17 Nov. 1904, *Letters*, 452.

139. Stoddard to London, 10 Aug. 1905, JLE 3312, HEH.

140. London to Brett, 31 Mar. 1905, *Letters*, 1:474.

141. London, *The Game*, 16.

142. Helen Dare, "The Conquering Hero as He Sees Himself," *San Francisco Call*, 14 May 1905, n.p.

143. The report was brief and probably for that reason has never been reprinted. See "Jack London a Critic," *Columbus Dispatch*, 20 Dec. 1904, Jack London Scrapbooks, vol. 5, HEH. This article appeared in other papers as well.

144. One reporter strenuously objected to London's unconventional reporting: "London gave us a philosophical dissertation which might have been written before the fight, and much of his descriptive matter would have been consigned to the Editor's basket if it had been written by a thirty dollar a week reporter." The Saunterer, "The Eloquent Parallel," *Town Talk*, n.d. (though probably mid-September 1905).

145. London, "Brain Beaten by Brute Force: Dane's Perpetual Motion More Effective Than Britt's Mental Superiority, Says Jack London," *San Francisco Examiner*, 10 Sept. 1905, 1. London provided the headline. See London, Britt [Nelson prizefight]: [article], JL 493, HEH.

146. London, letter to the editor, *New York Saturday Times*, 18 Aug. 1905, *Letters*, 512–13.

147. London to Brett, 19 Nov. 1904, *Letters*, 1:453.

148. London, *Martin Eden*, 279.

149. Jimmy Britt, "Jimmy Britt Reviews 'The Game,' Jack London's Story of the Ring: Tale of Pugilist Is True to the Life," *San Francisco Examiner*, 27 Aug. 1905. London summed up his reviews to Cloudesley Johns, which sound in general like those he received for *The Sea-Wolf*; see London to Johns, 2 Aug. 1905, *Letters*, 1:508.

150. Brochure included in London, *The Game*, HEH 337698. See London to Anna Strunsky, 19 Sept. 1904, *Letters*, 1:444.

151. London, "Britt: [notes for prizefight story]," JL 492, HEH. The Huntington cataloguer has mislabeled a folder; nothing in these notes indicates that "Britt" would be fictional.

152. See London to Johns, 8 Dec. 1904, *Letters*, 1:456.

153. London, "Article on Squeeze: [note]," JL 453, HEH.

154. "Fifteen Minutes of Socialism with Jack London," *Chicago Inter-Ocean*, 26 Nov. 1905, 1, Jack London Scrapbooks, vol. 5, HEH.

155. London, "Marlowe—A Play," JL 921, HEH.

156. London to Partington, 16 Aug. 1904, *Letters*, 1:438.

157. London to Partington, 19 Sept. 1904, *Letters*, 1:443.

158. London to Kittredge, 4 Oct. 1904, *Letters*, 1:447.

159. London to Partington, 4 Oct. 1904, *Letters*, 1:447.

160. London to Strunsky, 13 Oct. 1904, *Letters*, 1:450.

161. London, "The Scorn of Women," *Complete Short Stories*, 424.

162. London, marginalia, in Stewart Edward White, *The Silent Places*, HEH.

163. Edfrid A. Bingham, "Nance O'Neil, Ethel Barrymore, Mrs. Fiske and the New 'Carmen' Divide New York Interest," *Denver Post*, 4 Dec. 1904, Jack London Scrapbooks, vol. 5, HEH. See also Sarah Connell, "California Literature," *Town Talk*, Christmas 1904, Jack London Scrapbooks, vol. 6, HEH, "Ethel Barrymore's Plans," *The Wasp*, 10 Dec. 1904, Jack London Scrapbooks, vol. 6, HEH, and unsigned, "A Klondike Drama," *Town Talk*, n.d., Jack London Scrapbooks, vol. 5, HEH.

164. Charmian Kittredge, diary, 1904, JL 217, HEH.

165. London to Brett, 10 Oct. 1904, *Letters*, 1:448.

166. See London, "The Scorn of Women," typescript, JL 1140, HEH.

167. See Charmian Kittredge, diary, 1904, JL 217, HEH.

168. See London, diary, 1904, JL 594, HEH.

169. London to Strunsky [2 Dec. 1904], *Letters*, 1:454.

170. London to Johns, 21 Dec. 1904, *Letters*, 1:458. See Charmian London, *The Book of Jack London*, 2:13, where she says London saw a San Francisco production of the play.

171. "Fifteen Minutes of Socialism with Jack London," *Chicago Inter-Ocean*, 26 Nov. 1905, 29, Jack London Scrapbooks, vol. 5, HEH.

172. Quoted at en.wikipedia.org/wiki/Mrs._Warren%27s_Profession. The source is a letter Shaw wrote to the *Daily Chronicle*, 28 Apr. 1898.

173. London, "Jack London, Dramatist," interview by Ashton Stevens, *San Francisco Examiner*, 27 Aug. 1905, 47.

174. Bates to London, Jan. 1905, JL 2181, HEH.

175. London to Charmian Kittredge, 2 Feb. 1905, *Letters*, 1:466.

176. Jack London, "Jack London's 'Call of the Wild' Draws Him to Poetry and Song," interview with Constance Skinner, *Los Angeles Examiner*, 8 Jan. 1905, Jack London Scrapbooks, vol. 6, HEH. Skinner, "poet, historian and novelist, [was] at that time drama and music critic of the *Los Angeles Examiner*" (Johns, "Who the Hell *Is* Cloudesley Johns?," no. 5, 118). She lived for a time with Johns's mother in Los Angeles, but before that, in 1901, she had been a member of the Camp Reverie group, along with Jack, Bessie, Joan London, Charmian, and others. She was friends with Sophie Treadwell, who during this time had an affair with Maynard Dixon. There are many other connections making up the social network of turn-of-the-century bohemian Bay Area.

177. Charmian Kittredge, diary, JL 218, HEH.

178. See Minnie Maddern Fiske to London, 24 Apr. 1905, JL 6135, HEH.

179. Minnie Maddern Fiske to London, 24 July 1905, JL 6139, HEH.

180. London to Minnie Maddern Fiske, 2 Aug. 1905, *Letters*, 1:507–8.

181. See Brett to London, 17 May 1905, JL 3035, HEH.

182. Ada Lee Bascom Marsden to London, 7 May 1905, JL 14758, HEH.

183. London to Brett, 26 June 1906, *Letters*, 2:586.

184. Brett to London, 6 July 1906, JL 3071, HEH.

185. See London to Brett, 17 July 1906, *Letters*, 2:592.

186. See Brett to London, 13 Sept. 1906, JL 3075, HEH. Brett mentions a letter from London authorizing Macmillan to publish the play, but that letter seems not to exist. See also Brett to London, 22 Oct. 1906, JL 3079, HEH.

187. Blanche Partington, "London's Play Is a Success," *San Francisco Call*, 22 Aug. 1905, n.p., Jack London Scrapbooks, vol. 6, reel 3, HEH.

188. Bascom Marsden, 23 Aug. 1906, JL 2167, HEH.

189. London, "Jack London, Dramatist," interview by Ashton Stevens, *San Francisco Examiner*, 27 Aug. 1905, 47.

190. London, letter to Ada L. Bascom Marsden, 27 Apr. 1905, *Letters*, 1:477.

191. Ada Lee Bascom Marsden to London, 20 Jan. 1905, JL 14755, HEH.

192. See Bascom Marsden, letter to London, 19 May 1905, JL 14759, HEH.

193. See Helen McCaffry to London, 4 Mar. 1906, JL 14181, HEH.

194. See Harrison Grey Fiske to London, 5 Oct. 1905, JL 6133, HEH. See especially London to Marbury, 11 Dec. 1906, JL 12599, HEH, in which he describes Kauser as "my agent." Marbury took over in February 1906 after a Mr. Presbrey dropped his interest in London's plays.

195. London to Charmian Kittredge, [5 Dec. 1904?], *Letters*, 1:455. See also London to Brett, 5 Dec. 1904, *Letters*, 1:454.

5. REVOLUTION, EVOLUTION, AND THE SCENE OF WRITING

1. Collier to Jack London, 14 Dec. 1904, JL 5059, HEH.

2. London to Brett, 15 Aug. 1903, *Letters*, 1:379.

3. London, "The American Abyss: [Notes for a Sociological Study of New York and Chicago]," JL 438 and the typescript of these notes, JL 437, HEH. He wrote some of these notes on the back of his newspaperman's business card, which read "Jack London New York Journal New York American Chicago American San Francisco Examiner Los Angeles Examiner."

4. Charmian Kittredge, "Books I Have Read," JL 171, HEH.

5. London, "Great Socialist Vote Explained," *San Francisco Examiner*, 10 Nov. 1904, n.p., Jack London Scrapbooks, vol. 6, HEH. London wrote to Anna Strunsky after the article appeared, saying, "Austin Lewis called the Socialist-Vote article in *Examiner*, 'socialism of 1860'" and then humorously remarked, "I'm afraid I've grown old and crystallized" (London to Strunsky [2 Dec. 1904], *Letters*, 1:454). Austin thought Proudhonianism was outdated and favored a centralized state apparatus to control the economy, not local community control.

6. London, "Revolution," *Revolution, and Other Essays*, 8-9.

7. "The Socialist Campaign," *San Francisco Call*, 15 Nov. 1904, Jack London Scrapbooks, vol. 6, HEH.

8. Joan London, *Jack London and His Times*, 284-85.

9. Martinek, *Socialism and Print Culture in America*, 1.

10. London, "Jack London to University Students: The Socialist Revolution Is Here; There Has Been Nothing Like It in the World Before," *People's Paper*, 18 Feb. 1905, 1. Thanks to Dan Wichlan for providing me with this text.

11. "Mother Strangles Her Two Babies: Tried to Kill a Third and Drank Poison— Crazed by Her Hunger," undated, uncited newspaper clipping, Jack London Scrapbooks, vol. 27, HEH. See also "Asked Vagrancy Sentence," undated, uncited newspaper clipping, and "Gas Ends the Life of a Man Who Would Not Beg, Steal nor Starve," undated, uncited newspaper clipping, Jack London Scrapbooks, vol. 27, HEH.

12. Johns, "Who the Hell *Is* Cloudesley Johns?" 5:123.

13. Quoted in Zamen, *Standing Room Only*, 104. This quotation from the reporter on the scene may be a combination of what London said after his speech and what he said in the speech. In "Revolution," we find this line: "They [members of the capitalist class] are like the drones clustered about the honey-vats when the worker-bees spring upon them to end their rotund existence."

14. Veblen, *Theory of the Leisure Class*, 43.

15. London to Frederick L. Bamford, 8 June 1905, *Letters*, 1:491.

16. John Brisben Walker to London, 28 Apr. 1905, JL 19841, HEH. See also James Randolph Walker to London, 5 Apr. 1905, JL 19840, HEH.

17. Mott, *A History of American Magazines*, 4:491–92.

18. London, letter to the editor, *Collier's Weekly*, 1 Aug. 1905, *Letters*, 1:506.

19. London, letter to the editor, *Atlantic Monthly*, 6 May 1905.

20. McClure to London, 25 Apr. 1905, JL 14225, HEH.

21. McClure to London, 11 May 1905, JL 14226, HEH.

22. Perry to London, 25 May 1905, JL 1972, HEH.

23. Cosgrave to London, 21 July 1905, JL 5173, HEH.

24. Wilshire to London, 5 Sept. 1905, JL 20526, HEH.

25. Collier to London, 30 Aug. 1905, JL 5062, HEH.

26. See London, letter to the editor, *Collier's Weekly*, 1 Aug. 1905, *Letters*, 1:506n1.

27. Hapgood to London, 19 Mar. 1906, JL 7269, HEH.

28. See James Randolph Walker to London, 28 July 1906, JL 19845, and James Randolph Walker to London, 1906, JL 19849, HEH; there is no readable day and month on the telegram.

29. Upton Sinclair to London, 3 Oct. 1906, JL 18274, HEH.

30. See London to Bamford, 15 Dec. 1905, *Letters*, 1:539.

31. London to James Randolph Walker, 21 Aug. 1906, *Letters*, 2:602.

32. London to Collier, 21 Sept. 1906, *Letters*, 2:610.

33. See "Child Labor," unknown publication, 1912, JLE 1550, "Socialism," Jack London Subject File, box 555, HEH.

34. See Marcy to Ninetta Wiley Eames Payne Springer, 28 July 1909, JL 14725, HEH.

35. Marcy to London, 24 Aug. 1909, JL 14721, HEH.

36. "London Talks on Socialism," *Berkeley Daily Gazette*, 13 Apr. 1905.

37. London, "Persistence of the Established: [Notes for Book]," JL 1050, HEH.

38. Connolly, "The Public Good and the Problem of Pluralism," 125–47.

39. John Brisben Walker, editorial, *Twentieth Century* (Feb. 1906), 1; see London, "Persistence of the Established: [Notes for Book]," JL 1049, HEH.

40. See "Insurance Companies Employ Lobbying Counselors Openly Instead of Secretly—Coal Operators Establish Press Bureau," *Pandex* (Apr. 1906), 343–46, in London, "Persistence of the Established: [notes for book]," JL 1050, HEH. The article quotes Ray Stannard Baker, "Railroads on Trial," *McClure's Magazine* 26 (Mar. 1906): 535–49.

41. London, "Persistence of the Established: [notes for book]," JL 1049, HEH. Although undated, this clipping appears to come from *Appeal to Reason* from 1905; the back of the clipping has lines from Sinclair's *The Jungle*, which began serialization in *Appeal to Reason* on 26 February 1905.

42. See Landers, *Improbable First Century of "Cosmopolitan Magazine,"* 133–34, for the most accurate assessment of Hearst's role in the matter.

43. "Senator Depew and 'Equitable' Finance," *Literary Digest*, 22 July 1905, in London, "Persistence of the Established: [notes for book]," JL 1050, HEH. Depew's malfeasance and Phillips's articles led to the passage of the Seventeenth Amendment to the Constitution, the direct election of senators by the people.

44. London, "Persistence of the Established: [notes for book]," JL 1049, HEH. Most likely, this article, entitled "Nicholas, Tzar of Ruffians," was from the summer of 1905. The "tzar," of course, was an easy stand-in for American corporate "royalty." London even saved Mark Twain's "The Czar's Soliloquy" for possible use in his essay. See Twain, "The Czar's Soliloquy," 321–26.

45. London, "Persistence of the Established: [notes for book]," JL 1049, HEH. The article is entitled "Capitalistic Journalism" and is undated and the title of the publication is missing.

46. George Jr., *Menace of Privilege*, ix. This line from George finds its echo in *The Iron Heel* when Ernest Everhard tells Avis that the press will not print one word of Bishop Morehouse's Christian Socialist speech because the editors' "policy is to print nothing that is a vital menace to the established" (86). All but one of London's notes in George's book were taken for the composition of "Persistence"; on the inside back cover, he listed three page numbers for quotations to be used for "Persistence," all of which occur in the two chapters on the press and the university.

47. London to Brett, 2 Dec. 1905, *Letters*, 1:538.

48. "Criminal Newspaper Alliance," *Collier's*, 8 July 1905, in London, "Persistence of the Established: [notes for book]," JL 1050, HEH.

49. London, "Persistence of the Established: [notes for book]," JL 1050, HEH. Patent-medicine producers were allied with food and drug industries to prevent pure-food legislation and other reforms aimed at their occupations. See also the footnote in *The Iron Heel* about patent medicines and the corruption of which they are symptomatic.

50. London, marginalia, in Allan W. Ricker, "The Political Economy of Jesus," *Wayland's Monthly*, no. 45 (Jan. 1904): 27, JL 1041, HEH.

51. London, "Persistence of the Established: [notes for book]," JL 1050, HEH.

52. London, "Persistence of the Established: [notes for book]," JL 1049, HEH. See Veblen, *Theory of Business Enterprise*, 385–86, HEH 336149.

53. George D. Herron, "The Misinformation of the World," *Wayland's Monthly*, no. 64 (Aug. 1905): 3, in London, "Persistence of the Established: [notes for book]," JL 1050, HEH.

54. This quotation comes from a Collar Starcher, "A Collar Starcher's Story," *Independent*, 10 Aug. 1905, 310, JLE 579, box 541, HEH.

55. London, "Persistence of the Established: [notes for book]," JL 1049, HEH.

56. London, "Persistence of the Established: [notes for book]," JL 1050, HEH.

57. Steffens, *The Shame of the Cities*, 6, HEH 259464.

58. London, "Persistence of the Established: [Notes for Book]," JL 1050, HEH.

59. London, "Grit of Women," *Complete Short Stories*, 468.

60. London, "The Yellow Peril," 350.

61. London, "Klondike: How an Indian Could Not Understand the Innermost Traits of the White Man: [Notes for Short Story]," JL 849, HEH.

62. Johnson to London, 12 May 1905, JL 8497, HEH.

63. London to Johnson, 18 May 1905, *Letters*, 1:482.

64. London to Johnson, 18 May 1905, *Letters*, 1:482–83.

65. Johnson to London, 3 June 1905, JL 8498, HEH.

66. Johnson to London, 3 June 1905, JL 8498, HEH.

67. See McClure to London, 20 May 1905, JL 14227, HEH.

68. London, "The Unexpected," *Complete Short Stories*, 998.

69. London, "The Unexpected: [Short Story]," JL 1346, HEH.

70. London, letter to the editor, *Seattle Post-Intelligencer*, 2 Aug. 1906, *Letters*, 2:599.

71. After he had completed "Planchette," which I discuss below, he created a table of contents for a volume tentatively entitled "California Stories": "Planchette," "All Gold Canyon," "The Shadow and the Flash," "Minions of Midas," "Local Color," "Amateur Night," "Moon-Face," and "The Leopard Man's Story" (London, "Magazine Sales: No. 3, Feb. 1903–July 1907," JL 934, HEH). It totaled 49,597 words, roughly the amount that London aimed at when constructing a volume of short stories. In July 1905, he told Brett that he was "three-quarters of the book of short stories already written," when in fact he had just completed "Planchette" two days previous. Obviously he was still ready to write another story but abandoned the idea in 1906. He was too engrossed in researching and composing, first, *The Iron Heel*, then *The Road*, and then his futuristic socialist short stories.

72. L. Scott, *Walking Delegate*, 99.

73. London, review of *The Walking Delegate*, JL 1117, 4, HEH; London, notes in Scott, *The Walking Delegate*.

74. Edward Ross, "New Varieties of Sin," *Atlantic Monthly*, May 1905, 595.

75. London to Johns, 23 June 1899, *Letters*, 1:89.

76. London to Johns, 7 June 1899, *Letters*, 1:81.

77. London to the Central Labor Council, Alameda County, 25 Aug. 1905, *Letters*, 1:515.

78. London, review of *The Walking Delegate*, JL 1117, 32–33, HEH.

79. London didn't feel the need of footnoting this story, as he had done with "The Unexpected" and others, but he could have. After his death, Charmian wrote a note to herself, "'Planchette' was based on a personal observation of mine. Jack pounced on it!" Charmian London, "Planchette: [Note]," JL 350, HEH. She might have revealed what the observation had been—did it involve the horse? the planchette?—in her biography, but she plays coy: "'Planchette'—the material for this last was founded upon an incident that had once come under my observation, and I passed it on to him" (Charmian London, *The Book of Jack London*, 2:56).

80. London, "Planchette," *Complete Short Stories*, 1065; my emphasis. This passage shows how London found Spencer's *Principles of Psychology* inadequate.

81. Ellenberger, *The Discovery of the Unconscious*, 44.

82. London also owned Binet, *Psychology of Reasoning*, HEH 336271. Binet's work was originally published by Carus in 1889; London owned the 1905 reprint.

83. Ellenberger, *Discovery of the Unconscious*, 145.

84. Ellenberger, *Discovery of the Unconscious*, 146.

85. *Oxford English Dictionary*, s.v. "obsession."

86. Ellenberger, *Discovery of the Unconscious*.

87. Derrida's essay turns away from the kinds of concerns I am raising here; but see Derrida, "Freud and the Scene of Writing," 196–231.

88. London to Johns, 7 June 1905, *Letters*, 491. He finished "All Gold Canyon" just the next day. He must be referring to "The Sun-Dog Trail," "The White Man's Way," "The Unexpected," "All Gold Canyon," and "Planchette." On 7 June he received his $500 check for "The Sun-Dog Trail," and on 26 May he had received his $655 for "The Unexpected." If he really were desperate for money he would have continued cranking out stories, or he would have signed up for Collier's gravy train, but of course he wasn't, and he didn't; he was poor-mouthing again.

89. McClure to London, 6 Oct. 1905, JL 14230, HEH.

90. Hall to London, 1 Feb. 1906, JL 7063, HEH.

91. Sterling to London, 25 May 1906, JL 19047, HEH.

92. See Millard to London, 5 Mar. 1906, JL 15375, HEH.

93. Its immediate publication in June helped London; once Brett saw the announcement that it would be published in *Cosmopolitan* in June, he authorized the publication date of 10 October for *Moon-Face, and Other Stories*; see Brett to London, 14 May 1906, JL 3064, HEH. Then he heard from *Outing* about their plans to publish *White Fang*, which allowed Brett to speed up the book publication of *White Fang* to 10 October 1906 and move *Moon-Face, and Other Stories* to September, thus allowing the company to bring out the ideal pair of books from a single author. Brett would try to continue this publication plan of one novel and one collection of stories per year for the rest of their relationship. See Brett to London, 22 May 1906, JL 3065, HEH, and London to Brett, 28 May 1906, *Letters*, 2:577.

94. London to unnamed correspondent, 9 Mar. 1905, *Letters*, 1:472.

95. London, *White Fang*, 195.

96. White, *Silent Places*, 17, 37.

97. Jean Laplanche and J.-B. Pontalis, *The Language of Pyscho-Analysis*, s.v. "death instinct."

98. London to Brett, 5 Dec. 1904, *Letters*, 1:454.

99. London to Maurice, 26 Mar. 1914, *Letters*, 3:1313.

100. London to Bamford, 8 May 1905, *Letters*, 1:480.

101. London to Johns, 4 Oct. 1905, *Letters*, 1:532.

102. See Pfeifer, "United States," 199.

103. Pfeifer, "United States," 199.

104. See London to Johns, 22 July 1899, *Letters*, 1:96.

105. London to Johns, 6 Sept. 1899, *Letters*, 1:108.

106. London to Johns, 12 Sept. 1899, *Letters*, 1:110–11.

107. London to Johns, 20 Sept. 1899, *Letters*, 1:113–14.

108. London, "Ways of the World," pt. 3, interview with John D. Barry, *San Francisco Bulletin*, 10 June 1914, JL 517, HEH, scrapbook vol. 13.

109. See the interview with London by Sophie Treadwell in the *San Francisco Bulletin*, 28 Feb. 1914, "Is Jack London a Capitalist? No! But Is Certainly 'Magnifique, by Gosh!'" Reproduced and edited by Jay Williams in *Jack London Journal* 3 (1996): 200.

110. Jeffrey, "Historical Development of Criminology," 366–67.

111. Ferri, *Criminal Sociology*, 9, 10–11, 24–25.

112. London's notes are on the flyleaf of his copy of Ferri's *Criminal Sociology*, 336698, HEH.

113. London read two works that discuss homologous relation between physical and social disease. See Lydston, *Diseases of Society*, esp. page 13, and Nitsche and Wilmanns, "The History of the Prison Psychoses," esp. p. 82. London considered Lydston a friend and admired his work in sexology. See London to Lydston, 26 Mar. 1914, *Letters*, 3:1312.

114. London to More, 2 Oct. 1913, *Letters*, 3:1244; the editors of *Letters* misspell her name as Moore.

115. London, "The Life of the Convict: [Notes for a Book]," JL 891, HEH. These notes took up two pages on a note pad London used for jotting down story ideas. The next idea was similar: "Book Trace life of a slum and jungle beast, such as Owen Kildare, and the power of love and changing and elevating—a new force in environment."

116. See London to Brett, 7 Mar. 1905, *Letters*, 1:470.

117. See London to Brett, 4 Dec. 1904, *Letters*, 1:454.

118. See Flora Haines Loughead, "The Call of the Tame: An Antithesis," *San Francisco Chronicle*, 4 Dec. 1904, Jack London Scrapbooks, vol. 5, reel 3, HEH.

119. London to Brett, 5 Dec. 1904, *Letters*, 1:454–55.

120. London to Larsen-Ledet, 5 Nov. 1915, JL 12339, HEH.

121. London to Charmian Kittredge [5 Dec. 1904?], *Letters*, 1:455.

122. See London to Brett, 21 Feb. 1905, *Letters*, 1:468. As a result of this trip, Johns became active in the Socialist Party and gave his first lecture that summer.

123. See London to Bamford, 8 May 1905, *Letters*, 1:480.

124. See London to Brett, 11 May 1905, *Letters*, 1:481. London explains that because *Outing* does "not expect to publish it in the magazine until the first part of 1906. . . . while I am all ready to begin it, I have put back beginning it for a month or so, in the meantime turning out some short stories." If he really was ready to write it, he would have jumped on it, for he had just asked for half payment upon receipt of manuscript and half "when publication begins" (London, handwritten note at bottom of Whitney to London, 18 Apr. 1905, JL 20301, HEH). Instead, he was still trying out ideas for the novel in the stories he was writing. That, and he was deep into stories of the Southland, not ready to return to the North.

125. See Charmian Kittredge, diary, 1905, JL 218, heh. See London to Brett, 27 June 1905, *Letters*, 1:495: "To-day I have completed the first thousand words of my *White-Fang* story—the companion-story to *The Call of the Wild*, which I mentioned to you some time ago."

126. See London, sales notebook, JL 934, HEH.

127. London, "*White Fang*: [Novel]," JL 1407, HEH. I have no explanation for the discrepancies. Maybe he simply lost track of the date. He mailed out "Planchette" on 2 July, the day after Charmian finished typing it on 1 July. Maybe he went back to the first page of the manuscript at some later date and wrote the wrong date and guessed at the correct date when he wrote his entry in his sales notebook.

128. Brett to London, 15 Dec. 1904, JL 3021, HEH.

129. London to Brett, 22 Dec. 1904, *Letters*, 1:458. Brett concurred: "a very striking and effective title" (Brett to London, 27 Dec. 1904, JL 3024, HEH).

130. London to Applegarth, *Letters*, 1:518.

131. London to Brett, 11 Oct. 1905, *Letters*, 1:533.

132. Brett to London, 5 July 1905, JL 3044, HEH. Small wonder that London stayed with Brett for so long.

133. Brett to London, 16 Nov. 1905, JL 3053, HEH.

134. London to Brett, 26 Nov. 1905, *Letters*, 1:536.

135. Brett to London, 3 Apr. 1906, JL 3059, HEH. He also mentioned hard economic times for book publishers: "During the last year or so there has been a decided falling off in the sales of novels," resulting in losses between 25 and 50 percent of sales. He expected the situation to improve and *White Fang* to be immune.

136. See Brett to London, 22 Aug. 1906, JL 3073, HEH.

137. See Brett to London, 4 Nov. 1906, *Letters*, 2:630n1.

138. Brett to London, 22 Nov. 1906, JL 3083, HEH.

139. Brett to London, 7 Dec. 1906, JL 3084, HEH.

140. London to Brett, 15 Dec. 1906, *Letters*, 2:649.

141. Brett to London, 24 Dec. 1906, JL 3085, HEH.

142. Brett to London, 8 Feb. 1905, JL 3027, HEH.

143. London to Brett, 7 Mar. 1905, *Letters*, 1:470.

144. Whitney to London, 4 Aug. 1903, JL 20295, HEH.

145. See Whitney, *On Snow-Shoes to the Barren Grounds*.

146. See Whitney to London, 17 Feb. 1915, JL 20311, HEH.

147. "Exploring Unknown America: Caspar Whitney in the Jungle," *Outing* 48 (June 1906): 359–60.

148. Mott, *History of American Magazines*, 4:637, 4:638.

149. "The Author of 'White Fang,'" *Outing* 48 (June 1906): 361.

150. Whitney to London, 5 Jan. 1905, JL 20296, HEH.

151. Whitney to London, 5 Jan. 1905, JL 20297, HEH. London's correspondence to Whitney is incomplete.

152. Whitney to London, 7 Feb. 1905, JL 20299, HEH.

153. London to Brett, 21 Feb. 1905, *Letters*, 1:468.

154. See Brett, letter to London, 27 Feb. 1905, JL 3029, HEH.

155. Whitney to London, 17 Feb. 1905, JL 20300, HEH.

156. Reeve to London, 6 Mar. 1905, JL 16850, HEH.

157. Whitney to London, 18 Apr. 1905, JL 20301, HEH.

158. Whitney to London, 12 May 1905, JL 20302, HEH.

159. Whitney to London, 24 Aug. 1905, JL 20303, HEH.

160. Whitney to London, 14 Nov. 1906, JL 20307, HEH.

161. Whitney to London, 30 Nov. 1906, JL 20308, HEH.

162. Brett to London, 24 Dec. 1906, JL 3085, HEH.

163. See London to Whitney, 8 Dec. 1906, *Letters*, 1:646.

164. Whitney to London, 19 Dec. 1906, JL 20309, HEH.

6. THE JACK LONDON SHOW GOES ON THE ROAD

1. London to George Brett, 8 Oct. 1903, *Letters*, 1:393.

2. See London to Brett, 20 Nov. 1903, Macmillan Company Records, NYPL.

3. Bamford, *Mystery of Jack London*, 69.

4. London to Johns, [30] Apr. 1899, *Letters*, 1:71.

5. Curl, *For All the People*, 4, 5.

6. Curl, *For All the People*, 129.

7. See Joan London, *Jack London and His Times*, 183, and Hine, *California's Utopian Colonies*, 78, 79. Two members, in their memoirs, cited the preponderance of vegetarians, raw-food advocates, and other "cranks" (quoted in Hine, 84). See Hine, *California's Utopian Colonies*, 114–31, and Greenstein, Lennon, and Rolfe, *Bread and Hyacinths*, 22.

8. Some newspaper sources give the address as 918 Washington. Apparently, it was a long warehouse-type building, the top floor of which Becker leased out to various concerns. Other groups besides the SLP held meetings in Becker's Hall, including various unions, reform groups, and Christian Socialists.

9. "Mr. and Mrs. Jack London Given a Large Reception by the Members of the Ruskin Club," *Oakland Enquirer*, 7 Apr. 1906, p. 7, Jack London Scrapbooks, vol. 7, HEH.

10. London to Nichols, 10 Jan. 1913, *Letters*, 3:1111; the editors of *Letters* misidentify Hauch as Edward F. Hauch, but clearly the letter is a reference to Halvor Hauch, who was close friends with both Bamford and Wilson.

11. London to Johns, [30] Apr. 1899, *Letters*, 1:71.

12. See O'Connor, "On the Road to Utopia," 147. See Elsie Martinez Whitaker, "Jim Whitaker," for the information that her father was hired by Hauch.

13. Charmian London, 13 May 1906, diary, JL 219, box 13, HEH. This was at a time that they were trying to buy more land to expand the ranch.

14. A. Walter Tate, "Jack Loudon [*sic*], Socialist: The Adventurous Career of an Oakland Boy Who Traversed the Continent on a Breakbeam and Shipped as a Stowaway," *San Francisco Examiner*, 25 Dec. 1895. See "Have Not Room Enough: High School Graduates Object to the Exercise Plans," *Oakland Tribune*, 16 Dec. 1895, 1, and "Disciples of Clay," *Oakland Tribune*, 13 Jan. 1897, 6.

15. "Jack London, the Boy Socialist: Once an Industrial Tramp, Now a High-School Student and Street Orator," *San Francisco Chronicle*, 16 Feb. 1896, 20.

16. Hale, *James Russell Lowell*, 102.

17. D. M. Scott, "The Popular Lecture," 793.

18. Hale, *James Russell Lowell*, 102, 104.

19. Hale, *James Russell Lowell*, 106, 107.

20. D. M. Scott, "The Popular Lecture," 802.

21. Bode, *American Lyceum*, 252.

22. Millner, "'The Feels,'" 112.

23. "Slayton Lyceum Bureau," *Chicago Tribune*, 25 Sept. 1881, 18.

24. H. H. Fuller to Jack London, 30 Jan. 1908, JL 6386, HEH.

25. Slayton Lyceum Bureau to London, 17 Nov. 1904, JL 18509, HEH.

26. See London to Clink, 25 May 1906, *Letters*, 576–77.

27. Slayton Lyceum Bureau, *Jack London: Author and Lecturer*, pamphlet, Jack London Scrapbooks, vol. 6, p. 126, HEH. See also Slayton Lyceum Bureau to London, 17 Nov. 1904, JL 18509, HEH: "We have two ways of dealing with attractions; one, we pay a stated sum and all expenses; the other way, we sell the man for all we can get and take 20% commission." London chose the former.

28. See Slayton Lyceum Bureau to London, 17 Nov. 1904, JL 18509, and Slayton Lyceum Bureau to London, 17 Dec. 1904, JL 18511, both HEH.

29. Slayton Lyceum Bureau, *Jack London: Author and Lecturer*, pamphlet, Jack London Scrapbooks, vol. 6, p. 126, HEH.

30. P. S. Williams, "Jack London, Lecturer," *Overland Monthly*, Oct. 1906, 345.

31. H. R. B., "London in Private: Heart to Heart Talk with Author and Lecturer," *Herald* (Oskaloosa IA), 3 Nov. 1905. He had lectured in Oskaloosa on 1 November.

32. "Jack London Says He Hates Clothes: Novelist Appears before Women's Club in Negligee Shirt Last Night," *Des Moines Daily News*, 3 Dec. 1905.

33. Quoted in "Socialism in a New Dress: A Lecture by Jack London Clothes Old Ideas in New Phases," *Kansas City Star-Times*, 23 Oct. 1905, 2. Even when a newspaper reporter recounted London's ideas, he or she couldn't unconsciously refrain from referring to London's clothes.

34. Slayton Lyceum Bureau to London, 4 Jan. 1905, JL 18512, HEH. See P. S. Williams, "Jack London, Lecturer," *Overland Monthly*, Oct. 1906, 345, and "Jack London Says He Hates Clothes: Novelist Appears before Women's Club in Negligee Shirt Last Night," *Des Moines Daily News*, 3 Dec. 1905.

35. "Jack London Sees Social Revolution: Socialist Writer Predicts Wage-Earners Will Resort to Force," *Boston Post*, 20 Dec. 1905.

36. An anonymous, untitled, undated article (though, most likely, from the fall of 1905 because it appears in the London scrapbooks surrounded by articles from that time period) from Jack London Scrapbooks, vol. 7, HEH.

37. Slayton Lyceum Bureau to London, 8 Nov. 1904, JL 18508, HEH.

38. Slayton Lyceum Bureau, *Jack London: Author and Lecturer*, pamphlet, Jack London Scrapbooks, vol. 6, p. 128, HEH.

39. P. S. Williams, "Jack London, Lecturer," *Overland Monthly*, Oct. 1906, 345.

40. P. S. Williams, "Jack London, Lecturer," *Overland Monthly*, Oct. 1906, 345.

41. P. S. Williams, "Jack London, Lecturer," *Overland Monthly*, Oct. 1906, 346.

42. Gunning, "Cinema of Attractions," 59.

43. Gunning, email to author, 24 Dec. 2015.

44. Gunning, "Cinema of Attractions," 59.

45. P. S. Williams, "Jack London, Lecturer," *Overland Monthly*, Oct. 1906, 250.

46. The bureau did manage those who wanted to appear on the Chautauqua circuit, and Wagner offered to do so with London; but it never came about. See Slayton Lyceum Bureau to London, 8 Nov. 1904, JL 18508, HEH.

47. See "Slayton Lyceum Bureau: Jack London's Lecture Engagements," JL 1548, HEH.

48. Williams noted that Manyoungi's presence excited censure. One observer jokingly thought London hired a servant so that he could devote more time to the cause, which is exactly the rationalization London used.

49. See London to Ferguson and Goodnow, 15 Oct. 1910, *Letters*, 2:935–36, and Slayton Lyceum Bureau "[Agreement with Jack London to Manage Lecture Tours]," JL 21230, HEH.

50. See "Slayton Lyceum Bureau: Jack London's Lecture Engagements," JL 1548, HEH. London's diary for 1905 lists these figures: "Sent money to Slayton Nov. 4th $53.55 Nov. 7 $175.00 Nov. 13th 225.00 Nov. 20th 215.10 Nov. 28th 366.50," for a total of $1,035.15 (London, diary, 1905, JL 596, HEH). The same source details his daily expenses down to the tips he gave porters (usually a quarter). London tracked his expenses in the same way he tracked everything, including his manuscript submissions—meticulously.

51. See "Jack London: 'One More That Counts,'" *Slayton Courier* 1 (Mar. 1905): 1, and Fannie K. Hamilton, *The Reader*, Aug. 1903, 223, 279–83, Jack London Scrapbooks, vol. 6, HEH.

52. See brochures pasted into the Jack London Scrapbook, vol. 7, HEH.

53. Charmian Kittredge London, diary, 19 Nov. 1905, JL 217, box 13, HEH.

54. Charmian Kittredge London, diary, 31 Jan. 1906, JL 219, box 13, HEH.

55. Freeman to London, 13 Nov. 1905, JL 6299, HEH.

56. Slayton Lyceum Bureau [Agreement with Jack London to Manage Lecture Tours], 23 Jan. 1905, JL 21230, HEH.

57. At the very beginning of his negotiations with Slayton, he had stipulated that he needed time off in the middle of the tour in order to write. See Slayton Lyceum Bureau to London, 17 Nov. 1904, JL 18509, HEH. He planned to write a series of stories entitled *Created He Them*, but he quickly found (by the beginning of December) that he could not sustain his writing schedule. He wrote only two pieces during this time, including a newspaper account of a visit to a physical culture event. See London, "Jack London Sees Physical Culture Boom in Holy Jumper Stunts," *Hearst's Boston America*, 19 Dec. 1905, 3; rpt. *Jack London Journal* 5 (1998): 67–71, edited by Jay Williams. He also wrote "What Life Means to Me" while on tour, but not during this stipulated window of opportunity.

58. Galvin to London, JL 6421, HEH.

59. See Galvin to London, 7 June 1905, JL 6420, HEH.

60. Galvin to Charmian London, 25 Nov. 1916, JL 6418, HEH.

61. Galvin to London, undated, HEH.

62. See Balch to London, 27 Dec. 1906, JL 2098, HEH.

63. Upton Sinclair had trouble raising money for the Grand Central Palace event because of the content of London's speech. See Sinclair to Morris Hillquit, 30 Jan. 1905, folder T-5, box 1, correspondence, Morris Hillquit Papers, WSHS.

64. McMahon to London, 26 Jan. 1906, JL 14424, HEH. McMahon wrote a novel entitled *Toilers and Idlers* that London promoted successfully to Gaylord Wilshire, who published it in 1907, even though he had initially rejected it. London's enthusiasm for the work won him over. See McMahon to London, 16 Mar. 1906, JL 14425, HEH.

65. See Slayton to London, 20 Jan. 1906, JL 18536, HEH.

66. See Charmian London, diary, 1906, JL 217, HEH.

67. See "Author London Talks about Revolution: Tells of His Recent Trip in the East and How He Dined with the Rich," *Oakland Tribune*, 19 Mar. 1906, Jack London Scrapbooks, vol. 7, p. 123, HEH.

68. See "Display of the Red Flag Starts Riot on Market Street," *San Francisco Call*, 9 Apr. 1906, 2.

69. For an account of the first Noroton Conference, organized by Robert Hunter, see Hillquit, *Loose Leaves from a Busy Life*, 56–59. For the X Club, see *Loose Leaves from a Busy Life*, 68–70. For the second Noroton Conference, see Ross, *Socialist Party of America*, 84–87. Ghent says that London probably read Berger's speech: "Berger . . . must have been fairly well known to him; Hillquit was assuredly so, and

I should guess that there were few prominent Socialists that he did not meet at one time or another" (Ghent to Joan London Miller, 27 Aug. 1937, MI 473, HEH). True, but Ghent's letter confirms that London was for the most part an outsider among the eastern and midwestern socialists.

70. Simons to London, 8 Feb. 1906, JL 18235, HEH.

71. See London, "Magazine Sales: No. 3, Feb. 1903 to July 1907," JL 934, HEH: "Presented, via A. M. Simons, to daily newspaper run by Chicago socialists in fall campaign of 1906. Published in 'Chicago Daily Socialist,' November 4, 1906."

72. London to William English Walling, 30 Nov. 1909, Letters, 2:844.

73. Untermann to Joan London, 11 Jan. 1938, frame 27, microfilm, Ernest Untermann Papers, WSHS. Joan had written to Untermann in the middle of writing her biography, so she had the opportunity to include his assessment. But she did not, partly because it conflicted with Austin Lewis's assessment and her own. Lewis knew London well early in his career, Untermann in his mid to late career.

74. Quoted in Boylan, Revolutionary Lives, 169. The quotation is from a letter to Walling, probably written by his friend Stokes, who was advising him to stay out of party politics.

75. William English Walling to Willoughby Walling, 19 Jan. 1910, William English Walling Papers, correspondence, box 1, folder 17, WSHS.

76. In the file folder JL 20722, HEH, there is a printed version of a work attributed to London called "Things Alive." The publication is the Yale Monthly Magazine for March 1906. In what could very well be London's hand, at the top of the work, appears this note: "A new phase of literary effort. A Yale student projects himself into the work of Jack London and writes 'Things Alive by Jack London.'" Below that note, appears, in a different hand, "Jack Rawlston [sic], author" (JL 20722, HEH). Jack Ralston was an undergraduate at Yale in 1906; after London's speech at Yale, London, Ralston, and others retired to Ralston's dorm room to continue the discussion. For a reprint of this essay, see The Portable Jack London, 483–85, which incorrectly identifies the author as London.

77. See Mother Jones to London, 17 May 1906, JL 15622, HEH. Charmian had sent this letter to Anna Strunsky with a handwritten note: "Jack and I had returned from West Indies (honeymoon) full of dangue fever. He pulled himself together for the big greeting in N. Y. night of our arrival. I had to stay in bed at hotel. Mother Jones walked the length of the great hall, and embraced Jack. Isn't this letter lovely?"

78. "Jack London Talks to Big Crowd," Boston Globe, 27 Dec. 1905, Jack London Scrapbooks, vol. 7, p. 36, HEH, and "Tells of Child Labor: Jack London Speaks to Great Audience at Faneuil Hall," Traveller (Boston), 27 Dec. 1905.

79. Mother Jones to London, 17 May 1906, JL 15622, HEH. She must have wanted a more elaborated treatment of child labor in Southern textile mills, for "Revolution" takes up this issue emphatically, though briefly.

80. See "Jack London's Speech on the Social Revolution at the University of California," Socialist Voice (Oakland), n.d., n.p., Jack London Scrapbooks, vol. 6, pp. 18, 21, HEH, and London, "Jack London to University Students: The Socialist Revolution

Is Here; There Has Been Nothing Like It in the World Before," *People's Paper*, 18 Feb. 1905, 1. Thanks to Dan Wichlan for calling my attention to this latter publication. London's synopsis of "Revolution" appeared in "Jack London in Oakland, Sunday," *Socialist* (Toledo OH), 18 Mar. 1905, p. 1, Jack London Scrapbook, vol. 6, p. 55, HEH.

81. See "Two Distinguished Men Address Unitarian Club: Professor Dixon, Lately of Japan, Tells of that Nation's Rise [and] Jack London, California Author, Talks on 'The Revolution,'" *San Jose Mercury*, 26 Jan. 1905, Jack London Scrapbooks, vol. 6, p. 19, HEH. As far as I know, there is no transcription or newspaper account of the Ruskin speech, which is not surprising given that the press were probably not in attendance.

82. There is a fairly detailed account of this event in "Jack London's Sophism," *Stockton Daily Independent*, 28 Feb. 1905, Jack London Scrapbook, vol. 6, p. 52, HEH.

83. The transcription of this speech is the first that I have found for the period after the Stockton speech; see "Lecture by Jack London: Delivered at the Dewey Theatre, Oakland, Cal., March 12, 1905," *Socialist Voice* (Oakland), 18 Mar. 1905, 1.

84. See "Jack London on the Cave Men," *Waterbury (CT) American*, 28 Dec. 1905, Jack London Scrapbooks, vol. 7, p. 45, HEH. The article reported that Harvard University professor T. M. Carver pointed out that since cavemen never lived nearly as long as modern-day humans, they were in fact worse off. Modernity prolongs the lives of the destitute. So the question for Carver was how to "further ameliorate [the] conditions" of the poor. "It is because some of us believe that Socialism would not ameliorate, but deepen [them], that we do not adopt [London's] program."

85. They appeared in the *Boston Herald*, the *Boston American* (page A12 in Jack London Scrapbook vol. 7), a pamphlet-sized reprinting of the *Herald* report (several pages in the same scrapbook later, titled "Choice Preprint," selected by Marie Julia Burkhardt with an endnote that says, "from the Boston Herald, important omissions added"), and in a pamphlet by Alexander Irvine, state secretary of the Socialist Party of Connecticut entitled *Jack London at Yale* (JL 20722, HEH), taken from the *Yale Alumni Weekly*, 31 Jan. 1906.

86. See "Revolution Is Theme of Novelist London: Socialists Hear Author Tell of the Oppression of Labor by Capital," *San Francisco Call*, 17 Apr. 1905, Jack London Scrapbook, vol. 6, HEH.

87. "London Talks at Harvard Union," *Boston Herald*, 22 Dec. 1905, Jack London Scrapbooks, vol. 7, HEH.

88. "Lawson-London Talk Panaceas: Financier and Socialist Discuss Their Pet Problems for Four Hours at Young's Hotel Apartments," *Boston Herald*, 21 Dec. 1905.

89. "Jack London Speaks to Harvard Students: Attacks Newspapers, Claiming They Are Not Fair to Him," *Boston Journal*, 22 Dec. 1905.

90. London, "Revolution," 36.

91. "Author London Talks about Revolution: Tells of His Recent Trip in the East and How He Dined with the Rich," *Oakland Tribune*, 19 Mar. 1906, Jack London Scrapbooks, vol. 7, p. 123, HEH. See Sinclair, *Brass Check*, 341–43, for his account of the press's mistreatment of London in 1905-6.

92. See "London Tells of Prison Stripes: Young Author Addresses Gather of Socialists and Explains How and Why He Became One," *Boston Herald*, 21 Dec. 1905, Jack London Scrapbooks, vol. 7, 12, HEH.

93. London, "How I Became a Socialist," 276–77.

94. London, "Experience: [notes for autobiographical lecture]," JL 649, HEH. See also London, "Klondike . . . experience[s]: [notes for lecture]," JL 848, HEH, which is a collection of handwritten notes of which JL 649 is the typed version, with minor variations, though JL 848 is missing the final page.

95. For a brief recounting of the various topics covered in "Experience," see "Jack London's Lecture Last Night," *Newark Evening News*, 11 Nov. 1905, Jack London Scrapbooks, vol. 6, p. 235, HEH.

96. "'Jack' London Is in Error Journal Want Ad. Proves. Work Plenty in Boston," *Boston Journal*, 21 Dec. 1905, 1, Jack London Scrapbooks, vol. 7, p. 7, HEH.

97. "Assassination Pet Joy of Mr. London: 'Jack' Warms up for Today's Effort before University Students by Delivering Blood Curdling Diatribe to Socialists on West Side," *Inter-Ocean* (Chicago), 29 Jan. 1906, Jack London Scrapbooks, vol. 7, 69, HEH .

98. London, "Fanueil Hall lecture," JL 653, HEH, and "Jack London Talks to Big Crowd," *Boston Globe*, 27 Dec. 1905, Jack London Scrapbooks, vol. 7, p. 36, HEH. A reporter for a different paper (the clipping in London's scrapbook was pasted in without any bibliographic information) wrote a similar account of the speech, quoting it at length and ending with this telling point, which is not present in the *Globe* report, though it is in London's notes: "As to the argument about survival, we Socialists think that under present arrangements there is survival of the unfit rather than survival of the fit. The time has come for us to remove the power of the man of money and to develop a better type of the strong man, who in the coming Socialistic state will be powerful for good and not for hurt." Following the three points he had laid out about the Malthusian law, his notes read: "Survival of the Fittest. State the law, its misapplication and then its application. Many men say 'We will always have the strong man.' I grant it—shearing the strong of his strength. The entering for the race—the money-getter wins." Then he launched into his vision of the new man, the good man who comes in out of the rain, whose work is really play.

99. P. S. Williams, "Jack London, Lecturer," *Overland Monthly*, Oct. 1906, 346.

100. "Jack London Reiterates His Arraignment of Slavery in Chicago: 'Sweatshop Taskmasters Are Like Wild Beasts,'" *Chicago Evening American*, 30 Jan. 1906, 3, Jack London Scrapbooks, vol. 7, 63, HEH. See also "Women *Do* Toil in Chicago for $1 a Week!: Jack London's Charge Is Proved by Visits to the City's Sweatshops," *Chicago Evening American*, 29 Jan. 1906, n.p., Jack London Scrapbooks, vol. 7, 65, HEH (misdated "January 21" in unknown handwriting at top of clipping). London made the charge in his version of "Revolution" delivered at the West Side Auditorium on 28 January, coming just after his comparison of modern-day, starving workers and the cavemen of the Bone Age: "A garment worker in Chicago, according to the figures compiled by Miss Nellie Mason Aton, a settlement worker, gets an average of 90 cents per week, ordinary sewing" ("Assassination Pet Joy of Mr. London: 'Jack'

Warms up for Today's Effort before University Students by Delivering Blood Curdling Diatribe to Socialists on West Side," *Chicago Inter-Ocean*, 29 Jan. 1906, Jack London Scrapbooks, vol. 7, 69, HEH).

101. "Chat with a Noted Author," *St. Paul Dispatch*, 1 Feb. 1904, n.p., Jack London Scrapbooks, vol. 7, 82, HEH.

102. "London Says He Is Misrepresented: Author Sure He Is Married and Proclaims He Is Victim of Too Keen Reporters," *Oakland Herald*, 10 Feb. 1906, n.p., Jack London Scrapbooks, vol. 7, 105, HEH. Actually, it wasn't Bell who said it, but rather Major Thomas McClelland, the judge advocate of the Colorado National Guard. Sherman Bell was the commander of the Colorado National Guard. In "Revolution," London puts the phrase in the mouth of a workingman who finds traditional American exempla of freedom such as the Constitution hollow when "his head is broken by a policeman's club, his union treasury bankrupted by a court decision, or his job taken away from him by a labor-saving device. . . . Nor are this particular workingman's hurt feelings soothed by reading in the newspapers that both the bull pen and the deportation [of Moyer, Haywood, and Pettibone] were preeminently just, legal, and constitutional. 'To hell, then with the Constitution!' says he, and another revolutionist has been made—by the capitalist class" (London, "Revolution," 32). It's a brilliant piece of rhetoric partly because when accused of being the original author of the phrase he could point to the unconstitutionality of the federal government's actions.

103. London, "Lecture trip: [notes]," JL 881, HEH.

104. Strobell to London, 11 Dec. 1905, JL 19156, HEH.

105. Quoted in Horn, *Intercollegiate Socialist Society*, 3.

106. Rudd, *My Life with SDS and the Weathermen*, 13–14.

107. Sinclair, *Autobiography of Upton Sinclair*, 113. See Horn, *Intercollegiate Socialist Society*, 1–10.

108. Horn, *Intercollegiate Socialist Society*, 3–5.

109. Quoted in Karnoutsos, "Harry W. Laidler and the Intercollegiate Socialist Society," 40.

110. See Karnoutsos, "Harry W. Laidler and the Intercollegiate Socialist Society," 6.

111. See "Intercollegiate Socialist Society [statement]," JL 801, HEH.

112. Easley, "Socialists Seek to Inflame the Mind of American Youth," 9–10. This article, or others like it, triggered a correspondence between Easley and Morris Hillquit, which the latter republished as a pamphlet. See Hillquit and Easley, *Socialism and the National Civic Federation*.

113. For more biographical information about Triggs, focused principally on his marriages, divorce, and children, see Claudia Keenan, "Edmund, Oscar, Laura," a two-part blog post at *Through the Hourglass*, http://www.throughthehourglass.com/2016/03/edmond-oscar-laura-1.html, and Mike Allen, "Working Class Thought Leader," *Splintercat: Copy with Impact*. http://www.splintercatcopy.com/working-class-thought-leader-oscar-lovell-triggs/. These blog posts triggered responses from Triggs's granddaughter, Heidi Lovell Triggs Clausen. For Sandburg's profile of Lon-

don, see Charles Sandburg, "Jack London: A Common Man," *To-Morrow Magazine* 2 (Apr. 1906): 35–39.

114. Quoted in Easley, "The Origin of 'The Intercollegiate Socialist Society' Disclosed," 20, 11.

115. Oscar Lovell Triggs, "Oscar Lovell Triggs, in *Triggs's Magazine*, for September," in untitled pamphlet, Jack London Scrapbooks, vol. 7, p. 108, HEH.

116. Hayden, *Port Huron Statement*, 4–5.

117. I place *observation* in quotation marks because Shorey, in his 1909 convocation speech at the University of Chicago, remarked that "I once, feebly feeling after epigram, defined the university spirit as the 'passionate pursuit of passionless intelligence.' The reporter took from this what slight point it possessed by recording it as the 'passionless pursuit of passionless intelligence,' and in this form the poor little saying was worried and mangled by the bull-dogs of the strenuous life and repeatedly held up to scorn as the last word of decadence by no less a sociological authority than Mr. Jack London." See Paul Shorey, "The Spirit of Chicago," *University of Chicago Magazine* 1 (Apr. 1909): 234. I trust that Shorey actually was misquoted and that he was using "sociological authority" ironically. Nonetheless, his concept of passion would have excluded politically charged education.

118. I have stitched together Triggs's essay from two different sources because I was unable to locate the original; see Oscar Lovell Triggs, "Oscar Lovell Triggs, in *Triggs's Magazine*, for September," in untitled pamphlet, Jack London Scrapbooks, vol. 7, p. 108, HEH, and "Intercollegiate Socialism," *Public Opinion*, 4 Nov. 1905, 593. Triggs cites London's Berkeley speech in his last editorial for *To-Morrow*; see Triggs, "Universities and the People," *To-Morrow* 1 (Apr. 1905): 17.

119. "Socialist Club Names Jack London President," *Indianapolis News*, 13 Sept. 1906, Jack London Scrapbook, vol. 6, p. 185, HEH. According to Hillquit, William Ghent presided. See Hillquit, *Loose Leaves from a Busy Life*, 61. Among the attendees was Oscar Lovell Triggs. See Claudia J. Keenan, "Edmond, Oscar, Laura," *Through the Hourglass*, http://www.throughthehourglass.com/2016/03/edmond-oscar-laura -1.html.

120. See Sinclair, *Autobiography of Upton Sinclair*, 113, and Strobell to London, 12 Sept. 1905, JL 19154, HEH. Strobell's letter made clear that London's appointment was intended to end once "the regular officers should be nominated and elected by referendum." In no way should London's resignation be construed as an abandonment of the organization.

121. In "Jack London Tells Story: Author-Socialist Explains Why He Sought Adventure," *Boston Post*, 19 Dec. 1905, Jack London Scrapbooks, vol. 7, p. 34, HEH.

122. London, "Round Table: [notes for article]," JL 1132, HEH.

123. Seligman, *Economic Interpretation of History*, 93.

124. Seligman, *Economic Interpretation of History*, 95. See chapter 9 of the present work for Seligman's influence on the writing of *The Iron Heel*.

125. London, "Potentia," JL 1073, HEH. I discovered this text while researching this volume, and its discussion here is so detailed because no one has read it before. The

textual history of this essay is peculiar because it appears in the *Syracuse Herald*, minus its final paragraph, and partially in the middle of an interview with London published in the *Chicago Inter-Ocean*. He submitted it to a startup news service titled Potentia and received fifty dollars; London's sales notebook says that it was "sent to *Potentia* By Potentia Syndicated" (London, "Magazine Sales. No. 3 Feb. 1903 to July 1907," JL 934, HEH). *Potentia* was also the title of an annual, where London, I imagine, assumed the essay would appear as well as in newspapers that subscribed to the Potentia service. One of those newspapers, I suspect, was the *Syracuse Herald*, where it appeared sometime in December 1905; the clipping is pasted into London's scrapbook with just the year, no month, but surrounded by clippings from the first two weeks of December. Apparently, London showed the reporter for the *Inter-Ocean* in Chicago his carbon copy of the essay, for the reporter placed part of it in the middle of his interview, as if it were a summation of London's thought. See "Fifteen Minutes of Socialism with Jack London," *Chicago Inter-Ocean*, 26 Nov. 1905, 29, Jack London Scrapbooks, vol. 5, HEH. The manuscript of "Intercollegiate Socialist Society" has not been located.

126. "Fifteen Minutes of Socialism with Jack London," *Chicago Inter-Ocean*, 26 Nov. 1905, 29. I suspect that this quotation is also from the text of "Intercollegiate Socialist Society," but was cut in the *Syracuse Herald* printing.

127. As a teaser to this shared aesthetic vision, I will mention that Henry Meade Bland's 1906 profile of London was reprinted in Gustav Stickley's periodical the *Craftsman*. See Jack London Scrapbooks, vol. 7, pp. 112–16, HEH.

128. For the suggested titles to be read (which included, among many others, Marx, Kautsky, Veblen, Steffens, Shaw, Norris, and London), see the four-page brochure entitled *Books on Socialism: Recommended to College Students by the Executive Committee of the Intercollegiate Socialist Society*, Jack London Scrapbooks, vol. 7, pp. 110–11, HEH. The brochure ends with a call for submissions for an essay competition.

129. See Sinclair to London, 19 Feb. 1906, JL 18262, HEH. As Harry Laidler wrote in 1915, it was one of the "chief literary gems" the ISS circulated during this period (Harry Laidler, "Teaching the Collegians to Fight, Not Sleep," *New York Sunday Call*, 24 Oct. 1915, JLE 3149, HEH).

130. "The Intercollegiate Socialist Society [statement]," JL 800, HEH; yes, this title differs from JL 801 only in the matter of the initial article.

131. See Harry Laidler, "Teaching the Collegians to Fight, Not Sleep," *New York Sunday Call*, 24 Oct. 1915, JLE 3149.

132. See Reynolds, "Millionaire Socialists," 164.

133. See Sinclair, *My Autobiography*, 170.

134. See William English Walling to Anna Strunsky Walling, 7 Dec. [1913?], William English Walling Papers, correspondence, box 1, folder 1, WSHS.

135. Horn, *Intercollegiate Socialist Society*, 85.

136. "Words That Will Become Obsolete," *Socialist Voice*, 16 Mar. 1907, 1, Jack London Scrapbooks, vol. 8, n.p., HEH. Ellipses indicate words blurred in the microfilming of the scrapbook. The newspaper published London's cover letter that accompa-

nied the submission: "Dear Comrade Tuck: I am sending herewith a manuscript by Comrade Arthur George of Berkeley. You may . . . care to publish it in The Voice. If you don't, please return to me. Seems to me that there is quite a bit of propaganda in Comrade George's article. Yours for the Revolution, Jack London."

137. According to A. M. Simons, after London's speech at Mandel Hall at the University of Chicago, the question-and-answer session—as well as the speech itself—motivated almost twenty of "some of the brightest and best known men in the University" to form an ISS club. A. M. Simons, "'The Social Revolution': Socialism at the Chicago University," *Socialist Voice* (Oakland), 17 Feb. 1906, 1.

138. "Socialism at the University," *Socialist Voice* (Oakland), 1906, Jack London Scrapbooks, vol. 7 p. 143, HEH. This was most likely March 1906.

139. Hillquit, *Loose Leaves from a Busy Life*, 55.

140. Hillquit, *Loose Leaves from a Busy Life*, 61–62.

141. Karnoutsos, "Harry W. Laidler and the Intercollegiate Socialist Society," 2.

142. Upton Sinclair to London, 5 Jan. 1906, JL 18261, HEH.

143. "J. G. P. Stokes on Socialism: Takes Issue with Jack London," *Newark News*, 20 Feb. 1906.

144. See Karnoutsos, "Henry W. Laidler and the Intercollegiate Socialist Society," 87, where she cites Sinclair's letter to Laider, 30 Sept. 1906, ISS papers, Tamiment Library, NYU.

145. Karnoutsos, "Henry W. Laidler and the Intercollegiate Socialist Society," 87, ISS papers, Tamiment Library, NYU, 88, citing Mabel C. Willard's letter to Sinclair, 8 Apr. 1906, ISS papers, Tamiment Library, NYU. Edgar Burill, a professor of English at Lake Forest College, wrote to Ellis Jones that both Sinclair and London were likely to be unwelcome at his college—the former because Sinclair had antagonized Swift with *The Jungle*, and London was divorced, "hence an improper influence to come into contact with our innocent young ladies here!" (Karnoutsos, "Henry W. Laidler," 89).

146. Quoted in Horn, *Intercollegiate Socialist Society*, 197n5.

147. See London to Bamford, 24 Feb. 1906, 27 Feb. 1906, *Letters*, 2:554–55.

148. London to Bamford, 2 Oct. 1905, *Letters*, 1:531.

149. Slayton Lyceum Bureau to London, 29 Nov. 1904, JL 18510, HEH.

150. London to Bamford, 2 Oct. 1905, *Letters*, 1:531.

151. Mother Jones to London, 29 Sept. 1905, JL 15620, HEH.

152. Fahs, *Out on Assignment*, 176. Fahs rightly stresses how Richardson's newspaper work served as a rough draft for her novel, pointing out how paragraphs appeared word for word in both media.

153. London, review of Dorothy Richardson, *The Long Day*, JL 1075, HEH.

154. London, review of Dorothy Richardson, *The Long Day*, JL 1075, HEH.

155. Dorothy Richardson to London, 2 Nov. 1905, JL 17181, HEH. Interestingly, she had no problem with what Fahs would call London's "loopy," "sexualized" digression about "the threatened body of the heroine and race suicide" (Fahs, *Out on Assignment*, 185).

156. Mother Jones to London, 6 Nov. 1905, JL 15621, HEH.

157. See Niven, *Carl Sandburg*, 105; Niven discusses Sandburg's essay on London in *To-Morrow* on pages 105–6: "London was a dominant force in Sandburg's intellectual life" (106).

158. See Millard, *History of the San Francisco Bay Region*, 3 vols., 1:260. Millard relates that "so many San Francisco newspaper men went to New York in the 'nineties and later that at one time Manhattan seemed to be full of them. Hearst was accused of importing San Francisco journalists by the carload. Others went on their own initiative, and for a time San Francisco was nearly deserted by 'the talent'" (Millard, 1:258). Again it is worth noting that London did not leave his home state, thus marking him solidly as a western or Pacific Rim author.

159. London to Millard, 21 Feb. 1903, *Letters*, 1:345.

160. Millard to London, 8 Nov. 1905, JL 15372, HEH.

161. Millard to London, 24 Nov. 1905, JL 15373, HEH.

162. Frederick Upham Adams et al., "Are Great Fortunes Great Dangers?" *Cosmopolitan* 40 (February 1906): 392.

163. London, "What Life Means to Me," *Cosmopolitan Magazine* 40 (Mar. 1906): 530. As far as I can tell, the source for the "Frenchman's" quotation has never been located.

164. London, "What Life Means to Me," *Cosmopolitan Magazine* 40 (Mar. 1906): 529. London's sales notebook entry for the essay states, "Written in November 1905 and sold to Cosmopolitan. Received $345.00 in Jan. 1906" (London, sales notebook, JL 934, HEH).

165. Sinclair begins his contribution to the series in identical fashion, though with a different intended result: "I was born in what is called the upper middle-class." Whereas London's birth automatically qualified him for membership in the Socialist Party, Sinclair's birth is an obstacle to overcome before he can become a member. Upton Sinclair, "What Life Means to Me," *Cosmopolitan Magazine* 41 (Oct. 1906): 591–95.

166. London, "My Outlook upon Life: The Confession of a Climber," JL 964, HEH.

167. See Charmian London, diary, 1905, JL 218, HEH.

168. London, "Jack London Sees Physical Culture Boom in Holy Stunts. His Brand of Religion, When He Chooses," *Boston American*, 19 Dec. 1905, 3; rpt. *Jack London Journal*, no. 5 (1998): 67. Although the *Boston American* was a Hearst paper, presumably in tune with London's needs and desires as an author, they tried to gyp him by initially paying only twenty-five dollars. In July 1906 he finally received an extra seventy-five dollars. See London, sales notebook no. 3, JL 934, HEH.

169. He sent the story to *Everybody's Magazine* on 3 March 1906, John Cosgrave (who was back at the magazine) accepted it twenty-five days later, and London returned corrected proof sheets on 8 April. It appeared in August 1906. He received $750 for 5,900 words, and then he got twenty-five in pounds sterling in September for its publication in *Windsor Magazine* in England. See London, sales notebook no. 3, JL 934, HEH, and see Hall to London, 20 Apr. 1906, JL 7064, HEH, for the acceptance.

170. London to Brett, 3 July 1905, *Letters*, 1:497.

171. London, "Brown Wolf: [notes for a short story]," JL 494, HEH.

172. London, "Brown Wolf," *Lost Face, and Other Stories*, 191.

173. The notes read almost verbatim: "I know the ways of women. Their hearts is soft. When their hearts is touched they're likely to stack the cards, look at the bottom card, an' lie like the very devil" (London, "Dog story: [note for short story]," JL 611, HEH).

174. See Moore, *Universal Kinship*, 143.

175. London, comment on *The Jungle*, in the *Appeal to Reason*, 29 July 1905, http://dlib.nyu.edu/undercover/jungle-story-chicago-upton-sinclair-appeal-reason. According to Sinclair, this brief note netted him four thousand dollars from new readers of *The Appeal to Reason*. See Sinclair, *Brass Check*, 32.

176. Sinclair to London, 23 Sept. 1905, JL 18258, HEH.

177. London, notes for review of *The Jungle*, JL 1115, HEH.

178. London, "A Word to the Appeal Army from Jack London," *Appeal to Reason*, 18 Nov. 1905, 5. The analogy to *Uncle Tom's Cabin* as applied specifically to *The Jungle* was first made by Fred Warren in *Appeal to Reason* when he announced to his readers that his periodical would serialize Sinclair's novel: "It will be the Uncle Tom's Cabin of the Socialist movement" (unsigned editorial comment, *Appeal to Reason*, 4 Feb. 1905, 5). This analogy that might have had its roots in a comment in one of Leonard Abbott's editorials in the *Comrade*: "The author who succeeds in picturing the real pathos of the modern industrial tragedy may write the `Uncle Tom's Cabin' of a new emancipation." See Leonard Abbott, editorial, *Comrade* 1 (Dec. 1901): 64. Warren may well have been aware of Leonard Abbott's comment, and/or he may have been making the analogy based on his reading of Sinclair's first novel, *Manassas*, which in part depicts slave life in the South. See Harris, *Upton Sinclair*, 67, and Sinclair's *The Jungle*, edited by James R. Barrett, 351, note for page 317. See also Shore, *Talkin' Socialism*, 168, for the attribution to Warren.

179. Sinclair was well aware of this kind of attack. After Brett told him to cut out some of the more sensational material, he asked Lincoln Steffens for advice. Steffens told him, according to Sinclair, "The things you tell are unbelievable. I have a rule in my own work—I don't tell things that are unbelievable, even when they are true" (Sinclair, *Brass Check*, 32).

180. Upton Sinclair, *The Jungle*, 389. This is London's personal copy of his Sustainer's Editions inscribed by Sinclair: "To Jack London, with all my heart. Upton Sinclair. `When savage beasts through forest midnight roam, Seeking in sorrow for each other's joy!'" Sinclair typically wrote these lines from his own *The Journal of Arthur Stirling* in his gift copies.

181. London, "The Jungle," 516.

182. See Brett to London, 20 Sept. 1905, JL 3046, HEH, and London to Brett, 29 Oct. 1905, *Letters*, 1:533–34. The first letter in which London sent Brett his itinerary is apparently lost. But see Brett to London, 6 Oct. 1905, JL 3052, HEH, for Brett's acknowledgement of receiving London's itinerary. He mention in the latter that "I hope to be able to make some use of it that will benefit us both although several of the towns mentioned have no really good bookshops in which your books can be exhibited I think during your visit," meaning his tour. In the September letter he acknowledg-

es receipt of a "signed agreement," which is probably their annual contract, which hadn't changed in terms of royalties and production.

183. See Brett to London, 1 June 1905, 12 June 1905, and two items (letter and a receipt for sending London's check) from 13 June 1905, JL 3037-40, HEH, and Londons to Brett, 26 May 1905, 7 June 1905, and 20 June 1905, *Letters*, 1:483-84, 1:488-90, 1:492-94.

184. Brett to London, 11 July 1905, JL 3046, HEH.

185. See London to Brett, 1 Aug. 1905, *Letters*, 1:504-5, and Brett to London, 6 Sept. 1905, JL 3049, HEH.

186. See Brett to London, 20 Sept. 1905, JL 3051, HEH. Apparently, London's letter along with the contract—if indeed he wrote a cover letter—has been lost.

187. See London, sales notebook, JL 934, HEH, for the list of stories and word counts (usually he had a title in mind, but not for this collection). "The Story of Keesh," a mere 3,330 words, comes last, as a kind of filler and an attempt to collect as many of his published stories as possible. There is no thematic coherence to the collection.

188. London, "A Day's Lodging," *Love of Life, and Other Stories*, 45.

189. London, "When God Laughs," *Love of Life, and Other Stories*.

190. See Harry Cowell, "Rest: A Mood," *Town Talk*, 30 Jan. 1904, 7, and London to Blanche Partington, 19 Sept. 1904, *Letters*, 1:445.

191. Genthe, *As I Remember*, 69.

192. Cowell, "Rest: A Mood," 7.

193. Ninetta Eames called them that in "Haunts of Jack London," *Cosmopolitan* 40 (Dec. 1905): 227. London was now so famous that even his home life is of great interest to a national audience. The title may indicate Ninetta's understanding of London's relation to his imagination.

194. See London, "A Wicked Woman: [notes]," JL 1417, HEH. For some reason, four sheets of notes for "When God Laughs" are misfiled with the notes to "A Wicked Woman."

195. Interestingly, in London's notes it's the narrator who is described as Mephistophelean. London, "When God Laughs: [notes for short story]," JL 1397, HEH.

196. Reynolds to London, 28 Aug. 1906, JL 16941, HEH.

197. Reynolds to London, 4 Sept. 1906, JL 16943, HEH. See Reynolds to London, 12 Sept. 1906, JL 1694, HEH.

198. Reynolds to London, 26 Oct. 1906, JL 16945, HEH.

199. Gertrude B. Lane, note to F. Hayden Carruth, undated, stapled to Jack London, memo, box 7, Hayden Carruth Papers, NYPL.

200. Charmian K. London, 16 Feb. 1906, diary, JL 219, HEH. Vance and Carruth were soliciting a series of articles on child labor, which in time became a kind of "crusade"; see Mott, "Woman's Home Companion," of *History of American Magazines*, 4:767. Carruth told London at the end of March that he had just received Spargo's contribution. See Carruth to London, 29 Mar. 1906, JL 4760, HEH. See also Charm-

ian London, *Book of Jack London*, 2:117–19, and Joan London, *Jack London and His Times*, 317.

201. Jack London, memo, box 7, Hayden Carruth Papers, NYPL.

202. Quoted in Gorton V. Carruth, note dated May 1957, attached to Jack London, memo, box 7, Hayden Carruth Papers, NYPL.

203. Carruth to London, 13 Mar. 1906, JL 4757, HEH.

204. Carruth to London, 14 Mar. 1906, JL 4758, HEH.

205. Carruth to London, [14?] Mar. 1906, JL 4759, HEH.

206. London, "The American Abyss: [Notes for a Sociological Study of New York and Chicago]," JL 438, HEH.

207. See Kingman, *Jack London*, 52. It may seem odd that he would refer to "Revolution" as the "Ruskin Club talk" because he had delivered the speech multiple times on tour. Yet he had resigned from the club in July 1905; the last speech he gave before writing "The Apostate" was "Revolution" in January 1905. It seems, then, that he wrote these notes for "The Apostate" or "Rebel" sometime in 1905, just as he had composed notes for "Created He Them" and "A Wicked Woman," keeping them in reserve until he returned from his tour. London was careful to never leave himself facing a blank page with no preparation for another story to write.

208. Juliet Tompkins, "Turning Children into Dollars," *Success Magazine*, Jan. 1906, 15, 17.

209. Juliet Tompkins, "Turning Children into Dollars," *Success Magazine*, Jan. 1906, 15.

210. London, "The Apostate," *When God Laughs, and Other Stories*, 47–48.

211. Anon., "Child Labor Legislation: Owen R. Lovejoy's Address to Factory Inspectors," 17 Aug. [1905?], publication unknown, n.p. See London, subject file, "Socialism," box 555, JLE 1523, HEH. See also Owen R. Lovejoy, "The Modern Slaughter of the Innocents," *Men and Women*, Oct. 1905, 3–4, where Owen retells, in briefer form, the story of the little boy in the glass factory, which London again circled in pencil. See London, subject file, "Socialism," box 555, JLE 1554, HEH.

212. Gronlund, *Co-Operative Commonwealth*, 84.

213. Gronlund, *Co-Operative Commonwealth*, 80.

214. London, "The Apostate: [notes for short story]," JL 448, HEH.

215. See Charmian Kittredge London, 23 Mar. 1906, diary, 1906, JL 219, HEH. See entry for 28 March where she mentions the title change. A number of pages of London's notes for the story are headlined "Rebel" or "The Rebel." See London, "The Apostate: [notes for short story]," JL 448, HEH.

7. RED ATAVISMS AND REVOLUTION

1. London to Cloudesley Johns, 24 Aug. 1899, *Letters*, 1:104.

2. Allen, "The Backslider," 228.

3. London, "Jack London, Dramatist," interview by Ashton Stevens, *San Francisco Examiner*, 27 Aug. 1905, 47.

4. Wells, *Mankind in the Making*, 16. See Charmian London, diary, 1906, HEH.

5. See Ellenberger, *Discovery of the Unconscious*, 85–101.

6. See Satter, *Each Mind a Kingdom*, 49–56.

7. See Satter, *Each Mind a Kingdom*, 83–85.

8. See Hudson, *Law of Psychic Phenomenon*, 288. London's copy has no markings. See Hudson, *Law of Psychic Phenomenon*, 336253, HEH. There is a slight variation in the subtitle between the copy I examined and London's own, but the pagination is the same.

9. For biographical information on Moore, see Claudia J. Keenan, "The Anguish of J. Howard Moore," *Through the Hourglass*. http://www.throughthehourglass.com /2016/07/the-anguish-of-j-howard-moore.html; "Scorning Man, He Ends Life to Thrushes' Call: Prof. J. Howard Moore Goes Back to Nature by the Cruel Artifice of Suicide," *Chicago Tribune*, 18 June 1916, 11; and Darrow, *In the Clutches of the Law*, 499.

10. George N. Caylor owned the first socialist bookstore in Philadelphia and was a prominent socialist, writer, and food activist. In his autobiography, he wrote: "Joe [Joseph E. Cohen, a friend] and I had become vegetarians as the result of reading a couple of books by J. Howard Moore. The one that principally influenced us was The Universal Kinship. I remained a vegetarian for about 10 years, but Joe much longer. During these days I patronised vegetarian restaurants, especially one run by Bernarr McFadden. I ate their protose and other meat substitutes and their bean concoctions. I especially enjoyed their medley. This was a bowl of raw rolled oats, chopped nuts, raisins, dates, and figs. Milk or cream slightly softened the oatmeal but still one had to Fletcherize." At one point in life he and Cohen joined Scott Nearing and the Arden community and were in residence when Upton Sinclair and his wife came there to live with their son David. Caylor offered a scathing commentary on Sinclair's eating habits and marital relations (George N. Caylor, *If My Memory Serves Me Right: The Autobiography of George N. Caylor*, 136–37, folder 1, box 1, George N. Caylor Papers, WSHS).

11. See Kerr to London, 6 Mar. 1906, JL 8730, HEH.

12. London to [Charles Kerr?], 28 Apr. 1906, in Hamilton, *"The Tools of My Trade,"* 208. See London, "Book Reviews: A Letter from Jack London," *To-Morrow* 2 (May 1906): n.p. The book was reviewed by Sercombe and Charles Sandburg as well. See Parker H. Sercombe, "Universal Kinship," *To-Morrow* 2 (July 1906).

13. Weismann, *Germ-Plasm*, 468.

14. Moore, *Universal Kinship*, 24.

15. Richards, *Tragic Sense of Life*, 123; Mazzeo, introduction to August Weismann [iii]. See Weismann, *Germ-Plasm*, 19.

16. Haeckel, postcard to London, 7 July 1907, pasted inside front cover of London's personal copy of *Before Adam*, 5714, HEH. Another European writer, George Bernard Shaw, was a fan of the book as well; he was quoted in the *New York Times*, "I see that Jack London has written a book full of interest, entitled 'Before Adam'" (*New York Times*, 4 May 1907, clipping in London, scrapbook, vol. 8, HEH).

17. Otis, *Organic Memory*, 2–3.

18. Otis, *Organic Memory*, 2.

19. See London to Johns, [30] Apr. 1899, *Letters*, 1:72.

20. London to Hamilton, 15 July 1906, *Letters*, 2:590

21. Jordan, *Foot-notes to Evolution*, 342.

22. Jack London to Johns, 24 Aug. 1899, *Letters*, 1:106.

23. See Churchill, *August Weismann*.

24. Weismann, "The Duration of Life," *Essays upon Heredity*, 33.

25. See Moore, *Universal Kinship*, 144.

26. G. Morris, *The Pagan's Progress*, 52. Inscribed by Austin Lewis: "To Jack the Fighter from a Brother in Arms Austin Lewis Sept. 1904." The book was published in September 1904.

27. Stocking, *Victorian Anthropology*, 299.

28. Tylor, *Anthropology*, 122.

29. See London to Johns, 17 Apr. 1899, *Letters*, 1:62. Johns had sent him a review of the novel, and London replied that the mother of Ab "must have been" "a delightful, fascinating woman." See also London to the editor, *Life*, 15 Dec. 1906, *Letters*, 2:651, in which he says he first read Waterloo in 1900. London also read another novel by Waterloo, *A Man and a Woman*. See London to Johns, 10 Mar. 1900, *Letters*, 1:168–69. He thought it good.

30. London to B. W. Babcock, 3 Dec. 1906, *Letters*, 2:644. See Babcock to London, 27 Nov. 1906, JL 2069, HEH.

31. London to B. W. Babcock, 3 Dec. 1906, *Letters*, 644.

32. Waterloo, *Story of Ab*, 72. Weirdly enough, Moon Face is the name of "the richest man in the tribe" in Gouverneur Morris's *The Pagan's Progress*. His white whiskers encircled his baboonlike face.

33. See London to Waterloo, 20 Oct. 1906, *Letters*, 2:623–25. By citing Kipling, London is referring to poems like "The Story of Ung" and "In the Neolithic Age." See Pearson, "Primitive Modernity," 58–74.

34. Though later in the year when the novel was being serialized, after declaring *Before Adam* a poor work of literature in a number of letters, George Sterling tells London to read "A Story of the Stone Age" to see how London should have written the novel. And then he added, "I'm wondering what Wells will think of 'Everybody's' impudent (or ignorant) assumption of your pioneership in the fiction of the primitive" (Sterling to London, 28 Sept. 1906, JL 19058, HEH).

35. London read two children's book by Katherine E. Dopp called *The Tree-Dwellers* and *The Early Cavemen*. One of his notes says, "p. 82-tree-dwellers," where Dopp has two Stone Age boys in a tree being frightened by a noise. See Joan London, *Jack London and His Daughters*, 157.

36. London, *Before Adam*, 24.

37. Sterling to London, 7 July 1906, JL 19049, HEH.

38. London, "Before Adam: [notes for novel]," JL 505, box 37, HEH.

39. See Charmian London, 15 May 1906, diary, JL 217, HEH: "After supper, great discussion on Immortality between Jack and Edward." And again on 24 May: "Big discussion in evening–Edward and Mate."

40. London, *Before Adam*, 2.

41. London and Strunsky, *Kempton-Wace Letters*, 110.

42. Spencer, *Principles of Psychology*, 1:293. Spencer repeats and enlarges on his maxim in two other works: *Principles of Biology*, 1:99, and *First Principles*, 4th ed., 86. London may have run across the maxim and its discussion in one or all of these; his copies of Spencer's works are now lost.

43. London and Strunsky, *Kempton-Wace Letters*, 111.

44. London to Waterloo, 20 Oct. 1906, *Letters*, 2:624.

45. London, *Before Adam*, 1.

46. London, *Before Adam*, 1.

47. London, *Before Adam*, 13

48. See Charmian London, 13 May 1906 and 18 Apr. 1906, diary, JL 219, HEH.

49. See London to Bamford, 27 Feb. 1906, *Letters*, 2:555.

50. London to Bamford, 3 Apr. 1906, *Letters*, 2:560.

51. London to Bamford, 15 May 1906, *Letters*, 2:574.

52. London, *Before Adam*, 9.

53. London, "Before Adam: [notes for a novel]," JL 505, HEH.

54. See *Oxford English Dictionary*, s.v. "disassociation."

55. See *Oxford English Dictionary*, s.v. "projection," and Ellenberger, *Discovery of the Unconscious*, 532.

56. London, "Who Believes in Ghosts!" *Complete Short Stories*, 1:38.

57. London, "Before Adam: [notes for a novel]," JL 505, HEH.

58. "Catalogue of Books," in Bölsche, *Evolution of Man*, 9. See also "Publisher's Advertisement," in Bölsche, *Evolution of Man*, 4. Both these texts are published at the back of the volume, with separate pagination.

59. See Ruff, *"We Called Each Other Comrade,"* 167.

60. London, "Before Adam: [notes for a novel]," JL 505, HEH.

61. Charmian London, 10 Apr. 1906, diary, JL 219, HEH.

62. See London to Brett, 8 Apr. 1906, *Letters*, 2:563, Charmian London, entries for Apr. 1906, diary, JL 217, HEH, and Kingman, *Jack London*, 64.

63. London, manuscript of *Before Adam*, JL 506, box 37, HEH.

64. London, "Before Adam: [notes for novel]," JL 505, box 37, HEH.

65. Charmian London, *The Book of Jack London*, 2:137. She wrote the following entry in her diary: "Finished Before Adam—copying, everything. Jollied up Mate all day for fear he might get the blues" (Charmian London, 7 June 1906, diary, JL 217, HEH).

66. Jordan, *Foot-notes to Evolution*, 340.

67. Sterling to London, 22 Feb. 1906, JL 19044, HEH.

68. Sterling to London, 27 May 1906, JL 19048, HEH.

69. Charles Warren Stoddard felt the same way; see Stoddard to London, 3 July 1906, JL 19084, HEH.

70. Sterling to London, 7 July 1906, JL 19049, HEH.

71. London to Sterling, 9 June 1906, *Letters*, 2:579.

72. Sterling to London, 7 July 1906, JL 19049, HEH.

73. Sterling to London, 7 Aug. 1906, JL 19053, HEH.

74. Brett to London, 23 May 1906, JL 3066, HEH.

75. See McClure to London, 12 Nov. 1908, JL 14238, HEH. This is a form letter sent to all of McClure's authors notifying them of the change.

76. McClure to London, 1 Mar. 1905, JL 14224, HEH.

77. McClure to London, 31 Jan. 1906, JL 14232, HEH.

78. London to McClure, 25 Apr. 1906, *Letters*, 2:572.

79. McClure to London, 30 Apr. 1906, JL 14234, HEH.

80. Brett to London, 20 Mar. 1906, JL 3057, HEH.

81. See Reynolds to Brett, 23 May 1906, JL 16898, HEH. Will Irwin, who went to work for McClure in the middle of these negotiations, told London that "the offer of Mr. Ridgway is stunning, and it means at least a safeguard for your work." Irwin had met London in New York during the lecture tour, but still was working in "the newspaper game" (Irwin to London, 8 June 1906, JL 8256, HEH).

82. See Mott, *History of American Magazines*, 82.

83. See Ridgway to London, 1 Aug. 1906, JL 17192, HEH.

84. Reynolds to London, 6 June 1906, JL 16928, HEH. See London to Reynolds, 31 May 1906, JL 13260, HEH, and London to Brett, 31 May 1906, JL 11070, HEH, in which London tells both men that he has to honor his promise to McClure.

85. Reynolds to London, 23 June 1906, JL 16932, HEH.

86. Reynolds to London, 29 June 1906, JL 16933, HEH.

87. Reynolds to London, 5 Nov. 1906, JL 16946, HEH.

88. Reynolds to London, 18 June 1906, JL 16931, HEH.

89. London to Cosgrave, 21 Aug. 1906, *Letters*, 2:601.

90. London to McClure, 19 July 1906, *Letters*, 2:595.

91. Reynolds to London, 8 June 1906, JL 16929, HEH.

92. Brett to London, 19 June 1906, JL 3068, HEH.

93. London to Brett, 24 June 1906, *Letters*, 2:584.

94. London to Brett, 24 June 1906, *Letters*, 2:584. Perhaps, too, he was remembering that both Sterling and Charles Warren Stoddard loved *Tales of the Fish Patrol*. If grownups could enjoy a boy's story, perhaps boys could enjoy adult fiction.

95. London to Sterling, 28 Oct. 1915, *Letters*, 3:1511.

96. London to Walton, 23 Nov. 1906, *Letters*, 2:639.

97. London to Buck, 1 Mar. 1913, *Letters*, 3:1134.

98. See Wilshire to London, 9 Mar. and 14 Mar. 1906, JL 20528 and JL 20529, HEH.

99. "Author London Talks about Revolution: Tells of His Recent Trip in the East and How He Dined with the Rich," *Oakland Tribune*, 19 Mar. 1906, Jack London Scrapbooks, vol. 7, 123, HEH. The *Oakland Socialist Voice* ran the text of the entire

speech in four installments, from 24 March to 14 April. All but the last is in volume 7 of the scrapbooks.

100. Bergenhammer to London, 19 May 1913, JL 2276, HEH. Bergenhammer was inspired to write this letter during the serial publication of *John Barleycorn*, where London gives an inaccurate account of that evening.

101. "Fiery Lecture by Jack London: Denounces Capital; Scents Conspiracy; Predicts Revolt," *San Francisco Call*, 19 Mar. 1906, Jack London Scrapbooks, vol. 7, HEH. See also "London Talks on Socialism: Says Whole Power of Union Will Be Needed to Execute Miners of Boise," *San Francisco Call*, 19 Mar. 1906. The line about taking the whole U.S. Army to carry out the death penalty was picked up by one of the four speakers at the 8 April protest meeting: Franklin Jordan, George Holmes, P. H. McCarthy, and George Speed. See "Bloody Riot in Frisco: A Red Flag Causes Riot between Police and Mob," *Los Angeles Herald*, 9 Apr. 1906.

102. See Lukas, *Big Trouble*, 748, 727–28.

103. See "Display of the Red Flag Starts Riot on Market Street," *San Francisco Call*, 9 Apr. 1906, 2. A photograph taken before the riot shows that the banner read Workingmen of the World Unite. See Watkins and Olmstead, *Mirror of the Dream*, 176–77.

104. For the invitation, see Sandgren to London, 28 Mar. 1906, JL 17485, HEH.

105. "The Rising Tide of Revolution: Jack London on the Moyer-Haywood Outrage," *Oakland Socialist Voice*, 24 Mar. 1906, 1.

106. London to Jack Barrett, 7 Oct. 1906, *Letters*, 2: 615.

107. *San Francisco Examiner*, letter to London, early spring 1906 [HEH cataloguer incorrectly dates it 1907], JL 17469, HEH; the letter is actually signed by Barrett.

108. London to business manager of *San Francisco Examiner*, 11 Feb. 1907, JL 13370, HEH.

109. See *San Francisco Examiner* to London, 6 Mar. 1907, JL 17467, HEH. See London's response in which he asserts Barrett called him with, first, the offer to go to Boise, and, failing that, an offer to publish an essay. See London to Bogart [*San Francisco Examiner*], 7 Mar. 1907, JL 13372, HEH. See also London to Bogart, 2 Apr. 1907, JL 13373, HEH; *San Francisco Examiner* to London, 3 Apr. 1907, JL 17468, HEH; London to Hearst, 15 Jan. 1908; and London to Brisbane, 3 May 1909 and 2 Sept. 1909, *Letters*, 2:726–27, 2:802–3, and 2:833–34.

110. Barrett to London, 17 Aug. 1906, JL 2140, HEH.

111. London to Brisbane, 18 Sept. 1909, JL 11236, HEH.

112. London to Robert, 27 Mar. 1910, *Letters*, 2:880.

113. "Something Rotten" appeared twice in socialist newspapers: "Jack London Scores the Idaho-Colorado Conspirators," *Oakland Socialist Voice*, 19 June 1906, and "Something Rotten in Idaho," *Chicago Sunday Socialist*, 4 Nov. 1906.

114. According to Lukas, the question of their guilt "defies easy answers," for there is no documentation of the talks among the Boise Three, Harry Orchard, and Steve Adams. But Lukas's research turned up letters to and from prominent socialists, especially Fred Warren, after the trial. He concludes, "If, four years after the Boise trial, these prominent Socialists wrote freely to one another about the guilt of Haywood,

Moyer, and Pettibone, what does this tell us about who struck down the governor on that snowy night in Caldwell?" (754).

8. EARTHQUAKE APOCALYPSE

1. Sterling to London, 18 Apr. 1906, JL 19046, HEH.

2. See Associated Press, "Half the City Lies in Ruins," *Los Angeles Daily Times*, 19 Apr. 1906, 14.

3. See Unna, *Coppa Murals*, 54–55. The claim that London spent nights at Martinez's studio comes in Hagerty, *Life of Maynard Dixon*, 73. Hagerty also details some of the losses I repeat here.

4. Charmian London, diary, 1906, JL 217, HEH.

5. Menu, in Jack London Scrapbooks, vol. 8, reel 5, HEH.

6. See C. Morris, *San Francisco Calamity by Earthquake and Fire*, 54.

7. Fraser to London, 1 Oct. 1909, JL 17470, HEH. Arnold Genthe imperfectly recalled the scene of her coronation: "I have a faint picture of Gelette Burgess, who was then editing *The Lark*, sitting at the end of the table poring libations into an enormous loving-cup to toast our exalted guest of honor [Fraser]." Among the guests were "Porter Garnett, Will Irwin [who was now editing the *Wave*], Maizie Griswold, now Mrs. Edwin Emerson, and George Sterling" (Genthe, *As I Remember*, 55).

8. Not all of it was good art, of course, but all of it was sincere. For example, in *Sunset*'s summer of 1906 issue principally devoted to the event, the lead piece was Joaquin Miller's "San Francisco," which referenced his own volume, the Christian-themed *Building the City Beautiful*; see Joaquin Miller, "San Francisco," *Sunset Magazine* 17 (June–July 1906): 12. The same issue had good reporting by the editor, Charles Aiken, E. H. Harriman, Katherine Chandler, and others, as well as a serviceable short story by Charles Norris. Genthe's memories of the earthquake mix acute descriptions of people in shock, his calm demeanor, the altruism of the rich, taking breakfast at the St. Francis Hotel in the company of Enrico Caruso, and his walk through the city with a camera (Arnold Genthe, *As I Remember*, 87).

The Bohemian Club summer High Jinks was held in July. The grove play, written by Charles K. Field, was *The Owl and Care*. As Porter Garnett wrote in his history of the club, "The whole affair was in the nature of a defiance of Care who had so recently and so heavily laid his hand on the whole of the Western community." George Sterling wrote the next play for 1907; he entitled it *The Triumph of Bohemia*, which featured the subjugation of the Spirit of Fire by the tree-spirits (Garnett, *Bohemian Jinks*, 73–74, 78–92; London's copy is inscribed by Garnett).

9. In *Sunset Magazine*'s first issue after the fire, William Dallam Armes wrote a short essay on the history of the seal, and Theodor H. Hittell contributed a poem; see Armes, "The Phoenix on the Seal" *Sunset Magazine* 17 (June–July): 1906, and Hittell, "Phoenix Redivivus," *Sunset Magazine* 17 (June–July): 113–15, 115.

10. Millard, *History of the San Francisco Bay Region*, 1:499, 507, 509.

11. Millard to London, 23 July 1906, JL 15382, HEH.

12. Millard, "When Altruria Awoke," *Cosmopolitan* 41 (July 1906): 237.

13. Mother Jones to London, 17 May 1906, JL 15622, HEH.

14. Herman Whitaker, "Human Drama at San Francisco," *Harper's Weekly*, 19 May 1906, 698.

15. Millard, "When Altruria Awoke," *Cosmopolitan* 41 (July 1906): 237.

16. Sandburg, "Heroism at San Francisco," *To-Morrow Magazine* 2 (May 1906). He quotes London: "Jack London says, 'An enumeration of the deeds of heroism would stock a library and bankrupt the Carnegie medal fund.'"

17. Gorky, "To Stricken 'Frisco," *To-Morrow Magazine* 2 (May 1906).

18. Norris, "The Valley of the Shadow: A Tale of the San Francisco Fire and Earthquake," *Sunset Magazine* 17 (June–July 1906): 111, 108. This story was reprinted—but without the final two paragraphs—in P. Johnson, ed., *The Early "Sunset Magazine," 1898–1928*, 53, 50.

19. Wilshire to London, 20 Apr. 1906, JL 20530, HEH.

20. See Stasz, "Family, Friends, Mentors," 49; see also London to Sterling, 31 May 1906, *Letters*, 2:578, and Sterling to London, 7 July 1906, JL 19049, HEH. Sterling thought Whitaker's essay "pretty poor."

21. James Hopper, "Our San Francisco," *Everybody's Magazine* 14 (June 1906): 760.

22. Her husband also wrote an account. See Emerson, "Handling a Crisis: How Affairs in San Francisco Were Controlled by Men Who Knew Just What to Do," *Sunset Magazine* 17 (June–July 1906): 230–35. Emerson was on the East Coast lecturing during the earthquake and fire and donated his proceeds to the Red Cross.

23. Mary Edith Griswold, "Three Days Adrift: The Diary of a San Francisco Girl during the Earthquake and Fire," *Sunset Magazine* 17 (June–July 1906): 122, 120.

24. London to Winship, 17 May 1906, *Letters*, 2:575.

25. Charmian London, 29 May 1906, diary, JL 217, HEH.

26. At least Brett liked it, calling it "the most vivid account" he had read (Brett to London, 12 May 1906, JL 3063, HEH).

27. London, *Before Adam*, 235.

28. Quoted in Kurzman, *Disaster!*, 38. See Hopper, "Our San Francisco," *Everybody's Magazine* 14 (June 1906): 759.

29. Charmian London, *Book of Jack London*, 2:125.

30. Whitaker, "Human Drama at San Francisco," *Harper's Weekly*, 19 May 1906, 694.

31. See Pinker to London, 19 Apr. 1906, JL 16645, HEH. He may have been paid half the price quoted; there is an entry of "Paid 5/5 Dec. 2/07" in London's sales notebook, seemingly indicating a payment of five pounds, five shillings. So, in today's currency, he received either $4,000 or half that. Either way, it is an extraordinary payment.

32. London to the editor of *Editor* [Apr. 1907?], *Letters*, 2:684.

33. London, "The League of the Old Men: [statement regarding short story]," JL 876, HEH. See London, introduction to "My Best Story and Why I Think So," *Grand Magazine* 4 (Aug. 1906): 86.

34. London, "The League of the Old Men," *Complete Short Stories*, 822.

35. London, "These Bones Shall Rise Again," *Reader* 2 (June 1903): 31.

36. London to Brett, 26 Dec. 1904, *Letters*, 1:459.

37. London, "The Somnambulists," *Revolution, and Other Essays*, 42.

38. Eugene Debs to Theodore Debs, 23 Mar. 1908, *Letters of Eugene V. Debs*, 1:259.

39. See London, checkbook, 20 Sept–4 Oct. 1906, JLE 201, HEH. By the end of November, even with constant payments for labor and materials for the boat, his account stood at $8,038.58 in the black. See London, checkbook, 21 Oct.–22 Nov. 1906, JLE 201, HEH. See also London to Walter V. Holloway and Thomas Booth, 29 Aug. 1906, JL 7546, HEH. Both were prominent socialists in the Bay Area. Booth ran for mayor of Oakland on the socialist ticket in 1911, and Holloway, who would later ask London for a job on the ranch, wrote *The Supreme Court and the Constitution*. See Holloway to London, 12 June 1913, JL 7547, HEH. Holloway would team up with Cloudesley Johns in Los Angeles to run a free-speech campaign.

40. London to Brett, 3 July 1905, *Letters*, 1:497.

41. London to Brett, 2 Dec. 1905, *Letters*, 1:538.

42. He made a list of alternative titles for the collection: The Taste of Life; The Bitter and the Sweet; The Bitter Taste of Life; The Bitter-Sweet; The Fiber of Life; The Constitution of Life; Men and Women. See London, "Created He Them: [notes for short story collection]," JL 566, HEH.

43. London, "Created He Them: [notes for short story collection]," JL 566, HEH.

44. London, "Created He Them: [notes for a short story collection]," JL 565–66, HEH. My dating of the notes relies on two elements. First, among the typescript pages of notes, there are four pages on a larger, thinner paper than the other twenty-six. One of those four pages is the typescript of "Burton's fight with death," labeled "Smoke of Life or Created He Them." None of the twenty-six mentions "The Smoke of Life." Given his 1905 letters to Brett, I am dating anything not connected to "The Smoke of Life"—that is, the *Created He Them* series—as 1905. I believe he concocted the idea for "The Smoke of Life" post-1909, probably in 1911.

45. See Herny, Rideout, and Wadell, *Berkeley Bohemia*, 166. Thanks to Clarice Stasz for first turning me on to this book.

46. London, "Created He Them: [notes for short-story collection]," JL 565, HEH. The typescript is catalogued as London, "Aunt Netta: [notes for a novel]," JL 457, HEH.

47. London, "Created He Them: [notes for short story collection]," JL 566, HEH.

48. See London, "Dramatic sketches: [notes for plays]," JL 612, HEH. This is the handwritten version of the story idea. The typed version clearly indicates that it was meant to be a part of the short-story series, not a play.

49. These story ideas may be related to that of a consumptive, Doctor Burton. In a handwritten note, filed at the Huntington separately from the *Created He Them* and the *Smoke of Life* series, the two Burtons' stories appear on the same note page entitled "Dramatic Sketches": "Dr. Burton's struggle with death—describe trenchantly," and "Mrs. Burton's choice in one day, between her two children (divorce) Court allowed her one, and her husband one" (London, "Dr. Burton's Struggle with Death: [note for dramatic sketch]," JL 604, HEH).

50. The sheet on which this idea is typed is entitled "CREATED HE THEM"; see London, "Created He Them: [notes for short story collection]," typewritten, JL 566, HEH. The handwritten note from which this is typed is entitled "Dramatic Sketches" and is filed separately; see London, "The Consumptive: [notes for dramatic sketch]," JL 550, HEH.

51. For the handwritten version of these notes, see London, "The pair of free-lovers . . . [notes for dramatic sketch]," JL 1033, HEH.

52. See Bennion, *Equal to the Occasion*, 126–27, for the most complete biography available.

53. London, "Created He Them; [notes for short-story collection]," JL 566, HEH. London had typed out these notes in a slightly different version for something he first called "As between Men," which he thought he might use as an "opening for a novel"; later he cut out the paragraph of notes and pinned it to a notebook sheet labeled "Dramatic sketches." London was pulling ideas from earlier story-idea notebooks and rearranging them for the series *Created He Them* (London, "As between Men: [notes for a dramatic sketch or novel]," JL 455, HEH).

54. London, "Created He Them: [notes for short-story collection]," JL 566, HEH. The handwritten notes are catalogued separately from JL 565 as London, "Anna's mood. . . . : [notes for dramatic sketch]," JL 446. The typescript has additions in London's hand, again showing how he was elaborating the story idea as he typed it.

55. London, "Insane Asylum Sketch: [notes for short story]," JL 798, HEH.

56. See London, "Burton's fight with death: [notes for short story]," JL 503, HEH. London wrote out two manuscript notes for this story idea. This one is the longest and closest to the typescript, yet he wrote "Death took shape before him in a half delirium."

57. London, "Smoke of Life: [notes for short story]," JL 1208, HEH. This is the typescript of London, "Smoke of Life: [notes for short story]," JL 1207, HEH, the handwritten notes for the same set of story ideas.

58. London, handwritten note at bottom of John Fleming Wilson's letter to London, 23 Oct. 1906, JL 20557, HEH. See also London to Wilson, 26 Oct. 1906, JL 14013, HEH.

59. Wilson to London, 29 Oct. 1906, JL 20558, HEH.

60. London to Reynolds, 31 Oct. 1906, JL 1323, HEH.

61. London, "A Wicked Woman," *When God Laughs, and Other Stories*, 72.

62. Nietzsche, *Nietzsche contra Wagner*, 90–91. This passage, which London marked, appears in the epilogue, on the first page of which London wrote, "the whole epilogue," apparently a note for Charmian, to whom he had written in 1904, "Have been getting hold of some of Neitzsche [*sic*]. I'll turn you loose first on his *Genealogy of Morals*—and after that, something you'll like—*Thus Spake Zarathustra*" (London to Charmian Kittredge, 29 Sept. 1904, *Letters*, 446).

63. Sterling to London, 7 July 1906, JL 19049, HEH.

64. London, "A Wicked Woman (Curtain-Raiser): [1-act play]," JL 1415, HEH.

65. See *Smart Set* to London, 14 Aug. 1906, JL 18550, HEH. F. W. Splint was the editor of the *Smart Set*.

66. See London, "A Wicked Woman (Curtain-Raiser): [1-act play]," JL 1415, HEH. The play was published posthumously in *The Human Drift* (1917).

67. London, "The Wit of Porportuk," *Lost Face, and Other Stories*, 191–92.

68. Quirk, "Interviews with Editors," 10.

69. James Randolph Walker to London, 28 July 1906, JL 19842, HEH.

70. London to James Randolph Walker, 29 July 1906, *Letters*, 2:598.

71. See James Randolph Walker to London, 14 Aug. 1906, JL 19844, HEH.

72. See James Randolph Walker to London, 20 Aug. 1906, JL 19850, HEH. This is misdated as 1908 in the Huntington collection.

73. See James Randolph Walker to London, 4 Dec. 1906, JL 19846, HEH.

74. See Sinclair to London, 2 Jan. 1907, JL 18276, and 6 Mar. 1907, JL 18278, HEH.

75. See London to James Randolph Walker, 15 Dec. 1906, *Letters*, 2:653. London tells Walker that he can't sue the *Times Magazine* because he doesn't know the disposition of the magazine; a false excuse because, as Sinclair told him, he just had to threaten them with legal action in order to get his money, regardless of the standing of the magazine.

76. See James Randolph Walker to London, 14 Aug. 1906, JL 19845, HEH.

77. London to James Randolph Walker, 21 Aug. 1906, *Letters*, 2:602.

78. See Charmian London to Elwyn Hoffman, 24 Sept. 1909, box 1, Hoffman Collection, HEH.

79. London, "Dramatize Wit of Porportuk: [note]," JL 613, HEH.

80. Longstreth, *On the Edge of the World*, 119, 120. See Haughey and Johnson, *Jack London Homes Album*, 24.

81. See R. G. Wilson, "'Divine Excellence,'" 13. See also anon., "A Departure in Church Building—The Second New Jerusalem Church in California: By a Stranger," in Sanders, ed., *The Craftsman: An Anthology*, 181–83, with photographs of the altar and a central, enormous fireplace.

82. Longstreth, *On the Edge of the World*, 111.

83. Longstreth, *On the Edge of the World*, 112.

84. London to Johns, 23 Feb. 1902, *Letters*, 1:283.

85. London, interview with Hamilton, *Reader* 2: 283.

86. See Longstreth, *On the Edge of the World*, 3. Sterling became "good friends" with Ernest Peixotto at the 1907 High Jinx (Sterling to London, 6 Aug. 1907, JL 19061, HEH).

87. London to Hamilton, 14 Aug. 1903, *Letters*, 1:378.

88. Triggs, *Chapters in the History of the Arts and Crafts Movement*, 1.

89. Triggs, "Industrial Art," 13, 17. See also Triggs, "The New Industrialism," *Craftsman* 1 Oct. 1901; rpt in Sanders, ed., *The Craftsman*, 60–71.

90. Reproductions of the Morris and Ruskin plaques appear as the frontispiece and on page 24 of Boris, *Art and Labor*. The Carlyle plaque appears as the frontispiece to Triggs, *Chapters in the History of the Arts and Crafts Movement*.

91. See Boris, *Art and Labor*, 26.

92. Stone to London, 6 June 1906, JL 19097, HEH.

93. Mott, "House Beautiful," *History of American Magazines*, 5:156.

94. Quoted in Gatti, "Stone Hearths and Marble Babies," 44.

95. See Mott, "House Beautiful," in *History of American Magazines*, for the reproduction of the cover of *House Beautiful* and Boris, *Art and Labor*, 25.

96. It is hard to see beyond the cliché, but here it is anyway: "If you have built castles in the air, your work need not be lost; that is where they should be. Now put the foundations under them." Thoreau, *Walden*, 324.

97. London to Stone, 22 July 1906, *Letters*, 2:597.

98. Thoreau, *Walden*, 35,36, 40.

99. Charmian and Jack London to Sercombe, Jack London Scrapbooks, vol. 8, n.p., HEH.

100. Charmian London, 28–30 Feb., diary, 1906, JL 217, HEH. See also Jack London, 28–30 Feb., diary, 1906, JL 597, HEH. Simons published "The Economic Foundation of Art" in Gustav Stickley's first issue of the *Craftsman*. See A. M. Simons, "The Economic Foundation of Art," *Craftsman* 1 (Oct. 1901); rpt. in Sanders, ed., *The Craftsman*, 18–24.

101. Amy Lowell, "Is There a National Spirit in 'the New Poetry' of America?" *Craftsman* 25 (Dec. 1913); rpt in Sanders, ed., *The Craftsman*, 317. As Sanders says in his introduction, the *Craftsman* was "the principal journal for the dissemination of the Arts and Crafts philosophy in America" (vii).

102. Lambourne, *Utopian Craftsmen*, 124, 146

103. Triggs, *Chapters in the History of the Arts and Crafts Movement*, 145.

104. See Claudia J. Keenan, "Edmond, Oscar, Laura," *Through the Hourglass*, http://www.throughthehourglass.com/2016/03/edmond-oscar-laura-1.html.

105. Advertisement, *To-Morrow* 1 (Jan. 1905): i. After Triggs resigned from *To-Morrow* and Sercombe took over, the editorial offices moved to 2238 Calumet, where the Spencer-Whitman Center and the People's Industrial College were also established. Sercombe was secretary for the center, and Grace Moore, associate editor of the magazine, was chair of the center's roundtable discussion group.

106. Triggs, endorsement, *Conservator* 17 (June 1906): 1.

107. Debs to Reynolds, 10 Mar. 1900, *Letters of Eugene V. Debs*, 1:146. See also Debs to Traubel, 16 Nov. 1908, *Letters of Eugene V. Debs*, 1:290.

108. Joaquin Miller, selection from *Building the City Beautiful*, in the *Conservator* 17 (May 1906): 1.

109. See Martin, *Rebel Souls*, 184–85.

110. London to Stoddard, 13 Oct. 1906, *Missouri Review* 23, no. 2 (2000): 112.

111. London to Traubel, *Conservator* 16 (June 1905): 60.

112. London to Sercombe, Jan.–Mar. 1907 issue of *To-Morrow* 3, no. 3, in Jack London Scrapbooks, vol. 8, n.p. HEH.

113. Charles A. Sandburg, "Jack London: A Common Man," *To-Morrow* 2 (Apr. 1906): 35–39; rpt. *Jack London Newsletter* 5 (Jan.–Apr. 1972): 14–18.

114. Sandburg, "On Beatniks," CBS television news feature, 28 Oct. 1959.

115. A. M. Simons, "The Economic Foundation of Art," *Craftsman* 1 (Oct. 1901); rpt. In Sanders, ed., *The Craftsman*, 23.

116. Waterman, "My Castle in Spain," 38.

117. London, "The House Beautiful," *Revolution, and Other Essays*, 162.

118. Quoted in R. G. Wilson, "'Divine Excellence,'" 17.

119. London, "The House Beautiful," JL 763, HEH.

120. Corra Harris, "The Walking Delegate Novelist," *Independent*, 24 May 1906, 14–15.

121. London to Harris, 22 Jan. 1914, Corra Harris Collection, University of Georgia Library, Athens GA. Many thanks to Melissa Bush for tracking this letter down for me.

122. Harris, *My Book and Heart*, 216–17.

123. Holt to London, 28 Mar. 1907, JL 7570, HEH.

124. Holt to London, 9 Nov. 1909, JL 7571, HEH.

125. London to Harris, 17 Sept. 1906, *Letters*, 2:606.

126. Longstreth, *On the Edge of the World*, 308.

127. Thoreau, *Maine Woods*, 125.

128. Quoted in Haughey and Johnson, *Jack London Homes Album*, 36–37.

129. Quoted in Haughey and Johnson, *Jack London Homes Album*, 37.

130. London, *The Cruise of the* Snark, 10.

131. "As for the article on the starting out of 'The Snark,' I take it that this is one of the series to be covered by the advance which we made to you. You will be duly credited for the article" (Millard to London, 27 Aug. 1906, JL 15385, HEH).

132. Because the next line in his notes is "First article," the Huntington Library cataloguer mistitled this file as London, "[The Inconceivable and Monstrous:] [notes]," JL 786, HEH.

133. Charmian London, diary, 1905, JL 218, HEH. Jack may have already owned an 1894 edition of Slocum's first book, *Voyage of the* Liberade (1890), which is in his library at the Huntington. There has been some speculation that Charmian introduced Jack to Slocum's voyage; she saw the *Spray* when she visited the Buffalo fair in 1901. But Slocum's book was serialized in the *Century* in 1899, a time when London was reading magazines, including the *Century*, voraciously. Thanks to Susan Nuernberg for pointing this out to me.

134. See London to Brett, 12 Feb. 1903, *Letters*, 343, and London to Strunsky, 5 Sept. 1903, *Letters*, 386.

135. In March 1906, he told Sterling it was called the *Gull*; in July he told an editor that "We are going to call the boat the *Snark*." See London to Sterling, 22 Mar. 1906, *Letters*, 557, and London to Vance, 16 July 1906, *Letters*, 591.

136. In a playful letter to the editor of the *West Coast Lumberman*, a member of a "secret" society comprised of lumbermen called Hoo-Hoo, London said that "all hands wanted to be Bojum and Jabberwock." The society borrowed names from Carroll's poems for the titles of their officers. See London to Cole [Jan. 1907?], *Letters*, 1:666.

137. London to Robert Mackay, 11 Mar. 1907, *Letters*, 2:677.

138. London, "[The Inconceivable and Monstrous:] [notes]," JL 786, HEH.

139. See London to Bamford, 22 Apr. 1906, *Letters*, 2:571. Roscoe and Jack's arguments continued three weeks into the voyage on the *Snark*: "Uncle and Jack," writes

Charmian in her diary, "have hot argument on 'Inside Theory,' in cockpit. Uncle insults Jack in 700 different ways. Jack laughs. Uncle acts as if he expects to convert Bert" (Charmian London, diary, 1907, JL 220, HEH). Bert is Herbert Stolz, native-born Hawaiian whose father was killed by Koolau the leper, the subject of one of Jack's more famous Hawaiian stories.

140. London, "Finis: [short story]," JL 672, HEH.

141. London, "Finis: *The Turtles of Tasman*," 184.

142. London, "Finis: [short story]," JL 672, HEH.

143. London, "Finis: [notes for short story]," JL 671, HEH.

144. Maxwell to London, 27 Oct. 1906, JL 15220, HEH. Two and a half weeks later, a different editor or assistant editor sent a standard rejection letter. See *Cosmopolitan* to London, 14 Nov. 1906, JL 5190, HEH. This duplication could have only fueled London's already bubbling ire at Maxwell and the magazine over rate of pay and the proper way to count words in anticipation of London's contributions to the magazine during the *Snark* voyage.

145. See MacKay to London, 17 Nov. 1906, JL 14348, HEH: It was a short-and-sweet letter: "I should like very much to arrange with you for some short stories for 1907, and trust that you are in a position to send something our way." At the bottom of the letter, London wrote, "Offer to do short stories after first several months of 1907.—15 cents. Ask for an advance."

146. MacKay to London, 27 Dec. 1906, JL 14350, HEH.

147. MacKay to London, 5 Mar. 1907, JL 14351, HEH. To further cement his bona fides with London, he recounted a story of sailing in the South Seas in tune with London's talk of his impending trip, which involved sharks, a new and developing topic for London; see MacKay to London, 16 Mar. 1907, JL 14353, HEH. MacKay, London, and Ernest Untermann all should have gotten together over beers and recounted their South Sea adventures.

148. See advertisement for "Morganson's Finish," *Success Magazine*, Apr. 1907, 300.

149. MacKay to London, 3 Dec. 1906, JL 14349, HEH.

150. See London to the editorial department of *Cosmopolitan*, 12 Feb. 1907, *Letters*, 2:671.

151. See MacKay to London, 11 Mar. 1907, JL 14352, HEH. London of course agreed to the title change, but later he would regret it: "I must say that I cannot congratulate you upon the change. I still stick to the belief that 'Finis' is the better title" (London to MacKay, 28 Mar. 1907, *Letters*, 2680).

152. MacKay to London, 21 June 1907, JL 14355, HEH.

153. See Millard to London, 27 Aug. 1906, JL15385, HEH.

154. London to the editor of *Cosmopolitan*, 24 Nov. 1906, *Letters*, 2:639–40.

155. London to MacKay, 11 Mar. 1907, *Letters*, 2:677. Unfortunately, MacKay's name is misspelled in *Letters* as "McKay."

156. London to the editor of *Cosmopolitan*, 24 Nov. 1906, *Letters*, 2:639.

157. See London, "Just Meat: [notes for short story]," JL 829, HEH.

158. London, "Just Meat," *When God Laughs, and Other Stories*, 105.

9. FUTURE OF SOCIALISM, DEATH OF THE INDIVIDUAL

1. Untermann to Joan London, 8 Apr. 1938, Ernest Untermann Papers, WSHS.

2. See London, "Russian Revolution Short Story: [notes for a story]," JL 1138, HEH.

3. London to Strunsky, 4 Sept. 1905, *Letters*, 1:517.

4. Foner, *Jack London*, 88.

5. London, *The Iron Heel*, 126.

6. See London, subject file, "Socialism," box 555, JLE 1562, HEH.

7. London to MacKay, 28 Mar. 1907, *Letters*, 2:680.

8. Trotsky, introduction to *The Iron Heel*, by Jack London, vii. Trotsky's text is taken from a letter he wrote to Joan London in 1937.

9. McIntyre to London, 7 June 1906, JL 14347, HEH.

10. London to Buck, 19 July 1913, *Letters*, 3:1210.

11. London, "The Pessimism of Jack London," interview with Emanuel Julius, *Milwaukee County Leader*, 28 May 1913; rpt. in *Jack London Journal* 3 (1996): 190; rpt. *Western Comrade* (June 1913).

12. Charmian London, *Book of Jack London*, 2:139.

13. Pittenger, *American Socialists and Evolutionary Thought*, 162. Pittenger, however, neglects to mention that Spargo was grateful to have been included in *The Iron Heel*.

14. Charmian London, *Book of Jack London*, 2:139.

15. Bercovitch, *American Jeremiad*, 11.

16. London, "Twentieth Century machine-breakers: [notes for articles]," JL 1339, HEH.

17. See London to Brett, 16 Oct. 1906, *Letters*, 2:619.

18. Quoted in Joan London, *Jack London and His Times*, 313; quoted in Watson, *Novels of Jack London*, 119.

19. See Lowes, *The Road to Xanadu*.

20. I recently discovered a mention of this booklet in the guide to the collection at the Jack London State Park. The booklet was circulated by the Socialist Party of America. It's presence in London's library means that he did in fact read, if only ten pages, *Capital*.

21. Gronlund, *Co-operative Commonwealth*, 80–81.

22. We don't know when London read Edwin Seligman's *The Economic Interpretation of History*, but in it London marked various long quotations from Marx's works, including a passage from the third volume of *Capital* in which he wrote, "It is always the immediate relation of the owner of the conditions of production to the immediate producers . . . in which we find the innermost secret, the hidden basis of the entire social structure, and thus also of the political forms" (Seligman, *The Economic Interpretation of History*, 48). Thus we can call London a Marxist in his unwavering commitment to class struggle and the necessity of the proletariat to own the means of production. Seligman was professor of political economy and finance at Columbia University. Seligman was not interested in Marx's economics—specifically, the theory of surplus value—and London's principal concern in *The Iron Heel* is with exactly

that theory. It is important to note that London concurred with Seligman that "we understand, then, by the theory of economic interpretation of history [which Seligman calls Marx's original creation], not that all history is to be explained in economic terms alone, but that the chief considerations in human progress are the social considerations, and that the important factor in social change is the economic factor. Economic interpretation of history means, not that the economic relations exert an exclusive influence, but that they exert a preponderant influence in shaping the progress of society" (Seligman, 67). London not only drew a line along this passage but placed an X next to it as well.

23. See Gronlund, *Co-Operative Commonwealth*, 9-26, 56.

24. London, "What Socialism Is," *San Francisco Examiner*, 25 Dec. 1895.

25. Gronlund, *Co-Operative Commonwealth*, 188-89.

26. Martinek, *Socialism and Print Culture in America*, 35,

27. See Charmian London, 19 July 1906, diary, JL 219, HEH. The entry reads simply, "Read in Mankind in the Making." This does not necessarily mean that Jack was reading it, too, but it is very likely that he had already read it and was now going back to it and that Charmian was reading it for the first time. They shared nearly every book they each read. Not every book they read in the summer contributed to the making of *The Iron Heel*; Charmian notes she was reading Clyde Fitch's *The Girl with the Green Eyes*, Connie Skinner's gift of *Fenris, the Wolf* in July, and Eden Phillpots's *The Portreeve*. Sometimes they read for relaxation, as we all do. But sometimes I sense that Charmian is reading in socioeconomics per instruction from her husband; if she is to participate in his authorial tasks, then she needs to be as fluent as he in the current literature.

28. Wells, *Mankind in the Making*, 19.

29. Untermann, *Science and Evolution*, 5, 14.

30. London to Hamilton, 15 July 1906, *Letters*, 2:590.

31. Ghent, *Mass and Class*, 9. As a monist, however, he did acknowledge the importance of the spiritual.

32. See Untermann to Joan London, 22 Jan. 1938, WSHS.

33. London, "The Iron Heel: [notes for novel]," JL 833, HEH.

34. See Pittenger, *American Socialists and Evolutionary Thought*, where he calls John Spargo and Arthur M. Lewis "less original" than Untermann.

35. Pittenger, *American Socialists and Evolutionary Thought*, 136.

36. Pittenger, *American Socialists and Evolutionary Thought*, 135.

37. See Charmian London, 30-31 Jan. 1906, diary, JL 219, HEH.

38. Ernest Untermann to Frauenglass, 23 Nov. 1938, WSHS.

39. See Charmian Kittredge London, 10 Aug. 1906, diary, JL 219, HEH. London's letters to Untermann were destroyed in a fire in Idaho in which Untermann lost his manuscripts as well, or they have gone missing, or they are held in private hands.

40. See Ernest Untermann, "How I Became a Socialist," *Comrade* (Dec. 1902): 62-63, and Roger Hansen, "Ernest Untermann, Dinosaur Artist and Socialist," http://

rogerdhansen.wordpress.com/2010/12/20/utahs-socialist-dinosaur-artist/. Hansen quotes Kirk Johnson and Ray Troll's book *Cruisin' the Fossil Freeway* on Untermann.

41. Charmian Kittredge London, 24 Aug. 1906, diary, JL 219, HEH.

42. Anon., "The International Socialist Review," in Liebknecht, *Karl Marx*, 182.

43. See Spargo, *Socialism*, 4–5.

44. London to Johns, 12 June 1899, *Letters*, 1:85–86.

45. For a good discussion of Spencer's common-sense philosophy, see Francis, *Herbert Spencer and the Invention of Modern Life*, chap. 10, "Common Sense in the Mid-Nineteenth Century."

46. Spencer, *First Principles*, 11.

47. Spencer, *First Principles*, 22.

48. Francis, *Herbert Spencer and the Invention of Modern Life*, 360n1, reads Spencer's work at this point in a different way, calling the Knowable and Unknowable "symbiotic." I would agree that at the most abstract level, the level at which both religion and science acknowledge that there are things about the world that remain unknown to each discipline, they are symbiotic.

49. Spencer, *First Principles*, 131.

50. Francis, *Herbert Spencer and the Invention of Modern Life*, 111.

51. Francis, *Herbert Spencer and the Invention of Modern Life*, 170.

52. James to Frances Rollins Morse, 12 Apr. 1900, In James, *Correspondence of William James*, 9:185–86.

53. James, preface to *Varieties of Religious Experience*, 17.

54. London to Johns, 15 Mar. 1900, *Letters*, 1:170.

55. London, "The Iron Heel: [notes for a novel]," JL 833, HEH.

56. Ghent to Joan London Miller, 8 Aug. 1937, MI 472, HEH.

57. See London to Brett, 25 Oct. 1904, *Letters*, 1:450.

58. Ghent, *Mass and Class*, vi, vii. London must have been favorably inclined toward Ghent's new book after he read the footnote on page 62 to his own essay, "The Class Struggle," which Ghent called "a striking summary of the present phases" of the class struggle.

59. London, "The Iron Heel: [notes for a novel]," JL 833, HEH.

60. London, "The Iron Heel: [notes for a novel]," JL 833, HEH.

61. Ghent, *Mass and Class*, 1.

62. See Ghent, *Mass and Class*, 30, with London's marginal markings.

63. Ghent, *Mass and Class*, 80.

64. Alexander Tille, introduction to Nietzsche, *Thus Spake Zarasthustra*, xiv.

65. One can't help recalling London's poignant letter to Charmian from 1903 about the difference between his public life—his love of "prizefights and kites and one thing and another"—and his private life. To live "placidly and complacently," that is, to watch sports or play with kites is "to fool my inner self pretty well" by not engaging in serious contemplation—absorption—of one's private self. "Poor inner self! I wonder if it will atrophy, dry up some day and blow away" (London to Charmian Kittredge, 18 June 1903, JL 12426, HEH). Given London's famous deployment of

various clothing and outfits to play the roles of hobo, down-and-outer, lecturer, and famous author, he knew all too well how disguise could lead to personal disintegration and the death of the self.

66. London, *Iron Heel*, 5-6.

67. London to Greer, 4 Aug. 1915, *Letters*, 3:1485. Sometime in 1916 he made the following note to himself: "SHORT STORY (Dandy) Nietzsche Confutation of Neitzsche? [*sic*] and Individualism See article 'A MIGHT-HAVE-BEEN' in Sing Sing The Literary Digest for February 19, 1916. Look up my war clips for German interpretation of Nietzsche" (London, "Nietzsche: [notes for short story]," JL 995, HEH). See also London, "Confrontation of Nietzschean and Individualist: [note for short story]," JL 549, HEH, which is the handwritten earlier version of JL 995.

68. London to Charmian Kittredge, 29 Sept. 1904, *Letters*, 1:446.

69. London, *People of the Abyss*, 168-69.

70. Nietzsche, *A Genealogy of Morals*, 43.

71. London, "How I Became a Socialist," 269.

72. Watson, *Novels of Jack London*, 69. Watson gives the best rationale for arguing that London was familiar with Nietzsche's work in early 1903. London's letter to Charmian in 1904—"Have been getting hold of some of Nietzsche"—is proof to some that London first read Nietzsche in 1904. It is, after all, the earliest mention of Nietzsche in the letters we have. But Watson takes this letter apart to show how it more than likely means that London is gathering books by Nietzsche for Charmian, not himself: "By playing the role of mentor, London seems to be saying that he was 'getting hold of some of Nietzsche' not for himself but for Charmian, since he obviously knows enough about Nietzsche's writings to be able to determine which book she should read first and which one she will like best." Watson concludes perspicaciously that given that Wolf Larsen is not "a precisely faithful incarnation" of the superman is not proof that London had not read Nietzsche (Watson, "Nietzsche and *The Sea-Wolf*," 34-35). See also Watson, *Novels of Jack London*, 259-60n29.

73. Payne, "Recent Fiction: *The Sea-Wolf*," 105.

74. "Literature: A Nietzsche Novel," in *The Critical Response to Jack London*, 106.

75. Ratner-Rosenhagen, *American Nietzsche*, 112.

76. Nietzsche, *Genealogy of Morals*, 42.

77. Rattner-Rosenhagen, *American Nietzsche*, 113.

78. Shaw, *The Revolutionist's Handbook*, 217, 218.

79. Quoted in Bridgwater, *Nietzsche in Anglosaxony*, 62

80. See Silver, *Bernard Shaw*, 153.

81. Silver, *Bernard Shaw*, 120.

82. See London, "The Question of the Maximum," and London, *The Iron Heel*, chapter 9. In his notes for the novel, he wrote, "Iron Heel Developing Question of the Maximum, that it is a struggle between nations, as to which shall first be driven into Socialism" (JL 833, HEH); note how he now sees the worldwide implications of his essay. See also Horwitz, "'See Things in New Ways,'" 527-30. In a summary statement that London agreed with, Untermann wrote, "Marx's 'Capital,' . . . revolutionized

political economy through his theory of surplus . . . and thus opened an impassable chasm between bourgeois and proletarian science" (Untermann, *Science and Evolution*, 123). Clearly, London's political philosophy was consistent in these important respects from 1898 to 1906.

83. London, "The Iron Heel: [notes for novel]," JL 833, HEH.

84. Shaw, *Man and Superman*, 2. Everhard uses a passage from "Revolution" in his speech to the Philomath Club; see London, *Iron Heel*, 64. In 1902, on his return from London and while writing *The Call of the Wild*, he collected newspaper and magazine articles about the middle class and its predicted disappearance. He wanted to write an essay entitled "The Disappearing Class," which would focus on the plight of the American farmer. Instead of completing the essay, he gave Everhard much of the information he gathered when he fights the Philomaths. See London, "Disappearing Class: [notes for collection of essays]," JL 601–2, HEH; these are both the handwritten and typed versions of his notes.

85. Shaw, *Man and Superman*, 125.

86. Silver, *Bernard Shaw*, 152.

87. The Londons received a copy of Charles Klein's novelization of Arthur Hornblow's play *The Lion and the Mouse* from Bamford in the first week of October, which Charmian read and while reading the beginning told Jack he should "read it once, in relation to my own novel" (London to Bamford, 10 Oct. 1906, *Letters*, 2:616–17). At this point he was two months from completing *The Iron Heel*. According to her marginal commentary, which is quite acute and remorseless, Charmian became disenchanted with the novel, which was a Christian Socialist's indictment of the railroad trusts and the general greed and corruption of American business practices; Bamford's inscription testifies to its political philosophy: "This, (in which we Ruskin men are,) for you, dear Jack and Charmian, with my love." It is unlikely that Jack read it at all. See Klein and Hornblow, *Lion and the Mouse*, HEH 331725.

88. Karl Marx called Lincoln "the single-minded son of the working class" and explained the Civil War as "the American anti-slavery war" that will empower "the working classes." Quoted in McPherson, *Battle Cry of Freedom*, 550.

89. Kipnis, *American Socialist Movement*, 167.

90. See Spargo, *Socialism*, 79.

91. London, "The Iron Heel: [notes for novel]," JL 833, HEH. Robert Hunter had given a signed copy of *Poverty* to London ("to Jack London with the sincere regards of the Author"), but a comparison between it and *The Iron Heel* reveals no real contribution other than a footnote by Meredith saying that Hunter in *Poverty* had put the total number of poor people in America in the ten million range. See London, *Iron Heel*, 65, and Hunter, *Poverty*.

92. See Spargo, *Bitter Cry of the Children*, 142, and London, *Iron Heel*, 65.

93. Spargo, *Bitter Cry of Children*, xiv; see also 293.

94. Charmian Kittredge London, *Book of Jack London*, 2:341.

95. Spargo to Charmian London, 8 Dec. 1921, JL 18844, HEH. No such letter from London to Spargo is known. Charmian's list is an odd one because it doesn't include

such obvious and more significant names like Jim Whitaker, Austin Lewis, Ernest Untermann, and Frank Strawn-Hamilton.

96. See Spargo's review of *The Iron Heel* in the *International Socialist Review* 8 (1908): 628-29; and London, *Iron Heel*, 27. See also Pittenger, *American Socialists and Evolutionary Thought, 1870-1920*, 161-62, 280-81. Spargo condemned London's "cataclysmic theory" of socialism's success and his disparagement of political action. Spargo recommended the novel to all socialists who wanted to know why London's socialist principles would fail. On a bibliographic note, Spargo's book is not included in London's library at the Huntington; however, it may be the copy that was digitized from the University of California. See books.google.com/books?id=TdM4AQAAIAAj &printsec=frontcover&source=gbs_ge_summary_r&cad=0#v=onepage&q&f=false, where the passages from Spargo's book that are quoted are among a number of marked passages, marked in a way similar to the way London marked up his books.

97. Twain, *Adventures of Huckleberry Finn*, 167. See Auerbach, introduction to *The Iron Heel*, vii.

98. London, "Christ Novel: [notes]," JL 532, HEH.

99. George Sterling, inscription of front flyleaf of Bierce, *The Cynic's Word Book*.

100. Graff, *Professing Literature*, 83.

101. Van Dyke, *Essays in Application*, 189; see page 201 for the quotation London uses.

102. London, "Anarchy: [notes for a lecture]," JL 442, HEH; the handwritten version of the notes is JL 444. See Sterling Heilig, "Louise Michel: The Daughter of the Commune," *Pearson's Magazine* 13 (June 1905): 601-7; and Watson, *Novels of Jack London*, 266n25.

103. Lydston, *Diseases of Society*, 229. His long account of the Haymarket affair concludes simply with an admonition that "the murderer or fanatic of to-day is the hero or martyr of to-morrow" and that were those charged with the bomb-throwing "tried again to-day, they would not be executed" (244). London would have seen how Lydston's criminal anthropology was disinterested in sociopolitical theoretical constructions and the most effective forms of social action, though he recognized how Lydston's science lent credence to his own political philosophy. Later, in the teens, London would praise Lydston's medical research, especially his sexology. See London to Lydston, 13 Feb. 1912 and 26 Mar. 1914, *Letters*, 2:1069, 3:1312.

104. Roulston was a Socialist Labor Party activist. That London was not on particularly close terms with Roulston is clear from a 1914 letter he wrote to Charmian, saying that he was planning lunch with "Jane Rolston (or however name is spelled)" (London to Charmian K. London, 29 Jan. 1914, *Letters*, 3:1294).

105. Joan London, *Jack London and His Times*, 181.

106. Sterling Heilig, "Louise Michel: The Daughter of the Commune," 606.

107. See "A Suppressed Incident," *Socialist Spirit* 1 (Sept. 1901): 10. Although this was the first issue of the *Socialist Spirit*, it was a seasoned publication, formerly titled *Social Crusader*. George Herron and John Spargo, among others, comprised its editorial "fellowship." In its first several pages, in double columns, it published news

items with commentary and then essays. The item from the *Candid Friend* appeared as just another news item. London wrote to *Vanity Fair* (probably not realizing that Harris was the editor), having recently returned from the South Seas, "I went up to my ranch, and in the barn resurrected a large box labeled on the outside with 'IRON HEEL CLIPPINGS.' Running through these clippings I found the one Mr. Harris said I lied when I stated I possessed it. Here is the clipping, with my marks on it, and my notes made at the time when I utilized it for *The Iron Heel*."

108. Frank Harris, "Mr. Jack London Again," *Vanity Fair*, 27 Oct. 1909, 519; this clipping accompanies London, letter to *Vanity Fair*, 16 Aug. 1909, JL 13863, HEH. Harris reproduced the page from the *Socialist Spirit*, with London's handwritten notes, that London had sent him.

109. "A Suppressed Incident," *Socialist Spirit*, 9.

110. London to *San Francisco Examiner*, 1 July 1909, *Letters*, 2:812.

111. London to *San Francisco Examiner*, 1 July 1909, *Letters*, 2:813.

112. Frank Harris, "How Jack London Writes a Novel," *Vanity Fair* (London), 14 Apr. 1909, 454.

113. See Baskett, "A Source of *The Iron Heel*," 269. Baskett presents other instances of supposed borrowing, but this is the only persuasive case. See London, "The Iron Heel: [notes for novel]," JL 833, HEH, where he writes, "at the beginning—a third dinner—in which ernest locks horns with a churchman—quote from Austin Lewis[.] Churchman—It is true, we have lost the—what you call the proletariat—to the working class."

114. See "The Great American Fraud: *Collier's Weekly* Makes a Comprehensive Assault upon Patent Medicines," the *Pandex*, in London, "Persistence of the Established: [notes for book]," JL 1049, HEH. In the same file, London placed a copy of the *Collier's Weekly* article, "The Great American Fraud" by Samuel Hopkins Adams.

115. See N. A. Richardson, "Methods of Acquiring National Possession of Our Industries," *Wayland's Monthly*, no. 38 (June 1903): 4–5, and "The Eleven Groups of Men Who Control," *Twentieth Century*, n.d., 24–25; both can be found in London, "Disappearing Class: [notes for collection of essays]," JL 602, HEH.

116. Note that when Everhard addresses the Machine-Breakers, the bourgeois middle-class business owners, the first one Avis lists as being in the audience is "Owen, of Silverberg, Owen and Company—a large grocery firm with several branch stores."

117. London, "The Iron Heel: [notes for novel]," JL 883, HEH. There are other notes for the foreword as well, notes made once his characters and narrative were more firmly in mind.

118. London, "The Apostate: [notes for short story]," JL 448, HEH.

119. London, "The Apostate: [notes for short story]," JL 448, HEH. Interestingly, London calls Johnny's departure from home and work the "Last Revolt," a harbinger for the last revolt in *The Iron Heel* when the socialists finally conquer the oligarchy. Again, the short story is less about becoming a tramp than it is about the triumph of socialism. As London says in his notes, when Ardis is built, "there were no more tramps in the U.S." It was built by "slave[s]," or former tramps.

120. London, "The Iron Heel: [notes for novel]," JL 833, HEH.

121. London, "The Iron Heel: [notes for novel]," JL 833, HEH. These notes may have been made in March 1906, when he first announced to Brett that "I think I shall write this summer a book to be entitled *The Iron Heel*" (London to Brett, 26 Mar. 1906, *Letters*, 2:558).

122. "The Socialist Party: National Platform, Resolutions at National Convention, National Constitution, Directory of Socialist Locals," in London, subject file, "Socialism," box 555, JLE 1572, HEH. See also London, "Disappearing Class: [notes for collection of essays]," JL 601, HEH.

123. See Kipnis, *American Socialist Movement*, 263.

124. Charmian K. London, diary, 1906, JL 219, HEH.

125. See London, "The Iron Heel," JL 834, HEH.

126. London to Radcliffe, 29 Aug. 1906, *Letters*, 2:604.

127. See London to Reynolds, 18 Sept. 1906, *Letters*, 2:607. He tells Reynolds he has completed twenty thousand words.

128. London to Johns, 12 Sept. 1906, *Letters*, 2:605.

129. See London to Reynolds, 18 Sept. 1906, *Letters*, 2:607.

130. London to Brett, 19 Sept. 1906, *Letters*, 2:608. Coincidentally, in the same month he was pushing Robert Collier to publish "Revolution" or explain why he could not. See chapter 5.

131. London to Brett, 28 Sept. 1906, *Letters*, 2:611.

132. See London to Reynolds, 16 Nov. 1906, JL 13264, HEH.

133. London to Bamford, 10 Oct. 1906, *Letters*, 2:617.

134. Brett to London, 8 Oct. 1906, JL 3078, HEH.

135. London to Brett, 16 Oct. 1906, *Letters*, 2:619.

136. Brett to London, 22 Oct. 1906, JL 3079, HEH.

137. Brett to London, 22 Oct. 1906, JL 3079, HEH. See also Brett to London, 24 Dec. 1906, JL 3085.

138. London to the *Appeal to Reason*, 22 Nov. 1906, *Letters*, 2:638.

139. See London to Whitney, 19 Nov. 1906, *Letters*, 2:637.

140. London to Brett, 15 Dec. 1906, *Letters*, 2:649.

141. London to Reynolds, 15 Dec. 1906, JL 13265, HEH.

142. London to *Appeal to Reason* [A. M. Simons], 15 Dec. 1906, JL 10901, HEH.

143. London to Brett, 15 Dec. 1906, *Letters*, 2:649.

144. See Brett to London, 24 Dec. 1906, JL 3085, HEH.

145. London, "The Iron Heel," JL 834, HEH.

146. London to Brett, 28 Jan. 1907, *Letters*, 2:665. Lochner v. New York—the case involving bakers' hours—was a seminal case, prompting a famous dissent from Oliver Wendall Holmes, representing the minority opinion of four judges.

147. Brett to London, 9 Jan. 1907, JL 3086, HEH.

148. London to Brett, 16 Jan. 1907, *Letters*, 2:663.

149. Brett to London, 9 Jan. 1907, JL 3086, HEH.

150. London to Brett, 16 Jan. 1907, *Letters*, 2:663.

151. Brett to London, 23 Jan. 1907, JL 3090, HEH.

152. See MacKay to London, 5 Mar. 1907, JL 14351, HEH.

153. See MacKay to London, 16 Mar. 1907, JL 14353, HEH.

154. See Reynolds to Brett, 4 Nov. 1907, JL 16899, HEH.

155. Macmillan's first printing totaled 12,472, showing Brett's faith in the work. This amount is over twice the amount printed of London's next work, *The Road*. Oddly enough, *Appeal to Reason* and Wilshire Book Company both brought out editions in the same month and year as Macmillan. It is possible that the arrangement the two socialist publishers made with Brett took the place of serialization. It is unknown whether London knew about these arrangements. See Sisson and Martens, *Jack London*, 123-24, 38.

156. Untermann to Joan London, 22 Jan. 1938, WSHS. Untermann gives a long and convincing explanation for what Joan had called the inconsistency between what Jack wrote in *The Iron Heel* about going to war against Germany and his support for the Allies. According to Untermann, given London's poor health, he could not afford to go to jail like Debs for protesting the war. Also, he did not want to alienate the Anglo-American book market, not so much for financial reasons but for maintaining an audience for his socialist principles; see Untermann to Ettie Frauenglass, 23 Nov. 1938, WSHS. Many a good socialist advocated for the war, following a preexisting split in the party, accepting the futility of ever organizing a general international strike like that pictured in *The Iron Heel*.

157. London to Harris, 26 October 1914, pasted in London, *The Iron Heel*, HEH 337696.

158. Henry to London, 10 Mar. 1911, pasted in London, *The Iron Heel*, HEH 337696.

10. THE ROAD NEVER ENDS

1. The back-cover copy for the Penguin edition of the novel hedges its bets by calling it "part science fiction, part dystopian fantasy, part radical socialist tract."

2. See Hay, "Jack London's Sci-Fi Finale," 356.

3. C. W. Saleeby, *The Cycle of Life According to Modern Science: Being a Series of Essays Designed to Bring Science Home to Men's Business and Bosoms* (New York: Harper, 1904), 40. Saleeby, a Fellow of the Royal Society of Edinburgh, became a prominent eugenicist, nudist, and proponent of nuclear energy. His daughter was tutored by D. H. Lawrence.

4. John Morris, "Food-Production of the Future," *Arena* 36 (Aug. 1906): 173. Interestingly, London wrote at the top of the first page of the article, not "The Iron Heel," but rather "Farthest Distant," a note telling him and/or Charmian how to file the article.

5. This newspaper article from early 1907 from the Sunday *American-Examiner* was titled "Like the Unseen Fingers of Ghosts: How an Electric Wizard, M. Georgia Knap, Does the Most Uncanny Miracles with Electricity in His Extraordinary New Mansion in Troyes." When dealing with the future, even those technological inno-

vations that aimed to simply make our lives easier or more efficient, science and the metaphysical were inseparable, if only by metaphor.

6. His copy is not marked. Other books, however, are or are referenced in his notes, including Ball on geology and Saleeby's *Cycle of Life*. As far as I can tell he read just one book in which he marked notes for "Farthest Distant": Irving, *How to Know the Starry Heavens*. Irving inscribed this volume for London on 10 December 1906. On the back flyleaf, London wrote "Farthest Distant" next to page 113, which discusses "stellar drift"; p. 176, which discusses solar eruptions and its effects on the Earth's atmosphere; and pp. 219-20 "for behavior of a comet in space."

7. See "Lowell Observatory: History," *Lowell Observatory*, lowell.edu/history/.

8. See Claire Evans, "The Canals of Mars," *ScienceBlog*, http://www.scienceblogs .com/universe/2012/09/28/the-canals-of-mars/.

9. Because some of the articles he collected are from 1911—I do not discuss those here—it is possible that he wrote and then typed up notes for the novel in that year and perhaps beyond. But I am assuming that his initial burst of creativity in 1906-7 led him to write up all his notes for the novel and that after he returned from the South Seas he turned once again to collecting data, but not reaching a point when he felt like adding to his narrative. I am also making an educated guess about the ordering of his notes and the grouping of them into first and second iterations. None of the pages are dated—though three are numbered consecutively—but my grouping is based on their content and the typed pages' relationship to handwritten notes on various notepads. For example, we can date the typed pages about telepathic speech as January or February 1907 because they were written on the music program. And by using the content of those notes I grouped other, similar yet undated notes to form what I am calling the second iteration. I admit that there is no evidence to say that this iteration came second. I am assuming that since he was collecting data in 1906, he was also writing notes, and those formed what I am calling the first iteration. Those handwritten notes are catalogued as "The Last Novel," and the typed version consists of the three consecutively numbered sheets; those handwritten notes, however, are simply titled "The Last Novel at [sic] All," meaning he only added "Farthest Distant" later and that these are almost beyond doubt the first iteration of his idea.

10. London, "Farthest Distant: [notes for science fiction novel]," JL 655-56, HEH.

11. London to Rogers, 16 Sept. 1915, *Letters*, 3:1502.

12. All quotations from London's notes for the novel come from his typescript: London, "Farthest Distant: [notes for science fiction novel]," JL 656, HEH. All his magazine and newspaper clippings, as well as his preliminary, handwritten note taking can be found in London, "Farthest Distant: [notes for science fiction novel]," JL 655, HEH. The typewritten version of those handwritten notes includes sentences he composed while typing.

13. Thoreau, *Maine Woods*, 45.

14. London, "Eternal Enemy: [notes for psychological study]," JL 642, HEH.

15. Arthur Symons, "On the Value of a Lie: The Intellectual Somersaults of Oscar Wilde," *Vanity Fair*, Nov. 1916, 49; in London, "Eternal Enemy: [notes for psycholog-

ical study]," JL 643, HEH. When London was writing notes for his "Christ novel," he instructed himself to reread Wilde's "Salome." Both "Salome" and the Bible provided appropriate patterns of speech for London's biblical characters. Wilde's influence on London was as deep as it is surprising.

16. London, "Pictures [. . .] from my own life: [autobiographical notes]," JL 1054, HEH. London typed up these handwritten notes while adding to them; see London, "Pictures [. . .] from my own life: [autobiographical notes]," JL 1055, HEH. See Prison Reform League, *Crime and Criminals* (Los Angeles: Prison Reform League Publishing Company, 1910). This book was copyrighted by the secretary and treasurer of the Prison Reform League, Griffith J. Griffith, and most likely written by him.

17. Smith to London, 27 Dec. 1905, JL 18574, HEH.

18. London, "A Tramp novel: [notes]," JL 1321, HEH. The typed version is London, "A tramp novel: [notes]," JL 1322, HEH.

19. London, "Tramping: [note for lecture]," JL 1324, HEH. The cataloguer's title is somewhat misleading. There are two note sheets in this folder: the one that I quote in its entirety and one that is labeled "Lectures—Tramping—Riding all night—underneath—man at window who in morning gave me two dollars [around fifty dollars today]." The kindnesses of strangers is a suitable topic to include in a lecture to strangers, but not for *The Road*. The typescript of the former can be found at London, "[The Road]: [Note for short story collection]," JL 1128, HEH.

20. Charmian London, 14 Dec. 1906, diary, JL 219, HEH.

21. London to the Editorial Department, *Cosmopolitan*, 17 Dec. 1906, *Letters*, 2:654. On Sunday, the sixteenth, Charmian wrote that she had typed nearly two thousand words of "Confession."

22. Charmian London, 31 Dec. 1906, diary, JL 219, HEH.

23. Charmian London, 1 Jan. 1907, diary, JL 220, HEH.

24. London to Brett, 16 Jan. 1907, *Letters*, 2:663. See *Cosmopolitan* to London, 11 Jan. 1907, JL 5195, HEH.

25. London to Brett, 7 Feb. 1907, *Letters*, 2:669.

26. Brett to London, 28 Jan. 1907, JL 3088, HEH.

27. Brett to London, 28 Feb. 1907, JL 3092, HEH.

28. London to Brett, 7 Mar. 1907, *Letters*, 2:675–76.

29. Brett to London, 17 June 1907, JL 3099, HEH.

30. London to Brett, 11 July 1907, *Letters*, 1:693.

31. Charmian London, 17 Dec. 1906, diary, JL 219, HEH.

32. See M. G. Wilson, "Northern California" and Reed, "Southern California Pictorialism," in *Pictorialism in California*, 1–22, 67–88.

33. Pasted on the back of one of the photographs and opposite the page describing London buying two beers in the incident of the barkeep telling him "You've got scabs on your nose," a postcard from "an ex-member of the United Brew Workers Union" tells London that the barkeep's puzzling invective simply meant that he was not selling to men who thought he was selling beer made by scabs. "Cheap breweries

were putting on the market a beer made by nonunion labor" at that time, the anonymous postcard writer explained.

34. London to Brett, 16 Jan. 1908, *Letters*, 2:728.

35. London to Wood, [early 1907 or late 1906], Jack London Scrapbooks, vol. 8, n.p., HEH, in clipping from unknown publication but probably *Appeal to Reason*.

36. The typescript is "Competition: [Speech delivered at the Ruskin Club dinner]," JL 547, HEH. The cataloguer's title comes from the title of the latter, which is actually accompanied by a question mark—"Competition (?)"—and not authoritative.

37. London, "Goliah: [notes for short story]," JL 711, HEH. London also began with a story idea that George Sterling gave him. Among all the other notes for the story, there are five sheets titled "Short Story Greek's idea." They inform the content of the second and third paragraphs of Goliah's first letter. Sterling told London about "two methods" (in London's words in the story) "whereby man may become the master of society." The first, as London's notes has it, "every man, or the majority, must reform before they can have a higher government. (2) Serfs of government are the majority. They do not make it but are made by it, etc." Then he wrote down Sterling's plot: "Socialism is failing benevolent feudalism is being established right now. the master mind comes along Controls radium, or some other terrific force. From his island summons 10 captains of industry to him—public summons. If do not come, on certain day they die. Amusement in papers, cartoons—etc. Then forgotten. On the appropriate day the ten die. Second summons—ten die. 3rd summons. They come in fleet (trouble to fleet). Then summons scientists. They go forth and do his bidding and slay the multitudinous drudges—the 'abysmal fecundity.' Compel humanity to be his slave in order to institute higher civilization. Splendid" (JL 711, HEH). Note that Sterling's idea is all about the amoral necessity of eliminating the masses that will never rise up or better themselves so that the rest of society can. It's a revenge story that London turned into a jeremiad.

38. It could also be a play on Goliath. The revelation that Goliah is actually a schlub named Percival then becomes a funny conflation of Goliath with David, with a political twist. David slays the giant named capitalism.

39. Originally, London likened the island to Midway or Fanning. See JL 711, HEH.

40. See JL 711, HEH.

41. London, "Goliah," *Revolution, and Other Essays*, 78.

42. See also London's notes for the story where he writes, "First letter contains; mastery of matter—time has come for food and shelter to be automatic." JL 711, HEH.

43. London, "Goliah: [notes for short story]," JL 711, HEH.

44. London, "Goliah: [notes for short story]," JL 711, HEH.

45. London to Bamford, 20 June 1906, *Letters*, 2:584.

46. London, "The Passing of Marcus O'Brien," *Lost Face, and Other Stories*, 163.

47. MacKay to Jack London, 29 Apr. 1907, JL 14354, HEH.

48. London, "The Unparalleled Invasion," *The Strength of the Strong*, 72.

49. London, "The Unparalleled Invasion: [notes for short story]," JL 1348, HEH.

50. London to Phillips, 25 Aug. 1909, *Letters*, 2:830.

51. Phillips to London, 15 [or 14] Sept. 1909, folder 12, box 5, USU.

52. London, "The Enemy of All the World," *The Strength of the Strong*, 101.

53. See London to Lloyd, 21 Jan. 1907, Jack London Scrapbooks, vol. 8, reel 5, HEH.

54. Weininger, *Sex and Character*, 258.

55. London to Bram Norsen, 10 Sept. 1914, *Letters*, 3:1368-69. See Hamilton, "'The Tools of My Trade,'" 284-85.

56. See Charmian London, 9 Mar. 1907, diary, JL 220, HEH. London devotes a full paragraph to Gluck's controversial suggestion made in that book that couples could start a "trial marriage" to see if a longer one would work. How quaint! But London's point is that for this seemingly sensible yet unconventional proposal Gluck was publicly humiliated, thus establishing his antagonistic relationship with the press and public.

57. London, "The Dream of Debs: [notes for short story]," JL 615, HEH.

58. London, "The Dream of Debs," *The Strength of the Strong*, 134.

59. London, "The Dream of Debs: [notes for short story]," JL 615, HEH.

60. London, "A Curious Fragment," *When God Laughs, and Other Stories*, 259.

61. Simon to London, 27 Aug. 1906, USU. Joan London emphasizes the displeasure many socialists felt, though they seem to have been split in their attitude. Oakland's *Socialist Voice* published a hail-and-farewell notice, saying "The Snark, flying the red flag, weighed anchor April 22. . . . To us Comrade London's departure is a source both of congratulation and regret," and noted his new venture into international socialism ("Goodbye, Jack, Goodbye!" *[Socialist Voice (Oakland)]*, 27 Apr. 1907). See Joan London, *Jack London and His Times*, 320-21.

62. See London, "Denied Admittance to U. S. Because He Loves Liberty," *Oakland Herald*, 29 Dec. 1906, 1, and Noel to London [31 Dec. 1906], Jack London Scrapbooks, vol. 8.

63. "Red Flag Floats from the Topmast of Jack London's Ketch, Snark," *San Francisco Examiner*, 23 Apr. 1907.

BIBLIOGRAPHY

ARCHIVAL COLLECTIONS

Anna Strunsky Walling Papers, Henry E. Huntington Library, San Marino, California

Corra Harris Collection, University of Georgia Library

Elwyn Hoffman Papers, Henry E. Huntington Library, San Marino, California

Ernest Untermann Papers, Wisconsin State Historical Society, Library Archives Division

F. Hayden Carruth Papers, New York Public Library

Franklin Walker Papers, Henry E. Huntington Library, San Marino, California

George N. Caylor Papers, Wisconsin State Historical Society, Library Archives Division

Harry Ransom Center, University of Texas-Austin

Henry E. Huntington Library, San Marino, California

Holman Collection, Jack London State Park, Sonoma, California

Intercollegiate Socialist Society Papers, Tamiment Library, New York University

Irving Stone Papers, Bancroft Library, University of California-Berkeley

Jack London Collection, Utah State University

Jack London Collection, Oakland (California) Public Library

Jack London Papers, Huntington Library, San Marino, California

Joan (London) Miller Papers, Huntington Library, San Marino CA

Macmillan and Company Collection, New York Public Library

Morris Hillquit Papers, Wisconsin State Historical Society, Library Archives Division

Tamiment Library, New York University

Theodore Roosevelt Papers, Library of Congress Manuscript Division

University of Georgia Library

William English Walling Papers, Wisconsin State Historical Society, Library Archives Division

PUBLISHED SOURCES

Adney, Tappan. *The Klondike Stampede of 1897–1898*. New York: Harper, 1900.

Allen, Grant. "The Backslider." *Twelve Tales with a Headpiece, a Tailpiece, and an Intermezzo*. London: Grant Richards, 1899.

Arthur, Anthony. *Upton Sinclair: Radical Innocent*. New York: Random House, 2006.

Auerbach, Jonathan. Introduction to *The Iron Heel*, by Jack London. Edited by Jonathan Auerbach. Penguin: Harmondsworth UK, 2006.

———. *Male Call: Becoming Jack London*. Durham NC: Duke University Press, 1996.

Bamford, Georgia Loring. *The Mystery of Jack London*. Oakland CA: Georgia Loring Bamford, 1931.

Barry, Richard Hayes. *Port Arthur: A Monster Heroism*. New York: Moffat, Yard, 1905.

Baskett, Sam S. "A Source of *The Iron Heel*." *American Literature* 27 (May 1955).

Bennion, Sherilyn Cox. *Equal to the Occasion: Women Editors of the Nineteenth-Century West*. Reno: University of Nevada Press, 1990.

Bercovitch, Sacvan. *The American Jeremiad*. Madison: University of Wisconsin Press, 2012. First published 1978.

Berwick, Arnold. *The Abraham Lincoln of the Sea: The Life of Andrew Furuseth*. Santa Cruz CA: Odin Press, 1993.

Bierce, Ambrose. *The Critical Reception of Jack London*. Edited by Susan Nuernberg. Westport CT: Greenwood Press, 1995.

———. *The Cynic's Word Book*. New York: Doubleday, Page, 1906.

Bilgrami, Akeel. "What Is a Muslim? Fundamental Commitment and Cultural Identity," *Critical Inquiry* 18 (Summer 1992).

Binet, Alfred. *On Double Consciousness: Experimental Psychological Studies*. Translated by the publisher, 1889. Chicago: Open Court, 1905.

———. *The Psychic Life of Micro-organisms*. Translated by the publisher, 1888. Chicago: Open Court, 1903.

———. *The Psychology of Reasoning Based on Experimental Researches in Hypnotism*. Translated by Adam Gowans White. Chicago: Open Court, 1899.

Bishop, Isabella Lucy (Bird). *Korea and Her Neighbors: A Narrative of Travel, with an Account of the Recent Vicissitudes and Present Position of the Country*. New York: Fleming H. Revell, 1898.

Bode, Carl. *The American Lyceum: Town Meeting of the Mind*. Oxford: Oxford University Press, 1956.

Bölsche, Wilhelm. *The Evolution of Man*. Translated by Ernest Untermann. Chicago: Charles H. Kerr, 1905.

Boris, Eileen. *Art and Labor: Ruskin, Morris, and the Craftsman Ideal in America*. Philadelphia: Temple University Press, 1986.

Boylan, James. *Revolutionary Lives: Anna Strunsky and William English Walling*. Amherst: University of Massachusetts Press, 1998.

Bretschneider, Emil. *Map of China and the Surrounding Regions*. Shanghai: Kelly and Walsh, 1900.

Bridgwater, Patrick. *Nietzsche in Anglosaxony: A Study of Nietzsche's Impact on English and American Literature*. Leicester UK: Leicester University Press, 1972.

Brooks, John Graham. *The Social Unrest: Studies in Labor and Socialist Movements*. New York: Macmillan, 1903.

Buchanan, Joseph R. *The Story of a Labor Agitator*. New York: Outlook, 1903.

Carpenter, G. R. "A Reader's Report for *The Call of the Wild*." *Jack London Journal* 1 (1994): 231–32.

Casson, Herbert N. *Organized Self-Help: A History and Defense of the American Labor Movement*. New York: Peter Eckler, 1901.

Chamberlain, Basil Hall. *A Handbook for Travellers in Japan Including the Whole Empire from Yezo to Formosa*. London: John Murray, 1901.

Churchill, Frederick B. *August Weismann: Development, Heredity, and Evolution*. Cambridge MA: Harvard University Press, 2015.

Coleridge, Samuel Taylor. *Biographia Literaria*. Vol. 7 of *The Collected Works of Samuel Taylor Coleridge*, edited by James Engell and Walter Jackson Bate. Princeton NJ: Princeton University Press, 1983.

Connolly, James J. "The Public Good and the Problem of Pluralism in Lincoln Steffens's Civic Imagination." *Journal of the Gilded Age and Progressive Era* 4 (Apr. 2005).

Conrad, Joseph. *Youth: A Narrative and Two Other Stories*. Edinburgh: William Blackwood and Sons, 1902.

Coodley, Lauren. *Upton Sinclair: California Socialist, Celebrity Intellectual*. Lincoln: University of Nebraska Press, 2013.

Curl, John. *For All the People: Uncovering the Hidden History of Cooperation, Cooperative Movements, and Communalism*. Oakland CA: PN Press, 2009.

Darrow, Clarence. *In the Clutches of the Law: Clarence Darrow's Letters*, edited by Randall Tietjen. Berkeley: University of California Press, 2013.

Darwin, Charles. *The Descent of Man*. In *Darwin*, edited by Philip Appleman. New York: W. W. Norton, 1970.

Davidson, Arnold I. "The Horror of Monsters." In *The Boundaries of Humanity: Humans, Animals, Machines*, edited by James J. Sheehan and Morton Sosna. Berkeley: University of California Press, 1991.

Debs, Eugene. *Letters of Eugene V. Debs*, edited by J. Robert Constantine. 3 vols. Urbana: University of Illinois Press, 1990.

de Cordova, Richard. *Picture Personalities: The Emergence of the Star System in America*. Urbana: University of Illinois Press, 1990.

Del Mar, Walter. *Around the World through Japan*. New York: Macmillan, 1902.

"A Departure in Church Building—The Second New Jerusalem Church in California: By a Stranger." In *The Craftsman: An Anthology*. Edited by Barry Sanders. Santa Barbara CA: Peregrine Smith, 1978.

Derrida, Jacques. "Freud and the Scene of Writing." In *Writing and Difference*. Translated by Alan Bass. Chicago: University of Chicago Press, 1978.

Doctorow, E. L. Introduction *The Call of the Wild*, by Jack London. New York: Random House, 1998.

Dyer, Daniel, ed. *The Call of the Wild by Jack London, with an Illustrated Reader's Companion*. Norman: University of Oklahoma Press, 1995.

Easley, Ralph M. "The Origin of 'The Intercollegiate Socialist Society' Disclosed: Its Defense by Thomas Wentworth Higginson, in 'Harper's Weekly' Analyzed and Refuted." *National Civic Federation Review* 2 (July–Aug. 1905).

———. "Socialists Seek to Inflame the Mind of American Youth." *National Civic Federation Review* 2 (June 1905).

Ellenberger, Henri F. *The Discovery of the Unconscious: The History and Evolution of Dynamic Psychiatry*. New York: Basic Books, 1970.

Fahs, Alice. *Out on Assignment: Newspaper Women and the Making of Modern Public Space*. Chapel Hill: University of North Carolina Press, 2011.

Ferri, Enrico. *Criminal Sociology*. New York: D. Appleton, 1898.

Fischer, Victor, and Lin Salamo. Introduction to *Adventures of Huckleberry Finn*, by Mark Twain. Edited by Victor Fischer, Lin Salamo, and Walter Blair. Berkeley: University of California Press, 2003.

Foner, Philip, ed. *Jack London: American Rebel*. New York: Citadel Press, 1947.

Foster, John. *American Diplomacy in the Orient*. Boston: Houghton Mifflin, 1903.

Francis, Mark. *Herbert Spencer and the Invention of Modern Life*. Ithaca NY: Cornell University Press, 2007.

Frankfurt, Harry G. *On Bullshit*. Princeton NJ: Princeton University Press, 2005.

Frémont. John Charles. *Memoirs of My Life: Including in the Narrative Five Journeys of Western Exploration*. Chicago: Belford, Clarke, 1887.

Fried, Michael. *Courbet's Realism*. Chicago: University of Chicago Press, 1990.

Gair, Christopher. *Complicity and Resistance in Jack London's Novels: From Naturalism to Nature*. Lewiston NY: Edwin Mellen, 1997.

Garnett, Porter. *The Bohemian Jinks: A Treatise*. San Francisco: Bohemian Club, 1908.

Gatti, Susan. "Stone Hearths and Marble Babies: Jack London and the Domestic Ideal." *Jack London Journal* 3 (1996): 43–56.

Genthe, Arnold. *As I Remember*. New York: Reynal and Hitchcock, 1936.

George, Henry Jr. *The Menace of Privilege: A Study of the Dangers to the Republic from the Existence of a Favored Class*. New York: Macmillan, 1905.

Ghent, W. J. *Mass and Class: A Survey of Social Divisions*. New York: Macmillan, 1904.

———. *Our Benevolent Feudalism*. New York: Macmillan, 1902.

Gifford, Daniel L. *Every-Day Life in Korea*. Chicago: Fleming H. Revell, 1898.

Graff, Gerald. *Professing Literature: An Institutional History*. Chicago: University of Chicago Press, 1987.

Graham, Loren R. *Between Science and Values*. New York: Columbia University Press, 1981.

Greener, William Oliver. *Greater Russia: The Continental Empire of the Old World*. New York: Macmillan, 1903.

Greenstein, Paul, Nigey Lennon, and Lionel Rolfe. *Bread and Hyacinths: The Rise and Fall of Utopian Los Angeles*. Los Angeles: California Classics Books, 1992.

Griffis, William Elliot. *Corea: The Hermit Nation*. New York: Charles Scribner's Sons, 1902.

Griscom, Lloyd C. *Diplomatically Speaking*. London: John Murray, 1941.

Gronlund, Laurence. *The Co-Operative Commonwealth: An Exposition of Modern Socialism*. London: Modern Press, 1885.

Gunning, Tom. "The Cinema of Attractions: Early Film, Its Spectator, and the Avant-Garde." In *Early Cinema: Space, Frame, Narrative*, edited by Thomas Elsaesser and Adam Barket. London: BFI Publishing, 1990.

Hackett, Alice Payne, and James Henry Burke. *Eighty Years of Best Sellers, 1895–1975*. New York: R. R. Bowker, 1977.

Hagerty, Donald J. *The Life of Maynard Dixon*. Layton UT: Gibbs Publishing, 2010.

Hale, Edward Everett. *James Russell Lowell and His Friends*. New York: AMS Press, 1965. First published 1899.

Haller, Mark H. *Eugenics: Hereditarian Attitudes in American Thought*. New Brunswick NJ: Rutgers University Press, 1984.

Hamilton, David Mike. *"The Tools of My Trade": The Annotated Books in Jack London's Library*. Seattle: University of Washington Press, 1986.

Harris, Corra. *My Book and Heart*. Boston: Houghton Mifflin, 1924.

Harris, Leon A. *Upton Sinclair: American Rebel*. New York: Thomas Y. Crowell, 1975.

Haughey, Homer L., and Connie Kale Johnson. *Jack London Homes Album*. Stockton CA: Heritage Publishing, 1987.

Hay, John. "Jack London's Sci-Fi Finale." In *The Oxford Handbook of Jack London*, edited by Jay Williams. Oxford: Oxford University Press, 2017.

Hayden, Tom. *The Port Huron Statement: The Visionary Call of the 1960s Revolution*. New York: Avalon, 2005.

Hearst, William Randolph. "Seven Rules." In *Newsmen Speak: Journalists on Their Craft*, edited by Edmond D. Coblentz. Freeport NY: Books for Libraries Press, 1954.

Hensley, Dennis E. "Jack London's Use of Maritime History in *The Sea-Wolf*." *Pacific Historian* 23 (Summer 1979).

Herny, Ed, Shelley Rideout, and Katie Wadell. *Berkeley Bohemia: Artists and Visionaries of the Early Twentieth Century*. Salt Lake City: Gibbs Smith, 2008.

Heuffer, Oliver Madox. "Jack London: A Personal Sketch." *Living Age* 292 (Jan.–Mar. 1917).

Hillquit, Morris. *Loose Leaves from a Busy Life*. New York: Macmillan, 1934.

Hillquit, Morris, and Ralph M. Easley. *Socialism and the National Civic Federation*. New York: n.p., 1911.

Hine, Robert V. *California's Utopian Colonies*. San Marino CA: Huntington Library Press, 1953.

Hodge, John W. *Corean Words and Phrases: Being a Handbook and Pocket Dictionary for Visitors to Corea and New Arrivals in the Country*. Seoul: Seoul Press, 1902.

Horn, Max. *The Intercollegiate Socialist Society, 1905–1921: Origins of the Modern American Student Movement*. Boulder CO: Westview Press, 1979.

Horwitz, Howard. "'See Things in New Ways': Jack London, Socialism, and the Conversionary Model of Politics." In *The Oxford Handbook of Jack London*, edited by Jay Williams. Oxford: Oxford University Press, 2017.

Howells, William Dean. *A Traveler from Altruria*. New York: Harper, 1894.

Hudson, Tomson. *The Law of Psychic Phenomenon: A Working Study of Hypnotism, Spiritism, Mental Therapeutics, Etc*. Chicago: A. C. McClurg, 1902.

Hulbert, Homer. *The Passing of Korea*. New York: Doubleday, Page, 1909.

Hunter, Robert. *Poverty: Social Conscience in the Progressive Era*. New York: Macmillan, 1904.

Irving, Edward. *How to Know the Starry Heavens*. New York: Frederick A. Stokes, 1904.

James, Elizabeth. "Letters from America: The Bretts and the Macmillan Company of New York." In *Macmillan: A Publishing Tradition*, edited by Elizabeth James. Basingstoke, Hampshire UK: Palgrave Macmillan UK, 2002.

James, William. *The Correspondence of William James*. Edited by Ignas K. Skrupskelis, Elizabeth M. Berkeley, and Wilma Bradbeer. Charlottesville: University of Virginia Press, 2001.

———. *The Varieties of Religious Experience*. New York: Collier Books, 1969.

Jeffrey, Clarence Ray. "The Historical Development of Criminology." In *Pioneers in Criminology*, edited by Hermann Mannheim. Chicago: Quadrangle Books, 1960.

John, Arthur. *The Best Years of the "Century": Richard Watson Gilder, "Scribner's Monthly," and "Century Magazine," 1870–1909*. Urbana: University of Illinois Press, 1981.

Johns, Cloudesley. "Who the Hell *Is* Cloudesley Johns?" Edited by Jay Williams. *Jack London Journal* 1–6 (1994–99).

Johnson, Donald Leslie. *Frank Lloyd Wright versus America: The 1930s*. Cambridge MA: MIT Press, 1990.

Johnson, Kirk, and Ray Troll. *Cruisin' the Fossil Freeway: An Epoch Tale of a Scientist and an Artist on the Ultimate 5,000-mile Paleo Road Trip*. Golden CO: Fulcrum, 2007.

Johnson, Paul C., ed. *The Early "Sunset Magazine," 1898–1928*. San Francisco: California Historical Society, 1973.

Jordan, David Starr. *Foot-notes to Evolution: A Series of Popular Addresses on the Evolution of Life*. New York: D. Appleton, 1898.

Karnoutsos, Carmela Ascolese. "Harry W. Laidler and the Intercollegiate Socialist Society." PhD diss., New York University, 1974.

Kingman, Russ. *Jack London: A Definitive Chronology*. Middletown CA: David Rejl, 1992.

Kipnis, Ira. *The American Socialist Movement, 1897–1912*. New York: Greenwood Press, 1968.

Klein, Charles, and Arthur Hornblow. *The Lion and the Mouse: A Story of American Life*. New York: G. W. Dillingham, 1906.

Kowner, Rotem. "Becoming an Honorary Civilized Nation: Remaking Japan's Military Image During the Russo-Japanese War, 1904–1905." *Historian* 64 (2007).

———. *Historical Dictionary of the Russo-Japanese War*. Lanham MD: Scarecrow, 2006.

Krausse, Alexis. *The Far East: Its History and Its Question*. London: Grant Richards, 1903.

Kuehl, Warren F. *Hamilton Holt: Journalist, Internationalist, Educator*. Gainesville: University of Florida Press, 1960.

Kurzman, Dan. *Disaster! The Great San Francisco Earthquake and Fire of 1906*. New York: William Morrow, 2001.

Lambourne, Lionel. *Utopian Craftsmen: The Arts and Crafts Movement from the Cotswolds to Chicago*. Salt Lake City: Peregrine Smith, 1980.

Landers, James. *The Improbable First Century of "Cosmopolitan Magazine."* Columbia: University of Missouri Press, 2010.

Laplanche, Jean, and J.-B. Pontalis. *The Language of Pyscho-Analysis*. Translated by Donald Nicholson-Smith. New York: W. W. Norton, 1974.

Liebknecht, Wilhelm. *Karl Marx: Biographical Memoirs*. Translated by Ernest Untermann. Chicago: Charles H. Kerr, 1901.

"Literature: A Nietzsche Novel." In *The Critical Response to Jack London*, edited by Susan Nuernberg. Westport CT: Greenwood, 1995.

London, Charmian K. *The Book of Jack London*. 2 vols. New York: Century, 1922.

———. *Jack London and Hawaii*. London: Mills and Boon, 1918.

London, Jack. "The Apostate." In *When God Laughs, and Other Stories*. New York: Macmillan, 1911.

———. "Bâtard." In *The Complete Short Stories of Jack London*, edited by Earle Labor, Robert C. Leitz, and I. Milo Shepard. Redwood City CA: Stanford University Press, 1993.

———. *Before Adam*. New York: Macmillan, 1908.

———. "The Boy Socialist." In *The San Francisco Chronicle Reader*, edited by William Hogan and William German. New York: McGraw-Hill, 1962.

———. "Brown Wolf." In *Lost Face, and Other Stories*. New York: Macmillan, 1910.

———. *The Call of the Wild*. New York: Macmillan, 1903.

———. "A Camera and a Journey." In *In Many Wars, by Many War Correspondents*, edited by George Lynch and Frederick Palmer. Baton Rouge: Louisiana State University Press, 2010.

———. "The Class Struggle." In *War of the Classes*. New York: Macmillan, 1905.

———. "A Classic of the Sea." In *The Human Drift*. New York: Macmillan, 1917.

———. *The Complete Short Stories of Jack London*. Edited by Earle Labor, Robert C. Leitz, and I. Milo Shepard. 3 vols. Redwood City CA: Stanford University Press, 1993.

———. "A Curious Fragment." In *When God Laughs, and Other Stories*. New York: Macmillan, 1911.

———. "A Day's Lodging." In *Love of Life, and Other Stories*. New York: Macmillan, 1907.

———. "The Dream of Debs." In *The Strength of the Strong*. New York: Macmillan, 1914.

———. "The Enemy of All the World." In *The Strength of the Strong*. New York: Macmillan, 1914.

———. "Explanation of the Great Socialist Vote of 1904." In *Jack London: American Rebel*, edited by Philip Foner. New York: Citadel Press, 1947.

———. "The House Beautiful." In *Revolution, and Other Essays*. New York: Macmillan, 1910.

———. "How I Became a Socialist." In *War of the Classes*. New York: Macmillan, 1905.

———. "How Jack London Got in and out of Jail in Japan." In *Jack London Reports: War Correspondence, Sports Articles, and Miscellaneous Writings*, edited by King Hendricks and Irving Shepard. New York: Doubleday, 1970.

———. "Husky—Wolf Dog of the North." In *Jack London: The Unpublished and Uncollected Articles and Essays*, edited by Daniel Wichlan. 3rd ed. Virginia Beach VA: Createspace Publishing, 2018.

———. *The Iron Heel*. New York: Macmillan, 1908.

———. *Jack London on the Road*. Edited by Richard Etulain. Logan: Utah University Press, 1979.

———. *Jack London: The Unpublished and Uncollected Articles and Essays*. Edited by Daniel Wichlan. 3rd ed. Virginia Beach VA: Createspace Publishing, 2018.

———. *John Barleycorn*. New York: Century, 1913.

———. "The Jungle." In *The Social Writings of Jack London*, edited and with an introduction by Philip S. Foner. Seacaucus NJ: Citadel, 1964.

———. "Just Meat." In *When God Laughs, and Other Stories*. New York: Macmillan, 1911.

———. "The League of the Old Men." In *The Complete Short Stories of Jack London*, edited by Earle Labor, Robert C. Leitz, and I. Milo Shepard. 3 vols. Redwood City CA: Stanford University Press, 1993.

———. "The Leopard Man's Story." In *The Complete Short Stories of Jack London*, edited by Earle Labor, Robert C. Leitz, and I. Milo Shepard. 3 vols. Redwood City CA: Stanford University Press, 1993.

———. *The Letters of Jack London*. Edited by Earle Labor, Robert C. Leitz, and I. Milo Shepard. 3 vols. Redwood City CA: Stanford University Press, 1998.

———. *Love of Life, and Other Stories*. New York: Macmillan, 1907.

———. "Negore, the Coward." In *The Complete Short Stories of Jack London*, edited by Earle Labor, Robert C. Leitz, and I. Milo Shepard. 3 vols. Redwood City CA: Stanford University Press, 1993.

———. *No Mentor but Myself: Jack London on Writers and Writing.* Edited by Dale L. Walker and Jeanne Campbell Reesman. Stanford CA: Stanford University Press, 1999.

———. "A Northland Miracle." In *The Complete Short Stories of Jack London,* edited by Earle Labor, Robert C. Leitz, and I. Milo Shepard. 3 vols. Redwood City CA: Stanford University Press, 1993.

———. "The Passing of Marcus O'Brien." In *Lost Face, and Other Stories.* New York: Macmillan, 1910.

———. *The People of the Abyss.* New York: Macmillan, 1903.

———. *The Portable Jack London.* Edited by Earle Labor. Harmondsworth UK: Penguin, 1994.

———. "The Question of the Maximum." In *War of the Classes.* New York: Macmillan, 1905.

———. "A Review." In *War of the Classes.* New York: Macmillan, 1905.

———. "Revolution." In *Revolution, and Other Essays.* New York: Macmillan, 1910.

———. "The Road." In *Jack London Reports: War Correspondence, Sports Articles, and Miscellaneous Writings,* edited by King Hendricks and Irving Shepard. New York: Doubleday, 1970.

———. *The Road.* New York: Macmillan, 1907.

———. "The Scab." In *War of the Classes.* New York: Macmillan, 1905.

———. *The Scorn of Women.* New York: Macmillan, 1906.

———. *The Sea-Wolf.* New York: Macmillan, 1904.

———. *The Sea-Wolf.* Edited by John Sutherland. Oxford: Oxford University Press, 1992.

———. "The Somnambulists." In *Revolution, and Other Essays.* New York: Macmillan, 1910.

———. "Too Much Gold." In *The Faith of Men, and Other Stories.* New York: Macmillan, 1904.

———. "The Tramp." In *Jack London on the Road,* edited by Richard Etulain. Logan: Utah University Press, 1979.

———. "Travel in Korea." In *Jack London Reports: War Correspondence, Sports Articles, and Miscellaneous Writings,* edited by King Hendricks and Irving Shepard. New York: Doubleday, 1970.

———. "The Unparalleled Invasion." In *The Strength of the Strong.* New York: Macmillan, 1914.

———. *War of the Classes.* New York: Macmillan, 1905.

———. "What Life Means to Me." *Cosmopolitan Magazine* 40 (Mar. 1906).

———. "When God Laughs." In *Love of Life, and Other Stories.* New York: Macmillan, 1907.

———. "Where the Trail Forks." In *The Complete Short Stories of Jack London,* edited by Earle Labor, Robert C. Leitz, and I. Milo Shepard. Redwood City CA: Stanford University Press, 1993.

———. "A Wicked Woman." In *When God Laughs, and Other Stories.* New York: Macmillan, 1911.

———. "The Wit of Porportuk." In *Lost Face, and Other Stories*. New York: Macmillan, 1910.

London, Jack, and Anna Strunsky. *The Kempton-Wace Letters*. New York: Macmillan, 1903.

London, Joan. *Jack London and His Times: An Unconventional Biography*. New York: Doubleday, Doran, 1939.

Longstreth, Richard. *On the Edge of the World: Four Architects in San Francisco at the Turn of the Century*. Berkeley: University of California Press, 1998.

Lorimer, George Horace. *Letters from a Self-Made Merchant to His Son*. Boston: Small, Maynard, 1902.

Lowes, John Livingston. *The Road to Xanadu: A Study in the Ways of the Imagination*. Boston: Houghton Mifflin, 1927.

Lukas, J. Anthony. *Big Trouble: A Murder in a Small Western Town Sets off a Struggle for the Soul of America*. New York: Simon and Schuster, 1997.

Lydston, G. Frank. *The Diseases of Society: The Vice and Crime Problem*. Philadelphia: J. B. Lippincott, 1905.

Martin, Justin. *Rebel Souls: Walt Whitman and America's First Bohemians*. Boston: Da Capo, 2014.

Martinek, Jason. *Socialism and Print Culture in America, 1897–1920*. London: Pickering and Chatto, 2012.

Mazzeo, Joseph A. Introduction to *Essays upon Heredity and Kindred Biological Problems*, by August Weismann. Translated by Arthur E. Shipley et al. Oxford: Clarendon Press, 1977. First published 1889.

McCarthy, Justin. *History of Our Own Times*. 7 vols. London: Chatto and Windus, 1881–1905.

McDevitt, William. *Jack London as Poet and as Platform Man*. San Francisco: Recorder-Sunset Press, 1947.

McKenzie, Frederick A. *From Tokyo to Tiflis: Uncensored Letters from the War*. London: Hurst and Blackett, 1905.

McPherson, James M. *Battle Cry of Freedom: The Civil War Era*. Oxford UK: Oxford University Press, 1988.

Meynell, Alice. "The Spirit of Place." In *The Spirit of Place, and Other Essays*. London: John Lane, 1899.

Micheaux, Oscar. *The Wind from Nowhere*. New York: Book Supply Co., 1941.

Millard, Bailey. *History of the San Francisco Bay Region*. 3 vols. Chicago: American Historical Society, 1924.

Miller, Joaquin. *Building the City Beautiful*. Chicago: Stone and Kimball, 1893.

Milner, Michael. "'The Feels': Jack London and the New Mass Cultural Public Sphere." In *The Oxford Handbook of Jack London*, edited by Jay Williams. Oxford: Oxford University Press, 2017.

Moore, J. Howard. *The Universal Kinship*. Chicago: Charles H. Kerr, 1906.

Morgan, Charles. *The House of Macmillan (1843–1943)*. London: Macmillan, 1944.

Morris, Charles. *The San Francisco Calamity by Earthquake and Fire.* Urbana: University of Illinois Press, 2002. First published 1906.

Morris, Gouverneur. *The Pagan's Progress.* New York: A. S. Barnes, 1904.

Mosby, Thomas Speed. *Causes and Cures of Crimes.* St. Louis: C. V. Mosby, 1913.

Mott, Frank Luther. *Golden Multitudes: The Story of Best Sellers in the United States.* New York: Macmillan, 1947.

———. *A History of American Magazines.* 5 vols. Cambridge MA: Harvard University Press, 1957.

The New Testament of Our Lord Saviour Jesus Christ. Arranged in the Order in Which Its Parts Came to Those in the First Century Who Believed in Our Lord. Edited by Ernest Rhys. Chronological arrangement by Thomas N. Lindsay, Everyman's Library. London: J. M. Dent, 1906.

Nietzsche, Friedrich. *A Genealogy of Morals.* Vol. 10 of *The Works of Friedrich Nietzsche.* Translated by William A. Hauseman. Edited by Alexander Tille. New York: Macmillan, 1896.

———. *Nietzsche contra Wagner.* Vol. 11 of *The Works of Friedrich Nietzsche.* Translated by Thomas Common. Edited by Alexander Tille. New York: Macmillan, 1896.

Nitobe, Inazo. *Bushido, the Soul of Japan: An Exposition of Japanese Thought.* Tokyo: Shokwabo, 1899.

Nitsche, Paul, and Karl Wilmanns. "The History of the Prison Psychoses." Translated by Francis Barnes. *Nervous and Mental Disease Monograph Series,* no. 13. New York: Journal of Nervous and Mental Disease Publishing Co., 1912.

Niven, Penelope. *Carl Sandburg: A Biography.* New York: Charles Scribner's Sons, 1991.

Nuernberg, Susan, ed. *The Critical Response to Jack London.* Critical Responses in Arts and Letters, issue 19. Westport CT: Greenwood, 1995.

"O." *The Yellow War.* New York: McClure, Phillips, 1905.

O'Connor, Richard. *Jack London: A Biography.* Boston: Little, Brown, 1964.

O'Connor, Shaun. "On the Road to Utopia: The Social History and Spirituality of Altruria, an Intentional Religious Community in Sonoma County California, 1894–1896." PhD diss., Graduate Theological Seminary, Berkeley CA, 2000.

Otis, Laura. *Organic Memory: History and the Body in the Late Nineteenth and Early Twentieth Centuries.* Lincoln: University of Nebraska Press, 1994.

Palmer, Frederick. *With Kuroki in Manchuria.* New York: Charles Scribner's Sons, 1904.

———. *With Mine Own Eyes: A Personal Story of Battle Years.* New York: Bobbs-Merrill, 1933.

Payne, William Morton. "Recent Fiction: *The Sea-Wolf.*" In *The Critical Response to Jack London,* edited by Susan Nuernberg. Westport CT: Greenwood, 1995.

Pearson, Richard. "Primitive Modernity: H. G. Wells and the Prehistoric Man of the 1890s." *Yearbook of English Studies* 37, no. 1 (2007).

Pfeifer, Edward J. "United States." In *The Comparative Reception of Darwinism*, edited by Thomas F. Glick. Chicago: University of Chicago Press, 1988.

Pittenger, Mark. *American Socialists and Evolutionary Thought, 1879–1920*. Madison: University of Wisconsin Press, 1993.

Poe, Edgar Allan. *Letters of Poe and His Friends*. Vol. 17 of *The Complete Works of Edgar Allan Poe*. Edited by James Harrison. New York: Society of English and French literature, 1902.

Proctor, Ben. *William Randolph Hearst: The Early Years, 1863–1910*. Oxford: University of Oxford Press, 1998.

Quirk, Leslie W. "Interviews with Editors: James Randolph Walker, of the *Cosmopolitan* and *Twentieth-Century Home*." *Editor* 20 (Dec. 1904).

Rattner-Rosenhagen, Jennifer. *American Nietzsche: A History of an Icon and His Ideas*. Chicago: University of Chicago Press, 2012.

Rauschenbusch, Walter. *Christianity and the Social Crisis*. New York: Macmillan, 1907.

Reade, Winwood. *The Martyrdom of Man*. New York: Peter Eckler, 1872.

Reed, Dennis. "Southern California Pictorialism: Its Modern Aspects." In *Pictorialism in California: Photographs, 1900–1940*, edited by Michael G. Wilson and Dennis J. Reed. Malibu and San Marino CA: J. Paul Getty Museum and Henry E. Huntington Library and Art Gallery, 1994.

Renan, Ernst. *Life of Jesus*. Edited by Joseph Henry Allen. Boston: Little, Brown, 1903.

Reynolds, Robert Dwight Jr. "The Millionaire Socialists: J. G. Phelps Stokes and His Circle of Friends." PhD diss., University of South Carolina, 1974.

Richards, Robert J. *Darwin and the Emergence of Evolutionary Theories of Mind and Behavior*. Chicago: University of Chicago Press, 1987.

———. *The Tragic Sense of Life: Ernst Haeckel and the Struggle over Evolutionary Thought*. Chicago: University of Chicago Press, 2008.

Richardson, Peter. *No Simple Highway: A Cultural History of the Grateful Dead*. New York: St. Martin's Griffin, 2015.

Ross, Jack. *The Socialist Party of America: A Complete History*. Lincoln: University of Nebraska Press, 2015.

Rudd, Mark. *My Life with SDS and the Weathermen*. New York: William Morrow, 2009.

Ruff, Allen. *"We Called Each Other Comrade": Charles H. Kerr and Company, Radical Publishers*. Urbana: University of Illinois Press, 1997.

"Russia's Answer to Japan's Final Note Is a Refusal: Both Nations Contract for War Supplies in America." *San Francisco Call*, 29 Dec. 1903.

Said, Edward W. *Beginnings: Intention and Method*. New York: Basic Books, 1976.

Saleeby, C. W. *Evolution: The Master-Key: A Discussion of the Principle of Evolution as Illustrated in Atoms, Stars, Organic Species, Mind, Society and Morals*. London: Harper, 1906.

Sanders, Barry, ed. *The Craftsman: An Anthology*. Santa Barbara CA: Peregrine Smith, 1978.

Satter, Beryl. *Each Mind a Kingdom: American Women, Sexual Purity, and the New Thought Movement, 1875–1920*. Berkeley: University of California Press, 1999.

Scott, Donald M. "The Popular Lecture and the Creation of a Public in Mid-Nineteenth-Century America." *Journal of American History* 66 (Mar. 1980).

Scott, Leroy. *The Walking Delegate*. New York: Doubleday, Page, 1905.

Seligman, Edwin. *The Economic Interpretation of History*. New York: Columbia University Press, 1902.

Shaw, George Bernard. *Man and Superman*. New York: Brentano's, 1904.

———. *The Revolutionist's Handbook*. In *Man and Superman*. New York: Brentano's, 1904.

Shore, Elliott. *Talkin' Socialism: J. A. Wayland and the Role of the Press in American Radicalism, 1890–1912*. Lawrence: University Press of Kansas, 1988.

Shulman, Robert. *The Power of Political Art: The 1930s Literary Left*. Chapel Hill: University of North Carolina Press, 2000.

Silver, Arnold. *Bernard Shaw: The Darker Side*. Stanford CA: Stanford University Press, 1982.

Sinclair, Upton. *American Outpost: A Book of Reminiscences*. New York: Farrar and Rinehart, 1932.

———. *The Autobiography of Upton Sinclair*. New York: Harcourt, Brace, and World, 1962.

———. *The Brass Check: A Study in American Journalism*. New York: A. and C. Boni, 1936.

———. *The Jungle*. New York: The Jungle Publishing Company, 1906.

Sisson, James E., III, and Robert W. Martens. *Jack London First Editions: A Chronological Reference Guide*. Oakland CA: Star Rover House, 1979.

Skrine, Francis Henry Bennett. *The Expansion of Russia: 1815–1900*. Cambridge UK: Cambridge University Press, 1903.

Smith, Arthur. *China in Convulsion*. 2 vols. New York: Fleming H. Revell, 1901.

Sonnichsen, Albert. *Deep Sea Vagabonds*. New York: McClure, Phillips, 1903.

Spargo, John. *The Bitter Cry of Children*. New York: Macmillan, 1906.

———. *Socialism: A Summary and Interpretation of Socialist Principles*. New York: Macmillan, 1906.

Spencer, Herbert. *First Principles*. 4th ed. New York: D. Appleton, 1898.

———. *Principles of Biology*. 2 vols. London: Williams and Norgate, 1864.

———. *The Principles of Psychology*. 2 vols. London: Williams and Norgate, 1870.

Stasz, Clarice. *American Dreamers: Charmian and Jack London*. New York: St. Martin's Press, 1988.

———. "Family, Friends, Mentors." In *The Oxford Handbook of Jack London*, edited by Jay Williams. Oxford: Oxford University Press, 2016.

———. *Jack London's Women*. Amherst: University of Massachusetts Press, 2001.

Steffens, Lincoln. *The Shame of the Cities*. New York: McClure, Phillips, 1904.

Stevenson, Robert Louis. "A Note on Realism." In *R. L. Stevenson on Fiction: An Anthology of Literary and Critical Essays*, edited by Glenda Norquay. Edinburgh: Edinburgh University Press, 1999.

Stocking, George W. Jr. *Victorian Anthropology*. New York: Free Press, 1987.

Stone, Irving. *Sailor on Horseback: The Biography of Jack London*. Cambridge MA: Houghton Mifflin, 1938.

Tebbel, John. *George Horace Lorimer and "The Saturday Evening Post."* Garden City NY: Doubleday, 1948.

Thomas, George. *William L. Price: Arts and Crafts to Modern Design*. New York: Princeton Architectural Press, 2000.

Thoreau, Henry David. *The Maine Woods*. Edited by Joseph J. Moldenhauer. Princeton NJ: Princeton University Press, 1972.

———. *Walden*. Edited by William L. Howarth. Princeton NJ: Princeton University Press, 1971.

Tichi, Cecilia. *Jack London: A Writer's Fight for a Better America*. Chapel Hill: University of North Carolina Press, 2015.

Tille, Alexander. Introduction to *Thus Spake Zarasthustra: A Book for All and None*, by Friedrich Nietzsche. Translated by Alexander Tille. New York: Macmillan, 1896.

Tooker, L. Frank. *The Joys and Tribulations of an Editor*. New York: Century, 1924.

Trachtenberg, Alan. *The Incorporation of America: Culture and Society in the Gilded Age*. New York: Hill and Wang, 1982.

Triggs, Oscar Lovell. *Chapters in the History of the Arts and Crafts Movement*. Chicago: Bohemia Guild of the Industrial Art League, 1902.

———. "Industrial Art." *Jack London Journal* 3 (1996): 13–20.

Trotsky, Leon. Introduction to *The Iron Heel*, by Jack London. Edinburgh: Rebel Inc, 1999.

Twain, Mark. *The Adventures of Huckleberry Finn*. Vol. 8 of *The Works of Mark Twain*, edited by Walter Blair et al. Berkeley: University of California Press, 1988.

———. "The Czar's Soliloquy." *North American Review* 43 (Mar. 1905).

Tylor, Edward B. *Anthropology: An Introduction to the Study of Man and Civilization*. New York: D. Appleton, 1897.

Unna, Warren. *The Coppa Murals: A Pageant of Bohemian Life in San Francisco at the Turn of the Century*. San Francisco: Book Club of California, 1952.

Untermann, Ernest. *Science and Evolution*. Chicago: Charles H. Kerr, 1905.

Van Dyke, Henry. *Essays in Application*. New York: Charles Scribner's Sons, 1905.

Veblen, Thorstein. *The Theory of the Leisure Class: An Economic Study in the Evolution of Institutions*. New York: Macmillan, 1899.

———. *The Theory of Business Enterprise*. New York: Charles Scribner's Sons, 1904.

Walker, Franklin. *Jack London and the Klondike: The Genesis of an American Writer*. Seattle: University of Washington Press, 1966.

Waterloo, Stanley. *The Story of Ab: A Tale of the Time of the Cave Man*. Chicago: Way and Williams, 1897.

Waterman, Nixon. "My Castle in Spain." In *A Book of Verses*. Boston and Chicago: Forbes, 1900.

Watkins, T. H., and R. R. Olmstead. *Mirror of the Dream: An Illustrated History of San Francisco*. San Francisco: Scrimshaw Press, 1976.

Watson, Charles N. *The Novels of Jack London: A Reappraisal*. Madison: University of Wisconsin Press, 1983.

———. "Nietzsche and *The Sea-Wolf*: A Rebuttal." *Jack London Newsletter* 9 (Jan.-Apr. 1976).

Weininger, Otto. *Sex and Character*. Translation authorized by the publisher. London: William Heinemann; New York: G. P. Putnam's Sons, 1906.

Weintraub, Hyman. *Andrew Furuseth: Emancipator of the Seamen*. Berkeley: University of California Press, 1959.

Weismann, August. *Essays upon Heredity and Kindred Biological Problems*. 2 vols. Edited by E. B. Poulton, Selmar Schönland, and A. E. Shipley. Oxford: Clarendon Press, 1892-93.

———. *The Germ-Plasm: A Theory of Heredity*. Translated by W. Newton Parker and Harriet Rönnfeldt. London: Walter Scott, 1893.

Wells, H. G. *Mankind in the Making*. New York: Charles Scribner's Sons, 1904.

———. "A Story of the Stone Age." In *Tales of Space and Time*. London and New York: Harper, 1900.

———. *When the Sleeper Wakes*. New York: Harper, 1899.

Whitaker, Elsie Martinez. "Jim Whitaker." Online Archive of California. http://www.oac.cdlib.org/view?query=Hauch&docId=hb6j49p1b8&chunk.id=div00005&toc.depth=1&toc.id=0&brand=oac4&x=18&y=12.

White, Stewart Edward. *The Silent Places*. New York: McClure, Phillips, 1904.

Whitney, Caspar. *On Snow-Shoes to the Barren Grounds: Twenty-Eight Hundred Miles after Musk-Oxen and Wood Bison*. New York: Harper, 1896.

Wilde, Oscar. "The Soul of Man under Socialism." In *The Soul of Man under Socialism, the Socialist Ideal Art, and the Coming Solidarity*, by Oscar Wilde, William Morris, and W. C. Owen. New York: Humboldt, 1892.

Williams, Jay. *Author under Sail: The Imagination of Jack London, 1893-1902*. Lincoln: University of Nebraska Press, 2014.

———. "Corrections to *The Letters of Jack London*." *The Call* 25-26 (Fall/Winter 2014-Spring/Summer 2015).

———. "A Critical Edition of *The Star Rover*." PhD diss., Columbia University, 1989.

———. "Editor's Introduction: On Art and the Machine." *Jack London Journal* 3 (1996).

———. Editor's introduction to William Morris, "How I Became a Socialist." *Jack London Journal* 3 (1996).

———. "Life in Jewish Oakland: A Lost Short Story by Jack London." *Studies in American Naturalism* 10 (Summer 2015).

Wilson, Michael G. "Northern California: The Heart of the Storm." In *Pictorialism in California: Photographs, 1900-1940*, edited by Michael

G. Wilson and Dennis J. Reed. Malibu and San Marino CA: J. Paul Getty
 Museum and Henry E. Huntington Library and Art Gallery, 1994.
Wilson, Richard Guy. "'Divine Excellence': The Arts and Crafts Life in California."
 In *The Arts and Crafts Movement in California: Living the Good Life*, edited by
 Kenneth R. Trapp. New York: Abbeville Press, 1993.
Zamen, Mark. *Standing Room Only: Jack London's Controversial Career as a
 Public Speaker*. New York: Peter Lang, 1990.

INDEX

Abbott, Leonard, 39, 41, 322, 323, 593n3, 597n7, 632n178
Abbott, Tarnel, 538
Abrams, M. H., xvi
absorption: and cinema, xiv, 300; definition of, xv–xviii; fiction and, 19, 25, 33, 37, 121, 137, 194, 203, 228, 244, 250, 267, 279, 362, 370, 386, 388, 397, 399, 400, 413, 429, 431, 443, 444–47, 472, 474, 481, 580; from Fried, xiv; ghosts and, 228; Gunning's use of, xiv, 299–300; horror and, 107; imagination and, xx; interest and, 84, 148, 407; London's work and, xv–xviii, xx, 38, 474; painting and, xv–xvi, xvii, 229; photography and, xiv, xvii, 148; print culture and, xvi; psychology and, 398; self-identity and, 567, 650n65; sincerity and, 85; theatricality and, 19, 39, 92, 101, 141, 155, 171, 210, 212, 226, 227, 299, 338, 346, 354, 356, 369, 388, 530, 574; timelessness and, 398
The Abysmal Brute (London), 189
abyss: absence of, 355; green, xi, 245–48, 350; imagination and, xi, 22, 355; proletariat and, 16, 43, 152, 184, 314, 342–43, 368, 477, 487, 518, 537–38; white, xi, 350, 501. See also *The People of the Abyss*
Adams, Ansel, 152
Adams, Frederick Upham, 341
Addams, Jane, 307, 321, 376
Advance, 57
advances and advice to authors, 76; from Brett, 5–6, 8, 180, 353, 533; from Houghton Mifflin, 586n9; increase in, 177–78; from McClure, 237
adventure, 26, 84, 93, 101, 115, 122, 167, 169, 205, 225, 284, 287, 298, 312–13, 389–90, 391, 412, 465, 505, 539, 545, 547, 551, 558–59, 560, 561, 562, 563, 573
Adventure, 337, 588n56
Aegis, 100, 162, 559

African Americans, 167, 257
"Again the Literary Aspirant" (London), 74, 75, 87, 594n6
Allen, E. F., 565, 567
Allen, Grant, 371, 387
"All Gold Canon" (London), xi, 126, 238–39, 241–42, 244–45, 248, 254, 256, 258, 261, 280, 597n50, 616n71, 617n88
Althusser, Louis, 561
Altruria, 289, 290, 291, 419–20, 432, 450, 599n79
American Federation of Labor, 50, 55, 306
"The American Abyss" (London), 204, 211, 363, 368
Anglo-Saxons. See whiteness
animality. See monsters and monstrousness
Anthropology (Tylor), 384
Anti-Capital Punishment Society, 273
The Antichrist (Nietzsche), 207
Anticipations (Wells), 487
"The Apostate" (London), 307, 343, 352, 362–69, 370, 372, 430, 438, 525, 526, 562, 574, 634n207
Appeal to Reason, 57, 336, 350, 534, 535, 537, 632n178, 655n155
Applegarth, Mabel, xii
Archer, Alison. See More, Margaret
"Are Great Fortunes Great Dangers?" (Adams), 341
Arena, 302, 322, 541
Argonaut, 115, 147, 418
The Art of Controversy (Schopenhauer), 224
Arts and Crafts movement, 322, 323, 331, 418, 448–54, 456–59, 460–62, 463, 645n101
Ashbee, Charles Robert, 453
"Atavism" (O'Hara), 14
Atherton, Frank, 125
Atlantic Monthly, 9, 52, 105, 158, 215, 242, 410, 442, 597n47
"At Rainbow's End" (London), 227

Atropos, 186

Austin, Alfred, 357

Austin, Mary, 574

author figures: "The Apostate" and, 368; *Before Adam*, 233, 389, 398; "Brown Wolf" and, 347–49; *The Call of the Wild* and, xii, 15, 17, 24–25; Christ novel and, 62–63; *Created He Them* and, 432, 433, 435; "Created He Them" and, 439; critic as, 99; "A Curious Fragment" and, 581; "A Day's Lodging" and, 355–56; dreaming and, 233; "The Enemy of All the World" and, 578, 579; false authors as, 194, 244, 256, 257, 467–68, 575; *The Game* and, 188; ghosts as, xx, 20, 21, 23; historian as, 552; hoboes as, xxi; the imagination and, xii, 79, 102, 105, 251, 389, 551, 579; *The Iron Heel* and, 478, 525, 526, 527, 529; "The Leopard Man" and, 91–92; Malemute Kid as, 228; *Martin Eden* and, 63; miners as, 21, 23, 29, 137; "Morganson's Finish" and, 467–68; newspapermen as, 132; "A Nose for the King" and, 194; "An Odyssey of the North" and, 23; "The Passing of Marcus O'Brien" and, 575; "Planchette" and, 251, 257; *The Road* and, 550; sailor as, 1, 95, 98–99, 102; *The Sea-Wolf* and, 94–96, 98–99, 506; Sitka Charley as, 228–29; "The Sun-Dog Trail" and, 233; vision and, 63, 373; "When God Laughs" and, 357; "Where the Trail Forks" and, 21; *White Fang* and, 267, 277; "The Wit of Porportuk" and, 445–46; women as, 94–95, 108–9, 355–56, 432, 433, 435, 445–46, 527, 529

authorship: beginnings of, 74, 88–90, 348; bohemianism and, 107–8, 429, 464; canonicity and, 98, 105, 106, 113; duties of, 350; economics of, 30, 38, 51, 78, 181, 266, 281, 300–301, 416, 557; essays on, 39, 73–80, 82–88, 89–90, 120; experimentation and, 278, 533, 555; fundamental commitments for, xviii, xix, 75, 165, 370; *The Game* and, 188; genre and, xviii; hack writing and, 82, 120; horror and, 87; identity and, 27, 34, 144, 153, 478; imagination and, xx, 15–17, 78–80, 115, 137, 370,

381, 389, 397, 473; incomplete work and, 73; influences on, 94; job as, 89; models of, xix, 75, 95, 156, 286, 514, 557; newspapers and, 135, 145, 196–97; race and, 152; readers and, xx, 25, 84, 111–12, 120–21, 388, 389; reading and, 137, 483; representation of, 15, 196, 479, 556, 562; romantic genius as, 95, 553; *The Sea-Wolf* and, 95; sex and, 433, 436; sincerity and, 84; socialism and, xviii, xix, 41, 337, 339, 344–45, 413, 474, 518; as a solace, 407, 533; theatricality and, 145, 388; tragedy of, 436; travel, 144, 370; women and, 514. *See also* author figures; London, Jack

Author's League of America, 45

automatic writing, xx, 246, 247, 250, 251, 254

Aveling, Edward, 435

"The Backslider" (Allen), 371

Bacon, Francis, 488

Balch, William Lincoln, 303

Bamford, Fredrick: London's friend, 47, 214, 217, 289, 290, 337, 350, 392, 407, 533, 573; reading suggestions for London, 69, 263, 280, 466, 593n73, 652n87; residence in Burke's Sanitarium, 436; Ruskin Club, 67, 68, 322, 336; Social Gospel and, 66, 70

"The Banks of the Sacramento" (London), 129, 135

Barker, Elsa, 339

Barrett, Jack, 2, 338, 414, 415

Barrymore, Ethel, 196, 197

Barthelme, Donald, 554, 555

Barthes, Roland, 80

Barton, Mr. (character), 253, 256, 257

"Bâtard" (London), 8, 12–13

Bates, Blanche, 199, 227, 431

Baudelaire, Charles, xvi

beasts: boxer as, 182, 189; horror of, 103–4, 107, 114; London as, 460; no-work, 16; primordial, 24, 269, 505; slum, 18, 338; work, 16, 17, 42, 43, 77, 339. *See also* blond beast; Buck (character); monsters and monstrousness

the Beats, 455

Beauty Ranch, 291, 353, 460

Becker, Fred, 289, 620n8

Before Adam (London): absorption and, 398; alternate titles, 401; atavism and, 297, 404, 413; author figure in, 233, 389, 398; beginning of, 369, 370, 404; bohemianism and, 402-3; Charmian London and, 406; cinema and, 23, 400; as companion to *White Fang*, 370; composition of, 370, 371, 388-89; 404-6; cover, 412-13; dreaming in, 233, 368, 391, 399; first readers of, 407-8, 411-12; as ghost story, 102, 397; imagination and, 356, 389, 393-94, 397, 400, 407; mother and, 398; multiple personality disorder and, 396; 1906 earthquake and, 405; psychological themes in, 258, 260, 264, 370, 375, 389, 391-93, 394-97, 399-401; reading for, 377-88, 390-91; relation to Native American story, 172; serialization of, 361, 407-11; socialism and, 211, 308, 351, 396-97, 401-2; spiritism and, 389, 398; technology and, 401-2; time and, 372, 397-98; time travel in, 368, 394

Beginnings: Intention and Method (Said), 88, 97

Be Good to Yourself (Marden), 469

Bercovitch, Sacvan, 479

Bergenhammer, Chris "The Dane," 413, 639n100

Berger, Victor, 305, 332, 334, 538, 623-24n69

Bergson, Henri, 511

Better World Philosophy (Jennie Darrow), 376

Bible, 61, 62, 69, 492, 527, 593n73, 602n105, 658n15

Bierce, Ambrose, 87, 105, 435, 518, 552

Bigelow, James, 293

"Big Socialist Vote Is Fraught with Meaning" (London). *See* "Great Socialist Vote Explained"

Bilgrami, Akeel, xviii

Bill the miner (character), 241, 244-45, 256, 257, 261

Binet, Alfred, 248-51, 375, 395, 396

Binford, Jessica, 307

The Birth of Tragedy (Nietzsche), 97

The Bitter Cry of the Children (Spargo), 516

The Black Cat, 78, 91, 102, 112, 193, 246, 303, 577

Black Power movement, 210

Blanchard and Venter, 294-95

Blatchford, Robert, 42

blindness, 87, 110, 218, 265, 492, 498

blond beast, 117, 313, 503-5, 506, 507, 508, 509, 526, 560, 573, 598n59

Bloody Sunday, 240, 328

body: celebration of, 185, 188, 190, 266; mind over, 192; testing limits of, 551; violence to, 180, 207, 338, 345, 359, 429

bohemia: *Before Adam* and, 407; destruction of, 417-18; history of, 184; lifestyle of, 190, 212, 214, 266, 447, 462, 568, 574; 1906 earthquake and, 417-26

Bohemia Guild of the Industrial Art League (Chicago), 450

Bohemian Club, xi, 157, 418, 441, 463, 640n8

bohemianism: antibohemian, 128; architecture and, 1, 77, 123-24, 343, 445, 448-52, 454; body and, 359; difficulty of, 184-86, 358, 561; economics and, 26, 51, 76, 212, 213-14, 305, 318, 329, 348, 361, 369, 416, 573; excess and, 19, 144, 154; hobo and, 18, 557, 559, 562; imagination and, 43, 105, 107-8, 111, 228-29; play and, 182, 183, 198, 329, 403, 464, 573; race and, 142; socialism and, 42, 189, 305, 455, 526; sprezzatura and, 193; travel and, 205

the Boise Three. *See* Haywood, William; Moyer, Charles; Pettibone, George; "Something Rotten in the State of Idaho"

Bölsche, Wilhelm, 401

Bonaparte, Napoleon, 505, 506, 507, 512

book covers, xiii, 34-35, 139, 174, 186, 201, 297, 355, 412, 413, 419, 450, 451, 456, 463, 537-38, 567-68

Bookman, 43, 260

A Book of Verses (Waterman), 456

The Bostonians (James), 126

Boston Journal, 315

bourgeois, 16, 59, 115, 142, 176, 259, 271, 299, 305, 320, 429, 445, 450, 477, 491, 505, 508, 509, 518, 522, 529, 565, 568

boxing, 182, 185-92, 198, 270, 414, 429, 564

Bracken, Julia, 450

Brady, Matthew, 150

Burning Daylight and, 337; critique of, 42, 61, 116, 192, 204–5, 211–12, 220, 239, 242, 297, 309–10, 320, 420, 434, 472, 516, 530, 531, 535, 568; evolution of, 482–83, 485–86, 496, 498; global nature of, 49–50, 169–70; as health crisis, 569–71, 575; 1906 earthquake and, 423; primitivism and, 338, 427–28, 444; religion and, 47–48, 72, 222, 243, 401, 519, 522, 525, 551; in *The Silent Places*, 259; *Snark* trip and, 583–84; surplus labor and, 550; trade unionism and, 43; vs. socialism, 219, 369, 452, 479, 518, 539. *See also* child labor; Christianity

Carlyle, Thomas, 67, 450, 644n90

Carnegie, Andrew, 52, 224, 226, 428

Carnegie Hall, 302, 303, 332

Carpenter, George R., 28, 32, 54, 322, 589n61

Carroll, Lewis, 463, 646n146

Carruth, F. Hayden, 362–63, 440

Carus, Paul, 248

The Case of Wagner (Nietzsche), 207

Cashel Byron's Profession (Shaw), 198

Casson, Henry, 50–51

castle in Spain, 451, 456

"The Castle of Indolence" (Thomson), 451

Central Labor Council of Alameda County, California, 242

Century Magazine: *Huckleberry Finn* and, 600n87; rival to *McClure's*, 138, 602n109; *The Sea-Wolf* and, 34, 125–29, 130–31, 172, 601n97, 602n105; "The White Man's Way" and, 235–37

Chabot Park, 288, 289

Chants Communal (Traubel), 455

Chapters in Workshop Reconstruction and Citizenship (Ashbee), 453

Charcot, Jean-Martin, 373, 393

Charles Kerr and Company, 51, 218, 376, 401, 486

Chautauqua movement, 300

child labor, 307, 310, 352, 362, 363–64, 367, 369, 480, 517, 520, 536, 557, 572. *See also* labor

"A Child of the Phalanstery" (Allen), 371

Children of the Frost (London): London's opinion of, 428; publication of, 27, 138;

586n9; reception of, 160; themes of, 139, 172, 228; word count of, 9

Chinese, 141, 153–54, 163, 167, 169, 172, 422, 458, 473, 476–77

Christianity: capitalism and, 223, 525, 551; Native Americans and, 259; primitivism and, 371; psychology and, 374, 384; socialism and, 65–66, 69, 53

Christianity and the Social Crisis (Rauschenbusch), 69

Christian Register, 119

Christian Science, 253

Christian Socialist movement. *See* Social Gospel movement

Christ novel (London), 61–72

cinema: absorption and, xiv; dreaming and, 230, 400; novel as, 194; representation and, 179–80, 299, 394, 494, 536, 554

cinema of attractions: absorption and, xiv; 179–80, 299–300, 554

City Hall Park, 289

Civil War, 515, 569, 652n88

class consciousness, 45, 56, 60, 401, 477, 499

class struggle: and biology, 150, 170; as civil war, 53, 515; as history of humans, 540; Marxism and, 648–49n22; religion and, 61; in *The Sea-Wolf*, 118; socialism and, 58–59, 176, 211, 328; unions and, 45, 55–56; *War of the Classes* and, 175

"The Class Struggle" (London): Brett and, 54; serialization of, 52–53; sources for, 56–59; themes of, 53–54, 55–56; works of London and, 37, 38, 48

Clough, Edwin "Yorick," 2, 604n18

Clubland, 115, 187, 395, 396, 580–81

Coburn, Frank, 318

Coleridge, Samuel Taylor, xv, xvi, 80–82, 83, 84, 91, 137, 483

collar-starchers, 224, 243, 337

Collectivist Society, 323

Collier's Weekly, 147, 148, 216–18, 254

Commons, John R., 322

The Communist Manifesto (Marx and Engels), 59, 176

Comrade, 39, 40, 41, 450, 590n3, 591n13

Conrad, Joseph, 3, 92–93, 95–96, 101, 110, 111, 122, 197, 387, 426, 595n27 consciousness: and animals, 45; of class, 56, 60, 68, 401, 477, 499; as double, 248–51; and ghosts, 103; and imagination, 84–86, 229; of the Pacific, 25; and perception-consciousness system, 252; and race, 229, 230; and spiritism, 389; and unconsciousness, 262–63, 277, 375

Conservator, 454–55

"Contradictory Teachers" (London). *See* Brooks, John Graham; Ghent, W. J.; "A Review"

Cooke, John Willis, 326

Coolbrith, Ina, 418

The Co-operative Commonwealth (Gronlund), 484–85

cooperative communities, 288, 452

Coppa's Restaurant, 417–18, 449

Cosgrave, John O'Hara, 216, 254–55, 285, 411, 561, 599n81

Cosmopolitan: copyediting and, 471; "Finis" and, 468–69; foreword to *The Cruise of the* Snark and, 462; future relationship with London, 473; hoboes and, 562; "Just Meat" and, 470–72; London's rates and, 470; "Love of Life" and, 137–38; Phillips and, 221; "Planchette" and, 255; "Revolution" and, 214–15, 415, 446; *The Road* and, 562–64, 565, 567–68; "The Scab" and, 52; socialism and, 473; "The Unparalleled Invasion" and, 577; "What Communities Lose by the Competitive System" and, 61, 220, 446; "What Life Means to Me" and, 332, 339–42; "When Altruria Awoke" and, 419. *See also* Maxwell, Perriton; Millard, Bailey; Walker, James Randolph; Walker, John Brisbane

Courbet, Gustave, xvi, xviii

Cowell, Harry, 356, 357–58

Coxhead, Ernest, 448

Craftsman, 453, 459, 629n127

"Created He Them" (London): genre of, 439–40; London's other work and, 429–30, 467; notes for, 430, 438–39; relationship to *Before Adam*, 430; relationship to *Created He Them*, 430; relationship to *When God Laughs, and Other Stories*, 431; serialization of, 440; word count of, 431

Created He Them (London), composition of, 429–44; genre of, 392, 444; relationship to *Smoke of Life*, 437–38

Crime and Criminals (Prison Reform League), 554, 658n16

Crimes of the Profit Furnace (Wood), 568–69

criminality: capital punishment and, 275–77; and criminal studies, 274; environmental factors, 276–77; evolutionary theory and, 270; heredity and, 271, 276–77; hoboes and, 559–60; primitivism and, 270; reform of, 276

Criminal Sociology (Ferri), 134, 273

Critic, 43, 90, 125, 600n85

The Cruise of The Dazzler (London), 3, 94

The Cruise of the Snark (London), 286, 313, 440, 597n52; foreword to (London), 430, 461–67, 471, 559

Cunniff, M. G., 317

"A Curious Fragment" (London), 476, 581

Curtis, Edward S., 152

Curtis, G. W., 293

The Cycle of Life According to Modern Science (Saleeby), 540, 597n44

The Cynic's Word Book (Bierce), 518

Dall, William H., London's realism and, xvi, 85–86, 95, 386, 428

Dana, Richard, 92, 95

Dare, Helen, 187

Darling, Ernest, 182

Darrow, Clarence, 322, 323, 376

Darrow, Jennie, 376

Darwin, Charles, 381, 505

Darwinism, 376

A Daughter of the Snows (London), 4, 5, 12, 14, 28, 40, 108, 595n12

Davidson, Arnold I., 109

Davis, L. Clare, 19

Davis, Richard Harding, as bourgeois writer, 259; Theodore Roosevelt and, 159, 605n37, 607n66; as war correspondent, 147, 148, 159, 161, 165, 166, 204

Dawson Weekly News, 160

"A Day's Lodging" (London), 354–56, 361

Debs, Eugene, 222; Clarence Darrow and, 322; compared to Hearst, 134; conversion of, 311; Dorothy Richardson and, 339; "The Dream of Debs" and, 580; Ernest Untermann and, 490; Horace Traubel and, 454; *The Iron Heel* and, 489, 538; ISS and, 321; Job Harriman and, 290; 1900 election, 205; 1904 election and, 173–74, 204, 206, 215; opinion of "The Somnambulists," 429; Paris Commune and, 475; religion and, 222; William Haywood and, 414

"The Decay of Lying" (Wilde), 83, 553

Deep Sea Vagabonds (Sonnichsen), 95–96, 119, 596n36

Denison, A. A., 67

De profundis (Wilde), 582

Derrida, Jacques, 252

de Ville, Peter, 91

"The Devil's Dice Box" (London), 22, 231, 355

Dickens, Charles, 486, 510

Diderot, Denis, xiv, xv

dipsychism, 249, 252

Dirigo, 140

"The Disappearing Class" (London), 59, 60, 522, 592n35, 652n84

The Diseases of Society (Lydston), 519–20

disassociation of personality, 322, 394, 395–96

Disassociation of Personality (Prince), 395

The Discovery of the Unconscious (Ellenberger), 247, 253, 373

Dixon, Lillian, 418, 422

Dixon, Maynard, 417, 418, 419, 422, 612n176

Donnelly, Ignatius, 514, 515–16

Doubleday, Page, and Company, 408

Doyle, Arthur Conan, 90, 426

dreaming: *The Call of the Wild* and, 23–24; cinema and, 230; the primitive and, 230, 233, 384, 387, 399; as psychological concept, 33; the unconscious and, 260; *White Fang* and, 260, 263

"The Dream of Debs" (London): absorption and, 580; authorship and, 476; communication and, 581; plot of, 580–81; relation to "The Enemy of All the People," 581; title of, 580

Drummond, Freddie (character), 329

Dubois, W. E. B., 334

Dunbar, Chris (character), 246, 247–49, 250, 251, 252, 253, 254

Dunn, Allan, 418

Dunn, Robert L., 153, 155, 158, 165, 608n83

Dynamic Sociology (Ward), 377

Eames, Ninetta Wiley: married to Edward Payne, 290, 599n79; member of Ruskin Club, 67; "Planchette" and, 430–31; "A Wicked Woman" and, 444

Eames, Roscoe: captain of *Snark*, 432; as member of Ruskin Club, 67

Easley, Ralph, 323–24, 326, 331, 332

Eccentricities of Crime (Burnside), 577

The Economic Interpretation of History (Seligman), 327, 498, 648–49n22

Editor, 40, 90, 135, 285, 427, 446, 594n7

"Editorial Crimes" (London), 87, 550

Eisenstein, Sergei, 300

Ellenberger, Henri, 247, 252, 253, 373, 374

Ely, Richard T., 322

Emerson, Edwin, 144, 147

Emerson, Ralph Waldo, 293, 300, 422, 488

The End of the World (Max Meyer), 466

"The Enemy of All the World" (London): criminality and, 579 as "future stunt," 476; imagination and, 580; theme of, 577–78; Weininger and, 578

Engels, Frederick, 68, 256, 484, 570

Eppingwell, Mrs. (character), 196

Essays in Application (Van Dyke), 518–19

Essays upon Heredity (Weismann), 271, 371, 380, 381

"The Eternal Enemy" (London), 552

eugenics, 271, 276, 317, 514

Everhard, Avis (character): as author figure, 367, 406, 483, 493, 524–25, 526; as hero, 538; Second Revolt and, 476, 538

Everhard, Ernest (character): "The Apostate" and, 524–25, 526; "The Dream of Debs" and, 581; Friedrich Nietzsche and, 501, 508–9, 511–12, 560; ghost as, 501–2; "Goliah" and, 572, 573; Herbert Spencer and, 491–95; as hero, 538; H. G. Wells and, 487; Jesus and, 72; monologues by, 530; "The Persistence of the Established" and, 320; Philomath Club speech and, 299, 517, 530; proletarian science and, 488–89; Second Revolt and, 476, 499; surplus value and, 485, 513; W. J. Ghent and, 497, 499–500

Charles Warren Stoddard's response to, 185-86; composition of, 8, 171, 175, 195, 411-12; contract and, 177-78; fame, 186, 187; ghosts and, 184, 186; illustrations for, 186; James Britt and, 187, 189-92; length of, 255; life and, 190; notes for, 181-82; nudity and, 185-86; payment for, 227; race and, 182; sales of, 35, 181; serialization of, 179-80, 255, 284; theatricality and, 186-87, 202; as tragedy, 182, 184-85; violence and, 186, 391; war as game, 184; women and boxing, 187-88; working class and boxing, 188-89

Garland, Hamlin, 136, 298

Garnet, Porter, 407, 417, 418, 640n8

Garrison, William Lloyd, 293, 322

The Gay Science (Nietzsche), 441

A Genealogy of Morals (Nietzsche), 97, 207, 503, 505, 506, 507, 598n59

genre: *Before Adam* and, 386, 388; *The Black Cat* and, 193, 246; the bricklayer and, 99; Britt-Nelson fight, 337; *The Call of the Wild* and, 9, 10, 13; concept of, 478; contract and, 4-6; experimentation and, 94, 194, 198, 199, 255, 278, 341-42, 501; fact and, 371, 383, 478; familiarity with, 202; "A Farthest Distant" and, 544, ghost and, 250, 251, 478, 501; history of cinema and, 299; horror as, 88; human document and, 74; identity as author and, 219, 444; *The Iron Heel* and, 227, 474, 496, 500, 539, 544; jeremiad and, 478, 572; *The Jungle* and, 481; London's mastery of, 140, 219, 278; melodrama and, 481; moving-picture novel as, 194; oscillation between, xviii, 37, 337, 444; pictorialism and, 567; "Planchette" and, 255; playwriting and, 198-201; prehistoric fiction and, 388; science fiction and, 383, 539; *The Sea-Wolf* and, 94, 121; supernatural and, xvi; "What Life Means to Me" and, 341 *White Fang* and, 337. *See also* authorship; *and individual titles of London's work*

Genthe, Arnold, 357, 418, 567, 640n7, 640n8

George, Arthur, 333

George, Henry, 41, 44, 221, 453, 520

"Getting into Print" (London): advice in, 75-78; alternate titles, 74; bohemianism, 77; compared to "Again the Literary Aspirant," 75; ghosts and, 83; inspiration and, 78-83; Jesus and, 77; machine and, 78; other works by London and, 31; payment for, 74; poor-mouthing and, 75; sincerity and, 83; work and, 77

germ-plasm, 370-71, 383

The Germ-Plasm (Weismann), 376, 385

Ghent, W. J., 43-48, 54, 59, 74, 139, 174, 176, 213, 322, 477, 479, 488-89, 497-99, 500, 537, 591n14, 623n69, 650n58

ghosts: absorption and, 203, 228, 398; beginnings and, 102; the bricklayer as, 102, 104; Buck as, xii, xx, 23, 24, 25, 43, 79, 82, 103, 115, 203, 250; dreaming and, xx, 250, 393, 400; fact and, xii; genre and, 478; ghost story, 228, 231, 248, 255, 382, 396, 397, 432, 463, 502; hobo-author and, xxi, 556, 558-59; horror and, 83, 86, 90, 102; human ancestors, 412; identity and, xiii, 16, 184, 405; imagination and, xi-xii, xx, 11, 15-17, 23, 90, 99, 102, 104, 106, 115, 121, 203, 228, 244, 246, 250, 355, 393, 396-97, 400, 406-7, 461, 468-69, 495, 502, 559, 579; Klondike stories and, xi, xx, 39, 139, 231, 238, 259, 258-63, 278, 355, 359, 467, 556; Koreans and, 151, 153, 194, 228; London's encounters with, 102-3, 104; London's work and, xx-xxi; manuscript as, 73; Nietzsche and, 501-2, 526; psychology and, xx, 16, 248, 250-51, 254, 263, 268, 373-74, 397; reader as a, xxi, 121; sex and, 359; socialism and, 219; Southland and, xi-xii, 238, 278, 501; as spirit, 43, 99, 246, 250-51, 253, 254, 258, 261, 267, 268, 463; theatricality and, xx, 155, 176, 294, 393; Wolf Larsen as, 99, 100, 104, 115. *See also individual titles of London's works*

Gibson, Henry, 291

Gilded Age, 316, 326

Gilder, Jeannette Leonard, 125-26

Gilder, Richard Watson, 34, 125, 126-29, 130-31, 235, 600n87, 601n97, 602n109

Gilman, Charlotte Perkins, 322, 323

Goddard, Charles, 194

Mark Hopkins Institute of Art, 418
"The Marriage of Lit-Lit" (London), 39
Mars: in *Brown Wolf*, 539; in *A Farthest Distant*, 543-44 in *The Iron Heel*, 539; the Mars boy, 546-47; in *The Road*, 550-51; study of, 542-43; in *White Fang*, 269, 539
Mars and Its Canals (Lowell), 542
Marsden, Ada Lee Bascom, 201
Martin Eden (London), xxi, 45, 63, 78, 95, 110, 112, 113, 191, 206, 218, 233, 291, 331, 313, 342, 343, 358, 359, 390, 434, 493, 494, 496, 503, 508, 543, 549, 579, 590n82
Martinek, Jason, 210
Martinez, Xavier, 111, 357, 417, 418
Marx, Aveling, 435
Marx, Eleanor, 435
Marx, Karl, 59, 66, 67-68, 97, 117, 256, 327, 348, 401, 435, 485, 488, 490, 496, 557, 570, 648-49n22
masculinity, 108, 197
Mass and Class (Ghent), 139, 488, 497-99, 500, 650n58
"Material Gain" (London), 569-70
Maxwell, Perriton, 468-69, 471, 473
Maybeck, Bernard, 418
McCaffry, Helen, 203
McClelland, Thomas, 299, 627n102
McClure, S. S., 26, 78, 138, 179-80, 215, 216, 254-55, 408-10, 411, 412, 430, 565, 602-3n109, 610n123
McClure and Phillips Company, 5, 565
McClure's Magazine, 84, 135, 136, 217, 219, 237, 407, 442, 446, 522, 543, 477
McDevitt, William, 304-5, 414
McDonald, J. K., 135, 136, 137
McIntyre, Clara F., 477
McKenzie, F. A., 154, 155
McNamara brothers, 289
memory: the Goth's, 62; the imagination and, 80-81, 91, 107, 120, 231, 368, 578; London's, 2; psychology and, 16, 252, 263, 374-75, 381, 392, 578; race-memory, 368, 371, 374, 381, 383, 388-89, 392, 394, 395, 398; William Wordsworth and, 587n37; wolves and, 264-65, 266, 267-68. *See also* imagination
The Menace of Privilege (George), 221, 520

"The Men of Forty-Mile" (London), 227
The Mercy of the Sea (London), 99, 177
Meredith, Anthony (character), 452, 475, 476, 481, 482-83, 487, 488, 491, 496, 498, 499, 501, 502, 503, 511, 516, 517-18, 520, 523, 524, 525, 526, 527-28, 529, 532, 533, 535-36, 539, 540, 541, 544, 545, 551-52, 571, 573-74, 575, 579, 582
Merrie England (Blathford), 42
Meserole, Mrs. Darwin J., 326
Metropolitan Magazine, 180, 181, 186, 284, 609n112
Meyer, Frederick H., 418
Meyer, Max, 466
Michel, Louise, 519, 520
Mill, John Stuart, 499
Millard, Bailey: *Cosmopolitan* and, 169, 215, 255, 339-40, 470-71, 473; 1906 earthquake and, 419-20, 421, 423, 424, 426, 462; *San Francisco Examiner* and, 169, 345
millennialism, 70
Miller, Joaquin, 2, 435, 454, 458
Mills, C. Wright, 325
Milton, John, 80, 82, 83, 97-98, 110, 118, 367-68, 401, 542, 560, 597n50
mining, 1-3, 245, 248, 281, 423
mission design, 449
Moby-Dick, or The White Whale, 111
A Model of Christian Charity (Winthrop), 479
monsters and monstrousness: the Bricklayer and, 103-4; "The Enemy of All the World" and, 577; Friedrich Nietzsche and, 505, 506-7, 509; Frona Welse and, 94; *The Iron Heel* and, 482; "The Leopard Man" and, 91-92; London's understanding of, 111, 113-16, 132; 1906 earthquake and, 428; outer space and, 548; *The Sea-Wolf* and, 107-10, 112, 121; socialism and, 175-76, 220, 568, 571
Moody, Dwight, 290
Moon-Face, and Other Stories (London), 256, 353, 354, 405, 407, 617n93
Moore, John Howard, 349, 375-81, 383, 384, 393, 455, 635n10
Moran of the Lady Letty (Frank Norris), 92
More, Margaret, 275-76. *See also* Archer, Alison

"Morganson's Finish." *See* "Finis"

Morris, Governeur, 384, 385, 388

Morris, Madge, 435

Morris, William, 40, 67, 68, 450, 453, 454, 456, 457, 461, 510, 644n90

Mott, Frank Luther, 35–36, 284, 451

Moyer, Charles, 304, 306, 405, 413, 414, 415, 416, 467, 525, 531

Mrs. Warren's Profession (Shaw), 198

The Mutiny of the Elsinore (London), 597n41

"My Best Story and Why I Wrote It" (London), 467

My Dogs in the Northland (Young), 14

Nancy school of psychology, 373

National Child Labor Committee, 366

National Civic Federation Review, 323, 331, 332

National Grange, 288

Native Americans: encounters with whites, 22, 139–40, 166–67; and medicine men, 372, 518; nature and, 230; possible stories about, 172–73; representation of, xvi–xvii, 85, 211, 230, 257–58, 309, 384, 428, 452; systems of justice and, 161, 233–35, 393

nature: architecture and, 448–49; Buck and, 25; capitalism and, 239, 248, 575; chance and, 97, 98; death drive and, 260, 263; Goth and, 62; imagination and, 110; Native Americans and, 230; vs. nurture, 271, 276–77; voice of life and, 95

"Negore, the Coward" (London), 139–40, 171, 354

Nelson, Oscar "Battling," 189, 237, 270–71, 280, 337

News from Nowhere (Morris), 40

newspapers: authorship and, xii, 105, 144, 145, 157, 159, 161, 189–90, 194–95, 197, 277, 319, 343, 345, 581; fame and, 291–92, 521; as publishing outlet, 1, 2, 5, 14–15, 133–34, 164; quotidian life and, 16; socialism and, 210, 211, 312, 318–19; source for fiction, xii, xvii, xx, 14–15, 20, 25, 55, 57, 59, 81, 85, 87, 135, 173, 211, 219, 221, 243, 279, 358, 364, 367, 375, 430, 437–38, 523. *See also* journalism

New Thought, 252–53, 345, 373, 469

"New Varieties of Sin" (Ross), 242

New York American, 156

New York Herald, 147, 361

New York Tribune, 235

Nietzsche, Friedrich, 97, 117, 118, 207, 441, 443, 481, 496, 500, 501–9, 510, 511, 513, 514, 515, 526, 528, 547, 549, 560, 567, 572–73, 582, 598n59, 643n62, 651n67, 651n72

1906 earthquake and fire, 305, 356, 392, 405, 407, 417–26, 640n8. *See also History of the San Francisco Bay Region* (Millard); "Human Drama at San Francisco" (Whitaker); "Our San Francisco" (Hopper); "Story of an Eye-Witness" (London); "Three Days Adrift" (Griswold); "The Valley of the Shadow" (Norris); "When Altruria Awoke" (Millard)

Nitobe, Inazo, 168

Noel, Joseph, 583

Noroton Conference, 305

Norris, Charles, 421

Norris, Frank, xvi, 68, 92, 204, 567, 594n6

North American Review, 503

Northland. *See* Klondike

"A Nose for the King" (London), 171, 192–94, 196, 227

"A Note on Realism" (Stevenson), 88

"Note on the Mystic Writing Pad" (Freud), 252

"A Northland Miracle" (London), 21

Oakland Chronicle, 165

Oakland Enquirer, 67

obsession, 246, 247, 251–52, 349, 372, 396, 445

"An Odyssey of the North" (London), 9, 10, 22, 23, 138, 350, 355, 490

Offenbach, Jacques, 348

O'Hara, John, 14–15, 32, 587n38

"The One Thousand Dozen" (London), 125

On Liberty (Mill), 499

On the Double Consciousness (Binet), 248–51

"On the Value of a Lie" (Symons), 552

"On the Writer's Philosophy of Life" (London), 87

Oppenheimer, Jacob (character), 277

Organized Self-Help (Casson), 50

The Origin of Species (Darwin), 97

Orpheus in the Underworld (Offenbach), 348

Otis, Laura, 381

prison reform, 205, 258, 268, 269-70, 271

Prison Reform League, 554

Progress and Poverty (George), 41

Progressivism, 369

proletarian science, 488, 489

prophecy, 65, 215, 477, 478, 479, 482, 522

prostitution, 117-18, 198, 237

The Psychic Life of Micro-organisms (Binet), 248

psychoanalysis, 248, 253, 374

psychology: anthropology and, 383, 393, 395, 400; biology and, 258, 278; Christianity and, 374; competing schools in; dissociation of personality, 249; evolutionary science and, 245, 258, 383-84, 388, 394, 395, 400, 544; history of, 249, 374; imagination and, 494; London's career and, 248, 251, 370; Macmillan and, 3; as metaphysics, 490; obsession, 251-52; opposed to metaphysics, 252-54, 389; Spencer, 495

The Psychology of the Unconscious (Jung), 553

public sphere, 39, 293

"A Publisher's View" (Mabie), 7

Pushing to the Front (Marden), 469

"The Question of a Name" (London), 87

"The Question of the Maximum" (London), 138, 217, 287, 292, 410, 480, 485, 513

race, xxi, 59, 61, 142, 145, 146-47, 150, 152, 162-63, 166-70, 172, 173, 175, 209, 229, 230, 232-33, 235, 238, 243, 257-58, 378, 427, 436, 458, 504, 507, 509, 528, 576, 577

Radcliffe, Zoe Greene, 531

Ralston, Henry, 334, 574

Rank, Otto, 249

Rauschenbusch, Walter, 66, 69-70, 222-23

realism: as hybrid mode of writing, 85-86, 88, 127, 128, 160, 191, 226, 313, 338, 367, 435, 481, 522; vs. idealism, 95; photography and, 127, 180, 200, 400, 423, 435; vs. romanticism, 120, 230; science and, 382; traditional concept of, xiv-xviii, 127, 255, 537, 567

"The Red Game of War" (London), 184

The Red Hot Dollar, and Other Stories (Umbstaetter), 78

redness, 261-62, 426, 428

Reeve, James Knapp, 285, 295

Reimers, Johannes, 19-20

"The Rejuvenation of Major Rathbone" (London), 112

Renan, Ernest, 65, 71-72

"Rest: A Mood" (Cowell), 356

"Retrogressive Development in Nature" (Weismann), 272

"A Review" (London), 44-47

review of *The Jungle* (London), 336, 350, 351-53, 354, 413, 415, 481

review of *The Long Day* (London), 280, 307, 336, 337-39

review of *The Walking Delegate* (London), 239-42, 245, 248, 280

revolution: altruism and, 117, 270, 569-70; anarchy and, 571, 578; art and, 40, 172, 450, 452, 456, 459, 511; biology and, 273, 317, 486, 489; bourgeois publications and, 215, 218; child labor and, 211; as class struggle, 176, 219, 329, 489, 500, 508; color of, 174, 413; conversion to, 343-44; cooptation of, 516; electoral politics and, 208; future of, 523; vs. individualism, 118; internationalism, 209, 476, 500; Jesus and, 66, 69, 490; materialism and, 488; Mexico and, 184; of the mind, 225; 1960s radicals and, 321-22; physical strength and, 176, 209; print culture and, 210; prison reform and, 273; promotion of, 240, 244, 297, 322, 401, 583-84; rhetoric and, 221, 335, 479, 500; Social Gospel movement and, 66-67, 290, 511, 515, 516; Socialist Labor Party and, 306, 334, 517; vs. trade unionism, 67; violence and, 477; women and, 528-29. *See also* Paris Commune; Russian Revolution

"Revolution" (London): authorship and, 175, 206, 207-8, 213, 220, 444, 480, 513; bohemian economics, 212-13; caveman and, 379-80; electoral politics and, 208; epigram for, 413; internationalism and, 209; Keynes and, 213; lecture version of, 294, 298-99, 302, 307, 364, 453; print culture and, 210-11; publication history of, 215-18; rhetoric of, 214; sale of, 415-16,

446–47; "Something Rotten in the State of Idaho" and, 414–15, 627n102; as summation of London's work, 213; theatricality and, xix, 292; versions of, 307–12, 325, 335, 336; violence and, 475

Revolution, and Other Essays (London), 35, 310, 459, 571

The Revolutionist's Handbook (Shaw), 512, 514

Reynolds, Paul, 361, 407, 409–11, 440, 470, 533, 534–35, 536, 537

Reynolds, Stephen, 429

Ribot, Théodule-Armand, 249

Richards, Robert J., 381

Richardson, Dorothy, 337, 338–39

Richardson, Frederick A., 446–47

Ricker, Allan, 65, 222

Ridgway, E. M., 361, 407, 409–10

Riis, Jacob, 224, 567

"The Rime of the Ancient Mariner" (Coleridge), 483

The Ring and the Book (Browning), 438

The Rise of Silas Lapham (Howells), 126

"The Rise of Socialism" (London). *See* "Intercollegiate Socialist Society"

"The Rising Tide of Revolution" (London). *See* "Something Rotten in Idaho"

The Road (London): authorship and, xi, 83–84, 550–52, 560; autobiography and, 567; bohemianism and, 557; book publication of, 567–68; Brett's opinion on, 564, 565–66; *The Call of the Wild* and, 20; collage and, 555; composition of, 561–63; ghosts and, 558–59; *The Iron Heel* and, 465, 503, 552; Mars and, 550, 551; photography and, 554–56; sales of; scene of writing and, 286; serialization of, 473, 563–64; socialism and, xiv, 557–61; structure of, 553–56, 557–61; theatricality of, 556; travel and, 549; violence in, 556

"The Road" (London), 18

Roberts, Charles G. D., 33, 339

Roberts, Jeremiah, 291

Robinson, H. Perry, 8, 9, 27

Roosevelt, Theodore, 146, 147, 158, 159, 284, 286, 414

Rose Valley Colony (Pennsylvania), 460

Ross, Edward, 242, 592n35

Roulston, Jane, 520, 653n104

Roycrofters community, 452

Rudd, Mark, 321, 324

"A Run Across" (London), 100

Ruskin Club, 67–68, 287, 289, 290, 308, 309, 322, 364, 405, 449, 533, 569, 571

Ruskin, John, 67, 68, 450, 463

Russell, Clark, 119–20

Russian Review, 221

Russian Revolution, 474–75

Russians, 139–44, 146, 152, 307

Russo-Japanese War writings, 140–52, 153–69

Said, Edward W., 88, 89, 90, 96, 97, 98

Saint Louis Declaration, 334

Saleeby, C. W., 540, 597n44, 656n3

The Salt of the Earth (London), 54, 173–74. See *War of the Classes*

"The Salt of the Earth" (London), 167, 173, 175

Saltus, Edgar, 553

Sandburg, Carl, 323, 339, 376, 420, 452, 453, 455

San Francisco Call, 146, 147, 149, 187, 195, 209, 399, 421

San Francisco Examiner, 1, 43, 133, 159, 189, 191, 202, 206, 211, 215, 306, 338, 339, 342, 414, 415, 418, 542

Satter, Beryl, 373

Saturday Evening Post, 11–12, 25–26, 27, 30, 32, 43, 75, 462, 522–23, 536, 588n56

"The Scab" (London), 38, 47–52, 55, 59, 213, 287

The Scarlet Plague (London), 549

Schopenhauer, Arthur, 97, 224, 508, 510

Schwind, Max, 288, 289

Science and Evolution (Untermann), 487–89, 490, 491

Scientific American, 542

The Scorn of Women (London): actresses and, 197, 198–201; authorship and, 196–97, 444; book publication and, 201, 444, 481; composition of, 195–98, 202, 509; theatricality and, 194, 227

"The Scorn of Women" (London), 171, 196, 227, 354, 444

Scott, Leroy, 239–40, 241, 332

61; food and, 289, 290, 291; as ghost, 256–57; history of, 321, 414, 499; individualism and, 116–17; internationalism, 209, 328–29, 337; liberalism and, 487, 516, 569–70; marriage and, 116–17; materialism and, 488; millionaire socialists, 177, 572; 1906 earthquake and, 425, 429; principles of, 341, 367, 484–85, 517, 569; print culture and, 41, 210–11, 213, 485–86, 582; promotion of, 40, 44, 294, 306, 473; race and, 170; telos of, 317, 498, 556, 573; as theater, 304, 341, 524; unions and, 49–51, 55–58; utopianism and, 170, 288, 289, 291, 344; violence and, 556; wage slavery and, 367, 524; war and, 401–2; World War I and, 334, 517. *See also* revolution; theatricality; *and individual titles of London's works*

Socialism (Spargo), 516, 517

Socialist Call the, 303

Socialist Labor Party, 289, 290

Socialist Party of America, 39, 332, 334

Socialist Spirit, 56, 521, 653n107

Socialist Voice, 308, 310, 333, 430

The Social Unrest (Brooks), 43, 45–46, 49, 59, 60, 174

sociology: art and, 496; authorship and, xix; biology and, 273–74; education in, 271, 559; Macmillan Co. and, 3; prehistory and, 383, 399; socialism and, 327, 495–96

"Something Rotten in the State of Idaho" (London), 304, 414–15

somnambulism, 252

"The Somnambulists" (London), 428–29

A Son of the Sun (London), 70

A Son of the Wolf (London), 75, 228, 555, 586n9

Sonne, Edgar, 133–35

Sonnichsen, Albert, 95–96, 112, 119–20, 122, 596nn36, 38

Sophie Sutherland, 93, 94, 101, 102, 466, 601–2n103

The Soul of Man under Socialism (Wilde), 116

Spargo, John: friendship with London, 590n3, 590n5; "How I Became a Socialist" and, 39–40, 306; influence of, 516–17, 538; liberalism of, 363, 478, 491, 516, 653n96; originality of, 489; Paris Commune and, 475; Socialist Party and, 305, 528–29

species: dogs and humans, 15, 19, 90, 267; perfection of, 528; permeability of, 268; recapitulation theory, 271; reproduction of, 513

Speed, George, 289, 560, 561

Spencer, Herbert, 70, 271, 288, 330–31, 371, 379, 381, 382, 390–91, 490–96, 518, 542, 555, 569

Spencer-Whitman Institute (Chicago), 454, 645n105

spirit. *See* ghost; imagination; socialism

spiritualism, 250, 252–54, 370, 400

Spray, 122, 123, 125, 129, 280, 463, 646n133

ss *Siberia*, 146, 148, 153, 171

Standing, Darrell, 2, 262, 267, 277, 297, 493

The Star Rover (London), 2, 102, 135, 150, 153, 252, 262, 267, 276, 277, 368, 372, 480, 493, 548, 549, 554

Steffens, Lincoln, 219–20, 225, 226, 632n179

Sterling, George: bohemianism and, 123–24, 574, 640n8; as a character, 359, 441; collaboration with London, 129, 194, 438, 518, 602n105, 636n34, 659n37; 1906 earthquake and, 417, 418, 421; origin of nickname, 441; reading London's work, 255, 387, 388, 407, 441–42, 568; Ruskin Club member, 67; *Snark* and, 463; socialism of, 308, 569

Stevenson, Robert Louis, xv, 88, 92, 95, 123, 204

Stickley, Gustav, 449, 451, 453, 460, 629n127

Stoddard, Charles Warren ("Dad"), 14, 73, 185–86, 418, 454–55, 638n94

Stokes, J. G. Phelps, 307, 322, 323, 324, 326, 332, 334, 335, 517

Stone Age, 374, 386, 387; as the Bone Age, 309, 310, 338, 349, 380, 385, 394, 397, 411, 444

Stone, Herbert, 450–51, 459

Story, Lute (character), 245, 246–47, 248, 251, 253, 254, 255

The Story of Ab (Waterloo), 370, 385–87

The Story of a Labor Agitator (Buchanan), 519

"Story of a Typhoon off the Coast of Japan" (London), xiv, 99, 425, 574

"The Story of an Eye-Witness" (London), 419, 423–26

Tolstoy, Leo, 44, 453, 510
To-morrow Magazine, 323, 420
Tompkins, Juliet Wilbor, 364, 365
"To the Man on Trail" (London), 34
Tooker, L. Frank, 130–31
"Too Much Gold" (London), 138–39
tourism, 464
Town Talk, 108
Trachtenberg, Alan, 41
"The Tramp" (London), 17, 18, 20, 25, 59, 213, 550
Tramping with Tramps (Flint), 562
Traubel, Horace, 454, 455
travel, 92, 144, 153, 205, 225, 319, 547, 550–51, 583
The Treason of the Senate (Phillips), 221
Triggs, Oscar Lovell, 307, 322, 323–26, 328, 329–30, 331, 376, 450, 452, 453–54, 455, 462
Trigg's Magazine, 323
Trotsky, Leon, 477, 481
"Turning Children into Dollars" (Tompkins), 364–65
trusts, 46, 49–50, 55, 221, 289, 472, 519, 652n87
Tucker, Amy, xiii
Turgenev, Ivan, 304
Turner, Frederick Jackson, 55
The Turtles of Tasman (London), 468
Twain, Mark, 75, 126, 435, 600n87
Twentieth Century, 220, 522
"Two Children of Israel" (London), 60, 62, 63, 291
Two Years before the Mast (Dana), 95, 111
Tylor, Edward B., 384, 385, 387
Typee: A Peep at Polynesian Life (Melville), 111

Umbstaetter, H. D., 78, 91
Uncle Tom's Cabin (Stowe), 351, 481, 632n178
unconsciousness, xx, 16, 80–81, 97, 247, 249, 254, 257, 258, 260, 262–64, 268, 270, 277, 278, 375, 401, 403, 490, 508. *See also* cinema; dreaming; imagination; memory
"The Unexpected" (London), 227, 237–38, 241, 242, 244, 248, 255, 354, 617n88
unions, 45, 49–51, 55–58, 65–66, 67, 243, 288, 336, 497, 521, 527, 530, 580, 581
The Universal Kinship (Moore), 349, 375–80, 635n10
universities, 2, 55, 223, 224, 311, 325–26, 328, 329–30, 331, 344, 628n117

University Settlement House, 332
"The Unparalleled Invasion" (London), 167, 476, 575–77
Untermann, Ernest, 306, 401, 474, 475, 487–91
"Up the Slide" (London), 113, 114, 115, 595n12
"Uri Bram's God" (London), 339
ut picture poesis, xiv, xv, 153, 231

Vagabond, 578
The Valley of the Moon (London), 43, 208, 248, 260, 412, 508, 531
Van Dyke, Henry, 518–19
Van Weyden, Humphrey (character), 92, 94, 98–100, 105, 106, 108–10, 115, 116, 117, 118, 128, 130, 137, 189, 506, 530
The Varieties of Religious Experience (William James), 494
Veblen, Thorstein, 44–45, 162, 213–14, 223, 322, 608n78. *See also* bohemianism
Vischer, Edmund, 448
Vision. *See* imagination; London, Jack

Wace, Herbert (character), 95, 127, 128, 390, 514
Wagner, Charles, 294, 295, 296, 298, 300, 337
Wagner, Harr, 435
Walden (Thoreau), 451, 452
Walker, James Randolph, 214–15, 446, 447
Walker, John Brisbane, 78, 137–38, 214–15, 217, 220, 255, 473
The Walking Delegate (Scott), 239–41, 332
"The Walking Delegate Novelist" (Harris), 459
Walling, Anna Strunsky, 8, 240, 478, 520
Walling, William English, 240, 306, 322, 323, 332, 334, 458, 478, 517, 608n78
"Wanted: A New Law of Economic Development" (London), 40, 43
Ward, Lester, 377
War of the Classes (London), 46, 51, 53, 54, 58, 171, 172, 173–77, 204, 206, 209, 213, 322, 351, 369, 391, 401, 455, 536
Waterloo, Stanley, 370, 385–87, 388, 391, 394, 399, 401
Waterman, Nixon, 456
Watson, Charles, 506, 519, 588n59, 651n72
Watson, William, 226
Wayland's Monthly, 222, 223, 522
Weininger, Otto, 578

CPSIA information can be obtained
at www.ICGtesting.com
Printed in the USA
LVHW091306290121
677828LV00014B/53/J